ALMANAC·OF·SEAPOWER
1988

THE·ALMANAC·OF·SEAPOWER

12

34

90

A key player on your ASW team–

the CAE MAD system that gives their subs...

CAE AIMS* — The First Inboard MAD System for Helicopters. Now Fully Developed and in Production.

AIMS was the world's first, and is the only proven MAD system capable of fixed installation on helicopters . . . and is still the one and only true **inboard** MAD system.

CAE AIMS offers unrivalled sensitivity and accuracy combined with ease of operation . . . including fast compensation at all altitudes — even in a hover mode.

...nowhere to hide.

AIMS has auto detection capability, eliminates false detections and has a superior detection range.

CAE AIMS Offers a Host of Important Benefits for Both Fixed and Rotary Wing ASW Aircraft.

AIMS is cost-effective, reliable, compact and lightweight. And it's worth remembering that CAE has been supplying MAD equipment to the armed forces of 10 nations in the free world for over 25 years.

*Advanced Integrated MAD System [AN/ASQ-504 (V)]

CAE ELECTRONICS LTD.

A subsidiary of CAE Industries Ltd.

C.P. 1800 Saint Laurent, Québec, Canada H4L 4X4

122

196

218

SEAPOWER FACTS AND FIGURES

Jack H. Morse, *National President*
William G. Sizemore, *Executive Director*
Kenneth E. Cornell, *Director of Administration/Controller*

Staff for this book

Editor, Vincent C. Thomas, Jr.
Editorial Advisor, James D. Hessman
Assistant Editor, Mary L. Tuthill
Contributing Editor, Brooke Nihart
Editorial Assistants: John Slinkman, Susan Higman, Margaret M. Skekel
Director of Advertising, George K. Smith
Assistant Director of Advertising, Margaret M. Skekel
Art Director, John Kaljee
Typographer, Earl E. Thomas

Authors of Essays

Trevor Armbrister
Peter J. Finnerty
Thomas B. Hayward
Isaac C. Kidd, Jr.
John E. Moore
L. Edgar Prina
Sidney A. Wallace
Don Walsh
Francis J. West, Jr.

ISBN 0-944433-00-6
ISSN 0736-3559

MagneTek ALS has gone to sea to conquer space.

No matter what your application—land, sea or air—chances are one of your problems is space. No military facility, aircraft, computer room, vehicle or vessel ever has enough of it. Seventeen years of military power systems experience has taught ALS the value of space. And it was the pressing need to reduce deck-space consumption and loading in naval vessels that led ALS to one of the most dramatic technological advances ever made in power conversion technology.

The ALS Standard Family of PACE Frequency Converters.

One half the size and two thirds the weight of all other converters of comparable power! That describes the ALS Standard Family of PACE frequency converters in 5, 15, 40, 75 and 150 KVA models. Using a new ALS technology called VPSW (variable pulse synthesized waveform) in combination with our unique transistorized power conversion techniques, ALS has been able to provide high quality 400 Hz power while reducing the deck space/loading required by 50%. In some naval vessels this can mean a reduction of as much as eight tons! And it's done while improving efficiency, speeding load response and increasing overload capability.

ALS MK 84 powers the AEGIS weapons system.

While your application may not require an eight-ton weight reduction, chances are the kind of innovation and advanced technology which created PACE converters can help solve your power problems. That's ALS' specialty—power solutions. Call ALS today. MagneTek ALS, 1400 North Baxter Street, P.O. Box 66006, Anaheim, California 92806-0606, (714) 956-9200, TELEX 182283.

"DOUBLE TROUBLE."

© 1987 McDonnell Douglas Corporation

"They offered me the chance to go back to another plane, but I didn't take it. No way. Once I strapped this plane on I didn't want to fly anything else.

"Right away I loved everything it gave me to work with. Air-to-air, air-to-ground all wrapped up in one tight little package.

"But it wasn't until this strike exercise up in Fallon, Nevada, that I learned I could really trust this bird to bring me back alive.

"Fourteen Hornets are heading into the target area, six of them strikers. Those six are split into three groups of two. I'm leading

"Geez, it was just beautiful. In one precise, fluid motion I'd gone from air-to-ground to air-to-air and back again."

the third group. We're carrying Mark 82 bombs, 500 pounders, plus a couple of Sidewinders and Sparrows.

"The first section is off and egressing the area. The second section is just into its run.

"I'm coming into the target area now, doing about 500 knots right on the deck. Five miles out, I pull my nose up about 45 degrees. Right then I spot a bogie. He's up there circling the target at about ten, maybe 15 thousand feet. I hit the button and immediately I'm air-to-air as I pull up to greet him.

"A little thumb action and I've got it locked up. I shoot off a Sidewinder—and *nail him!* Still have the mission to complete so I switch back to air-to-ground. I pull upside down, roll over and come in at about 45 degrees, drop my bombs—bull's eye! Geez, it was just beautiful. In one precise, fluid motion I'd gone from air-to-ground to air-to-air and back again. I've got a dead bogie and my bombs off—double trouble for the bad guys from one pilot, one plane. It's only taken a few seconds and virtually no effort. It couldn't be easier."

THE F/A-18. FAMILIARITY BREEDS AWE.

The F/A-18 strike fighter is a highly effective force multiplier—one plane with one pilot capable of flying more tactical missions more effectively than any other Naval aircraft. Hornet Tales are taken from actual F/A-18 pilot interviews. Do you have a true Hornet Tale? Write to: McDonnell Douglas, Hornet Tales, P.O. Box 4105, Hazelwood, MO 63042.
McDonnell Douglas prime contractor, Northrop principal subcontractor.

MCDONNELL DOUGLAS

"Sea power in the broad sense . . . includes not only the military strength afloat that rules the sea or any part of it by force of arms, but also the peaceful commerce and shipping from which alone a military fleet naturally and healthfully springs, and on which it securely rests."

Alfred Thayer Mahan

The Almanac of Seapower is dedicated—with the sincerest respect and greatest affection—to the men and women of the U.S. sea services and their families.

PREFACE

The sixth edition of the Navy League's *Almanac of Seapower* continues to reflect additions to, as well as modifications of, and other changes to the U.S. sea-service hardware inventories. It is published at the end of a seven-year period that for the most part has been favorable to the sea services, with the exception of the merchant marine, and which has led to marked improvement in the overall capabilities of the Navy, the Marine Corps, and—to a lesser extent—the Coast Guard. The apparent ending of this cycle signals defense-budget reductions which are certain to lead to, at least, stagnation within the sea services and in turn to a decline in their capabilities.

The 600-ship Navy is close to reality. But even as that goal is approached, Congress is struggling over how, and whether, to keep that Navy properly manned, supplied, and fully operable. That debate couldn't come at a more difficult time. And while it continues, the additional funding needed to operate and maintain naval forces in the Persian Gulf, over and above those normally deployed elsewhere, totals nearly a million dollars a day. As it has done in recent years, the Navy meets the immediate crisis by stripping funds from other programs which are no less essential, and by postponing scheduled maintenance and overhauls of ships and aircraft. Unfortunately, such postponements almost always lead to much higher long-term costs. And, unless there is adequate additional funding provided, such false economies also will result, without doubt, in lessened operational readiness.

As one reads and studies the sixth edition of the *Almanac,* one cannot escape the thoughts of the happenings and events which both singly and collectively can, and undoubtedly will, impact adversely on those elements that combine to make up our nation's seapower. Among the more noteworthy of those "happenings and events" are the missile attack on the frigate *Stark,* the administration's decision to provide U.S. naval escorts for the reflagged Kuwaiti tankers now sailing under U.S. colors in the Persian Gulf, Gramm-Rudman-Hollings and all its ramifications, the INF treaty, the October stock-market plunge, and the recent issuance of a most discouraging report from the Commission on Merchant Marine and Defense. (The fact that we now have nearly lost our merchant fleet, not through enemy action but as a result of our own lethargy, may rank as one of the greatest economic and military blunders our country has been guilty of since World War II.) If all those matters collectively leave a negative impression of vulnerability, whether operational or fiscal, or a deficiency of courage and will, then our sea services could, ultimately, suffer greatly from a lack of moral as well as fiscal support.

So I urge you to take time to read carefully the essays in this edition of the *Almanac,* so that you may better understand the seapower challenges of today and tomorrow. For only the informed person can truly understand—and perhaps institute action to counter—the problems posed, for example, by Third World conflicts in which we might become embroiled, the dramatic expansion of the Soviet navy, the economic war on the high seas against American shipping interests, the inability of the underfunded Coast Guard to cope with all the additional responsibilities thrust upon it, and the unquestionable harm that will result from additional reductions in sea-service budgets. None of these are easy problems to solve, but their solution can't even be attempted without an understanding of what they are, and of their likely effect on national defense as well as on the U.S. economy.

The Almanac of Seapower is, without question, an unusually helpful and credible reference book. I suggest you keep it on your desk, where it will be always available for instant use. And raise your voice in support of what its learned and highly qualified essayists urge in order that we may continue to remain, as we should be, the world's unquestioned No. 1 maritime power.

Jack H. Morse

JACK H. MORSE, *National President*

NAVY

After the INF Treaty
Should Become Mor

By Francis J. West, Jr.

From 1981 until 1986, the U.S. Navy benefited from a substantial growth in resources. Although as a share of the defense budget the Navy/Marine Corps declined from 37 percent in FY 1977 to 34 percent in FY 1987, over that same time frame the trend in force structure improved markedly. For the 1990s the current projection is for a 600-ship Navy, with 15 deployable carriers and 27 Aegis cruisers. Compared with the outlook in 1978, the turnaround in the force-structure fortunes of the Navy has been remarkable.

An issue in 1988 is whether this buildup will be sustained. The American body politic supports resources for defense on a cyclical, if not rollercoaster, basis. When resources become too thin, this is communicated by great unease throughout the national-security community and a resource correction follows. By the beginning of this decade, the services were receiving a generous level of resources. Now the nation is entering a period when resources will be less. If we go too far, there will be another correction. Unfortunately, our allies in Western Europe and Japan exhibit no such cyclical corrections, and the United States has no intention of matching the brute-force spending approach of the Soviet Union. It is in the nature of democracies not to sacrifice for the common defense until faced with a clear and present danger.

The FY 1988 defense budget request may be reduced substantially by Congress, but whether the reductions will be coherent or will force the Navy (and the other services) to choose among forces for different missions is far from clear. Six years ago, the current administration broadened the tenets of defense planning. A conventional conflict with the Soviet Union was assumed to be global, not limited to the European theater; this increased the case for naval, amphibious, and mobility forces. The window of nuclear vulnerability was to be closed; this required increased resources

for strategic forces, command, control, communications, and intelligence. With a former Supreme Allied Commander, Europe, installed as Secretary of State, the administration made sure the modernization of forces earmarked for NATO continued at a rapid pace. While the Air Force received the largest share of the defense budget, all services and DOD agencies experienced several years of large growth. Ambitious strategic assumptions were matched by impressive budget increases.

Former Secretary of Defense James Schlesinger warned at the outset that the buildup could not be sustained. It was imprudent, he said, to reduce taxes, increase defense spending, and assume economic growth would generate enough revenues to reduce the deficit. Five years later, alarmed by the deficit, Congress curtailed defense spending amidst charges that the Pentagon had no strategy, the implication being that when there was an agreed-on strategy end-state, it could be sustained with significantly lower defense spending. That debating point was reinforced by two years (1986 and 1987) of Department of Defense reorganizations, announced with trumpets and accomplished with scarcely any shift in defense leadership. It was not reasonable to expect Secretary of Defense Caspar W. Weinberger, Deputy Secretary William H. Taft, Under Secretary Fred Ikle, or even National Security Advisor Frank Carlucci to admit their strategic choices of five years ago were incorrect. After all, given that the United States was lagging in several defense areas, it made sense to increase resources across the board rather than to presume that strategic cleverness could substitute for resources.

An analogy to, say, two football teams who have not played one another is not exact, but it may be illustrative. One team is large and bulky and persists in weightlifting; one year its line averages 250 pounds, the next year 260, and so on. The other team is lighter, faster, capable of executing many different plays. One year the latter team

he Maritime Strategy
mportant Than Ever

In September 1987 an Iranian landing craft, the Iran Ajr, with a cargo of mines was intercepted and boarded in the Persian Gulf by U.S. naval forces. An aerial view of the deck of the craft, with many of its mines still aboard, is shown left. A closer view of the improved 1908-model mines which detonate upon contact with their "horns" also is shown. In October, after a U.S.-flagged Kuwaiti tanker had been struck by an Iranian missile in Kuwaiti waters, U.S. naval forces shelled an Iranian command and control platform near Rashadat in the Persian Gulf. The shelling set the tower afire. A warship stands by as it continues to burn.

will increase its weight and its speed, the next year it will not; then it will again be concerned about the growing bulk of the other team, and so on. The fans of the lighter team like to believe it could offset bulk by better play selection—by better strategy. Perhaps.

In any event, any budget of any size is an exercise in setting priorities. This can be done without ever addressing strategic choices, but over several years a pattern will form.

The selection of U.S. naval forces at present shows one pattern: 15 deployable carriers, about 2,300 carrier aircraft, about 100 nuclear attack submarines, the introduction of the new SSN-21, measured ballistic-missile submarine and amphibious programs, and increased emphasis upon ASW. This program suggests a careful, traditional approach under which the year 2000 would not look very much different than the year 1988 in terms of broad balance among mission areas.

This pattern of tradition could be affected by the decision

F.J. "BING" WEST, JR., is president of Gama Corporation, specializing in gaming and analysis. He has served as Assistant Secretary of Defense for International Security Affairs and as Dean of Research at the Naval War College, and is a frequent contributor to naval journals. He directed the Navy force-planning study "Operation 2000" in the 1970s.

of the next administration to follow any one of five different paths. The first path relates to strategic defense. Three years ago, the President presented the concept as a centerpiece of defense policy, without staffing from inside the Pentagon. The Soviet response indicates they are seriously concerned that they could not compete with U.S. defense efforts in space. It is not clear, however, how to exploit that concern to American advantage. Opinions range from those who view SDI as a research and development effort which should be used immediately as a bargaining chip to those who wish to deploy some defenses in order to then negotiate significant reductions in offensive weapons to those who advocate a phased, incremental SDI to those who envision a full-fledged "astrodome" defense.

The problem with any deployment is that it is eight to 15 years away and will require steadfastness and funding constancy in the interim. It also requires, in order to test weapons in space, abrogation of the ABM treaty. While President Reagan believed the treaty was not in the best interests of the country and SDI was, he was not willing to abrogate it. Excepting egregious Soviet misbehavior, it is not clear why the next President will be willing to break that treaty.

Further, if the Soviets hold firm in linking no SDI in space to central-systems arms reductions, the SDI program is at a great disadvantage in American politics. To the extent

that arms control prevents strategic defense or any other major strategy, then arms control in itself becomes a strategic path. The current administration has been reported as offering up to a 10-year moratorium on weapon testing in space. How can any successor administration offer less? And, since the offer was not sufficient, SDI testing and deployment are held hostage to Soviet concurrence, if a central-systems arms agreement is essential. The question, then, is whether the body politic of the United States is willing to go 10, 20, or more years without another SALT agreement? On the other hand, it is not credible to the author that space will remain free of weapons, any more than the oceans are free of weapons. With hundreds of surveillance and communications satellites, space long has been militarized. It is the only passageway for the ballistic missile—most terrible weapon in the world's arsenal. Sooner or later, probably later, probably after 2000 or 2010, there will be weapons in space to destroy satellites and missiles, although they may not be in large numbers or largely effective.

SDI Costs Will Be Large Indeed

All we know now is that the process is slow-moving, that there is no American political consensus about SDI, that various schemes are competing for favor, and that the Soviets, fearing the results, want to use the American desire for arms control to veto any deployment.

Given these uncertainties and the certainty that SDI costs will be very large indeed, the services and the chairman of the Joint Chiefs of Staff have been guarded in their public enthusiasms. There is no evidence that an acceleration in strategic defense would come with any new administration, or that the Navy would reallocate resources to provide a larger funding wedge for such a defense.

A second, alternative strategic path would emphasize a strengthening of U.S. forces in Europe. Because of the interaction between SDI and arms control, this path looks assured. There is an irony here. The Reagan administration criticized the Carter administration for overemphasizing NATO, yet there is a good chance the Reagan administration will conclude its eight years with the same emphasis.

The West Europeans have expressed some anxiety about the U.S.-Soviet theater nuclear arms agreement. The American systems at issue—the cruise missiles and Pershing IIs—have the range to hit the western Soviet Union, and so they serve as the visible symbol which ties the North American continent to the European continent in terms of nuclear destruction. In a war, if NATO forces struck the Soviet Union, then American territory would be hit in return. Because this linkage has a symbolic effect, any reductions will require symbolic compensation. Most likely this will lead to an expanded naval role in theater nuclear matters.

This may not lead to more force deployments; it will, however, force the U.S. Navy to review its thinking about the concept of theater nuclear deterrence and conflict.

The theater nuclear treaty also will mean an increase in U.S. conventional capabilities, with emphasis upon the "emerging technologies," mainly air-to-surface surveillance and capabilities and air-to-surface anti-armor weapons. In response to a perceived overemphasis upon SDI, the Congress has mandated a CDI, or Conventional Defense Initiative. There also is a web of strategic defense agreements with European governments and countries, focused on land-based systems which will provide a sophisticated defense against aircraft and cruise missiles. Given the attitudes of the Senate and House Armed Services Committees, strategic defense R&D cannot be advanced without advancing conventional R&D. The Army and the Air Force are in the lead in the CDI, and it presages a return to a NATO conventional emphasis. What remains to be seen is whether Congress will stipulate that the CDI systems must be built to weight/ transport specifications which permit mobile deployment on a worldwide basis versus fixed deployment in a theater. But whatever the case, the initial conventional defense of Europe is going to receive a resurgence of American attention.

The U.S. Navy's contribution to the initial conventional defense of NATO's Central Front, many will argue, is to give up resources.

The criterion for additional resources should be whether the result will be a marked increase in confidence in the initial defense or a continuation of the current belief in NATO inferiority.

Most informed observers do not believe the West could carry out its declared strategy of an initial forward defense by conventional forces. To be sure, the threat of initiating nuclear war is a powerful deterrent, but it rests on the premise that Americans are willing to commit suicide for Europeans who spend comparatively less of their wealth for the common defense.

Political Strategy Is Sound

The Europeans fought their last great civil war almost a half century ago. One consequence of World War II was that all the nations of Europe gave up the ambitions, dangers, and burdens of being global powers. The long-term trend in Western Europe is disengagement from the global competition of the two superpowers. It is therefore doubtful that these same West European nations will be motivated to make the financial sacrifices necessary to have high confidence in their conventional forces. The Europeans may promise to do a little more, too, but it would be strategically imprudent for the United States to increase spending for NATO at the expense of our other forces. Resources alone are not the solution to the Soviet edge in mass and firepower along the inner-German border.

We would have to spend two or three times more than the Soviets to have confidence in our politically-driven military strategy of forward defense along a Maginot Line without physical barriers. For alliance cohesion, the political strategy is sound and should endure. The requirement, however, to defend the edge of West German territory deprives our land forces of strategy and of manpower and leaves them with only firepower to stop Soviet firepower and mass. The United States does not have a realistic strategy for fighting the Soviet Union in a major conventional war.

The Navy has a maritime strategy for fighting its piece of the war. But the unified commanders and the services as a joint body do not have a strategy. Why? The major reason is that a realistic strategy must come from the Commander in Chief, U.S. Forces, Europe; but that same man is also SACEUR, and he must be careful not to propose military contingency plans, no matter how sensible, which may weaken the political alliance.

So there is a problem with our military strategy.

A fourth strategic path is to pursue initiatives which force the Soviets to shift resources from offensive to defensive programs. This notion of cost-imposing strategies long has been a favorite of defense intellectuals and appears annually in the posture statement of the Secretary of Defense. The two classic examples are that the U.S. strategic bomber threat in the 1950s forced the Soviets to erect a costly and ineffective air defense, while today the U.S. submarine threat has forced the Soviets into costly ASW programs. If the examples are anywhere near the true story, the concept sounds ideal. The practical questions are whether the United States has several other such programs, whether the concept is responsible for the program or is a side-benefit claimed after the fact, and whether in the event of war we would regret the peacetime cost-imposing strategy. Intuitively, the class of low-observable aircraft, drones, and cruise missiles has the potential to be deployed so as to induce the Soviets into some costly, ineffective, and defensive responses.

It is instructive to note, however, that while the posture statement of the Secretary of Defense cites U.S. ASW as a classic example of our cost-imposing strategy, the Chief of Naval Operations in his 1988-1989 posture statement singled out ASW as a mission area where the challenge of the future was particularly pressing. So, most likely any strategy chosen to impose costs upon the Soviets will be controversial and will not be a future choice of U.S. naval forces.

The fourth strategic path is to reinforce and expand the Navy's maritime strategy. The major problem with the strategy is that it is associated with one service. It should be called the conventional strategy because, strained of its salt water, it is a set of campaign concepts, derived from fleet exercises and war games, for fighting Soviet forces—without resorting to nuclear weapons. This is done by husbanding resources and fighting sequential, rather than simultaneous, campaigns. In other words, this is done by fighting a protracted war.

Threat of Nuclear War Still Deterrent

That raises another serious problem. Most likely a protracted war, even assuming NATO had the supplies, would not be fought in trenches along the inner-German border. It is even less likely the ground war would initially be fought in the People's Democratic Republic of Germany (East Germany). The very reason for the American nuclear linkage was to deter conventional war which would be fought in Western Europe. A protracted conventional war would

Surface Ship Comparisons

USSR

New Class Aircraft Carrier

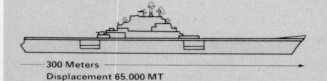

—— 300 Meters ——————→
Displacement 65,000 MT

KIEV-Class Guided-Missile VSTOL Aircraft Carrier

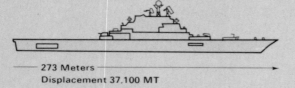

—— 273 Meters ————→
Displacement 37,100 MT

KIROV-Class Nuclear-Powered Guided-Missile Cruiser

—— 248 Meters ————→
Displacement 28,000 MT

SLAVA-Class Guided-Missile Cruiser

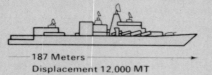

—— 187 Meters ——→
Displacement 12,000 MT

UDALOY-Class Guided-Missile Destroyer

—— 162 Meters ——→
Displacement 8,000 MT

SOVREMENNYY-Class Guided-Missile Destroyer

—— 156 Meters ——→
Displacement 7,300 MT

US

NIMITZ-Class Aircraft Carrier

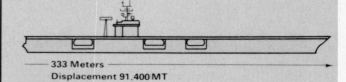

—— 333 Meters ——————→
Displacement 91,400 MT

IOWA-Class Battleship

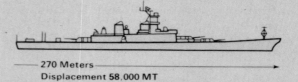

—— 270 Meters ————→
Displacement 58,000 MT

VIRGINIA-Class Guided-Missile Cruiser

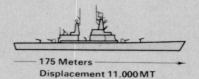

—— 175 Meters ——→
Displacement 11,000 MT

TICONDEROGA-Class Guided-Missile Cruiser

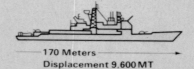

—— 170 Meters ——→
Displacement 9,600 MT

ARLEIGH BURKE-Class Guided-Missile Destroyer

—— 142 Meters —→
Displacement 8,300 MT

OLIVER HAZARD PERRY-Class Guided-Missile Frigate

—— 130 Meters —→
Displacement 3,900 MT

bring massive destruction. Therefore, it is difficult to believe West European leaders can in peacetime endorse the concept, even as an option. It seems to add uncertainty to the already uncertain nuclear linkage.

The United States does not have a unified conventional-war strategy—as distinct from unofficial war-college efforts—because, to be realistic, it would have to take into account initial setbacks. To do so is politically unacceptable. Yet not to do so leaves us without a realistic conventional strategy. This condition was perhaps marginally acceptable when we possessed nuclear superiority, making credible the threat of the United States' first use of nuclear weapons. The threat of nuclear war remains an extraordinary deterrent. But I also believe the Joint Chiefs of Staff should take the lessons from the global war series at the Naval War College, Newport, R.I.; take the work from the Army and Air War Colleges, and from the National Defense University; take the dozens of major exercises by the unified commanders, and—quietly but firmly—craft a strategy for protracted conventional war.

The maritime strategy is an important step in that direction and it does have certain strengths. The foremost is that it is conventional, despite West European reservations. In the highly unlikely event war did break out in Western Europe, before responding to a SACEUR request for the release of nuclear weapons, a President would ask the Chairman of the JCS: What are our other alternatives? The Chairman could scarcely reply that the Navy and Marine Corps had seriously worked on a conventional war strategy but, for that very reason, the other services ignored it and he as Chairman dropped the issues. So, it is likely that in some form or another the JCS will pursue the premises of the maritime strategy, although under a different title and without screen credits.

A second strength of the strategy is that it is optimistic and should reinforce deterrence. It basically says that, regardless of how well the Soviets do in the initial land battles, they cannot stop the defense buildup 6,000 miles away in the United States and in other nations. No matter how well they have done in one theater, the Soviets face one major adversary, and if they cannot stop the conventional and nuclear buildup of the United States, then they have entered a war with a battle plan but no strategy. The NATO threat of initiating nuclear war in order to deter Soviet conventional attack is becoming less credible; the United States has proposed negotiations which include the possibility of major reductions in U.S. long-range missiles in Europe. Efforts to strengthen NATO's initial forward defense wax and wane. They now are about to see a resurgence with emphasis upon American technology. But confidence in the initial defense always will be strained by the political and societal requirement that the defense be at the very edge of the West German territory, thereby depriving NATO's commanders of maneuver and of strategy. So, it seems reasonable that the JCS would quietly proceed with plans for how they would fight a conventional war, despite initial setbacks and losses.

The allies—and we—will not invest heavily enough to have a credible initial war strategy. It is like a lightheavyweight boxer, with good speed, endurance, and adapability, decid-

ing to knock out or be knocked out by a super heavyweight in the first round. If we do develop a protracted war option as we bargain down our nuclear forces in Europe, then we must keep our naval superiority, if we are to continue to fight. The carriers do two things: they provide the mobile air umbrellas which defend our movement of supplies anywhere in the world, and they deliver munitions ashore, from the beach to 500 miles inland.

12 or 13 Deployed Carriers Needed

Since 1974, and in Sea Plan 2000 in 1977, the Navy has argued for 600 ships, about 15 carriers, and an offensive battle plan. Why 15 carriers? If fighting the Soviets, in any theater we would have to mass three to four battle groups. There are five major theaters: Atlantic, Norwegian Sea, Mediterranean, Southwest Asia, and the West Pacific (with the Caribbean a minor sixth theater). Given that two carriers would be in overhaul or workup at any given time, and given that losses would occur, a series of exercises and war games year after year have shown that 12 or 13 deployed carriers are needed, if used in prudent, sequential campaigns, to gradually assert allied control over those maritime theaters.

Since by definition a democracy during peacetime will not dedicate the resources necessary for such a conflict, parallel with the conventional strategy there must be a mobilization plan. DOD and FEMA are institutionally capable of developing and gaming such a plan, just as the war colleges game military plans.

The fifth strategic path would begin to research, game, and develop strategic-planning principles for a serious U.S.-Soviet conflict which did not include fighting in Western Europe. In 1984, both the Supreme Allied Commanders, Atlantic and SACEUR, publicly stated (Commander in Chief, Pacific, and Commander in Chief, Central Command have been more guarded in their statements) they could not envision such a conflict without war in Europe. That is our current planning scenario. But we should seriously look at an alternative.

Why? There are several reasons. First, we frequently are challenged militarily outside Western Europe, and respond by using force, which we have never done in the NATO context. Some of these challenges, as in the April 1986 raid against Libya, involve Soviet forces and equipment on the other side.

Chances of Direct U.S.-USSR Conflict Low

In the world outside Western Europe, we see high instabilities—"Arcs of Crises"—and the intermingling of Soviet forces with their allies and of U.S. forces with our allies and friends. The chances of a direct U.S.-Soviet conflict are low anywhere, but they are higher outside Western Europe. However, U.S. forces are in the dominant position. We have an edge anywhere in the world where the Soviets must rely upon sea or air lines of communication.

This force mismatch is reassuring to American interests. We take it for granted but, if one stops and thinks about it, it is rather remarkable. The Soviets can build for 10, 15, 20 years in Syria, Cuba, Libya, or wherever, and in a week to two we can mass three or four battle groups or bomber

groups and take out any target set we want. We can land our troops where we want. We can go anywhere we want across the oceans. We debate sharply whether, in a war, we should strike the Kola Peninsula; the question is whether it would be worth the cost. But it is worth noting that both we and the Soviets know we could do it if we wanted to. Our internal debates are about how long it will take us to destroy Soviet naval and projection power, how long Soviet SSBNs can survive before we sink them, how long before we shut down the Soviet Far East C3 and bomber forces, how quickly we can deploy to northern Norway, etc. In essence, our debates are not about whether we have naval superiority, but about how we should apply it.

This is preferable to the debates of the 1970s, when the issue during the Yom Kippur War was whether the Sixth Fleet could hold station against the Soviet fleet in the Eastern Mediterranean and, in Asia, Chinese and Japanese leaders were asking whether the United States could, in war, maintain a link to their countries.

A second reason is that the Reagan-Gorbachev meeting at Reykjavik, Iceland, in 1986 was a watershed. A conservative American President established that the United States would reduce sharply its nuclear systems in Europe, if the Soviet Union did likewise. Third, the long-term secular trend in Western Europe has been toward a disengagement from the global competition of the two superpowers. Poll after poll, year after year, has reflected this trend. Fourth, non-nuclear technologies are increasing the damage and shock which can be achieved in less than a full-scale war: the penetration capabilities of low-observables, the lethality of the next generation of non-nuclear explosives, the U.S. Air Force decision that its new fighter will have a 1,000-mile combat radius, etc. Fifth, the Western Hemisphere, and above all Central America, is unfortunately emerging as a fourth active strategic theater which will require continuous deployments and attention. These trends, when taken together—violence outside Western Europe, a loosening of the nuclear coupling with NATO, de-emphasis of nuclear systems as a deterrent to conventional aggression, the West European trend toward disengagement, the increase in long-range, accurate, lethal conventional systems, a fourth strategic theater to our south, absence of real growth in funds for conventional defense—suggest a future decline in the commitment of U.S. land and air power to the defense of continental Europe. Stated differently, it is quite possible that the United States will shift gradually towards a defense posture that moves away from large, geographically-tied forward deployments and towards the maintenance of a large pool or central reserve of forces that could be lifted and committed anywhere. An additional, related consideration is the reality that conflict, whether or not the Soviet Union is involved, is more likely outside Europe, in regions characterized by far less mature and stable security regimes.

To what extent will naval forces and budgets be driven by alternative strategies?

While the maritime strategy and the deterrence of the Soviet Union received the media attention and controversy in the early and mid-1980s, what is now emerging and will persist are the non-European cases, such as involving the Persian Gulf. There, U.S. forces have deployed and have conducted themselves effectively on an operational level, bringing in special equipment from all the services, to protect the seaborne export of oil and to box in the violent radicalism of Khomeini's Iran. The U.S. Navy's professionalism in these tense and quasi-combat operations, combined with the clear economic and geopolitical imperatives for the deployment around the globe of U.S. naval forces, probably will offset any tendency to return to the 1977-78 period and reduce U.S. naval forces in order to increase the U.S. contribution to the initial defense of the Central Front.

In 1980 there was a genuine strategic debate about conventional forces—the NATO Central Front school versus the Globabst school. There is no major strategic debate in 1988 about conventional forces—there is, unfortunately, a lack of appropriated funds. So far, Congress has not reduced funding in keeping with any sort of strategic plan. Nor, as far as can be discerned, has the administration. Instead, each service has taken a serve of cuts and adjusted its programs as best it could.

That pattern probably will hold until there is a serious crisis—a shock to the domestic body politic—or until the restiveness on the part of the national security community —civilian and military alike—grows as it did in 1979 and 1980, and resources are increased.

In summary, these points deserve mention.

1. Nuclear weapons, with their terrifying destructiveness, do deter and have greatly inhibited the resort to major conventional conflict. There is strong deterrent merit in the NATO doctrine of flexible response. However, the threat to use nuclear weapons is the threat to commit mutual suicide. By accident as much as by design, as witnessed by World War I, deterrence can fail.

2. Therefore, in addition to the deterrent threat of nuclear war, the United States should develop a realistic conventional war strategy. This can be done quietly by the JCS. But it should be done.

3. In parallel with the conventional strategy, we need a mobilization strategy and a trust fund for putting in place a base from which to mobilize.

4. As we reduce nuclear weapons in Europe there will be a tendency to compensate by increasing our NATO conventional budget. We should be careful we do not pay for this by trading off forces where the United States has superiority to reinforce an area where the political strategy and the attitudes of our allies place the United States militarily in a disadvantageous position which cannot be overcome by modest budgetary increases.

5. We should treat the allied military deficit—the refusal of others, especially Japan, to do their fair share—as seriously as we treat the trade deficit.

6. We should recognize that the military competition with the Soviet Union is shifting outside Western Europe, and should maintain flexible projection forces superior to those of the Soviets.

7. The basic Navy force structure is certainly traditional. This invites the presentation of new and alternative concepts. But the balance of the forces is driven by a balance among missions. None of those missions is less applicable in the 1990s than in the 1980s. ∎

The Heart of Mission Success

Military Leaders Know They Need Precise Navigation

After five complete generations of navigation advancements and more than 25,000 systems delivered, *pilots and engineers, mission analysts and avionics specialists* have learned to rely on the world leader, Litton, for innovative, superior inertial navigation technology.

Litton systems are currently on all U.S. Navy, U.S. Air Force, and U.S. Army high-performance aircraft in addition to many international aircraft.

For information write Guidance and Control Systems, 5500 Canoga Avenue, Woodland Hills, 91365 CA.

Litton
Guidance & Control Systems

The Corps' Fiery New
to Improv

By L. Edgar Prina

Looking back a few years hence one may very well conclude that the most important thing that happened to the United States Marine Corps in 1987 was the appointment of General Alfred M. Gray, Jr., as Commandant.

Although he has spent less time in Washington than many of his fellow generals, Gray came to his new assignment last July full of plans and ideas. He hit Marine Corps Headquarters like a Kansas twister and left the staff breathless with the major changes he was eager to make. He plainly is not satisfied with things as they are. It's not that he believes the situation is bad; rather, he knows it could be better.

Hailed as a "warrior" and "mud Marine," his image as a rough, tough, and hard-to-bluff type is enhanced by his preference for camouflaged fatigues and chewing tobacco. He came determined to shake up what he obviously thinks has become too comfortable a Corps.

A former enlisted man, Gray recognizes that the Marines have an overall image problem, a problem more serious than the one that flowed from the boot-camp brutalities of the 1970s. The bombing of the Marine barracks in Lebanon, the Moscow embassy security disaster, and the Iran-Contra affair in which a Marine officer was so heavily involved, have led to ridicule and a public perception that perhaps the Corps was not as good as it claimed to be.

Clearly, Gray is not convinced in his own mind that the Corps is that good, or he would not have told Marines at Camp Pendleton, Calif., shortly after succeeding General P.X. Kelley as Commandant, that "if you know anything at all about gunslinging and warfighting or anything at all about training or being a warrior, then you know in your heart we are not as good as we ought to be."

Not surprisingly, therefore, one of Gray's main efforts is being directed at personnel—individual and unit training; education, officer assignments, and new standards for command.

He has vowed to eliminate what are known in the Corps as "careerism," "homesteading," and the "zero defects mentality." Let this most colorful and quotable member of the Joint Chiefs of Staff in years elaborate in his own words in talks to his officers and enlisted personnel.

On careerism: "We have too much careerism creeping into the officer corps. What do I mean by careerism? Officers who worry more about themselves and how they are going to get ahead than they do about the people they are privileged to lead. We're going to stamp out careerism."

On zero-defects mentality: "We have a corps of Marines who are afraid to make mistakes. It takes guts to turn someone loose to go out and make mistakes where you are accountable. We are going to create an environment where people can do things, seek challenges 'way beyond what we're letting them do today. People must be free to grow."

On homesteading or the settling in for a long, comfortable assignment: "My recommendation is that if you've been (stationed) somewhere for four years, don't send out your laundry. ... We have a new policy now. They (officers) are going to go where I want them to go and do what I want them to do for the length of tour that I prescribe, based on the needs of the country and the needs of the Corps. ... If you go where you want to go, you've lucked out."

Marine training is in for some important changes, with a greater emphasis placed on urban-area operations, realism, and nightfighting. The Corps has had a goal of doing half its training at night, but has yet to achieve it. Gray has pledged to see that it is done.

High on the new Commandant's planning list is a return

eader Is Determined
ts Image

to the day when every Marine went through infantry training after completing boot camp. He concedes that this will be difficult in a time of budget squeezes, because it will cost lots of money and manpower—for facilities, equipment, and additional training personnel. Nevertheless, he says he is adamant on the matter and will realign the Corps to see that it's done. Congress, of course, could derail this plan during the appropriations process.

"I believe that every Marine, regardless of rank, male or female, must consider themselves [sic] to be a rifleman first," he said. "You've got to be able to defend yourselves. You have got to be able to shoot, move, and communicate. Pick it up, lay it down, and get moving. Whether you're along the flight line, in supply, or in the infantry or whatever . . . there are no rear areas in the battlefield of the future."

The Commandant has let it be known that he wants, and is determined to get, "one high standard of excellence" for all Marines regardless of rank. "I don't care if we have to reduce our strength in half, you're going to live my standards of excellence and they are going to be higher than you thought possibly could exist," he told the Corps.

The "every Marine a rifleman" program will see changes in the 11-week recruit regimen at boot camp as certain time-eating "frills" are removed so that combat training may be substantially increased. After recruit training is completed, the new Marine will go to the School of Infantry on the East or West Coast, probably for four weeks.

New Warfighting Center Being Created

The Corps has succeeded in increasing significantly the number of recruits in the higher mental categories in recent years, and Marine leaders have mentioned this over and over again in public speeches and reports. Gray believes such talk as "best quality ever" ought to be dropped, because the really important thing is what is done with the quality after it's acquired.

"For 10 years we've been bragging about how great all of you are because you have high school education . . . and you won three letters in East Cupcake, Nebraska, and all of that. And that's good," he told Marines at the Yuma, Ariz., air station. "I believe that we need that. But we need to understand that a high school diploma doesn't make you a warrior, it doesn't make you a leader, it doesn't make you a follower, it doesn't make you a gunslinger, it doesn't make you a great aviation technician or [skilled in] supply, logistics, or communications."

What does make young Marines these things is training, studying, the kind of leadership given them, and the opportunities to grow, he said.

Physical fitness is another area in which Gray has taken a keen interest. He is not opposed to jogging or running; he

does some himself. But he clearly thinks a number of Marines overdo it and he wants balance. He plans to continue with the formal Physical Fitness Test (PFT), but he is not looking for any Marine track stars.

"When I see people running half the day or half the night in their pretty silk shorts and their $200 Adidas [shoes], I wonder about the training. . . . That doesn't have a damn thing to do with the kind of preparedness I'm talking about."

The Commandant said he was more interested in whether a Marine could carry a wounded buddy 75 or 100 yards across a battlefield under fire and not kill him before he could find a corpsman to treat him.

"So, we are going to go back to combat-type conditioning," he said. "We're going to introduce the old-fashioned physical-readiness training that we used to have in our Corps. I'm talking about obstacle courses, confidence courses, load-bearing forced marches—the kind of things that build strength and stamina. If you can't saddle up and go, I don't need you. If you want to run for 15 or 20 miles, that's fine. You do it on your time, not mine."

As part of the overall drive to standardize and improve training, Gray has moved quickly on a pet project to make the base at Quantico, Va., a super "think-tank" or, as he puts it, the "crossroads of the Corps." Specifically, he is taking the training department out of headquarters and combining it with Quantico's Education Center and other parts of the Marine Corps Development/Education Command, to form a Training and Education Center.

In addition, a new Warfighting Center is being created around the present Doctrine Center and the concepts and analysis experts now in the Development Center. "It will be the home of our new ideas, doctrinal improvement, and tactical examination," Gray said.

Finally, a new Research, Development, and Acquisition Command will be set up at Quantico by moving the rest of the acquisition business and research and development effort from HQMC.

These consolidations are expected to save manpower, but more important to Gray, they will remove from the chain of command a great many officers who have been able to say "no" and, thus, delay decisions on proposals that come to headquarters from major Marine commands outside Washington.

According to press reports last summer, Gray told his headquarters staff he wanted to eliminate exhaustive examination of issues by large staffs on behalf of general officers.

"We are going to eliminate a lot of these people who, up to now, have been able to say 'no,'" he said. "Within reason, we will eliminate the requirement for majors and lieutenant colonels to have to rush in before a meeting and pump up some general so he can vote. That's what we do too much of."

A little more than three years ago, Admiral James D. Watkins, Chief of Naval Operations, and Kelley directed Vice Adm. W.F. McCauley, Commander Surface Force, Atlantic Fleet, and Gray, then Commanding General, Fleet Marine Force Atlantic, to see what could be done about improving the capabilities of the amphibious forces in special operations.

Within eight months, the PHIBRON/MAU-SOC (amphibious squadron/Marine amphibious unit-special operations

---

L. EDGAR PRINA has served as a defense correspondent for the *Washington Star* and later the *Copley Press* for more than 30 years. For seven years he also was Washington Bureau Chief for the Copley News Service. He now is senior correspondent for that news organization.

Mountain-warfare training and obstacle courses are just two of the many kinds of training Marines will receive as readiness and physical fitness are improved.

capable) was created and sent to sea. The forward deployed amphibious forces were augmented with attachments from Marine force reconnaissance, air/naval gunfire liaison company (ANGELICO), Navy SEAL units, radio battalions, etc. Special equipment was provided such as small boats, forward-area support-team ropes, submachine guns, sniper weapons, silencers, backpack satellite communications, and other items to these units.

Before the PHIBRON/MAU-SOC deployed, it underwent six months of training so that the Navy and Marine elements could be properly worked up together and evaluated.

Commandant An Advocate of Cohesion

Gray is a strong advocate of one vital training element he feels had been missing for too long a time: cohesion. The Navy and Marine components of the PHIBRON/MAU now are organized and equipped to train together long enough to develop that cohesion, and even carrier battle groups are becoming involved. The Commandant wants this sort of coordinated training and exercising adapted by the Pacific Fleet amphibious forces. Perhaps a joint suggestion by Adm. Carlisle A.H. Trost, CNO, and Gray to Adm. Ronald J. Hays, Commander in Chief, Pacific, calling for integrated carrier battle group-amphibious force operational workups, would be timely.

In this connection, it might be mentioned that it has been demonstrated in the Mediterranean that sailors and Marines aboard amphibious ships have been surprisingly helpful in collecting intelligence of value to carrier battle group commanders.

Major General Carl E. Mundy, director of operations at HQMC, noted during an interview that a carrier battle group and an amphibious ready group had deployed together for the first time last October.

"We've got to tie together better the amphibious forces and the carrier battle groups, because the carrier battle groups don't just chase submarines," he said. "Just 10 years ago that's all a carrier admiral would talk to you about—keeping the sea lines of communication open and strike warfare. Now the *Saratoga* battle group that just went out with the amphibious force—they train together before they get to the Med."

Mundy said that a year ago one would have seen the carrier deploy with its escorts, then a few weeks later the logistics ships and, finally, the amphibs. Now it appears they are all on the same cycle, at least in the Atlantic Fleet.

The Marines believe the general public does not understand the value of amphibious forces to carrier battle groups. Brigadier General Michael K. Sheridan, director of the plans division at HQMC, said that is one reason the Marines have been assigned to strengthen the northern flank of NATO and bolster deterrence.

"We would fight the naval campaign ashore in Norway," he said. "If we lose the airfields in northern Norway, we lose air superiority over the Norwegian Sea. When we lose air superiority, we end up with our ships getting sunk with Exocet-type [cruise] missiles. Air superiority is absolutely essential to maintain both our surface and subsurface campaigns."

Sheridan's point was that, with air superiority, U.S.

Navy P-3 maritime reconnaissance aircraft and other NATO planes would be freer to drop their sonobuoys and aid in the detection and alternate destruction of Soviet submarines.

Marine airborne radars in Norway could see out 200 miles to detect Soviet Backfire bombers and other missile-shooting aircraft heading West from their bases in the northern part of the Soviet Union. The Marine aircraft could data-link their information to carrier-based E-2C Hawkeye early warning aircraft, Aegis anti-missile cruisers, and Air Force AWACS planes in microseconds. And Marine air tankers could refuel U.S. carrier-based aircraft.

Greater Use of Reserves Sought

In the late 1970s a Defense Department study group concluded that a rapidly deployed brigade could help deter a Soviet grab for air bases in northern Norway. Later, a bilateral agreement was worked out calling for the prepositioning in Norway of equipment for 13,000 Marines. This equipment is being stored underground, much of it under hundreds of feet of solid rock. By last October, more than 40 percent of the equipment had been delivered and stored. The initial operational capability to deploy the airlifted Marine Amphibious Brigade is slated for 1989. The plan, of course, would be for the Marines to fly to airfields near the equipment. The Norwegians would provide the transport for the battle-ready Marines to the far north.

Gray says he wants infantry battalions, aircraft squadrons, gunfire liaison companies, force reconnaissance, and "a few other big ticket" units manned up to 100 percent of peacetime allowance.

With total Marine manpower now at approximately 199,500, and unlikely to go higher in view of the shrinking military budget, the Commandant's manpower-costly plans will be difficult to carry out. His proposal to give every new Marine extended combat training in the school of infantry reportedly would require 1,500 additional officers and enlisted personnel to run the program.

Meanwhile, the Corps still is in the process of reversing its decision of a few years ago—a decision driven by manpower limitations—to reduce the size of the infantry squad from 13 to 11 men. And, like the other services, it must reduce the number of active duty officers by 2 percent in the current fiscal year and by 3 percent in fiscal 1989 unless Congress is persuaded to amend the law to drop the requirement.

Nor are these the only pressures on manpower the Commandant faces. The Marines are being called upon to provide more officers for joint-command assignments and increased numbers of enlisted personnel for U.S. embassy security.

In face of this grim prospect on manpower, Gray thinks he may have an answer. For more than a decade he has advocated a greater integration of regulars and reserves. In his new, more influential, billet, he is in a position to speak with greater authority. His aim: to free up a significant number of active duty personnel by turning over additional capabilities to the reserve or, as he puts it, "by further amalgamating" the Selected Marine Reserve with the regulars.

"We think the reserve offers unique possibilities not only to provide another Marine Amphibious Force on mobiliza-

Three LCACs unload their heavy cargo on an Australian beach after speeding to the landing area at 50 knots, and the crew of a Marine amphibious vehicle gets their bearings after swimming ashore.

tion, but also to provide depth in specific capabilities which may be better maintained in the reserve than in the active force," Gray said. "For example, we are looking at the potential for moving active structure of heavy armor, engineer, and maintenance capabilities into the reserve. That contributes to a truly 'total force' concept in which the active forces are prepared for those contingencies short of general war and, on mobilization, reserve forces contribute individuals and units for depth of capability."

"We're going to shed some logistic functions most appropriate to general war to the reserve and use that structure and valuable manning for things such as light armor units, more depth in our infantry battalions, and increased support capability in communications units."

The Commandant added that he was ready "to take a key step" by assigning the drilling reserve to the Fleet Marine Forces for operational and training matters.

Unlike the Army, which under its total force concept relies heavily on its National Guard and reserve for entire units in any contingency, the Marine Corps' three divisions and three air wings do not require augmentation by units, although they might need individual reservists as fillers, depending upon the size of the operation. Marine reserves are attached to the 4th Marine Division and 4th Marine Air Wing and would form a 4th Marine Amphibious Force if it were mobilized.

Questions being asked in this connection include the following: Are four or five 155mm howitzer battalions needed in each of the three Marine divisions? Does each of the three FSSGs (Force Service Support Groups) need three-force motor transport battalions? With the Seabee capabil-

ity available, are three-force engineer battalions in each of the FSSGs really needed?

Although Gray has announced more changes than any other incoming Commandant in memory, it should not be inferred that the Marine Corps is not ready for combat. As a matter of fact, Kelley has probably turned over a more potent, higher quality, better equipped and supplied outfit than any in the peacetime history of the Corps.

"The Marine Corps is in extremely good shape," Mundy asserted as the current fiscal year started. He pointed to the three Maritime Prepositioning Ship (MPS) squadrons in place in the Atlantic, Pacific, and Indian Oceans with fully loaded equipment and supplies to sustain a 16,000-man brigade for 30 days.

Mundy noted, too, that the special operations capable Marine Amphibious Units can now, on six hours' notice, plan and execute a mission in the daytime or at night, good weather or bad, thanks to better training and more sophisticated equipment.

Marines Pleased with LCACs—So Far

Picking up on the same readiness theme, Sheridan said, "We can sustain our people for 60 days." A number of NATO nations find this difficult to believe, he added, because they could keep their forces supplied in battle for only a couple of weeks.

Sheridan also commented on the big plus the Marines get with the addition of two new aviation support ships now in the fleet. These 24,000-ton converted roll-on, roll-off ships, designated TAVB-3 and TAVB-4, provide transportation for a Marine intermediate maintenance activity and aviation supply detachment in support of the rapid deployment of fixed-wing and rotary aircraft. They can support MPS brigades and Marine Air Ground Task Forces (MAGTFs). They each carry 300 Marines, aviation spares, supplies, and mobile facility vans.

According to Lieutenant General Keith A. Smith, then deputy chief of staff for aviation at HQMC, the ships will take the place of a large number of Military Airlift Command C-141-equivalent sorties and will be "far more economical" than the airlift. The big advantage: The ships will permit the Marines to deploy the IMA at the same time the troops are deployed. Once under way to the objective area, the IMA will be able to 'warm up' its maintenance capability.

While the budgets of all the military services have been reduced once again, they are far higher than they were in the years of the Carter administration. As Kelley was the beneficiary of large appropriations in the early 1980s, Gray will be on watch as the munitions, aircraft, and weapons contracted for in the last couple of years flow into the Corps' inventory.

Two new vehicles, one in hand, the other in development, are expected to revolutionize amphibious warfare in the 1990s by making possible an over-the-horizon assault against a strongly held base ashore. These are the LCAC (landing craft, air cushion), and the MV-22A Osprey, a tilt-rotor aircraft that combines the features of the fixed-wing plane and the helicopter.

Gray will see a sizeable number of LCACs delivered to the Navy, but perhaps only one operational Osprey before

his four-year tour is up June 30, 1991. Ten LCACs had been delivered as of late last October and four were under construction. President Reagan requested funds for nine more in fiscal 1989. A total of 107 are programmed.

The job of the LCAC, which rides on a cushion of air atop the ocean's surface, is to transport, from ship to shore and across the beach, personnel, weapons, equipment, and cargo of the assault elements of the MAGTF. It can do so at up to 50 knots while carrying a payload of more than 70 tons. Its range is in excess of 200 nautical miles.

The Marines are quite pleased with the LCAC so far, according to Sheridan.

"In a recent exercise off Australia we used three LCACs and offloaded the ships so fast everyone was amazed," he said. "We just were not used to things operating at 52 miles per hour between the ship and the shore. The LCAC was almost back before we were ready to load anything else into it, before we had anything piled up to put into it. They are even better than we thought they were."

As for the Osprey, which can carry 24 combat-loaded Marines or five tons of cargo 200 nautical miles at speeds up to 300 knots, the Marines are cautiously optimistic that Congress will not stretch out the program because of the budget crunch. First flight for the revolutionary aircraft is scheduled for this summer. Initial operational capability is due in fiscal year 1991, which begins 1 October 1990.

Smith sees the Osprey, which is the Marine Corp' highest priority this year, as "the most dramatic capability improvement" in this decade.

"The big advantage is the extended range it gives us and the flexibility that comes from that range, to say nothing of the payload it can carry," he said. "It will be the next great leap in modern warfare, much like the heliborne assault was over the airborne assault and the jet over the reciprocating engine."

1987 Good Year for Recruitment, Retention

The Corps is in the middle of a modernization of its aviation. New AV-8B Harrier vertical/short takeoff and landing (V/STOL) aircraft and F/A-18 Hornet strike-fighters continue to join the active force, and a vastly improved A-6 Intruder medium-range attack plane (A-6F) is in development. Four Harrier squadrons of 20 planes each and nine Hornet squadrons of 12 planes each were in the active force as of late last year. Current plans are for eight Harrier and 12 Hornet squadrons. Last year, for the first time, two six-plane AV-8B detachments were assigned to forward-deployed Marine Amphibious Units aboard ship.

Marine aviation's night-attack development program is ahead of schedule. The first night attack AV-8B made its initial flight in 1987 with a wide, fixed-field-of-view navigational forward-looking infra-red (FLIR) system, a digital moving map display, and night vision goggles for the pilot. Smith said the night attack package "gives us an immense improvement in darkness conditions."

Adequacy of naval gunfire support has always been of concern to Marine leaders. But 1988 will be a good-news year as the battleship *Wisconsin* completes modernization and joins the fleet. *Wisconsin* is the fourth and final ship of the 58,000-ton Iowa-class in active service. She gives the fleet nine more 16-inch guns for a total of 36.

Amphibious shipping is another story. Progress is being made, but too slowly in the view of HQMC. Although the first LHD multi-purpose assault ship was launched last year, the pace of amphibious ship construction is not likely to allow the Navy/Marine Corps to reach their goal—the capability to lift simultaneously the assault elements of a MAF and a MAB—in the foreseeable future. The 40,000-ton LHD is 844 feet long and has a speed of 22 knots. It will be able to carry LCACs, the Harrier and the Osprey. A contract to build the second LHD was awarded in 1988, and President Reagan has requested funds for two more of these ships—one this fiscal year, the other in FY 1989.

There are 63 amphibious ships in the amphibious Navy today. Planners figure it would take 76 ships of the right types to achieve a MAF-MAB lift. Gray believes it is a mistake to base requests to Congress on what he calls "a programmatic fleet approach," that is, on the one-MAF, one-MAB line. He plans to base his pitch on what the contingency plans of the various commanders in chief of the unified commands—the warfighters—require. It will be interesting to see the congressional reaction to the Gray approach and what effect it might have on the overall naval shipbuilding program.

Recruitment and retention had another very good year in 1987. Recruiters signed up more than 100 percent of their goal despite the shrinking pool of young Americans, and the vast majority of recruits were in the upper three mental categories. Retention of first-tour Marines hit a very respectable 34.7 percent while those with six to 10 years of service re-enlisted at 68 percent and careerists at 92.8 percent. Smith said pilot retention "was the best I've ever seen it."

Even the fears of a deleterious effect of the new Defense Reorganization Act, which Kelley and the Corps opposed with true Marine vigor, were eased as ways were found to address the concerns.

What had worried Kelley most was a provision of the law that consolidated the civilian secretariats and military staffs of the various services. The law gave the Secretary of the Navy sole responsibility for seven functions: acquisition, auditing, comptroller work, information management, inspector general duties, legislative affairs, and public affairs. Kelley feared that, if implemented improperly, the reorganization would prevent the Commandant from effectively managing the Corps.

Sheridan said, in effect, "not to worry," that "all of it was worked out to the total satisfaction of General Kelley" a week before John F. Lehman, Jr. departed as Secretary of the Navy.

Gray, whose appointment as Commandant was strongly advocated by James Webb, Lehman's successor, apparently has established a satisfactory staff relationship with the new secretary and his Pentagon team.

To sum up: Gray has inherited a very good Marine Corps, well-armed and supplied, but he believes it can be better trained and led and its war-winning capabilities enhanced. He has lots of plans, and some of them have high pricetags. Can he achieve them in an era of budget austerity? Can he do "more with less"? He has a little more than three years in which to make the effort. As they say, only time will tell. ∎

MORE BAD NEWS FOR THE BAD GUYS.

New, more powerful engines. More speed. More range. New, more advanced radar, avionics and weaponry. The new Grumman Tomcat – still the *only* fighter in the nation's defense arsenal with the Phoenix missile. Grumman Aircraft Systems Division, Bethpage, Long Island, NY 11714.

Only GRUMMAN

GRUMMAN®

The Role of the Coast
Maritime Strategy Mus

Guard Within the
Not Be Overlooked

By Sidney A. Wallace

Two years ago the U.S. Naval Institute published "The Maritime Strategy" as a supplement to its magazine *Proceedings.* This slim publication—less than 50 pages—contained articles under the by-lines of the Chief of Naval Operations, Commandant of the Marine Corps, and Secretary of the Navy, together with a bibliography oriented to contemporary U.S. naval strategy. While bits and pieces of developing maritime strategy previously had appeared in various unclassified periodicals, this was the first authoritative exposition on the public record of a strategy, carefully developed over several years, that was intended to shape programmatic decisions affecting naval forces.

This unclassified version of the nation's maritime strategy caught the attention of the national press, especially the disclosure that attacks on Soviet submarines armed with nuclear ballistic missiles would be vigorously prosecuted in a non-nuclear war. This and other features of the maritime strategy have been subject to public debate ever since. Little attention has been paid, however, to the role of the U.S. Coast Guard in support of certain features of the maritime strategy. Clearly the Coast Guard has a role to play, given its tasking with respect to the Maritime Defense Zone (MDZ) commands and its other missions to be pursued in wartime as extensions of peacetime functions. And if the maritime strategy is a key element in shaping programmatic decisions for the Navy and Marine Corps, it is reasonable to conclude that it should be a key element for Coast Guard programs as well, at least those programs directly relevant to Coast Guard missions that have strong national defense orientation.

How should concepts of the maritime strategy be applied

to Coast Guard programs? When they are applied retrospectively, how do Coast Guard programs measure up in light of strategic goals? What needs to be done to improve the situation? This essay seeks answers to these questions.

The chain of programmatic decision making that starts with program sponsors in the warrens of Coast Guard headquarters culminates in Congress with enactment of appropriations bills. Seeing the Coast Guard through the process has become particularly agonizing for its leaders in recent years. The very setting promotes the agony: the Department of Transportation budget basket (function 400) contains grant programs that the administration wants to shut down and the Congress wants to nourish. Result: the Coast Guard comes up short so rapid transit and Amtrak can flourish. Is the function 400 problem getting worse, endangering the health of the service, or is it a chronic condition merely to be endured? Does it affect the Coast Guard in ways that impair military readiness and capabilities? A look at the FY 1988 budget may provide some clues.

From the budget, the discussion will turn to two other topics, the Maritime Defense Zones (MDZs) and the U.S. icebreaker fleet. Both embody the melding of peacetime and defense functions of the Coast Guard, and thereby illustrate the dynamic relationship between Coast Guard and DOD, and especially the Navy.

While an examination of these issues may not disclose wholly new directions that should be taken by DOD, Navy, and Coast Guard in working out the Coast Guard defense role, some arguments for change emerge. These are presented as conclusions, to be viewed, as the preceding discussion should be viewed, in light of the maritime strategy.

Excruciating problems peculiar to the Coast Guard's budget process afflict its champions year after year; yet, in

the end, sufficient funds somehow become available to run the service and even make occasional modest improvements. Participants in the process suffer through it, often staring into the face of disaster and seldom allowing themselves the luxury of confidence that "it will all work out." Indeed, one of these years a confluence of negative forces may occur and it will *not* work out, with major reductions in operating forces the result. Should that happen, the nation would be the poorer for it, for few institutions on the American scene offer the return on the taxpayer's investment that the multimission Coast Guard delivers. Worse yet, a comparatively small but very sensitive component of the national defense structure will be weakened.

From the perspective of maritime strategy, the test of the Coast Guard budget at first blush is sufficiency in those functional areas where the Coast Guard plays a unique defense role. The Coast Guard must be equipped with armaments and the command, control, and communications facilities necessary to function in iis defense assignments, but, more broadly, it must maintain a critical mass of personnel, cutters, aircraft, shore facilities, and peacetime missions if it is to perform effectively in event of hostilities. Sufficiency of the Coast Guard budget is, therefore, an issue with national security implications and maritime strategy importance, an issue with dimensions beyond guns, sensors, and secure communications equipment funded by the Navy.

Budget Picture Vastly Complicated

The Coast Guard budget for FY 1988 has progressed at this writing to the stage where both Houses of Congress have acted individually, but are delaying enactment of a final appropriations bill to deal with cosmic economic forces that afflict the federal budget as a whole. A snapshot of the FY 1988 process to date, together with 1986 and 1987 for comparison, may be found in Table 1. The figures are not as comforting as they may appear at first glance.

The President's 1988 budget proposes $1,906,000,000 for operating expenses (OE), which is the central source of funding year by year for operating ships and aircraft and paying people. The House reduced this amount by $123 million, adding commensurately to mass transit, highway, and Amtrak accounts and assuming that the Coast Guard's shortfall would be made up at least in part by transfers from DOD appropriations. The Senate restored part of the House reduction to Coast Guard OE by levying an across-the-board cut on other Department of Transportation accounts, and refused to assume that any help would be forthcoming from DOD funds. But the Senate also specified that the Coast Guard would absorb the costs of the January

RADM SIDNEY A. WALLACE, an aviator and a lawyer, was chief of Coast Guard Public and International Affairs and later maritime policy advisor to the Secretary of Transportation before retiring in 1979. Subsequently, he served as counsel to the House Merchant Marine and Fisheries Commission. He now is counsel in the Washington office of a New York admiralty firm, and consults on maritime affairs and international relations.

1988 pay raise and operation of two aerostat units transferred from the Customs Service without promised support funding "out-of-hide" adjustments totalling as much as $40 million.

The President's budget for acquisition, construction, and improvements (AC&I) was $278 million, considerably below previous years which had been richly augmented with transfers from DOD appropriations. AC&I is five-year money provided to build buildings, overhaul and refit ships, and purchase new vessels and aircraft. Both House and Senate made adjustments for projects cancelled or delayed, but did no major damage to an obviously austere AC&I budget request.

The $123 million reduction made in OE by the House illustrates a major budgetary problem that goes along with the Coast Guard's status as an agency in DOT. The culprit has been identified earlier as function 400, a budgetary basket that includes all DOD accounts. The congressional budget process places ceilings on all "functions," within which appropriation committees must work. In this case, the House Appropriations subcommittee on transportation decided on funding levels for mass transit, highways, and Amtrak that were considerably higher than those proposed by the President. The subcommittee, constrained by a ceiling based largely on 1987 function 400 appropriation figures (*not* on the President's budget), had to make corresponding adjustments elsewhere within the function. Coast Guard OE came out of this exercise with $123 million less than the President had proposed.

There are two ways to look at the House action on Coast Guard appropriations. From the Coast Guard's point of view, the President's proposed budget was the starting point, and any congressional action that resulted in lower funding was a cut. From the House Appropriations Committee's point of view, the starting point was established by 1987 appropriation levels within function 400. The President's FY 1988 budget constituted a proposal, not a standard against which House actions must be measured. FY 1988 appropriations under function 400 should not be increased to reflect FY 1987 transfers from DOD (function 050).

Regardless of point of view, the House action was a severe blow, and the Coast Guard could only hope for relief from: (1) the Senate within function 400; (2) function 050, courtesy of the House or Senate; or (3) a supplemental appropriation bill some months later. This time the Senate helped, thanks to a higher function 400 ceiling than the House, but the Senate is not always the rescuer; two years ago the Senate cut Coast Guard appropriations $230 million, an action rectified only by infusions of DOD dollars. As to relief this year from function 050, neither the House nor Senate authorized any DOD funding for Coast Guard and no support for such a transfer has surfaced in either appropriations committee. Finally, supplemental appropriations bills are always late and often chancy; this year the prospects are especially uncertain. There are no easy escapes when the function 400 trap springs. For a graphic portrayal of the effects of that trap on Transportation budgets 1984-88, see Figure 1.

This year the federal budget picture is vastly complicated

COAST GUARD BUDGET SUMMARY
(dollars in millions)

	FY 86 Actual	FY 87 Final Approval	FY 1988		
			President's Budget	House	Senate
OE	1,747	1,906	1,965	1,912	1,948
AC&I	594	531	273	269	271
RT	59	65	69	65	66
RDT&E	18	20	20	19	20
Other	379	391	407	408	423
Total	2,797	2,913	2,739	2,673	2,728

NOTES:

Appropriation Accounts:

    OE = Operating Expenses
    AC&I = Acquisition, Construction, and Improvements
    RT = Reserve Training
    RDT&E = Research, Development, Testing, and Evaluation
    Other = Retired pay and miscellaneous small accounts

For FY 1988 OE, the House figure includes $70 million on assumption that amount will be transferred from DOD appropriations. Senate assumes no transfer from DOD.

DOD funding transfers in previous fiscal years:

    OE: $115M in 1986 and $75M in 1987.
    AC&I: $300M in 1982; $300M in 1984; $375M in 1986; and $200M in 1987.

Figure 1

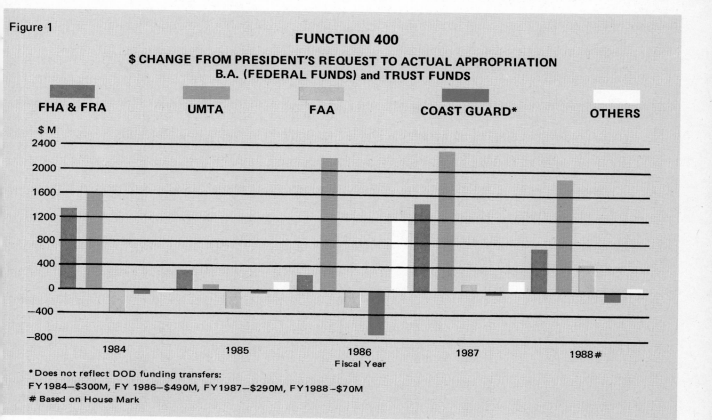

FUNCTION 400
$ CHANGE FROM PRESIDENT'S REQUEST TO ACTUAL APPROPRIATION
B.A. (FEDERAL FUNDS) and TRUST FUNDS

FHA & FRA   UMTA   FAA   COAST GUARD*   OTHERS

Fiscal Year

*Does not reflect DOD funding transfers:
FY 1984—$300M, FY 1986—$490M, FY 1987—$290M, FY 1988—$70M
Based on House Mark

by two developments, an amendment to the Gramm-Rudman-Hollings legislation and negotiations between the President and Congress on deficit reductions. The effect and interaction of these developments cannot be described here, and in any event, their results will be on record by the time this is published. But they are representative of the perils in the obstacle course Coast Guard officials must run when seeking sufficient funds to operate the service and maintain its effectiveness. The lot of Coast Guard leaders is made even more difficult by two facts beyond those mentioned thus far. First, the Coast Guard budget is a very complicated one, especially considering the size of the service. Vigilance is required against tinkering with accounts during the legislative melee that has dire results unanticipated by the tinkerers. Second, with the bulk of appropriations in operations, serious reductions in funding almost always means that ships will be decommissioned, stations will be closed, and personnel will be affected in ways that ransom the future: premature release, stagnation in grade and assignment, curtailed recruiting, and limited opportunities for training.

Finally, it is fair to observe that DOD and Navy do not ordinarily press their appropriations subcommittees to come to the Coast Guard's rescue with infusions of funds from function 050. From one standpoint, that is readily understandable: Defense appropriations are hard won, and transferring function 050 funds to the Coast Guard to make up for function 400 shortfalls means, in effect, that DOD dollars sustain mass transit, Amtrak, and highways. While the House Transportation subcommittee looks at it differently, this critical view is buttressed by press reports that the subcommittee initially planned much larger cuts from the Coast Guard budget on the assumption that they would be made up from defense appropriations. This action was averted by the message from the defense subcommittee that no such largesse was available in FY 1988, notwithstanding the claimed "precedent" of previous years. All this means that the Coast Guard budget process is now so skewed by the function 400 trap that rescue can no longer be expected as a matter of course from DOD deep pockets.

MDZs Are Navy Commands

The CNO's article in "The Maritime Strategy," cited earlier, describes the establishment of Maritime Defense Zones as an "example of cooperative efforts to correct combat deficiencies." Under the Memorandum of Agreement between Coast Guard and Navy, "Coast Guard units combined with naval forces, both active and reserve, will defend harbors and shipping lanes along our coasts in time of war." In another context, the CNO states that "an early decision to place the Coast Guard under Navy command and control will have a major impact on the rapidity with which the strategy can be implemented."

MDZs are Navy commands, headed by Coast Guard area commanders who report to Atlantic and Pacific Fleet commanders when activated for operations and for planning and exercise purposes during normal peacetime, MDZ responsibilities include contingency planning, exercising the plans with regular and reserve forces, and operational command of designated Navy and Coast Guard forces when mobilization occurs.

The MDZ area of operations includes the navigable waterways, port areas, harbor approaches, and ocean areas from the coast seaward to 200 miles. MDZ staffs have a nucleus of active-duty officers from both Navy and Coast Guard, to be augmented upon mobilization by reservists of both services. Forces destined for MDZ operational control when the command is fully activated include most Coast Guard ships, aircraft, and port security units; naval mine warfare units not deployed overseas; airborne mine-countermeasures squadrons; inshore undersea warfare units; explosive-ordnance and salvage detachments as available; and a limited number of frigates, destroyers, and maritime patrol aircraft.

The MDZ mission is illustrated by the following assignment to MDZ Atlantic by CINCLANTFLT:

Plan for and, when directed, conduct, coordinate, and control operations in the area designated as the Maritime Defense Zone Atlantic, as required, in order to ensure the integrated defense of the area, to protect coastal sea lines of communications, and to establish and maintain necessary control of vital coastal sea areas, including ports, harbors, navigable waters, and offshore assets of the United States, exercising both statutory and naval command capability.

The objective of the MDZs, consistent with the maritime strategy, is to ensure the success of the following: (1) SSBNs successfully sortie in accordance with contingency plans; (2) battle groups, amphibious groups, submarines, and support ships deploy unimpeded from U.S. ports when hostilities are imminent; (3) reinforcement and resupply shipping in support of forward deployments safely departs U.S. ports and coastal areas; and (4) safe and secure water transportation of economic cargoes continues from U.S. ports and coastal areas.

The threat with which the MDZ must deal includes the entire spectrum of covert and overt hostile actions that could compromise a port or sink a ship at sea. This ranges from mine and submarine warfare to terrorist attacks to intelligence gathering and special operations.

In the face of these challenges, the Coast Guard must take advantage of every opportunity and every available resource in peacetime to develop expertise and amass experience doing the kinds of things that can readily be applied to MDZ operations in the event of hostilities. This reflects a principle expressed by the secretary of the Navy in "The Maritime Strategy": we train as we intend to fight.

In that context, a major and highly visible mission for the Coast Guard in the 1980s has been enforcement of laws and treaties (ELT), especially the prevention of entry into the United States of illegal drugs through transportation by sea. The scope of operations is illustrated by results over the five-year period, 1982-86: the Coast Guard confiscated over 12.5 million pounds of marijuana and 15,500 pounds of cocaine, seized 886 vessels from drug smugglers, and arrested over 400 persons for activities involving illegal drugs. In FY 1987, over $800 million was spent for the ELT mission, with drug interdiction claiming the major portion. Increasingly, since enabling legislation in 1981, the Navy has participated in drug-interdiction efforts, and joint Navy/Coast Guard operations have yielded excellent results.

An ideal platform for SIGINT, ELINT, ESM, COMINT, et al.

When an air force decides it needs a new airplane to perform a certain mission, it draws up criteria the airplane must satisfy.

In the case of high altitude surveillance and reconnaissance missions, the criteria are certain to include these features:

• The highest levels of technology, such as computerized flight management systems integrated with electronic flight instruments, autothrottles, laser-driven inertial reference systems, and other advanced state-of-the-art systems, so the aircraft and flight crews will perform at peak efficiency and productivity.

• A big cabin, with room for all the electronic and optical sensors required for the most effective gathering of intelligence data, plus the specialists to manage the consoles and the systems.

• Long endurance and high cruise speeds, so missions can last 8, 9, even 10 hours, and cover as great an area as possible.

• Reliable turbofan engines with excellent fuel efficiency.

• High operating altitudes, certainly a minimum of 45,000 feet, so the airplane can operate unrestricted by other traffic.

Now, it may sound as if we're beginning to describe the Gulfstream IV, newest generation of our legendary long range business jets.

We are.

In fact, we can describe in detail how a derivative of the Gulfstream IV will match your criteria for a surveillance/reconnaissance aircraft almost exactly. What's more, we can give you performance data, specifications, price and a delivery date. And you could save your government time and money by talking to us about the Gulfstream IV.

You see, we not only have the platform you're looking for, but we also have it in production.

For more information about maximizing Gulfstream jet aircraft in military applications, contact: Larry O. Oliver, Regional Vice President, Military Requirements, Gulfstream Aerospace Corporation, 1000 Wilson Blvd., Suite 2701, Arlington, Virginia 22209. Telephone: (703) 276-9500.

Gulfstream Aerospace
A CHRYSLER COMPANY

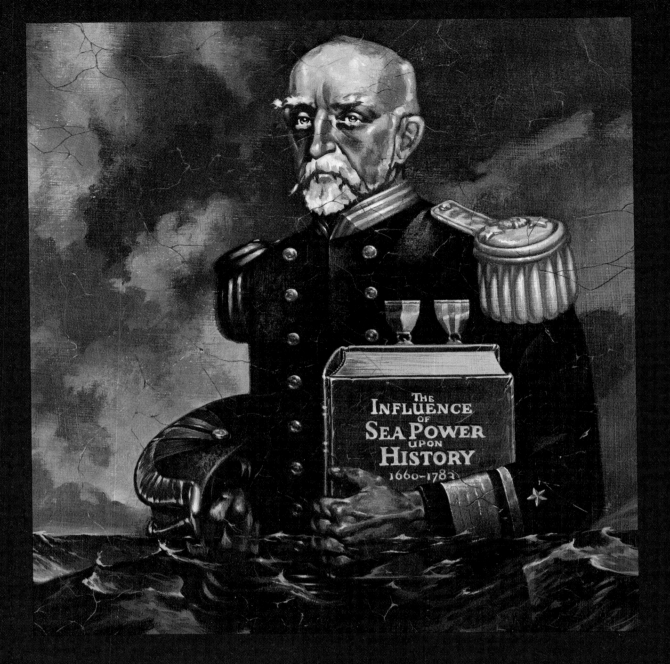

First came the influence of sea power upon history. Now comes the influence of technology upon sea power.

Admiral Alfred Thayer Mahan (1840-1914). A brilliant strategist, whose writings first defined the importance of sea power in the modern world.

It is a tribute to Mahan that his ideas still live, not only in navy tradition and history, but also in the minds of those who will help build tomorrow's navies.

At Autonetics Marine Systems Division, we appreciate the importance of sea power. That's why we're so proud of the technologies we're developing for the U.S. Navy. Our precision navigation and control systems. Our cost-effective shipboard information management. And our innovative undersea warfare programs.

We'd like to tell you more about our commitment to sea power. Write or call Autonetics Marine Systems Division (DA41), 3370 Miraloma Avenue, Anaheim, CA 92803, (714) 762-7775. And be sure to ask for a copy of this specially commissioned portrait of Admiral Mahan.

Autonetics Marine Systems Division
Autonetics Electronics Systems

 Rockwell International

...where science gets down to business

Aerospace / Electronics / Automotive
General Industries / A-B Industrial Automation

Drug-interdiction operations in many ways constitute ideal training to fulfill military readiness requirements in general and prepare for MDZ duties in particular. Operations are fast-paced and continuous; command, control, communications, and intelligence (C³I) functions are exercised in demanding conditions, where the unexpected is the norm and tight security is the standard. Multiunit, multiagency task-force operations are planned, conducted, and analyzed on a regular and frequent basis; force, including use of weapons, is frequently required. Vessels, aircraft, and their crews are tested in all-weather, high-demand, and often unforgiving conditions, and all the while the enemy is real, dangerous, and anxious to elude detection and apprehension. In short, the drug war at sea in many ways qualifies as the real thing. Certainly drug interdiction, properly conducted, requires the application of military principles, skills, and hardware in real time and conditions, and its training value in preparing forces for hostilities is immense.

Sen. Sam Nunn (D-Ga.), chairman of the Senate Armed Services Committee and of the Permanet Subcommittee on Investigations (PSI) (Governmental Affairs Committee), sponsored an amendment to the defense authorization bill, passed in the fall of 1986, that required the President to focus on what the Senator called "a war going on at federal level, federal agencies against one another," by assigning lead agencies in the several areas of responsiblity. In a speech to a law-enforcement group in Atlanta, Nunn described disputes between the Drug Enforcement Administration (DEA) and the Customs Service about respective roles in law enforcement, both domestic and international, and between the Customs Service and the Coast Guard about respective roles in the maritime area. Nunn's recommendation was that DEA should have responsibility for foreign and domestic law enforcement, Customs responsibility for the border, and the Coast Guard responsibility for offshore. He described the Coast Guard, a military organization with law-enforcement powers and expertise, as the "perfect link" between assigned DOD assets and the national drug-enforcement effort. He said that the idea behind the legislation was not to create a new agency, but properly to organize those already in the business.

Opportunities Lost to Coast Guard

The President's designation of lead agencies in the maritime area, based on a 11 May Memorandum of Understanding (MOU) between Customs and Coast Guard, fell far short of the goals Nunn had in mind in proposing his amendment. It failed to bring order out of the chaos among federal agencies that impelled the amendment in the first place.

From the military readiness perspective, the accommodation made last May between the Customs Service and Coast Guard seemed to be rife with lost opportunities. The main features of the arrangement are as follows:

• Coast Guard to be lead agency in the maritime area from the shoreline seaward, but Customs jurisdiction is recognized in the contiguous zone.

• Customs to be lead agency for the land border of the United States.

• Joint responsibility for airspace. Rotating command

for the Miami air C³I center, staff to be provided on a 50-50 basis (surface command centers remain under agency control). Coast Guard lead agency for detection assets. Customs lead agency for tracking and apprehension assets. [Note: Customs detection assets (aerostats, E-2Cs, and P-3s) ostensibly are for use on the U.S.-Mexican land ("southwest") border. When aircraft are no longer needed for the southwest, they will be turned over to the Coast Guard. Coast Guard will provide eight HU-25 Falcon aircraft for use as tracker/interceptors.]

In sum, the Coast Guard does not have sole responsibility for the maritime area. Far from it. Customs expects to range far offshore in its air-interdiction role, and has operations on the surface that extend far outside customs waters. Air interdiction in the maritime area is to be controlled by a joint C³I center, operating independently of Coast Guard command.

The 11 May MOU was the culmination of a contest between the two agencies over which would do what in the drug-interdiction realm. The dispute had been elevated to the cabinet-level National Drug Policy Board (NDPB), but the board apparently preferred not to decide the case on the merits, but charged the agency heads with finding a solution. The MOU displays the characteristics of a deal cut between contestants of equal strength, with some features more optically appealing than they are functionally effective, and some ambiguities that paper over problems rather than solve them. The MOU does contain some provisions on how resources are to be provided and managed. How well that works will be demonstrated in time, and will depend on how well the parties live up to the deal that was struck.

The opportunities were lost to the Coast Guard, to the MDZ commands, and ultimately to the DOD and the cause of national defense. In a non-political world driven by national security needs and principles of rational management of limited federal resources, the drug-interdiction assignment in the maritime area would have gone to the Coast Guard, on the sea, over the sea, and, as the need arises, under the sea. The decision would have been based on the area of responsibility (AOR) concept and on the nature of the problem measured against the character and capability of the agency. As it turned out, the MOU split responsibilities for the maritime area, and did it in ways that guarantee involvement of both agencies in similar tasks both on the surface of the sea and in the air over it. One could argue that nothing is changed, the turf fight continues, but now it is more formal, and resolution is delayed indefinitely.

The blame for the fact that the Coast Guard was not assigned complete and unalloyed responsibility for drug interdiction in the maritime area cannot be laid at the Coast Guard's door. It seems evident from press reports alone that the Coast Guard fought the good fight, but received insufficient support from the right quarters to carry the day. Strong support from DOD could have made all the difference.

The assignment of the maritime area to the Coast Guard as a drug-interdiction AOR when it is already an MDZ AOR, makes eminent good sense. Putting maritime law enforce-

The Soviet research icebreaker Otto Schmidt. The Soviets have a fleet of four nuclear-powered icebreakers, with three more under construction, and a large number which are conventionally powered. Their already formidable capability to operate with great effectiveness in the polar regions continues to grow rapidly.

ment surveillance and tracking resources in the hands of the agency that, at a stroke, could devote them to maritime defense purposes, seems inescapable as a good management decision. But this was not to be. No officials, other than Coast Guard leaders, made the national defense argument in favor of assigning the Coast Guard entire responsibility for drug interdiction in the maritime area. No such official offered convincing argument on the Coast Guard's MDZ role; on its status as an armed force; on its military character with all that implies as to methods, management, and means of problem solving, on the best bang for the taxpayer's buck. It is difficult to believe, had DOD insisted on purely national defense grounds that the Coast Guard get the maritime area assignment, that the matter would not have been resolved accordingly.

There can be no doubt that the Arctic Ocean is an important operating area for the Soviet navy. The Northern Fleet, based on and around the Kola Peninsula, has one-half of the Soviet navy's submarines, including over one-half of its SSBNs, and about one-fourth of the navy's surface fleet, aircraft, and personnel. With the Soviet's intimate familiarity with Arctic operations, and its warships augmented by an imposing fleet of icebreakers, it was inevitable that the Arctic, affording natural protection from surveillance and ASW, would become a bastion for Soviet ballistic missile submarines.

The Soviet nuclear-powered icebreaker *Arktika* was in 1977 the first surface ship in history to reach the North Pole. This feat was matched in May 1987 by *Sibir*, a sister ship of *Arktika*. A third ship of the class, *Rossiya,* now is in service, and a fourth is under construction. The continuous, level icebreaking ability of the Arktika-class ships is eight feet at three knots. The journeys of *Arktika* (since renamed *Leonid Brezhnev*) and *Sibir* to the Pole are noteworthy for more than the records set. They demonstrate the abilities of these ships and their crews to navigate through extremely difficult conditions of ice and weather, to do so on a sustained basis toward specific predetermined positions, and to employ a highly effective means of ice reconnaissance.

The Soviets still operate the older nuclear-powered icebreaker *Lenin,* and are building at least two new icebreakers with nuclear power, longer but with shallower draft than the Arktika-class ships. This Soviet nuclear-powered fleet will have immense capability and versatility, year-round and in heavy ice. The nuclear fleet is backed up by a large number of oil-powered icebreakers, some of which are classed as polar and others as sub-Arctic. All told, this fleet should be able to maintain a presence virtually anywhere in the Arctic the Soviets really want to be. In early configurations, the Arktika-class ships had weapons installed. Armed or not, their ability to work with and for the Northern Fleet in a variety of military assignments is abundantly obvious.

The CNO's article in "The Maritime Strategy" takes note of Soviet activities in the Arctic. Indeed, while no mention is made of details like icebreakers, a chart depicts a large section of the Arctic, well north from the Kola Peninsula, as an area where Soviet naval exercises take place on a frequent basis. Included later is a statement that the United States has begun exercising its submarines in the Arctic where they might be called upon to execute portions of the maritime strategy.

The early history of the U.S. icebreaker fleet is not particularly germane to this discussion except for one point: The U.S. national interest in the polar regions has never been doubted, and for many years after World War II the size of the icebreaker fleet kept pace with demands for services. At some undefined point, perhaps in 1965 when the Navy and Coast Guard agreed that the Coast Guard would operate all polar icebreakers for the United States (then eight in number), national interest in sustaining the strength of the icebreaker fleet began to flag. A hard look at polar icebreaking requirements was taken in the early 1980s, manifested by an interagency report in 1984, but since then the icebreaker fleet has slid into steep decline.

The interagency study recommended that the United States operate four polar icebreakers in order to meet re-

quirements in both Arctic and Antarctic regions. The Coast Guard felt that five were required to allow for contingencies, but received no support for that view, even from the Navy. With the decommissioning of *Glacier* in 1987, the size of the fleet is now four. Two of the ships, *Polar Sea* and *Polar Star,* were commissioned in the 1970s, but the two Wind-class ships date from World War II. The Wind-class ships will require massive infusions of funds to keep them running, and, even so, estimates that they will last five more years are admittedly brave. As no funds for new icebreakers have yet been appropriated, it seems likely that the Winds will pass from the scene before their replacements appear. Look for a two-ship icebreaker fleet in the early 90s.

NSF Sought A New Deal

That is not the worst of it. Getting the money to buy two new icebreakers to round out the U.S. fleet at four will not be easy. OMB [Office of Management and Budget] continues to look at the world through glasses focused on one year at at time, and money for one icebreaker equals Coast Guard AC&I in a good year (without DOD transfusions). Furthermore, there may be other ways than buying a ship for the Coast Guard to obtain one, like leasing, an idea that flourished for a while in 1987. Leasing sounds good to

OMB because it stretches out the capital costs over a long period, probably to be paid out of OE, instead of shocking the budget system with whopping AC&I requests added to whatever else the Coast Guard needs to buy that year. The Coast Guard, of course, prefers its own design and prefers to own and operate the ship in the traditional style, although Coast Guard officials say they will look at the leasing alternative if significant cost savings can be shown to result.

All of this slows down the icebreaker acquisition process. The general budget crunch makes it easier to justify keeping the Winds going just a few years longer, and, after all, taking a look at the leasing idea takes a while, and it can hardly be dismissed out of hand. Result: to date no President's budget request for funding for a new icebreaker, although one suspects the Coast Guard has been urging OMB to let it happen in order to meet the congressional mandate to get going on two new icebreakers that was included in an authorization bill soon after the 1984 report was released.

Enter the National Science Foundation. The NSF is in charge of scientific efforts in the Antarctic region, and was a member in good standing of the interagency group that studied polar icebreaker requirements. NSF supported the conclusions found in the 1984 report: four icebreakers needed, Coast Guard to operate them, users to pay according to a schedule related to demand.

In 1987 the NSF sought a new deal. It now wants its own icebreaker. Through a surrogate, ITT Antarctic Services Inc., a request for proposal was published, seeking to lease a research vessel with icebreaking capabilities. Operation under U.S. flag is preferred, but other flags may be proposed by the bidder. The ship will operate exclusively in the Antarctic, and will be expected to serve scientific purposes only. Space, facilities, accommodations, and support systems for scientists and their pursuits must be fully commensurate with the ship's purpose—i.e., first class.

The Coast Guard hopes the efforts by the NSF to get its own icebreaker will not derail Coast Guard plans to replace the Winds. NSF says the Polar-class ships are not suited for the NSF mission, neither are the Winds, and programs cannot wait for new Coast Guard ships to enter service. Sailing in a Coast Guard ship is not that great anyway, because of its missions that interfere with scientific programs, inadequate science facilities, and a crew too numerous and too authoritarian for comfortable relations to develop.

The U.S. Navy, which was, of course, a member of the interagency study and signed off on the 1984 report, does not seem to insist on very much. At a July hearing on icebreakers before the House Subcommittee on Coast Guard and Navigation, the principal Navy witness made a number of important points, including: (1) the two Polar-class icebreakers meet Department of Defense needs in the Arctic, for resupply and research tasks now and for whatever comes in wartime; (2) four polar icebreakers will satisfy national requirements; i.e., defense in the Arctic, non-military purposes in the Antarctic; (3) the Navy prefers that U.S.-flag ships be used for scientific purposes, but will in this case defer to the NSF, which has the lead in the Antarctic; and (4) the Soviet Union has the largest polar ice-

breaker fleet in the world with over 10 ships; the United States comes in second with four.

Summing up, the situation today may be described as follows. The 1984 interagency report concluded that the United States needs four polar icebreakers (the Coast Guard said five). The size of the icebreaker fleet now is four, two of which are suffering from over four decades of heavy wear and tear. DOD says that the two newer Polar-class ships will suffice for defense purposes in the Arctic. The Coast Guard wants two new ships to replace the old ones. NSF wants to lease its own icebreaker for the Antarctic. OMB thinks leasing should be considered by the Coast Guard, but the Coast Guard is reluctant. Prospects for buying new ships are dim because money is very tight. If icebreakers are important, the United States is in trouble.

What to do? One thing that should be done is to re-examine the level of icebreaker support needed to satisfy the maritime strategy, given Soviet capabilities in the Arctic theater and U.S. operations there. If that re-examination discloses that the icebreaker fleet, given its prospects for the immediate future, will fall short, the DOD should crank that into its program-analysis process. Out of that should come a programmatic decision: fund icebreakers or do without.

DOD Should Focus on Arctic

The foregoing discussion drives at two related main points. First, the support of the Coast Guard by the Department of Defense and the U.S. Navy falls short when viewed through the glass of the maritime strategy. Second, whoever pays the bill, the maritime strategy should be taken into account when making programmatic decisions affecting the U.S. Coast Guard. A third point, implicit rather than explicit, is that change is needed before senseless, long-term damage is done.

The Coast Guard is a force in being, funded mainly for its peacetime missions, notwithstanding its permanent status as one of the armed forces of the United States. If the Coast Guard is equipped and funded to cope fully with peacetime assignments, it requires very modest additional means (minuscule by DOD standards) to be ready for war. In its area of capabilities and expertise, the Coast Guard offers high-quality defense services at bargain basement prices. If those defense services can correct combat deficiencies that would otherwise exist, DOD should pay the increment, and be glad of the bargain.

DOT, OMB, and appropriations committees should face up to the Coast Guard's defense role. A way out of the function 400 trap should be found so that the budget for the Coast Guard and its interrelated missions *can be viewed as a whole*. The Coast Guard's part in effecting maritime strategy should not be held hostage to grant programs. The question should not be how much to take from this or that function, but how much the Coast Guard needs to do its total integrated job. This does *not* imply that analysis of proposed program funding should be any less rigorous than today.

The strength of the U.S. icebreaker fleet, in light of the maritime strategy, is an issue demanding renewed attention at DOD, preferably as part of a broader concern: the Arctic as a theater of operations. Certainly, DOD needs will not be entirely met by U.S. icebreakers in coming years unless something is done. Perhaps it will take a notorious event to demonstrate the perils of allowing the U.S. icebreaker fleet to atrophy. In any event, DOD should focus on the Arctic, and soon. In the meantime, Coast Guard efforts to obtain funding for replacement icebreakers need real support from DOD, not just views hedged to avoid the inference that DOD should help pay the bill.

The Coast Guard survives year after year of budget battles and occasional interagency struggles, but survival requires extraordinary efforts by its officials and its supporters in both the executive branch and Congress. Lately, budget calamities have loomed almost as often as appropriation hearings, and disputes about agency jurisdiction have arisen where logic and precedent suggest there should be no contest. Perhaps that state of affairs will continue, as change in the order of things is so hard to effect in Washington, but surely the possibility of change for the better should not be dismissed out of hand.

What about OMB review of the Coast Guard? Presently the Coast Guard budget falls under the authority of the associate director for economics and government. Another associate director presides over national security and international affairs. Where does the Coast Guard best fit? It simply makes more sense for the Coast Guard to be considered in light of national security and international issues than within the mix of transportation and commercial issues.

A broader proposal for change was recently advanced by Rep. Robert W. Davis (R-Mich.), who is ranking minority member of the Committee on Merchant Marine and Fisheries (the authorizing committee for Coast Guard) and a member of the Armed Services Committee. Davis introduced H.R. 3299, a bill that would establish a "Federal Maritime Administration" in the Department of Transportation and place within it the Coast Guard, which would be expanded to include NOAA's marine functions, and the present Maritime Administration. The new administration would be headed by an undersecretary for maritime affairs and readiness, who would serve as the primary liaison to DOD for maritime readiness matters relating to DOT. The bill provides that DOT, in consultation with OMB, shall recommend methods for consolidating in a single budget function all budget authority relating to the Federal Maritime Administration, including the military programs conducted by the Coast Guard.

Davis, introducing the bill, spoke of his concern that the defense-readiness mission of DOT is not getting the attention it deserves within DOT and of his parallel concern that DOD is not sensitive to the important defense role played by DOT agencies.

The ideas behind H.R. 3299 are powerful, and Davis's concerns are shared by many in Congress. "If it ain't broke, don't fix it" does not apply where something is clearly broken. Perhaps hearings on the Davis bill will highlight the problems and pave the way for constructive change. Here is an instance in government where a little corrective action applied in a timely manner will pay rich dividends, for maritime defense and for an overtasked Coast Guard. ∎

Marine Excellence

The Cincinnati Gear Company has set the standards for high performance marine gears by specializing in surface hardened and precision ground epicyclic and parallel shaft diesel and gas turbine driven marine propulsion gears.

Product Leadership

PHM

JETFOIL

H.M.S. SPEEDY

- The PHM/Jetfoil/H.M.S. Speedy, (with CODOG drive) made by Boeing Marine Systems, all have gas turbine drives. For the LM-2500 or 501.

- The American Enterprise crewboat was built by Halter Marine, Inc., with a 501 gas turbine drive.

- The T-AO 187 class fleet oiler made for use by the Rapid Deployment Force has the largest carburized and hardened and precision ground gears in the U.S. Navy.

- AOE-6, built by NASSCO, features two Cincinnati Gear dual input locked train reduction gears incorporating a hydraulic reversing coupling. This marks the first reversing reduction gear of its size in a U.S. Navy surface ship.

- Each LCAC produced utilizes 8 gas turbine powered gearboxes and 24 couplings and clutches provided by CGCO.

CREWBOAT

SURFACE HARDENED AND PRECISION GROUND

T-AO 187

AOE-6   LCAC

Facility and Equipment

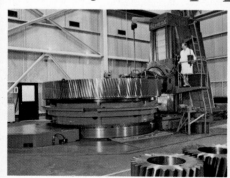

- Precision gear hobbing machine can cut class 14 gears up to 200" in diameter.

- Internal hobbing head attachment for internal gears up to 220" pitch diameter.

- Precision gear grinder for class 15 surface hardened gears up to 158" in diameter by 63" face.

The **Cincinnati Gear** Company 5657 Wooster Pike • Cincinnati, OH 45227 • (513) 271-7700 • telex 21-4568

Now there are three new place
IBM mainframe performance can g

Anywhere you take it, our System/MIL-3
deployable information system gives you
IBM mainframe software compatibility and
proven performance.

Lightweight yet rugged, this militarized
tem satisfies C^{3}I requirements on aircraft,
military vehicles, shelters and ships. Indust
standard mounting features permit it to be

asily installed in a variety of racks or user-transport-
ble cases.

Wherever it goes, System/MIL-370 offers compatible
ardware and software between fixed-site command
enters and deployed systems. System/MIL-370 is a
ew militarized processor, derived from the IBM 9370
nformation System, an IBM MIL PC-AT workstation,
nd other input/output devices — including a remov-
ble media disk drive, magnetic cartridge tape drive
nd printers. The system provides cost-effective data

processing and delivers balanced performance.

Commercial off-the-shelf (COTS) software may be
used with System/MIL-370 to construct applications in
areas such as mission planning, intelligence fusion,
combat information processing, and data reduction.

For further information, contact your IBM marketing
representative or write: Director of Marketing,
IBM Federal Systems Division,
Owego, NY 13827.
Phone: (607) 751-3130.

Federal Systems Division

SOVIET NAVY

Are External Force
Inch Ahead or

Helping the Soviets to the High Seas?

By John E. Moore

Comparisons have been described as odious but, far more importantly from a naval viewpoint, they often are impossible or misleading. This is rarely appreciated by those not directly involved, and this fact is underlined by the frequent question, "Which is No. 1, the U.S. Navy or the Soviet Navy?" When such a query is answered by comparison of the total tonnage of the ships of each navy, comparison of numbers of each ship type, and other equally crass mathematical approaches one can only cry in pain at the depth of ignorance or self interest that prompts these approaches. Any attempt to evaluate the rival merits of two navies must take account of many factors: political and strategic background; intelligence available; command, control and communications (C^3); personnel and training; research and development capability; design and construction capability; deployment and sustainability. These are among the more important elements.

All these must be set against the background of far less tangible matters which reach back into history: morale, determination, and natural reaction to events that are based on a long maritime tradition. When British losses in the Mediterranean were at their peak in World War II, Lord Cunningham, then the Commander in Chief of that station, remarked that while ships could be built in a few years it took hundreds to establish a tradition of naval service. How far such a tradition affects the navies of the two superpowers, both of whom established their fleets in the 18th century, is of importance. The Soviet Union inherited a varied collection of ships at the time of the October Revolution, did little to organize a modern fleet during the subsequent decade, destroyed the senior command in the 1930s, and emerged from World War II with a heterogeneous collection of outdated vessels and little to be proud of in the naval sphere. Thus the tradition of the Red Fleet had scant foundations other than the exploits of a few recent heroes, a rigid political system, and a gulf between the volunteers (the officers and most senior ratings) and the huge bulk of conscripts which are reminiscent of the divide that existed in Tsarist days. This situation has been somewhat modified in the ensuing 42 years, but the basic fact is that a man still is judged on his political reliability as much as his professional prowess.

Because political inclination is considered a matter of individual choice in democracies, the tradition of the U.S. Navy has grown on the basis of its operations during more than two centuries, a far firmer basis than any political ideology. It is a maritime tradition based on service to one's country, one's ship, and one's messmates—a simpler tradition with far more appeal and yielding far superior results than the call to patriotic duty imposed by the followers of a system whose amorphous tenets can mean very little to a three-year conscript from Central Siberia. Pride in oneself and one's service is a powerful impulse and is evident in abundance in the U.S. Navy of 1988. It is a long time since the overall standard of the men and women has been as high as it is today. No question who is No. 1 here.

But tradition is only the skeleton that supports any disciplined service. The flesh and blood and the directing brain must be kept fit and healthy, a task that requires unremitting attention from those in charge. If the funds and facilities granted for this task are inadequate or intermittent, the whole corpus will suffer. Once the Soviet leadership had been persuaded of the value to the state of a considerable fleet, an adequate budget was forthcoming. Once the plan was agreed there was no sudden change of political direction. The aim was accepted and pursued without frequent variations every four or five years. Dissenters are not popular in the Soviet Union and, although the blight of bureaucracy is no less in that country than in democratic lands, a continuity of purpose has produced the goods.

In the United States a band of potential dissenters of great power and influence exists. Congress, with its thousands of staffers and lobbyists, has the power to wreck, alter, support, or delay the best laid plans. As the administration can change every four years and the composition of Congress every two, the goal of continuity is necessarily illusive. Funds for defense, acknowledged by those who framed the Constitution as the prime task of those selected to govern, can be withheld at the whim of a few. Alterations to plans which have taken many professionals many months to produce can be forced through by amateur strategists, tacticians, and ship designers; the pay and conditions of those who are the inheritors of the service tradition can be allowed to deteriorate by a process of default. None of these actions is theoretical; all have happened, to the detriment of the country's defense and will, undoubtedly, happen again. In this sphere the U.S. Navy is very definitely No. 2.

During the last 40 years three tenets of American thinking have been evident, not shared by all but prompted by the size, power, and success of the United States. These are, basically, "Others should be like us," "Others should act as we do," and "Others should be duly grateful for what we do for them." But, unfortunately, "others" frequently don't appreciate American cuisine nor pine after affluence; their religious and cultural backgrounds prompt a very different reaction to events, and gratitude is not one of the world's besetting virtues. Strategy, whether it be political or military, must be based on understanding of the myriad disparate threads that make up the world's design, and it is in this business of "understanding" where many non-Americans sense a weakness. No two countries are truly similar, and within many lie fiery divides. Military strategy depends upon that of the politicians and, if these directors of the country's affairs vacillate, as yet another crisis erupts, the task of the military planners becomes— well, not impossible, but damned difficult. And in the navy those who suffer are the people in the ships. Some 25 years ago Lord Stockton, then Harold Macmillan, Prime Minister in London, used to issue to the service planners a list of 10 planning assumptions designed to cover the next 10 years. They were infinitely valuable, but in those days it was a little easier to forecast the future.

The Soviets have problems similar to those of the United States in understanding other nations and races. The first wave of Soviet troops into Afghanistan used their lorries to ship countless copies of the Koran to their brethren over the border. Perhaps the Soviets have done no better than the Americans in understanding the world's myriad races. It may be an intractable problem, but until it is addressed strategy will be at fault and the ships and people of the two navies will be in the wrong place at the right time.

Ninety years ago George Curzon, a rising and, later, suc-

CAPT. JOHN E. MOORE spent most of his Royal Navy career in submarines. He circled the globe several times in pursuit of information about the world's navies for inclusion in *Jane's Fighting Ships,* which he edited for 15 years, until retiring from that post upon completion of the 1987-88 edition. He also is the author of numerous books and articles about sea power.

cessful politician, commented to the British House of Commons, "I do not exclude the intelligent anticipation of facts even before they occur." This is an extension of the "understanding" problem; "intelligent anticipation" depends on a great deal of hard work spent on the analysis of every available snippet of information culled from a variety of sources, both covert and overt. Intelligence analysis is a highly professional occupation not to be taken on lightly by all and sundry. "Give me the facts and I'll make up my own mind" may be a necessary approach when instant decisions are called for, but it is too often a recipe for disaster under normal conditions. The gathering, collation, and analysis of intelligence precede the final estimation of the probable course of events, the "intelligent anticipation" referred to by Curzon. But the road to success is strewn with hazards, not least of which is the built-in secrecy of many intelligence organizations and the dangers of overclassification of the final product so that it fails to reach the user most in need. This process can be compounded if a number of agencies are involved and their various estimates are not adequately integrated. There are few things more confusing for a user than to find, once he has laid hands on the product, that he is faced with a variety of estimates. In certain cases such diversity of views is not surprising but the end result should at least show some measure of unanimity; otherwise, the agencies are bucking their responsibilities. The reasons for this are not hard to find; some are variations in approach and expertise, vested interests, and lack of communication during the processes of analysis and estimation. The larger the number of agencies, the bigger each is allowed to become, the greater the danger of this undesirable situation arising.

No Love Lost Between GRU and KGB

The Soviets have two main agencies, the GRU and the KGB. No love is lost between the two, but each has its own task to perform. In the United States, apart from the six major agencies concerned with providing estimates, a number of smaller ones deal with more specialized subjects. This very large and diverse community, designed to provide background for both political and military strategy and initiatives, has become unwieldy, bringing the danger of clogged channels and less than timely intelligence.

But, and it is a very important "but," when a coordinated estimate of future trends is reached, the community has no means of ensuring that the users do, in fact, take note of what has been so laboriously produced. The process of selective employment of intelligence, in which use is made of only those sections of an estimate that support a pre-determined course of action, is not uncommon. The result is a lowering of intelligence morale and the encouragement in some areas of individual initiatives, either of dissemination beyond normal bounds within the country or to the agents of other states. Whichever way the cards fall the main sufferer is the country's security. Polygraph tests may help in plugging the leaks but, until there is a coordinated approach to intelligence, until the necessity of secrecy at controlled levels is acknowledged, until those charged with physical and document security are presented with a manageable task, then efficiency will suffer. A distinguished Chief of

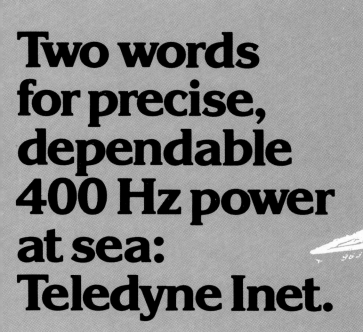

Two words for precise, dependable 400 Hz power at sea: Teledyne Inet.

Teledyne Inet has air cooled, solid state Frequency Converters to support your shipboard electrical requirements — 10 kW to 20 kW and 110 kW to 210 kW.

When the U.S. Navy selected our new 110 kW air cooled 60/400 Hz Frequency Converters for their DD963, 993, FFG, BB, AOE-6, LSD and LHD classes of combat vessels, we were proud — but hardly surprised. Because our entire family of Frequency Converters are the most reliable converters on the market, with demonstrated MTBF of 90,000 hours in fleet operation — more than twenty times greater than the U.S. Navy's specification requirement.

But more importantly, Teledyne Inet Frequency Converters have a low acquisition cost, and a low life cycle cost due to their high efficiency, reliability, and easily-maintainable modular design.

With these and other advantages like parallelability for increased power and redundancy and an established logistics support network, it's no wonder the U.S. Navy selects Teledyne Inet.

Proud? Of course we're proud of our new family of air cooled Converters. But we're Teledyne Inet. And we're already working on the next challenge.

▼ TELEDYNE INET   ...the precise power people

Making certain of where they are and who and what is around them are Soviet naval officers on the bridge of a Petya I-class frigate.

Naval Operations once remarked, "If Congress continues to castrate the Navy I must have more and better intelligence to provide a basis for future protrams and current deployments."

The second of these requirements leads the argument into the field of command, control, and communications (C^3). Reams have been written on this subject but the main requirement of C^3 remains the same today as it has been for generations: a timely response to an expected or actual situation. The nub of the problem is "timely," and the increased speed of everything connected with naval affairs, the swollen number of individual states whose reactions to situations are uninhibited by the accepted standards of international behavior, the huge number of small but lethal terrorist groups, all combine to reduce the time available for decision making. Whereas an admiral once had minutes to make up his mind, today this period often can be measured in seconds. Delay can be fatal.

The Soviet system of command has been evolving steadily, but their methods still are inhibiting to initiative. On land they have an organization based on military districts with a series of "fronts" for use in war. Coordination of operations relies on internal lines of communication and, although there is a fair measure of redundancy in radio nets, the land-line system is far from satisfactory. At sea the fleets have access to all standard methods of modern communications ranging from ELF to VHF, but the prime question is how much freedom of action would be delegated down

the line. There are reports of greater freedom for commanding officers, but habits die hard and those who might benefit from such relaxations are, and will be for a generation, those who were brought up under the old restrictive practices.

In the past, in the U.S. Navy the command system exercising control over the fleets at sea was tolerably well known. Today a proliferation of commands has encouraged the new designation "Commander in Chief of the month." Operations in the Persian Gulf are supplied with ships from many sources as requirements increase. The overall command within the Gulf is that of a Marine general in the southern states while, beyond Hormuz, Commander in Chief, Pacific holds sway. Overall surveillance of affairs rests with a number of high-placed officers of state and the military forces in Washington. What is important here is that the magnificent and instant web of communications available to these people should not be used for micro-management of those who are eight or nine time zones away, in the midst of a sandstorm and uncomfortably hot and tired. This has ocurred in other areas in the past and probably will not be repeated by the present hierarchy. But the danger exists, and any such interference would produce a cause and effect. The cause would be doubts as to the aim and the rules of engagement; the effect, a dampening of initiative and morale. If there is no repetition of what has gone before, command, control, and communications should be to the advantage of the U.S. Navy.

Soviets Well Placed in Personnel Area

One area in which the Soviet authorities are reasonably well placed is that of personnel. With a large population and a three-year conscription period for junior ratings, there is not only a steady intake but a considerable reserve of recently trained men. The first six months of service constitute the normal training period, but a significant proportion of the intake, all of whom have been brought up from kindergarten (with deviations from the norm in areas more distant from Moscow) in the worship of Lenin and military arms, will have been through preliminary courses with the military youth program of DOSAAF. The remaining 2½ years probably will be spent in one surface ship, although the cream will be drafted to submarines. The amount of sea experience which these men will receive during their service will vary markedly. The submariners may well top the bill, while surface sailors will come far lower in the program. Despite the high visibility of foreign deployments, these employ only a small proportion of the total numbers, while recent exercises have been conducted much closer to home waters than was the case a few years ago.

Lack of experience is probably of more significance for the volunteer element, the officers, warrant officers, and senior chief petty officers. The load on this group is considerable because of the inexperience of almost all the junior ratings. Maintenance can be entrusted to only a small proportion of the personnel and must be supplemented by base staffs to a marked degree. The officers are highly trained technically but are, necessarily, very specialized in their approach. Long periods in the same ship narrow their vision and the previously mentioned curb on initiative prob-

ably results from uncertainty about the reaction of individuals to freedom of action. One Soviet ship observed entering harbor had an admiral, the captain, the executive officer, and the previous captain on the bridge simultaneously, each with his own view of the arrival plan. Where the navigating officer fitted in is not recorded.

Personnel problems in the U.S. Navy stem from very different causes. Recruitment and retention of enlisted men and women is the nub of the problem. No matter how good the officer corps, a ship relies very largely on the skill and enthusiasm of the lower deck. With a steady increase in the Navy from 479 ships in 1980 to 555 in 1987 and 600 by 1989, there is an urgent call for an equally impressive rise in personnel numbers. This includes the Reserves. This has been managed satisfactorily since the disastrous levels of pay and other conditions were dealt with around 1980. However, service pay raises currently lag behind the average civilian increases and other elements are on the borderline. Any fall in recruitment and retention rates resulting from congressional cheese-paring will start a vicious circle of inefficiency: fewer men to man increasing numbers of ships in the fleet, fewer ships at full operational readiness, greater domestic separation, further reductions in recruitment and retention, and a fall in personnel efficiency.

Two congressional initiatives may yet blight the officer structure. The call for an increase of representation in the Joint Staff billet has resulted in legislation that will decrease overall efficiency by providing an element in the Navy in which staff work will override the need for sea experience for an unacceptable proportion of naval and marine officers. Combined with proposed cuts in the total number of officers in both services this could have a serious effect on the operational strength and efficiency of the fleet. All aspects could suffer; lack of practical operational experience in staff planning, reduced complements in ships and Marine Corps units, reduction in training capability, reduction of the number of recently experienced officers for the fleet and Marine Corps in a crisis, are only some of these. A high proportion of time on a shore staff with 3½-year assignments is a sure recipe for reducing the operational capability of a fighting service.

When this congressional action runs concurrently with the second plan, to diminish the overall numbers of officers by two and three percent in the next two fiscal years, there could well be trouble ahead. The proportion of officers to enlisted men is 1-7 in the Navy, 1-9 in the Marine Corps, 1-6 in the Army and 1-4½ in the Air Force. To apply an arbitrary percentage reduction in such circumstances will cause far greater disturbance to the naval and Marine forces than to the other services, and this will come at a time when there are more ships to man than today. As the Joint Staff legislation will be biting into seagoing strength by removing officers to Washington for long stints, those who remain to man the fleets will be in danger of longer periods of family separation than now. At present an average of only six percent of Air Force officers are absent for more than six months in the year, less than nine percent of Army officers, and more than 22 percent of Navy officers. In the lower two officer grades the proportions are even more significant —five percent Air Force, 11 percent Army, 15 percent Marines, and over 30 percent Navy. It is up to Congress to reconsider its ideas, to abjure rule-of-thumb decisions, and to realize that it is pushing the Navy into second place.

Technology Advances Many and Rapid

Needs for experience and training of the people in a navy are directly linked with the technological state of the fleet. A flotilla of canoes with outboard engines requires marginal skills; a flotilla of modern ships with increasingly complex propulsors and weapon systems calls for maximum ability. But, in a rapidly changing technical world, there is no place for complacency and the comfortable feeling, "Haven't we done well?" While self-congratulation is inhibiting advance, the likely opposition is stealing the good ideas, developing them and marrying them to his own discoveries. The Soviet Union is adept at this process, and only a cursory inspection of the advances made in the Red Fleet during the last 20 years will show how far and how fast advances have been made. Research and development must be among the top priorities of the U.S. Navy if it is to maintain its present undoubted technological lead.

Well-Tested Design Has Many Advantages

A number of points emerge during the editing of a book such as *Jane's Fighting Ships.* Those that spring clearly to mind—the increasing complexity and capability of the ships, and their vastly increased prices—overshadow the problems that some navies have in deciding what the tasks of their fleet might be and, therefore, the types and numbers of ships that are needed. That this is a vital area of decision making is underlined by the fact that the period between conception and commissioning of a new class of ship may be anything from 10 to 15 years and the life of that ship may be 30 to 45 years. If a large number of ships of a particular class are built over, say, a 10-year period the validity of the original concept and design will be tested over a period of 55 to 70 years. This would be manifestly absurd if the original equipment and weapon systems were retained, so each class undergoes a major modernization/conversion at various points in its career. In the case of aircraft carriers this is understandably expensive as new and heavier aircraft have to be accommodated, with resultant improvement in elevator, launching, and landing facilities. But modern technology has reached the point where modular equipment of advanced capability can be and is being produced to replace older systems within the same spaces; these range from propulsive machinery to computers and communications.

The point here is that a basic hull with its associated machinery may be used for a number of purposes. These two items cost less than 40 percent of the total outlay in the majority of shipbuilding countries and, if they do not, they should. Thus a basic and well-tested design which has a comfortable margin for top-weight variations, an internal capacity adequate for sufficient fuel for long ranges and variations in weapon load, and good sea-keeping capabilities, would result in considerable savings in design and construction effort as well as spares and stores. Not only would a class of this description be of value to the building country, but it would also provide a source of revenue for exports, with an inevitable reduction in unit costs.

Babcock & Wilcox. Earning our stripes in America's defense.

...ponents and control systems ...the USS Nautilus, the world's ...nuclear powered ship.

...On the morning of January 17, ...5, the Nautilus cast off all lines ...radioed her historic message, ...derway on nuclear power."

Within months she would break virtually every submarine speed and endurance record. Her global odyssey would carry her under the seven seas and on the first voyage in history across the top of the world passing submerged beneath the North Pole.

During 25 years of service, the Nautilus would steam half a million miles on nuclear energy, making the fantasy of Jules Verne come alive. And Babcock & Wilcox would help make the saga possible . . . every league of the way.

Babcock & Wilcox

goal of building and maintaining a strong defense. That's the B&W defense team. Earning our stripes for the Army, Navy, Air Force, and Marine Corps.

For more information, write Babcock & Wilcox, Manager, Defense Marketing, 1735 Eye Street N.W., Washington, D.C. 20006. Or call (202) 296-0390. Babcock & Wilcox, a McDermott International company.

...ey "Network 90®" provides state-of-...art monitoring and control for defense

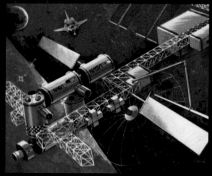

B&W is developing space and ground based reactor designs for military and commercial

While this approach has not been adopted by the Soviet Navy, the Soviets have, at times, produced large classes of ships designed for specific purposes. In some cases these have been modified to include new weapon systems, but the general trend has been towards larger hulls carrying increased loads of more diverse sensors and weapons systems. Whether this tendency will change if the allocation of funds for naval construction is more limited in the future remains unclear but the proliferation of types and classes has become a habit that may be difficult to break.

Soviet Submarines: Formidable Fighting Vehicles

This is particularly true of the Soviet submarine program in which improvements on basic originals such as the Yankee and Victor classes have given way to the side-by-side development of a whole crop of new designs. These are now running parallel to improvements on earlier classes while the purpose of such a variety remains an enigma. Were there major differences in size it might be thought that some were designed for specific tasks such as anti-submarine warfare, but three smaller submarines recently completed are, apparently, trials boats for various purposes. One of the areas in which considerable effort has been expended is that of propulsion allied with new methods of boundary-layer and turbulence control. The use of gasification and polymers long has been evident, while compliant coatings on the hull have increased in thickness and complexity during the last 20 years. Using double hulls has provided two advantages; protection for the inner hull and the damping of sound emissions. The combination of the results of a mass of scientific inquiry has resulted in a major reduction of sound signatures, and increases in speed, diving depth and weapons capacity. The modern Soviet submarines are formidable fighting vehicles; the main query as to the effective use of this force is the quality of the crews that man them.

ASW at Forefront of Any Commander's Considerations

The main task of the U.S. Navy lies in providing counters to this Soviet force. This is essential if the merchant shipping on which the industry and armed forces of the country depend are to be protected, a fact that is too often forgotten. A navy's job is to protect shipping whether the cargoes be mercantile, troops, or amphibious forces, and to inhibit the ability of the opposition to use the oceans for the same purposes. Because the stealth of submarines renders their destruction the most difficult part of this protective task, ASW remains at the forefront of any commander's considerations. From the strategic viewpoint the deployment of fleets, submarines, and aircraft must place those elements in the most advantageous positions for mutual cooperation and for the use of available sensors and weapons. Overcrowding in restricted sea areas can well result in interference with one's own forces. Major carrier forces are not designed as effective ASW groups and need to be routed accordingly. Anti-submarine hunting groups can be wasted in the pursuit of a quarry whose position is uncertain and whose existence is problematical. The surest methods of detection are to concentrate the most effective ASW platforms, submarines, on the likely transit routes and the surface and air forces in the vicinity of likely targets.

The area around a convoy or major force that requires investigation is probably about 300 miles in radius, and this requires a major concentration of ships and aircraft. The nuclear-propelled cruise-missile and torpedo-attack submarines that threaten the target will have a speed advantage over all current surface ships, although use of this speed will provide a sound source for passive sensors. This will provide initial contact, but the ships with towed arrays streamed are themselves speed limited, and the prosecution of such contacts will fall to the lot of other, unencumbered, ships and aircraft, both fixed-wing and rotary. Improved silencing and higher quiet speeds have made this task increasingly difficult; constant training under operational conditions is essential if success is to be achieved. The current world situation in which global deployments disrupt such programs does nothing but harm to ASW teamwork.

The three prongs of the ASW trident all have their problems in the U.S. Navy. A proportion of the shortage of 470 nuclear trained officers from lieutenant commander through captain affects the submarine force, which also is suffering a reduction in the retention of petty officers. In the air world as of late 1987, there are 142 too few ASW helicopter pilots and, in the fixed-wing arena, had a shortfall of 28 carrier ASW pilots and 171 maritime patrol pilots. Although all sea-going billets in surface ships are fully manned, these figures show little veer-and-haul and a precious small back-up.

The conclusion from these figures is that the ASW problem is suffering from over-stretch, which militates greatly against efficiency. All these facts are available to the Soviet planners who must view with satisfaction present congressional plans to reduce the naval officer corps, an action that will, if fully implemented, reduce the total to less than that of FY 1983 despite the addition of 46 ships and 15 air squadrons since that year.

Surface/tactical air operations are two aspects of naval warfare that have been inextricably linked for 45 years, a lesson the Soviet Navy has been slow to assimilate. The spindle on which the surface-action element of the U.S. Navy rotates is the requirement for 15 deployable aircraft carriers. The impetus behind the new construction program associated with these ships is the protection of these essential centers of naval air power against attack from the air, the surface, and the subsurface. By the very nature of ships all types and classes are vulnerable if struck by large explosive charges. They will sink if they lose stability or buoyancy. The ultimate aim is to prevent their being struck, and in this respect the advent of Aegis has placed the U.S. Navy in an unrivaled position to detect and repel surface and air threats. Subsurface problems already have been mentioned, but these need close integration with all other aspects, and one returns, inevitably, to the necessity for effective and well trained C^3. In all these respects the Soviet navy is lagging and this must be of concern to the Kremlin.

Small Wars Will Continue to Erupt

Ten years of this century have been occupied by wars on a global scale, 14 years by limited but vicious conflict in the circumscribed areas of Korea and Vietnam, while, in the last 45 years, some 250 local wars have taken place. In 80

USSR Attack Submarines

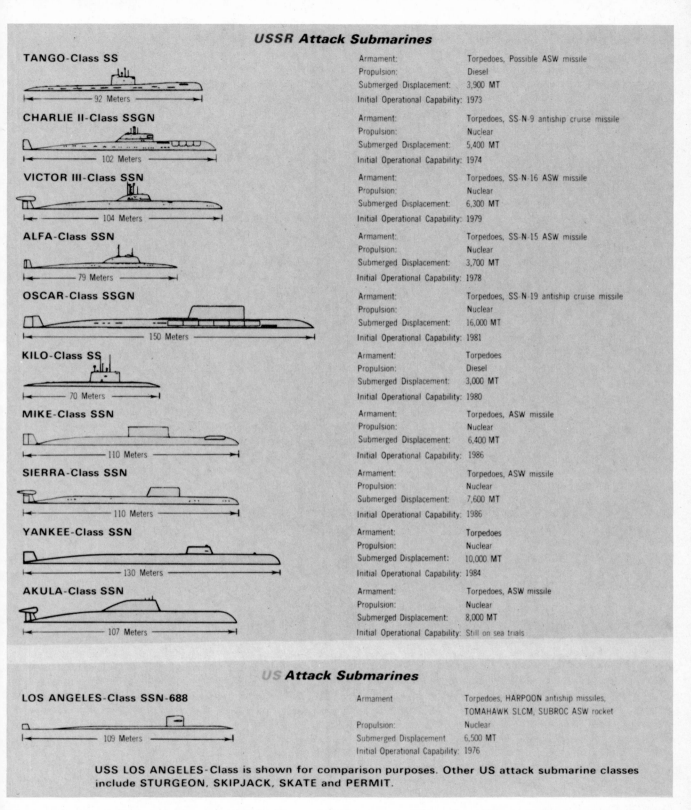

TANGO-Class SS — 92 Meters		
Armament:	Torpedoes, Possible ASW missile
Propulsion:	Diesel
Submerged Displacement:	3,900 MT
Initial Operational Capability:	1973

CHARLIE II-Class SSGN — 102 Meters		
Armament:	Torpedoes, SS-N-9 antiship cruise missile
Propulsion:	Nuclear
Submerged Displacement:	5,400 MT
Initial Operational Capability:	1974

VICTOR III-Class SSN — 104 Meters		
Armament:	Torpedoes, SS-N-16 ASW missile
Propulsion:	Nuclear
Submerged Displacement:	6,300 MT
Initial Operational Capability:	1979

ALFA-Class SSN — 79 Meters		
Armament:	Torpedoes, SS-N-15 ASW missile
Propulsion:	Nuclear
Submerged Displacement:	3,700 MT
Initial Operational Capability:	1978

OSCAR-Class SSGN — 150 Meters		
Armament:	Torpedoes, SS-N-19 antiship cruise missile
Propulsion:	Nuclear
Submerged Displacement:	16,000 MT
Initial Operational Capability:	1981

KILO-Class SS — 70 Meters		
Armament:	Torpedoes
Propulsion:	Diesel
Submerged Displacement:	3,000 MT
Initial Operational Capability:	1980

MIKE-Class SSN — 110 Meters		
Armament:	Torpedoes, ASW missile
Propulsion:	Nuclear
Submerged Displacement:	6,400 MT
Initial Operational Capability:	1986

SIERRA-Class SSN — 110 Meters		
Armament:	Torpedoes, ASW missile
Propulsion:	Nuclear
Submerged Displacement:	7,600 MT
Initial Operational Capability:	1986

YANKEE-Class SSN — 130 Meters		
Armament:	Torpedoes
Propulsion:	Nuclear
Submerged Displacement:	10,000 MT
Initial Operational Capability:	1984

AKULA-Class SSN — 107 Meters		
Armament:	Torpedoes, ASW missile
Propulsion:	Nuclear
Submerged Displacement:	8,000 MT
Initial Operational Capability:	Still on sea trials

US Attack Submarines

LOS ANGELES-Class SSN-688 — 109 Meters		
Armament	Torpedoes, HARPOON antiship missiles, TOMAHAWK SLCM, SUBROC ASW rocket
Propulsion:	Nuclear
Submerged Displacement	6,500 MT
Initial Operational Capability:	1976

USS LOS ANGELES-Class is shown for comparison purposes. Other US attack submarine classes include STURGEON, SKIPJACK, SKATE and PERMIT.

percent of these the U.S. Navy has been involved to some extent. Today 100 of the medium and smaller states operate tactical jet aircraft, half that number operate ships and craft with anti-ship cruise missiles, and half again (24) possess non-nuclear submarines. Terrorist gangs now have access to varied arsenals ranging from missiles downwards. Thus any embroilment in localized conflict involves heightened danger of severe damage and the forces involved require a

considerable war-fighting capability. The operations off Libya in 1986 went far to prove this point. However, the British involvement with Iceland in the so-called Cod Wars resulted in damage to front-line ships in engagements that were properly the task of armed trawlers. Somewhere between these extremes lies the possibility of a design which, while having sufficient effectiveness for a high proportion of low-intensity conflict could, with rapid enhancement of its equipment, play a significant role in major war. This is by no means an untried policy; several European and Warsaw Pact navies have adopted this line, not only for use in coastal waters but also for global deployment. The result could be the provision of a major hull and propulsion package capable of carrying Aegis (the *Spruance* (DD-963) design is an example) and a second design of some 2,500/3,000 tons which, taking advantage of modern technology, would have a far lower through-life cost than normal and whose loss or damage would have a much reduced impact on the Navy's overall capability. This approach has been examined by the U.S. Navy in the past and discarded, but since then more capable hull forms which are cheaper to build have been evolved and shipbuilding costs restrained by competitive tendering. Maybe the cash is unavailable and Congress would fight shy of such an approach. But small wars will continue to erupt, the responsibility of the U.S. Navy will not diminish, and highly competent and extremely expensive ships will be in positions of risk. Such an outcome could be to the satisfaction of any potential foe.

Marine Corps A Fully Integrated Force

The Soviet Navy has a very different approach to amphibious operations from that of its American counterparts. The Naval Infantry is less than one tenth the size of the U.S. Marine Corps and makes use of a much smaller number of far less sophisticated landing ships and craft. This results from a philosophy of use in which the Naval Infantry is maintained as an elite force for comparatively small intervention operations by the groups attached to the four widely dispersed fleets. While training for such tasks, they also act as a training cadre for specially selected army units which would provide the bulk of any major landing force. The transport of such a force would fall to a proportion of some 100 merchant vessels of the ro-ro, ro-flow, barge-carrier, lash type ships which have been built during the last 13 years to naval standards of communications, weight-carrying, wash-down, ECM/ESM etc. This is a formidable force with a total lift capability of about 10 divisions if all ships were available simultaneously. However this is rarely, if ever, the case, and any major concentration of these ships would be a sure indicator of the likelihood of amphibious action.

The U.S. Marine Corps, on the other hand, with an unbroken tradition of intervention operations spread over 200 years, is a fully integrated force with a personnel strength outstripping that of most standing armies, a modernization plan which has replaced a high proportion of equipment over the last five years, and with imaginative plans over the next 10 years for extra equipment ranging from the V-22A Osprey tilt-rotor aircraft to reverse-osmosis water purification units and man-packed satellite navigators. From the amphibious-lift viewpoint, naval programs are advancing toward the goal of transporting simultaneously a Marine Amphibious Force of some 50,000 Marines and sailors and a Marine Amphibious Brigade of some 16,000. With the ongoing procurement of the 40-knot, 60-ton-load Landing Craft Air Cushion (LCAC) towards a target of 90 such craft and the introduction of the 250-knot Osprey in the 1990s to replace the medium assauult helicopters, the MAF and the MAB will have an unequalled capability for over-the-horizon operations on 80 percent of the world's coastlines. The new Wasp-class LHDs and Whidbey Island-class LSDs are vital elements in an amphibious lift which has fallen from 162 active ships in 1967 to 63 in 1987, all of which currently would be required for the simultaneous MAF/MAB lift. The use of the three Maritime Prepositioning Squadrons in the Indian Ocean, Pacific, and North Atlantic, with associated CH-53E heavy lift helicopters, and the eventual introduction of equipment storage sites ashore in Norway will significantly reduce deployment time, probably from weeks to days. When to this mobility is added the firepower of the fleet, ranging from improved 16-inch bombardment by battleships to the hoped-for introduction of 5-inch semi-active laser-guided projectiles, as well as the devastating capability of the carrier air wings and the Marines' own squadrons of AV-8B Harriers, F/A18 Hornets, A6E Intruders, AH-1W Sea Cobra helicopters, supported by EW, reconnaissance, and tanker aircraft, it is apparent that the combination of U.S. Marine Corps and naval capability is unrivaled. The Soviet forces are lacking one essential element, embarked air. But it must be remembered that, in the event of operations against the northern and southern flanks of NATO, Alaska, Japan, and Southeast Asia, Soviet shore-based aircraft could fulfill a number of these tasks. The balance is heavily weighted toward the American side but the capability of the Soviets is by no means negligible.

Mines Can Remain Lethal for 70 Years

The use of sea mines has been a characteristic of both the Imperial and Soviet Navies for well over a century. Today the Soviet inventory is estimated at more than 300,000 mines of different types. These vary from simple horned contact mines to modern and highly complex weapons that can be laid by ships, submarines, aircraft, merchant ships, or, as has been proved in the Red Sea and the Persian Gulf, suitably converted small ships and craft. Delay mechanisms applied to many varieties, including those actuated by means of pressure, acoustic or magnetic signatures, pro-

The warships depicted in the three photographs right typify the constant progress being made by the Soviet Union in creating a modern, highly capable, formidable blue-water navy. From the top are a Kirov-class cruiser, one of the most powerful warships afloat in the world today; an artist's concept of the aircraft carrier Leonid Brezhnev, now under construction; and an Akula-class nuclear-powered submarine, one of many new classes of submarines built in recent years.

NATO and Warsaw Pact Maritime Forces in the North Atlantic and Seas Bordering Europe 1986*

Category	NATO	Warsaw Pact
Aircraft Carriers VSTOL Carriers	11	—
KIEV-Class Ships	—	2
Helicopter Carriers	6	2
Cruisers	16	22
Destroyers, Frigates, Corvettes	310	201
Coastal Escorts and Fast Patrol Boats	267	586
Amphibious Ships – Ocean-going	57	24
– Other Ships/ Coastal Craft	71	188
Mine Warfare Ships/Craft	270	330**
Total Submarines (All Types)	206	258
– Ballistic Missile Submarines	35	44
– Long-Range Attack Submarines	68	145
– Other Types	103	69
– % Submarines Nuclear Powered	50%	51%
Sea-based Tactical ASW and Support Aircraft Including Helicopters	832	205
Land-Based Tactical and Support Aircraft Including Helicopters	389	527
Land-Based Anti-Submarine Warfare Fixed-Wing Aircraft and Helicopters	462	209

Excludes France and Spain
* US Estimate of 1986 NATO data
** Excludes minesweeping boats and drones

US and Soviet Procurement of Major Weapon Systems 1977-1986

	US	USS
ICBMs and SLBMs	850	3,0
IRBMs and MRBMs	200	1,0
Surface-to-Air Missiles *	16,200	140,0
Long- and Intermediate-range Bombers	28	3
Fighters **	3,450	7,1
Military Helicopters	1,750	4,6
Submarines	43	
Major Surface *** Combatants	89	
Tanks	7,100	24,4
Artillery	2,750	28,2

* Includes naval SAMs
** Excludes ASW and combat trainers
*** Excludes auxiliaries

Naval Ship Construction USSR and NATO *

Ship Type	USSR			NATO		
	1984	1985	1986	1984	1985	
Submarines	9	8	8	12	8	
Major Combatants	9	8	9	19	16	
Minor Combatants	50	50	50	34	30	
Auxiliaries	5	5	6	11	5	

* Revised to reflect current total production information. Inc United States; excludes France and Spain.

Source: "Soviet Military Power 1987"

vide a means of sowing fields long before the date at which their actuation is required. Mines can remain lethal for at least 70 years, as bitter experience in the North Sea has shown.

With these capabilities in mind the Soviet Navy has in service more than 350 mine countermeasure vessels (MCMVs) of varied capabilities, a total larger than the entire NATO force. The years following the Korean War brought an extraordinary flush of MCMV building, triggered by the discovery of a new type of Soviet mine. Hundreds of these vessels were completed for Western navies, but since then many have been transferred to other fleets, broken up, or sold as pleasure craft. The result was that, when these largely wooden-hulled craft were reaching the end of their lives, major gaps appeared in this vital but ignored element of NATO's naval forces. The U.S. Navy was as guilty as any of her allies, and it was not until June 1982 that the first of a new class of MCMVs was ordered. By the end of 1986 the United States had only 21 30-year-old MCMVs, of which only three were on the active list, and seven MSBs, as well as 23 Sea Stallion MCM helicopters. But mine-countermeasures tasks are manifold; clearance of approaches to civilian ports and naval bases, the maintenance of swept channels and feeder routes, and searching offshore in intervention areas and merchant ship channels in foreign waters. For all these tasks U.S. forces are manifestly inadequate, and this fact is based on a dual heresy: that the U.S. Navy will provide the big ships and their allies the small, and that that waters of the continental United States are likely to be immune from a major mining campaign. Because of this process of indefensible rationalization the United States is now vulnerable to a pre-war mining campaign using merchant ships, trawlers, and submarines laying long-delay mines of many types. In such a circumstance the European allies would be in no position to help. If this scenario is considered fanciful, it must be remembered what chaos resulted in the Persian Gulf area from a few antique mines laid in important areas. The awful truth about this form of warfare is that the presence of a few known mines can presage larger fields, thus crippling a whole carefully planned sailing schedule. It doesn't call for large numbers of specialized minelayers to cause untold damage, as those who had business on the east coast of Britain in World War II can vouch. The magnetic mines there were laid by E boats, aircraft and submarines; the result was almost disastrous. In this category of warfare the Soviet Navy holds the whip hand.

Deployment and Sustainability Closely Linked

These two factors are closely interlinked. A simple fact that is too often ignored is that the ratio of support ships to those of the naval force being sustained rises steeply as the distance from base increases. As a fairly typical example, the 36 surface ships of the Royal Navy that took part in the 1982 Falklands campaign, which lasted for 2½ months 8,000 miles from the United Kingdom, were supported by 15 Royal Fleet Auxiliary ships, six RFA manned landing ships, and a helicopter training ship as well as 42 merchant ships taken up from trade—a ratio of almost two support ships for each naval ship.

As has been pointed out earlier, the Soviet Navy has placed great reliance on the merchant shipping of the USSR for support, and the same is true in the field of tanker numbers. Although they maintain some 30-40 support tankers which are mostly short-haul ships, they have only 13 small replenishment tankers, eight large replenishment tankers, and seven replenishment ships. Any gaps in requirements are made up from merchant tankers, although these can do little more than refuel at anchor.

Other forms of afloat support, all of which must be carried out in harbour, include 16 submarine tenders, 17 missile-support ships, 36 repair ships, and 12 miscellaneous support ships. Among the many auxiliaries listed are 85 transports, the great majority of which are coastal vessels. Thus the Soviet fleets have considerable flexibility in support because they have a large number of tenders of various kinds but, most importantly, a firm grip on a merchant navy which is now appreciably larger than that of the United States.

American authorities have appreciated the decline in numbers of both the merchant ships and men sailing under the flag of the United States, and the Ready Reserve Force has been instituted to deal with this growing gap. At present there are about 85 ships which have been purchased and are kept at 5-10 days readiness with a goal of 122 by FY 1992. The stumbling block is whether there will be enough seafarers to man those ships by that date.

This problem does not apply to the Military Sealift Command with its 122 ships, of which 100 are assigned to strategic or direct fleet support. It is these ships which must be available to transport the fuel, stores, and spare parts on which the fleets depend, and it is the provision at base of all these necessities on which the operations of the U.S. Navy finally depends. Stocks have improved markedly since 1981, in some cases by 90 percent. But their provision in the future depends entirely on adequate funding, which in the past has been hostage to congressional quirks. Though screws and spanners hit the headlines only when subject to overcharge, they are vital elements and, if their provision is limited, the U.S. Navy's efficiency will be in question. Sustainability has increased but there is still some way to go. The capacity is there, but fiscal restraints could play havoc with the program.

Congress Has Role in Defense of Country

While it is impossible to make overall comparisons between two navies whose roles and tasks vary widely, there are specific areas in which some conclusions can be reached. In all these cases the Soviet Navy has maintained two notable advantages, political continuity and a steady allocation of funds. An all-volunteer navy such as the U.S. Navy has a far firmer base than the Soviet conscript fleets if recruiting and retention are maintained at a high level. The American building program is providing the right ships in most cases, but no ship can perform adequately unless properly manned. As things stand the U.S. Navy occupies a sound position, but such complex matters as ASW and MCM require unremitting attention. It is up to members of Congress to appreciate their role and to consider how best to discharge their primary task, which is not self-enhancement but the defense of their country.

■

SOVIET GLOB

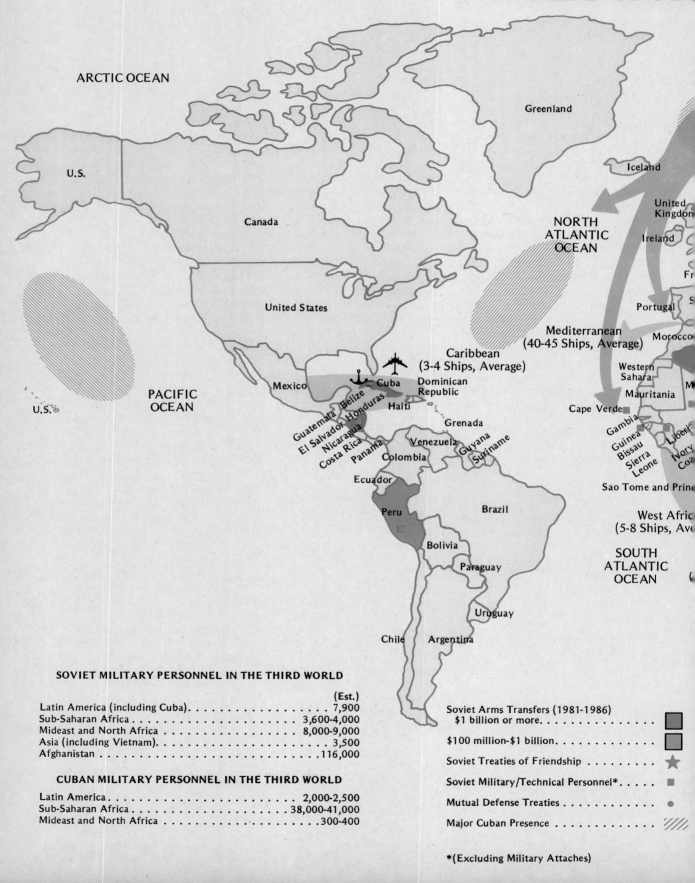

ARCTIC OCEAN

Greenland

Iceland

U.S.

United
Kingdom

Canada

Ireland

NORTH
ATLANTIC
OCEAN

Fr

United States

Portugal

Morocco

Mediterranean
(40-45 Ships, Average)

Western
Sahara

Mexico

Cuba

Caribbean
(3-4 Ships, Average)

Dominican
Republic

Mauritania

Cape Verde

PACIFIC
OCEAN

Guatemala
El Salvador Honduras
Nicaragua
Costa Rica

Belize

Haiti

Gambia

Guinea
Bissau
Sierra
Leone

Liberi

U.S.

Grenada

Ivory
Coa

Panama

Venezuela

Colombia

Guyana
Suriname

Sao Tome and Prin

Ecuador

West Afric
(5-8 Ships, Ave

Peru

Brazil

SOUTH
ATLANTIC
OCEAN

Bolivia

Paraguay

Uruguay

Chile

Argentina

SOVIET MILITARY PERSONNEL IN THE THIRD WORLD

	(Est.)
Latin America (including Cuba)	7,900
Sub-Saharan Africa	3,600-4,000
Mideast and North Africa	8,000-9,000
Asia (including Vietnam)	3,500
Afghanistan	116,000

CUBAN MILITARY PERSONNEL IN THE THIRD WORLD

Latin America	2,000-2,500
Sub-Saharan Africa	38,000-41,000
Mideast and North Africa	300-400

Soviet Arms Transfers (1981-1986)
$1 billion or more. . . . .

$100 million-$1 billion. . . . .

Soviet Treaties of Friendship . . . .

Soviet Military/Technical Personnel* . . . . .

Mutual Defense Treaties . . . .

Major Cuban Presence . . . .

*(Excluding Military Attaches)

OWER PROJECTION

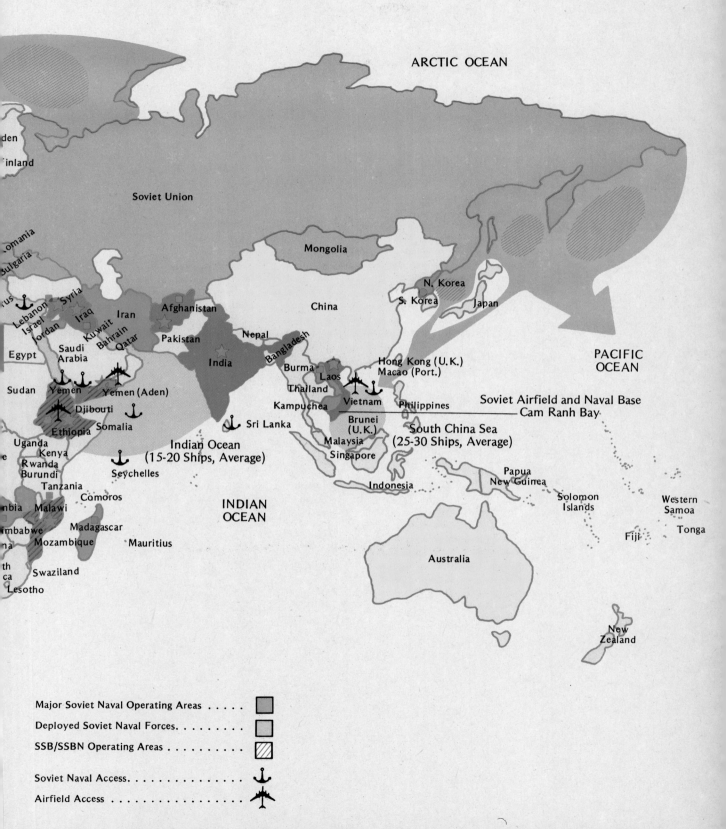

ARCTIC OCEAN

Soviet Union

Mongolia

China

N. Korea
S. Korea   Japan

PACIFIC
OCEAN

Afghanistan

Nepal

Pakistan

India

Bangladesh

Burma

Laos

Hong Kong (U.K.)
Macao (Port.)

Iran

Iraq

Kuwait
Bahrain
Qatar

Saudi
Arabia

Egypt

Sudan

Yemen   Yemen (Aden)

Djibouti

Ethiopia

Somalia

Lebanon
Israel
Jordan
Syria

Thailand

Kampuchea

Vietnam   Philippines

Soviet Airfield and Naval Base
Cam Ranh Bay

Brunei
(U.K.)

Malaysia

Singapore

South China Sea
(25-30 Ships, Average)

Sri Lanka

Indian Ocean
(15-20 Ships, Average)

Seychelles

INDIAN
OCEAN

Uganda
Kenya
Rwanda
Burundi
Tanzania

Comoros

Malawi

Madagascar

Mozambique   Mauritius

Swaziland

Lesotho

Indonesia

Papua
New Guinea

Solomon
Islands

Western
Samoa

Fiji   Tonga

Australia

New
Zealand

Romania
Bulgaria

Finland

den

Major Soviet Naval Operating Areas . . . . .

Deployed Soviet Naval Forces. . . . .

SSB/SSBN Operating Areas . . . .

Soviet Naval Access. . . . .

Airfield Access . . . .

As Its Dynamism Grows, an Upgrading of the Stature of the Pacific is Long Overdue

By Thomas B. Hayward

A consistent feature of America's national security strategy over the years has been its commitment to build and maintain forces adequate to *deter* an attack upon the United States and our vital interests abroad or, failing that, to assure that our forces are capable of fighting and *winning* any ensuing conflict so as to provide an outcome favorable to basic U.S. interests. It is difficult to take issue with a strategic policy as fundamental as this. As a former member of the U.S. Joint Chiefs of Staff, I endorsed this guidance year after year. One can be confident that the current set of chiefs do likewise.

Yet an analysis of the major conflicts in which we have become embroiled over the past few decades suggests that either we do not understand what the guidance really says (which is highly unlikely), or, in order to meet domestic needs perceived to be of higher priority, we prefer to rationalize force-adequacy in terms that understate the level of risk involved and cause us to pursue policies that either do not deter or produce outcomes that meet national interests:

• In 1950, for instance, conflict erupted on the Korea Peninsula which found us with neither policies nor forces consistent with the strategy. We did not deter the North Korean invasion, nor did we win the ensuing battle on terms that achieved U.S. objectives. As a consequence, today we are compelled to station sizeable forces on the territory of the Republic of Korea, expending enormous sums to maintain our forces in a state of combat readiness sufficient to deter, or win, next time around.

• In August 1964, U.S. naval forces conducting what

U.S. Navy sailors enjoy liberty in the Chinese port city of Qingdao. The November 1986 port call by three Navy ships was the first in China in almost 40 years.

was perceived to be a deterrent mission in the Gulf of Tonkin were attacked (though this fact has been strenuously refuted by some, even some who were there), drawing us into the longest war in U.S. history. Can we argue that our presence in Southeast Asia and the policies we pursued there were consistent with the national strategy? It hardly seems so, especially when one is compelled to take into account our ignominious withdrawal in the spring of 1975.

• More recently, in May 1987, we were confronted with the "inadvertent" attack on the guided missile frigate USS *Stark* (FFG-31) while it was conducting a deterrent mission focused on one of the two adversaries in the Persian Gulf war; a war with strategic implications not only to the U.S. vital interests but those of the entire free world. The number of ships attacked in those waters now has passed 330. Of those, more than 50 have either been sunk, run aground to avoid sinking, or scrapped. Ship victims of both Iranian and Iraqi aggressiveness cover the geopolitical spectrum—from the United Kingdom to the Soviet Union, the United States, Japan, and Australia. Consequently, naval forces representing more than six nations sortied to the Persian Gulf in an extraordinary display of collective concern over a long-established strategic principle: freedom of shipping in international waters. Is this the beginning of yet another "limited" commitment of U.S. forces, this time in circumstances that have the superpowers commingled in a precarious way? Is this commitment consistent with the national strategy, and, if so, do we have forces adequate to meet our objectives?

It is not the intention of this essay to explore or critique the application or adequacy of the national military strategy to this latter situation. But given that each of the above conflicts has been or is of direct relevance to Asia-Pacific security, is well to examine these events in light of the importance of a viable U.S. maritime strategy to U.S. and

allied interests in the region. Also of considerable importance is the emerging circumstance in which the U.S. Navy finds itself today—at the onset of being "stretched thin" once again while facing congressional action to reduce further the defense budget, thereby assuring four consecutive years of level or declining financial support at the very time that our maritime strategy takes on more and more significance.

There are factors other than military, of course, that exert a profound influence on the strategic balance in Asia today which merit our intense scrutiny and awareness, namely, regional and domestic geopolitical events as manifested in the unique democratization movement that is evolving (if not erupting) throughout Asia, and the major influence of the economy as seen in the remarkable achievements of Korea, Japan, and Taiwan in particular, with the nettlesome byproducts of trade protectionism and competition of concern to all.

Economic Resurgence Once More Is Evident

A year ago there was an air of credibility to the rationale of those who projected optimism about the strategic situation in the Asia-Pacific region. Ferdinand Marcos and his cronies had been ousted from the Philippines. President Corazon Aquino had acquired a national following that had been unimaginable six months earlier, and signs of an economic recovery already were becoming visible. Korea continued its extraordinary display of economic vitality while President Chun Doo Hwan showed unanticipated willingness to make accommodation with the vocal opposition. Even the Middle East had struck a certain status-quo stance that did not appear especially threatening to the vital interests of regional neighbors. Most analysts justifiably were looking toward increasing economic and political gains progressing in a reasonably stable environment.

The "baker" flag of warning flies much higher on the yardarm today. The 28 August coup attempt by Col. Gregorio Honason in the Philippines not only was much too close to being successful, but became the catalyst that energized other disparate and competitive groups within the Philippine political structure to initiative independent moves for power and influence. In Korea, Chun struggled to maintain cohesion in the government in the face of student and labor factions whose frequently violent actions provided succor and leverage to the political opposition. Meanwhile, the escalation of activity in the Persian Gulf generated ramifications and linkages to East Asian policy that could not be overlooked.

Nevertheless, these factors appear to be attenuated, at least tentatively, by the proposed INF [intermediate-range nuclear force] treaty between the superpowers, which promises the elimination of the threatening SS-20s in Soviet Asia. The Chinese Party Congress, held in late October, reaffirmed

ADMIRAL THOMAS B. HAYWARD commanded the Seventh Fleet in the Far East and the Pacific Fleet before becoming Chief of Naval Operations in 1978. He retired from the Navy in 1982 and now heads his own Honolulu-based consulting firm on Asia/Pacific matters. He travels extensively throughout that vast area.

a course of action perceived to be beneficial to Sino-Western relations. Relaxation of martial law and further "Taiwanization" of the government bureaucracy by President Chiang Ching-Kuo of the Republic of China portends increased liberalization at a time when economic growth continues its remarkable course. Economic resurgence once again is in evidence throughout the ASEAN region. And, despite the severity of trade relationships between the United States and Japan, there is a constructive awareness among many in leadership positions of the importance of containing the rhetoric and reactionary policies—though one must heavily discount the reckless penchant toward politicizing this critical issue by many in the U.S. Congress.

The sum of this leads one to the obvious:

• the Asia-Pacific region continues to be in the forefront of world news.

• it is a major factor in U.S. global strategy as we gain a deeper appreciation of Asia's importance to our long-term national interests.

• it continues to be the most dynamic region of the world in a variety of dimensions.

• it presents enormous potential for providing constructive role models to the Third World in terms of both economic and political development.

The region is so dynamic that it reminds us that the United States must continually reevaluate its national security policies to assure ourselves and our friends that our leadership is not only wise but responsive to *their* interests, as well.

A striking aspect of this Asia-Pacific overview surely must be the sparse reference to the Soviet Union. After all, the Soviets are a major Pacific and Asian power. Their military strength is without question the most pronounced in the region, and concern with that power has dominated U.S. foreign policy. Yet, it is not without good reason that the influence of the Soviet Union on Asian matters has been slighted to this point, for 1987 was a disappointing year for the Soviets in Asia. General Secretary Mikhail Gorbachev's July 1986 Vladivostok speech had been heralded as a major policy statement promising numerous benefits to the wanting countries of East and Southeast Asia. Ironically, none of these countries really has held its breath in the interim; the absence of Soviet impact in Asia over the past 18 months had not gone unnoticed.

This is especially true in Japan. In 1986, Soviet Foreign Minister E.A. Shevardnadze visited Tokyo to lay the groundwork for a basic improvement in relations between these two major powers. He openly implied that Gorbachev soon would be traveling to Japan to confer with then-Prime Minister Nakasone, a projection that has yet to materialize and is unlikely to do so. Not only has the Soviet Union amply demonstrated that it has no economic or political leverage over Japan, but its inept geopolitical savvy is all too evident as it shuts off all prospect of being perceived as negotiating in good faith over the four northern islands claimed by Japan by simultaneously reinforcing its military units occupying this contested territory. Nor can Russia hope to woo the Japanese away from the U.S. mutual security agreement while brandishing its Pacific fleet and Far East air force in exercises clearly directed at Japan, although such crude attempts at coercion could possibly bring

<table>
<tr><th colspan="2" align="center">The Problem of Distances
(in miles)</th></tr>
<tr><td colspan="2">United States to Persian Gulf by shortest air route:</td></tr>
<tr><td>from East Coast</td><td>7,450</td></tr>
<tr><td>from West Coast</td><td>8,150</td></tr>
<tr><td colspan="2">Charleston, S.C., to Strait of Hormuz:</td></tr>
<tr><td>through Suez</td><td>8,250</td></tr>
<tr><td>around Africa</td><td>11,500</td></tr>
<tr><td colspan="2">San Diego to Strait of Hormuz — 11,477</td></tr>
<tr><td>to Singapore</td><td>7,736</td></tr>
<tr><td>to Manila</td><td>6,604</td></tr>
<tr><td>to Sydney</td><td>6,530</td></tr>
<tr><td colspan="2">Lajes Field (Azores):</td></tr>
<tr><td>to Cairo</td><td>3,155</td></tr>
<tr><td>to Dhahran</td><td>4,325</td></tr>
<tr><td>Torrejon Air Force Base (Spain) to Cairo</td><td>1,960</td></tr>
<tr><td>Aswan (Egypt) to Strait of Hormuz</td><td>1,304</td></tr>
<tr><td>Berbera (Somalia) to Strait of Hormuz</td><td>1,350</td></tr>
<tr><td>Mombasa (Kenya) to Strait of Hormuz</td><td>2,500</td></tr>
<tr><td colspan="2">Diego Garcia:</td></tr>
<tr><td>To Dhahran</td><td>2,600</td></tr>
<tr><td>to Strait of Hormuz</td><td>2,500</td></tr>
<tr><td>to Tehran</td><td>2,959</td></tr>
<tr><td>to Freemantle (Australia)</td><td>2,850</td></tr>
<tr><td>to Singapore</td><td>2,227</td></tr>
<tr><td>to Clark Field (Philippines)</td><td>3,445</td></tr>
<tr><td colspan="2">Singapore:</td></tr>
<tr><td>to Honolulu</td><td>5,881</td></tr>
<tr><td>to Al Basrah (Iraq)</td><td>3,916</td></tr>
<tr><td>to Port Said</td><td>5,018</td></tr>
<tr><td colspan="2">Cape of Good Hope:</td></tr>
<tr><td>to New York</td><td>6,801</td></tr>
<tr><td>to Sundra Strait</td><td>5,164</td></tr>
<tr><td>to Straits of Florida</td><td>6,784</td></tr>
</table>

Source: Distances from Ports, Defense Mapping Agency

the Japanese to think less comfortably about its American security arrangement. There is little prospect of a major improvement in the Japanese outlook towards the Soviet Union as long as Gorbachev continues to pursue the policies of his predecessors while professing glasnost to the politically naive.

Russian Objectives Seen to Be Missing the Mark

Most analysts suggest that Gorbachev's Vladivostok enunciations were directed largely towards China in anticipation that, through token accommodation of the "Three Obstacles," the Chinese could be drawn into a revitalized relationship with their Socialist brothers. In truth, despite Gorbachev's offer to negotiate the disputed border issue on the Amur-Ussuri rivers, as well as to make some cosmetic withdrawal of Soviet troops from Mongolia, nothing of merit has been achieved, nor do the Chinese believe it likely for the future. Expectations in Beijing initially may have been high in some circles, that Gorbachev's overtures constituted a serious initiative, but the discussions and negotiations with the Soviets throughout 1987 convinced most Chinese leaders that little has changed. Consequently, China is now in the driver's seat with respect to the pace of improved relations between these two giants, given the urgency with which Gorbachev evinces a need to "buy some time" to

direct his priorities internally. The Soviets must be prepared to undertake significant force reductions along the common border, a reduction of at least 20 divisions, if they are to prevail in their desire for greater Sino-Soviet harmony. Such an accommodation hardly is likely in the current setting.

Where the Soviet Union seems to have made some visible progress and attracted the attention of many Pacific nations has been in its policies toward the South Pacific island nations. Kiribati and Vanuatu are cases in point. Not exactly household words in the American lexicon in years past, they rapidly are becoming so as Soviet successes become ever more apparent. Consequently, there is a much greater awareness of the strategic importance of these island states to western interests today—finally. Almost as a direct result of the cooperative fishing agreement between the Russians and Kiribatis in 1985-86, the United States became serious about amending an inflammatory policy which had protected U.S. tuna seiners poaching in South Pacific EEZ waters by ultimately negotiating a reasonably sensible compensation package. All in all, Soviet influence to date has not caused undue alarm, but it is enough to alert Australia, New Zealand, and the United States that these traditionally friendly nations, long considered aligned with the Western world, no longer can be so assumed. The Soviets unwittingly have done us a favor while gaining little in the process. Our task now is to keep it that way.

Elsewhere, Russian objectives are seen to be missing the mark. On the Korean peninsula, the Soviets have been noticeably unproductive in their relationships with the Democratic People's Republic of Korea, where by virtue of adding to North Korea's military strength they weaken North Korea in its feeble efforts to project a more positive image to the rest of the world. Vietnam continues to be a substantial economic drain and draws frequent criticism from the ASEAN countries, inhibiting Soviet overtures to improve relationships there. And in Afghanistan, Soviet promises to begin the withdrawal process are seen as a sham and lead to further distrust of Russian proclamations that they desire to "do better in Asia."

In essence, 1987 was not the year for Gorbachev to gloat over Soviet achievements in the Asia-Pacific region. However, of one thing he can remain certain—the Soviet Union is an Asian power, and a mighty one. The Soviets continue to invest heavily in its enormous military structure in the region, both conventional and nuclear. This fact is lost on no one, especially those in China, Japan, and the United States. A bankrupt economic system and an ideology that has lost its attractiveness thus are offset by persistent efforts to pose as a major military force to be reckoned with. Significantly, herein lies the justification and rationalization for major U.S. forward presence, in consort with effective alliances. Though it is seldom stated these days by the Asia-Pacific nations, it is well understood that it is the U.S. military presence, and especially naval power, counter-balancing Soviet posturing that has accounted for at least two decades of relative security during which the nations of Asia have been able to exploit their economic talents, accounting much for the dramatic record of economic development achieved throughout the region.

While "Japan bashing" became a favorite pastime of the

U.S. Congress in 1987, as agitation over the trade imbalance mounted, with little sign of abatement despite the dramatic adjustment of the yen-dollar exchange ratio, the Japanese body politic became highly sensitive to the adverse fallout from the "Toshiba Affair" and the crescendo of American and European criticism. Consequently, Japan's emerging sense of nationalism, framed by its recently acquired pride in advanced technology accomplishments, and its widely heralded superiority in manufacturing expertise, struggled for adequate expression against the realization that, with its emergence as the world's second largest economic power and dominant creditor nation, Japan must take on heftier "international" responsibilities, like it or not. Nakasone had a clear sense of this obligation. Thus, for instance, he called upon the Japanese people to share financially in keeping the sea lanes open in the Persian Gulf (not that this sacrifice did not serve Japan's self-interests as well), hoping thereby to deflect almost certain complaints that once again Japan was getting a "free ride."

Simultaneously, however, he was wise enough to recognize that Japan's obligations had certain limits, that direct employment of elements of the Japanese Self Defense Force in the Persian Gulf, as some suggested, would have set off alarm bells everywhere. For what has become increasingly obvious is that, though required by constitutional mandate to adhere to a non-belligerent status, Japan has, with considerable U.S. encouragement, developed "self-defense" forces increasingly able to respond to situations elsewhere though designed solely to meet national defense needs. It is, in fact, this very increase in military capability that stirs concerns in Asian capitals regarding Japan's ultimate intentions, and leads to the refrain well known to U.S. military planners, "How much is enough?"

Annually, the Japanese Defense Agency submits to the government a defense white paper, "Defense of Japan—19XX." It is available for all to peruse, much as the U.S. secretary of defense's annual report is circulated worldwide. In it the Japanese have made it clear what threat they are up against and what forces are considered appropriate to meet self-defense obligations. U.S. concurrence has been implicit. Thus, widespread public discussion through much of 1987 on such investments as Japan's next-generation fighter, FSX, its rumored plans to acquire the Boeing AWACS, and the desire of the JMSDF to initiate construction of a new class of air-defense-capable (AAW) destroyer equipped with the Aegis-like weapon system, all at enormous cost, accentuate the relevance of the how-much-is-enough debate.

The principal issue is, of course, the "remilitarization" of Japan claimed by some as explicit in the 1987 breach of the "1 percent Gross National Product barrier" which had for so long been a political nemesis. The 1 percent GNP limit decided by the National Defense Committee and the Cabinet in November 1976, and long endorsed by the Japanese public, had been meticulously adhered to by successive governments. The policy attracted persistent U.S. criticism that Japan was not contributing its "fair share" and thereby was being subsidized by the American taxpayer while Japan's economy was unleashed to become the most dynamic in the world. U.S. Pacific military commanders were not hesitant to put frequent pressure on the Japanese to expand its level of investment beyond 1 percent, more specifically to meet the defense objectives espoused in the white paper on a much more aggressive schedule than generally apparent. Nakasone astutely recognized that failing to address valid U.S. concerns on this issue would only compound the difficulties confronting Japan and the United States. Consequently, breach of the 1 percent barrier was permitted to occur, albeit by only the narrowest of margins, (1.004 percent), with its implied commitment to continue modernization of the Japanese armed forces.

But within hours after public notification by the Japanese government that the 1987 Defense Agency budget would surpass 1 percent the likes of no less a strategic guru than former Secretary of State Henry Kissinger, in a profoundly alarming op-ed article, decried the move—"The Japanese are Coming!" It could come as no surprise when the Russians capitalized on the opportunity to denounce Japan's reversal of its long-held security policy, criticizing the United States for abetting it, and drumming up further international concern over aggressive U.S. policies in Asia. The Chinese were much less visible in their evaluation of this move, but the tenor of their comments took on a distinctively more negative tone than before. Even privately, the Chinese no longer were prepared to suggest that Japan's armed forces were not troubling. The remilitarization of Japan has become a real issue, one we anticipate will be frequently debated in the months and years ahead.

1987 Not An Easy Year for South Korea

As long as the remilitarization question remains visible and debatable by all parties with a valid interest in security and stability in Asia, the more likely the Japanese Self Defense Force will retain its *defensive* characteristics and the less likely the Japanese will be perceived as threatening to their neighbors.

From a balance-of-power perspective, it is difficult to do other than applaud this policy shift by the Japanese government, given the commonly accepted and overriding strategic policy objective of "deterrence first" on which the Western strategy has so long depended. Certainly from a U.S. perspective, we would find it difficult indeed not to endorse a policy that virtually assures Japan's continued emphasis on major modification and improvements to its air defense, for example.

Over-The-Horizon-Radar [OTHR], AWACS, getting on with design and construction of an FXS in consort with U.S. industry, upgrading command-and-control systems, including the use of space, all make eminently good sense and are properly focused on the threat sector to the north and northeast. In the context of the maritime strategy, can there be any doubt remaining that U.S. naval forces are overcommitted and undersupported when one considers the national demands in Northeast Asia, Southeast Asia, and far into the Indian Ocean? A Japanese Maritime Force that can do much towards fulfilling its pledge to meet its vital sea lane defense out to 1,000 miles while becoming ever more interoperable with the U.S. 7th Fleet can only be encouraged. In this context, Japanese attainment of an Aegis-variant destroyer is of tremendous importance toward improving its

The submarine-based Exocet deterrent.

Anti-surface warfare credibility now begins below the surface — if you're equipped with the new SM39 Exocet.

Housed in an underwater launch module, the SM39 can be fired from a standard submarine torpedo tube.

The SM39 orients itself towards the target while submerged.

Then it leaves the water, pops up just 30 meters while separating from its launch module, and skims to its target at a height of less than 5 meters.

Payoff? Dramatically reduced vulnerability to enemy detection and countermeasures.

And the same combat-tested accuracy that has made Exocet the most celebrated weapons system of its type in the world.

aerospatiale

DIVISION ENGINS TACTIQUES
2, rue Béranger - 92322 Châtillon Cedex - France

CYALUME® LIGHTSTICKS...ON STATION

Damage Control: With an Allowance Change Request that puts 50 into each ship's Damage Control Repair Stations, 6″ Hi-Intensity lightsticks deliver 360° of instant bright light — without batteries or electricity.

NSN 6260-01-074-4230

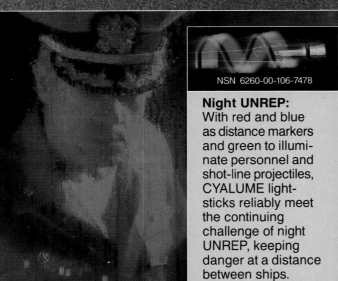

NSN 6260-00-106-7478

Night UNREP: With red and blue as distance markers and green to illuminate personnel and shot-line projectiles, CYALUME lightsticks reliably meet the continuing challenge of night UNREP, keeping danger at a distance between ships.

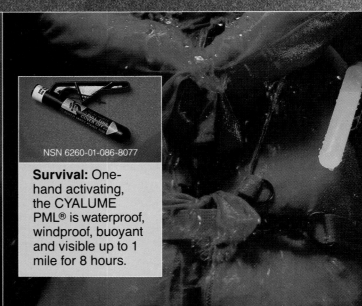

NSN 6260-01-086-8077

Survival: One-hand activating, the CYALUME PML® is waterproof, windproof, buoyant and visible up to 1 mile for 8 hours.

CYANAMID
Illuminating Solutions
For Naval Operations

air control of sea areas. One element remains to be addressed, however: naval airborne early warning (AEW&C). Relying solely on American carrier air power may have been a "nifty idea" some time ago, but the good old days of 9-12 U.S. aircraft carriers in the Pacific Fleet are not likely to be seen again, while national demands on those that exist can be predicted to remain high indeed, if not excessive. Thus, an armed AEW&C aircraft, operating in direct support of JMSDF forces, in conjunction with tactical information derived from OTHR and other sources, could provide that essential dimension with the Aegis destroyers to project a truly capable AAW defense-in-depth in the maritime defense zones.

Can there be any doubt that deterrence in Northeast Asia is gaining increased credibility?

The Korea Peninsula remained one of the most potentially explosive and destabilizing regions of the world. How often has that statement been made over the past couple of decades? So often that we have become inured to its true meaning? Hopefully not, and probably not. Despite long-time North Korean leader Kim Il Sung's ploy this past year to upstage Chun by suggesting a willingness to unilaterally draw down his armed forces by 100,000 troops and enter negotiations for mutual concessions in the threatening posture of both sides, nothing really has changed. Suspicion and distrust is every bit as apt a description of the relations between these two entities today as it has been for the past several years. Kim is in the unenviable position of daily being made aware of the economic bankruptcy of his policies and of the disdain with which most nations regard the Democratic People's Republic. While Asia's socialism enters a phase of major change, even in as unexpected a place as Vietnam, there is little evidence of any effective movement towards openness or reform on the part of North Korea. Instead, military expenditures continue to exceed 15 percent GNP, and Kim turns more and more towards the Soviet Union for material as well as ideological support.

At the same time, 1987 has not been an easy year for South Korea. With an economy booming at an unprecedented pace, education levels of Koreans at home and abroad setting ever higher standards of accomplishment, employment thriving, and Korean products and athletes receiving greater and greater acclaim, one would not have been quick to predict that Chun would have lost control of the domestic political situation so emphatically. Student violence and labor unrest are not conditions that Chun looked forward to in his final year in office, especially in view of the substantial concessions he made to the political opposition over the past year or more. We are witnessing a growing desire on the part of the vast majority of the South Korean people for markedly increased political participation, concomitant with a fresh awareness of their many accomplishments, in juxtaposition with their long-standing distrust of a militarily controlled government. Of singular importance is what major change in security policy is likely, if any, when the new leadership assumes responsibility. Happily, the prevailing judgment is that, whichever party wins the election, the political transition will proceed in an evolutionary way, and the leadership will recognize the compelling need to continue to modernize and reinforce its military capabilities,

given the absence of any reassurance that the situation on the peninsula has lessened in its war-making potential.

By virtue of its technological advancements and industrial expansion, in combination with a national policy accentuating self-reliance and industrial "localization," the ROK armed forces will be increasingly able to deal independently with the threat from the north. Such a capability induces at least two issues which have been emerging gradually: (1) The overall command structure and relationship with U.S. military forces; and (2) The requirement for a maritime capability that relies less upon the U.S. Seventh Fleet for its viability.

Though difficult to deal with, the issue of national command authority and responsiblity inevitably must be readdressed by both the U.S. and ROK governments. The democratization process, which has full American support, carries with it profound seeds of nationalism, already strongly imbedded in South Korean thinking and motivation. The armed forces modernization programs being encouraged by the United States simply speed along the movement towards self-reliance. Thus, mounting pressure to address the issue of command relationships is almost certain to become more immediate.

Two Significant Deficiencies Need Attention

As for the ROK navy, one can begin to say that it finally is entering the modern age. It is well known that Korea has not only been an army-dominated political arena but that the army long has controlled the budget allocation process as well—for good and logical reasons. The navy generally has struggled to obtain a portion sufficient for more than simply maintaining the status quo, with modest modernization. However, in recent years a greater awareness of the importance of maritime strength to the achievement of national security objectives has penetrated the upper echelons of the ROK Joint Chiefs and the Defense Ministry. Not only has a fine new frigate been constructed in numbers, the Ulsan class, but detailed design soon should commence on the next generation Korean destroyer. The two-fleet system is in place, and command-and-control network problems are being addressed. Given the possession of some 20 or more diesel submarines by North Korea, and the proximity of large numbers of Soviet submarines in the Sea of Japan, recognition of the need for a much more competent and capable ASW force is emerging, both within the ROK royal hierarchy itself as well as the U.S. Pacific Fleet.

Even as a more aggressive modernization program is pursued, two significant deficiencies need attention: (1) Harbor defense/close-in SLOC control, and (2) Maritime air power. Given the enormous demand for the immediate influx of combat consumables on the outbreak of any hostilities on the Korean peninsula, it long has been puzzling as to why this particular dimension of a maritime strategy has been so routinely overlooked. Regrettably, harbor defense and close-in SLOC control is not one of the U.S. Navy's strengths. It falls somewhat below that of mine warfare, which means it is likely to be eased off the edge of the budget table year after year. Even so, that does not provide any solace, or excuse, for the Koreans to dismiss the requirement as primary, clearly falling on the shoulders of the host

country. A joint effort to advance the technologies and systems available to turn this situation around is very much in order.

Of even greater importance is the need for the ROK navy to modernize aviation. It has been painfully slow to recognize the benefits to be gained from coastal surveillance and vital sea area control with a dedicated, capable maritime air force. The existing S-2 Tracker naval air arm simply is inadequate for the task and has been unsuccessful in spawning a tradition of naval air advocates sufficiently talented and schooled in naval air warfare to break into the senior ranks of the navy or to influence appropriate circles in the JCS or Ministry of Defense. There are hopeful signs, however, that this situation is about to be reversed with the procurement of a modern, capable maritime patrol aircraft, which has been under study for a year or more, and with the advent of ASW-capable helicopters.

The 13th Party Congress, held in late October 1987, almost surely will be recorded as of signal importance in the evolution of Deng Xiaoping's reform strategy, both for its reassurance that the economic policies will maintain their momentum and that the political policies directed at significant party reform will parallel the economic progress. It is obviously far too early to measure the results, though not too risky for the less informed to chance predictions.

Thus, the assumption is made that the Party Congress will have produced no startling change to the reform course set by Deng and that the leadership changes will enhance Deng's basic development strategy. Geopolitically, this suggests that on the short term Deng will continue to probe improved relationships with the Soviet Union along the lines of China's self-interests entirely, and that no major accommodation to Soviet interests is likely. A tilt towards the West still will dominate policy actions and fundamentally leave the balance-of-power equation in Northeast Asia favorable to Western interests.

Soviet Military Capability Will Remain Impressive

On their part, the Soviets are likely to make token drawdowns in their military strength in Asia. But one would be foolhardy indeed to interpret such movement as strategically significant. Soviet military capability will remain impressive in all of its conventional dimensions and confront the United States with a force structure that remains substantially larger than any reasonable estimate of Soviet-Asia defense needs. Consequently, the U.S. military is almost certain to continue to look for ways to enhance gradually the military capability of the People's Republic of China, and Chinese interest in modernizing its forces will be all the more evident as its economy provides flexibility for such investments. There is no dearth of those who are anxious to help. The Chinese industrial landscape is cluttered with arms salesmen from all of Europe—and the United States. Obtaining modern equipment is not going to be China's major obstacle. Paying for it and maintaining it will be, as well as leveraging the opportunity in a political context. The major policy issue confronting Western governments with respect to Chinese military modernization is the pace at which it is prudent to assist in this modernization. If there are concerns about Japanese remilitarization that

trouble some of the Asian nations, the tremors that would be felt with a substantially rearmed Chinese military, however appropriately marketed as anti-Soviet, would cause the Japanese problem to pale in comparison.

In a maritime context, assisting the Chinese to develop capabilities that would enhance Western interests in a confrontation involving the Soviet Union in the Pacific would seem to be a logical extension of U.S. policy towards normalization and transfer of technology. The U.S. Navy's success in developing practical and fruitful navy-to-navy relations with allies around the globe suggests that a policy which takes advantage of this special talent could serve useful purposes.

There is a huge hooker, however: the Republic of China on Taiwan. Though the United States no longer retains full diplomatic relations with the ROC, we have firm commitments to the government and its people that must not be sacrificed for political "chips" to play in the Sino-Soviet competition. In this context, one of the major shortcomings that has evolved as U.S. activity has expanded on the mainland and lessened on Taiwan has been the atrophying of U.S. strategic thinking regarding the continued importance of Taiwan to U.S. interests in our Asia-Pacific strategy vis-a-vis the Soviets.

The United States has, as a matter of policy, made it abundantly clear that, while it supports the one-China policy and will not interfere with the internal issues that confront China and Taiwan, it rules out the use of force as an accept-

able means of settling their differences. That being so, it is time for the United States to strive to cause *both* the PRC and ROC to acknowledge that each would play a significant role in any major confrontation involving the superpowers and that their interests would be parallel. Were it possible to entice the three parties—China, the Republic of China, and the United States—to sit down and address this issue

South Korean and U.S. forces train together annually in many phases of warfare. In Operation Team Spirit '87, repair of the radar on a fighter aircraft and paradrops were only two of the joint training missions undertaken.

head on, it could follow that substantial enhancement of the strategic significance of Taiwan in the context of a Pacific strategy would ensue. It has been much too long since U.S. military personnel were present in Taiwan and engaged in sensible discussions and strategic planning related to optimization of attractive Taiwanese geostrategic advantages—those that face to the East and not the West. Regrettably, such a cooperative initiative is not likely to be seen soon.

Indian Ocean Maritime Balance Being Hid Under A Bushel

This brings us to the Philippines, the last regional player about which this essay has room to contemplate. But, before going into the Philippine imbroglio, passing acknowledgment is necessary related to three strategic movements afoot that cannot help but have a growing impact on the maritime strategy of the Pacific-rim nations, and especially the United States.

• The coup in Fiji led by Lt. Col. Sitivini Rabuka is illustrative of the growing awareness by indigenous populations in the South Pacific Islands of their conflicting and perhaps incompatible interests in independence and economic viability. Nationalism of a sort is rampant and runs headlong into arguments favoring popularly elected governments, party coalitions, and the vulnerability to encroachment from unwanted outsiders such as Libya and the Soviet Union. A movement is afoot that deserves close and intelligent watching; it also bears with it the trappings of nascent racism, long ignored in South East Asia and the Pacific.

• Successful acceptance of the sentiment favoring ostracizing nuclear weapons from the South Pacific was accomplished in 1987 with the passage of the Treaty of Rarotonga. Treaty signatories accept the obligation that they will not manufacture, station, or test nuclear explosive devices in the South Pacific Nuclear Free Zone. France, Great Britain, and the United States have refused to sign, while the Soviet Union and China gain political chips through their prompt willingness to accede. Our friends in Australia, who put so much effort into crafting a treaty they thought would be acceptable to the United States, were hardly pleased with U.S. priorities. The United States is right. Proliferation of agreements of this nature elsewhere can only work to the detriment of peace and stability in a practical context, a feature which regional states seldom are willing to take into account, or have the capacity to judge. The Southeast Asia Nuclear Free Zone concept being advocated by several ASEAN members can only exacerbate the situation and lead to highly detrimental outcomes if ever adopted by the group.

• The Indian Ocean maritime balance is being hid under a bushel, distracted by such dominant events as the Japan-American trade imbalance and the protectionist consequences therefrom on the one hand, and the Persian Gulf military buildup on the other. Naval strategists have an obligation not to become so distracted with other major concerns as to miss the implications of something as dramatic and dynamic as is unfolding with the Indian Ocean forces, especially India's navy. Not only do the Indians now fly two squadrons of MiG-29 Fulcrum fighters, have eight Bear long-range ASW aircraft coming, are already building the

MiG-27 Flogger, and have plans to initiate construction of the light air combat aircraft (LCA) and the advanced light helicopter (ALH), but the Navy has put the converted HMS *Hermes* to sea with Sea Harriers on board, and will be accepting Kashin II guided-missile destroyers and Kresta II guided-missile cruisers. The Russians have promised the sale of at least a half dozen Kilo-class diesel-electric submarines and the Germans are helping out with type 1500 submarines. The major new fleet base at Karwar has been constructed, command-and-control networks have been modernized, and an Indian navy that will one of these days alarm some of its neighbors will emerge ready to dominate the situation in South Asia.

Meanwhile, as the year 1987 unfolded in the Philippine archipelago, it became increasingly clear that U.S. policy objectives were not being met and that Aquino's grasp of her responsibility and grip on the leadership were on a slippery slope. The two are closely interrelated, as the United States continues to espouse total support for Aquino and her democratically elected government. But the viability of that government is increasingly questioned by analysts and political experts everywhere—and certainly by the disparate opposition that is growing unchecked throughout the country. (Many predict that by the time of the publication of the 1988 edition of *The Almanac of Seapower*, Aquino might no longer be in office.)

Among the characterizations articulated by the opponents and uneasy supporters of Aquino in the days prior to the 1986 election was the common perception that as worthy an individual as she obviously is, Aquino would be unable to deal with the various power cells in the political structure and would have too little experience to understand how to get the economy moving, as it must. It was also contended she was from a background of too much wealth and comfort to properly institute the necessary reforms needed to touch the common Filipino, and would be soft on Communism. Also commonly expressed to the many American visitors and teams of analysts that poured through Manila in those days was the emphatic enunciation by the Philippine military leadership that one need not fear a coup on the part of the Philippine armed forces. No, they said, the Philippine armed forces had no tradition of supporting coups; quite the contrary, they were strong supporters of the existing government. How ironic that 18 months later these collective concerns have proved all too prophetic, and how crucially disturbing that the military has become one of the more destabilizing elements of society.

Not A Healthy Situation from ASEAN Perspective

The rebellion of Col. Honasan set off flares that sounded alarms throughout the capitals of much if not all the Pacific rim, including the United States, with his substantial coup attempt, the fifth such effort since Aquino was swept into the presidency. The military implications and concerns of this growing turmoil in the Philippines are obvious: the continued viability of the U.S. base structure at Clark Air Base and Subic Bay, and the mounting insurgency of the Communist New People's Army throughout the country.

• A year ago there was good reason to feel reasonably optimistic that the base renegotiation discussions would begin in 1988 with fair prospects of success, and that both sides would sit down and negotiate in good faith a plan of approach that would permit the continued utilization of these vital facilities. Reasons for thinking this way were largely dependent on an understanding that the key Philippine leaders were growing ever more practical in their assessment of the importance of the bases to the Philippines themselves, beyond the historic rhetoric that these were simply "U.S. bases promoting U.S. interests." Fortunately, several ASEAN leaders have been known to have taken forthright stands with the Philippine government arguing for continued U.S. presence as of vital strategic importance to all of Southeast Asia. The strategic linkage is almost too obvious to comment on; yet it has been all too evident by its absence from the debate. Meanwhile, the Soviet Union keeps careful watch on the developments and continues to create more permanent facilities that support Soviet naval and air activities in Cam Ranh Bay. It is not a healthy situation from an ASEAN or U.S. perspective. Much work lies ahead if all of Southeast Asia is not to find itself faced with a shift in the balance of power in the region of major proportions.

• The trouble now is knowing just who the leaders will be when the real negotiating gets under way. Having Joker Arroyo out of the picture as executive secretary is a favorable development, but that is offset by the appointment of Sen. Raul Manglapus as foreign minister replacing Salvador Laurel, who has developed an alliance of sorts with former Defense Chief Juan Ponce Enrile, which is perplexing and probably not helpful. Highly regarded and respected, Manglapus is known to oppose continued U.S. presence on the bases, a position that must be reversed in the very near future. Two other politicians of growing stature and importance are Sen. Jovito Salonga, president of the Senate, and Ramon Mitra, speaker of the House, neither of whom is known to look kindly on the U.S. position.

• Consequently, as the time draws nearer to commencement of the negotiations, regional interests must be forced to center stage if the strong nationalistic proclivities of these Philippine players are to be balanced in favor of keeping the bases viable. Furthermore, not only must obvious balance-of-power factors pertaining to the Soviet presence at Cam Ranh Bay be viewed with greater objectivity, but the potential impact on Japanese, Korean, and Chinese policies must receive more erudite analysis. Consider, for example, the logical Japanese interest in SLOC security beyond 1,000 nautical miles if the U.S. 7th Fleet is perceived to be no longer handily available and forward deployed. This is but one of many strategic ramifications bearing regional markings that deserve far greater awareness than is presently apparent.

• With regard to the insurgency, Aquino was convinced she had to give the rebels an opportunity to "come down out of the hills" in order to have a cease fire in which reasonable men could find reasonable solutions, only to be compelled to firm up her position the hard way—perhaps too late. While the issues that confront the domestic scene in the Philippines today are manifold and difficult, it is hard to imagine any that is more dangerous than the current Communist offensive. Now she faces a reinvigorated

The U.S. Navy's strategically located, versatile, capable, and politically controversial base at Subic Bay in the Philippines.

NPA, some 23,000 strong, refurbished with additional arms and supplies, confident that time is on their side.

Increasing numbers of critics now share the belief that Aquino had her chance to get tough with the Communist insurrection but has lost it. The heavy bloodshed in the villages as well as the cities, the mounting assassinations and threats, and the deep split within the military, encompassing the reform officers movement as well, do not speak well of the effectiveness of her anti-communist campaign.

There is a partner yet to be counted in all this downside disillusionment, one to whom history is not likely to be lenient—the United States. It wasn't enough that we hung in there with Marcos well beyond the point of intellectual reasonableness, that we failed to have appropriate intelligence on his activities and to understand the depth of corruption and distrust that pervaded his government. But now, having been given a second chance to help democracy prevail in this fragile country, so emotionally and figuratively part of us, we now show the depth of our support by reneging on promises made by some of our most senior statesmen and legislators, and continue to only sporadically elevate the Philippine crisis to the level of priority it deserves. We are as responsible for the lack of preparedness of the AFP to deal with the Communist insurgency as the Filipinos themselves. It surely can come as no surprise that

the Philippine armed forces are poorly led, poorly trained, and inadequately equipped. We have been aware of that for years. And we have stated officially on more than one occasion that we were going to help fix that. Eighteen months after Marcos, the AFP remains sadly equipped, and lacks good communications, mobility, the basics of firepower, and effective training, all of which the United States could provide with relative ease. Even if it weren't easy, it is our moral and national obligation! Furthermore, the Japanese should be enticed to join in with assistance, probably supervised by some joint committee with the United States and the Philippines. Who then will answer up when the cry comes forth, "Too little and too late"? Will the Congress of the United States? Will the Government of Japan? Will the candidates for the presidency of the United States?

"On the Whole, There Are Grounds for Optimism"

When no less an authority than the prestigious Professor Robert Scalapino, director of the Institute for East Asian Studies at the University of California, is prepared to conclude on the basis of his latest analysis of Asia's future that "on the whole, there are grounds for optimism," one is compelled to take heart. He contends that

• Economic strategies being pursued in Asia are producing remarkable results (if one can overlook the Philippines and Vietnam);

• Greater political freedom and individual participation are prevalent characteristics on the upswing in their influ-

ence on national policies;

• Regionalism is growing as nations tend to relate better towards one another while finding increased independence from both superpowers; and

• Danger of large-scale war is declining and prospects for peaceful evolution are stronger.

On the other hand, it is fair to point out that there are disquieting rumblings not to be overlooked or treated lightly:

• Nationalism is producing its own shades of gray, leading to unsettling and unstable trends, especially where governments are relatively inexperienced and are pursuing politically immature concepts. Violence in different forms is in evidence as well as simmering just below the boiling point.

• Chaos in the Middle East, as manifested by the seven years of warfare between Iran and Iraq, is certain to have a lasting effect upon Asia, though in various ways in different countries. Likewise, racism is not a concept unknown to Asia. And,

• The potential for a demoralizing trade confrontation between Japan and the United States refuses to go away. If it is not resolved in a way that ameliorates the damaging potential to Asia's developing countries, it is almost certain to produce highly destabilizing results.

Additionally, several external pressures must be constantly borne in mind:

• The arms limitations/arms reduction negotiations ongoing between East and West;

• The international financial crisis, and

• The many significant changes in leadership certain to take place in the next few years, if not immediately.

Taken together, these several factors produce an environment which compels the United States to consider their implications on U.S. policy towards the Asia-Pacific nations in consonance with our national strategy. In sum:

• American and Asian friends must be deliberate and pragmatic in evaluating recent policy announcements by Gorbachev. The Asiafication of glasnost has yet to generate much more than rhetoric. The Soviet Union must buy time to turn inward to address its failing economy. Soviet overtures towards Asia in 1987 should be seen for what they are—a facade, papering over a decade or more of inept foreign policy directed to the region. If Russia intends to become an effective Pacific player, she must earn her way in with deeds, not words. Constructive movement for real peace in Afghanistan and Cambodia would gain the Soviet Union more credibility than all the high-level Asian visits she can muster. However, there is little likelihood of real progress in either country in the immediate future to assuage the deep suspicions that most Asia-Pacific nations have towards the Soviet Union.

• The United States must take measures to retain strong alliances in Asia, especially with Japan and Korea, and to assure that the ANZUS alliance does not erode further in our relationships with Australia. Fears will be enunciated from time to time by some in the Soviet Union and the PRC that the triangularization of military relationships between the United States, Japan, and Korea are destabilizing and threatening to Northeast Asia security. Similar allegations will be made that an alliance is being developed between the United States, China, and Japan. Persistent efforts should be expended to keep these relationships harmonized.

• The U.S. Congress and administration must become far more concerned in assessing the vitality of the Communist insurgency in the Philippines and the growing danger that the United States may find itself looking for a new home for its forward-based forces in Southeast Asia. For its part, ASEAN likewise must finally become realistic on these matters and openly endorse the presence of U.S. forces in the Philippines, appreciating that regional security is very much at stake.

• While the U.S. Pacific maritime strategy will properly continue to focus heavily on Northeast Asia, given the proximity and magnitude of Soviet East-Asia military forces, the Indian Ocean and littoral must be recognized for its growing importance in global security. Strategies and policies of the West must reflect this recognition.

• U.S. naval forces, now highly visible in the Persian Gulf, could well find themselves becoming a more permanent feature than ever envisioned. In this context, the U.S. unified-command structure proves daily that the role of maritime forces was never adequately understood or visualized when the U.S. Central Command was conceived.

• Preparation for conventional, "more-likely" wars always has been difficult to assimilate in the process of planning for and expending billions to deter or fight the major, "least-likely" war. Hence, Third World kinds of threats tend to receive insufficient analysis, leading to such anomalies as U.S. surface combatants compelled to present themselves as lucrative targets while being inadequately equipped to deal confidently with today's anti-ship missile threat, and with mine warfare, which continues to be grossly underappreciated as a means of supporting maritime strategies.

The Atlantic Ocean long has held a position of pre-eminence in American and European strategic thought, as it should have. The time is well behind us, however, when the Pacific deserved promotion to equal stature. Platitudinous phrases uttered from time to time by prominent U.S. leaders meant to assuage our Far Eastern friends and allies of serious U.S. interest are insufficient to overcome our sad performance supporting democracy in the Philippines, our relative disinterest in promoting economic development in Southeast Asia, and demonstrable failings in the South Pacific, which together belie the integrity of our Pacific strategy. Consequently, U.S. naval forces can look forward to greater demands on operational tempo in response to exigencies yet visualized. Policymakers in Washington will continue to be quick to ask for maritime power to undergird American commitments worldwide but will be equally as facile in belittling the "600-ship Navy" when asked to ante up the wherewithal.

Scalapino has strong justification for viewing Asia's prospects optimistically. But U.S. prescience and resolve must measure up to the challenge if this optimism is to materialize. The Asia-Pacific region remains extraordinarily dynamic with an abundance of encouraging signs. Yet turbulence and instability are ever present and must be contained. U.S. naval forces will play a decided, if not decisive, role on more than one occasion in the unfolding of this vibrant panorama.

■

SPACE TRANSPORTATION SYSTEMS

A dynamic unit in the aerospace spectrum.

Space Transportation Systems (STS) is a unit of United Technologies Corporation. STS is using the experience of its personnel, specialized facilities and management know-how to aid in the exploration of space.

Built on a solid foundation, the STS organization includes:

▶ Chemical Systems... a world leader in aerospace propulsion systems research, development and production.

▶ Space Flight Systems (SFS)... which is providing program management and systems integration and is currently performing study contracts on the Advanced Launch System and Shuttle C programs.

▶ USBI Booster Production Company... which employs extensive experience in transporting, handling and assembling large space components, and recovering and refurbishing spent space hardware.

STS is supported by other UTC divisions, including Pratt & Whitney, a leader in jet engines and space propulsion systems; Sikorsky Aircraft, producer of helicopters and advanced structures; Hamilton Standard, eminent in electronic guidance and flight control systems, environmental control systems, and satellite attitude control propulsion systems; Norden Systems, a major manufacturer of radar and command and control systems, displays, and computers and fire control systems; and UTC's Research Center, renowned for optical components and systems, and advanced sensor technologies.

SPACE TRANSPORTATION SYSTEMS
Colonial Plaza, 2111 Wilson Blvd., Eighth Floor, Arlington, Virginia 22201. (703) 284-1826

UNITED TECHNOLOGIES SPACE TRANSPORTATION SYSTEMS

MARITIME LOGISTICS

For Our Nation
Combat and

By Isaac C. Kidd, Jr.

". . . Thou dost assume away too much."
—Shakespeare

History has been completely uncompromising in its documentation of the outcome of every war, campaign, battle, confrontation—or whatever the term in current fashion—wherein the planners and strategists have found it convenient to set aside hard-nosed practicality and fundamentals in favor of offering an assessment or prediction which best, or better, fits the perceived needs of the moment. These needs often find themselves so rooted in the unhealthy soil of political expedience, wishful thinking on the part of theoretical strategists, inexperience, selfishness, and, from time to time, plain stupidity, that the outcomes which follow adoption of such faulty ideas should really come as no surprise. But the fact remains that they do—over and over again. "How could such a calamity happen to such a nice guy as I," is the repeated refrain running through the minds of those caught short every time one of the building blocks necessary to military success has ended up on the proverbial cutting-room floor. President Truman best summed it up in his ascerbic comment on those determined to turn their backs on the lessons of history. "Is there an assured remedy?" The safe answer seems most likely to be, "Probably not." Man has simply not changed much over the centuries. Determined to learn for himself with the thought that, ". . . it could never be that bad again," he assumes away the lessons of the past and ends up writing his own example of just how bad it might be. He is then shocked at the outcome.

Antiques such as I continue to attempt to resurrect the past—usually too late to be of much good—but since all of us are born optimists, we continue to try. With each turn of the capstan bringing up the chain of "lessons learned" for periodic wire brushing and red-leading, there are, hopefully, a few links noted as being weak, kinked, or otherwise badly in need of attention before the bridge orders those on the foc'sl to "Let go" again.

The bridge across the Rhine at Remagen has been called "A Bridge Too Far." Our Army found themselves overreached, despite the best planning available, and it was comparatively pragmatic planning at that. We had been at war for several years. It should have been well done. But there were overly optimistic assumptions. There always are. Depending upon whose diary or analysis one reads, opinions vary as to where things began to fray around the edges. Hannibal experienced the very same trouble in his campaign in Italy. His on-scene requirements had not changed from the outset. Things had to come together on time at sites of his choice if the campaign were to be effective. The object of the exercise was to defeat Rome. Those on the "bridge" —powers at home—saw fit to change the rules on him. His letter to Carthage sums up rather well his judgments on that War Too Far—

". . . having been obliged to embark on this campaign without adequate transport, it has been necessary to walk to the war at hand. We are some 24 months without reinforcement. We are some 30 months without resupply of the sinews of war itself. We are fed by foraging. We are armed today largely with the weapons of the vanquished. These weapons, unfamiliar to your army, oblige us to make do. The efficacy of adaptation is attested to by the two bushels of gold rings forwarded herewith—one each from the finger of a leader in the enemy's ranks killed in the battle concluded successfully yesterday afternoon. I have today one-half the number with which I set out. Your indecisive procrastination leaves the outcome of this campaign in doubt unless immediate resupply is forthcoming."

/s/ Hannibal   (216 B.C.)

here Must Be Both
taying Power

As a matter of passing interest, on the day before his scribe took that letter, 30,000 Carthagenians had slaughtered some 80,000 Romans on the plains of Cannae. Now, in the sophisticated thinking found in capitals 2,203 years later, one could expect some snide comment to the effect that Hannibal had "made do" very well indeed, and that he was lucky he had no environmental impact statement to prepare, and no worries with the tasks facing an office of graves registration. All to validate the wisdom in their decision to let the man in the field fend for himself, that he had asked for much too much at the outset, that there would certainly be no supplementary budget to pay for this too-long and too-far-away war while more pressing matters of trade and business as usual demanded the national leader's attention at home. Of course, because things moved much more slowly in those days, from the movements of the elephants across the Strait of Gibraltar on very large rafts to the movement of information itself, it took longer for the insidious creeping paralysis called logistic inadequacy to make itself felt. It came to pass as predictable. It was only in 1951 that French archaeologists found Carthage, the Romans having done such a thorough job of razing the city, sowing the earth with salt, and burying all that was left.

The Northern Flank is a Distant War Indeed

Time, distance, and the environment are the most unforgiving of ingredients impacting the outcome of any military undertaking. It was just over 100 short years between the time that Napoleon confirmed that winters are miserable for armies, and quite capable of being a campaign's deciding factor, and the time that another group of environmentally insulated men, the Nazi Germany high command, decided those rules did not apply to them and decided to take on Moscow without providing proven safeguards against low temperatures, deep mud, very long, completely exposed logistic lines, and the mentally numbing impact of cold. We, too, managed to do exactly the same thing to ourselves in Korea as we galloped up to the North Korea-China border, only to rediscover the German findings as we then advanced to the rear from the Chosin Reservoir. This remarkable revalidation of the strengths of those common enemies called cold, mud, and exposed logistic lines took place less than 10 years from the German confirmation.

Just what is this motivator in the minds of leaders that insists "It could not be that bad again," or, that "It can't happen to me." Norway, a very long and very slender nation, comes to mind. The northern third, roughly, is well

north of the Arctic Circle. It is cold in north Norway, even colder than in south Norway. But south Norway is where "orientation visits" are made. Such visits to north Norway are usually made up and back in the same day. The total time actually outside in the natural environment was roughly a 52-minute average during my visits, with no single exposure running to more than 15 minutes. Enough to identify the likely impact on the reinforcing forces Supreme Allied Commander, Atlantic is expected to deliver—feet dry and ready for sustained operations? Of course not! Had it not been for the many days and nights at sea in the rampaging environment off Norway's shore during World War II, there could have been completely inadequate appreciation of what NATO is up against.

A cliche advises that when all else fails, read the instruction book. In such instances, ask the man who lives there just how he copes. Two great warriors, Gens. Zeiner Gundersen and Svere Hamre, both chiefs of defense for Norway for whom I served, answered the question: "How do you move and fight in this environment?" in exactly the same way. "You do it very, very slowly, and this is what your people do not understand." We now understand much better, thanks to splendid initiatives taken by Adm. Ralph Cousins, Gen. Robert Barrow, and others. Do we have a good, firm handle on this matter? Unlikely. It is not the environment we are accustomed to, although we now train a bit more in north Norway. And thanks to Gen. Frederick Weyand, the Army chief of staff, and his successors, we now freeze locally at Army facilities at Fort Drum in upstate New York. This is less expensive. We can train more soldiers and Marines. It is not north Norway, but it is better than a poke in the eye with a sharp stick, as Adm. Walter Boone used to say to describe a questionable compromise.

Like many other parts of NATO, the northern flank is a distant war indeed, akin in many respects to the far eastern end of the Mediterranean, where our national needs and treaty arrangements have tied us to Turkey, Greece, Israel, and Egypt, and, today points even farther east than they are. The temperatures are much higher. More pleasant in which to serve, to fight if need be? That becomes a purely subjective question.

Length of Logistic Pipeline Boggles the Mind

Most are well aware of the dangers to be guarded against in an area cold enough to freeze flesh in contact with metal surfaces long exposed to very low temperatures. The reverse is true in those hot areas of the Middle and Near East. The ill-defined area of southwest Asia can reach temperatures of up to 160 degrees Fahrenheit inside parked automobiles after but 30 minutes in the sun. Think of this in terms of the combat environment of a tank crew. Much has been written of the rapid degradation of combat efficiency experienced by anyone suited up in the protective clothing required for chemical warfare, an assured loss of 50 percent efficiency no matter what the occupation, military or civilian. If the same or near same impacts occur from merely normal ambient temperatures in the area when in a closed vehicle, must we then plan on taking twice as many troops to do the same job in any given period of time, or do we

ADMIRAL ISAAC C. KIDD, JR., retired in 1978 after serving for three years as Supreme Allied Commander, Atlantic, and Commander, U.S. Forces, Atlantic. During his 40-year career, which included 28 years in sea assignments, he was heavily involved in maritime logistics, including naval procurement, and planning for and meeting short- and long-range air- and sea-lift requirements. Since retirement he has served as an advisor to the Defense and State Departments, the General Accounting Office, and the Contress, and as a member of the Defense Science Board.

plan on having to stay twice as long to do the same job?

Is, then, the Arabian Gulf a venue too far for prudent planning in conventional form? We are learning this to be the case. New texts for new environments have become the order of the day. Of the many professional soldiers who have had to take a new and very hard look at the elements quickly identifiable as potential war-losers in such a debilitating theater, our infantrymen, Army and Marines, require the most attention simply because the environment's extremes hit men the hardest. There are more of them (infantrymen) than any other kind. We can adapt and build into ships and planes available offsetting filters for the sand and grit, and cooling for the overheating electronics before we ever send the platform to the theater. But people are quite a different matter. The evolutionary characteristics of each man are tailored to our natural habitats. The work of millions of years of natural selection is not changed either quickly or easily. These very simple facts of life have combined to generate a logistics nightmare for areas east of the Suez—different uniforms, different shoes and socks, different lubricating oils, and far different failure rates for the tools of war. The length of the logistic pipeline boggles the mind. It has become so long that entirely new methods of computation have become necessary because there is so much tied up in inventory in transit that is unavailable for use until it gets there. The supply systems of our several services and the Defense Supply Agency are having to work several miracles each day. We can all thank the unsung heroes of the moment, and likely for a long time to come, those in the air and sea-lift commands. They now are extended. Should widespread escalation occur in the local area of just the Arabian Gulf itself, we could quickly find ourselves overextended locally there, and most certainly overcommitted as far as lift is concerned as we are expected to be able to perform elsewhere in the world—NATO, for example.

One Never Knew Where Fleet Might Turn Up

This business of being ready to wage a war and a half, or a major war and a brush-fire war, is an area of arithmetic legerdemain I'm afraid I've never fully understood. Our oilers, our beef boats, our stores and spare-parts ships are all in very short supply. They can only go just so fast. They can only be in one theater at a time. When we take the few we have, ask them to go twice as far to do their job, thus extending their turn-around times, we end up with the de facto burden of tying units of the fleet to some designated local port, hopefully with an adequate airhead, which then becomes that ship's permanently fixed "underway replenishment unit." Subic Bay filled this role for our time in Vietnam. I've yet to find a welcome mat in the Persian Gulf approximating the quality of that in the Philippines. One of the vaunted national advantages of balanced sea power has been its far-ranging flexibility as an instrument of national policy. One never knew just where the fleet might turn up next, in order to settle turbulence just by being there 24 hours a day, dependent upon no one. Overly heavy dependence upon any friendly state for such critical support must indeed weigh heavily on the minds of those in authority. One quickly finds vast reaches of the world's oceans to be denied by too much dependence upon

a very short logistical leash. This can quickly become very bad news when the intentions of the one on the other end of the leash begin to waver, or become unclear.

Among the many studies and reviews of available options in the Gulf area, there runs a common thread of political opportunism cropping up every step of the way wherein those who live there want a handsome price for their accommodations. At the other extreme, there are those who want a substantial U.S. presence close by for both moral and actual support. But then when we get there, we are so often told, "Please, not quite that close." Their reasons go back over centuries of sensitivities. They are understandable. They are frustrating. We find ourselves in a no-win situation. Perhaps Adm. Chester B. Nimitz had it about right for that region in the way he handled his island-hopping strategy in the Pacific. We would like to be as independent as possible in the Gulf. We would like to avoid heavy investment in permanent infrastructure ashore which we would have to leave, as we did in France when she withdrew active military support from NATO, and as we did in Vietnam on departure. In the Pacific, we could not afford to build so much at each step of the way. Moreover, it took too long to build with brick and mortar before an advanced base became usable. Lions and Cubs came into being—floating mobile large advanced base packages (Lions), and smaller versions of the same (Cubs). Floating machine shops, hospitals, warehouses, tankers, SATS airfields, and like platforms, mostly in barges, made it possible to quickly move in behind the landing force, set up shop, and be in business within two or three days. Like Barnum and Bailey, they could fold up and be on the move within a few days, on to the next island or atoll. All that was needed was an open, or preferably a protected roadstead with good holding ground on the bottom. To a layman, identification of Lions and Cubs was a simple matter; the size of the floating drydock was the key. Lions had the very large one—battleship and carrier size. Cubs had the middle-sized dock for cruisers and smaller ships.

Diego Garcia is the Best We Have

Like the Greek who said he could move the world if he had a lever arm long enough and a place to stand, we in the Indian Ocean, like the Pacific headquarters in 1942, are finding we need two places to stand—one quite close to the scene of actual or potential military activity, while the other can be farther back and less susceptible to daily attack, much as was Pearl Harbor. Diego Garcia is the best we have, yet it is far removed from the stadium where we might have to fight. Moreover, the long sea route from the Strait of Hormuz to the Suez Canal could quickly become an exposed line of vulnerability to both sea and air attacks. The most casual glance at any map makes the point well when we note the choke points en route to Yemen, for example. The last choke point northbound is, of course, Suez itself. On the several occasions when it has been closed by sinking a dozen or so ships in selected spots, this has been done in roughly 12 hours. Each time, this half day's work has taken one year to clean up the mess, move the wrecks, and reopen the Canal. It has taken every piece of heavy salvage equipment in the Free World to do the job in

The magnitude of the task of moving ships and supplies to Southwestern Asia was dramatized by the voyage of the salvage ship Grapple (ARS-53). She departed Little Creek, Va., 6 September 1987 with the minesweepers Fearless (MSO-442), Illusive (MSO-448), and Inflict (MSO-456) in town and arrived in the Persian Gulf 2 November, taking 58 days for the voyage of more than 8,000 miles.

12 months. On each occasion, the salvage environment has been completely benign. Could anyone count with confidence on the willingness of owners to assemble such an international commercial salvage effort in a combat zone? It must be marked as "doubtful." This eventuality quickly establishes an almost doubled transit time from the eastern seaboard around Africa. Few have any appreciation of just how far away Hormuz really is. There are just 360 degrees in any circle, our own equator included. Hormuz lies some 180 degrees west of Oakland, or some 150 degrees east of Galveston. It could not be much farther away, no matter which direction we chose to sail. We have had no hard experience fighting a war or conducting a campaign of preventive actions that far away before. We are learning the hard way, and we are doing a very good job of it. We lost most of our Asiatic Fleet in the early days of World War II off Java. The British and Royal Netherlands navies suffered the

same fate at the same time in the same area. Four years later, however, remembering that bitter lesson in overly long logistic lines we could not defend, we assaulted Okinawa with a combat force of over 1,300 men of war. We had come to stay, but it took almost four full years to get ready. Britain, too, had kept her logistic experiences close at hand when she looked at the options in the Falklands. Britain's staying power, the depth of her bench, as it were, was most impressive. Of the 110-odd ships involved on any given day of the campaign, there averaged some 75 support ships for 35 men of war. But we Americans do not own that kind of supporting numbers. I would commend to you the splendid book by Hansen Baldwin, the distinguished former military correspondent for the *New York Times*, entitled *SeaFights and Shipwrecks*. In the last chapter he recounts the Okinawan campaign in vivid terms. The staggering logistic demands for an effort of that magnitude that far from home bases will sober any reader as he contemplates the very heavy and unexpected losses encountered from the religious fanatics in cockpits flying one-way trips. Such fanaticism appears to be in evidence again, this time from Iran. The possibilities are most unsettling.

The crystal-clear, obvious-to-all readiness to both deliver and to absorb punishment on scene with enough power on

the bench to stay until the job is done is called deterrence, and this is where we are perceived as being of doubtful resolve. Our long record of shortchanging logistics and lift therein over the years has been a source of puzzlement to friend and potential foe alike. We have been so fat for so long in our ability to count upon someone else taking care of those essentials that perhaps we've sent the wrong message to the world. While we are very strong indeed, if we can no longer get to a war in time with enough to do a good job, an enemy could ask, "Whom are you fooling, America, other than yourself?"

The Alliances Own 6,000 Bottoms

NATO and the myriad obligations for concurrent actions from the North Cape of Norway to the eastern end of the Mediterranean which are promised combine to beggar the mind as to support demands. The allies expect to welcome some 1 million men from the United Kingdom and the North American continent (U.S. and Canadian forces) in the first 30 days—preferably before the first bullet has been fired. Since levitation is not yet in hand, these forces must move by air and sea—10 and 90 percent, respectively. Assuming we will behave as we have in the past and not turn our national backs on the civilian populations of the European allies, we will have to plan on assuring that they are fed, kept warm (energy), and otherwise supported. Certainly while they can't be at peacetime levels of supply, let us assume we must deliver but one-half of Europe's peacetime needs until the war is won. We must then look at the gross requirements for air and maritime movement of monstrous tonnages.

• We must reinforce, and then resupply, our troops that are there now plus those million in the reinforcing wave; and

• We must resupply the civilians who live there. We must expect losses at levels far exceeding those of World War II, simply because Soviet forces in being, and able to inflict losses, are some six times the German submarine force levels at the start of World War II.

Very rough computations suggest 6,000 shiploads would be needed per month for offloading in Europe. In 1975 the alliance owned, including flags of convenience, some 10,000 merchant bottoms of all types. This was somewhat comforting, since it allowed for losses. Today, shipping industries are in chaos. Tonnages have been on a toboggan for 10 years, and the alliance owns some 6,000 bottoms.

Our planning analysts have solved the problem—read "deficiency"—by tinkering with the numbers once again. "Losses could never again be as bad as in the past," they say. We will, therefore, just assume fewer than 1 percent losses and the problem goes away. As an aside, we lost 66 percent trying to resupply Malta in the early days of World War II. We did improve as the war progressed and we learned how to better sink submarines. But the issue can and will be decided in the early months. Sir Winston Churchill wrote that Britain's fate was in grave doubt at the outset. There were but a handful of U-Boats at sea—less than a dozen—early on. Yet the Soviet navy has well over 150 available for such a war of attrition just in the Atlantic. Is it indeed prudent to make such rash assertions and assumptions in the face of such sobering historic evidence of the efficacy of Germany's unrestricted submarine campaign?

"We have More Fight than You Can Ferry"

Our Army and our Marines have not been fooled by such dangerous doings. Gen. David M. Shoup, former commandant of the Marine Corps, said it well when he blasted the Navy with, "We have more fight than you can ferry." Our Navy is now buying merchant bottoms to have them ready to help with troop movement. These are steps in the right direction, but it is indeed a sad commentary when the Navy has to put up warfighting dollars to cover Maritime Administration and congressional neglect over so many years. While it was no well-kept secret that MARAD and the industry itself were in default, our NATO allies were busy taking our business in sealift of their own, so we talked ourselves into it being acceptable to have our troops take someone else's ferry to the front.

Carl Vinson, the wise former chairman of the old Naval Affairs Committee and later the Armed Services Committee in the House of Representatives, established well our need as a nation to be able to haul one-half of what needs to be hauled in an American ship to support ourselves. We are now down to the embarrassing level of having enough tonnage to move but 10 percent. The most recent action

that forced the diversion of warship money into heretofore merchant-type lift occurred when our allies began to lose their individual and collective shirts to shipbuilders and ship operators in the Orient. Congress recently ordered an investigation of just how bad things are. A Commission on Merchant Marine and Defense was formed, with former Sen. Jeremiah Denton in the chair. The report was reassuring in that the commission discovered nothing new, but neither did it come up with anything particularly useful. This was not the commission's fault. But we as a nation have been doing so well in so many ways since 1945 that it has been possible to devote most of our efforts to making a profit. There have been no global thundering wars. Deterrence has worked. What wars we have had have been far-distant and reasonably well localized. We have become so sophisticated we no longer call them wars; that's not fashionable. Profit motives have driven sealift from our shores, first to Europe, and now to Japan, Korea, China, and Taiwan. Can we count with confidence on always getting what we must have to get to the "theater of the moment" with enough staying power at hand to be convincing? I am not certain. It is a bad spot to be in where one is so totally dependent upon cooperative builders, owners, and operators to make our diplomatic demarches convincing and credible.

Laboratories Create New Engines of Destruction

Adm. Cousins, Supreme Allied Commander, Atlantic at the time, summed up NATO's maritime dilemma most eloquently. When NATO was established, there was plenty of seapower. Forces in Europe, allied and our own, had adequate stocks left over from the war just ended to last for 90 days with some few exceptions. Naval commanders at the time opined they could have a clean sweepdown fore and aft in the Atlantic in about 60 days, clear the seas of Soviet predators (submarines), and then begin to sail the resupply ships across a sanitized ocean. In the interim, the ground and air forces in place would be able to feed off of the 90 days of stocks in place with but a few selected needs to be satisfied. This arithmetic provided 30 days of slack to crank up the convoys and get them to Europe in time before our own and the alliance forces ran out. "Keep in mind," cautioned Cousins, that there was "a cement of fear common in all capitals which held the entire network together." The clock began to tick and all went as planned. With the passage of time, though, the cement of fear began to dry and crack. National interests and priorities turned elsewhere. Economies were needed in each nation to pay new bills in other areas. Defense departments began to shrink along with the forces they controlled. Laboratories created new engines of destruction. Old stocks in Europe had to be updated. Stock levels began to drop as new items arrived. They were newer, better, and much more expensive. The same happened to military platforms themselves—planes, ships, and armor. Platforms, too, came down in number, gradually at first, then more rapidly as they went to scrap or to other parts of the world—Korea, the Republic of China off-shore island area, and later to Southeast Asia. Until, in 1975, NATO found itself with but some 30 days of stocks in place, U.S. forces dual-based—home base in the

U.S., having to move rapidly back to Europe to marry up with their prepositioned combat tools of their trade, and NATO navies shrunken to one-half the numbers of ships and planes needed to do all of the missions expected to be done simultaneously.

Losses Are Going to be Staggering

This litany was quite logical and predictable. Clearly we had all been doing something correctly because the deterrence desired had come to pass. The time table had, however, changed drastically. To get the U.S.-based Army forces back to Europe, they would have to fly to be in time to help. With so few days of stocks, resupply would have to begin at once; there was no time for the clean sweepdown envisioned at the outset. With the logistic hydrant in North America and the nozzle in the soldier's hands in Europe, we had to build up the logistic pressure in the hose connecting the two so that there would be no interruption in flow. The answer was quite simple: plan to roll over the enemy on and under the Atlantic from day one. Losses are guaranteed to be staggering under such a plan, considering the navies with the job of keeping the pressure up had been cut to one-half of the numbers needed. This is not a particularly pretty picture, but obviously one accepted as worth the risks involved by those in NATO capitals.

All of the foregoing, hopefully, will bring into somewhat sharper focus some of the cliches and grand numbers being tossed about these days. A 600-ship Navy, for example, can be bumped against the 1,000-ship Navy we had at the height of the Vietnam War. There was no evidence that Hanoi was terrified of 1,000 ships to the point of abject surrender. And, how do 600 ships compare with the 1,300 needed to take Okinawa? Six hundred of what? What kinds of ships are we counting these days? And, 600 does not seem to have any noticeable impact on those wild-eyed pirates racing about in store-bought speed boats in the Gulf where they seem to have a license to shoot everything in sight. One wonders what Stephen Decatur would have said about these pirates of a different age and time, but still pirates. On the matter of acceptable risks and credibility in the balance, Gen. Creighton Abrams opined, 'There's no sense sitting down at a poker game when everybody at the table knows you don't have any money." For our great nation, there must be balanced power—combat power and staying power. No one is ever sure just how long we might have to "stay," so we cannot afford to invite an opponent to simply wait us out. Such specious reasoning invites the lazy thinkers to too easily conclude that the issue is too hard, so we'll just have to "go nuclear" early. That is among the dumbest thoughts on the bill of fare these days because logistic adequacy is such a bargain. Further, it is so persuasive and so absolutely necessary. It is my conviction that any possible opponent, just like a scout for a football team, will first size up the depth and staying power of the next opponent's bench. When it is clear that the owners have invested wisely in size, talent, and numbers, the capability of that team to stay on the field as long as needed to win will be as much or more of a strategic deterrent than any missile in any silo, any submarine, or any bomber.

CONVOY!

U.S. military sealift assets operated by private sector U.S.-flag firms and manned by civilian American seafarers—a reliable combination for U.S. defense in national emergency.

DISTRICT 2

**DISTRICT 2
MARINE ENGINEERS
BENEFICIAL ASSOCIATION
—ASSOCIATED MARITIME
OFFICERS**

☆

AFFILIATED WITH
THE AFL-CIO MARITIME
TRADES DEPARTMENT

650 FOURTH AVENUE
BROOKLYN, NEW YORK 11232
(718) 965-6700

☆

RAYMOND T. McKAY
PRESIDENT

JOHN F. BRADY
EXECUTIVE VICE PRESIDENT

**DISTRICT 2
MEBA-AMO
AFL-CIO**

CENTRAL AMERICA

Consequences of Diplomatic Ineptitude in Central America Could Burden Us for Years

By Trevor Armbrister

With no warning at all, the Soviets attack. Quickly, their tank columns advance across a broad European front. NATO armies retreat and call for reinforcements from the United States. At ports along the East Coast and the Gulf of Mexico, ships take on men and material. Will that cargo reach the front lines in time? Will it arrive at all?

This scenario is imaginary, of course, but the questions are germane to an understanding of why Central America is so vital to us in a maritime sense. During the first five months of World War II, Nazi submarines sank 114 Allied merchant ships—more than 560,000 gross tons—in the Caribbean Sea. Those diesel subs were slow, and were operating far from home. Soviet submarines today are more capable, and more difficult to detect. Further, they would have Cuban support facilities and, in 1988, new facilities at the port of El Bluff on Nicaragua's Caribbean coast. Now, consider the targets they'll enjoy.

"One-half of U.S. foreign trade goes through the Panama Canal or the Gulf of Mexico," a Heritage Foundation analysis explains. "Two-thirds of U.S. imported oil and one-half of its strategic minerals pass through the Panama Canal. In addition, many of our allies in Europe, Asia, and Latin America depend even more heavily than the United States on the Canal for their external commercial activities. Further, the ability of the United States to resupply its forces in Europe in time of conflict or crisis would be hampered substantially if the Canal were to be inoperable.

"For decades," the analysis continues, "the United States has been able to fulfill its security-related obligations to its allies without having to be greatly concerned about its own borders. If this were to change, the United States might well need more military forces in this hemisphere."

Now, strip away the dry prose and focus solely on oil. The United States imports 42 percent of the oil it consumes, and Mexico and Venezuela combine to supply 1.437 million barrels a day—or 23.1 percent—of that total amount. Even more important, at least 70 percent of that overall total is processed in the Caribbean area. This means it's likely to traverse the Gulf of Mexico, a wide expanse that used to be known as an "American lake." And what happens if these sea lanes are cut? Says Joseph Lastelic, a spokesman for the American Petroleum Institute in Washington, D.C.: "Big Trouble."

Given the region's importance and vulnerability to attack, it would be reasonable to assume that the United States spent 1987 trying to reduce the enemy threat, bolster its allies, and guarantee the safety of those sea lanes. That, however, would not be accurate, because four separate events intervened to deter Washington from focusing on the ball. First was the fallout from the President's weakened political authority after the Republicans lost control of the Senate in the 1986 election. Next came the disclosures of the Iran-contra affair. That led to a decision not to request new aid for the "freedom fighters" in Nicaragua. Finally, the United States embraced a peace accord that swapped clear concessions for Communist promises to behave, and that left the contras high and dry.

"It's a catastrophe," a senior U.S. official told me over lunch one day last fall. "We have snatched defeat from the jaws of victory. People here are hanging crepe." The official paused to make sure I understood his next point: "It isn't that we were outfought. We were *out-thought*."

America's friends had trouble understanding these self-inflicted wounds. Visiting Washington last fall, the prime minister of an old ally was surprised to find that U.S. policy makers still were debating Soviet *intentions* in Central America. "What they (the Soviets) are up to is very simple," he told an assistant secretary of state. "You saved Grenada and you should have saved Nicaragua, and you're going to

pay, and pay, and pay, for your failure to do so."

On the surface the idea seems preposterous. Nicaragua? A threat to the United States? Why should we worry about a country of three million people where the inflation rate ranges between 1,000 and 1,500 percent each year and a 20,000 cordoba note is worth $1.20; where students have to take their own desks to school, and where toilet paper is a luxury? A poverty-stricken state whose only abundance is need. A former U.S. intelligence official brings me back to reality. "The *first* problem of Central America is Nicaragua," he explains. "So long as all the other governments of the area feel themselves under attack by an expansive, heavily armed Marxist revolutionary regime, supported and encouraged by the Soviet Union and Cuba, political and economic progress along democratic and individualistic lines is impossible."

Flow of Armaments Became A Flood

The links to Cuba and the Soviet Union are critical. "From these sources come the arms, the experts, the world-wide propaganda and influence network, and the prestige of power—the sense of the course of history being set from Moscow. Without their allies, the Sandinistas are only a group of assertive and uncertain young men (who) might as well be in charge of Bolivia. With them, they appear to be the crest of the wave of the future."

That's not how we saw them initially. In 1979, after dictator Anastasio Somoza fled and the Sandinistas took power, almost everyone rejoiced. Somoza had been a tyrant; he or members of his family had ruled for 46 years and Nicaraguans were glad to be rid of them. As for the Sandinistas, no one could say for sure because no one knew much about them. Quickly, they reassured the Organization of American States (OAS). They would organize a "truly democratic government," they vowed, and hold free elections as soon as possible. They would maintain a mixed economy along with a non-aligned foreign policy. Finally, they said they would respect the rights of free speech and assembly.

Helped by thousands of Cuban advisers, the Sandinistas consolidated their hold. Within weeks after taking power, they issued a bill of rights. It paid homage to individual liberties, equality before the law, and freedom of speech, religion, and assembly. But there was a catch. Any of the bill's provisions could be suspended for reasons of "public order" or "national security." This was followed by a state of emergency law that restricted meetings, allowed censorship of the press, and curbed political activity.

Washington didn't object. In September 1979, when Nicaraguan President Daniel Ortega led a delegation to the United States, he was welcomed effusively. The Carter administration was dispensing the first installments of the $118 million in aid that it would provide the new govern-

ment. This after the Sandinistas had labeled the United States "an enemy of mankind." Then the State Department urged Congress to allocate even more funds to push Managua "in the direction of a democratic regime." And just to make sure they understood his concerns about human rights, President Carter suggested that Sandinista troops could train at U.S. bases in Panama.

Ortega had different ideas. In New York City that fall, he told a United Nations audience that Managua wouldn't pay its debts; the rest of the world would have to shoulder them. He castigated the United States and called for independence for Puerto Rico. Then he returned home where he and his colleagues proceeded to crack down on internal dissent, and funnel large quantities of arms from Cuba and Vietnam to Marxist forces on the move in El Salvador.

The internal repression—one target was the church, another was the press—intensified each year. Catholic priests and Protestant pastors were harassed. Newspapers, radio, and television stations were shut down. "Las Orejas"—literally, the ears—told the kinds of stories that sent people to jail. Cuban-style "block committees" formed in every city and town to decide who held jobs and, more importantly, who received ration cards. The schools introduced new textbooks from Cuba and East Germany. Anyone who objected to their content was taking a huge risk. Private enterprise collapsed under the weight of regulations that deeded almost everything to the state. Labor unions and political parties functioned only in name.

The flow of armaments from the Soviet Union and Eastern Europe soon became a flood. In 1982, when U.S. assistance to *all* of Central America totaled only $80 million, the Soviets and their allies were dispensing $1.810 *billion* worth of hardware just to Cuba and Nicaragua. (This is to say nothing of the $4.775 *billion* they allocated that year in economic aid.) By 1985, the value of Soviet bloc arms unloaded at Cuban and Nicaraguan ports had increased to $2.4 billion.

In 1986 and the first six months of 1987—an 18-month period during which the Russian word 'glasnost,' or openness, entered our consciousness and Soviet leader Mikhail Gorbachev considered a summit meeting with President Reagan in Washington—arms deliveries actually *increased*. In 1986, the Soviets sent 23,000 metric tons of military aid to Nicaraguan ports. Between January and June 1987, a six-month period, those shipments totaled nearly 16,000 metric tons. Talk of peace notwithstanding, that's a sizable jump.

"For every dollar of economic aid provided by the United States to Central America during the 1980s," a State Department publication notes, "Cuba and Nicaragua received $10 worth from the Soviet Union and its East European allies. Soviet bloc military deliveries—weapons, ammunition, vehicles—exceed the cumulative value of U.S. military assistance by 8-to-1." Then the publication discusses the threat: "Nicaragua, like Cuba, has the potential to become a strategic asset to the Soviet bloc by providing seaports on both the Atlantic and Pacific coasts, a mainland base for military and intelligence networks, and a training and supply depot for Marxist-Leninist guerrillas seeking to topple democratic governments in neighboring countries."

TREVOR ARMBRISTER, former Washington bureau chief for the old Saturday Evening Post, is a senior editor at the Reader's Digest. Since 1962 he has made 28 reporting trips to Central or South America.

Modern Soviet military equipment is put on display in Managua, Nicaragua.

While they were battling Somoza, the Sandinistas never mustered more than 5,000 troops. Today they boast an active force of 75,000 men with another 60,000 in the trained militia and reserves. (Costa Rica, by contrast, has no army at all; Honduras has a force of 22,000 men.) These numbers don't include an estimated 8,000 advisers from the Soviet Union and the Soviet bloc. Cubans—military and civilian—account for 6,500 of them, but there are also delegations from East Germany, Bulgaria, North Korea, Vietnam, Libya, and the PLO.

Central America's biggest army also is its best equipped. When they seized power in 1979, the Sandinistas inherited three obsolete WWII tanks, 25 Staghound armored cars, and three 105mm howitzers. Today their arsenal includes at least 150 Soviet T-54, T-55, and PT-76 tanks, more than 200 armored vehicles, 450 surface-to-air missiles, 24 100mm howitzers that can fire a 96-lb. shell almost 11 miles, and at least 56 combat helicopters. These include 16 Mi 25/HIND "flying tanks" of the sort that proved so lethal in Afghanistan. Late last October, a State Department official told me that the Sandinistas had obtained cluster bombs from Panama and were using them against contra formations in remote areas of Honduras.

Weapons Sale Raised Only $4 Million

Why this enormous buildup of military strength? The Sandinistas always have maintained that they need adequate supplies of arms to repulse the U.S. "invasion" that they expect momentarily. Paranoia may play a role. An even better explanation is simply that they determined long ago to expand their revolution as fast and as far as possible by intimidation and brute force. In a region with five countries and 25 million people, they wanted to become "numero uno." That they have become.

In this space last year, I cited construction activity at El Bluff on Nicaragua's Caribbean coast. According to a *Miami Herald* report, Bulgarian and East German engineers were building breakwaters, drydocks, and piers while they dredged and deepened the bay from less than 10 to more than 60 feet. The area, the *Herald* explained, was a likely spot for a base to service Soviet submarines. Work contin-

ued there in 1987 and is scheduled to be completed later this year. Similarly, at Punta Huete near Lake Managua, Nicaragua's largest military air base has become operational. Its 10,000-foot runways can accommodate the most modern aircraft the Soviets possess. By last November, these runways had handled some reconnaissance flights. They seemed ready for more.

Earlier, I wrote that Punta Huete was important because it gave the Soviets a platform from which they could launch TU-95 Bear reconnaissance planes to monitor the western United States in much the same way that aircraft based in Cuba have been monitoring the coast between Maine and Florida. My sources were correct; they just underestimated the threat.

"Sandinistas using MiGs in Cuba," claimed the headline in the *Miami Herald* last 14 June. Nicaraguan pilots who had been trained in Bulgaria, the article explained, were operating MiG-21 jets from the San Julian air base at Cuba's western tip. From there a MiG-21 could fly as far north as Savannah, Ga., or as far south as San Jose, Costa Rica, then turn around without refueling and return to base. Punta Huete changed all that. It let the MiGs refuel while flying to or from the Panama Canal. And there is little doubt that, in the event of war, the Sandinistas would strike at the canal.

As recently as 1979, all but one—Costa Rica—of the five nations of Central America were controlled by military or military-dominated governments of the right or left. Once it assumed power in Washington, the Reagan administration moved swiftly to promote democracy throughout the region. And with some success. In 1984, voters in El Salvador elected Jose Napoleon Duarte, a 62-year-old graduate of Notre Dame, as their new civilian president. He took steps to bolster the nation's war-torn economy while keeping leftist guerrillas off balance and on the move. In 1985 bvoth Honduras and Guatemala held honest elections, and the triumphs of Jose Aszona and Vinicio Cerezo completed transitions from military rule. In 1986, Costa Ricans elected Oscar Arias to a five-year term and democracy seemed to be on the march.

Except in Nicaragua, where totalitarianism reigned. From the moment the Sandinistas marched into Managua in 1979,

there has been no doubt about their implacable hostility toward the United States. ("Let us fight against the Yankee, the enemy of humankind," one stanza of their national anthem begins. And an early policy paper referred to the United States as the "rabid enemy" of peoples struggling for "national liberation" everywhere.) Facing that hostility, on might have expected the United States to reciprocate. But Washington preferred to turn the other cheek. "They are at war with us and we just aren't recognizing it," a retired general fumed. "If we don't recognize it, we're going to lose it."

In 1981, merely by making some threats and being seen as willing to follow through on them, Washington persuaded the Sandinistas to cut the flow of arms to Marxist guerrillas in El Salvador. But—and this is important—policymakers never seemed to ask themselves what America's vital interests in the region were. They never defined how far they were willing to go to advance their goals. Almost from day one, their response to the growing threat that Nicaragua posed to the rest of Central America has been disorganized, haphazard, not at all well thought out.

When the contras emerged as a fighting force in 1981, for example, the White House arranged for Argentinian officers to train them at secret camps in the Honduran countryside. (No one seemed to know—or care—that the Argentinians had gained their experience battling urban terrorists and that associating the contras with them risked disaster from a public-relations point of view.) That lasted

U.S. forces find rough terrain in Honduras tough going during training exercises. But there's always time to explain to fascinated youngsters why they're there and how their equipment works.

until the United States sided with Britain—against Argentina—in the Falklands War.

Next the United States gave the task of running the contra campaign to the Central Intelligence Agency, which proceeded to mine Nicaragua's harbors and to produce a training manual that detailed assassination techniques. When Congress objected to that, the CIA deferred to the National Security Council and the enthusiasms of Marine Corps Lt. Col. Oliver North. The resulting sale of weapons through Israel to Iran may indeed have been "a nifty idea"—as North believed and testified—but it raised only $4 million for the contra cause and unleashed a flood of negative publicity. "The contras are on their own," stated Rep. Dave McCurdy (D-Okla.), a moderate who had long supported their requests for aid. "The power of the president, the personality of the president, is not going to carry the day for them again." Agreed Sen. David Durenberger (R-Minn.), the outgoing chairman of the Senate Intelligence Committee: it would be "a cold day in Washington" before the contras received another dime.

Administration Had A Different Plan

Since 1979, Soviet assistance to the Sandinistas has been uninterrupted and dependable. "As regular as rain," one U.S. official says. Contrast that with U.S. assistance to the contras, which has been scattershot. Between 1982 and 1984, for example, Congress voted $62 million in aid. Then, upset by disclosures of CIA activities, it ceased this aid and decreed that the contras could receive $27 million for "humanitarian" purposes. In 1986, by a margin of just 12 votes in the House of Representatives and six in the Senate, lawmakers deposited another $100 million in the contras' account, but proclaimed that $30 million had to go for "non-lethal" expenditures. Obtaining this aid was like climbing aboard a roller coaster; no one could predict the ups or downs or even the length of the ride.

In October 1986, the Sandinistas shot down a U.S. C-123K cargo plane near the Costa Rican border and captured crew member Eugene Hasenfus. Supply flights had been taking off from El Salvador's Ilopango Air Force base for months, the plane's logs revealed. Then came the revelation that the United States had sold arms to Iran. Finally, there were reports that high-ranking officials had persuaded the Saudi Arabians and the Sultan of Brunei to contribute to the freedom fighters in Central America. When the questions multiplied, Congress appointed committees to investigate. This triggered the four events that combined to put the United States in its present box. Consider event number one.

As he neared the end of his sixth year as leader of the Free World, Ronald Reagan lost a sizable chunk of his political authority. In the mid-term elections of 1986, the Democrats regained control of the Senate. This enabled Sen. Christopher Dodd (D-Conn.), a fervent foe of contra aid, to take over as chairman of the Western Hemisphere Affairs subcommittee of the Foreign Relations Committee. And it allowed Sen. Claiborne Pell (D-R.I.)—who often had referred to the contras as "our terrorists"—to replace Sen. Richard Lugar (R-Ind.) as full committee chair. Not a single Democrat on that full committee, observers pointed out, ever had cast a pro-contra vote.

Long before the hearings began on Capitol Hill, the Iran-contra affair dominated the news. The almost daily disclosures deepened the Oval Office gloom and even the appointment of new officials—Frank C. Carlucci to replace Navy Vice Adm. John Poindexter as director of the NSC, and former Sen. Howard Baker (R-Tenn.) to take Donald Regan's place as White House chief of staff—failed to reverse the impression that Regan had been weakened badly. That perception of weakness led to these results:

• In Honduras, President Azcona halted a contra commander's meeting in the capital of Tegucigalpa. Then he called in the U.S. ambassador and got him to agree that the main contra camps would be closed by July 1987 and that the contras themselves would be fighting on *Nicaraguan* soil.

• In Costa Rica, officials at Puerto Limon refused to allow crewmen from the guided missile destroyer USS *Luce* (DDG-38) ashore for a routine visit. The skipper's certification that his men carried no contagious disease wasn't good enough. Officials said they wanted to check each crew member for AIDS. This insulting decision, it turned out, had been made by senior officials in the capital of San Jose.

• In Mexico, the government reversed policy and resumed shipments of petroleum to oil-starved Nicaragua. The Iran-contra scandal "has created a new political space," one official explained, "in which Latin American nations can maneuver in opposition (to the United States) and we must take advantage of that."

That was event number two.

In the fall of 1986, the contras had begun to receive the first increments of the money Congress had voted them a few months earlier. And what a difference those funds made. By the end of June 1987, the contras no longer resembled the "cross-border raiding party" that a military critic had called them earlier in the year. Politically, they had recovered from the resignation of their former leader, Arturo Cruz, and were united again as a viable, independent force. Economically, the fighters and their families had enough to eat and their communications were computerized. Militarily, they had neutralized the Sandinistas' advantage in the air by using Red-Eye missiles to knock helicopter gunships from the sky. In the last month or two, they had infiltrated thousands of men into northern Nicaragua without detection by enemy troops—an amazing accomplishment—and were just about to seize the initiative for the first time in the war.

Arias Plan Considers Region As A Whole

Then, in Washington, Oliver North took the witness stand. Public-opinion polls tracing contra support suddenly shot up; the American people, it seemed, had finally figured out who the "good guys" were and were backing them. The $100 million that had done so much good would expire 30 September. Wasn't this the right moment to go before Congress and request additional funds?

Because it didn't think it had the votes, the White House didn't even send up another aid request. That meant funding would die at the end of the fiscal year. That was event number three.

The administration, it turned out, had a different plan. Sensitive to complaints that it was interested only in a vic-

tory on the battlefield, and anxious to prove to a skeptical Congress that it was willing to follow a negotiations track that might lead to peace, it persuaded House Speaker Jim Wright (D-Tex.) to "co-author" a peace plan with the President. That's the genesis of the Reagan-Wright plan which was announced to the world last August. The Sandinistas, administration strategists were sure, would reject the plan. That would enable them to return to Capitol Hill, say "we tried," and request more aid.

The trouble with this approach was that it was too clever by half. It boomeranged on its creators. That failure was event number four. Meeting in Guatemala City on 7 August, the presidents of all five Central American nations rejected Reagan-Wright and instead embraced a plan that Costa Rican President Arias first had proposed six months earlier. Their action took Washington completely by surprise—not a single expert in or out of government had predicted this would happen—and U.S. officials could only hope that the game wasn't already lost.

"Feet People" Have Fled The War Zone

That's the problem now, for even a cursory glance at the two accords shows the Arias plan to be soft. No wonder the Sandinistas agreed to it. Under Reagan-Wright, there would be an immediate 60-day cease-fire, reconciliation talks, and amnesty for contra forces in the field. Soviet and Cuban advisers would have to return home. The Sandinistas would restore civil liberties and schedule elections as soon as possible. In return for these positive steps, the United States would suspend military aid to the contras, halt maneuvers in neighboring Honduras, and withdraw its forces from the area.

Whereas Reagan-Wright focuses on Nicaragua, the Arias plan considers the region as a whole. While calling for the end of contra aid, it has nothing to say about arms or personnel from the Soviet bloc. It assumes a false symmetry: the contras, in its view, are just as legitimate in a moral sense as the Marxist troops who are trying to overthrow the democratically elected government of El Salvador. Finally, it contains no penalties or enforcement provisions against signatories who break its rules. So what will make the Sandinistas adhere to the plan? Fear, Arias volunteered. If they fail to comply, "they will be morally isolated by the whole world."

"Reagan's Bay of Pigs," the *Wall Street Journal* alleged. "Barring some dramatic event, Nicaragua was lost once and for all to the Communist empire during the past week, just as Cuba was lost when the exile invasion failed." "Folly," complained *New York Times* columnist William Safire about "the blundering that led to the unconscionable sellout of our national interest in preventing further Communist penetration of this hemisphere." Summed up columnist Charles Krauthammer in the *Washington Post:* "Ten years from now when Oscar Arias takes his vanity and his Nobel Peace Prize into Miami exile, Americans will ask who lost Central America. The answer will be that the Democrats thought of the idea, but they never could have swung it without Ronald Reagan."

As the two sides approached the plan's initial deadline of 7 November, the Sandinistas made well-publicized efforts to comply with parts of the accord. They allowed *La Prenza*—shut down for 15 months—to publish again without censorship. They authorized Radio Catolica to broadcast religious programs—but not to carry news—and welcomed a handful of priests back from exile abroad. They even asked Cardinal Miguel Obando y Bravo to mediate talks they said they agreed to hold with the contras.

"Nobody Thinks We're Serious"

Yet that was about as far as they were prepared to go. They wouldn't grant total amnesty—as called for by the the plan—or let all prisoners out of jail. There were other things they just wouldn't do. "Let no one harbor illusions that we are going to trade the principles of the revolution," Interior Minister Tomas Borge told a group of textile workers in Managua last fall. Soon it became clear. The Sandinistas would allow the symbols—but not the substance—of opposition to appear. They could—and would—take back these "concessions" any time they chose. "I suspect the Arias plan will buy a kind of peace," says Curtin Winsor Jr., the former U.S. ambassador to Costa Rica, "but come the next presidency and it's all over. The Sandinistas will feel free to go at it again, and we won't have the contras. We'll have no other option than the U.S. Marines."

The consequences of our diplomatic ineptitude, Winsor and others maintain, will burden us for years. By embracing—or being perceived as embracing—the Arias plan, the United States has legitimized the Sandinista regime, abandoned the contras to a perilous fate, forsaken whatever remained of the Reagan Doctrine, and placed our Central American allies in dire jeopardy.

Already, the "feet people"—400,000 strong—have fled the war zone and settled in refugee camps throughout Central America. Let another domino fall—Honduras, say, or El Salvador—and that number could quadruple overnight. Those people won't march south. They'll head north to America.

"The reason we haven't succeeded with our policy is that nobody *thinks* we're serious," former National Security Adviser Zbigniew Brzezinski has pointed out. "We don't *act* like we're serious." The United States can remedy that without dispatching Marines. One step would be to cut diplomatic relations with the Sandinista regime. Another would be to exert pressure on our hemispheric allies to have the OAS withdraw recognition of Managua until it fulfills the promises it made in 1979—and made again in 1987. A third would be to recognize the Nicaraguan Democratic Resistance—the contras—as that country's only legitimate government and to support it both economically and politically.

"It is the Resistance that has given Nicaragua a chance for true freedom," Reagan told the United Nations Assembly in New York City last October. "We must not abandon these courageous men and women. So let me promise: Nicaragua will have its freedom. And we will help the Resistance carry on its brave fight until freedom is secure."

As the new year began, the Soviets and the Sandinistas alike were wondering if the President and the American people were willing to place steel and resolve behind those lofty words.   ∎

E-Systems AN/WSC-3(V) LOS UHF Shipboard Radio.
The Standard of the Free World.

More than 6,000 WSC-3s are currently in service, providing ,000-hour MTBF reliability to e United States Navy and to umerous international navies Europe, Asia, Africa and the ideast.

Advanced modular architecture nsures that every new WSC-3 presents the latest in technol-gy. Advanced modular design ermits a configuration to meet ur current operational require-ents, then reconfiguration to eet future requirements, all in a st-effective manner. The WSC-3 a true growth radio.

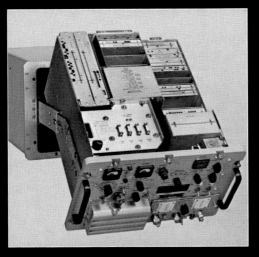

The radio can be configured for AJ operation or for parallel or serial (MIL-STD-1553, MIL-STD-188) remote control. No other line-of-sight (LOS) communications equipment can match the record of the WSC-3 for reliability and versatility. Let E-Systems show you how the AN/WSC-3 (V) can be tailored to your exact specifications. E-Systems, Inc., Corporate Headquarters, P.O. Box 6600248, Dallas, Texas 75266-0248.

E-SYSTEMS
The science of systems.

MERCHANT MARINE

Despite Helpfu
the Outlook for th

By Peter J. Finnerty

As the United States and global markets attempt to comprehend the full importance of dramatic fluctuations in the stock market, a treaty with the Soviet Union to eliminate medium and short-range nuclear missiles, and wide variations of opinion about what course of action to follow to reduce the enormous federal budget deficits, the relatively small U.S. merchant marine shrinks even further, a victim of political neglect. And as the privately owned, U.S.-flag merchant fleet contracts, the nation's vulnerability at sea grows.

The reduction in U.S. merchant ships and in shipyards is so large that it finally has attracted the attention of the national media. National security planners also are said to be, at long last, recognizing that the disappearance of hundreds of U.S. merchant ships and thousands of trained merchant seafarers has reached a stage that is inadequate for defense and will require sweeping action to arrest. Sadly, no such remedy is on the horizon.

Events over the past year have demonstrated clearly that the United States remains dependent on maritime commerce, and that government policies concerning ships and the oceans upon which they transport international cargoes still constitute an important element of U.S. national interest. Attacks on merchant shipping in the Persian Gulf have been a daily reminder of the peril to western economic lifelines that grows as the United States needlessly allows U.S. maritime resources to contract and to shift to foreign countries.

The steady downward trend has been recognized for some time by many knowledgeable officials in the public and private sectors. Several years ago, Rep. Charles Bennett (D-Fla.), a wise and experienced legislator who chairs the Seapower Subcommittee of the House Armed Services Committee and serves on the Merchant Marine and Fisheries Committee, took action to address the worsening problem.

After conducting a Seapower Subcommittee hearing to explore the situation, Bennett sponsored legislation to name a presidentially appointed Commission on Merchant Marine and Defense to study the matter in depth. Though that legislation was enacted some years ago, an absence of appropriated funds held up action by the Commission until 1987.

The Commission on Merchant Marine and Defense, chaired by former Sen. Jeremiah Denton, issued a sobering report last October which documented the decline in the maritime industry's ability to perform its defense role. The report spells out in detail the well-advanced drop in merchant ships, shipyards, and trained personnel. Even the so-called effective control fleet of American-owned, foreign-registered ships has experienced a reduction. These declines also are matched by large drops in the numbers of merchant ships in the fleets of Europe.

Dwindling U.S. maritime resources should alarm responsible federal officials, but for too long they have not been faced with a mobilization emergency that would reveal to the nation and to the world just how bad things really are. If and when that happens, fingerpointing will do nothing to help the United States respond with adequate sealift in a short time. History will record of that future crisis that we Americans attained certain initial military and naval goals, but that inadequate commercial sealift was America's Achilles heel.

Repeated Warnings Have Been Ignored

Many thoughtful and alert naval officers have realized that the problem exists, but view it as a political one best left to various civilian officials to resolve. Tragically, those civilian officials are disinclined to heed repeated warnings unless the Defense Department really presses the case as representative of a risk to national security. Thus, another administration will complete its time in office and move on, while the basic maritime deficiency of the nation simply worsens. Former Chief of Naval Operations Adm. James Holloway, a member of the Commission on Merchant Marine and Defense, recently stated that the current Chief of Naval Operations should testify before Congress on the severity of the problem.

The Persian Gulf situation has focused some long-overdue attention on merchant shipping policies. In the Pentagon's first formal outline of the U.S. Persian Gulf mission provided to Congress, then Secretary of Defense Caspar Weinberger indicated that U.S. Navy protection of the 11 U.S.-flag Kuwaiti tankers "was not part of an open-ended unilateral American commitment to defend all nonbelligerent shipping in the Persian Gulf." At a 9 September news briefing, it also was noted that "we protect U.S.-flagged shipping throughout the world, wherever it is." The point of the explanation is that the men and women of the U.S.

Legislative Proposals,
Merchant Marine is Bleak

Navy risk their lives to protect only U.S.-flag merchant ships, not foreign-flag ships, whether U.S.-owned or not.

For some of us in the shipping business, these statements were thought-provoking, indeed. Consider the dire predictions of the Commission on Merchant Marine and Defense on the one hand and news reports of the need for U.S.-flag ships on the other. America's maritime resources still could be renewed, but it seems that even the current pro-defense administration prefers to treat the U.S.-flag merchant marine as an industry it can afford to neglect. Time will tell if this expediency will become a national regret.

According to the Maritime Administration, the size of the privately-owned merchant fleet was 450 ships as of October 1987, but only 360 were active. The Commission's report noted that the active dry cargo fleet, excluding Military Sealift Command charters, as of 1 November numbered 170 ships. But that number included many ships dedicated to domestic trades. It is the liner ships engaged in foreign commerce that are the best barometer of the U.S. merchant fleet. However, the specifics on those ships startle even the casual observer. There are only seven U.S.-flag liner carriers in foreign commerce: American President Lines, 23 containerships; American Transport Lines, seven containerships; Farrell Lines, six ships; Lykes Brothers Steamship Co., 27 ships; Sea-Land Service, 23 containerships; Top Gallant, two containerships, and Waterman Steamship Co., three LASH barge carrier ships. The total is 91 liner ships deployed in foreign commerce; in January 1987, they held a 14.9 percent share of the U.S. liner trade, down from 30 percent in 1975.

Lest anyone mistakenly take solace in the figure of 91 ships, consider the age and pending obsolescence of more than half of them. In the intensely competitive field of modern ocean shipping, only highly automated, large, diesel-powered ships are likely to survive. But almost all of the seven U.S. liner carriers still operate some old steam-turbine ships in foreign commerce. APL operates 14, Sea-Land seven, Lykes 27, Farrell six, and Waterman three, for a total of 57 which likely will leave active service within the next several years. APL plans to replace five in 1988 and Sea-Land reportedly will scrap nine old ships.

The Commission on Merchant Marine and Defense also documented the sharp drop in merchant seamen as the ships that are the source of their livelihood disappear. The total dropped from 48,000 seafarers in 1960, to 36,000 in 1970, to 23,000 in 1980, to 13,400 in 1987. There is doubt as to whether adequate personnel will be available to provide crews for the growing Ready Reserve Fleet. And if that weren't enough of a problem, technology and international competition are reducing crew sizes on automated foreign ships to levels of 14 and even nine per ship. U.S. Coast Guard requirements now are held at higher levels by such statutory rules as three watch crews and no crossover between deck and engine personnel; those requirements therefore result in crew sizes of 19 to 21 on modern U.S. ships. Soon foreign competition, with both lower wages and much smaller crew sizes on modern ships, will require Congress to lower Coast Guard manning requirements in order for U.S.-flag ships to remain competitive. That, of course, would lead to a further diminution of the numbers of personnel available to man U.S. ships in the reserve fleets. Conversely, fewer U.S. seafarers per vessel would be required to crew the modern, automated ships in active service.

Changes in Federal Policies Needed

This grim review of the downward trend need not constitute the last chapter of a depressing period in U.S. merchant marine history. Actually, for a few of the U.S. carriers, there are some exciting, positive indications. Just as the U.S. Navy must renew its fleet with periodic infusions of new tonnage, so also must private U.S. ship operators marshal private capital resources to deploy modern, efficient ships able to effectively engage in foreign competition on the high seas. APL, American Transport Lines, and Sea-Land all have made substantial capital commitments to modernizing their fleets. Billions of dollars of private—not government—capital now are invested and further vessel replacements are expected during 1988. By year end, more than four dozen very large, automated, fuel-efficient containerships will be operating under U.S. flag.

Equally important, these same three carriers have developed extensive shoreside intermodal transport networks involving trains, trucks, and terminals. Sea-Land alone manages a complex global system of over 100,000 containers in service in more than 60 countries. Highly sophisticated computer systems tie the ocean and landside activities together in a carefully orchestrated, profitable system that is in perpetual motion. That enterprise represents not only a significant contribution to the U.S. balance of trade, but constitutes a vital resource in the defense industrial base.

Although this and other U.S. liner systems are among the most modern in the world, they alone aren't enough to support defense efforts in time of crisis. They would be more useful if the Defense Department would accelerate its use of commercial, privately-operated containerization for much more of its sealift needs.

In order for the modern and competitive portion of the U.S. merchant marine to expand, a variety of basic changes are needed in federal policies. Many of the changes are obvious and have been under discussion for many years. However, for a variety of competitive and political reasons, reforms have not been made. Federal statutes impose numerous costly requirements on U.S. ship operators. U.S. laws specify how American ships must be built, crewed, taxed, and maintained. Statutes require U.S.-citizen crews and even spell out how the crews must be fed each day. U.S.-flag carriers also must comply with antipollution, safety, and defense requirements. All of these federal rules impose added costs that do not apply to the same extent, if at all, to foreign-flag competition.

The major area of cost difference is that of crew cost.

PETER J. FINNERTY, who holds a third mate's license, is vice president, public relations, for Sea-Land Corporation and vice president, maritime affairs, for CSX Corporation, Sea-Land's parent corporation. He also is the Navy League's vice president for maritime affairs.

U.S. crew wage costs are higher than those of Japan and Europe and, naturally, much higher than those of other countries in Asia and of developing countries. As the numbers of Asian competitors has grown on major trade routes, the crew cost disadvantage increased for nonsubsidized U.S.-flag carriers—Sea-Land, American Transport Lines, and Top Gallant. To attempt to compensate, U.S. crew sizes were reduced to 21, and U.S. maritime unions agreed to reduce some fringe benefits and other costs. However, U.S. statutes prevent further reductions in crew size. The 59 liner vessels under federal operating subsidy, those operated by APL, Lykes, Farrell, and Waterman, most with large crew sizes, enjoy the advantage of having the government pay most of the crew costs. The 34 nonsubsidized liner ships of necessity have smaller crews, since their operators must bear the entire cost.

If America is to achieve its goal of a healthy, competitive U.S. merchant fleet, the federal operating-differential subsidy (ODS) program must be revised. Efforts at ODS reform have been under way in Congress for the past four years, but the administration would not engage in serious discus-

The Sea-Land Anchorage is one of three ships built by Bay Shipbuilding, of Sturgeon Bay, WI, for service in the domestic trades under the Jones Act. This 20,965-ton, 710-foot-long ship, capable of carrying 1,402 containers at 20 knots, entered service in August 1987. The three ships, which will ply between the ports of Anchorage, Kodiak, and Tacoma, together cost approximately $200 million to build.

sions about statutory revision until 1987. Following a May hearing before the Senate Merchant Marine subcommittee, it was learned that the administration planned to release a new policy statement. It was presented in early July in a letter to Congress and represented the first major change in ODS policy since 1982.

The most significant change of position was a willingness to enter into new ODS contracts with all seven U.S.-flag liner carriers for a total of about 100 ships. This new acknowledgment that the ODS program should be available to all U.S. liner carriers, and not just the four lines that have held contracts for many years, is essential to leveling the competitive playing field among U.S. carriers. Current policies limit ODS to mostly older ships, and force many new ships of the nonsubsidized carriers to operate under the double handicap of low-cost foreign competition and subsidized U.S. competition. This double standard is simply bad policy. The sooner Congress enacts an efficient and equitable ODS program to foster more modern U.S. liner ships, the sooner the U.S. fleet will attract added investment capital and expand.

Legislative Proposal Sent to Congress in October

The Department of Transportation/OMB legislative reform proposal includes a list of limits and rule changes that are intended to reduce the government's costs. In fact, the main criticism is that the proposal is overly concerned with cost cutting. The list of changes would:

1. Limit ODS payments per ship to no more than the

comparable cost of the most efficient U.S. management-labor contract in 1987, with provisions included for cost-of-living increases over time;

2. "Grant" new 10-year contracts to presently unsubsidized U.S. liner carriers, not "entitlements." Further, those contracts should be subject to congressional authorization and appropriations. Existing ODS contracts which are entitlements would become amended contracts with a duration of 10 years. Under Gramm-Rudman-Hollings budget cuts, entitlements are firm obligations of the federal government not subject to reduction through sequestration;

3. Limit each large U.S. liner carrier to a maximum under the bill of 20 ships operating with ODS, but each carrier would be permitted to purchase additional ODS shipyear rights from other carriers. The smaller lines would each be provided with 10 shipyears of ODS rights, and could use or sell them. The administration thus proposes to reduce existing U.S.-flag vessel operations under ODS of the two larger ODS carriers and legislatively increase the ODS authority of the two smaller ODS lines, as well as the three nonsubsidized lines. That, however, doesn't help the U.S liner fleet to grow. If focuses, instead, on budget limits;

4. Limit the subsidizable crew size on each ship to present Coast Guard manning scales. On modern, automated U.S. ships, this level is now about 17 people. legislative changes in Coast Guard statutes would be necessary to bring crew sizes down to foreign minimum levels authorized by the International Maritime Organization in London. IMO allows about 12 to 16 people depending upon ship type. The administration package fails to address further reductions in manning, although that could reduce ODS expenses and carrier operating costs;

5. Eliminate "double subsidy" by requiring reductions in ODS in proportion to an ODS vessel's revenue derived from U.S. government-impelled, U.S.-flag preference cargoes. For example, if a subsidized liner vessel earned a gross revenue on a foreign commerce voyage of $2.5 million and 20 percent of that revenue was derived from U.S.-flag preference cargoes, then the ODS due for that voyage would be reduced by one-fifth. If the ODS for the voyage were $200,000, the governmeng ODS payment would be reduced by $40,000 to a total of $160,000. Thus the federal government wouldn't pay the carrier once for the transport of the U.S.-flag preference cargoes and a second time for the ODS. American President Lines agreed to such change for its five automated containerships entering service in 1988;

6. Eliminate current trade route restrictions. These rules now limit competition by the ODS lines, but smaller U.S. carriers do not want to allow open competition by the larger U.S. carriers;

7. Authorize foreign-flag feeder ships for ODS carriers to operate abroad in order to increase the utilization of the U.S.-flag "line haul" ships. U.S.-flag line haul ships are larger transoceanic ships. Feeder ships provide pickup and delivery service between major "hub" ports and outports; and

8. "Grandfather" domestic services in existence to avoid section 805 hearing delays. Long-standing rules prevent any domestic ship operations by an ODS carrier unless approved under such lengthy section 805 hearings. These domestic trades include Alaska, Hawaii, and Puerto Rico.

This detailed legislative proposal for broad reform was sent to Congress in late October by Acting Secretary of Transportation James V. Burnley, IV. It is expected that Congress, before commencing consideration of it, first will solicit the views of carriers, shippers, and labor. Accordingly, no final action on it is anticipated until 1988, if then. But the chances of such a sweeping proposal becoming law in toto are unlikely because of strong opposition to many of the reform positions by some liner companies and shipboard unions representing licensed and unlicensed personnel. They represent formidable legislative obstacles.

Three Carriers Have Proposed Compromise Bill

It is encouraging, though, that the government finally is recognizing that it needs to eliminate the arbitrary designation of some ships to receive operating subsidy, while others that often are more modern and efficient are denied eligibility. Reshaping policy to encourage additional modern ships with smaller crews and lower operating costs is the essential ingredient to a competitive U.S. liner fleet.

The three U.S. liner carriers operating most U.S.-flag ships (American President Lines, Lykes, and Sea-Land Service) have proposed a compromise bill in an attempt to break the current impasse. It would provide eligiblity to operate as ODS ships to all U.S.-flag liner vessels, would phase out trade-route restrictions in three years, and would amend the section 805 domestic hearing rules for domestic carriers Matson and Tote. Congress will evaluate these and other proposals during 1988.

Another important area of opportunity to strengthen the competitiveness of U.S.-flag shipping is in U.S. tax law. The Tax Reform Act of 1986 substantially increased the tax burden of U.S.-flag vessels engaged in foreign commerce. Depreciation periods were doubled from five to 10 years, investment tax credits were eliminated, foreign tax-credit rules became more restrictive, foreign sourcing-of-income rules were narrowed, and the alternative minimum tax rules were applied. Such tax changes for companies in the domestic U.S. economy are much less consequential because the new tax rules apply to all competitors in the domestic trades. In international shipping, this is not the case. Foreign-flag ships now carry more than 85 percent of the liner cargoes in U.S. foreign commerce. Most foreign countries do not impose a tax on their ships in international commerce. Such shipping activity in international commerce is properly viewed as an export of services from a foreign country's national economy, with a contribution to their balance of trade.

International Trade Laws Are Increasingly Important

To impose taxes on U.S. shipping in foreign commerce is to handicap the competitive position of U.S. ships versus their foreign competition. The solution would be to provide tax deferral to the U.S.-flag foreign commerce ships, much like domestic ships are treated under the Capital Construction Fund. A proposal by U.S. carriers to establish a Merchant Marine Account to allow U.S.-flag ships in foreign commerce to defer taxes in order to accumulate capital for vessel replacement is a much needed reform. U.S. carriers

WILL THIS BE AMERICA'S LAST COMMERCIAL VESSEL?

The 710' oceangoing containership shown above and its two sister vessels represent the last non-military ships constructed by a U.S. shipyard. Unless current maritime policy changes immediately, the domestic commercial shipbuilding industry may cease to exist.

FRESHWATER AND SALTWATER CAPABILITIES ...IN A COMPETITIVE, QUALITY SHIPYARD!

With access to the world's oceans through the St. Lawrence Seaway, Bay Shipbuilding is both a freshwater <u>and</u> saltwater shipyard. Recognized as one of America's most progressive shipyards, Bay Shipbuilding has the facilities and capabilities to construct saltwater vessels up to 760' in length and Great Lakes vessels to 1,100' in length. Our facilities include 5 major building berths, 15 repair/outfitting berths, a 1,158' graving dock, 7,000-ton floating dry dock, 200-ton overhead gantry crane, plus numerical-controlled lofting and plasma burning equipment.

Our highly-skilled workforce, with more than 80 years' experience in steam and diesel propulsion systems, is complemented by complete in-house capabilities to design, build, repair, convert, re-power, retrofit, and jumboize <u>any</u> type of vessel.

Since 1902, Bay Shipbuilding has constructed a wide variety of vessels, including containerships, oil tankers, derrick ships, passenger ships, and stern trawlers. Bay Shipbuilding has also constructed more self-unloading vessels than any other shipyard in the United States...and has converted numerous straight-bulk vessels to self-unloaders as well. Additionally, Bay Shipbuilding is equally qualified in all facets of barge construction as it has built tug/barge units, notch barges, hydro-dump barges, and self-unloading barges for the bulk, chemical, and petroleum industries.

PUT BAY'S PROVEN RECORD OF EFFICIENCY, ON-SCHEDULE DELIVERIES, AND QUALITY WORKMANSHIP TO WORK FOR YOU...

BAY SHIPBUILDING CORP.
Subsidiary of The Manitowoc Company, Inc.
605 North 3rd Avenue, Sturgeon Bay, WI 54235
Phone: 414-743-5524 • Telefax: 414-743-2371

©MANITOWOC 1987

The DOD gives nod to AT&T for powerful gallium arsenide "super chips."

That old standby, the silicon chip, is in for stiff competition.

The Defense Advanced Research Projects Agency (DARPA) has awarded AT&T a four-year, $19.8 million contract for the development and production of gallium arsenide (GaAs) integrated circuits.

Compared to silicon, GaAs chips provide higher speeds, lower power requirements, and resistance to radiation for tomorrow's military computer and telecommunications systems.

Until now, producing GaAs chips has been a slow, costly process. The Pentagon is counting on AT&T—working with GM Hughes and McDonnell Douglas—to change all that.

Land, sea and air: Navy calls AT&T for $92 million San Francisco telecommunications network.

The Navy has made a major move to serve its growing communications needs in San Francisco—homebase for 22 warships, 30,000 sailors, and 28,000 civilians.

A 10-year contract has been awarded to AT&T to engineer, install, and maintain a state-of-the-art network linking 14 Bay Area bases in the Navy's San Francisco Consolidated Area Telephone System (CATS). AT&T will replace the Navy's entire World War II network with System 85 PBXs, 3B15 and 3B2 computers, fiber optic cable, microwave radio and—for administrative functions—a Management Information System (MIS), designed by AT&T specifically for this project.

Clearly, the Navy knows how to ride the wave of the future.

The value of "value engineering": Navy names AT&T Contractor of the Year.

As a result of several AT&T Value Engineering (VE) initiatives, including a $1.4 million cost-cutting idea implement at AT&T's Burlington, NC manufacturing facility, the U.S. Navy recently named AT&T 1986 Contractor of the Year for Value Engineering.

AT&T's Burlington people, working on Navy towed arrays, came up with an idea replace an interconnection design for th Data Transmitter with a less expensive approach, proved it would meet all Navy performance standards, and saved $70,000 per array.

AT&T places heavy emphasis on VE an other cost avoidance/reduction program which are welcomed by the Defense Department. On VE cases, the contracto shares a portion of the savings with the Government.

New AT&T Security-Plus STU-III phone answers government call.

Government agencies can now order AT&T's new STU-III phone, making it possible for Federal personnel to achieve communications security with unprecedented ease and convenience.

AT&T's Security-Plus communications terminal meets or exceeds all government requirements for STU-III terminals, ensuring security of voice and data communications over the public switched network through desktop to desktop encryption.

Enhanced features include clear and secure voice and data transmission at both 2.4 Kb/s and 4.8 Kb/s. AT&T's STU-III is also the only terminal that can handle multiple programs or security levels.

New U.S. Navy communications systems achieve ISDN capability with off-the-shelf economy.

The U.S. Navy is utilizing AT&T's commercially available switching, distribution, and information systems products to meet its voice and data communications needs.

The AT&T 5ESS™ Switch and System 85 PBX, both with proven Integrated Services Digital Network (ISDN) capability, will be used extensively in the Navy's Base Enhancements Program.

Both of these state-of-the-art systems provide user-oriented features, operate in virtually any environment, and have the flexibility to grow to meet the needs of tomorrow's Navy.

For more about the items on this page, dial **1 800 424-2988, Ext. 7,** between 8 am and 4:45 pm EST. In metro Washington, dial **457-0177, Ext. 7.**

AT&T
The right choice.

LAST OCEANGOING COMMERCIAL SHIP DELIVERED

On 9 November 1987, Bay Shipbuilding Corporation, of Sturgeon Bay, WI, delivered the last of three 1,400 TEU containerships to Sea-Land Corporation. With that delivery, there were no oceangoing merchant ships being constructed in the United States.

This represented a sharp contrast to what was taking place in U.S. shipyards 10 years ago, when there were 155 ships—76 Navy and 79 merchant ships—under construction. As of mid-November 1987, there were no firm plans for building other merchant ships in U.S. shipyards.

The American President Line's President Eisenhower is an example of the kind of modern, automated ship U.S. carriers must operate if they are to compete effectively in international trade. This 55,000-ton ship is propelled at 23 knots by 44,700-horsepower slow-speed diesels that use one barrel of oil per mile, and manned by a crew of 21. She was built in Japan at a cost of $29 million.

hope that the tax change will be taken up by Congress in 1988.

International trade laws are increasingly important to the U.S. merchant marine. The recent U.S.-Canada Free Trade Agreement is an example of trade agreements applying to U.S.-flag shipping. The significance to U.S. seapower is that trade negotiators seemingly have tunnel vision focused on economics and pay little attention to national defense implications. In the Canada situations, the USTR people expressed the view that U.S. domestic shipping was "protected," as well as U.S. shipyards. They were intent upon creating rules that could have the effect of transferring U.S. domestic shipping markets to Canadian ships, rather than encourage new investments in the U.S. fleet.

Plight of U.S. Shipbuilders Is Worsening

Trade negotiators, like tax collectors, maintain that U.S.-flag shipping is someone else's problem. Their response to carrier explanations of the threats to U.S.-flag shipping posed by their policies is for the plaintiffs to tell their story to the Department of Defense. The lesson to this writer is that the Defense Department must recognize that the existing commercial sealift capability of the country, as manifested by the dwindling numbers of ships still operating, is being taxed and negotiated away at the behest of free trade. A prime example is the effort to export Alaskan oil to Japan and thereby wipe out the U.S. domestic tanker fleet. Other U.S. government agencies have similarly displayed antipathy toward, or ignorance of, defense implications when addressing laws and rules that otherwise would support the U.S. merchant fleet. This has been true not only with regard to government-impelled cargo, but also with regard to rules on user fees, anti-trust measures, and foreign state-controlled carriers. The net result of anti-shipping bureaucracy ultimately will result in a failure for democracy as the U.S.-flag fleet is rendered noncompetitive by that bureaucracy.

The state-controlled carrier issue is especially timely because the negotiations on the nuclear-missile limitation treaty with the Soviet Union have been accompanied by

renewed pressure from the Soviets to regain full access to U.S. ports and cargoes for their merchant marine. Since the Soviet invasion of Afghanistan, Russian ships have been excluded from carriage of cargo between the United States and countries other than the U.S.S.R. Soviet ships must request clearance 14 days in advance for U.S. port calls in the U.S.-U.S.S.R. commerce. U.S. Maritime Administra-

closed, 60 of them just in the past two years. As a consequence, over 52,000 shipyard production workers have lost their jobs. The Commission's observation about real costs is especially apt with regard to U.S. shipyards: "The rapidly deteriorating situation cannot be addressed without real costs in terms of national resources allocated to pay for the defense aspects of the maritime industries. Any successful course of action will have costs. The challenge is to develop and implant policies that meet the requirements in the most cost-effective manner possible."

U.S. commercial shipyards were dropped off the list of national priorities in 1981 when the Reagan administration took office. The funding for commercial ship construction subsidies was eliminated by then Office of Management and Budget Director David Stockman. That policy stands out in sharp contrast to the generous support provided shipyards in Asia and Europe by their governments. Just recently the European Economic Community agreed to a uniform policy of subsidizing shipbuilding in Europe up to 28 percent of the construction cost. That formula does not include tax incentives. In October, European builders petitioned the EEC to increase the maximum level of government subsidy to 30 percent; as of the time of publication of this essay no action had been taken on this petition. But even under existing EEC policies, the West German government is subsidizing the construction of five U.S.-flag American President Lines containerships for delivery in 1988. Denmark previously built three of the new U.S.-flag ships now operated by American Transport Lines. It is a dramatic example of how U.S. shipyard policy is out of step with the rest of the world, when the industrial economies of Denmark and West Germany see the wisdom of producing modern, automated ships for U.S. carriers, but the United States government chooses to build none.

In sum, deficient policies for the U.S. merchant marine must be addressed if the threat to U.S. defense sealift is to be corrected. As Lewis Carroll wrote in the 19th century:

> The time has come, the Walrus said,
> to talk of many things:
> of shoes—and ships—and sealing wax—
> of cabbages—and kings— . . .

His lines call up the centuries-old struggle for nations and leaders to allocate scarce resources to competing economic and defense purposes. It is time for such decisions on the U.S. merchant marine and related policies. The government and the political process must develop a responsive solution, or the unrelenting competitive pressure of market forces and aging ships will drive U.S.-flag shipping down and down.

American merchant ship operators prefer to operate U.S.-flag ships, crewed by U.S. citizens. But current federal policies are making that approach less and less viable. Continued government indecision amounts to a negative decision for U.S. commercial shipping and shipbuilding. The time has indeed come to stop the rhetoric and initiate realistic new approaches to U.S. maritime policy. Other foreign shipping interests and their governments, including the Soviet Union, will be delighted if the United States continues to withdraw from the playing field. ∎

tor John Gaughan held discussions in Moscow in mid-October 1987 with his counterpart in response to Soviet inquiries for a maritime agreement that might reinstitute Soviet access to U.S. ports and cargoes. Unrestricted Soviet access could be devastating to Western carriers trying to compete against Soviet government merchant ships. It was in the 1970s when Russian ships created commercial havoc with massive rate cutting. The Soviet objective was then, and is now, to earn hard Western currency and to contribute in the process to the expansion of the already huge, and still expanding, Soviet merchant marine. The hammer and sickle again may appear in U.S. ports in 1988.

It would be remiss not to address the worsening plight of U.S. shipbuilders. The Commission on Merchant Marine and Defense noted that since 1982, 76 U.S. shipyards have

Oceanographic Activity, Research are on the Rise but More Funding and Ocean Policy Needed

OCEANOGRAPHY

By Don Walsh

It is difficult to present accurate information about congressional and administration final actions on funding for support of oceanography. If Congress and the White House were doing their respective jobs in a timely manner, the federal budgets would be approved and allocated by 1 October. However, this has rarely happened and the author of "Oceanography 1988" can only offer the reader the past year's budget after the fact and a best guess as to what will be approved for the present fiscal year.

However, in general terms, it is fairly easy to review national funding for oceanography. Since 1980 there have been few significant changes in overall funding trends. These trends are:

1. Navy budget support for oceanography has grown as a general result of the Reagan administration's strong push to increase funding for the Department of Defense. Special emphasis has been in the areas of antisubmarine warfare (ASW) and undersea warfare (USW), both of which have a strong dependence on environmental knowledge (i.e., oceanography). The Navy's goal is to have 3 percent real (above the rate of inflation) growth per year in its budget. Depending on how you count what's "oceanography" in the Navy's Research, Development, Test & Evaluation (RDT&E) budget, the FY 1987 figure is $101.77 million, while that for FY 1988 will be roughly $109.32 million. The difference is about 7.5 percent, or about 3 percent after inflation is deducted. As will be discussed later, the Navy's ocean program for the past five years has been getting excellent high-level attention at the Secretary of the Navy level.

2. From the beginning the Reagan administration has declared strong support for basic research, and the overall budget trend for the National Science Foundation since 1980 has been comfortably ahead of the rate of inflation. In fact, funding for NSF's ocean programs have grown at an annual rate of more than 10 percent during the past two years. This is roughly 5-6 percent real growth over inflation.

3. By comparison, the ocean programs of the National Oceanic and Atmospheric Administration (NOAA, a part of the Department of Commerce), have suffered. Each year since 1980 the administration has proposed the termination of large segments of NOAA's programs. And each year Congress has balked at these proposals and has allocated funding for their continuance. Despite this annual 'salvation' by Congress, funding for NOAA's overall ocean program has not even kept up with inflation.

4. Very little national investment has been made in needed high-capital-cost facilities (ships, satellites, submersibles, shore facilities, etc.) for support of oceanography.

5. Congress and the administration have given little specific attention to the national ocean program as a whole. Thus a coherent 'road map' does not exist as the basis for determining priorities and resulting funding allocations.

For FY 1987, which ended 1 October 1987, there were few surprises. The overall administration budget reflected the pressures of the need to reduce the federal deficit. The "Gramm-Rudman-Hollings" legislation had some of its impact blunted when the courts found that some of its authorities were unconstitutional. Nevertheless, the sense of Congress was that strict measures would have to be taken to start to bring this dangerous fiscal situation under control. Thus Congress may be moving in the same direction as the administration in cutting some of the budgets for ocean programs, but for different reasons.

Few Funding Surprises Expected in FY 1988

The problem is that there is not much left in the federal budget, other than defense appropriations, that is large enough to make an impact in reducing the budget. The President threatens to veto any budget sent to him by Congress that has significant cuts in defense funding and has adamantly opposed the adoption of any new taxes. Combine all of this with an increasing concern about the size of the federal deficit, and the possibility of having much new 'wealth' appropriated for ocean programs seems bleak.

For FY 1988 it appears that there will be few surprises in the levels of federal support for oceanography. That is,

the prevailing trends of the past seven years will continue.

Although there was considerable controversy over many of his actions, with respect to support and expansion of ocean sciences and technology former Secretary of the Navy John Lehman was probably one of the most progressive men to hold this office in several years. Under Lehman's direction, in 1984 new policies for direction and support of the Navy's oceanographic program were issued and implemented. As part of the plan he established Navy-supported "Secretary of the Navy Chairs in Oceanography" at four oceanographic institutions as well as "Secretary of the Navy Fellowships in Oceanography" to provide for oceanographic studies for naval personnel. At present five Navy fellows are near graduation from this program.

Lehman also directed that an Institute for Naval Oceanography be established at the National Space Technology Laboratories at Bay St. Louis, MS. This also is the location of the Navy's Oceanographic Office and the Naval Oceanographic Research and Development Activity. INO began operation in 1987. This will be the Navy's primary in-house facility for the conduct of oceanographic research using numerical modeling techniques. Administration of INO will be handled by the University Corporation for Atmospheric Research (UCAR) at Boulder, CO.

Finally, he supported increases in the Navy oceanographic research budget and was an active supporter of the high-technology, at-sea exercise of Navy-developed equipment, one demonstration of which led to the dramatic location and visit to the steamship *Titanic* in 1985 and 1986.

Lehman resigned as Secretary of the Navy in April 1987. It's expected that the new Secretary, James H. Webb, Jr., will carry on with this major renaissance of naval oceanography that was carefully mapped out by his predecessor. Lehman's actions have given ocean science and technology a recognized and key role in support of the broad naval mission throughout the world ocean.

Japanese-U.S. ASW Research Program to Be Developed

In addition to the departure of Lehman in 1987, the Navy also lost, through retirement in September, one of its most oceanographic-experienced officers. Rear Admiral Brad Mooney served as Oceanographer of the Navy for three years and then as Chief of Naval Research for four more. Coming from oceanographic, deep-submergence, and submarine-warfare backgrounds, Mooney was a major factor in developing and carrying out many of the Navy oceanographic policies developed during the past seven years.

The Office of Naval Research recently has established a University Research Initiative Program which will emphasize studies related to remote sensing of the world ocean. At present five academic institutions have been granted a total of $33 million to be used over a five-year period.

DR. DON WALSH served 25 years in the Navy, during which time he was involved in many aspects of Navy oceanographic activity. In 1975, he founded and chaired the Institute for Marine and Coastal Studies at the University of Southern California. He left that post in 1983 to devote full time to international Maritime, Inc., which he founded in 1975 and now heads.

There are solid institutional reasons for all of this recent Navy activity. For several years both the Secretary of the Navy and the Chief of Naval Operations have stated that ASW and USW are among the highest priority concerns of the Navy. Clearly, knowledge of the marine environment is a major factor in ASW, and this emphasis has now resulted in more support for mission-related oceanography.

The recent actions of Japan's Toshiba Company and Norway's Kongsberg Vaapenfabrik which sold advanced machine tools and operating software to the Soviet Union for submarine propeller manufacture, have created a major scandal. This equipment will permit Soviet submarines to be fitted with even quieter propellers. Estimates of how much added U.S. research funding will be required to regain the lost advantage run as high as five billion dollars.

As a result of embarrassment and a lack of diligence in processing export permits, the Japanese government has agreed to develop a joint ASW research program with the United States. The added stimulus of Japanese participation should promote added activity in ocean-related research and development.

Over the years of the Reagan administration the National Science Foundation also has enjoyed continuing increases in its program budgets for ocean sciences and technologies. Although much of its new program emphasis has been on the development and support of regional/global scale programs, it still allocates nearly 50 percent of its approximately $60-million-a-year funding to small, individual projects. As noted earlier, NSF's ocean program funding is growing at the rate of more than 10 percent per year.

The interaction of the oceans and the atmosphere takes place over three-fourths of the Earth's surface. These interactions have a profound effect on man's environment. Abnormal heating or cooling of the oceans in certain regions can cause global problems. The recent "El Nino" events in the Pacific were evidence of this. More recently a National Academy of Sciences study reported that the sea level of the world ocean was rising at an increasing rate. Within 100 years many coastal cities will face some difficult problems. We need to understand more about this process and be able to accurately predict the consequences.

The new NSF program emphasis on "global geosciences" recognizes that the only way large, regional ocean processes can be understood is to simultaneously study the oceans and atmosphere, and their interactions, over large regions. This is a 'holistic' approach to ocean studies requiring the cooperation of many institutions in many nations. The advent of the operational ocean-sensing satellite has provided a powerful tool in being able to study many ocean processes on a real-time basis.

Today we have under way the most comprehensive and extensive studies of the world ocean ever undertaken. Some of the programs falling under the general category of global geosciences are:

WOCE: World Ocean Circulation Experiment.
TOGA: Tropical Ocean Global Atmosphere program.
GOFS: Global Ocean Flux Study.
EPOCS: Equatorial Pacific Ocean Climate Study.
STACS: Sub Tropical Atlantic Climate Studies.
This is not intended to be a catalog for all such large-

The venerable, but still active, research submarine Alvin, commissioned in 1964, survived almost a year on the bottom of the sea. In October 1968, her support cables parted as she was being lowered into the sea preparatory to a mission off Wood's Hole, MA, and she went to the bottom in 1,535 fathoms of water. Recovered in September 1969, she has since then been modernized, refurbished, and lengthened. Her propeller assembly fared poorly when she hit bottom, as this unusual photograph, taken from the experimental aluminum submarine Aluminaut, shows.

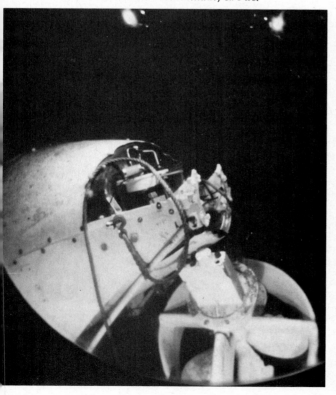

scale research efforts, but rather a sample of some of them. NSF, NOAA, and the Navy, the three major U.S. ocean-research-supporting agencies, all have roles in one or more of these programs. In addition, many have extensive participation by research assets of foreign countries.

By comparison with Navy and NSF, NOAA has had an uneven year. As with every year since 1980, the Reagan administration has proposed cutting major ocean program elements from this agency's budget. Some of these proposed actions are:

- National Sea Grant Program to be terminated.
- Coastal Zone Management Program to be terminated.
- NOAA Underwater Research Program to be terminated.
- Approximately one-half (12 vessels) of NOAA's research fleet to be taken out of service, including all the fisheries research vessels. In their place would be the use of lower-cost chartered vessels on an 'as-needed' basis.

If all these terminations were approved by Congress, then NOAA's ocean-program budget would be decreased by nearly half. But Congress will not, and has not, approved cuts of these programs. Each year Congress restores proposed cuts and the NOAA program has another year of grace. Clearly this sort of start-stop program history obstructs the conduct of effective management of this agency. Admittedly, within NOAA, internal plans are made and certain longer-lead-time actions are taken. Yet, when the congressional budget cycle begins it is almost certain that none of this advance-planning work will have any relation to the outcome. The net result is a measurable waste of time and resources as NOAA zigzags through this annual drill.

Use of Manned and Unmanned Submersibles is Rising

With respect to the almost 50 percent reduction of NOAA's in-house fleet, the question is whether it's more efficient to own or to charter research vessels. The ships that would be retained by NOAA would be their large research, mapping, and charting vessels, since it's difficult to find these specialized hulls in the private-sector charter fleet. Congress was not persuaded by the administration's arguments for this action. In addition, an assessment of the general proposal by the General Accounting Office (an arm of Congress) came to the same conclusion. NOAA was directed to study the problem and to come back to Congress with more convincing data. This study now is being done by the Marine Board of the National Research Council (of the National Academy of Sciences), an advisory group independent of government agencies. The study results will be given to NOAA early in 1988.

Adding to NOAA's many problems was the short-notice resignation of its experienced Administrator, Dr. Anthony Calio (who had the rank of Undersecretary of Commerce), in September 1987. Calio had been with NOAA since 1981 and had served in the top job since late 1985.

As of late October it was not clear who would be nominated by the President for this important position. First, it will be difficult to find a qualified person who wants to preside over any federal agency for the final 12 months of a presidential administration. This is especially true in the

case of this administration, which has consistently attempted to greatly reduce NOAA's ocean programs. Second, it's hard to see how any individual could accomplish much more than routine, ongoing administration of NOAA. There will be no time for, nor interest in, bold new initiatives.

In 1987 there was a real increase in the use of manned and unmanned submersibles for *in situ* marine research.

In manned submersibles, the pioneering work of Woods Hole's *Alvin* and the Harbor Branch Foundation's *Johnson Sea Link* I and II submersibles continues to confirm the utility and uniqueness of this approach. Every year an increasing number of marine scientists is using these small submarines to make major discoveries in the deep oceans. For example, in 1987:

• At Bermuda, Project Beebe, a program supported by NOAA and the National Geographic Society, made 35 dives using the submersibles *Pisces IV* and the *Johnson Sea Link I.* The project was named after Dr. William Beebe, the first deep-diving marine scientist who worked off Bermuda with his *Bathysphere* in the late 1920s and early 1930s. The 1987 dive series provided research opportunities for scientists from 10 different universities and research institutions. NOAA and NGS intend to continue Project Beebe as an annual program, if NOAA's budget for its Undersea Research Program holds up.

• At the Cayman Islands two submersibles, *Pisces IV* and *PC-1802,* leased from Research Submersibles Limited, were used over the course of the year for studies of deep-dwelling sharks. Nearly a dozen dives, each lasting several hours, were made between depths of 1,000 and 5,000 feet. From this work a new species of shark was found and observed.

• Off New York City the submersible *Delta* worked in the Hudson Submarine Canyon at depths between 200-300 feet studying and assessing commercial scallop beds for the Northeast Fisheries Laboratory of NOAA's National Marine Fisheries Service.

• The venerable *Alvin* spent the year operating in the Pacific. A major exploration was on the slopes of the Marianas Trench, the same geographic feature where the deepest point in the ocean (the challenger Deep) is located. On these dives *Alvin*'s scientists found new bottom-dwelling animals as well as unique geological structures. One of the more exciting diving operations during the Pacific operation was into the crater of a submarine volcano, a first in deep-submergence science. Later in the year *Alvin* made dives on the Juan de Fuca Ridge along the coast of Oregon and Washington. This area is a potential source of valuable ocean mineral deposits as well as a site of unique biological and geological activity.

• The French deep submersible *Nautile* completed an overhaul and spent the summer months participating in an expedition at the wreckage of the *Titanic.* This was the third year that this site had been visited. In 1985 the ship was located by a joint U.S.-French expedition where a deep towed camera system was used to photograph the wreckage field. The next year a U.S. expedition from Woods Hole used the *Alvin* and its tethered ROV, *Jason,* to explore and photograph *Titanic.* In 1987 the *Nautile* and its mothership, *the Nadir,* were chartered by a British-French group to go to the *Titanic* site for further exploration, photogra-

phy, and recovery of selected artifacts. A total of 27 dives were made that resulted in extensive photographic documentation, together with numerous artifacts that were successfully recovered. In October a television special was broadcast which gave an overview of the operation and showed some of the materials recovered. Undoubtedly this is just the beginning of the story on this remarkable deep-sea salvage operation.

• Meanwhile in the North Atlantic the Soviet Union now is testing its first 20,000-foot-depth-capable research submersible. Built by the Rauma-Repola shipyard in Finland, this vehicle is probably the *Akademik,* which will be used by the P.P. Shirshov Institute of Oceanology, headquartered in Moscow. This institute already has four operational submersibles. There is also a second 20,000-foot submersible completing construction at R-R that probably will be operated by the USSR Ministry of Geology.

• In Japan Mitsubishi Heavy Industries is building the *Shinkai 6500,* a submersible with a 21,000-foot depth capability. It should be completed within 2-3 years. The titanium pressure hull was sent to the United States in the fall of 1987 for pressure testing in the giant test complex at Annapolis, MD.

• The U.S. Navy's *Sea Cliff* and *Turtle* submersibles finally will get a dedicated mother ship that will give these vehicles a realistic 'go anywhere' capability for the first time. This vessel, *Laney Chouest,* presently is being converted from an offshore-diving-support vessel to a submersible mother ship. The conversion will be so comprehensive that the vessel will not be able to be used for support of offshore oil and gas operations again.

• RLS of Grand Cayman also has sold one of its Perry submersibles, a PC-8B, to the Institute of Oceanology at Varna in Bulgaria. The vehicle will be used for research studies in the Black Sea.

USNS Bowditch Rammed in Rio de Janeiro Harbor

In the area of *unmanned* submersibles, especially important were the first real projects involving the use of remotely operated vehicles (ROVs). These tethered, surface-controlled submersibles have been in active use for commercial work in the oceans since the mid-1970s. Today more than 1,100 of them have been built, ranging from $10,000 swimming TV cameras to multi-million-dollar work vehicles capable of working in sea conditions where divers and manned submersibles could not operate. However, it was only about three years ago that the low-cost ROV (LCROV) was developed. This put the inspection type ROV (swimming cameras) into a price range ($10,000-$50,000) that could be afforded by whole new sectors of ocean operators. These operators covered the spectrum from small commercial diving companies to recreational divers and from merchant ship operators to oceanographic research institutions. Before the LCROV, the inspection type ROVs were priced in the hundreds of thousands of dollars, well beyond the reach of these users.

An example of a successful LCROV is the Phantom series of LCROVs built in Oakland, CA, by the Deep Ocean Engineering Company (DOE), one of the largest manufacturers of LCROVs. There are eight models in the Phantom family in a price spectrum from $10,000 to $55,000. More than 83 have been sold since production began three years ago.

The other major U.S. builder is Deep Submergence Systems International (DSSI) of Woods Hole, MA, whose LCROVs, the MiniRover series, are priced between $20,000 and $50,000 depending on how they are equipped.

Nearly 200 LCROVs have been manufactured. Between them, DOE and DSSI have built over 150 LCROVs in the past four years. But until this year few have been used for oceanographic research for other than demonstrations of vehicle capabilities.

In Crater Lake, CA, a *Super Phantom* LCROV was used to explore the bottom of this ancient volcanic crater. Researchers found and studied ocean-like 'seafloor features' similar to the vents and fissures seen by the manned submersible *Alvin* during its dives in the Pacific and Atlantic oceans. These features were found and recorded during the brief operation at Crater Lake, and plans are being made to undertake longer and more extensive operations.

At the end of 1988 a Phantom will be used in the Antarctic to do research work under the ice and in some of the lakes found on land there.

A DSSI MiniRover was used in May for a week in the Great Lakes to support scientific studies for the Center for Great Lakes Studies. This work, sponsored by NOAA's Undersea Research Program, also had used a *Johnson-Sea-Link* submersible there the past two summers.

In January, the Navy's USNS *Bowditch* (TAGS-21) was rammed twice while at anchor in the port of Rio de Janeiro, Brazil. During stormy conditions two ships broke loose from their moorings and drifted into the helpless research ship. The resulting damage was so great that the Navy has decided to scrap the ship. She was old and planned for replacement, but retirement was not anticipated this early, nor in this way.

On the other hand, this event offered some new opportunities for the NOAA research fleet. To help compensate for the loss of *Bowditch* the Navy contracted to have the NOAA vessel *Discoverer* cover some of the Ocean Survey Program requirements in the Pacific.

This is good news for the NOAA fleet operators, coming at a time when the existence of a large part of this fleet is under pressure to be discontinued. The Navy is pleased with the services it's getting from the NOAA fleet, and there may be additional tasks given this sector.

Conversion of Tuna Clippers Makes Sense

The Navy and the National Science Foundation essentially provide the majority of the research vessels used by academic institutions. The average age of the 22-vessel academic fleet is about 20 years, while the retirement age generally is given as 30 years. So it is very important that both these federal agencies soon begin to design and construct the next generation of research vessels which will be the backbone of the academic research fleet. Even if these agencies begin serious planning at this time, it will take from three to five years to put replacement vessels into the academic fleet.

In 1987 the Navy was given funds to construct a new oceanographic research ship which will replace one of its seven vessels on loan to civilian oceanographic institutions. The five-year plan is to build four more of these ships, although funds have not been appropriated yet. The service

also is building two new ocean survey ships, the *Maury* and the *Tanner*. Both will be delivered in 1988. There are also plans to convert two tuna purse seiners to coastal survey ships.

The first conversion of this type is the RV *Osprey;* it is being converted by the private University of Southern California's (USC) Institute for Marine and Coastal Studies. *Osprey* is 11 years old, but as a research vessel she will have nearly two-thirds of her effective life available to support USC's marine programs. While this work is being done with private funds, the conversion project has attracted a great deal of interest from federal offices concerned with research ship assets.

Conversion of a 'tuna clipper' vessel makes a lot of sense. Good vessels recently have been on the market at greatly discounted prices because of economic problems with the U.S. tuna fishing industry. These long-range vessels are designed to stay at sea for up to two months, and have excellent habitability, low maintenance, good riding qualities, low fuel consumption, lots of space, and plenty of electrical power. All of these characteristics are highly prized in research vessels.

In recent times of financial difficulty in the U.S. tunaboat fleet, a new purse seiner which had been built for a selling price of over $11 million was offered for less than half that price. While the economic situation has improved powerfully in this industry, there will continue to be bargains in good used vessels which can be converted to research vessels at a fraction of the cost of new construction. This may be a cost-effective means for upgrading large parts of the academic fleet.

This year the Navy instituted a novel means to reduce the cost of operating its in-house research fleet. The Lovino Corporation was awarded the contract to be the fleet operator for 12 USN research vessels which were formerly operated by the Navy's Military Sealift Command.

In 1987 NASA selected one naval officer and one Coast Guard officer, both oceanographers, to be mission specialist candidates for the Space Shuttle. It may be several years before they fly a mission but at least more oceanographers will be getting into space.

In December 1986 Secretary of the Navy Lehman cancelled the program for the Navy's dedicated ocean sensing satellite, N-ROSS (Navy Remote Ocean Sensing Satellite) because of growth of program costs, reportedly from an estimated $270 million to $470 million, and the question of its 'value added' to the Navy's missions. Subsequent vigorous negotiations between Lehman and pro-N-ROSS advocates resulted in his reversing this decision in April 1987 shortly before he left office. However, his approval was conditioned on the development of evidence that the satellite would be of significant benefit to the Navy. Right now it appears that N-ROSS will be built and be operational by the early 1990s.

This is not a particularly fast-track development for the United States' first operational oceanographic satellite. This author was among the first oceanographers in the United States to be involved in ocean remote sensing during the time he was a graduate student at Texas A&M in the mid-1960s. At that time we (and NASA) were confident that

an operational oceanographic satellite would be in orbit by the end of that decade. When N-ROSS becomes operational, it will be a quarter of a century later.

The world's first oceanographic satellite was the U.S. SEASAT, which flew for a brief 100 days in 1978. The experimental SEASAT was not an operational system. It was designed to help engineers and oceanographers learn more about how to sense the oceans, in terms of orbit paths, what sensors could measure, and how to process the formidable volume of data outputs from a dedicated satellite system. Unfortunately, a mechanical failure resulted in a greatly abbreviated lifetime for this first and only ocean satellite until 1987.

In February 1987, Japan launched the free world's first operational ocean satellite, MOS-1 (Marine Observation Satellite). Plans are being made to launch MOS-2, probably before the N-ROSS operational date.

In addition, the European Space Agency (ESA) is planning to launch an oceanographic satellite, ERS-1 (European Remote Sensing satellite), in late 1989, also earlier than the U.S. N-ROSS launch. ERS-1 will be used for remote sensing over the oceans, coastal areas and polar ice masses.

In the USSR, its space agency claims that it has had ocean-sensing versions of its COSMOS satellites in service for the past several years.

This does not mean that ocean sensing is not being done. Many of the meteorological, geophysical, and land-observing satellites do provide oceanographers with considerable useful data. For example, NOAA's GEOSAT has had its orbit adjusted to follow that of SEASAT, thus giving oceanographers much excellent data on ocean surface conditions. But satellites for ocean applications have specialized requirements in terms of orbital paths, types of sensors, resolution of the sensors, and timing of passes over geographic regions. In general, these specialized sensor, resolution, temporal, and spatial requirements are highly ocean-specific. Therefore, other types of satellites do not fully meet oceanographic requirements. Dedicated ocean satellites are required for effective remote sensing of the world ocean, which covers 71 percent of the planet.

As stated in previous years' versions of this annual report, a coherent national ocean policy is absolutely vital for the support of national seapower (defined as the sum of all national uses of the world ocean). The United States has a plethora of micro-ocean policies, but there is no unifying structure. The result is overlap, duplication, and oversight. If this were a building, it might be said we have the outside and inside walls, the floors, and most of the wiring and plumbing. But we have neither foundations nor roof for the structure. A coherent national ocean policy will help government set overall priorities and allocate resources for the national interest in the world ocean.

The pre-election year of 1987 saw continued moderation of congressional interest in national ocean programs. The handful (and their numbers are decreasing) of representatives and senators who are 'ocean people' continued to do their best to make a difference. But they were outnumbered, and the overall trends of the past few years continue. At the other end of Pennsylvania Avenue, the White House continued to overlook ocean issues in terms of policy and/or budgets.

At the beginning of FY 1987, the National Advisory Committee on Oceans and Atmosphere (NACOA) was terminated by joint action of the Congress and the administration. No substitute organization was proposed to replace a body that had provided nearly 15 years of continuous, impartial advice and the hundreds of advisory communications to government.

During the present session of Congress, a bill to create a "National Ocean Policy Commission" (NOPC) was reintroduced (with some minor changes) for a third time in as many years. Both the House and the Senate have versions. Even if the House passes the bill, it appears unlikely that the Senate will act on it before the current session adjourns.

NOPC Designed to Be Ad Hoc

The NOPC is a good idea. It establishes a commission, whose members are named jointly by the President and Congress, which will study national ocean policy issues. The Commission will have a 'life' of two years; in its final report it is to make specific recommendations to the President and Congress for a national ocean policy, its development, implementation, and management. This is an ocean policy focus that is long overdue.

However, the NOPC is not the same thing as an NACOA-type advisory committee. By the terms of its charter, its two-year life and a specified final product, NOPC is designed to be *ad hoc*. On the other hand, NACOA was a continuing advisory body whose advisory products were not specified in its statutory authority. The two organizations would have had complementary functions.

It's unfortunate that congressional and governmental proponents of both organizations have claimed that they would serve the same purposes. In fact, our government should have both committees, considering how poorly our national ocean policies have fared in recent years.

We should not expect any significant changes in this situation until 1989, when a new Congress and President begin the next quadrennial cycle. In the meantime it is important for those outside government who believe the oceans are important to our nation's future to make sure they get their views before the most promising candidates for elective national offices. The efficiency of such petitioning is not very high, but a vocal minority of the electorate (the 'ocean people') still can make a difference. Besides, unless one tries, it is absolutely assured that nothing will happen.

Some readers who follow ocean sciences and technology in other publications will notice that some 1987 events have been left out of this summary. This does not mean that they were not important nor interesting. It was a busy year for oceanography, and the author had to choose from a mass of events those that would be the most interesting for the space available. Those projects and programs which are ongoing and significant will be described in future annual contributions to this series. The primary intent in this series is not simply to provide a chronological listing of events; it is to develop, analyze, and describe important worldwide trends in ocean sciences and technology.

SEAPOWER
FACTS&FIGURES

A MULTIPLE CHOICE TEST HE CAN'T AFFORD TO FAIL.

TAKE MAGNAVOX... OR TAKE A GUESS!

It's twenty-two hundred zulu. Thirty minutes left on-station. His search has spanned 15,000 square miles of ocean. It's been a routine day ... hundreds of signals have crossed his monitor. Painstakingly he's tried to analyze the origin of each. Now, there's one more. A new acoustic signature. Quickly, he must advise — hostile sub, or not? His analysis is critical to national security, but it's a heavy burden for one man to shoulder. At this point we can't afford a mistake.

At Magnavox, we understand his needs. With twenty-five years of experience in "wet" and "dry" end electronics, we know the job is tough. We know the equipment is sophisticated. That's why we've developed post-processing techniques to support the operator. A new system to enhance his decision-making abilities.

An example is Update IV. The team is Boeing Aerospace Company and Magnavox. As the acoustic subsystem integrator, Magnavox will help operators take the guesswork out of locating and classifying submarines. We have the proven expertise and performance. Take Maganvox ... or take a guess.

A Subsidiary of Magnavox Government & Industrial Electronics Co.
1313 Production Road, Fort Wayne, IN 46808 USA
Telex 22-8472 • TWX 810-332-1610

Magnavox
Electronic Systems Company

SEA POWER: *CONGRESS*

Pehaps the most significant feature of the first session of the 100th Congress was its inaction with regard to enacting budgetary legislation for FY 1988 for the various departments of the government. As of mid-November, well after the start of the fiscal year which began 1 October, not one major appropriations bill had been passed; as a result, the government once more was forced to operate under a business-as-usual Continuing Resolution, which simply continued government operations at FY 1987 levels, but without permitting new initiatives that would be authorized and funded as part of the FY 1988 budget.

Many factors contributed to Congress's lack of action. Among them were the lengthy Iran-Contra hearings, a Republican filibuster in the Senate over proposals by the Democrats to prohibit the use of funds for the development and testing of space-based anti-ballistic missile systems without congressional approval, and debates in both the House and the Senate over proposed legislation that would require the President to invoke the controversial War Powers Act. The latter debate stemmed from the President's decision to authorize the flagging as U.S. ships of 11 Kuwaiti tankers and to escort these ships to and from the Persian Gulf. It was intensified by the inadvertent missile firing on the frigate *Stark* by an Iraqi aircraft, the tanker *Bridgeton* hitting a mine planted by Iranian forces, and the discovery of many other mines, and attacks by Iranian patrol boats on a number of tankers in the Persian Gulf.

But what finally galvanized Congress into action in November was "Black Monday," 19 October, on Wall Street, when the Dow-Jones averages plummeted more than 500 points, and markets around the world also fell sharply, and legislation that would have required sequestration of funds commencing 20 November under the Gramm-Rudman-Hollings Act. When both the markets and the dollar continued to fall, the administration and Congress were forced to face the fact that all the major industrial nations were waiting to see if action finally would be taken to reduce the huge federal deficit, and to do so with a program that would not be as indiscriminately hurtful as across-the-board sequestration.

UNITED STATES SENATE

COMMITTEE ON APPROPRIATIONS

JOHN C. STENNIS, Mississippi, Chairman

Democrats	Republicans
ROBERT C. BYRD, West Virginia	MARK O. HATFIELD, Oregon
WILLIAM PROXMIRE, Wisconsin	TED STEVENS, Alaska
DANIEL K. INOUYE, Hawaii	LOWELL P. WEICKER, JR., Connecticut
ERNEST F. HOLLINGS, South Carolina	JAMES A. McCLURE, Idaho
LAWTON CHILES, Florida	JAKE GARN, Utah
J. BENNETT JOHNSTON, Louisiana	THAD COCHRAN, Mississippi
QUENTIN N. BURDICK, North Dakota	ROBERT W. KASTEN, JR., Wisconsin
PATRICK J. LEAHY, Vermont	ALFONSE M. D'AMATO, New York
JIM SASSER, Tennessee	WARREN RUDMAN, New Hampshire
DENNIS DeCONCINI, Arizona	ARLEN SPECTER, Pennsylvania
DALE BUMPERS, Arkansas	PETE V. DOMENICI, New Mexico
FRANK R. LAUTENBERG, New Jersey	CHARLES E. GRASSLEY, Iowa
TOM HARKIN, Iowa	DON NICKLES, Oklahoma
BARBARA A. MIKULSKI, Maryland	
HARRY REID, Nevada	

COMMITTEE ON ARMED SERVICES

SAM NUNN, Georgia, Chairman

Democrats	Republicans
JOHN C. STENNIS, Mississippi	JOHN W. WARNER, Virginia
J. JAMES EXON, Nebraska	STROM THURMOND, South Carolina
CARL LEVIN, Michigan	GORDON J. HUMPHREY, New Hampshire
EDWARD M. KENNEDY, Massachusetts	WILLIAM S. COHEN, Maine
JEFF BINGAMAN, New Mexico	DAN QUAYLE, Indiana
ALAN DIXON, Illinois	PETE WILSON, California
JOHN GLENN, Ohio	PHIL GRAMM, Texas
ALBERT E. GORE, JR., Tennessee	STEVEN D. SYMMS, Idaho
TIMOTHY E. WIRTH, Colorado	JOHN McCAIN, Arizona
RICHARD C. SHELBY, Alabama	

COMMITTEE ON COMMERCE, SCIENCE, AND TRANSPORTATION

ERNEST F. HOLLINGS, South Carolina, Chairman

Democrats	Republicans
DANIEL K. INOUYE, Hawaii	JOHN C. DANFORTH, Missouri
WENDELL H. FORD, Kentucky	BOB PACKWOOD, Oregon
DONALD W. RIEGLE, JR., Michigan	NANCY LANDON KASSEBAUM, Kansas
J. JAMES EXON, Nebraska	LARRY PRESSLER, South Dakota
ALBERT E. GORE, JR., Tennessee	TED STEVENS, Alaska
JAY ROCKEFELLER, West Virginia	ROBERT W. KASTEN, JR., Wisconsin
LLOYD BENTSEN, Texas	PAUL S. TRIBLE, JR., Virginia
JOHN F. KERRY, Massachusetts	PETE WILSON, California
JOHN B. BREAUX, Louisiana	JOHN McCAIN, Arizona
BROCK ADAMS, Washington	

An obvious target for a sizeable reduction in FY 1988 was the proposed defense budget, which had been under fire since it first was submitted in January 1987 and which had been termed "dead on arrival" by one member of Congress. The President was seeking $312 billion in new budget authority; however, that total was reduced sharply by Congress, which also finally concurred in the two-year

$75 billion deficit-reduction package that had been agreed upon by White House-Congress conferees just before the automatic sequestration deadline.

There was growing concern in Congress over the extent of the present and future U.S. commitment in the Persian Gulf, where Navy ships regularly were escorting the U.S.-flagged Kuwaiti tankers in and out of the Persian Gulf and teaming with minecoun-

termeasures ships of five other NATO countries to seek out and destroy mines planted by Iranian forces. There was general agreement that Persian Gulf waters and those adjacent to it must be kept open and free for international shipping, but not in the manner this should be accomplished. But since there, no firm proposals that would delineate the extent of involvement of U.S. forces, Congress had little choice but to adopt a "wait-and-see" position. However, there was worry over the high cost of the U.S. commitment, and particularly to the Navy, which was bearing the brunt of it.

In sharp contrast to what transpired during the last session of the 99th Congress with regard to the enactment of controversial legislation affecting the Department of Defense, there was none passed in 1987 that had anything like the impact, for example, of that which brought about a reorganization of the Joint Chiefs of Staff. In fact, the services were most concerned over the continuing deleterious effect of legislation passed in 1986 that would, over a three-year period, require a cut of 6 percent in officer personnel strengths. That legislation, which was vigorously supported by Senator John Glenn (D-Ohio), was having particularly serious consequences for the Navy, which was adding to its totals of ships and aircraft squadrons and would need more officers and enlisted personnel to man and support them. However, by year's end all attempts to bring about a moratorium on such cuts had failed, although the severity of them was somewhat reduced. Next to the Navy, the Marine Corps was hardest hit by the mandated reductions.

The Navy and the Marine Corps also were strongly opposed to provisions of the JCS reorganization act that would require lengthy periods of duty in joint-staff billets in order for personnel to qualify for promotion to flag- and general-officer rank. Both services, which have lower ratios of officers to enlisted personnel than do the Army and the Air Force, worried that the skills of outstanding personnel would be dulled by excessive periods of staff duty that would minimize tours of duty at sea or with combat forces. There were indications that Congress agreed, and that certain of these requirements might be relaxed.

One of the issues greatly affecting those in uniform was legislation providing education benefits to members of

U.S. HOUSE OF REPRESENTATIVES
COMMITTEE ON APPROPRIATIONS
JAMIE L. WHITTEN, Mississippi, Chairman

Democrats

EDWARD P. BOLAND, Massachusetts
WILLIAM H. NATCHER, Kentucky
NEAL SMITH, Iowa
SIDNEY R. YATES, Illinois
DAVID R. OBEY, Wisconsin
EDWARD R. ROYBAL, California
LOUIS STOKES, Ohio
TOM BEVILL, Alabama
BILL CHAPPELL, JR., Florida
BILL ALEXANDER, Arkansas
JOHN P. MURTHA, Pennsylvania
BOB TRAXLER, Michigan
JOSEPH D. EARLY, Massachusetts
CHARLES WILSON, Texas
LINDY (MRS. HALE) BOGGS, Louisiana
NORMAN D. DICKS, Washington
MATTHEW F. McHUGH, New York
WILLIAM LEHMAN, Florida
MARTIN OLAV SABO, Minnesota
JULIAN C. DIXON, California
VIC FAZIO, California
W.G. "BILL" HEFNER, North Carolina
LES AuCOIN, Oregon
DANIEL K. AKAKA, Hawaii
WES WATKINS, Oklahoma
WILLIAM H. GRAY III, Pennsylvania
BERNARD J. DWYER, New Jersey
STENY H. HOYER, Maryland
BOB CARR, Michigan
ROBERT J. MRAZEK, New York
RICHARD J. DURBIN, Illinois
RONALD B. COLEMAN, Texas
ALAN B. MOLLOHAN, West Virginia
(one vacancy)

Republicans

SILVIO O. CONTE, Massachusetts
JOSEPH M. McDADE, Pennsylvania
JOHN T. MYERS, Indiana
CLARENCE E. MILLER, Ohio
LAWRENCE COUGHLIN, Pennsylvania
C.W. "BILL" YOUNG, Florida
JACK F. KEMP, New York
RALPH REGULA, Ohio
VIRGINIA SMITH, Nebraska
CARL D. PURSELL, Michigan
MICKEY EDWARDS, Oklahoma
BOB LIVINGSTON, Louisiana
BILL GREEN, New York
JERRY LEWIS, California
JOHN EDWARD PORTER, Illinois
HAROLD ROGERS, Kentucky
JOE SKEEN, New Mexico
FRANK R. WOLF, Virginia
BILL LOWERY, California
VIN WEBER, Minnesota
TOM DELAY, Texas
JIM KOLBE, Arizona

COMMITTEE ON ARMED SERVICES
LES ASPIN, Wisconsin, Chairman

Democrats

MELVIN PRICE, Illinois
CHARLES E. BENNETT, Florida
SAMUEL S. STRATTON, New York
BILL NICHOLS, Alabama
DAN DANIEL, Virginia
G.V. "SONNY" MONTGOMERY, Mississippi
RONALD V. DELLUMS, California
PATRICIA SCHROEDER, Colorado
BEVERLY B. BYRON, Maryland
NICHOLAS MAVROULES, Massachusetts
EARL HUTTO, Florida
IKE SKELTON, Missouri
MARVIN LEATH, Texas
DAVE McCURDY, Oklahoma
THOMAS M. FOGLIETTA, Pennsylvania
ROY DYSON, Maryland
DENNIS M. HERTEL, Michigan
MARILYN LLOYD, Tennessee
NORMAN SISISKY, Virginia
RICHARD RAY, Georgia
JOHN M. SPRATT, JR., South Carolina
SOLOMON P. ORTIZ, Texas
GEORGE "BUDDY" DARDEN, Georgia
TOMMY F. ROBINSON, Arkansas
ALBERT G. BUSTAMANTE, Texas
BARBARA BOXER, California
GEORGE J. HOCHBRUECKNER, New York
JOSEPH E. BRENNAN, Maine
OWEN B. PICKETT, Virginia

Republicans

WILLIAM L. DICKINSON, Alabama
FLOYD SPENCE, South Carolina
ROBERT E. BADHAM, California
BOB STUMP, Arizona
JIM COURTER, New Jersey
LARRY J. HOPKINS, Kentucky
ROBERT W. DAVIS, Michigan
DUNCAN L. HUNTER, California
DAVID O'B. MARTIN, New York
JOHN R. KASICH, Ohio
LYNN MARTIN, Illinois
HERBERT H. BATEMAN, Virginia
MAC SWEENEY, Texas
BEN BLAZ, Guam
ANDY IRELAND, Florida
JAMES V. HANSEN, Utah
JOHN G. ROWLAND, Connecticut
CURT WELDON, Pennsylvania
JON KYL, Arizona
ARTHUR RAVENEL, JR., South Carolina
JACK DAVIS, Illinois

armed services. Military personnel who contribute $100 per month for 12 months will receive $300 a month from the government for a period of 30 months to be applied toward a college or vocational education. The legislation, named after its author, Rep. G.V. "Sonny" Montgomery (D-MS), passed with only two dissenting votes in the House and none in the Senate. It strengthens the all-volunteer force greatly by providing young men and women an incentive first to serve in the armed services, and then to further their education upon their return to civilian life.

The budget submitted by then Secretary of Defense Caspar Weinberger in January was the first two-year defense budget submitted to Congress and seemingly represented a long forward step in reducing the turmoil brought about by the annual submission of one-year budgets, and the usual failure to pass them by the start of the fiscal year for which they were designed. However, it soon became obvious that Congress had no desire to commit itself to a two-year budget cycle, and as a result there was consideration only of the FY 1988 budget. Whether DOD will try again next year to gain approval of a two-year budget remains to be seen.

The past year saw Senator Sam Nunn (D-Ga.) not only become chairman of the Senate Armed Services Committee but also emerge as the paramount authority on defense matters, and principal force with which to be reckoned, in the Senate and perhaps in the entire Congress as well. Certainly it appeared that he has a far stronger base of support

COMMITTEE ON MERCHANT MARINE AND FISHERIES
WALTER B. JONES, North Carolina, Chairman

Democrats

MARIO BIAGGI, New York
GLENN M. ANDERSON, California
GERRY E. STUDDS, Massachusetts
CARROLL HUBBARD JR., Kentucky
DON BONKER, Washington
WILLIAM J. HUGHES, New Jersey
MIKE LOWRY, Washington
EARL HUTTO, Florida
W.J. "BILLY" TAUZIN, Louisiana
THOMAS M. FOGLIETTA, Pennsylvania
DENNIS M. HERTEL, Michigan
ROY DYSON, Maryland
WILLIAM O. LIPINSKI, Illinois
ROBERT A. BORSKI, Pennsylvania
THOMAS R. CARPER, Delaware
DOUGLAS H. BOSCO, California
ROBIN M. TALLON, South Carolina
LINDSAY THOMAS, Georgia
SOLOMON P. ORTIZ, Texas
CHARLES E. BENNETT, Florida
THOMAS J. MANTON, New York
OWEN B. PICKETT, Virginia
JOSEPH E. BRENNAN, Maine
GEORGE J. HOCHBRUECKNER, New York

Republicans

ROBERT W. DAVIS, Michigan
DON YOUNG, Alaska
NORMAN F. LENT, New York
NORMAN D. SHUMWAY, California
JACK FIELDS, Texas
CLAUDINE SCHNEIDER, Rhode Island
HERBERT H. BATEMAN, Virginia
H. JAMES SAXTON, New Jersey
JOHN R. MILLER, Washington
HELEN DELICH BENTLEY, Maryland
HOWARD COBLE, North Carolina
MAC SWEENEY, Texas
JOSEPH J. DioGUARDI, New York
CURT WELDON, Pennsylvania
PATRICIA SAIKI, Hawaii
WALLY HERGER, California
JIM BUNNING, Kentucky

than does his counterpart in the House, Les Aspin (D-Wis.) who had to withstand a challenge to his chairmanship by Marvin Leath of Texas. However, both Nunn and Aspin were members of the joint Senate-House committee which conducted the Iran-Contra hearings, and as a consequence were unable to devote as much of their time to defense matters as they would have wished. It apparently was Nunn's threat to delay confirmation hearings of the administration's first nominee for a Supreme Court seat that led to the ending of the filibuster on the defense-budget legislation and made possible an acceleration of its consideration.

The depth of the reductions in proposed spending for defense made it clear that the services faced hard times ahead. Regrettably, it also appeared that there was an absence of full understanding of the impact of such reductions not only on both short- and long-term readiness, but also on the cost to the government and the taxpayer of stretch-outs and cancellations of defense programs. In many respects, what was happening in late 1987 with regard to cuts in the defense budget was in many respects reminiscent of what transpired in the late 1970s under President Carter, and which led in turn to the massive build-up of the early 1980s.

KEY CONGRESSIONAL PHONE NUMBERS*

House Committees
Appropriations Subcommittee on Defense 225-2847
Armed Services Committee 225-4151
Merchant Marine and Fisheries Committee 225-4047
Coast Guard and Navigation Subcommittee 225-8204

Senate Committees
Appropriations Subcommittee on Defense 224-7258
Armed Services Committee 224-3871
Commerce, Science, and Transportation Subcommittee
on Merchant Marine (also Coast Guard) 224-4766

Members of Congress 224-3121

Cloakroom Announcements
(For running accounts of proceedings on
House and Senate floors)

House: Democratic 225-7400
        Republican 225-7430
Senate: Democratic 224-8541
        Republican 224-8601

When writing to a member of Congress use
the following addresses:

Documents
(For information/copies of bills and reports)
House 225-3456
Senate 224-4321

Government Printing Office
(For copies of committee reports, etc.) 783-3238

Legislative Information
(For information on status of legislation, either House
or Senate, name of committee to which bill was
referred, number of committee report, etc.) 225-1772

Military Liaison
Navy/Marines: House 225-7124
               or 225-4395
               Senate 224-4681
Coast Guard: House 225-4775
               Senate 224-2913

*Area code for all numbers: 202

SENATOR:

The Honorable_____
U.S. Senate, Washington, D.C. 20510

REPRESENTATIVE:

The Honorable_____
U.S. House of Representatives
Washington, D.C. 20515

SEA POWER: *DEFENSE*

"Most citizens realize that the safeguarding of our nation and our vital interests must be our first priority. Budget deficits and domestic program cuts can be rectified, but security shortfalls carry the risk of irreversible losses. Together, we must look beyond the immediate present. We must understand that America's security begins well beyond our shores, and that our interests are worldwide.

"We must realize, too, that we cannot do the task alone, and that we need allies and friends in all parts of the world. We must recognize also the long-term consequences if our allies and friends perceive us waning in military strength and in resolve to protect our shared interests. Many would not notice the subtle erosion of our security as once-friendly nations drifted toward neutralism, or worse, accommodation to the pressures of our adversaries. But both such unfavorable developments are possible consequences of inadequate American

strength and leadership. Any neglect of our own security has global consequences.

"In sum, American defense budgets should be based on defense needs, not on political expediency or short-term fiscal goals. To this end, this FY 1988 *Annual Defense Report to Congress* analyzes America's defense needs at a prudent and efficient pace. Our goal is to keep America safe and free, not just as safe or as free as short-term fiscal and political goals allow.

"Anyone who says we cannot afford to do what we must to keep our freedom is halfway along the road to losing it."

So then Secretary of Defense Caspar W. Weinberger, on 12 January 1987, concluded the philosophical opening to his seventh defense-budget presentation to Congress. Yet even before he had finished his first day of testimony on Capitol Hill, it had been made unmistakably clear by members of Congress that his budget had no

chance of being passed in its original form, and that the major question pertaining to it was: "How much would it be cut?" By 1 December, more than 10 months later, senior military officials of all the services still would not know for sure how severe the cuts would be or how much they would be authorized by Congress to spend in FY 1988, Weinberger himself would be gone, and a defense appropriations bill approved by Congress still would be weeks away. For those who might take Weinberger's sober philosophy to heart, these were indeed discouraging developments.

Weinberger resigned in November, after having served longer as Secretary of Defense than all except one of his predecessors. He failed by four months to equal the record of Robert S. McNamara, who served Presidents Kennedy and Johnson. During his almost seven years in office he presided over the greatest peacetime military build-up in the nation's history, a build-up

Table D-1

FEDERAL BUDGET TRENDS

(Dollars in Millions)

Fiscal Year	Federal Outlays as a % of GNP	DoD Outlays as a % of Federal Outlays	DoD Outlays as a % of GNP	Non-DoD Outlays as a % of Federal Outlays	Non-DoD Outlays as a % of GNP	DoD Outlays as a % of Net Public Spending[1]
1950	16.0	27.5	4.4	72.5	11.6	18.5
1955	17.6	51.5	9.1	48.5	8.6	35.6
1960	18.2	45.0	8.2	55.0	10.0	30.3
1965	17.5	38.8	6.8	61.2	10.7	25.2
1970	19.8	39.4	7.8	60.6	12.0	25.5
1971	19.9	35.4	7.0	64.6	12.8	22.4
1972	20.0	32.6	6.5	67.4	13.5	20.6
1973	19.1	29.8	5.7	70.2	13.4	19.0
1974	19.0	28.8	5.5	71.2	13.5	18.3
1975	21.8	25.5	5.6	74.5	16.2	16.5
1976	21.9	23.6	5.2	76.4	16.7	15.4
1977	21.1	23.4	4.9	76.6	16.2	15.5
1978	21.1	22.5	4.7	77.5	16.4	15.2
1979	20.5	22.8	4.7	77.2	15.8	15.4
1980	22.2	22.5	5.0	77.5	17.2	15.3
1981	22.7	23.0	5.2	77.0	17.5	15.8
1982	23.7	24.5	5.8	75.5	17.9	16.7
1983	24.3	25.4	6.2	74.6	18.2	17.3
1984	23.1	25.9	6.0	74.1	17.1	17.5
1985	24.0	25.9	6.2	74.1	17.8	17.7
1986	23.8	26.8	6.4	73.2	17.4	18.1
1987	23.0	27.0	6.2	73.0	16.8	17.8
1988	21.7	28.2	6.1	71.8	15.5	18.1
1989	21.1	28.4	6.0	71.6	15.1	18.1

[1] Federal, State, and Local net spending excluding government enterprises (such as the postal service and public utilities) except for any support these activities receive from tax funds.

Table D-2

100 BIGGEST DEFENSE CONTRACTORS

(The 100 defense contractors receiving the largest dollar volume of prime contract awards from the Department of Defense during fiscal 1986.)

(in thousands of dollars)

1. General Dynamics Corp.	8,012,975	51. Massachusetts Institute of Technology	368,010
2. General Electric Co.	6,847,079	52. Burroughs Corporation	339,918
3. McDonnell Douglas Corp.	6,586,311	53. Johns Hopkins University	317,626
4. Rockwell International Corp.	5,589,681	54. The Mitre Corporation	310,011
5. General Motors Corp.	5,069,296	55. Olin Corporation	306,631
6. Lockheed Corporation	4,896,318	56. Morrison Knudsen Corporation	303,599
7. Raytheon Company	4,051,573	57. The Aerospace Corporation	301,781
8. The Boeing Company	3,556,026	58. Gould Inc.	300,379
9. United Technologies Corporation	3,527,014	59. Mobil Corporation	299,599
10. Grumman Corporation	2,967,495	60. Sun Company Inc.	294,442
11. Martin Marietta Corporation	2,935,397	61. The Penn Central Corporation	292,101
12. Honeywell Inc.	1,846,445	62. Computer Sciences Corporation	288,086
13. Westinghouse Electric Corporation	1,713,190	63. Bahrain National Oil	282,720
14. Textron Incorporated	1,671,046	64. Emerson Electric Company	278,543
15. Litton Industries Incorporated	1,663,274	65. Soberbio Inc.	275,924
16. Sperry Corporation	1,556,731	66. Draper Charles Stark Laboratory	265,983
17. The LTV Corporation	1,444,587	67. Rolls Royce Inc.	262,846
18. Texas Instruments Inc.	1,434,886	68. Control Data Corporation	255,029
19. International Business Machines	1,359,218	69. The Coastal Corporation	247,962
20. Eaton Corporation	1,068,071	70. Sanders Associates Inc.	246,472
21. TRW Inc.	1,052,560	71. Ashland Oil Inc.	242,802
22. Allied-Signal Inc.	1,042,812	72. Oshkosh Truck Corp.	242,113
23. GTE Corporation	1,041,218	73. Dynalectron Corp.	241,240
24. Royal Dutch Petroleum Company	985,796	74. Science Applications International	236,319
25. American Telephone & Telegraph Company	913,650	75. Morton Thiokol Inc.	235,705
26. The Singer Company	870,564	76. Figgie International Holdings	234,484
27. FMC Corporation	863,022	77. Lear Siegler Inc.	232,658
28. ITT Corporation	799,376	78. The Gates Corporation	232,595
29. Chevron Corporation	794,485	79. Hewlett Packard Company	224,163
30. Ford Motor Company	752,083	80. Chrysler Corporation	218,393
31. Northrop Corporation	742,022	81. Tracor Inc.	193,662
32. Harsco Corporation	707,087	82. E Systems Inc.	192,146
33. Gencorp Inc.	643,344	83. Amerada Hess Corporation	186,191
34. Atlantic Richfield Company	642,079	84. Pacific Resources Inc.	180,969
35. Harris Corp.	541,587	85. Zenith Electronics Corporation	176,095
36. Exxon Corporation	531,990	86. Todd Shipyards Corporation	175,776
37. Bell Boeing Joint Venture	514,908	87. United Industrial Corporation	172,445
38. CFM International Inc.	512,272	88. Colt Industries Inc.	170,758
39. Motorola Inc.	510,155	89. Steuart Investment Company Inc.	170,165
40. Goodyear Tire & Rubber Company	498,896	90. Sundstrand Corporation	168,070
41. Teledyne Inc.	487,625	91. Digital Equipment Corporation	165,722
42. Tenneco Inc.	477,187	92. Eastman Kodak Company	164,921
43. Pan Am Corp.	476,708	93. Texaco Inc.	163,652
44. United States Philips Trust	474,363	94. Holly Corporation	161,126
45. Bath Iron Works Corporation	464,928	95. GEC Inc.	160,480
46. Hercules Inc.	423,350	96. BDM International Inc.	159,031
47. Avondale Industries Inc.	394,675	97. Electrospace Systems Inc.	153,619
48. Motor Oils Hellas Corinth Ref.	380,628	98. ITT & VARO Joint Venture	152,867
49. Loral Corporation	377,037	99. Transamerica Corporation	152,803
50. Amoco Corporation	371,079	100. Brunswick Corporation	148,972

Source: Defense '87 Almanac

necessitated in large measure by the rapid decline in U.S. military strength that began during President Ford's tenure in office and accelerated rapidly during President Carter's four years in the White House. When he departed, the pace of the build-up had slowed almost to a halt, and the outstanding peacetime readiness of all the services was in jeopardy.

Preceding Weinberger in returning to civilian life was the equally controversial and colorful John F. Lehman, Jr., perhaps the most influential Secretary of the Navy since James Forrestal. Lehman, who resigned in April 1987, led the way in persuading Congress to authorize and fund a 600-ship Navy, up in numbers that totaled only slightly more than 450 when President Reagan took office. He also was responsible for bringing competition into the Navy's, and ultimately the military's, procurement practices to an unprecedented degree, and with former Chiefs of Naval Operations Thomas B. Hayward and James D. Watkins would contribute tremendous-

ly to the stemming of the "hemorrhage of talent" that cost the Navy thousands of skilled personnel during the late 1970s and early 1980s.

The defense budget would, unfortunately, become a pawn in the intense deliberations aimed at reducing the national budget deficit that followed the 19 October "Black Monday" stock-market decline. The defense authorization bill that finally was passed by Congress in mid-November actually specified a high and a low level of military spending, with the prevailing level dependent upon final deficit-reducing decisions. The legislation signed by the President authorized a national defense budget of $296 billion, well below the $312 billion in TOA initially sought by Weinberger.

The Navy's share, in TOA, would be $96.3 billion, down from the original request of $101.7 billion. In outlays, although the appropriations bill still had not been enacted, it appeared the Navy would be given a pro rata reduction, down from $86 billion, and the Marines $9.2 billion. The Navy-Marine Corps share of the overall DOD budget was 33 percent. As a matter of fact, final approved figures, line item by line item, would have, as one senior Navy specialist put it, only a "casual resemblance" to those initially submitted to Congress by Weinberger.

As was the case in FY 1987, emphasis was on those programs such as shipbuilding where initial outlays were quite small. Only 6-7 percent of the estimated cost of a new ship is expended in the first year of its construction. That philosophy enabled the Navy to fare well with its overall ship-construction program, with 15 new ships and four conversions approved. In contrast, proposed personnel and operations and maintenance accounts all were reduced, in some areas substantially. These are accounts where almost all expenditures take place during the current budget year.

Perhaps the most unusual action taken by Congress was in the shipbuilding program, where the Navy's request for authorization to construct two Ticonderoga-class cruisers was increased to five, with the request to build three Burke-class guided missile destroyers being reduced from three to zero. It was Congress' view that, with considerable difficulties being encountered by Bath Iron Works in the construction of Burke (DDG-51), and the Navy therefore being in no position to immediately award construction contracts for future

We're On A U.S. Navy Alert

Around the clock, in all types of weather, systems from Eaton help keep the U.S. Navy in readiness.

As if all this wasn't enough, we pioneered in the design of the ALQ-99 support jamming system. This combat proven, state-of-the-art ECM system, installed in every EA-6B Prowler provides unparalleled protection for strike aircraft while operating in hostile radar environments.

And whether it be in the darkness of a mid-Atlantic Ocean night, a rain squall in the South Pacific or a land-based air station, our SPN-41 microwave landing system provides accurate landing guidance.

Our automated air traffic control systems are an important part of the Carrier Air Traffic Control Center (CATCC). They are providing safe and efficient control to the various aircraft operating from the carriers.

This past and present experience combines at Eaton to respond to the Navy's future needs every day. We are proud of our association with the U.S. Navy and are constantly seeking opportunities to help solve problems.

At Eaton—
the Originator is still the Innovator.

For more information contact:
Eaton Corporation, Commack Road
Deer Park, New York 11729
(516) 595-3094

Kollmorgen is ready.

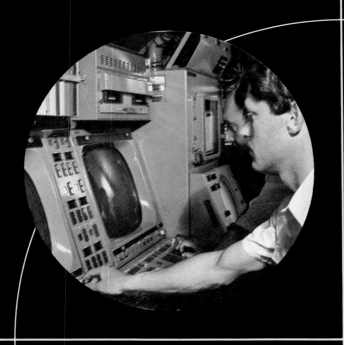

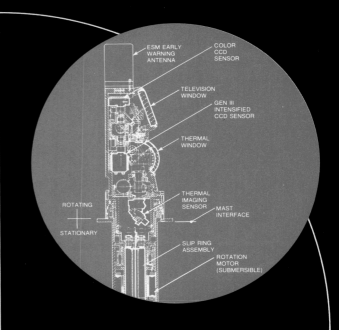

- **Thermal Imaging**
- **Television**
- **Stabilization**
- **ESM**
- **Communications**
- **Stealth**
- **AN/BSY Interface and Control**

DDG-51s until existing problems had resolved, it would be wiser to complete the 27-ship CG-47 program by authorizing construction of the final five ships in it. The authorizing committees were not so lavish, however, with funding; they authorized the expenditure of funds for construction of only four cruisers, but with a proviso that if funds could be found elsewhere to build the fifth ship there would be no objection. That presumably left the door open for the appropriations committees to include enough dollars in the shipbuilding account to make that possible.

Although it might have been assumed that increased minesweeping requirements resulting from the mining of the Persian Gulf by Iran would have resulted in increased appropriations for more minecountermeasures ships, such was not the case. In fact, Congress refused to authorize construction of the final three MCMs in that 14-ship program pending resolution of problems encountered in the early ships of the class. Only one of these has been completed and is out of the Great Lakes; a second is nearly complete but is icebound until the spring of 1988. Six others are under construction, and a contract still is to be awarded for building MCM 9-11, which were funded in FY 1985. And, although there had been some earlier grumbling in Congress about the Navy's plans to build 17 coastal minehunters (MHC) with glass reinforced plastic (GRP) hulls using Italian techniques and expertise, no strong opposition materialized, and those plans were not changed. The first ship of this class is about to start construction.

Two SWATH-hulled surveillance ships (TAGOS) were added to the Navy's shipbuilding account; since three had been programmed in both FY 1989 and FY 1990 and two in FY 1991, that simply represented a step-up in the overall program.

Weinberger had caught Congress by surprise by requesting funding for long-lead-time items for two nuclear aircraft carriers in his proposed FY 1988-1989 budget, after telling Congress earlier that no such requests would be forthcoming until 1990s budgets. However, after hearing the Navy's principal reasons for getting construction underway earlier —the deteriorating condition of the ancient and rapidly aging *Midway* (CV-41) and *Coral Sea* (CV-43)— Congress approved the funds re-

Table D-3
SPECIAL OPERATIONS EXPANSION

	FY 1981	FY 1988	FY 1992
MAJOR SOF UNITS			
Special Forces Groups[1]	7	8	9
Ranger Battalions	2	3	3
Psychological Operations Battalions	3	4	4
Civil Affairs Battalions	1	1	1
SEAL Teams	2	5[2]	6[2]
SEAL Delivery Vehicle (SDV) Teams	0	2[2]	2[2]
Special Operations Wings	1	1	3
Special Operations Aviation Brigade	0	0	1
Total	**16**	**24**	**29**
PRIMARY AIRCRAFT			
Air Force			
MC-130E/H Combat Talons	14	14	38
AC-130A/H/U Gunships[3]	20	20	22
MH-53H/J Pave Low Helicopters	9	19	41
CV-22 Ospreys[4]	0	0	6
EC-130E Volant Solos	4	4	4
HC-130 Tankers (SOF-dedicated)	0	8	31
C-141s Special Ops Low Level II (SOLL-II)	0	0	13
C-130s SOLL-II	0	0	11
Total	**47**	**65**	**166**
Army			
MH-60X Helicopters	0	0	23
MH-47E Helicopters (Pave Low equivalent)	0	0	17
MH-60 FLIR (SOF-dedicated) Helicopters	0	16	21
M/UH-60 (SOF-dedicated) Helicopters	0	29	17
CH-47D (SOF-dedicated) (10 with FLIR) Helos	0	16	0
UH-1 (SOF-dedicated) Helicopters	0	23	23
A/MH-6 (SOF-dedicated) Helicopters	29	54	29
Total	**29**	**138**	**130**
PRIMARY NAVAL EQUIPMENT			
Seafox (Special Warfare Craft, Light)	12	36	36
Sea Viking (Special Warfare Craft, Medium)	0	0	19
High Speed Boat	0	0	7
Dry Deck Shelters (DDS)	0	2	6
Submarines modified to accommodate DDS	0	5	7
SEAL Delivery Vehicles (SDVs)	18	19	19
Advanced SDVs	0	0	1
Total	**30**	**62**	**95**

[1] Includes four Reserve Component Groups.

[2] Includes two Underwater Demolition Teams redesignated in 1983.

[3] Includes ten AC-130A Air Force Reserve gunships in FYs 1981-87. FY 1992 number reflects decommissioning of AC-130As and addition of 12 AC-130U aircraft.

[4] Includes programmed procurement through FY 1992. Actual deliveries will not begin until FY 1994. Total to be procured for SOF will be 55.

Source: Department of Defense

quested in the FY 1988 budget for the items for the first carrier, and included $20 million for the commencement of acquisition of long-lead items for the second.

Also approved were three more Los Angeles-class attack submarines, another Trident strategic missile submarine, an amphibious assault ship (LHD), cargo-variant version of the Whidbey Island-class of LSD, and two more of the Henry J. Kaiser class of fleet oilers. Funding for the service life extension program for the carrier *Kitty Hawk* (CV-63) also was approved, as were the conversions of two merchantmen into crane ships (TACS), and the jumboization of another Cimarron class of fleet oiler.

The major controversy in aircraft

Table D-4

WHERE THEY SERVE
(As of 31 March 1987)

Countries/regional areas where 100 or more United States military members are assigned.
Area totals include countries with less than 100 assigned United States military members.

REGIONAL AREA/COUNTRY	TOTAL	ARMY	NAVY	MARINE CORPS	AIR FORCE
United States, United States Territories, Special Locations					
Continental United States	1,340,674	470,674	274,702	152,945	442,674
Alaska	21,510	8,298	2,050	189	10,973
Hawaii	46,900	18,968	12,754	9,060	6,118
Guam	8,970	38	4,476	405	4,051
Johnston Atoll	142	135	—	—	7
Puerto Rico	3,652	435	2,911	270	30
Transients	47,703	14,577	13,587	4,965	14,574
Afloat	190,622	—	189,271	1,351	—
Total	1,660,306	512,880	499,789	169,185	478,452
Western & Southern Europe					
Belgium	3,418	1,304	133	32	1,949
Germany (Federal Republic & West Berlin)	250,168	208,168	318	91	40,817
Greece	3,490	558	525	15	2,392
Greenland	305	—	—	—	305
Iceland	3,161	3	1,758	88	1,312
Italy	14,911	4,269	4,441	309	5,892
Netherlands	3,130	1,039	19	10	2,062
Norway*	219	33	38	23	125
Portugal	1,645	63	366	14	1,202
Spain	9,027	22	3,704	203	5,098
Turkey	4,964	1,180	112	19	3,853
United Kingdom	29,669	222	2,360	373	26,714
Afloat	19,020	—	17,081	1,939	—
Total	343,423	217,696	30,890	3,262	91,575
East Asia & Pacific					
Australia	753	10	441	11	291
Japan (including Okinawa)	47,204	2,135	7,462	20,397	17,210
Philippines	16,290	64	5,932	1,223	9,071
Republic of Korea	43,886	31,206	394	720	11,566
Thailand	115	60	11	13	31
Afloat	22,637	—	20,481	2,156	—
Total	131,113	33,517	34,807	24,585	38,204
Africa, Near East & South Asia					
Bahrain	120	3	104	5	8
British Indian Ocean Territory (includes Diego Garcia)	1,280	8	1,268	—	8
Egypt	1,368	1,246	26	31	63
Saudi Arabia	439	158	39	22	220
Afloat	10,369	—	10,369	176	—
Total	14,357	1,827	11,679	639	412
Other Western Hemisphere					
Bermuda	1,139	—	1,058	81	—
Canada	540	8	397	11	124
Cuba (Guantanamo)	2,497	—	1,886	609	2
Honduras*	1,072	1,045	3	14	10
Panama	10,386	6,977	507	197	2,705
Afloat	2,139	—	2,139	—	—
Total	18,524	8,306	6,137	1,162	2,919
Antartica					
Total	94	—	94	—	—
Eastern Europe					
Total	201	69	5	107	20
Worldwide					
Ashore	1,923,393	774,104	344,389	193,318	611,582
Afloat	244,787	—	239,165	5,622	—
Total	2,168,180	774,104	583,554	198,940	611,582

*Includes military personnel on TDY for planning and conduct of exercises.

Source: Defense '87 Almanac

Table D-5

WHERE MILITARY DOLLARS ARE SPENT

(FY 1986 Estimated)
($ in thousands)

	PERSONNEL COMPENSATION					PRIME CONTRACT AWARDS		
	Civilian Pay	Military Active Duty Pay	Reserve & National Guard Pay	Retired Military Pay	Total Compensation	Civil Functions Contracts More Than $25,000	Military Functions Contracts More Than $25,000	Total Contracts More Than $25,000
Alabama	839,890	511,794	170,578	411,533	1,933,795	40,703	1,563,148	1,603,851
Alaska	154,892	386,130	21,519	57,711	620,252	9,203	555,473	564,681
Arizona	271,757	482,293	53,799	451,305	1,259,154	2,322	2,530,077	2,532,399
Arkansas	170,908	190,730	55,655	226,039	643,332	32,446	854,251	886,697
California	3,877,041	5,597,902	378,611	2,632,755	12,486,309	78,242	27,659,508	27,737,750
Colorado	331,486	759,520	71,257	473,460	1,635,723	4,137	1,892,848	1,896,985
Connecticut	143,756	270,560	37,126	116,779	568,215	2,005	5,439,058	5,441,063
Delaware	44,624	84,357	20,726	52,402	202,109	3,000	221,478	224,478
District of Columbia	562,807	360,573	59,279	45,292	1,027,951	9,253	947,540	956,793
Florida	898,325	1,966,074	118,348	1,785,186	4,770,933	34,751	5,629,387	5,664,138
Georgia	1,082,200	1,103,654	230,186	583,681	2,999,721	36,110	3,727,999	3,764,109
Hawaii	647,556	1,127,513	42,640	153,261	1,970,970	854	561,989	562,843
Idaho	36,822	105,272	22,132	82,896	247,122	9,573	53,337	62,910
Illinois	847,017	774,230	135,350	274,778	2,031,375	124,138	1,610,614	1,734,752
Indiana	405,741	138,349	132,316	166,671	843,077	5,874	2,484,268	2,490,142
Iowa	52,566	11,898	45,814	72,358	182,636	17,681	562,138	579,819
Kansas	176,664	460,103	105,332	164,194	906,293	3,824	1,950,682	1,954,506
Kentucky	404,529	641,584	87,651	179,593	1,313,357	59,280	1,497,908	1,557,188
Louisiana	302,183	454,829	89,608	285,277	1,131,897	227,279	1,270,377	1,497,656
Maine	275,266	156,388	25,280	99,215	556,149	589	583,606	584,195
Maryland	1,253,919	782,320	114,421	463,374	2,614,234	26,455	4,510,060	4,536,515
Massachusetts	1,353,815	209,442	134,883	221,811	1,919,951	8,014	8,726,846	8,734,860
Michigan	372,142	183,812	89,921	189,790	835,665	28,955	2,324,147	2,353,102
Minnesota	106,046	25,422	78,400	113,229	323,097	26,534	2,328,062	2,354,596
Mississippi	551,508	395,831	70,903	208,936	1,227,178	80,143	1,553,596	1,633,739
Missouri	650,881	272,793	150,978	277,530	1,352,182	29,977	5,517,604	5,547,581
Montana	36,547	69,035	20,293	52,187	178,062	2,069	59,931	62,000
Nebraska	169,703	298,617	30,832	110,988	610,140	12,253	213,342	225,595
Nevada	51,992	179,302	12,748	167,594	411,636	365	141,054	141,419
New Hampshire	62,037	94,801	19,596	98,115	274,549	1,863	469,308	471,171
New Jersey	747,366	324,143	132,745	258,059	1,462,313	25,390	3,201,064	3,226,454
New Mexico	285,056	343,965	24,481	198,242	851,744	2,924	562,148	565,072
New York	549,120	407,128	174,869	295,118	1,426,235	30,183	9,878,201	9,908,384
North Carolina	413,181	1,765,949	97,138	554,871	2,831,139	29,161	1,019,872	1,049,033
North Dakota	50,496	199,849	18,792	23,033	292,170	5,450	195,301	200,751
Ohio	990,537	310,155	123,208	324,792	1,748,692	30,366	5,170,561	5,200,927
Oklahoma	758,645	549,182	99,482	300,409	1,707,718	19,767	754,849	774,616
Oregon	191,652	27,018	47,231	183,386	449,287	57,207	282,862	340,069
Pennsylvania	1,452,046	250,805	267,688	393,893	2,364,432	38,121	4,153,542	4,191,663
Rhode Island	132,870	134,012	25,387	67,104	359,373	1,153	392,419	393,572
South Carolina	539,881	1,138,473	120,779	443,380	2,242,513	13,728	507,345	521,073
South Dakota	47,429	109,531	19,379	34,766	211,105	4,230	123,728	127,633
Tennessee	1,262,907	192,936	87,198	336,527	1,879,568	29,707	1,126,894	1,156,601
Texas	1,683,768	2,463,382	252,244	1,788,554	6,187,948	92,436	10,847,791	10,940,227
Utah	607,154	127,314	48,339	94,612	877,419	1,085	713,063	714,148
Vermont	17,136	2,666	15,902	27,598	63,302	1,158	122,453	123,611
Virginia	3,215,244	3,778,162	148,863	1,253,996	8,396,265	31,758	5,370,268	5,402,026
Washington	888,637	966,056	115,195	617,535	2,587,623	37,620	2,487,630	2,525,250
West Virginia	86,048	11,101	29,030	77,215	203,394	7,948	97,497	105,445
Wisconsin	91,918	27,684	139,677	109,389	368,668	8,308	973,108	981,416
Wyoming	30,362	71,993	10,357	33,180	145,892	295	91,857	92,152
Total U.S.	**28,156,274**	**31,299,832**	**4,624,160**	**17,633,499**	**81,713,765**	**1,408,892**	**134,617,236**	**136,026,128**
Guam	104,071	550,624	2,687	11,152	668,534	30	60,670	60,700
Puerto Rico	53,207	205,643	38,693	50,803	348,346	25,033	389,314	414,347
Other U.S. Possessions	5,306	7,087	16,508	3,194	32,095	43	310,897	310,940
Total U.S. Possessions	**162,584**	**763,354**	**57,888**	**65,149**	**1,048,975**	**25,106**	**760,881**	**785,987**

Source: Defense '87 Almanac

procurement centered on acquisition of Navy attack aircraft. The Navy sought to produce its first A-6Fs, an improved, but more costly, version of the A-6E. However, the two Armed Services Committees finally elected not to authorize construction of A-6Fs, but rather to approve 11 A-6Es and continued development of the Advanced Tactical Aircraft, which would be used by both the Air Force and the Navy. That was a welcome compromise for the Navy, which feared neither A-6Es nor A-6Fs would be authorized, and that as a consequence it would run out of A-6Es long before the ATA reached the fleet. Subsequently, however, the two Appropriations Committees elected not to fund acquisition of A-6Es and instead added $587 million for construction of an estimated 12 A-6Fs. They also funded continued development of the ATA. The full Congress approved, and the President signed, both pieces of legislation.

Another casualty was the AV-8B program. Procurement of 32 Harriers had been requested in FY 1988, but that number was reduced by eight. Any reduction at all was a blow to the Marines, but the loss of that relatively small number from the original request was far better than having the entire 32 eliminated, which at one stage of deliberations appeared to be the course that might be followed.

With two exceptions, all other Navy and Marine Corps aircraft programs fared well. The request for three E-6A TACAMO aircraft was reduced by one, and that for AH-1W helicopters from 22 to 17. Surprisingly, all 84 F/A-18s requested were approved; in years past the large numbers requested of this aircraft had been a prime target for cuts. Twelve F-14s, a mixture of existing F-14A versions and improved F-14D versions, were approved, as were 14 CH-53E, six SH-60B, and 18 SH-60F helicopters. No additional MH-53Es, the minesweeping version of the CH-53E, were added by Congress, despite the high rate of utilization of these aircraft in the Persian Gulf and their relatively small numbers. Six more of the tremendously effective E-2C early-warning aircraft also were authorized, as were the first 12 of the new and long-needed T-45TS training aircraft.

Navy missile programs survived the budget-cutting axe quite well; in fact, Congress authorized the Navy to procure an additional six Trident D-5 missiles, up from the original request of 66, if it could negotiate a better

Table D-6

DEPARTMENT OF DEFENSE AIRLIFT AND SEALIFT FORCES HIGHLIGHTS

	FY 1980	FY 1984	FY 1986	FY 1987	FY 1988	FY 1989
Intertheater Airlift (PAA)[1]						
C-5A	70	70	66	66	66	66
C-5B	—	—	5	14	32	44
C-141	234	234	234	234	234	234
KC-10A	—	25	48	57	57	57
C-17	—	—	—	—	—	—
Intratheater Airlift (PAA)[1]						
Air Force						
C-130	482	520	504	559	521	513
C-123	64	—	—	—	—	—
C-7A	48	—	—	—	—	—
Navy and Marine Corps						
Tactical Support	97	85	88	88	92	92
Sealift Ships, Active						
Tankers	21	21	24	20	20	20
Cargo	23	30	40	41	41	41
Reserve[2]	26	106	122	135	144	151

[1] PAA = Primary Aircraft Authorized

[2] = Includes useful National Defense Reserve Fleet ships and the Ready Reserve Force

Source: Department of Defense

Table D-7

MAJOR WEAPONS AND COMBAT FORCES

(As of 1 July 1987)

Item	Number
Intercontinental Ballistic Missiles	1,000
Fleet Ballistic Missile Submarines	37
Submarine-Launched Ballistic Missiles	656
Strategic Bomber Squadrons	21
Interceptor Squadrons (11 Air National Guard)	15
Army Divisions (10 National Guard)	28
Marine Divisions (1 Reserve)	4
Air Force Tactical Fighter Wings (12 Air National Guard/Reserve)	36
Navy Carrier Air Wings (2 Reserve)	16
Marine Aircraft Wings (1 Reserve)	4
Aircraft Carriers (also, 1 in extensive overhaul)	13
Other Naval Surface Combatants	203
Navy Attack Submarines (4 Diesel)	100
Other Ships (60 Amphibious, 37 Naval Fleet Auxiliary, 41 Support and 78 Logistical and Auxiliary)	216
Ships in the Naval Reserve	43
Dry Cargo Ships	8
Tankers	22
Hospital Ship	1
Afloat Prepositioning Ships in the Military Sealift Command-Controlled Fleet	25
Strategic Airlift Aircraft	359
Air Force Tactical Airlift Aircraft (307 Reserve/Air National Guard)	557

Source: Defense '87 Almanac

SMALL THINGS CAN HIDE BIG PROBLEMS.

Some of the smallest creatures in the ocean make the most noise. More noise than most man-made vessels. That puts unprecedented demands upon defense electronics surveillance instruments to flawlessly detect quiet threats, like submarines, and differentiate them from countless other distracting sounds.

As a versatile prime contractor, DRS designs, develops and manufactures systems for a variety of applications: sonar signal processors, acoustic video displays, mission recorders and on-board trainers.

Currently operational on hundreds of U.S. and allied naval ships and aircraft, DRS systems are consistently chosen because they are unparalleled in sensitivity and sophistication.

Our reputation for getting the job done on time and within budget has made us a growing force in defense electronics. In fact, you won't find a stronger supplier of ASW defense, intelligence and surveillance products. And you won't overlook big problems because of small distractions.

For more information, contact Richard Ross, DRS Corporate Business Development, Dept. SPA, 16 Thornton Road, Oakland, NJ 07436, (201) 337-3800. Telex: 710-988-4191.

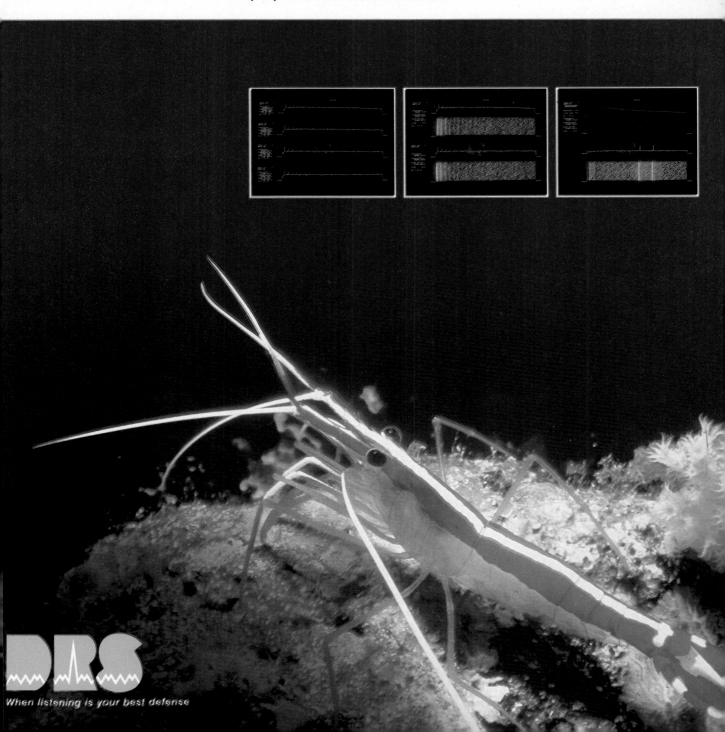

DRS
When listening is your best defense

USS Helena (SSN 725)

Submarine Technology in a League by Itself.

General Dynamics has been designing and building nuclear submarines for more than 30 years. We designed and are the builder of Trident ballistic missile submarines. We are building SSN688 Class submarines and are involved in the design of the Navy's new SSN 21. At our Electric Boat Division, we continue to set the standard of excellence in submarine technology.

GENERAL DYNAMICS
A Strong Company For A Strong Country

contract with the sole provider, Lockheed. Tomahawk, just a few years ago one of the most maligned missiles under development, has demonstrated such outstanding capabilities in recent tests that 475 missiles, a level of procurement up almost 50 percent over FY 1987, were approved. That cruise missile very likely will loom ever larger in its importance to the services as a result of the INF treaty. There were few reductions in the balance of Navy and Marine Corps requests for missiles.

The Navy did encounter rough seas in its request for sharply increased production of its Mark 50 advanced lightweight torpedo, principally because development of that weapon is behind schedule. As a consequence, funding for production of only 60 missiles, vice 153, was approved, and additional dollars had to be channeled into the development program. One hundred Mark 48 ADCAP torpedoes were approved, however, as were 260 vertical-launch ASROC weapons.

In the area of research and development, the Navy lost about 10 percent of its original request for $10.5 billion. However, continued high-level funding for development of two major programs, the SSN-21 and the V-22 tilt-rotor aircraft, was approved, as was funding for the highly sophisticated SSN-21 combat system. Throughout 1987 it appeared that the V-22 would prove vulnerable to criticisms from several corners, but Congress apparently became convinced that it would be worth the cost and that its development was on schedule, both with regard to time and money.

The O&M accounts for both the Navy and the Marine Corps were reduced, despite the fact that the Navy

Table D-8

DEPARTMENT OF DEFENSE STRATEGIC AND GENERAL PURPOSE FORCES, AND AIR AND SEALIFT HIGHLIGHTS

	FY 1980	FY 1984	FY 1986	FY 1987	FY 1988
Strategic					
Strategic Offense Land-Based ICBMs[1]					
Titan	52	32	7	—	—
Minuteman	1,000	1,000	998	973	954
Peacekeeper	—	—	2	27	46
Strategic Bombers (PAA)[2]					
B-52D	75	—	—	—	—
B-52G/H	241	241	241	234	234
B-1B	—	—	18	58	90
Fleet Ballistic Launchers (SLBMs)[1]					
Polaris	80	—	—	—	—
Poseidon (C-3 and C-4)	336	384	320	336	368
Trident	—	72	144	192	192
Strategic Defense Interceptors (PAA/Squadrons)[2]					
Active	127/7	90/5	76/4	54/3	36/2
Air National Guard	165/10	162/10	198/11	195/11	216/12

[1] Number on-line.

[2] Primary Aircraft Authorized.

	FY 1980	FY 1984	FY 1986	FY 1987	FY 1988
General Purpose					
Land Forces					
Army Divisions					
Active	16	16	18	18	18
Reserve	8	8	10	10	10
Marine Corps Divisions					
Active	3	3	3	3	3
Reserve	1	1	1	1	1
Tactical Air Forces (PAA Squadrons)[1]					
Air Force Attack/Fighter					
Active	1,608/74	1,734/77	1,764/78	1,812/81	1,762/79
Reserve	758/36	852/43	876/43	900/44	894/43
Navy Attack/Fighter					
Active	696/60	616/63	758/65	752/67	758/67
Reserve	120/10	75/9	107/10	101/10	120/10

Table D-9

HOW OLD THEY ARE

(As of 31 December 1986)

	ARMY Officers	ARMY Enlisted	NAVY Officers	NAVY Enlisted	MARINE CORPS Officers	MARINE CORPS Enlisted	AIR FORCE Officers	AIR FORCE Enlisted	TOTAL DoD Officers	TOTAL DoD Enlisted
20 and younger	49	152,256	4	101,884	0	52,490	4	73,410	57	380,040
21-25	18,145	241,746	11,983	192,757	3,820	74,691	16,019	183,247	49,967	692,441
26-30	26,783	130,001	17,899	101,934	5,537	28,805	27,279	107,000	77,498	367,740
31-35	24,012	77,775	15,042	57,550	4,419	12,527	23,614	66,738	67,087	214,590
36-40	22,344	48,760	13,972	36,264	3,776	7,198	22,315	51,205	62,407	143,427
41-45	11,336	14,624	7,801	12,542	1,644	1,908	14,070	14,159	34,851	43,233
46-50	5,069	3,629	3,348	3,441	633	502	4,550	2,429	13,600	10,001
Over 50	1,700	427	1,325	586	203	93	1,312	218	4,540	1,324
Unreported	620	753	276	203	1	12	15	1	912	969
Total	**110,058**	**669,971**	**71,650**	**507,161**	**20,033**	**178,226**	**109,178**	**498,407**	**310,919**	**1,853,765**

Source: Defense '87 Almanac

	FY 1980	FY 1984	FY 1986	FY 1987	FY 1988
Marine Corps Attack/Fighter					
Active	339/25	256/24	333/25	331/25	346/25
Reserve	84/7	90/8	94/8	96/8	96/8
Naval Forces					
Strategic Forces Ships	48	41	45	43	43
Battle Forces Ships	384	425	437	445	450
Support Forces Ships	41	46	55	59	61
Reserve Forces Ships	6	12	18	22	28
Total Deployable Battle Forces	**479**	**524**	**555**	**569**	**582**
Other Reserve Forces Ships	44	24	21	21	20
Other Auxiliaries	8	9	7	5	5
Total Other Forces	**52**	**33**	**28**	**26**	**25**

[1] PAA—Primary Aircraft Authorized.

	FY 1980	FY 1984	FY 1986	FY 1987	FY 1988
Airlift and Sealift					
Intertheater Airlift (PAA)[1]					
C-5A	70	70	66	66	66
C-5B	—	—	5	14	32
C-141	234	234	234	234	234
KC-10A	—	25	48	57	57
C-17	—	—	—	—	—
Intratheater Airlift (PAA)[1]					
Air Force					
C-130	482	520	504	559	521
C-123	64	—	—	—	—
C-7A	48	—	—	—	—
Navy and Marine Corps					
Tactical Support	97	85	88	88	92
Sealift Ships, Active					
Tankers	21	21	24	20	20
Cargo	23	30	40	41	41
Reserve[2]	26	106	122	135	144

[1] PAA—Primary Aircraft Authorized.

[2] Includes useful National Defense Reserve Fleet ships and the Ready Reserve Force.

Source: Secretary of Defense Annual Report to Congress

unquestionably is bearing the brunt of the cost of operations in the Persian Gulf and can be expected to for some time to come. Cuts will total about $1 billion. With a 3 percent pay increase for civilian personnel having to come from that account in addition to the increased costs of operating fleet units, it is obvious the Navy faces some difficult choices, unless a supplemental budget request is made and approved, and that appears unlikely at present. Dollars to meet added operating costs likely will come from deferring maintenance of real property, an action which may well haunt the Navy later, and a reduction in operational tempo of ships and aircraft not deployed, which in time will react adversely on readiness.

Congress refused to authorize increases in personnel strengths to the degree requested by the Navy and the Marines. The Navy had sought 6,200 to meet the demands being created by entry into the fleet of new ships and aircraft squadrons; Congress reduced that number to 5,600. The Marines received no additional personnel, nor did the Army, and the

Table D-10

ROTC UNITS

(1985-1986 School Year)

Army	317
Navy	64
Air Force	152
Total	**533**

Source: Defense '87 Almanac

Table D-9A
REENLISTMENT RATES (FY 1977-FY 1986)
(in percentages)

	FY 77	FY 78	FY 79	FY 80	FY 81	FY 82	FY 83	FY 84	FY 85	FY 86
FIRST TERM										
Army	33	36	43	51	55	59	45	43	43	41
Navy	37	40	38	37	42	50	56	58	55	57
Marine Corps	29	29	20	23	27	34	33	40	35	46
Air Force	39	41	38	36	43	57	66	62	54	58
DoD Overall	35	37	37	39	43	53	52	51	48	49
CAREER										
Army	70	69	66	69	73	86	86	88	85	85
Navy	68	64	62	67	73	79	82	80	79	79
Marine Corps	72	69	52	50	74	76	76	84	83	84
Air Force	86	82	82	82	86	90	92	90	89	88
DoD Overall	75	72	68	71	76	85	86	86	84	84

Source: Defense '87 Almanac

Air Force took a reduction in end strength in order to save dollars needed elsewhere. Still unresolved was the problem of continuing officer personnel cuts. A 1 percent cut was mandated in FY 1988 and 2 percent in each of FY 1989 and FY 1990; all efforts to bring about a moratorium failed. These cuts impact far more severely on the Navy and Marines, since their ratios of officers to enlisted personnel were much higher than those of the Army and Air Force. Also of concern were reductions in bonuses aimed at keeping key personnel, both officer and enlisted, in uniform. The aviation community in particular is likely to be weakened further because of reductions in Aviation Officer Continuation Pay combined with the continued growth of civilian airlines and their need for more pilots.

Congress did approve a 3 percent increase in pay for military personnel, but the gap between military and civilian pay for comparable skills continued to widen.

Table D-11

THE NAVY'S FORCE STRUCTURE GOALS

Ballistic Missile Submarines and
  Support Ships . . . . 20-40[1]
Deployable Aircraft Carriers. 15
Reactivated Battleships. 4
Antiair Warfare Cruisers
  and Destroyers 100
Antisubmarine Warfare Destroyers 37
Frigates. 101
Nuclear-Powered Attack Submarines. . 100
Mine Countermeasures Ships 14
Amphibious Ships
  (MAF-plus-MAB Lift) 75
Patrol Combatants 6
Combat Logistics Ships. 65
Support Ships and
  Other Auxiliaries 60-65

Deployable Battle Force Ships 600

[1] The force-level goal for strategic submarines has not been determined; the eventual force level will depend on arms reduction talks and other factors.

Table D-12

DOD'S BUDGET FOR RESEARCH, DEVELOPMENT, TEST, AND EVALUATION

($ in millions)

	TOTAL OBLIGATIONAL AUTHORITY		
	FY 1986 Actual	FY 1987 Estimate	FY 1988 Estimate
BY COMPONENT			
Army.	4,577.3	4,711.6	5,511.2
Navy	9,520.9	9,352.9	10,490.4
Air Force.	13,161.0	15,388.8	18,623.4
Defense Agencies	6,303.2	6,667.5	8,811.5
Defense Test and Evaluation.	113.7	119.9	178.2
Defense Operations Test and Evaluation	—	11.3	104.2
Total	**33,676.1**	**36,252.0**	**43,718.9**
BY R&D CATEGORY			
Research	953.7	891.7	918.0
Exploratory Development	2,278.7	2,341.6	2,502.7
Advanced Development	9,472.1	10,368.0	14,602.3
Engineering Development	9,215.4	10,114.9	13,112.0
Management and Support	2,689.4	2,673.2	2,711.1
Operational Systems Development	9,066.8	9,862.6	9,872.8
Total	**33,676.1**	**36,252.0**	**43,718.9**
BY BUDGET ACTIVITY			
Technology Base	3,232.4	3,233.3	3,420.6
Advanced Technology Development	4,066.8	4,930.1	7,163.2
Strategic Programs	7,509.0	8,124.7	9,990.0
Tactical Programs.	10,265.8	10,998.1	13,726.6
Intelligence & Communications.	4,525.1	4,922.8	5,262.1
Defensewide Mission Support	4,077.0	4,043.0	4,156.4
Total	**33,676.1**	**36,252.0**	**43,718.9**
BY PERFORMER			
Industry	24,186.6	25,443.9	31,556.4
Government In-house.	8,031.7	9,058.3	10,114.9
Federal Contract Research Centers	688.1	875.2	1,053.8
Universities	789.7	884.6	994.8
Total	**33,676.1**	**36,252.0**	**43,718.9**

Source: Defense '87 Almanac

Table D-13
WHERE THEY LIVE

(Total Dependents as of 30 September 1986)

Location	Army	Navy	Marine Corps	Air Force	Total DOD
Continental United States . . .	915,019	605,503	190,125	709,322	2,420,969
Alaska	10,622	1,351	80	15,224	27,277
Hawaii	15,739	19,761	8,182	9,746	53,428
U.S. Territories/ Special Locations	965	8,655	266	5,451	15,337
Foreign Countries.	208,055	38,109	7,848	146,994	401,006
Total	**1,150,400**	**674,379**	**206,501**	**886,737**	**2,918,017**

Source: Defense '87 Almanac

Table D-14

MILITARY TRAINING

TRAINING LOADS

(FY 1986)

"Training loads" are the average number of students and trainees participating in formal individual training and education courses during the fiscal year. For a full fiscal year, training loads are the equivalent of student/trainee man-years for their participants, including both those in temporary duty and permanent change-of-station status.

WHICH SERVICES TRAIN HOW MANY

Active Forces

Army	73,000
Navy	68,000
Marine Corps	19,000
Air Force	42,000
Reserve Components	37,000
Total	**239,000**

WHAT SKILLS ARE IMPARTED TO THOSE IN TRAINING

Recruit	52,000
Officer Acquisition	21,000
Specialized Skill	132,000
Flight	7,000
Professional Development	11,000
One-Station Unit Training	17,000
Total	**240,000**

Source: Defense '87 Almanac

Table D-15

SKILLS AND SPECIALTIES

Enlisted Personnel Assigned as of 31 December 1986 by Skill/Specialty Grouping

Skill/Specialty	Number
Electrical/Mechanical Equipment Repair	384,352
Administration & Clerks	298,017
Combat	265,784
Communications & Intelligence	176,696
Supply & Service Handlers	172,142
Electronic Equipment Repair	171,809
Health Care Specialists	88,720
Craftsmen	76,989
Other Technical	42,951
Other	176,305
Total	**1,853,765**

Source: Defense '87 Almanac

Table D-16

ACTIVE DUTY PEOPLE BY FUNCTION

(End Strength in Thousands)

	FY 1986 Actual	FY 1987 (Estimate)	FY 1988 (Estimate)
Strategic	**92.8**	**94.1**	**95.8**
Offensive Strategic Forces	72.3	73.8	76.2
Defensive Strategic Forces	5.8	5.3	4.3
Strategic Control and Surveillance	14.7	15.0	15.3
Tactical/Mobility	**1,019.6**	**1,050.0**	**1,056.3**
Land Forces	563.2	571.6	574.8
Tactical Air Forces	204.5	214.8	215.8
Naval Forces	211.9	224.0	227.2
Mobility Forces	40.0	39.7	38.5
Auxiliary Activities	**107.7**	**106.0**	**99.9**
Intelligence	33.3	36.1	36.7
Centrally Managed Communications	40.8	35.8	35.0
Research and Development	23.1	24.1	18.6
Geophysical Activities	10.5	10.3	9.6
Support Activities	**652.9**	**650.7**	**649.2**
Base Operating Support	306.6	299.2	299.7
Medical Support	44.5	45.5	45.7
Personnel Support	34.3	33.8	33.8
Individual Training	105.5	105.8	101.6
Force Support Training	53.6	54.5	51.1
Central Logistics	20.1	25.2	30.8
Centralized Support Activities	48.0	47.3	47.4
Management Headquarters	37.2	36.4	35.9
Federal Agency Support	3.1	3.1	3.1
Subtotal-Force Structure	**1,872.9**	**1,901.0**	**1,901.1**
Operating Strength Deviation	**0**	**−7.6**	**−8.1**
Individuals	**296.2**	**280.8**	**279.4**
Total	**2,169.1**	**2,174.2**	**2,172.4**

Source: Defense '87 Almanac

Table D-17

JOINT SERVICE SCHOOLS

Name	Location
National Defense University	Washington, DC
The National War College	
Industrial College of the Armed Forces	
Department of Defense Computer Institute	
Armed Forces Staff College	Norfolk, VA
Uniformed Services University of the Health Sciences	Bethesda, MD
Defense Institute of Security Assistance Management	Wright-Patterson AFB, OH
Defense Intelligence College	Washington, DC
Defense Mapping School	Ft. Belvoir, VA
Defense Equal Opportunity Management Institute	Patrick AFB, FL
Defense Systems Management College	Ft. Belvoir, VA
Defense Information School	Ft. Benjamin Harrison, IN
Defense Foreign Language Institute	Presidio of Monterey, CA
Defense Language Institute, English Language Course	Lackland AFB, TX
Defense Resources Management Education Center	Monterey, CA
Joint Military Packaging Training Center	Aberdeen Proving Ground, MD

Source: Defense '87 Almanac

Table D-18

MAJOR NAVAL ORGANIZATIONS

Organization **Location of Headquarters**

OPERATING FORCES

Pacific Fleet	Pearl Harbor, HI
—Third Fleet	Pearl Harbor, HI
—Seventh Fleet	Yokosuka, Japan
Atlantic Fleet	Norfolk, VA
—Second Fleet	Norfolk, VA
U.S. Naval Forces, Europe	London, England
—Sixth Fleet	Gaeta, Italy
Military Sealift Command	Washington, DC
Naval Reserve Force	New Orleans, LA
Mine Warfare Command	Charleston, SC
Operational Test and Evaluation Force	Norfolk, VA
Naval Forces Southern Command	Rodman, Panama
Naval Forces Central Command	Pearl Harbor, HI
—Middle East Force	Bahrain

SHORE ESTABLISHMENT

Naval Military Personnel Command	Washington, DC
Naval Air Systems Command	Washington, DC
Naval Facilities Engineering Command	Alexandria, VA
Naval Sea Systems Command	Washington, DC
Naval Supply Systems Command	Washington, DC
Space and Naval Warfare Systems Command	Washington, DC
Naval Medical Command	Washington, DC
Naval Telecommunications Command	Washington, DC
Naval Intelligence Command	Washington, DC
Naval Security Group Command	Washington, DC
Naval Education & Training Command	Pensacola, FL
Naval Oceanography Command	Bay St. Louis, MI
Naval Data Automation Command	Washington, DC
Naval Legal Service Command	Alexandria, VA
Naval Space Command	Dahlgren, VA
Naval Security and Investigative Command	Washington, DC

MAJOR MARINE CORPS COMMANDS

Fleet Marine Force, Atlantic	Norfolk, VA
Fleet Marine Force, Pacific	Camp H.M. Smith, HI
Marine Corps Development & Education Command	Quantico, VA
I Marine Amphibious Force	Camp Pendleton, CA
II Marine Amphibious Force	Camp Lejeune, NC
III Marine Amphibious Force	Camp Butler, Okinawa
Marine Corps Air Ground Combat Center	Twentynine Palms, CA

Source: Defense '87 Almanac

Table D-19

EDUCATION

(As of 31 December 1986)

OFFICERS

Below baccalaureate	16,128
Baccalaureate only degree received	169,114
Advanced degree received	105,848
Unknown	19,829
Total	**310,919**

ENLISTED

No high school diploma or GED	55,934
High school graduate or GED	1,448,277
1-4 years' college (no baccalaureate)	303,028
Baccalaureate degree	40,932
Advanced degree	2,773
Unknown	2,821
Total	**1,853,765**

Source: Defense '87 Almanac

Chart 1

DOD PERCENTAGE OF FEDERAL BUDGET

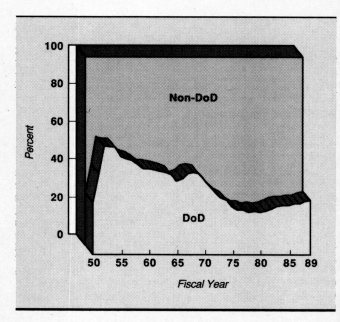

Source: Secretary of Defense Annual Report to Congress

Chart 2

FEDERAL SPENDING PROFILES

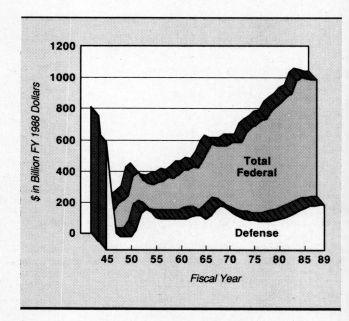

Source: Secretary of Defense Annual Report to Congress

Automatic Carrier Landing System (ACLS)

HIGH TECH ON THE HIGH SEAS

When it comes to superior performance and breakthrough technology, Bell Aerospace takes a back seat to no one. For decades we have been recognized as a leader in new technology. And we continue to lead, with revolutionary systems designed exclusively to enhance U.S. naval superiority.

Gravity Sensor System (GSS) reflects Bell's position as the world leader in real-time gravity measurement from moving platforms. This unique system allows precision inertial measurement of the magnitude and direction of gravity's forces near the earth's surface. These precise measurements, taken from moving ships, allow for major improvements in navigational accuracy.

Automatic Carrier Landing System (ACLS) AN/SPN-46(V) provides the capability to simultaneously and automatically control

two aircraft during the final approach and landing phase of carrier recovery operations. This automatic control capability enables pilots to make "hands-off" landings with minimum interference from severe weather and sea state conditions, and with no limitations due to low ceilings and visibility.

MILSTAR stabilized antenna/pedestal subsystems is a new generation of equipment for the U.S. military communications satellite program. The MILSTAR system will ensure survivable and reliable C^3I capabilities for U.S. strategic and tactical forces worldwide.

Get complete information on these revolutionary breakthroughs, available only from Bell Aerospace Textron. Call Lincoln C. Klabo, Vice President/Business Development at 716-297-1000.

Gravity Sensor System (GSS)

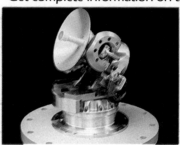

MILSTAR

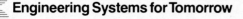

Engineering Systems for Tomorrow

Bell Aerospace TEXTRON
Division of Textron, Inc.
P.O. Box One, Buffalo, N.Y. 14240 U.S.A.

"We fight our country's battles in the air, on land and sea."

Marines

Table D-20

MINORITIES IN UNIFORM

(As of December 1986)

Enlisted	Black Americans		Hispanic Americans		Other*		Total	
	Number	Percent	Number	Percent	Number	Percent	Number	Percent
Army.	198,552	29.6	26,727	4.0	26,626	4.0	251,905	37.6
Navy	73,103	14.4	21,499	4.2	28,984	5.7	123,586	24.4
Marine Corps	36,678	20.6	9,343	5.2	5,376	3.0	51,397	28.8
Air Force.	85,635	17.2	18,582	3.7	16,860	3.4	121,077	24.3
Total DoD	393,968	21.3	76,151	4.1	77,846	4.2	547,965	29.6
Coast Guard	2,545	8.0	1,299	4.0	1,033	3.0	4,877	15.0

Officers	Black Americans		Hispanic Americans		Other*		Total	
	Number	Percent	Number	Percent	Number	Percent	Number	Percent
Army.	11,054	10.0	1,508	1.4	2,948	2.7	15,510	14.1
Navy	2,427	3.4	1,257	1.8	3,098	4.3	6,782	9.5
Marine Corps	948	4.7	353	1.8	287	1.4	1,588	7.9
Air Force.	5,777	5.3	2,166	2.0	2,700	2.5	10,643	9.7
Total DoD	20,206	6.5	5,284	1.7	9,033	2.9	34,523	11.1
Coast Guard	107	1.0	56	1.0	116	2.0	279	4.0

*Includes Native Americans, Alaskan Natives, and Pacific Islanders.

Source: Defense '87 Almanac

Table D-21

WOMEN IN UNIFORM

(As of December 1986)

OFFICERS	Number	Percent	ENLISTED	Number	Percent
Army.	11,436	10.4	Army.	71,343	10.6
Navy	7,210	10.1	Navy	46,195	9.1
Marine Corps	659	3.3	Marine Corps	9,172	5.1
Air Force.	12,595	11.5	Air Force.	61,640	12.4
Total DoD	30,476	10.3	Total DoD	188,350	10.2
Coast Guard	184	3.7	Coast Guard	2,304	7.6

Source: Defense '87 Almanac

SEA POWER: *NAVY*

The mission of the Navy, as set forth in the U.S. code, is "to be prepared to conduct operations at sea in support of U.S. national interests."

To do this, the Navy, with the strength of 581,200, maintains a sea force of 555 ships and an air force of some 5,389 planes, in conjunction with a Marine Corps with an authorized end strength of 198,800.

There's much more. The Navy also:

• Directs and maintains the Military Sealift Command, consisting of 121 strategic sealift, fleet auxiliary and special mission ships.

• Administers 36 naval air stations/naval air facilities and 22 naval stations/naval bases throughout the United States.

• Manages through its naval supply system $38 billion worth of equipment and acquires over $11.5 billion of material and services each year. It also stocks some 2.7 million line items of repair parts and components and fills more than 7.9 million demands from the fleet annually.

• Operates a world-wide "Resale System" consisting of five programs: Navy Exchanges, Commissary Stores, Uniform Stores, Navy Lodges, and Ships' Stores Afloat. The system has about 26,000 employees, most of whom are paid with non-appropriated funds.

• Operates 32 hospitals with over 4,000 beds. Fifty thousand military and civilian medical personnel annually treat over 12 million outpatients and admit more than 250,000 to in-patient care.

• Operates banks, homes, apartments, schools, radio and television stations, shipping ports, and motor pools.

• Builds bridges, hospitals, roads, and airfields.

• Designs missiles, ships, boats, and aircraft.

• Conducts research in mathematics, physics, materials, fluid and solid mechanics, biology, psychology, lasers, chemistry, electronics, ocean sciences and technology, arctic environment, acoustics, geology and geophysics, superconductivity, and atmospheric sciences. The Office of Naval Research manages two laboratories, an ocean research and development activity, an environmental prediction facility, the Naval Institute for Oceanography and two overseas offices, as well as numerous research-related field activities.

• Finances and operates eight shipyards, 150 printing plants, 10 ordnance stations, six aircraft overhaul facilities, seven public works centers, 17 research and experimental and test stations and laboratories; and six Poseidon/Trident activities.

• Operates a four-year, degree granting university, graduating about 1,000 naval officers annually.

• Administers Naval Reserve Officer Training Corps programs at 65 colleges and universities throughout the country. About 1,400 officers are commissioned annually in these programs.

• Operates a postgraduate school conferring a master's and doctoral degrees upon Navy, other service, civilian, and international military students annually.

• Participates in graduate programs in major colleges and universities throughout the United States. These programs lead to the award of additional advanced degrees to Navy officers.

• Operates a professional war college and medical school.

• Sponsors a two-year, associate degree granting program for eligible enlisted personnel in fields related to specific Navy ratings; also, an Enlisted Commissioning Program, which is an undergraduate program that provides enlisted personnel in the Navy or Naval Reserve an opportunity to earn a regular commission in a participating Naval Reserve Officers Training Corps upon completion of degree requirements for a non-technical degree in not more than 30 calendar months, or technical degree in not more than 36 calendar months.

• Administers approximately 4,740 recruiters in the field, six Navy recruiting areas, 41 recruiting districts, 61 recruiting processing stations and 197 part-time offices, to promote and man the U.S. Navy. Navy Recruiting Command personnel are located in the 50 states, Puerto Rico, the Virgin Islands, the Republic of the Philippines, Guam, Panama Canal Zone, and Europe.

U.S. NAVAL ACADEMY

The U.S. Naval Academy is the undergraduate professional college of the Navy. Founded in 1845, the academy today features beautiful and

U.S. Naval Academy

modern facilities on 322 acres along the Severn River in Annapolis, Md. About 1,200 men and 120 women enter USNA each year; nearly 80 percent of them complete the rigorous four-year program of moral, mental and physical development, and graduate with commissions in the Navy or Marine Corps.

Degrees and Majors: Midshipmen select one of 18 majors—eight in engineering, six in science and mathematics, and four in the humanities and social science. All must complete a core curriculum designed to give future naval officers a solid foundation in technical areas, the humanities, naval science, physical education, and leadership. Graduates are awarded Bachelor of Science degrees.

Costs: Tuition, room and board costs are borne by the government in return for at least five years' commissioned service by graduates. Midshipmen also are paid $480 a month to cover uniforms, books, equipment and personal needs.

Admission: Candidates must qualify scholastically, medically, and physically; meet general eligibility requirements as to citizenship, age, character and marital status; and obtain a nomination from a member of Congress or other source.

For detailed information, call 1-800 638-9156 toll-free, or write:
Director of Candidate Guidance
U.S. Naval Academy
Annapolis, Md. 21402

Table N-1

WHERE TO GO FOR NAVY INFORMATION

Need	Contact	Additional Contact
To get in touch with someone in the Navy	Naval Military Personnel Command (NMPC-05) Department of the Navy Washington, D.C. 20370-5005 (202) 694-5011, 694-3155, 694-9221	
To get in touch in an emergency	Contact closest Red Cross office and give rank and ship or unit address.	
Casualty assistance hot line Marine Corps hot line	Toll Free 1-800-368-3202 (703) 694-1787	
For verification and issuance of medals or unit awards	Special Assistant for Public Affairs Naval Medical Command (MEDCOM 00D4) Department of the Navy 2300 E St. N.W. Washington, D.C. 20372-5120 (202) 653-1315	National Personnel Records Center Navy Reference Branch 9700 Page Blvd. St. Louis, Mo. 63132 (314) 263-7141
For information on Uniformed Services Health Benefits Program (USHBP) or the Civilian Health and Medical Program of the Uniformed Services (CHAMPUS)		The health benefits counselor at the nearest Navy or Marine Corps command or Commander Naval Medical Command Department of the Navy Washington, D.C. 20372-5120 (202) 653-1081
For information on Servicemen's Group Life Insurance		Office of Servicemen's Group Life Insurance 213 Washington St. Newark, N.J. 07102 (201) 877-7676
For change of next of kin or beneficiary if you hold National Service Life Insurance or U.S. Government Life Insurance		The Veterans Administration office that maintains your insurance records
For assistance from the Navy Relief Society	The local chapter of the Navy Relief Society or The local chapter of the American Red Cross or Headquarters, Navy Relief Society Room 1228 801 N. Randolph St. Arlington, Va. 22203 (202) 696-4904	
For miscellaneous Navy retirement assistance		Retired Personnel Support Section Naval Military Personnel Command (NMPC-N643) Department of the Navy Washington, D.C. 20370-5643 (202) 694-3197
For list of all Navy Family Centers worldwide For Navy policy on drugs For Navy physical fitness standards	Naval Military Personnel Command (NMPC-014) Department of the Navy Washington, D.C. 20370-5000 (202) 694-1006	
Admission to the U.S. Naval Home		Governor U.S. Naval Home Gulfport, Miss. 39507 (601) 896-3110
For information on retired pay and allowances, SBP annuities, or arrears of pay		Navy Finance Center Retired Pay Department (Code 301) Anthony J. Celebrezze Federal Building Cleveland, Ohio 44199 Toll Free 1-800-321-1080
For information on Navy nutritional standards	Navy Food Service Systems Office Code FS1 Department of the Navy Washington, D.C. 20374-1662 (202) 433-3093	
Survivors of deceased retirees: whom to notify For assistance to survivors of deceased retirees		Casualty Assistance Branch Naval Military Personnel Command (NMPC-642) Department of the Navy Washington, D.C. 20370-5000 (202) 694-2926
For addresses and phone numbers of Navy bands	Head, Music and Arts Branch Community Relations Division Office of Information Department of the Navy Washington, D.C. 20350-1200 (202) 697-9344	
For application for headstone or grave marker		Director Monument Service (#2) Veterans Administration 1425 K St. N.W., Room 617 Washington, D.C. 20420 (202) 275-1480
To obtain a Navy speaker	Navy Speakers Bureau Office of Information Department of the Navy Washington, D.C. 20350-1200 (202) 697-0333	
Phone numbers of Navy information offices outside Washington, D.C.		Atlanta . . . . (404) 347-2101 Boston . . . . (617) 426-0490 Chicago . . . . (312) 353-5000 Dallas . . . . (214) 767-2553 Los Angeles . . . . . (213) 209-7481 New York . . . . (212) 826-4653 San Francisco . . . . (415) 765-9111 Norfolk . . . . (804) 444-2163 San Diego . . . . (619) 235-1984
For information on the Blue Angels	Community Relations Division Office of Information Department of the Navy Washington, D.C. 20350-1200 (202) 695-6915 or Navy Flight Demonstration Squadron (Blue Angels) Naval Air Station Pensacola, Fla. 32508-7801 (904) 452-2583	

Source: Department of the Navy, Office of Information

SHIP CLASSIFICATIONS

COMBATANT SHIPS

WARSHIPS
Aircraft Carriers:

Aircraft Carrier	CV
Aircraft Carrier (nuclear propulsion)	CVN
Aircraft Carrier (for anti-submarine warfare)	CVS

Surface Combatants:

Battleship	BB
Gun Cruiser	CA
Guided Missile Cruiser	CG
Guided Missile Cruiser (nuclear powered)	CGN
Destroyer	DD
Guided Missile Destroyer	DDG
Frigate	FF
Guided Missile Frigate	FFG

Patrol Combatants:

Patrol Combatant	PG
Patrol Combatant Missile (hydrofoil)	PHM

Submarines:

Submarine	SS
Auxiliary Submarine	SSAG
Guided Missile Submarine	SSG
Attack Submarine (nuclear propulsion)	SSN
Ballistic Missile Submarine (nuclear propulsion)	SSBN

AMPHIBIOUS WARFARE SHIPS

Amphibious Command Ship	LCC
Amphibious Assault Ship (general purpose)	LHA
Amphibious Cargo Ship	LKA
Amphibious Transport	LPA
Amphibious Transport Dock	LPD
Amphibious Assault Ship (helicopter)	LPH
Dock Landing Ship	LSD
Tank Landing Ship	LST

MINE WARFARE SHIPS

Mine Countermeasures Ship	MCM
Mine Hunter	MSH
Minesweeper Ocean	MSO

COMBATANT CRAFT

AMPHIBIOUS WARFARE CRAFT

Amphibious Assault Landing Craft	AALC
Landing Craft, Air Cushion	LCAC
Landing Craft, Mechanized	LCM
Landing Craft, Personnel, Large	LCPL
Landing Craft, Utility	LCU
Landing Craft, Vehicle, Personnel	LCVP
Light Seal Support Craft	LSSC
Amphibious Warping Tug	LWT
Medium Seal Support Craft	MSSC
Swimmer Delivery Vehicle	SDV
Side Loading Warping Tug	SLWT
Special Warfare Craft, Light	SWCL
Special Warfare Craft, Medium	SWCM

MINE WARFARE CRAFT

Minesweeping Boat	MSB
Minesweeping Drone	MSD
Minesweeper, Inshore	MSI
Minesweeper, River (Converted LCM-6)	MSM
Minesweeper, Patrol	MSR

PATROL CRAFT

Mini-Armored Troop Carrier	ATC
Patrol Boat	PB
River Patrol Boat	PBR
Patrol Craft (fast)	PCF
Patrol Gunboat (hydrofoil)	PGH
Fast Patrol Craft	PTF

AUXILIARY SHIPS

Destroyer Tender	AD
Ammunition Ship	AE
Store Ship	AF
Combat Store Ship	AFS
Miscellaneous	AG
Deep Submergence Support Ship	AGDS
Hydrofoil Research Ship	AGEH
Miscellaneous Command Ship	AGF
Frigate Research Ship	AGFF
Missile Range Instrumentation Ship	AGM
Oceanographic Research Ship	AGOR
Ocean Surveillance Ship	AGOS
Patrol Craft Tender	AGP
Surveying Ship	AGS
Auxiliary Research Submarine	AGSS
Hospital Ship	AH
Cargo Ship	AK
Vehicle Cargo Ship	AKR
Auxiliary Lighter	ALS
Oiler	AO
Fast Combat Support Ship	AOE
Gasoline Tanker	AOG
Replenishment Oiler	AOR
Transport Oiler	AOT
Transport	AP
Self-Propelled Barracks Ship	APB
Repair Ship	AR
Cable Repairing Ship	ARC
Repair Ship, Small	ARL
Salvage Ship	ARS
Submarine Tender	AS
Submarine Rescue Ship	ASR
Auxiliary Ocean Tug	ATA
Fleet Ocean Tug	ATF
Salvage and Rescue Ship	ATS
Guided Missile Ship	AVM
Auxiliary Aircraft Landing Training Ship	AVT

SERVICE CRAFT

Large Auxiliary Floating Dry Dock (non-self-propelled)	AFDB
Small Auxiliary Floating Dry Dock (non-self-propelled)	AFDL
Medium Auxiliary Floating Dry Dock (non-self-propelled)	AFDM
Barracks Craft (non-self-propelled)	APL
Auxiliary Repair Dry Dock (non-self-propelled)	ARD
Medium Auxiliary Repair Dry Dock (non-self-propelled)	ARDM
Deep Submergence Rescue Vehicle	DSRV
Deep Submergence Vehicle	DSV
Unclassified Miscellaneous	IX
Submersible Research Vehicle	NR
Miscellaneous Auxiliary (self-propelled)	YAG
Open Lighter (non-self-propelled)	YC
Car Float (non-self-propelled)	YCF
Aircraft Transportation Lighter (non-self-propelled)	YCV
Floating Crane (non-self-propelled)	YD
Diving Tender (non-self-propelled)	YDT
Covered Lighter (self-propelled)	YF
Ferryboat or Launch (self-propelled)	YFB
Yard Floating Dry Dock (non-self-propelled)	YFD
Covered Lighter (non-self-propelled)	YFN
Large Covered Lighter (non-self-propelled)	YFNB
Dry Dock Companion Craft (non-self-propelled)	YFND
Lighter (special purpose) (non-self-propelled)	YFNX
Floating Power Barge (non-self-propelled)	YFP
Refrigerated Covered Lighter (self-propelled)	YFR
Refrigerated Covered Lighter (non-self-propelled)	YFRN
Covered Lighter (range tender) (self-propelled)	YFRT

Rise to the top.

You're a nuclear-trained officer. It goes beyond special. It's elite! And your status reflects a job that demands your best. Proving your skills at the heart of today's nuclear-powered Navy.

Over half of America's nuclear reactors are in the Navy. That adds up to more years of experience with reactors than any company in the world, and it means working with the most sophisticated training and equipment anywhere.

College graduates get Officer Candidate School leadership training, and a year of graduate-level training in the Navy Nuclear Power School.

The rewards are top-notch, too. Generous bonuses upon commissioning and also upon completion of nuclear training. Sign up while still in college and you could be earning $1,000 a month right now.

Be one of the most accomplished professionals in a challenging field. Lead the Adventure as an officer in the Nuclear Navy.

Contact your Navy Officer Recruiter or call 1-800-327-NAVY.

NAVY ★ OFFICER.

LEAD THE ADVENTURE.

Harbor Utility Craft (self-propelled) . . . . .YFU
Garbage Lighter (self-propelled). . . . . .YG
Garbage Lighter (non-self-propelled) . . . . .YGN
Salvage Lift Craft, Heavy (non-self-propelled). . . . . . . .YHLC
Dredge (self-propelled) . . . . .YM
Salvage Lift Craft, Medium (non-self-propelled). . . . . . .YMLC
Gate Craft (non-self-propelled) . . . . .YNG
Fuel Oil Barge (self-propelled). . . . . .YO
Gasoline Barge (self-propelled) . . . . .YOG
Gasoline Barge (non-self-propelled). . . . . .YOGN
Fuel Oil Barge (non-self-propelled) . . . . .YON
Oil Storage Barge (non-self-propelled) . . . . .YOS
Patrol Craft (self-propelled) .YP
Floating Pile Driver (non-self-propelled) . . . . .YPD
Floating Workshop (non-self-propelled) . . . . .YR
Repair and Berthing Barge (non-self-propelled) . . . . .YRB
Repair, Berthing and Messing Barge (non-self-propelled). . . .YRBM
Floating Dry Dock Workshop (hull) (non-self-propelled) . . .YRDH
Floating Dry Dock Workshop
   (machine) (non-self-propelled) . . . . .YRDM

Radiological Repair Barge (non-self-propelled) . . . . .YRR
Salvage Craft Tender (non-self-propelled) . . . . .YRST
Seaplane Wrecking Derrick (self-propelled) . . . . .YSD
Sludge Removal Barge (non-self-propelled) . . . . .YSR
Large Harbor Tug . . . . .YTB
Small Harbor Tug . . . . .YTL
Medium Harbor Tug . . . . .YTM
Water Barge (self-propelled) .YW
Water Barge (non-self-propelled) . . . . .YWN

Letter prefixes to classification symbols may be added for further
identification. E: prototype ship in an experimental or developmental status. T: assigned to Military Sealift Command. F: being built
for a foreign government. X: often added to existing classifications
to indicate a new class whose characteristics have not been defined.
N: denotes nuclear propulsion when used as last letter of ship symbol.

Source: Shipbuilders Council of America

NAVY AND MARINE BASES
IN THE UNITED STATES
WITH 500 OR MORE PERMANENT PERSONNEL

ALASKA
NAS Adak, FPO Seattle 98791-1200

ARIZONA
MCAS Yuma 85369

CALIFORNIA
Naval Air Rework Facility, NAS Alameda 94501
NAS Alameda 94501
Marine Corps Logistics Base, Barstow 92311
MCB Camp Pendleton 92055
NH Camp Pendleton 92055-5008
NWC China Lake 93555-6001
NWS Concord 94520-5000
NAS Lemoore 93246-0001
NSY Long Beach 90822-5099
NH, 7500 E. Carson Street, Long Beach 90822
NS Long Beach 90822-5000
NAS, Miramar, San Diego 92145-5000
NAS Moffett Field 94035-5000
Naval Postgraduate School, Monterey 93943
NSC Oakland 94625-5000
NH Oakland 94627-5000
NPWC, Box 24003, Oakland 94623
NAS Point Mugu 93042
Pacific Missile Test Center, Point Mugu 93042
Naval Ship Weapon Systems Engineering Station, Port Hueneme
   93043-5007
Naval Construction Battalion Center, Port Hueneme 93043
Western Division, Naval Facilities Engineering Command, P.O.
   Box 727, San Bruno 94066-0720
NH San Diego 92134-5000
Fleet Combat Training Center, Pacific, San Diego 92147
Fleet ASW Training Center, Pacific, San Diego 92147
NS San Diego 92136-5000
Recruit Training Command, NTC San Diego 92133-2000
NAS, North Island, San Diego 92135
Naval Air Rework Facility, NAS, North Island, San Diego 92135
Naval Electronic Systems Engineering Center, P.O. Box 80337,
   San Diego 92138
NPWC, NB San Diego 92136-5113
NSC, 937 N. Harbor Drive, San Diego 92132-5044
NTC San Diego 92133-5000
Naval Ocean Systems Center, San Diego 92152-5000
Service School Command, San Diego 92133-3000
Naval Amphibious Base, Coronado, San Diego 92155
NS, Treasure Island, San Francisco 94130
MCAS El Toro, Santa Ana 92709
Marine Corps Recruit Depot, San Diego 92140
NWS Seal Beach 90740-5000
MCAS (Helicopter), Tustin 92710
Marine Corps Air-Ground Combat Center, Twentynine
   Palms 92278

Mare Island NSY, Vallejo 94592
Combat Systems Technical Schools Command, Mare Island,
   Vallejo 94592

CONNECTICUT
NSB New London, Box 00, Groton 06349-5000
New London Lab, Naval Underwater Systems Center Detachment,
   New London 06320
Naval Submarine School, Box 700, Groton 06349-5700
Naval Submarine Support Facility, Groton 06349

DISTRICT OF COLUMBIA
Military Sealift Command Headquarters, Washington Navy Yard
   20374
Naval Air Facility, Andrews AFB (Mail Address: Naval Air
   Facility 20390-5130)
Naval Air Systems Command Headquarters 20361-0001
Space and Naval Warfare Systems Command 20363-5100
Naval Sea Systems Command Headquarters 20362-5101
Naval Supply Systems Command Headquarters 20376-5000
Naval Military Personnel Command 20370
OPNAV Support Activity 20350
Naval Research Lab 20375
Naval District Washington, DC, Washington Navy Yard 20374-2002
Navy Regional Data Automation Center, Washington Navy Yard
   20374-1662
Naval Intelligence Support Center, 4301 Suitland Road 20390-
   5140
Marine Barracks 20390

FLORIDA
NAS Cecil Field 23315-5000
Naval Air Rework Facility, NAS Jacksonville 32212
NH Jacksonville 32214
NAS Jacksonville 32212-5000
NAS Key West 33040-5000
NS Mayport 32228
NAS Whiting Field, Milton 32570-5000
NH Orlando 32813
Naval Training Equipment Center, Orlando 32813-7100
NTC Orlando 32813
Recruit Training Command, Orlando 32813
Naval Coastal Systems Center, Panama City 32407-5000
Naval Air Rework Facility, NAS Pensacola 32508
Navy Technical Training Center, Corry Station, Pensacola
   32511-5000
Naval Education and Training Program Development Center,
   Pensacola 32509-5000
Naval Aerospace Medical Institute, NAS Pensacola 32508-5600
NPWC, NAS Pensacola 32508-6500
NAS Pensacola 32508

GEORGIA
Marine Corps Logistics Base, Albany 31704

HAWAII
Communication Area Master Station, Eastern Pacific, Wahiawa,
   Oahu 96786

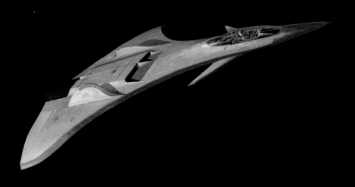

ASW.

Anti-submarine warfare and fleet protection are two of Loral's areas of concentration. Our capabilities span the broad range of underseas warfare, including guidance and training. Our technologies cover digital and hydro-acoustic signal processing, recognition, and simulation.

On-going R&D programs at Loral support these technologies and produce a steady stream of component improvements that enhance entire systems.

We also bring a bias to action to every project—a management emphasis on "no surprises," a reputation for bringing in projects on time, on budget, on spec.

And the same is true whether it's ASW, or self-protection, or C³, or simulation, or any of our other chosen areas.

Loral: It's a good synonym for *defense electronics.*

LORAL

Loral digital autopilot controller enables Vertical Launch ASROC missile to find its target.

CAPTOR mine can sense and confirm a target and fire a torpedo.

MK-30 training device simulates the "thumbprint" of adversary submarines.

VHSIC-based, fully militarized Associative Processor (ASPRO) allows real-time threat response.

DOUBLE FEATURE.

ASPJ—The first advanced electronic countermeasures system for both Navy and Air Force tactical aircraft.

AN/ALQ-165 Airborne Self Protection Jammer (ASPJ)...chosen by the United States Navy and Air Force to provide cost effective, high performance ECM protection for their front line aircraft, the F/A-18, F-14D, A-6E/F, AV-8B and F-16C... well into the nineties.

ASPJ...The new standard in electronic countermeasures technology...Successfully flight tested and ready to move forward.

ASPJ...Effective, affordable ECM protection from the ITT/Westinghouse team... defense leaders who blend technical excellence, sophisticated production technology and superior product support to help keep America strong.

For more information call or write.
ITT Avionics
500 Washington Avenue
Nutley, New Jersey 07110 • 201-284-5555

ITT
DEFENSE

NAS Barbers Point 96862
MCAS Kaneohe Bay 96863
NS Pearl Harbor 96860
Pearl Harbor NSY, Box 400, Pearl Harbor 96860
NSB Pearl Harbor 96860
NPWC Pearl Harbor 96860
NSC, Box 300, Pearl Harbor 96860

IDAHO
Nuclear Power Training Unit, P.O. Box 2751, Idaho Falls 83404

ILLINOIS
Service School Command
  Bldg. 520, NTC Great Lakes 60088-5400
NAS Glenview 60026-5000
NTC Great Lakes 60088-5000
NPWC, Bldg. 1A, Great Lakes 60088-5600
Recruit Training Command, NTC Great Lakes 60088-5300
NH Great Lakes 60088-5230

INDIANA
Naval Weapons Support Center, Crane 47522-5000
Naval Avionics Center, 6000 East 21st Street, Indianapolis
  46219-2189

KENTUCKY
Naval Ordnance Station, Louisville 40214

LOUISIANA
NAS New Orleans 70143-4000

MAINE
NAS Brunswick 04011

MARYLAND
Annapolis Lab
  D.W. Taylor Ship R&D Center, Annapolis 21402-1198
United States Naval Academy, Annapolis 21402-5000
Naval Medical Command, National Capital Region, Bethesda
  20814
D.W. Taylor Naval Ship R&D Center, Bethesda 20084-5000
Naval Ordnance Station, Indian Head 20640-5000
Naval Air Test Center, Patuxent River 20670-5304
White Oak Lab, Naval Surface Warfare Center, 10901 New
  Hampshire Avenue, Silver Spring 20903-5000

MASSACHUSETTS
NAS South Weymouth 02190-5000

MISSOURI
Marine Corps Finance Center, Kansas City 64197

MISSISSIPPI
Naval Oceanographic Office, National Space Technology Station
  Laboratory, Bay St. Louis 39522-5001
Naval Construction Battalion Center, Gulfport 39501-5000
NAS Meridian 39309

NEVADA
NAS Fallon 89406

NEW HAMPSHIRE
Portsmouth NSY, Portsmouth 03804-5000

NEW JERSEY
NWS Earle, Colts Neck 07722-5000
Naval Air Engineering Center, Lakehurst 08733-5000
Naval Air Propulsion Center, P.O. Box 7176, Trenton 08628-0176

NEW YORK
Nuclear Power Training Unit, P.O. Box 300, Ballston Spa 12020

NORTH CAROLINA
NH Camp Lejeune 28542
MCB Camp Lejeune 28542
MCAS Cherry Point 28533
Naval Air Rework Facility, Cherry Point 28533

OHIO
Navy Finance Center, Anthony J. Celebrezze Federal Building,
  Cleveland 44199-2055

PENNSYLVANIA
Navy Fleet Material Support Office, P.O. Box 2010, Mechanics-
  burg 17055-0787
Navy Ships Parts Control Center, P.O. Box 2020, Mechanicsburg
  17055-0788
Naval Ship Systems Engineering Station, NB Philadelphia 19112-
  5083
NH, 17th & Pattison Avenue, Philadelphia 19145
Naval Facilities Engineering Command, Northern Division, Phila-
  delphia 19112
Navy Aviation Supply Office, 700 Robbins Avenue, Philadelphia
  19111-5098
International Logistics Control Office, Philadelphia 19111-5095
NS Philadelphia 19112-5084
NSY Philadelphia 19112
Naval Air Development Center, Warminster 18974-5000

RHODE ISLAND
Naval Education and Training Center, Newport 02841-5000
Naval Underwater Systems Center, Newport 02841-5047

SOUTH CAROLINA
MCAS Beaufort 29902
NH Beaufort 29902
NH Charleston 29408-6900
NWS Charleston 29408
NS Charleston 29408-5100
NSC Charleston 29408-6300
NSY Charleston 29408
Polaris Missile Facility, Atlantic, Charleston 29408-5700
Marine Corps Recruit Depot, Parris Island 29905

TENNESSEE
Naval Air Technical Training Center, NAS Memphis,
  Millington 38054-5059
NAS Memphis, Millington 38054-5000
NH Millington 38054

TEXAS
NAS Chase Field, Beeville 78103-5000
NAS Corpus Christi 78419-5000
NAS Dallas 75211-9501
NAS Kingsville 78363

VIRGINIA
NAS Oceana, Virginia Beach 23460-5120
Headquarters Battalion, Headquarters USMC, Henderson
  Hall, Arlington 22214
Naval Facilities Engineering Command Headquarters, 200
  Stovall Street, Alexandria 22332-2300
Naval Surface Warfare Center, Dahlgren 22448-5000
FTC Norfolk 23511-6285
Naval Amphibious Base, Little Creek, Norfolk 23521
Naval Air Rework Facility, NAS Norfolk 23511
NAS Norfolk 23511
Naval Communication Master Station, Atlantic, Norfolk
  23511
Naval Facilities Engineering Command, Atlantic Division
  Norfolk 23511-6287
NPWC Norfolk 23511-6098
NS Norfolk 23511-6000
NSC Norfolk 23512-5000
NH Portsmouth 23708-5000
Norfolk NSY, Portsmouth 23709-5000
Marine Corps Development and Education Command, Quantico
  22134
Marine Corps Air Facility, Quantico 22134
Fleet Combat Training Center, Atlantic, Dam Neck, Virginia
  Beach 23461
Naval Guided Missiles School, Dam Neck, Virginia Beach 23461
NWS Yorktown 23691-5000

WASHINGTON
Puget Sound NSY, Bremerton 98314-5000
Naval Undersea Warfare Engineering Station, Keyport 98345-0580
NAS Whidbey Island, Oak Harbor 98278-5000
NSB Bangor, Bremerton 98315-5000
NH Bremerton 98314-5315
Strategic Weapons Facility, Pacific, Bremerton, Silverdale
  98315-5500
Trident Refit Facility, Bangor, Bremerton 98315-5300

NAVY AND MARINE BASES OVERSEAS
WITH 500 OR MORE PERMANENT PERSONNEL

BERMUDA
U.S. NAS, FPO New York 09560

CUBA (Guantanamo Bay)
U.S. NAS, FPO New York 09593
U.S. NS, FPO New York 09593

ICELAND (Keflavik)
U.S. NS, FPO New York 09571

JAPAN (Iwakuni)
U.S. MCAS, FPO Seattle 98764

MARIANA ISLANDS (Agana/Guam)
U.S. NAS, FPO San Francisco 96637-1200
U.S. NPWC, FPO San Francisco 96630-2937
U.S. Naval Ship Repair Facility, FPO San Francisco 96630-1400
U.S. Naval Communication Area Master Station, WESTPAC,
FPO San Francisco 96630-1800

OKINAWA (Kawasaki)
U.S. MCB, Camp Smedley D. Butler, FPO Seattle 98773

PUERTO RICO (Roosevelt Roads)
U.S. NS, FPO Miami 34051

REPUBLIC OF THE PHILIPPINES (Subic Bay)
U.S. NAS, FPO San Francisco 96654-1200

SICILY (Sigonella)
U.S. NAS, FPO New York 09523

SPAIN (Rota)
U.S. NS, FPO New York 09540-1000

DIEGO GARCIA
U.S. Navy Support Facility, FPO San Francisco 96685-2000

CHANGES IN SHIP FORCES OF THE U.S. NAVY INVENTORY
1 OCTOBER 1986 THROUGH 30 SEPTEMBER 1987

EFFECTIVE DATE	FLEET	SHIP TYPE	HULL NO.	SHIP NAME	FROM STATUS	TO STATUS
100186	PAC	AGDS	0002	POINT LOMA	ACTIVE	MSC NFSM
101386		TACS	0003	GRAND CANYON STATE	CONV	RRF
101586		TAKR	5064	CAPE MENDOCINO	NOSTAT	RRF
102586	LANT	CVN	0071	THEODORE ROOSEVELT	NEWCN	ACTIVE
103086		TAKR	5066	CAPE HUDSON	NOSTAT	RRF
110386	LANT	SSBN	0623	NATHAN HALE	ACTIVE	ISNAC
110886	LANT	SSN	0724	LOUISVILLE	NEWCN	ACTIVE
111486	PAC	SSN	0592	SNOOK	ACTIVE	STRIKE
111586	LANT	ARS	0053	GRAPPLE	NEWCN	ACTIVE
121086		TAKR	5068	CAPE HORN	NOSTAT	RRF
121186	PAC	AVM	0001	NORTON SOUND	ACTIVE	ISNAC
121586	PAC	TAH	0019	MERCY	CONV	MSC ROS
121586	LANT	SSBN	0636	NATHANAEL GREENE	ACTIVE	ISNAC
121986	LANT	TAO	0187	HENRY J KAISER	NEWCN	MSC NFAF
123186	PAC	AR	0006	AJAX	ACTIVE	ISNAC
013087	LANT	TAGOS	0010	INVINCIBLE	NEWCN	MSC NFAF
013087	PAC	FFG	0019	JOHN A MOORE	ACTIVE	NRF
013087	LANT	FFG	0020	ANTRIM	ACTIVE	NRF
021387		TAKR	5071	CAPE FLORIDA	NOSTAT	RRF
022187	LANT	CG	0053	MOBILE BAY	NEWCN	ACTIVE
022887	PAC	TAH	0019	MERCY	MSC ROS	MSC NFME
022887	LANT	FFG	0059	KAUFFMAN	NEWCN	ACTIVE
033087	PAC	SSN	0575	SEAWOLF	ACTIVE	ISNAC
033187	PAC	AR	0007	HECTOR	ACTIVE	ISNAC
040287		TAKR	5073	CAPE FAREWELL	NOSTAT	RRF
040287		TAOT	0149	MAUMFE	RRF	NDRF
040287		TAOT	0152	YUKON	RRF	NDRF
040387	LANT	TAO	0198	JOSHUA HUMPHREYS	NEWCN	MSC NFAF
041087		TAKR	5069	CAPE EDMONT	NOSTAT	RRF
050487		TAK	5001	CATAWBA VICTORY	RRF	NOSTAT
050987	PAC	FFG	0060	RODNEY M DAVIS	NEWCN	ACTIVE
052287	PAC	CG	0054	ANTIETAM	NEWCN	ACTIVE
060187	PAC	FF	1053	ROARK	ACTIVE	NRF
060187	PAC	FFG	0023	LEWIS B PULLER	ACTIVE	NRF
060587		TAKR	5070	CAPE FLATTERY	NOSTAT	RRF
062587	LANT	TAO	0189	JOHN LENTHALL	NEWCN	MSC NFAF
063087		TAKR	1001	ADM WILLIAM M CALLAGHAN	MSC CHLT	RRF
071087	PAC	TAH	0019	MERCY	MSC NFME	MSC ROS
071187	LANT	SSN	0725	HELENA	NEWCN	ACTIVE
080887	PAC	LSD	0043	FORT MCHENRY	NEWCN	ACTIVE
081887		TAVB	0004	CURTISS	CONV	MSC ROS
082287	LANT	CG	0051	THOMAS S GATES	NEWCN	ACTIVE
090587	LANT	CG	0055	LEYTE GULF	NEWCN	ACTIVE
091287	LANT	MCM	0001	AVENGER	NEWCN	ACTIVE
091384	LANT	SSN	0722	KEY WEST	NEWCN	ACTIVE
092487	LANT	TAH	0020	COMFORT	CONV	MSC ROS
092587	PAC	ARS	0039	CONSERVER	ISNAC	ACTIVE

CHANGES IN SHIP FORCES OF THE U.S. NAVY INVENTORY

EFFECTIVE DATE	FLEET	SHIP TYPE	HULL NO.	SHIP NAME	FROM STATUS	TO STATUS
092687	LANT	ARS	0008	PRESERVER	ISNAC	ACTIVE
092687	LANT	ATF	0159	PAIUTE	ISNAC	ACTIVE
092687	LANT	ATF	0160	PAPAGO	ISNAC	ACTIVE
093087	PAC	TAK	2043	LETITIA LYKES	MSC NFME	NOSTAT
093087		TAKR	5072	CAPE FEAR	NOSTAT	RRF
093087		TAKR	5074		NOSTAT	RRF
093087		TAKR	5075		NOSTAT	RRF
093087		TAKR	5076		NOSTAT	RRF

DEFINITIONS OF THE STATUS ABBREVIATIONS FOLLOW:

ACTIVE	ACTIVE FLEET
CONV	IN CONVERSION
ISNAC	INACTIVE SHIP IN NAVY CUSTODY
LEASE	LEASE
LOAN	LOAN
MSC NFAF	NAVAL FLEET AUXILIARY FORCE
MSC NFME	NAVAL FLEET MOBILITY ENHANCEMENT
MSC NFSL	MSC NUCLEUS FLEET—SEALIFT
MSC NFSS	MSC NUCLEUS FLEET—SCIENTIFIC SUPPORT
MSC ROS	REDUCED OPERATING STATUS
MSC CHLT	MSC CHARTER—LONG TERM
NDRF	RESERVED FOR NAVY—NATIONAL DEFENSE RESERVE FLEET
NEWCN	NEW CONSTRUCTION
NRF	NAVAL RESERVE FORCE
SCRAFT	SERVICE CRAFT
STRIKE	STRIKE FROM NAVAL VESSEL REGISTER
TNDRF	RESERVED FOR MSC—NATIONAL DEFENSE RESERVE FLEET
SLEP	SERVICE LIFE EXTENSION PROGRAM

ACRONYMS

AAW: Antiair Warfare
ABM: Antiballistic Missile
AC: Active Component
ACM: Advanced Cruise Missile
ACMR: Air Combat Maneuvering Range
ACIP: Aviation Career Incentive Pay
ADCAP: Advanced Capability (torpedo)
ADP: Automated Data Processing
AFATDS: Advanced Field Artillery Tactical Data System
AFQT: Armed Forces Qualification Test
AFR: Air Force Reserve
AFSATCOM: Air Force Satellite Communications
AGR: Active Guard and Reserve
AID: Agency for International Development
AIM: Air-Intercept Missile
ALCM: Air-Launched Cruise Vehicle
ALMV: Air-Launched Miniature Vehicle
AMRAAM: Advanced Medium-Range Air-to-Air Missile
ANG: Air National Guard
ANZUS: Australia-New Zealand-United States (Treaty)
AOCP: Aviation Officer Continuation Pay
AOE: Multipurpose Stores Ship
ASAT: Antisatellite
ASPJ: Airborne Self-Protection Jammer
ASROC: Antisubmarine Rocket
ASW: Antisubmarine Warfare
ATA: Advanced Tactical Aircraft
ATB: Advanced Technology Bomber
ATF: Advanced Tactical Fighter
ATM: Antitactical Missile, Automated Teller Machines
AUTOVON: Automatic Voice Network
AWACS: Airborne Warning and Control System

BA: Budget Authority
BCS: Battery Computer System
BFV: Bradley Fighting Vehicle
BMEWS: Ballistic Missile Early Warning System

C^3: Command, Control, and Communications
C^3CM: Command, Control, and Communications Countermeasures
C^3I: Command, Control, Communications, and Intelligence
CDE: Conference on Disarmament in Europe
CDI: Conventional Defense Improvements
CDIP: Combined Defense Improvement Projects
CELV: Complementary Expendable Launch Vehicle
CEM: Combined-Effects Munitions
CHAMPUS: Civilian Health and Medical Program of the Uniformed Services
CINC: Commander in Chief
COB: Collocated Operating Base
COMSEC: Communications Security
CONUS: Continental United States
CRAF: Civil Reserve Air Fleet
CSOC: Consolidated Space Operations Center
CY: Calendar Year or Current Year

DARPA: Defense Advanced Research Projects Agency
DCA: Dual-Capable Aircraft, Defense Communications Agency
DCAA: Defense Contract Audit Agency
DCIMI: Defense Council on Integrity and Management Improvement
DCS: Defense Communications System
DD/EFT: Direct Deposit/Electronic Funds Transfer
DDG: Guided Missile Destroyer
DDN: Defense Data Network
DDT&E: Director, Defense Test and Evaluation
DEW: Directed-Energy Weapons
DGSC: Defense General Supply Center

DIA: Defense Intelligence Agency
DLA: Defense Logistics Agency
DMSP: Defense Meteorological Support Program
DNA: Defense Nuclear Agency
DoD: Department of Defense
DoE: Department of Energy
DOT&E: Director, Operational Test and Evaluation
DPA: Defense Production Act
DPACT: Defense Policy Advisory Committee on Trade
DPC: Defense Planning Committee
DRB: Defense Resources Board
DSB: Defense Science Board
DSCS: Defense Satellite Communication System
DTSA: Defense Technology Security Administration

EC: Electronic Combat
ECM: Electronic Countermeasures
ELF: Extremely Low Frequency
EMP: Electromagnetic Pulse
EPA: Environmental Protection Agency
ESF: Economic Support Fund
EW: Electronic Warfare

FEMA: Federal Emergency Management Agency
FFG: Guided Missile Frigate
FLIR: Forward-Looking Infrared Radar
FMC: Fully Mission Capable
FMS: Foreign Military Sales
FMSCR: Foreign Military Sales Credit (Financing)
FSS: Fast Sealift Ships
FTS: Full-Time Support
FY: Fiscal Year

GAO: General Accounting Office
GLCM: Ground-Launched Cruise Missile
GNP: Gross National Product
GPS: Global Positioning System
GS: General Schedule
GWEN: Ground Wave Emergency Network

HARM: High-Speed Antiradiation Missile
HF: High Frequency
HLG: High-Level Group
HMMWV: High Mobility Multipurpose Wheeled Vehicle
HMO: Health Maintenance Organization
HNS: Host Nation Support

I-S/A AMPE: Inter-Service Agency Automated Message Processing Exchange
IAMP: Imagery Acquisition and Management Plan
IBP: Industrial Base Program
ICBM: Intercontinental Ballistic Missile
IFF: Identification Friend or Foe
IG: Inspector General
IIR: Imaging Infrared
IL: International List
IMA: Individual Mobilization Augmentees
IMP: Internal Management Control
IMET: International Military Education and Training
IMC: Internal Management Control
IMIP: Industrial Modernization Incentives Program
INCA: Intelligence Communications Architecture
INEWS: Integrated Electronic Warfare System
INF: Intermediate-Range Nuclear Forces
IR: Infrared
IR&D: Independent Research and Development
IRR: Individual Ready Reserve
IRS: Internal Revenue Service

JCS: Joint Chiefs of Staff
JCSE: Joint Communications Support Element
JSTARS: Joint Surveillance/Target Attack Radar System
JRMB: Joint Requirements and Management Board
JROC: Joint Requirements and Oversight Council
JTDE: Joint Technology Demonstrator Engine
JT&E: Joint Test and Evaluation
JTFP: Joint Tactical Fusion Program
JTIDS: Joint Tactical Information Distribution System

KEW: Kinetic Energy Weapons

LAMPS: Light Airborne Multipurpose System
LANTIRN: Low-Altitude Navigation and Targeting Infrared System for Night
LAV: Light-Armored Vehicle
LAV-AD: Light-Armored Vehicle, Air Defense
LCAC: Landing Craft, Air Cushion
LF: Low Frequency
LHX: Light Helicopter Experimental
LIC: Low-Intensity Conflict
LRINF: Longer Range Intermediate-Range Nuclear Forces
LVS: Logistics Vehicle System
LVT: Assault Amphibian Vehicle

MAB: Marine Amphibious Brigade
MAF: Marine Amphibious Force
MAP: Military Assistance Program
MAW: Marine Aircraft Wing
MBFR: Mutual and Balanced Force Reductions
MC: Mission Capable, Military Committee
MCC: Military Coordinating Committee
MCE: Modular Control Equipment
MCS: Maneuver Control System
MCTL: Military Critical Technology List
MFO: Multinational Forces and Observers
MiG: Mikoyan-Gurevich (aircraft)
MILCON: Military Construction
Milstar: Military Strategic and Tactical Relay System
MIRV: Multiple Independently Targetable Reentry Vehicle
MLRS: Multiple-Launch Rocket System
MMP: Master Mobilization Plan
MMWG: Military Mobilization Working Group
MNC: Major NATO Commander
MOA: Memorandum of Agreement
MOB: Main Operating Base
MOU: Memorandum of Understanding
MP: Military Personnel
MPS: Maritime Prepositioning Ship
MRT: Miniature Receive Terminal
MSE: Mobile Subscriber Equipment
MSO: Military Service Obligation
MYP: Multiyear Procurement

NAF: Nonappropriated Fund
NATO: North Atlantic Treaty Organization
Navstar: Navigation Satellite Timing and Ranging
NCA: National Command Authorities
NCS: National Communications System
NDS: Nuclear Detonation Detection System
NEACP: National Emergency Airborne Command Post
NFIP: National Foreign Intelligence Program
NIS: NATO Identification System
NMCC: National Military Command Center
NORAD: North American Aerospace Defense Command
NPG: Nuclear Planning Group
NPS: Nonprior Service
NRF: Naval Reserve Fleet, Naval Reserve Force
NSA: National Security Agency
NSDD: National Security Decision Directive
NTPF: Near-Term Prepositioning Forces

O&M: Operation and Maintenance
OJCS: Organization of the Joint Chiefs of Staff
OMB: Office of Management and Budget
OSD: Office of the Secretary of Defense
OSIS: Ocean Surveillance Information System
OTH: Over-the-Horizon
OTH-B: Over-the-Horizon Backscatter (radar)

P^3I: Preplanned Product Improvement
PARCS: Perimeter Acquisition Radar Attack Characterization System
PAVE PAWS: Phased-Array Radars
PCS: Permanent Change of Station
PECI: Productivity Enhancing Capital Investment
PGM: Precision Guided Munitions
PLRS: Position, Location, and Reporting System
PLSS: Precision Location Strike System
POL: Petroleum, Oil, and Lubricants
POMCUS: Prepositioning of Materiel Configured to Unit Sets
PRC: People's Republic of China

R&D: Research and Development
RC: Reserve Component
RDT&E: Research, Development, Test, and Evaluation
ROK: Republic of Korea
RO/RO: Roll-on/Roll-off
RPV: Remotely Piloted Vehicle
RRF: Ready Reserve Force
RSI: Rationalization, Standardization, and Interoperability

S&T: Science and Technology
SA/BM: Systems Analysis/Battle Management
SAC: Strategic Air Command
SALT: Strategic Arms Limitation Treaty, Strategic Arms Limitation Talks
SAM: Surface-to-Air Missile, Sea Air Mariner
SASC: Senate Armed Service Committee
SATKA: Surveillance, Acquisition, Tracking, and Kill Assessment
SCG: Special Consultative Group
SDAF: Special Defense Acquisition Fund
SDI: Strategic Defense Initiative
SDIO: Strategic Defense Initiative Organization
SEAL: Sea-Air-Land
SHORAD C^2: Short-Range Air Defense Command and Control
SINCGARS-V: Single-Channel Ground and Airborne System, VHF
SLBM: Submarine-Launched Ballistic Missile
SLC: Submarine Laser Communications
SLCM: Submarine-Launched Cruise Missile
SLEP: Service Life Extension Program
SLKT: Survivability, Lethality, and Key Technologies
SLOC: Sea Line of Communications
SM: Standard Missile
SNA: Soviet Naval Aviation
SNF: Short-Range Nuclear Forces
SOF: Special Operations Forces
SRAM: Short-Range Attack Missile
SSBN: Ballistic Missile Submarine, Nuclear-Powered
SSGN: Cruise Missile Attack Submarine, Nuclear-Powered
SSN: Attack Submarine, Nuclear-Powered
START: Strategic Arms Reduction Talks
Su: Sukhoy (aircraft)
SUBROC: Submarine Rocket
SURTASS: Surveillance Towed-Array Sonar System
SWA: Southwest Asia
SWS: Special Warfare Systems

T&E: Test and Evaluation
TACS: Auxiliary Crane Ship
TACTAS: Tactical Towed-Array Sonar
TAOC: Tactical Air Operations Center
TCAC: Technical Control and Analysis Center
TDAC: Training Data and Analysis Center
TFW: Tactical Fighter Wing
TGSM: Terminally Guided Submunitions
TIAP: Theater Intelligence Architecture Program
TIARA: Tactical Intelligence and Related Activities
TOA: Total Obligational Authority
TOW: Tube-Launched, Optically Tracked, Wire-Guided (antitank missile)
TRI-TAC: Joint Tactical Communications Program
UCA: Undefinitized Contractual Actions
UHF: Ultrahigh Frequency
USCENTCOM: United States Central Command
USCINCCENT: Commander in Chief, United States Central Command
USCINCEUR: United States Commander in Chief, Europe
USCINCLANT: Commander in Chief, United States Atlantic Command
USCINCPAC: Commander in Chief, United States Pacific Command
USCINCSOUTH: Commander in Chief, United States Southern Command
USSR: Union of Soviet Socialist Republics

VA: Veterans Administration
VHA: Variable Housing Allowance
VHF: Very High Frequency
VHSIC: Very High Speed Integrated Circuit
VLA: Vertical Launch ASROC
VLF: Very Low Frequency
VLS: Vertical Launch System
VLSI: Very Large Scale Integration
V/STOL: Vertical/Short Take-Off and Landing

WARMAPS: Wartime Manpower Planning System
WHNS: Wartime Host Nation Support
WWMCCS: Worldwide Military Command and Control System

CHART OF SEA STATE CONDITIONS

Sea State	(Beaufort Wind Force)	SEA—GENERAL Description	WIND Description	Range (knots)	Wind Velocity (knots)	WAVE HEIGHT Average	Significant	Average of One-Tenth Highest	Significant Range Periods (sec)	SEA — Periods of maximum Energy of Spectra $T_{max}=T_c$	Average Period T_z	Average Wave-length L_w (ft unless otherwise indicated)	Minimum Fetch (nautical miles)	Minimum Duration (hr unless otherwise indicated)
0	U	Sea like a mirror.	Calm	—	0	0	0	0	—	—	—	—	—	—
1	1	Ripples with the appearance of scales are formed, but without foam crests.	Light airs	1-3	2	0.04	0.01 0.01	0.09	1.2	0.75	0.5	10 in	5	18 min
2	2	Small wavelets; short but pronounced crests have a glossy appearance, but do not break.	Light breeze	4-6	5	0.3	0.5	0.6	0.4-2.8	1.9	1.3	6.7	8	39 min
3	3	Large wavelets; crests begin to break. Foam of glossy appearance. Perhaps scattered with horses.	Gentle breeze	7-10	8.5	0.8	1.3	1.6	0.8-5.0	3.2	2.3	20	9.8	1.7
					10	1.1	1.8	2.3	1.0-6.0	3.2	2.7	27	10	2.4
4	4	Small waves, becoming larger; fairly frequent white horses.	Moderate breeze	11-16	12	1.6	2.6	3.3	1.0-7.0	4.5	3.2	40	18	3.8
					13.5	2.1	3.3	4.2	1.4-7.6	5.1	3.6	52	24	4.8
					14	2.3	3.6	4.6	1.5-7.8	5.3	3.8	59	28	5.2
					16	2.9	4.7	6.0	2.0-8.8	6.0	4.3	71	40	6.6
5	5	Moderate waves, taking a more pronounced long form; many white horses are formed (chance of some spray).	Fresh breeze	17-21	18	3.7	5.9	7.5	2.5-10.0	6.8	4.8	90	55	8.3
					19	4.1	6.6	8.4	2.8-10.6	7.2	5.1	99	65	9.2
					20	4.6	7.3	9.3	3.0-11.1	7.5	5.4	111	75	10
6	6	Large waves begin to form; white crests are more extensive everywhere (probably some spray).	Strong breeze	22-27	22	5.5	8.8	11.2	3.4-12.2	8.3	5.9	134	100	12
					24	6.6	10.5	13.3	3.7-13.5	9.0	6.4	160	130	14
					24.5	6.8	10.9	13.8	3.8-13.6	9.2	6.6	164	140	15
					26	7.7	12.3	15.6	4.0-14.5	9.8	7.0	188	180	17
7	7	Sea heaps up, and white foam from breaking waves begins to be blown in streaks along the direction of the wind (spindrift begins to be seen).	Moderate gale	28-33	28	8.9	14.3	18.2	4.5-15.5	10.6	7.5	212	230	20
					30	10.3	16.4	20.8	4.7-16.7	11.3	8.0	250	280	23
					30.5	10.6	16.9	21.5	4.8-17.0	11.5	8.2	258	290	24
					32	11.6	18.6	23.6	5.0-17.5	12.1	8.6	285	340	27
7	8	Moderate high waves of greater length; edges of crests break into spindrift. The foam is blown in well-marked streaks along the direction of the wind. Spray affects visibility.	Fresh gale	34-40	34	13.1	21.0	26.7	5.5-18.5	12.8	9.1	322	420	30
					36	14.8	23.6	30.0	5.8-19.7	13.6	9.6	363	500	34
					37	15.6	24.9	31.6	6.0-20.5	13.9	9.9	376	530	37
					38	16.4	26.3	33.4	6.2-20.8	14.3	10.2	392	600	38
					40	18.2	29.1	37.0	6.5-21.7	15.1	10.7	444	710	42
8	9	High waves, Dense streaks of foam along the direction of the wind. Sea begins to roll. Visibility affected.	Strong gale	41-47	42	20.1	32.1	40.8	7-23	15.8	11.3	492	830	47
					44	22.0	35.2	44.7	7-24.2	16.6	11.8	534	960	52
					46	24.1	38.5	48.9	7-25	17.3	12.3	590	1110	57
9	10	Very high waves with long overhanging crests. The resulting foam is in great patches and is blown in dense white streaks along the direction of the wind. On the whole, the surface of the sea takes on a white appearance. The rolling of the sea becomes heavy and shock-like. Visibility is affected.	Whole gale*	48-55	48	26.2	41.9	53.2	7.5-26	18.1	12.9	650	1250	63
					50	28.4	45.5	57.8	7.5-27	18.8	13.4	700	1420	69
					51.5	30.2	48.3	61.3	8-28.2	19.4	13.8	736	1560	73
					52	30.8	49.2	62.5	8-28.5	19.6	13.9	750	1610	75
					54	33.2	53.1	67.4	8-29.5	20.4	14.5	810	1800	81
	11	Exceptionally high waves. Sea completely covered with long white patches of foam lying in direction of wind. Everywhere edges of wave crests blown into froth. Visibility affected.	Storm*	56-63	56	35.7	57.1	72.5	8.5-31	21.1	15	910	2100	88
					59.5	40.3	64.4	81.8	10-32	22.4	15.9	985	2500	101
	12	Air filled with foam and spray. Sea white with driving spray. Visibility very seriously affected.	Hurricane*	64-71	>64	>46.6	74.5	94.6	10-35	24.1	17.2	—	—	—

*For hurricane winds (and often whole gale and storm winds) required durations and reports are barely attained. Seas are therefore not fully arisen.

SHIPS/NAVY

The figures listed as the complement for each class of ship represent the average manpower requirements for those ships. However, actual manning may differ from the average requirement, depending on availability of personnel, specific mission requirements, etc.

STRATEGIC FORCES

BALLISTIC MISSILE SUBMARINES (SSBN)

Ohio Class

DISPLACEMENT: 18,700 tons dived.
LENGTH: 560 feet.
BEAM: 42 feet.
SPEED: 20-plus knots.
POWER PLANT: one nuclear reactor, two geared turbines, one shaft, 60,000 shaft horsepower.
ARMAMENT: 24 tubes for Trident missiles, four torpedo tubes.
COMPLEMENT: 155.
BUILDER: General Dynamics' Electric Boat Division.

Benjamin Franklin, Lafayette, and James Madison Classes

DISPLACEMENT: 8,250 tons dived.
LENGTH: 425 feet.
BEAM: 33 feet.
SPEED: 20 knots surfaced; approximately 30 dived.
POWER PLANT: one nuclear reactor, two geared turbines, one shaft, 15,000 shaft horsepower.
ARMAMENT: 16 tubes for Poseidon or Trident missiles, four torpedo tubes.
COMPLEMENT: 143
BUILDERS: SSBNs 616, 617, 623, 626, 628, 631, 633, 640, 643, 645, 655, 657, 659, General Dynamics' Electric Boat Division, 619, 624, 629, 634, 642, 658, Mare Island Naval Shipyard; 620, 636, Portsmouth Naval Shipyard; 622, 625, 627, 630, 632, 635, 641, 644, 654, 656, Newport News Shipbuilding.

BRIEFING: The Navy's SSBN program represents at one end of the spectrum perhaps the finest example in naval history of industry and government cooperation in the building of a ship, the creation of a weapons system, and the marriage of the two. The original 41-ship fleet, headed by *George Washington* (SSBN-598), came into being with a minimum of difficulty and has been a most credible deterrent force in the almost 30 years since the first SSBN was commissioned. Only eight years elapsed between the commissioning of *George Washington* and the last ship in the program, *Will Rogers* (SSBN-659). At the other end of the spectrum, the early days of the Ohio-class Trident SSBN program were marred by cost overruns, construction delays, protests by opponents of nuclear weapons, and questions about the capabilities of both the submarine and the missile system. However, over the years shipyard performance improved markedly, and the last seven Ohio-class submarines have been delivered ahead of schedule. The Navy now regards these ships as "the most effective warships of their kind in the world." Eight have been commissioned and five are under construction. It is anticipated that one ship will be funded each year until the current tentative goal of 20 is reached. The original Polaris missiles in the non-Trident submarines were replaced by the more advanced Poseidon missiles, and in 12 of the remaining 28 Poseidon submarines these missiles were in turn replaced by Trident C-3 missiles. *Sam Rayburn*'s missile tubes have been plugged. Commencing with the ninth Ohio-class ship, the advanced D-5 missile will be installed; the first eight ships ultimately will be refitted with it. Thirteen of the original Polaris SSBNs have either been withdrawn from service or converted to attack submarines. In 1986, the SSBN force completed 88 deterrent patrols, including 21 by Trident SSBNs.

Alexander Hamilton (SSBN-617)

Ohio Class

SSBN-726 Ohio; Bangor, WA (SE 98799-2093)
SSBN-727 Michigan; Bangor, WA (SE 98799-2096)
SSBN-728 Florida; Bangor, WA (SE 98799-2099)
SSBN-729 Georgia; Bangor, WA (SE 98799-2102)
SSBN-730 Henry M. Jackson; Bangor, WA (SE 98799-2105)
SSBN-731 Alabama; Bangor, WA (SE 98799-2108)
SSBN-732 Alaska; Bangor, WA (SE 98799-2111)
SSBN-733 Nevada; Bangor, WA (SF 98799-2114)

Benjamin Franklin Class

SSBN-640 Benjamin Franklin; Charleston, SC (MI 34091-2057)
SSBN-641 Simon Bolivar; Charleston, SC (MI 34090-2060)
SSBN-642 Kamehameha; Portsmouth, NH (09576-2063)
SSBN-643 George Bancroft; Charleston, SC (MI 34090-2066)
SSBN-644 Lewis and Clark; Charleston, SC (MI 34091-2069)
SSBN-645 James K. Polk; Portsmouth, NH (NY 09582-2072)
SSBN-654 George C. Marshall; Groton, CT (NY 09578-2075)
SSBN-655 Henry L. Stimson; Charleston, SC (MI 34093-2078)
SSBN-656 George Washington Carver; Groton, CT (NY 09566-2081)
SSBN-657 Francis Scott Key; Charleston, SC (MI 34091-2084)
SSBN-658 Mariano G. Vallejo; Charleston, SC (MI 34093-2087)
SSBN-659 Will Rogers; Groton, CT (NY 09586-2090)

Lafayette Class

SSBN-616 Lafayette; Groton, CT (NY 09577-2000)
SSBN-617 Alexander Hamilton; Bremerton, WA (NY 09573-2003)
SSBN-619 Andrew Jackson; Groton, CT (NY 09575-2006)
SSBN-620 John Adams; Charleston, SC (MI 34093-2009)
SSBN-622 James Monroe; Charleston, SC (MI 34092-2012)
SSBN-624 Woodrow Wilson; Charleston, SC (MI 34093-2018)
SSBN-625 Henry Clay; Charleston, SC (MI 34090-2021)
SSBN-626 Daniel Webster: Groton, CT (NY 09591-2024)

James Madison Class

SSBN-627 James Madison; Charleston, SC (MI 34092-2027)
SSBN-628 Tecumseh; Charleston, SC (MI 34093-2030)
SSBN-629 Daniel Boone; Charleston, SC (MI 34090-2033)
SSBN-630 John C. Calhoun; Charleston, SC (MI 34090-2036)
SSBN-631 Ulysses S. Grant; Groton, CT (NY 09570-2039)
SSBN-632 Von Steuben; Charleston, SC (MI 34093-2042)
SSBN-633 Casimir Pulaski; Charleston, SC (MI 34092-2045)
SSBN-634 Stonewall Jackson; Charleston, SC (MI 34091-2048)
SSBN-635 Sam Rayburn; Charleston, SC (MI 34092-2051)

Georgia (SSBN-729)

Simon Bolivar (SSBN-641)

SURFACE COMBATANTS

Nimitz (CVN-68)

AIRCRAFT CARRIERS (CVN, CV)

Nimitz Class

DISPLACEMENT: 91,487 tons full load (CVN-71, 96,358).
LENGTH: 1,040 feet.
BEAM: 134 feet.
FLIGHT DECK WIDTH: 252 feet.
SPEED: 30-plus knots.
POWER PLANT: two nuclear reactors, four geared steam turbines, four shafts, 260,000 shaft horsepower.
AIRCRAFT: 90-plus.
ARMAMENT: Sea Sparrow missiles, Phalanx close-in weapons systems—three on *Nimitz* and *Eisenhower,* four on *Vinson,* four to be installed on later ships of class.
COMPLEMENT: 3,150+ ship's company; 2,480 in air wing.
BUILDER: Newport News Shipbuilding.

Enterprise Class

DISPLACEMENT: 89,600 tons full load.
LENGTH: 1,040 feet.
BEAM: 133 feet.
FLIGHT DECK WIDTH: 252 feet.
SPEED: approximately 35 knots.
POWER PLANT: eight nuclear reactors, four geared steam turbines, four shafts, 280,000 shaft horsepower.
AIRCRAFT: approximately 90.
ARMAMENT: Sea Sparrow missiles, three Phalanx close-in weapons systems.
COMPLEMENT: 3,319 ship's company; 2,480 in air wing.
BUILDER: Newport News Shipbuilding.

John F. Kennedy Class

DISPLACEMENT: 82,000 tons full load.
LENGTH: 1,052 feet.
BEAM: 130 feet.
FLIGHT DECK WIDTH: 252 feet.
SPEED: 30-plus knots.
POWER PLANT: eight boilers, four geared steam turbines, four shafts, 280,000 shaft horsepower.
AIRCRAFT: approximately 85.
ARMAMENT: Sea Sparrow missiles, three Phalanx close-in weapons systems.
COMPLEMENT: 3,045 ship's company; 2,480 in air wing.
BUILDER: Newport News Shipbuilding.

Kitty Hawk (CV-63)

Kitty Hawk Class

DISPLACEMENT: 80,800 tons full load.
LENGTH: 1,046 feet.
BEAM: 130 feet.
FLIGHT DECK WIDTH: 252 feet.
SPEED: 30-plus knots.
POWER PLANT: eight boilers, four geared steam turbines, four shafts, 280,000 shaft horsepower.
AIRCRAFT: approximately 85.
ARMAMENT: Terrier missiles in *Constellation* to be replaced by Sea Sparrow missiles; Sea Sparrow missiles in *Kitty Hawk* and *America.* Three Phalanx close-in weapons systems.
COMPLEMENT: 2,970+ ship's company; 2,480 in air wing.
BUILDERS: CV-63, New York Shipbuilding; 64, New York Naval Shipyard; 66, Newport News Shipbuilding.

Forrestal Class

DISPLACEMENT: 75,900 to 79,300 tons full load.
LENGTH: 1,063 to 1,086 feet.
BEAM: 129 feet.
FLIGHT DECK WIDTH: 252 feet.
SPEED: 33 knots.
POWER PLANT: eight boilers, with *Forrestal*'s plant approximately 50 percent lower in psi (pounds per square inch) than those of other ships in class; four geared steam turbines, four shafts, 260,000 shaft horsepower for *Forrestal,* 280,000 for others.
AIRCRAFT: approximately 90.
ARMAMENT: Sea Sparrow missiles. Three Phalanx close-in weapons systems being installed in each during SLEP overhauls.
COMPLEMENT: 3,019 ship's company; 2,480 in air wing.
BUILDERS: CVs 59, 61, Newport News Shipbuilding; 60, 62, New York Naval Shipyard.

Midway Class

DISPLACEMENT: 62,000 tons full load.
LENGTH: 979 feet.
BEAM: 121 feet.
FLIGHT DECK WIDTH: 238 feet.
SPEED: 30-plus knots.
POWER PLANT: 12 boilers, four geared steam turbines, four shafts, 212,000 shaft horsepower.
AIRCRAFT: approximately 75.
ARMAMENT: Sea Sparrow missiles, three Phalanx close-in weapons systems.
COMPLEMENT: 2,890+ ship's company; 2,239 in air wing.
BUILDER: Newport News Shipbuilding.

America (CV-66)

Carl Vinson (CVN-70)

Night Fighters

For military personnel who must be ready to fight in the dark, Kollsman advanced infrared technology offers a vital tactical advantage.

Pod-mounted on aircraft or on tanks and anti-aircraft vehicles, these high-resolution IR imaging systems lift the cover of darkness for full-time combat readiness. Advanced IR systems attain new levels of thermal resolution and sensitivity, yet remain small, lightweight and rugged.

Finally, Kollsman IR systems come with the reliability and cost-effectiveness that make Kollsman a strong team player on any defense program. For the full Kollsman IR picture, call 603/889-2500 and ask for Marketing Manager, Kollsman Military Systems. Merrimack, NH 03054.

 Kollsman

...discovering the technology of tomorrow.

Dwight Eisenhower (CVN-69)

BRIEFING: USS *Ranger,* delivered in 1934, was the first ship designed as an aircraft carrier. However, carriers did not come into their own until World War II, when they became the most important ships in the fleet, particularly in the Pacific. Despite the fact that carrier task forces have been called upon hundreds of times since World War II to serve as the principal manifestation of U.S. strength and response in times of crisis, and acquitted themselves exceptionally well in Korea and Vietnam—although admittedly without the opposition encountered in World War II—carriers still are highly controversial because of their high cost and alleged vulnerability to modern long-range, high-speed, low-altitude missiles. The Navy considers 15 carrier battle groups (CBGs) the minimum it needs to meet the three-ocean defense requirement imposed by the numerous bilateral and multilateral treaties to which the United States is a party. *Forrestal* was the first carrier designed to operate jet aircraft; *Enterprise* the first with nuclear propulsion. Although *Enterprise* clearly demonstrated the inestimable value of nuclear propulsion in ships of this size and kind, two carriers laid down later were built with turbines driven by fossil fuel because the cost of nuclear reactors was deemed too high for the unquestioned operational advantages to compensate. However, all carriers constructed since 1964 have been nuclear powered. Funding for the two Nimitz-class ships was approved in the FY 1983 budget; this unusual funding of two carriers in the same budget has permitted more rapid construction and will enable them to join the fleet almost two years earlier than if they had been funded singly. *Theodore Roosevelt* (CVN-71) was commissioned last fall and became the 14th deployable carrier. *Abraham Lincoln* (CVN-72) becomes the 15th deployable carrier in 1989. *George Washington* (CVN-73) will replace *Coral Sea* (CV-43) in 1991. The Secretary of Defense caught Congress by surprise when he announced in January 1987 that funding was being sought in FY 1988-1989 for long lead-time items for two more Nimitz-class carriers, CVNs 74 and 75. Construction-contract awards would be sought in FY 1990 for CVN 74 and in FY 1993 for CVN 75; these two ships would replace *Midway* (CV-41) and *Saratoga* (CV-60). Despite predictions that Congress would refuse to fund procurement of the long-lead-time items and the ultimate construction of the carriers, both houses did support the request for funding. Meanwhile, carrier battle groups continued to be called upon whenever the U.S. interests were threatened in areas where CBGs could respond; when the frigate *Stark* (FFG-31) was struck and severely damaged in the Persian Gulf last May by Exocet missiles fired by an Iraqi aircraft, one of the first questions asked in the wake of the tragic accidental firing was: "Why wasn't there air cover?" At the time *Stark* was hit, *Kitty Hawk* (CV-63) had departed the Gulf for the Mediterranean, *Constellation* (CV-64) was en route to succeed her, and no carrier-based air cover was available. Carriers would remain on scene in that troubled area for the balance of the year, and would continue to be sent to other trouble spots when needed. Carrier aircraft loadings will vary according to their sizes and missions, but might well include: two fighter squadrons of F-14s; two attack squadrons of A-7s (until phased out) or F/A-18s and one of A-6s; one ASW squadron of SH-3 or SH-60F helicopters; EA-6B electronic-warfare aircraft; KA-6 tankers, and E-2C early-warning and control aircraft.

Nimitz Class

CVN-68 Nimitz; Bremerton, WA (SF 98780-2820)
CVN-69 Dwight D. Eisenhower; Norfolk, VA (NY 09532-2830)
CVN-70 Carl Vinson; Alameda, CA (SF 96629-2840)
CVN-71 Theodore Roosevelt; Norfolk, VA (NY 09599-2871)

Enterprise Class

CVN-65 Enterprise; Alameda, CA (SF 96636-2810)

John F. Kennedy Class

CV-67 John F. Kennedy; Norfolk, VA (NY 09538-2800)

Kitty Hawk Class

CV-63 Kitty Hawk; Philadelphia, PA (NY 09535-2770)
CV-64 Constellation; San Diego, CA (SF 96635-2780)
CV-66 America; Norfolk, VA (NY 09531-2790)

Forrestal Class

CV-59 Forrestal; Mayport, FL (MI 34080-2730)
CV-60 Saratoga; Mayport, FL (MI 34078-2740)
CV-61 Ranger; San Diego, CA (SF 96633-2750)
CV-62 Independence; SLEP

Midway Class

CV-41 Midway; Yokosuka, Japan (SF 96631-2710)
CV-43 Coral Sea; Norfolk, VA (NY 09550-2720)

BATTLESHIPS (BB)

Iowa Class

DISPLACEMENT: 58,000 tons full load.
LENGTH: 887 feet.
BEAM: 108 feet.
SPEED: 35 knots.
POWER PLANT: eight boilers, four geared turbines, four shafts, 212,000 shaft horsepower.
AIRCRAFT: one LAMPS MkIII helicopter.
ARMAMENT: nine 16-inch guns; 12 five-inch/.38-caliber guns; four Phalanx CIWSs, 20 40mm (in BB63 only); Tomahawk and Harpoon missiles.
COMPLEMENT: 1,518
BUILDERS: BBs 61, 63, New York Navy Yard; 62, 64, Philadelphia Navy Yard.

BRIEFING: The four Iowa-class battleships, the second largest battleships ever built (two Japanese BBs were larger) all saw action in World War II and Korea, then were "mothballed." *New Jersey* was activated for service in Vietnam, but again was decommissioned after less than 18 months in the fleet. All four ships either have been or are being completely modernized and provided with Tomahawk, Harpoon, and Phalanx weapons systems, the latest electronics and communications equipment, and accommodations for three helicopters. *New Jersey,* commissioned 28 December 1982 for the third time, first was deployed to the Pacific, thence to the Mediterranean, where on 14 December 1983 she fired her 16" guns for the first time since rejoining the fleet. Targets were gun emplacements in Beirut, Lebanon. *Iowa*'s modernization was expedited so she could be deployed to the Mediterranean as the relief for *New Jersey;* she was recommissioned 8 April 1984. *Missouri* was modernized in Long Beach Naval Shipyard and was recommissioned 10 May 1986 in San Francisco, where she ultimately will be homeported. *Wisconsin* is being activated by Ingalls Shipbuilding; her modernization began in October 1986 and is scheduled to be completed in October 1988. Funds for her activation were realized from savings in the FY 1986 shipbuilding budget. These behemoths can serve as integrated parts of carrier battle groups, spearhead assault forces, or lead their own surface-action groups. Still regarded by the Navy as virtually invincible, they will have an awesome array of weapons for use against targets ashore, at sea, or in the air. However, critics still argue that they are outdated, costly to operate, inaccurate and ineffective with their weapons and particularly with their 16" guns, and vulnerable to enemy missiles and bombs. The Navy has taken steps to improve upon the quality of both projectiles and powder for the 16" guns with the goal of improving upon accuracy. The Navy briefly tested RPVs (remotely piloted vehicles) aboard *Iowa* in the spring of 1987, but early results were marred by crashes of the RPVs against the sides of the ship or in the water during recovery operations. However, subsequent operations of RPVs from battleships appears likely.

Iowa Class

BB-61 Iowa; Norfolk, VA (NY 09546-1100)
BB-62 New Jersey; Long Beach, CA (SF 96688-1110)
BB-63 Missouri; Long Beach, CA (SF 96689-1120)

Iowa (BB-61)

New Jersey (BB-62)

CRUISERS (CG, CGN)

Ticonderoga Class

DISPLACEMENT: 9,600 tons full load.
LENGTH: 563 feet.
BEAM: 55 feet.
SPEED: 30-plus knots.
POWER PLANT: four gas turbines, two shafts, 80,000 shaft-horse-power.
AIRCRAFT: two LAMPS MkI helicopters (47, 48), LAMPS MkIII in 49 and later ships.
ARMAMENT: Tomahawk, Harpoon, and Standard missiles, anti-submarine rockets, two five-inch/54-caliber guns, two Phalanx CIWSs.
COMPLEMENT: 358.
BUILDERS: Ingalls Shipbuilding, CG 47-50, 52-56. Bath Iron Works, 51.

Virginia Class

DISPLACEMENT: 11,000 tons full load.
LENGTH: 585 feet.
BEAM: 63 feet.
SPEED: 30-plus knots.
POWER PLANT: two nuclear reactors, two geared turbines, two shafts, 100,000 shaft horsepower.
AIRCRAFT: one helicopter.
ARMAMENT: Tomahawk, Harpoon, and Standard missiles, anti-submarine rockets, two five-inch/54-caliber guns, two triple torpedo tubes, two Phalanx CIWSs.
COMPLEMENT: 562.
BUILDER: Newport News Shipbuilding.

California Class

DISPLACEMENT: 10,450 tons full load.
LENGTH: 596 feet.
BEAM: 61 feet.
SPEED: 30-plus knots.
POWER PLANT: two nuclear reactors, two geared turbines, two shafts, 60,000 shaft horsepower.
AIRCRAFT: none.
ARMAMENT: Harpoon and Standard missiles, anti-submarine rockets, two five-inch/54-caliber guns, six triple torpedo tubes, two Phalanx CIWSs.
COMPLEMENT: 595.
BUILDER: Newport News Shipbuilding.

Truxtun Class

DISPLACEMENT: 9,127 tons full load.
LENGTH: 564 feet.
BEAM: 58 feet.
SPEED: 30 knots.
POWER PLANT: two nuclear reactors, two geared turbines, two shafts, 60,000 shaft horsepower.
AIRCRAFT: one helicopter.
ARMAMENT: Harpoon and Standard missiles, anti-submarine rockets, one five-inch/54-caliber gun, four fixed torpedo tubes, two Phalanx CIWSs.
COMPLEMENT: 591.
BUILDER: New York Shipbuilding.

Bainbridge Class

DISPLACEMENT: 8,592 tons full load.
LENGTH: 565 feet.
BEAM: 58 feet.
SPEED: 30 knots.
POWER PLANT: two nuclear reactors, two geared turbines, two shafts, 60,000 shaft horsepower.
AIRCRAFT: none.
ARMAMENT: Harpoon and Standard missiles, anti-submarine rockets, two 20mm guns, two triple torpedo tubes, two Phalanx CIWSs.
COMPLEMENT: 558.
BUILDER: Bethlehem Steel.

Long Beach Class

DISPLACEMENT: 17,525 tons full load.
LENGTH: 721 feet.
BEAM: 73 feet.
SPEED: 30-plus knots.
POWER PLANT: two nuclear reactors, two geared turbines, two shafts, 80,000 shaft horsepower.
AIRCRAFT: deck for utility helicopter.
ARMAMENT: Harpoon and Standard missiles, anti-submarine rockets, two five-inch/38-caliber guns, two triple torpedo tubes, two CIWS.
COMPLEMENT: 958.
BUILDER: Bethlehem Steel.

Bunker Hill (CG-52)

Mississippi (CGN-40)

Belknap (CG-26)

Belknap Class

DISPLACEMENT: 7,930 tons full load.
LENGTH: 547 feet.
BEAM: 55 feet.
SPEED: 32.5 knots.
POWER PLANT: two geared turbines, two shafts, 85,000 shaft horsepower.
AIRCRAFT: one LAMPS MkI helicopter.
ARMAMENT: Harpoon and Standard missiles, anti-submarine rockets, two Phalanx CIWS, one five-inch/54-caliber gun, two triple torpedo tubes.
COMPLEMENT: 479.
BUILDERS: CGs 26-28, 32, 34, Bath Iron Works; 29, 31, Puget Sound Naval Shipyard; 30, San Francisco Naval Shipyard; 33, Todd Shipyards.

Leahy Class

DISPLACEMENT: 7,800 tons full load.
LENGTH: 533 feet.
BEAM: 55 feet.
SPEED: 32.7 knots.
POWER PLANT: four boilers, two geared turbines, two shafts, 85,000 shaft horsepower.
AIRCRAFT: none.
ARMAMENT: Harpoon and Standard missiles, anti-submarine rockets, two Phalanx CIWS, two triple torpedo tubes.
COMPLEMENT: 423.
BUILDERS: CGs 16-18, Bath Iron Works; 19, 20, New York Shipbuilding; 21, 24, Puget Sound Naval Shipyard; 22, Todd Shipyards; 23, San Francisco Naval Shipyard.

BRIEFING: The Navy's goal of 27 Aegis-equipped cruisers was brought to fruition in 1987 by the surprising action of Congress to authorize construction of the last five ships in the program, while at the same time deleting requests for three Burke-class destroyers. Congress' action culminates a remarkable reversal of opinion toward these cruisers, which only five years ago were being derided as top-heavy, gold-plated, and possessed of an ineffective air-defense system. However, the superlative performance of *Ticonderoga* and the second ship of the class, *Yorktown,* off Lebanon in 1983-84, during the intercept of the aircraft carrying the hijackers of the cruise ship *Achille Lauro* in 1985, and during the air strikes against Libyan targets in 1986 effectively laid these criticisms to rest. The Aegis air defense system has proven to be unusually capable; it gives ships of the class and other ships with which they might be operating an unprecedented defense capability against high-performance aircraft and surface-, air-, and submarine-launched missiles. Its radar enables it to control all friendly aircraft in its operating area and still have the capability for surveillance, detection, and tracking of enemy aircraft and missiles. Former Secretary of the Navy John Lehman praised the cruiser's performance thusly: "It has shifted the balance from where people thought we couldn't handle stream raids of missiles and Backfires to where nearly everyone is confident it is going to be an anomaly that is going to let a 'leaker' through our defenses." The vertical launch system was successfully tested in *Bunker Hill* in May 1986; it and the Tomahawk cruise missile will be installed in all later ships. Tomahawk also is to be installed in the four ships of the Virginia class, but not in ships of the Belknap and California classes because of weight constraints. There were no plans to install Tomahawk in the Leahy class, *Long Beach, Bainbridge,* or *Truxtun.* All cruisers not receiving Tomahawk will receive extensive radar and missile improvements under the New Threat Upgrade program. To date, the only shipyards building Ticonderoga-class ships are Ingalls Shipbuilding, the lead yard in the program, and Bath Iron Works.

Ticonderoga Class

CG-47 Ticonderoga; Norfolk, VA (NY 09588-1158)
CG-48 Yorktown; Norfolk, VA (NY 09594-1159)
CG-49 Vincennes; San Diego, CA (SF 96682-1169)
CG-50 Valley Forge; San Diego, CA (SF 96682-1170)
CG-51 Thomas S. Gates; Norfolk, VA (NY 09570-1171)
CG-52 Bunker Hill; San Diego, CA (SF 96661-1172)
CG-53 Mobile Bay; Mayport, FL (MI 34092-1173)
CG-54 Antietam; Long Beach, CA (SF 96660-1174)
CG-55 Leyte Gulf; Mayport, FL (MI 35091-1175)
CG-56 San Jacinto; Norfolk, VA (NY 09587-1176)

Virginia Class

CGN-38 Virginia; Norfolk, VA (NY 09590-1165)
CGN-39 Texas; Bremerton, WA (SF 98799-1166)
CGN-40 Mississippi; Norfolk, VA (NY 09578-1167)
CGN-41 Arkansas; Alameda, CA (SF 96660-1168)

California Class

CGN-36 California; Alameda, CA (SF 96662-1163)
CGN-37 South Carolina; Norfolk, VA (NY 09587-1164)

Truxtun Class

CGN-35 Truxtun; San Diego, CA (SF 96679-1162)

Virginia (CGN-38)

Halsey (CG-23)

Bainbridge Class

CGN-25 Bainbridge; Norfolk, VA (NY 09565-1161)

Long Beach Class

CGN-9 Long Beach; Bremerton, WA (SF 96671-1160)

Belknap Class

CG-26 Belknap; Gaeta, Italy (NY 09565-1149)
CG-27 Josephus Daniels; Norfolk, VA (NY 09567-1150)
CG-28 Wainwright; Charleston, SC (MI 34093-1151)
CG-29 Jouett; San Diego, CA (SF 96669-1152)
CG-30 Horne; San Diego, CA (SF 96667-1153)
CG-31 Sterett; Subic Bay, RP (SF 96678-1154)

CG-32 William H. Standley; San Diego, CA (SF 96678-1155)
CG-33 Fox; San Diego, CA (SF 96665-1156)
CG-34 Biddle; Norfolk, VA (NY 09565-1157)

Leahy Class

CG-16 Leahy; San Diego, CA (SF 96671-1140)
CG-17 Harry E. Yarnell; Norfolk, VA (NY 09594-1141)
CG-18 Worden; Pearl Harbor, HI (SF 96683-1142)
CG-19 Dale; Mayport, FL (MI 34090-1143)
CG-20 Richmond K. Turner; Charleston, SC (MI 34093-1144)
CG-21 Gridley; San Diego, CA (SF 96666-1145)
CG-22 England; San Diego, CA (SF 96664-1146)
CG-23 Halsey; San Diego, CA (SF 96667-1147)
CG-24 Reeves; Yokosuka, Japan (SF 96677-1148)

Bainbridge (CGN-25)

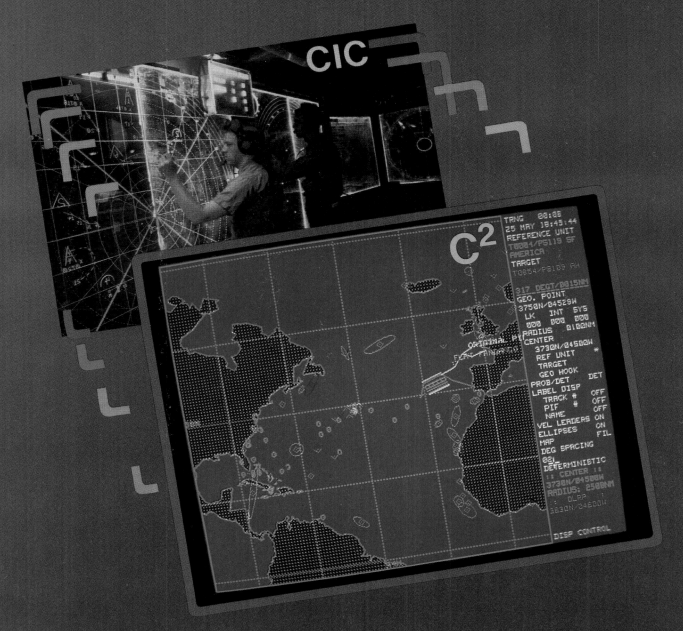

The New Dimension in Tactical Command and Control

- C² for Battle Group Commanders Warfare
- C² for Non-NTDS Ships
- Sensor Data Correlation

EDO's new mission-specific software and data acquisition capability are helping Naval Tactical Commanders in complex multi-warfare operations make time-critical decisions — quickly, correctly and confidently.

It is an entirely new dimension of EDO's continuing commitment to the U.S. Navy, shaping the future.

Contact: Marketing Department, EDO Corporation, Government Systems Division, College Point, NY 11356-1434, USA • Phone 718 445-6000 • Telex 127431

EDO CORPORATION GOVERNMENT SYSTEMS DIVISION

Where Technological Innovation Becomes Reality

Burke (artist concept)

DESTROYERS (DD, DDG)

Burke Class

DISPLACEMENT: 8,300 tons full load.
LENGTH: 466 feet.
BEAM: 59 feet.
SPEED: 30-plus knots.
POWER PLANT: four gas turbines, two shafts, 50,000 shaft horse-power.
AIRCRAFT: landing platform and handling facilities only.
ARMAMENT: Harpoon, Tomahawk, and Standard missiles, vertical launch ASROC, two vertical launch systems, anti-submarine rockets, two Phalanx close-in weapons systems, one five-inch/54-caliber gun, two triple torpedo tubes.
COMPLEMENT: 303.
BUILDER: Bath Iron Works, 51.

Spruance Class

DISPLACEMENT: 7,810 tons full load.
LENGTH: 563 feet.
BEAM: 55 feet.
SPEED: 33 knots.
POWER PLANT: four gas turbines, two shafts, 80,000 shaft horse-power.
AIRCRAFT: one Sea King or two LAMPS Mk I helicopters. (LAMPS III helicopters planned.)
ARMAMENT: Harpoon and NATO Sea Sparrow missiles, anti-submarine rockets, two Phalanx CIWS (on almost all ships), two five-inch/54-caliber guns, two triple torpedo tubes.
COMPLEMENT: 324.
BUILDER: Ingalls Shipbuilding.

Kidd Class

DISPLACEMENT: 8,300 tons full load.
LENGTH: 563 feet.
BEAM: 55 feet.
SPEED: 33 knots.
POWER PLANT: four gas turbines, two shafts, 80,000 shaft horse-power.
AIRCRAFT: two LAMPS I helicopters. (LAMPS III planned.)
ARMAMENT: Harpoon and Standard missiles, anti-submarine rockets, two Phalanx CIWS, two five-inch/54-caliber guns, two triple torpedo tubes.
COMPLEMENT: 346.
BUILDER: Ingalls Shipbuilding.

Charles F. Adams Class

DISPLACEMENT: 4,500 tons full load.
LENGTH: 437 feet.
BEAM: 47 feet.
SPEED: 30 knots.
POWER PLANT: four boilers, two geared turbines, two shafts, 70,000 shaft horsepower.
AIRCRAFT: none.
ARMAMENT: Harpoon and Standard missiles, anti-submarine rockets, two five-inch/54-caliber guns, two triple torpedo tubes.
COMPLEMENT: 360.
BUILDERS: DDGs 2, 3, 10, 11, Bath Iron Works; 4-6, 15-17, New York Shipbuilding; 7, 8, 12, 13, Defoe Shipbuilding; 9, 14, 23, 24, Todd Shipyards; 18, 19, Avondale Shipyards; 20-22, Puget Sound Bridge and Dry Dock.

RAM. The New Defense Against Anti-Ship Missiles.

There is now a new defense against cruise missiles — RAM, the Rolling Airframe Guided Missile Weapon System.

RAM, a fire-and-forget weapon system, reacts fast and puts high firepower accurately on target, countering single, simultaneous and multiple launched threats.

RAM is the first shipboard self-defense system to use dual mode passive RF/IR missile guidance. It is designed to use existing shipboard sensors and can operate in full automatic mode.

The key joint development of the United States, West Germany and Denmark, RAM has successfully completed initial developmental and operational testing. The U.S. Navy has approved RAM for initial production by General Dynamics Valley Systems Division and European industry.

RAM increases ship survivability by providing surface ships with a new dimension in firepower and terminal effectiveness.

GENERAL DYNAMICS
Valley Systems Division

Kidd (DDG-993)

Deyo (DD-989)

Farragut Class

DISPLACEMENT: approximately 5,800 tons full load.
LENGTH: 512 feet.
BEAM: 52 feet.
SPEED: 33 knots.
POWER PLANT: four boilers, two geared turbines, two shafts, 85,000 shaft horsepower.
AIRCRAFT: none.
ARMAMENT: Harpoon and Standard missiles, anti-submarine rockets, one five-inch/54-caliber gun, two triple torpedo tubes.
COMPLEMENT: 401.
BUILDERS: DDGs 37-39, Bethlehem Steel; 40, 41, Puget Sound Naval Shipyard; 42, San Francisco Naval Shipyard; 43, 44, Philadelphia Naval Shipyard; 45, 46, Bath Iron Works.

BRIEFING: The *Arleigh Burke* (DDG-51), first of a new and long-awaited class of guided-missile destroyers, is under construction, the contract to build it having been awarded in 1985 to Bath Iron Works after unusually keen competition for that contract among three shipyards. Funds were appropriated in FY 1987 for the next two ships of the class; at the same time, Congress directed that one of those two ships be built by a second shipyard, which will be Ingalls Shipbuilding. The other will be built by Bath. The Navy had requested funding for three ships in the 1988 budget; however, that request was ignored by Congress, which instead funded the last five ships of the Aegis-cruiser program. How the Navy will proceed to attain its goal of at least 29 DDG-51s remains to be seen, particularly since there are some in Congress who apparently would pre-

Thorn (DD-988)

Preble (DDG-46)

Ricketts (DDG-5)

fer to see cruiser construction continued at the expense of ships of the Burke class. Meanwhile, Spruance-class destroyers, the first large U.S. warships to employ gas turbines as their main propulsion systems, are undergoing modernization in a long-range program, during which they will receive, among other warfighting assets, Lamps III helicopters, Tomahawk missiles, and (for the handful of ships which do not yet have them on board) Phalanx CIWS. In addition, 24 ships of the class will receive the Vertical Launch System (VLS) and Vertical Launch Asroc (VLA). The modernization program, which got underway in 1985, will give the 31 ships of the class the capability of serving as effective ASW platforms well into the 21st century. The four Kidd-class guided-missile ships, also built on DD-963 hulls, generally have a greater warfighting capability; however, they, too, will receive extensive improvements to that capability. Three of the relatively venerable Adams-class guided-missile ships are scheduled for extensive modernization.

Spruance Class

DD-963 Spruance; Mayport, FL (MI 34093-1201)
DD-964 Paul F. Foster; Long Beach, CA (SF 96665-1202)
DD-965 Kinkaid; San Diego, CA (SF 96670-1203)
DD-966 Hewitt; San Diego, CA (SF 96667-1204)
DD-967 Elliot; San Diego, CA (SF 96664-1205)
DD-968 Arthur W. Radford; Norfolk, VA (NY 09586-1206)
DD-969 Peterson; Norfolk, VA (NY 09582-1207)
DD-970 Caron; Norfolk, VA (NY 09566-1208)
DD-971 David R. Ray; San Diego, CA (SF 96677-1209)
DD-972 Oldendorf; Yokosuka, Japan (SF 96674-1210)
DD-973 John Young; San Diego, CA (SF 96686-1211)
DD-974 Comte de Grasse; Norfolk, VA (NY 09566-1212)
DD-975 O'Brien; San Diego, CA (SF 96674-1213)
DD-976 Merrill; San Diego, CA (SF 96672-1214)
DD-977 Briscoe; Norfolk, VA (NY 09565-1215)
DD-978 Stump; Norfolk, VA (NY 09587-1216)
DD-979 Conolly; Norfolk, VA (NY 09566-1217)
DD-980 Moosbrugger; Charleston, SC (MI 34092-1218)

Buchanan (DDG-14)

DD-981 John Hancock; Mayport, FL (MI 34091-1219)
DD-982 Nicholson; Charleston, SC (MI 34092-1220)
DD-983 John Rodgers; Charleston, SC (MI 34092-1221)
DD-984 Leftwich; Pearl Harbor, HI (SF 96671-1222)
DD-985 Cushing; San Diego, CA (SF 96662-1223)
DD-986 Harry W. Hill; San Diego, CA (SF 96667-1224)
DD-987 O'Bannon; Charleston, SC (MI 34092-1225)
DD-988 Thorn; Charleston, SC (MI 34093-1226)
DD-989 Deyo; Charleston, SC (MI 34090-1227)
DD-990 Ingersoll; Pearl Harbor, HI (SF 96668-1228)
DD-991 Fife; San Diego, CA (SF 96665-1229)
DD-992 Fletcher; San Diego, CA (SF 96665-1230)
DD-997 Hayler; Norfolk, VA (NY 09573-1231)

Kidd Class

DDG-993 Kidd; Norfolk, VA (NY 09576-1265)
DDG-994 Callaghan; San Diego, CA (SF 96662-1266)
DDG-995 Scott; Philadelphia, PA (NY 09587-1267)
DDG-996 Chandler; San Diego, CA (SF 96662-1268)

Charles F. Adams Class

DDG-2 Charles F. Adams; Mayport, FL (MI 34090-1232)
DDG-3 John King; Norfolk, VA (NY 09595-1233)
DDG-4 Lawrence; Norfolk, VA (NY 09577-1234)
DDG-5 Claude V. Ricketts; Norfolk, VA (NY 09586-1235)
DDG-6 Barney; Norfolk, VA (NY 09565-1236)
DDG-7 Henry B. Wilson; San Diego, CA (SF 96683-1237)
DDG-8 Lynde McCormick; San Diego, CA (SF 96672-1238)
DDG-9 Towers; Yokosuka, Japan (SF 96679-1239)
DDG-10 Sampson; Mayport, FL (MI 34093-1240)
DDG-11 Sellers; Charleston, SC (MI 34093-1241)
DDG-12 Robison; San Diego, CA (SF 96677-1242)
DDG-13 Hoel; San Diego, CA (SF 96667-1243)
DDG-14 Buchanan; San Diego, CA (SF 96661-1244)
DDG-15 Berkeley; San Diego, CA (SF 96661-1245)
DDG-16 Joseph Strauss; Pearl Harbor, HI (SF 96678-1246)
DDG-17 Conyngham; Norfolk, VA (NY 09566-1247)
DDG-18 Semmes; Charleston, SC (MI 34093-1248)
DDG-19 Tattnall; Mayport, FL (MI 34093-1249)
DDG-20 Goldsborough; Pearl Harbor, HI (SF 96666-1250)
DDG-21 Cochrane; Yokosuka, Japan (SF 96662-1251)
DDG-22 Benjamin Stoddert; Pearl Harbor, HI (SF 96678-1252)
DDG-23 Richard E. Byrd; Norfolk, VA (NY 09565-1253)
DDG-24 Waddell; San Diego, CA (SF 96683-1254)

Farragut Class

DDG-37 Farragut; Norfolk, VA (NY 09569-1255)
DDG-38 Luce; Mayport, FL (MI 34091-1256)
DDG-39 MacDonough; Charleston, SC (MI 34092-1257)
DDG-40 Coontz; Norfolk, VA (NY 09566-1258)
DDG-41 King; Norfolk, VA (NY 09576-1259)
DDG-42 Mahan; Charleston, SC (MI 34092-1260)
DDG-43 Dahlgren; Norfolk, VA (NY 09567-1261)
DDG-44 William V. Pratt; Charleston, SC (MI 34092-1262)
DDG-45 Dewey; Charleston, SC (MI 34090-1263)
DDG-46 Preble; Norfolk, VA (NY 09582-1264)

FRIGATES (FFG, FF)

Oliver Hazard Perry Class

DISPLACEMENT: 3,585 tons full load.
LENGTH: 445 feet.
BEAM: 45 feet.
SPEED: 29 knots.
POWER PLANT: two gas turbines, one shaft, 41,000 shaft horse-power.
AIRCRAFT: two LAMPS Mk I helicopters (33 ships will have Mk III capability).
ARMAMENT: Harpoon and Standard missiles, one 76mm/62-caliber gun. One Phalanx CIWS.
COMPLEMENT: 206.
BUILDERS: FFGs 7, 8, 11, 13, 15, 16, 21, 24, 26, 29, 32, 34, 36, 39, 42, 45, 47, 49, 50, 53, 55, 56, 58, 59, Bath Iron Works; 10, 20, 22, 28, 31, 37, 40, 48, 52, Todd Shipyards, Seattle; 9, 12, 14, 19, 23, 25, 27, 30, 33, 38, 41, 43, 46, 51, 54, 57, 60, 61, Todd Shipyards, San Pedro.

Brooke Class

DISPLACEMENT: 3,426 tons full load.
LENGTH: 414 feet.
BEAM: 44 feet.
SPEED: 27.2 knots.
POWER PLANT: two boilers, two geared turbines, one shaft, 35,000 shaft horsepower.
AIRCRAFT: one LAMPS Mk I helicopter.
ARMAMENT: Tartar and Standard missiles, anti-submarine rockets, one five-inch/38-caliber gun, two triple torpedo tubes.
COMPLEMENT: 277.
BUILDERS: FFGs 1-3, Lockheed Shipbuilding; 4-6, Bath Iron Works.

Glover Class

DISPLACEMENT: 3,426 tons full load.
LENGTH: 414 feet.
BEAM: 44 feet.
SPEED: 27 knots.
POWER PLANT: two boilers, two geared turbines, one shaft, 35,000 shaft horsepower.
AIRCRAFT: one LAMPS Mk I helicopter to be installed.
ARMAMENT: anti-submarine rockets, one five-inch/38-caliber gun, two triple torpedo tubes.
COMPLEMENT: 280.
BUILDER: Bath Iron Works.

Knox Class

DISPLACEMENT: 3,877 tons full load FFs 1052-1077, 4,200 tons full load, remainder of class.
LENGTH: 438 feet.
BEAM: 47 feet.
SPEED: 27 knots.
POWER PLANT: two boilers, two geared turbines, one shaft, 35,000 shaft horsepower.
AIRCRAFT: one LAMPS Mk1 helicopter.
ARMAMENT: Harpoon missiles, Sea Sparrow missiles, anti-submarine rockets, one five-inch/54 caliber gun, four fixed torpedo tubes, one Phalanx CIWS being installed on all ships of the class.
COMPLEMENT: 288.
BUILDERS: FF 1052-1054, 1062, 1064, 1066, 1070, Todd, Seattle; 1055, 1058, 1060, 1067, 1071, 1074, 1076, Todd, San Pedro; 1057, 1063, 1065, 1069, 1073, Lockheed, Seattle; 1056, 1059, 1061, 1068, 1072, 1072, 1075, 1077-1097, Avondale Shipyards.

Ford (FFG-54)

Bradley (FFG-49)

Garcia Class

DISPLACEMENT: 3,403 tons full load.
LENGTH: 414 feet.
BEAM: 44 feet.
SPEED: 27.5 knots.
POWER PLANT: two boilers, two geared turbines, one shaft, 35,000 shaft horsepower.
AIRCRAFT: one LAMPS Mk1 helicopter.
ARMAMENT: anti-submarine rockets, two five-inch/38-caliber guns, two triple torpedo tubes.
COMPLEMENT: 270.
BUILDERS: 1040, 1041, Bethlehem Steel, San Francisco; 1043-1045, Avondale Shipyards; 1047, 1049, 1051, Defoe Shipbuilding; 1048, 1050, Lockheed Shipbuilding.

Bronstein Class

DISPLACEMENT: 2,650 tons full load.
LENGTH: 371 feet.
BEAM: 40 feet.
SPEED: 26 knots.
POWER PLANT: two boilers, two geared turbines, one shaft, 20,000 shaft horsepower.
AIRCRAFT: none.
ARMAMENT: anti-submarine rockets, two three-inch/50-caliber guns, two triple torpedo tubes.
COMPLEMENT: 286.
BUILDER: Avondale Shipyards.

BRIEFING: There are now more than 100 frigates in commission. However, the building program for the newest class, the FFGs, of which *Oliver Hazard Perry* (FFG-7) was the first, was curtailed by the Navy 10 short of its original goal of 60 of these ships. Subsequently, in FY 1983, Congress funded a 51st ship for construction in a west-coast shipyard in order to keep alive the rapidly dwindling combatant-ship construction capability on that coast. That ship is scheduled for delivery late this year. Although the FFG-7s are more versatile than their predecessors, they do have their limitations. The Navy's investigation into the extent of damage suffered by *Stark* (FFG-31) after it had been hit and set afire in May 1987 by two Exocet missiles fired by Iraqi aircraft pointed up many of the limitations resulting from building this class of ships on a "design to cost" basis. Although *Stark* did survive, in contrast to the British destroyer *Sheffield* which burned and sank after being hit by Exocets during the Falklands operation, the absence of certain materials and equipment that would have helped prevent the rapid spread of fire, and the presence of others of lesser quality, made it more difficult for her crew to cope with the blaze that cost the lives of 37 and decimated portions of the ship. The failure to install these materials and equipment during construction or during subsequent overhauls

Whipple (FF-1062)

resulted from initial financial constraints and the high cost of extensive refitting after construction. As of now, there are no plans for construction of another class of frigates.

Hepburn (FF-1055)

Sample (FF-1048)

Oliver Hazard Perry Class

FFG-8 McInerney; Mayport, FL (MI 34092-1466)
FFG-21 Flatley; Mayport, FL (MI 34091-1477)
FFG-22 Fahrion; Mayport, FL (MI 34091-1478)
FFG-23 Lewis B. Puller; Long Beach, CA (SF 96675-1479)
FFG-24 Jack Williams; Mayport, FL (MI 34093-1480)
FFG-25 Copeland; San Diego, CA (SF 96662-1481)
FFG-26 Gallery; Mayport, FL (MI 34091-1482)
FFG-27 Mahlon S. Tisdale; San Diego, CA (SF 96679-1483)
FFG-28 Boone; New Orleans, LA (MI 34093-1484)
FFG-29 Stephen W. Groves; Mayport, FL (MI 34091-1485)
FFG-30 Reid; San Diego, CA (SF 96677-1486)
FFG-31 Stark; (Mayport, FL (MI 34093-1487)
FFG-32 John L. Hall; Mayport, FL (MI 34091-1488)
FFG-33 Jarrett; Long Beach, CA (SF 96669-1489)
FFG-34 Aubrey Fitch; Mayport, FL (MI 34091-1490)
FFG-36 Underwood; Mayport, FL (MI 34093-1491)
FFG-37 Crommelin; Long Beach, CA (SF 96662-1492)
FFG-38 Curts; Long Beach, CA (SF 96662-1493)
FFG-39 Doyle; Mayport, FL (MI 34090-1494)
FFG-40 Halyburton; Charleston, SC (MI 34091-1495)
FFG-41 McClusky; San Diego, CA (SF 96672-1496)
FFG-42 Klakring; Charleston, SC (MI 34091-1497)
FFG-43 Thach; San Diego, CA (SF 96679-1498)
FFG-45 Dewert; Charleston, SC (MI 34090-1499)
FFG-46 Rentz; San Diego, CA (SF 96677-1500)
FFG-47 Nicholas; Charleston, SC (MI 34092-1501)
FFG-48 Vandergrift; Long Beach, CA (SF 96682-1502)
FFG-49 Robert G. Bradley; Charleston, SC (MI 34090-1503)
FFG-50 Taylor; Charleston, SC (MI 34093-1504)
FFG-51 Gary; Long Beach, CA (SF 96666-1505)
FFG-52 Carr; Charleston, SC (MI 34090-1506)
FFG-53 Hawes; Charleston, SC (MI 34091-1507)
FFG-54 Ford; Long Beach, CA (SF 96665-1508)
FFG-55 Elrod; Charleston, SC (MI 34091-1509)
FFG-56 Simpson; Newport, RI (NY 09587-1570)
FFG-57 Reuben James; Long Beach, CA (SF 96669-1511)
FFG-58 Samuel B. Roberts; Newport, RI (NY 09586-1512)
FFG-59 Kauffman; Newport, RI (NY 09569-1513)
FFG-60 Rodney M. Davis; Long Beach, CA (SF 96663-1514)

Brooke Class

FFG-1 Brooke; San Diego, CA (SF 96661-1459)
FFG-2 Ramsey; San Diego, CA (SF 96677-1460)
FFG-3 Schofield; San Diego, CA (SF 96678-1461)
FFG-4 Talbot; Mayport, FL (MI 34093-1462)
FFG-5 Richard L. Page; Norfolk, VA (NY 09582-1463)
FFG-6 Julius A. Furer; Philadelphia, PA (MI 34091-1464)

Glover Class

FF-1098 Glover; Norfolk, VA (NY 09570-1458)

Knox Class

FF-1052 Knox; Yokosuka, Japan (SF 96670-1412)

FF-1055 Hepburn; San Diego, CA (SF 96667-1415)
FF-1056 Connole; Newport, RI (NY 09566-1416)
FF-1057 Rathburne; Pearl Harbor, HI (SF 96677-1417)
FF-1058 Meyerkord; San Diego, CA (SF 96672-1418)
FF-1059 W.S. Sims; Mayport, FL (MI 34093-1419)
FF-1062 Whipple; Pearl Harbor, HI (SF 96683-1422)
FF-1063 Reasoner; San Diego, CA (SF 96677-1423)
FF-1064 Lockwood; Yokosuka, Japan (SF 96671-1424)
FF-1065 Stein; San Diego, CA (SF 96678-1425)
FF-1066 Marvin Shields; San Diego, CA (SF 96678-1426)
FF-1067 Francis Hammond; Yokosuka, Japan (SF 96667-1427)
FF-1068 Vreeland; Mayport, FL (MI 34093-1428)
FF-1069 Bagley; San Diego, CA (SF 96661-1429)
FF-1070 Downes; San Diego, CA (SF 96663-1430)
FF-1071 Badger; Pearl Harbor, HI (SF 96661-1431)
FF-1073 Robert E. Peary; Pearl Harbor, HI (SF 96675-1433)
FF-1074 Harold E. Holt; Pearl Harbor, HI (SF 96667-1434)
FF-1075 Trippe; Boston, MA (MI 34093-1435)
FF-1076 Fanning; San Diego, CA (SF 96665-1436)
FF-1077 Ouellet; Pearl Harbor, HI (SF 96674-1437)
FF-1078 Joseph Hewes; Charleston, SC (MI 34091-1438)
FF-1079 Bowen; Charleston, SC (MI 34090-1439)
FF-1080 Paul; Mayport, FL (MI 34092-1440)
FF-1081 Aylwin; Charleston, SC (MI 34090-1441)
FF-1082 Elmer Montgomery; Mayport, FL (MI 34092-1442)
FF-1083 Cook; San Diego, CA (SF 96662-1443)
FF-1084 McCandless; Norfolk, VA (NY 09578-1444)
FF-1085 Donald B. Beary; Norfolk, VA (NY 09565-1445)
FF-1086 Brewton; Pearl Harbor, HI (SF 96661-1446)
FF-1087 Kirk; Yokosuka, Japan (SF 96670-1447)
FF-1088 Barbey; San Diego, CA (SF 96661-1448)
FF-1089 Jesse L. Brown; Charleston, SC (MI 34090-1449)
FF-1090 Ainsworth; Norfolk, VA (NY 09564-1450)
FF-1092 Thomas C. Hart; Norfolk, VA (NY 09573-1452)
FF-1093 Capodanno; Newport, RI (NY 09566-1453)
FF-1094 Pharris; Norfolk, VA (NY 09582-1454)
FF-1095 Truett; Norfolk, VA (NY 09588-1455)
FF-1097 Moinester; Norfolk, VA (NY 09578-1457)

Garcia Class

FF-1040 Garcia; Philadelphia, PA (MI 34091-1402)
FF-1041 Bradley; San Diego, CA (SF 96661-1403)
FF-1043 Edward McDonnell; Mayport, FL (MI 34092-1404)
FF-1044 Brumby; Portland, ME (MI 34090-1405)
FF-1045 Davidson; Pearl Harbor, HI (SF 96663-1406)
FF-1047 Voge; Mayport, FL (MI 34093-1407)
FF-1048 Sample; Pearl Harbor, HI (SF 96678-1408)
FF-1049 Koelsch; Mayport, FL (MI 34091-1409)
FF-1050 Albert David; San Diego, CA (SF 96663-1410)
FF-1051 O'Callahan; Seattle, WA (SF 96674-1411)

Bronstein Class

FF-1037 Bronstein; San Diego, CA (SF 96661-1400)
FF-1038 McCloy; Norfolk, VA (NY 09578-1401)

If there are any hostile subs out there, they're about to mess with the wrong guys.

Those waves hide danger for our fleet. The U.S. Navy has a surefire defense.

SEAHAWK® helicopters.

They come in two varieties that send a shudder through the most sophisticated enemy submarines.

The newest SEAHAWK helicopter is the SH-60F CV-Helo.

It uses a dipping sonar (the bane of submarines) to patrol the inner zone of a carrier battle group, the bull's-eye within which a sub can strike. The CV-Helo has the sophisticated technology and weaponry to find, chase down and destroy the enemy before it can attack.

Blue water is the domain of the SH-60B LAMPS. It patrols the outer zone, defending against both enemy submarines and surface ships and providing early warning against aerial attack. Designed for diversity, this veteran is an indispensable member of the fleet. Its mission-flexibility is limited only by its crew's orders. It is ready for anything.

In short, if any enemy sub commanders happen to be reading this, consider it fair warning.

The Sikorsky SEAHAWK helicopters are on the job.

Chicago (SSN-721)

Honolulu (SSN-718)

Barb (SSN-596)

ATTACK SUBMARINES (SSN, SS)

Los Angeles Class

DISPLACEMENT: 6,900 tons dived.
LENGTH: 360 feet.
BEAM: 33 feet.
SPEED: 30-plus knots dived.
POWER PLANT: one nuclear reactor, two geared turbines, one shaft, approximately 35,000 shaft horsepower.
ARMAMENT: Harpoon and Tomahawk missiles, SUBROC (688-699), Mk48 torpedoes, four torpedo tubes, VLS.
COMPLEMENT: 143.
BUILDERS: SSNs 688, 689, 691, 693, 695, 711-718, 721-723, Newport News Shipbuilding; 690, 692, 694, 696-710, 719-720, 725. General Dynamics' Electric Boat Division.

Narwhal Class

DISPLACEMENT: 5,350 tons dived.
LENGTH: 314 feet.
BEAM: 38 feet.
SPEED: 30-plus knots dived.
POWER PLANT: one nuclear reactor, two steam turbines, one shaft, 17,000 shaft horsepower.
ARMAMENT: Torpedoes, four torpedo tubes; Harpoon; Tomahawk missiles to be fitted.
COMPLEMENT: 129.
BUILDER: General Dynamics' Electric Boat Division.

Glenard P. Lipscomb Class

DISPLACEMENT: 6,480 tons dived.
LENGTH: 365 feet.
BEAM: 32 feet.
SPEED: 25-plus knots dived.
POWER PLANT: one nuclear reactor, turbine-electric drive, one shaft.
ARMAMENT: SUBROC, torpedoes, four torpedo tubes; Harpoon; Tomahawk missiles to be fitted.
COMPLEMENT: 129.
BUILDER: General Dynamics' Electric Boat Division.

Ethan Allen Class

DISPLACEMENT: 7,880 tons dived.
LENGTH: 410 feet.
BEAM: 33 feet.
SPEED: 30 knots dived.
POWER PLANT: one nuclear reactor, two geared turbines, one shaft, 15,000 shaft horsepower.
ARMAMENT: torpedoes, four torpedo tubes (16 missile tubes used in earlier SSBN role now plugged).
COMPLEMENT: 132.
BUILDER: Newport News Shipbuilding.

Sturgeon Class

DISPLACEMENT: 4,640 tons dived.
LENGTH: 292 feet.
BEAM: 32 feet.
SPEED: 30-plus knots dived.
POWER PLANT: one nuclear reactor, two steam turbines, one shaft, 15,000 shaft horsepower.
ARMAMENT: Harpoon, SUBROC, torpedoes, four torpedo tubes; Tomahawk missiles to be fitted.
COMPLEMENT: 129.
BUILDERS: SSNs 637, 650, 667, 669, 673-676, 678, 679, 681, 684, General Dynamics' Electric Boat Division; 638, 649, General Dynamics' Quincy Shipbuilding Division; 639, 647, 648, 652, 680, 682, 683, Ingalls Shipbuilding; 646, 660, Portsmouth Naval Shipyard; 662, 665, 666, 672, 677, San Francisco Naval Shipyard; 651, 653, 661, 663, 664, 668, 670, 686, 687, Newport News Shipbuilding.

Spadefish (SSN-668)

Skate Class

DISPLACEMENT: approximately 2,500 tons full load.
LENGTH: 268 feet.
BEAM: 25 feet.
SPEED: 25-plus knots dived.
POWER PLANT: one nuclear reactor, two steam turbines, two shafts, 6,600 shaft horsepower.
ARMAMENT: torpedoes, eight torpedo tubes.
COMPLEMENT: 122.
BUILDERS: SSN-578, General Dynamics' Electric Boat Division; 579, 584, Portsmouth Naval Shipyard; 583, Mare Island Naval Shipyard.

Skipjack Class

DISPLACEMENT: 3,513 tons dived.
LENGTH: 252 feet.
BEAM: 31 feet.
SPEED: 30-plus knots dived.
POWER PLANT: one nuclear reactor, two steam turbines, one shaft, 15,000 shaft horsepower.
ARMAMENT: torpedoes, six torpedo tubes.
COMPLEMENT: 118.
BUILDERS: SSN-585, General Dynamics' Electric Boat Division; 588, Mare Island Naval Shipyard; 590, 592, Ingalls Shipbuilding; 591, Newport News Shipbuilding.

Permit Class

DISPLACEMENT: approximately 4,200 tons dived.
LENGTH: SSN-605, 297 feet; 613-615, 292 feet; others, 278 feet.
BEAM: 32 feet.
SPEED: 30-plus knots dived.
POWER PLANT: one nuclear reactor, two steam turbines, one shaft, 15,000 shaft horsepower.
ARMAMENT: SUBROC, torpedoes, four torpedo tubes; Harpoon missiles being fitted.
COMPLEMENT: 127.
BUILDERS: SSNs 594, 595, Mare Island Naval Shipyard; 596, 607, 621, Ingalls Shipbuilding; 603, 604, 612, New York Shipbuilding; 605, 606, Portsmouth Naval Shipyard; 613-615, General Dynamics' Electric Boat Division.

BRIEFING: Submarine warfare was revolutionized by the marriage of nuclear power and the submarine; it created what was viewed by most naval experts as the true submersible. That spectacular step forward in ship construction and propulsion was embodied first in *Nautilus* (SSN-571), the world's first nuclear-powered vessel. Her message on 17 January 1955, "Underway on nuclear power," was a milestone in naval history. The Navy initially experimented with two types of nuclear reactors—one cooled by liquid sodium, the other by pressurized water—before scuttling that cooled by liquid sodium. It also experimented with different sizes and shapes of hulls and with varying kinds of weapons and electronics systems. Permit-class SSNs, laid down in the early 1960s, were the first to be built in sizeable numbers; 13 remain in commission. The Sturgeon and Los Angeles classes, the latter still building, also were authorized and funded in large numbers. Even so, the U.S. Navy's undersea fleet is far smaller than that of the Soviet Union, which not only has a much greater capability for building nuclear-powered submarines, but has made maximum use of it. *Nautilus* predated the first Soviet SSN by five years, but the United States failed to maintain that early lead. Still, U.S. nuclear-powered submarines are considered the world's most advanced technologically, although the Soviets have made tremendous strides in this respect, particularly in the areas of hull strength, speed, and, most importantly, quieting. The Navy is seeking a total force of 66 Los Angeles-class submarines, of which 37 have been delivered. The improved SSN-688 class is, the Navy claims, twice as capable as early ships of the class. These ships have vertical launch systems, increased firepower, and major improvements in quieting and in combat systems. A new class of SSN, the first of which will be named *Seawolf*, will replace the Los Angeles class. The first funding for development was contained in the FY 1985 budget; initial funding for construction is contained in the FY 1989 budget. Despite problems with the development of its sophisticated combat system, SSN 21 development now appears to be on schedule with regard to design objectives. In the 18 years between the commissioning of *Los Angeles* in 1976 and the anticipated completion of *Seawolf*, the Soviet Union will have put to sea at least 14 different classes of nuclear-powered submarines. The Navy also has five diesel-powered submarines in commission, all of which are more than 25 years old.

Tullibee (SSN-597)

Los Angeles Class

SSN-688 Los Angeles; Pearl Harbor, HI (SF 96671-2368)
SSN-689 Baton Rouge; Norfolk, VA (NY 09565-2369)
SSN-690 Philadelphia; Groton, CT (NY 09582-2370)
SSN-691 Memphis; Norfolk, VA (NY 09578-2371)
SSN-692 Omaha; Pearl Harbor, HI (SF 96674-2372)
SSN-693 Cincinnati; Norfolk, VA (NY 09566-2373)
SSN-694 Groton; Groton, CT (NY 09570-2374)
SSN-695 Birmingham; Pearl Harbor, HI (SF 96661-2375)
SSN-696 New York City; Pearl Harbor, HI (SF 96673-2376)
SSN-697 Indianapolis; Pearl Harbor, HI (SF 96668-2377)
SSN-698 Bremerton; Pearl Harbor, HI (SF 96661-2378)
SSN-699 Jacksonville; Norfolk, VA (NY 09575-2379)
SSN-700 Dallas; Groton, CT (NY 09567-2380)
SSN-701 La Jolla; San Diego, CA (SF 96671-2381)
SSN-702 Phoenix; Norfolk, VA (NY 09582-2382)
SSN-703 Boston; Groton, CT (NY 09565-2383)
SSN-704 Baltimore; Norfolk, VA (NY 09565-2384)
SSN-705 City of Corpus Christi; Groton, CT (NY 09566-2385)
SSN-706 Albuquerque; Groton, CT (NY 09564-2386)
SSN-707 Portsmouth; San Diego, CA (SF 96675-2387)
SSN-708 Minneapolis-Saint Paul; Norfolk, VA (NY 09578-2388)
SSN-709 Hyman G. Rickover; Norfolk, VA (NY 09586-2389)
SSN-710 Augusta; Groton, CT (NY 09564-2390)
SSN-711 San Francisco; Pearl Harbor, HI (SF 96678-2391)
SSN-712 Atlanta; Norfolk, VA (NY 09564-2392)
SSN-713 Houston; San Diego, CA (SF 96667-2393)
SSN-714 Norfolk; Norfolk, VA (NY 09579-2394)
SSN-715 Buffalo; Pearl Harbor, HI (SF 96661-2395)
SSN-716 Salt Lake City; San Diego, CA (SF 96678-2396)
SSN-717 Olympia; Pearl Harbor, HI (SF 96674-2397)
SSN-718 Honolulu; Pearl Harbor, HI (SF 96667-2398)
SSN-719 Providence; Groton, CT (NY 09582-2399)
SSN-720 Pittsburgh; Groton, CT (NY 09582-2400)
SSN-721 Chicago; Norfolk, VA (NY 09566-2401)
SSN-722 Key West; Norfolk, VA (NY 09576-2402)
SSN-724 Louisville; Groton, CT (NY 09577-2402)
SSN-725 Helena; Groton, CT (NY 09573-2405)

Ethan Allen Class

SSN-609 Sam Houston; Pearl Harbor, HI (SF 96667-2321)
SSN-611 John Marshall; Norfolk, VA (NY 09578-2322)

Sturgeon Class

SSN-637 Sturgeon; Charleston, SC (MI 34093-2329)
SSN-638 Whale; Bremerton, WA (SE 98799-2330)
SSN-639 Tautog; Bremerton, WA (SF 96679-2331)
SSN-646 Grayling; Vallejo, CA (MI 34091-2332)
SSN-647 Pogy; San Diego, CA (SF 96675-2333)
SSN-648 Aspro; Vallejo, CA (SF 96660-2334)
SSN-649 Sunfish; Charleston, SC (MI 34093-2335)
SSN-650 Pargo; New London, CT (NY 09582-2336)
SSN-651 Queenfish; Pearl Harbor, HI (SF 96676-2337)
SSN-652 Puffer; Bremerton, WA (SE 98799-2338)
SSN-653 Ray; Charleston, SC (MI 34092-2339)
SSN-660 Sand Lance; Charleston, SC (MI 34093-2340)
SSN-661 Lapon; Norfolk, VA (NY 09577-2341)
SSN-662 Gurnard; San Diego, CA (SF 96666-2342)
SSN-663 Hammerhead; Norfolk, VA (NY 09501-2343)
SSN-664 Sea Devil; Charleston, SC (MI 34093-2344)
SSN-665 Guitarro; San Diego, CA (SF 96666-2345)
SSN-666 Hawkbill; Pearl Harbor, HI (SF 96667-2346)
SSN-667 Bergall; Vallejo, CA (SF 96661-2347)
SSN-668 Spadefish; Norfolk, VA (NY 09587-2348)
SSN-669 Seahorse; Bremerton, WA (SE 98799-2349)
SSN-670 Finback; Norfolk, VA (NY 09569-2350)
SSN-672 Pintado; San Diego, CA (SF 96675-2352)
SSN-673 Flying Fish; Bremerton, WA (SE 98799-2353)
SSN-674 Trepang; New London, CT (NY 09588-2354)
SSN-675 Bluefish; Norfolk, VA (NY 09565-2355)
SSN-676 Billfish; New London, CT (NY 09565-2356)
SSN-677 Drum; San Diego, CA (SF 96663-2357)

Pintado (SSN-672)

SSN-678 Archerfish; Groton, CT (NY 09564-2358)
SSN-679 Silversides; Norfolk, VA (NY 09587-2359)
SSN-680 William H. Bates; San Diego, CA (SF 96661-2360)
SSN-681 Batfish; Charleston, SC (MI 34090-2361)
SSN-682 Tunny; Pearl Harbor, HI (SF 96679-2362)
SSN-683 Parche; Vallejo, CA (SF 96675-2363)
SSN-684 Cavalla; Vallejo, CA (SF 96662-2364)
SSN-686 L. Mendel Rivers; Charleston, SC (MI 34092-2366)
SSN-687 Richard B. Russell; Vallejo, CA (SF 96677-2367)

Narwhal Class

SSN-671 Narwhal; Charleston, SC (MI 34092-2351)

Glenard P. Lipscomb Class

SSN-685 Glenard P. Lipscomb; Norfolk, VA (NY 09577-2365)

Skate Class

SSN-579 Swordfish; Pearl Harbor, HI (SF 96678-2302)
SSN-583 Sargo; Pearl Harbor, HI (SF 96678-2303)

Skipjack Class

SSN-585 Skipjack; Groton, CT (NY 09587-2305)
SSN-588 Scamp; Bremerton, WA (SF 98799-2306)
SSN-590 Sculpin; Groton, CT (NY 09587-2307)
SSN-591 Shark; Groton, CT (NY 09587-2308)

Permit Class

SSN-594 Permit; San Diego, CA (SF 96675-2310)
SSN-595 Plunger; San Diego, CA (SF 96675-2311)
SSN-596 Barb; San Diego, CA (SF 96661-2312)
SSN-603 Pollack; San Diego, CA (SF 96675-2316)
SSN-604 Haddo; San Diego, CA (SF 96667-2317)
SSN-605 Jack; New London, CT (NY 09575-2318)
SSN-606 Tinosa; New London, CT (NY 09588-2319)
SSN-607 Dace; New London, CT (NY 09567-2320)
SSN-612 Guardfish; San Diego, CA (SF 96666-2323)
SSN-613 Flasher; San Diego, CA (SF 96665-2324)
SSN-614 Greenling; New London, CT (NY 09570-2325)
SSN-615 Gato; Portsmouth, NH (NY 09570-2326)
SSN-621 Haddock; San Diego, CA (SF 96667-2328)

Tullibee Class

SSN-597 Tullibee; Portsmouth, NH (NY 09588-2313)

Darter Class

SS-576 Darter; Sasebo, Japan (SF 96663-3401)

Barbel Class

SS-580 Barbel; Sasebo, Japan (SF 96661-3402)
SS-581 Blueback; San Diego, CA (SF 96661-3403)
SS-582 Bonefish; Charleston, SC (MI 34090-3404)

Guardfish (SSN-612)

Aries (PHM-5)

PATROL COMBATANTS MISSILESHIPS (HYDROFOIL) (PHM)

Pegasus Class

DISPLACEMENT: 240 tons full load.
LENGTH: foils extended, 133 feet; foils retracted, 145 feet.
BEAM: 28 feet.
SPEED: foilborne, 48 knots; hullborne, 12 knots.
POWER PLANT: foilborne, one gas turbine, 18,000 shaft horse-power, waterjet propulsion units; hullborne, two diesels, 1,600 brake horsepower, waterjet propulsion units.
AIRCRAFT: none.
ARMAMENT: eight Harpoon missiles, one 76mm gun.
COMPLEMENT: 23.
BUILDER: Boeing Marine Systems.

BRIEFING: This class of ship was conceived originally as a NATO ship to be built jointly by Germany, Italy, and the United States; however, when the European countries withdrew from the project, only one six-ship squadron was authorized, funded, and, despite an attempt by the Department of Defense to have those funds rescinded, ultimately built. Those six ships now form a single squadron operating out of Key West. They are the Navy.s fastest ships, with good range on their diesels, excellent seakeeping qualities, amazingly fast response to requirements for speed, and a potent punch. In the more than three years they have operated as a unit, they have established an unusually high availability rate while participating in a variety of missions, including extensive involvement in the national drug-interdiction program. Their electronic-countermeasures suite and command-and-launch control system now are being upgraded to improve both their offense and defense. Although a second squadron would be welcomed by the Atlantic Fleet it is doubtful, in a day of declining budgets for shipbuilding, that funding for that squadron would be either sought or forthcoming.

Pegasus Class

PHM-1 Pegasus; Key West, FL (MI 34092-3408)
PHM-2 Hercules; Key West, FL (MI 34091-3409)
PHM-3 Taurus; Key West, FL (MI 34093-3410)
PHM-4 Aquila; Key West, FL (MI 34090-3411)
PHM-5 Aries; Key West, FL (MI 34090-3412)
PHM-6 Gemini; Key West, FL (MI 34091-3413)

AMPHIBIOUS ASSAULT SHIPS (LHA, LHD, LPH)

Wasp Class (LHD)

DISPLACEMENT: 40,500 tons full load.
LENGTH: 844 feet.
BEAM: 106 feet.
SPEED: 20+ knots.
POWER PLANT: two boilers, two geared turbines, two shafts, 70,000 shaft horsepower.
AIRCRAFT: mix of 30 helicopters and 6-8 AV-8B Harriers.
ARMAMENT: Sea Sparrow missiles, three Phalanx CIWS.
COMPLEMENT: 1,080 ship's company, 1,873 troops.
BUILDER: Ingalls Shipbuilding.

LHD (artist concept)

Guadalcanal (LPH-7)

Tarawa Class (LHA)

DISPLACEMENT: 39,300 tons full load.
LENGTH: 820 feet.
BEAM: 106 feet.
FLIGHT DECK WIDTH: 118 feet.
SPEED: 24 knots.
POWER PLANT: two boilers, two geared turbines, two shafts, 70,000 shaft horsepower.
AIRCRAFT: flight deck can operate a maximum of nine CH-53 Sea Stallion or 12 CH-46 Sea Knight helicopters. Mix of these and AV-8A V/STOL Harriers can be accommodated in LHA-2-5 but not in LHA-1.
ARMAMENT: three five-inch/54-caliber guns, two Phalanx CIWS.
COMPLEMENT: 843 ship's company; 1,703 troops.
BUILDER: Ingalls Shipbuilding.

Iwo Jima Class (LPH)

DISPLACEMENT: approximately 18,000 tons full load.
LENGTH: 602 feet.
BEAM: 84 feet.
FLIGHT DECK WIDTH: 104 feet.
SPEED: 23 knots.
POWER PLANT: two boilers, one geared turbine, one shaft, 22,000 shaft horsepower.
AIRCRAFT: hangar deck can accommodate 20 CH-46 Sea Knight or 11 CH-53 Sea Stallion helicopters, or combination of both. Seven Sea Knights or four Sea Stallions can take off simultaneously.
ARMAMENT: Sea Sparrow missiles, four three-inch/50-caliber guns. (Two Phalanx CIWS being fitted.)
COMPLEMENT: 684.
BUILDERS: LPH-2, Puget Sound Naval Shipyard; 3, 7, 9, 11, Philadelphia Naval Shipyard; 10, 12, Ingalls Shipbuilding.

BRIEFING: *Iwo Jima* (LPH-2) was the first ship designed and constructed specifically to operate helicopters. Each ship of the class can carry a Marine battalion landing team, its weapons and equipment, a reinforced squadron of transport helicopters, and support personnel. In addition to serving as platforms for V/STOL aircraft,

ships of the class also have served as sea-control ships and have demonstrated further versatility in providing platforms for mine-sweeping helicopters. There originally were to be nine LHAs of the Tarawa class, but the number was reduced to five after extensive cost overruns during an unusually long construction period. Those ships provide the Marine Corps with a superb means of ship-to-shore movement by helicopter in augmentation of movement of other troops and equipment by landing craft. They have extensive storage capacity for vehicles, palletized stores, and aviation and vehicle fuel. They also can accommodate four landing craft utility (LCUs). The new Wasp-class LHDs are scheduled to replace the Iwo Jima-class ships in the 1990s. With modifications to the basic LHA hull to permit accommodation of three LCACs (air-cushion landing craft) and the latest model Harrier V/STOL aircraft, as well as helicopters, the LHD can serve in the dual role of amphibious assault ship and small aircraft carrier. *Wasp,* first of the class, was funded in 1984 and is being built by Ingalls Shipbuilding; she is scheduled for delivery in March 1989. A contract for the second ship of the class, with fixed-price options for the third and fourth ships, was awarded to Ingalls in September 1986. Construction on LHD-2 is expected to commence in October 1988. Funding for the third ship was included in the FY 1988 budget request. The Navy hopes to build 12 of the class.

Tarawa Class

LHA-1 Tarawa; Long Beach, CA (SF 96622-1600)
LHA-2 Saipan; Norfolk, VA (NY 09549-1605)
LHA-3 Belleau Wood; San Diego, CA (SF 96623-1610)
LHA-4 Nassau; Norfolk, VA (NY 09557-1615)
LHA-5 Peleliu; Long Beach, CA (SF 96624-1620)

Iwo Jima Class

LPH-2 Iwo Jima; Norfolk, VA (NY 09561-1625)
LPH-3 Okinawa; San Diego, CA (SF 96625-1630)
LPH-7 Guadalcanal; Norfolk, VA (NY 09562-1635)
LPH-9 Guam; Norfolk, VA (NY 09563-1640)
LPH-10 Tripoli; San Diego, CA (SF 96626-1645)
LPH-11 New Orleans; San Diego, CA (SF 96627-1650)
LPH-12 Inchon; Norfolk, VA (NY 09529-1655)

Cleveland (LPD-7)

AMPHIBIOUS TRANSPORT DOCKS (LPD)

Austin Class

DISPLACEMENT: approximately 17,000 tons full load.
LENGTH: 570 feet.
BEAM: 84 feet.
SPEED: 21 knots.
POWER PLANT: two boilers, two steam turbines, two shafts, 24,000 shaft horsepower.
AIRCRAFT: up to six CH-46 Sea Knight helicopters.
ARMAMENT: four three-inch/50-caliber guns; two Phalanx CIWSs being fitted.
COMPLEMENT: 425 ship's company; approximately 900 troops.
BUILDERS: LPDs 4-6, New York Naval Shipyard; 7, 8, Ingalls Shipbuilding; 9, 10, 12-15, Lockheed Shipbuilding.

Raleigh Class

DISPLACEMENT: 13,600 tons full load.
LENGTH: 522 feet.
BEAM: 84 feet.
SPEED: 21 knots.
POWER PLANT: two boilers, two steam turbines, two shafts, 24,000 shaft horsepower.
AIRCRAFT: landing only.
ARMAMENT: six three-inch/50-caliber guns.
COMPLEMENT: 429 ship's company; 930 troops.
BUILDER: New York Naval Shipyard.

BRIEFING: These versatile ships replace amphibious transports (APA), amphibious cargo ships (AKA), and the older LSDs. Although their capabilities are less than those of the new Whidbey Island class of LSD, the 11 ships of the Austin class, built between 1965-1971, were considered sufficiently modern to have their service lives extended by a SLEP program commencing in 1988 that would have extended their service lives to 2005. However, Congress balked at funding the program, and as a result the ships will receive less extensive modernization during overhaul periods.

Austin Class

LPD-4 Austin; Norfolk, VA (NY 09564-1707)
LPD-5 Ogden; Long Beach, CA (SF 96674-1708)
LPD-6 Duluth; San Diego, CA (SF 96663-1709)
LPD-7 Cleveland; San Diego, CA (SF 96662-1710)
LPD-8 Dubuque; Sasebo, Japan (SF 96663-1711)
LPD-9 Denver; San Diego, CA (SF 96663-1712)
LPD-10 Juneau; San Diego, CA (SF 96669-1713)
LPD-12 Shreveport; Norfolk, VA (NY 09587-1714)
LPD-13 Nashville; Norfolk, VA (NY 09579-1715)
LPD-14 Trenton; Norfolk, VA (NY 09588-1716)
LPD-15 Ponce; Norfolk, VA (NY 09582-1717)

Raleigh Class

LPD-1 Raleigh; Norfolk, VA (NY 09586-1705)
LPD-2 Vancouver, San Francisco, CA (SF 96682-1706)

Saint Louis (LKA-116)

AMPHIBIOUS CARGO SHIPS (LKA)

Charleston Class

DISPLACEMENT: 20,700 tons full load.
LENGTH: 575 feet.
BEAM: 82 feet.
SPEED: 20 knots.
POWER PLANT: two boilers, one steam turbine, one shaft, 22,000 shaft horsepower.
ARMAMENT: six three-inch/50-caliber guns; two Phalanx CIWSs being fitted.
COMPLEMENT: 356 ship's company; 226 troops.
BUILDER: Newport News Shipbuilding.

BRIEFING: These ships, which carry heavy equipment and supplies for amphibious assaults, are the first class of ship designed specifically for this role. Four of the five ships in the class had been transferred to the reserve fleet in the late 1970s and early 1980s, even though they were just a decade old. However, the obvious need for additional sealift resulting from the 1979 upheaval in the Middle East and the possibility of U.S. involvement in that remote area resulted in all four being returned to the active fleet in 1982-83. They are among the first Navy ships to have a fully automated main propulsion plant.

Charleston Class

LKA-113 Charleston; Norfolk, VA (NY 09566-1700)
LKA-114 Durham; San Diego, CA (SF 96663-1701)
LKA-115 Mobile; Long Beach, CA (SF 96672-1702)
LKA-116 Saint Louis; Sasebo, Japan (SF 96678-1703)
LKA-117 El Paso; Norfolk, VA (NY 09568-1704)

AS THE QUESTIONS GET HARDER,

DO YOUR ANSWERS GET BETTER?

They'd better. Too much is at stake to base tomorrow's decisions, designs, and systems on yesterday's concepts and technologies. BDM knows how to build you a solid foundation on which you can act with confidence. We perform research and analysis to help you choose an optimum course of action. We can design systems, operations, and programs to implement the action. Then we can support the logistics to make it all come together and the training to make it work.

And we haven't even mentioned meeting your information systems needs. Information is more and more the key to making the right decisions and making the decisions right. Prepackaged information systems aren't the answer. What you need (if you're typical of BDM clients) is not raw data or prodigious printouts . . . but precise, timely information that puts you in effective charge of your world and keeps you there.

So as the questions get tougher, time gets shorter, and the answers are harder to find, call on BDM. We won't let you down, because we won't let up until we get your job done. Right. On time. On budget. BDM International, Inc., 7915 Jones Branch Drive, McLean, VA 22102. Phone (703) 848-5000. Telex 901103.

**MANAGING THE
COURSE OF CHANGE**

**CHANGING THE COURSE
OF MANAGEMENT**

DOCK LANDING SHIPS (LSD)

Whidbey Island Class

DISPLACEMENT: 15,726 tons full load.
LENGTH: 609 feet.
BEAM: 84 feet.
SPEED: 20+ knots.
POWER PLANT: four medium-speed diesels, two shafts, 34,000 brake horsepower.
AIRCRAFT: helicopter- and V/STOL-capable.
ARMAMENT: two Phalanx CIWS guns, two 20mm AA guns.
COMPLEMENT: 340 ship's company; 338 troops.
BUILDER: LSD 41-43, Lockheed Shipbuilding; 44-48, Avondale Shipyards.

Anchorage Class

DISPLACEMENT: 13,600 tons full load.
LENGTH: 553 feet.
BEAM: 84 feet.
SPEED: 22 knots.
POWER PLANT: two boilers, steam turbines, two shafts, 24,000 shaft horsepower.
AIRCRAFT: helicopter-capable.
ARMAMENT: six three-inch/50-caliber guns (2 Phalanx CIWS guns being fitted).
COMPLEMENT: 355 ship's company; 376 troops.
BUILDERS: LSD-36, Ingalls Shipbuilding; 37-40, General Dynamics' Quincy Shipbuilding Division.

Thomaston Class

DISPLACEMENT: 12,000 tons full load.
LENGTH: 510 feet.
BEAM: 84 feet.
SPEED: 22.5 knots.
POWER PLANT: two boilers, steam turbines, two shafts, 24,000 shaft horsepower.
AIRCRAFT: helicopter-capable.
ARMAMENT: six three-inch/50-caliber guns.
COMPLEMENT: 350 ship's company; 340 troops.
BUILDER: Ingalls Shipbuilding.

BRIEFING: *Whidbey Island* (LSD-41), commissioned in 1985, was the long-awaited first of a new class of the versatile, durable dock landing ships which first saw service during World War II but which really came into their own during the Korean War. Their ability to ballast down to flood a well deck makes possible loading at sea and transporting virtually any type of cargo that can be carried by utility landing craft (LCU) and smaller amphibious craft. LSDs can accommodate a sizeable number of troops. The Marine Corps long had sought replacement of the aging Thomaston class, only three of which remain in commission, but a decade passed before funding of *Whidbey Island* was approved. Three of that eight-ship class have been delivered, two others are scheduled for delivery later this year, and the remaining three are under construction. The Navy had planned to seek funding in FY 1988 for the first two of a variant of the LSD-41 which will have greater cargo-carrying capability, but budget constraints necessitated halving that planned request. Funding for the second of what the Navy hopes will be a 10-ship class will be sought in FY 1990. The LSD-41 class has far greater storage space than its predecessors, much improved facilities for embarked troops, greater operating range, and room for four of the Marines' new LCACs (air-cushion landing craft). Also notable is the ship's medium-speed-diesel propulsion system, considerably more economical than steam or gas turbines.

Whidbey Island Class

LSD-41 Whidbey Island; Little Creek, Norfolk, VA (NY 09591-1729)
LSD-42 Germantown; San Diego, CA (SF 96666-1730)
LSD-43 Fort McHenry; San Diego, CA (SF 96665-1731)

Anchorage Class

LSD-36 Anchorage; Long Beach, CA (SF 96660-1724)
LSD-37 Portland; Little Creek, Norfolk, VA (NY 09582-1725)
LSD-38 Pensacola; Little Creek, Norfolk, VA (NY 09582-1726)
LSD-39 Mount Vernon; Long Beach, CA (SF 96672-1727)
LSD-40 Fort Fisher; San Diego, CA (SF 96665-1728)

Thomaston Class

LSD-32 Spiegel Grove; Little Creek, Norfolk, VA (NY 09587-1720)
LSD-33 Alamo; San Diego, CA (SF 96660-1721)
LSD-34 Hermitage; Little Creek, Norfolk, VA (NY 09573-1722)

Whidbey Island (LSD-41)

San Bernardino (LST-1189)

TANK LANDING SHIPS (LST)

Newport Class

DISPLACEMENT: 8,450 tons full load.
LENGTH: 522 feet.
BEAM: 69 feet.
SPEED: 20 knots.
POWER PLANT: six diesels, two shafts, 16,000 brake horsepower.
ARMAMENT: four three-inch/50-caliber guns; Phalanx CIWS to be fitted.
COMPLEMENT: 290 ship's company; 400 troops.
BUILDERS: LSTs 1179-1181, Philadelphia Naval Shipyard; 1182-1198, National Steel and Shipbuilding.

BRIEFING: Ships of this class are larger and faster than earlier LSTs and are the first to depart from the bow-door design that characterized the workhorses of World War II. The hull form necessary for the attainment of the 20-knot speeds of contemporary amphibious squadrons would not permit bow doors. Accordingly, ships of this class offload cargo and vehicles by means of a 112-foot ramp over their bow. A stern gate also makes possible offloading amphibious vehicles directly into the water. The 20 ships of this class, all commissioned between June 1969 and August 1972, are the only LSTs remaining in the fleet.

Newport Class

LST-1179 Newport; Little Creek, Norfolk, VA (NY 09579-1800)
LST-1180 Manitowoc; Little Creek, Norfolk, VA (NY 09578-1801)

Blue Ridge (LCC-19)

LST-1181 Sumter; Little Creek, Norfolk, VA (NY 09587-1802)
LST-1182 Fresno; Long Beach, CA (SF 96665-1803)
LST-1183 Peoria; San Diego, CA (SF 96675-1804)
LST-1184 Frederick; San Diego, CA (SF 96665-1805)
LST-1185 Schenectady; San Diego, CA (SF 96678-1806)
LST-1186 Cayuga; San Diego, CA (SF 96662-1807)
LST-1187 Tuscaloosa; San Diego, CA (SF 96679-1808)
LST-1188 Saginaw; Little Creek, VA (NY 09587-1809)
LST-1189 San Bernardino; Sasebo, Japan (SF 96678-1810)
LST-1192 Spartanburg County; Little Creek, Norfolk, VA (NY 09587-1813)
LST-1193 Fairfax County; Little Creek, Norfolk, VA (NY 09569-1814)
LST-1194 La Moure County; Little Creek, Norfolk, VA (NY 09577-1815)
LST-1195 Barbour County; San Diego, CA (SF 96661-1816)
LST-1196 Harlan County; Little Creek, Norfolk, VA (NY 09573-1817)
LST-1197 Barnstable County; Little Creek, Norfolk, VA (NY 09565-1818)
LST-1198 Bristol County; San Diego, CA (SF 96661-1819)

AMPHIBIOUS COMMAND SHIPS (LCC)

Blue Ridge Class

DISPLACEMENT: 19,290 tons full load.
LENGTH: 596 feet.
BEAM: 82 feet.
SPEED: 23 knots.
POWER PLANT: steam turbine, two boilers, one shaft, 22,000 shaft horsepower.
ARMAMENT: Sea Sparrow missiles, four 3''/50-caliber anti-aircraft weapons, two Phalanx CIWS.
AIRCRAFT: None, although each ship has a helicopter landing area.
COMPLEMENT: Crew, LCC 19, 799; LCC 20, 821; Flag, LCC 19, 241; 20, 188.
BUILDER: LCC 19, Philadelphia Naval Shipyard; 20, Newport News.

BRIEFING: These are the only ships to be designed initially for an amphibious command ship role. Earlier amphibious command ships lacked sufficient speed to operate with a 20-knot amphibious force. Subsequently, both ships became fleet flagships. *Blue Ridge* became the Seventh Fleet flagship in 1979 and is homeported in Yokosuka, Japan; *Mount Whitney* became the Second Fleet flagship in 1981.

Blue Ridge Class

LCC-19 Blue Ridge; Yokosuka, Japan (SF 96628-3300)
LCC-20 Mount Whitney; Norfolk, VA (NY 09517-3310)

The world's most versatile mine countermeasure builde

224' MCM

112' MSI — M503 | 192' MSO — 520 | 144' MSC — 294

165' MSO — 522 | MCM FIBERGLASS TEST SECTION

Quality ships have been built for U.S. Navy and Navies throughout the world. We invite your inquiries for ships in wood/aluminum/steel/fiberglass.

PBi
PETERSON BUILDERS, INC.
SHIPBUILDERS
STURGEON BAY, WIS.
ZC 54235 USA

E. L. Peterson
President

Tel. (414) 743-5574

Telex 26-34

LCAC

LANDING CRAFT (AIR CUSHION) (LCAC)

DISPLACEMENT: 200 tons full load.
LENGTH: 88 feet.
BEAM: 47 feet.
SPEED: 40 knots with payload; 50 knots maximum.
CARGO CAPACITY: 60 tons.
POWER PLANT: four Avco-Lycoming gas turbines; 12,280 bhp; two shrouded reversible-pitch propellers; four double-entry fans for lift.
ARMAMENT: None.
RANGE: 200 miles at 50 knots with payload.
COMPLEMENT: 5.
BUILDER: Textron Marine Systems, Lockheed Shipbuilding.

BRIEFING: These speedy air-cushion vehicles, working with modern helicopters, are expected to literally revolutionize amphibious landing tactics. With LCACs in the fleet, an amphibious task force could be nearly 500 miles away from its objective at H-Hour minus 24 and still make a pre-dawn attack launched from beyond an enemy's horizon. The LCAC's air-cushion capability also allows it to proceed inland to discharge its cargo on dry, trafficable terrain, thus helping to avoid a significant build-up of troops, equipment, and material at the surf zone. With its speed, and because it is not restricted by tides, beach gradients, and surf conditions, the LCAC makes possible a four-fold increase in accessible beach areas. The first LCAC was delivered by Textron Marine Systems in 1984 and the first operational LCAC unit was activated at Camp Pendleton, CA, early last year, where its LCACs underwent extensive testing under the direction of Commander, Surface Force, Pacific Fleet. A number of changes and improvements were needed in the first LCACs. The delay in incorporating them meant that contracts for three of the craft funded in FY 1985 and for 12 funded in FY 1986 were not awarded until mid-1987. Further, the Navy did not seek procurement funds for LCACs in either FY 1987 or FY 1988, but will seek funding for 12 per year over the next several years. Lockheed Shipbuilding Corporation was selected as the second builder of LCACs.

MINE WARFARE SHIPS (MSO, MCM, MHC)

Avenger Class

DISPLACEMENT: 1,040 tons full load.
LENGTH: 224 feet.
BEAM: 39 feet.
SPEED: 14 knots.
POWER PLANT: four diesels, two shafts, 2,400 brake horsepower.
AIRCRAFT: none.
ARMAMENT: two .50-caliber machine guns.
COMPLEMENT: 72.
BUILDERS: MCM-1, -3, -5, -6, -8, Peterson Builders; -2, -4, -7, Marinette Marine Corporation.

Aggressive Class

DISPLACEMENT: 720 tons full load.
LENGTH: 172 feet.
BEAM: 36 feet.
SPEED: 14 knots.
POWER PLANT: two diesels, two shafts, 2,280 brake horsepower.
AIRCRAFT: none.
ARMAMENT: one 40mm or one 20mm.
COMPLEMENT: 76.
BUILDERS: MSO-443, Higgins; 448, Martinolich Shipbuilding; 490, J.M. Martinac Shipbuilding.

BRIEFING: For many years, the Navy paid scant attention to its mine-countermeasures program. The last MSO built by the Navy was included in the 1954 shipbuilding program and commissioned in 1958. Not until December 1982 was construction commenced on another MCM ship, when the keel was laid for *Avenger* (MCM-1). Because of various problems, including those with electromagnetic interference and main engines, *Avenger* was not delivered until the late summer of 1987. *Defender* (MCM-2) was to have been delivered later in 1987, but delivery has slipped to mid-1988. Ice in the Great Lakes, where *Avenger* and her sister ships are being built, poses delivery problems for the Navy, since ice normally forms in mid-November and precludes operations until the following spring. Six other MCMs are under construction, and contracts for three more may be awarded this summer. The Navy sought funds for the last three of the 14-ship class in the FY 1988 budget, but Congress did not authorize or fund their construction. Seventeen minesweeper hunters (MSH) also were in the Navy's plans, and the contract for the first of these was awarded to Textron Marine Systems in FY 1984. This class of ship was to have a surface-effect-ship hull and be built of glass-reinforced plastic (GRP) foam composite material; GRP technology is used by several European navies for their mine-warfare ships. The first MSH was scheduled for delivery in 1987; however, a test section undergoing shock tests failed to meet Navy expectations. Subsequently, in 1986, it was decided not to proceed further with the MSH program but to adopt a design perfected by Intermarine SPA, an Italian shipyard. Its Lerici-class minesweepers, monohull GRP ships, now are being used by three navies. A design contract for a coastal minehunter (MHC) was awarded to Intermarine SPA in August 1986, and a construction contract for the lead ship of a 17-ship MHC class was awarded to Intermarine USA in May 1987. That ship is to be constructed at its Savannah, GA, shipyard, and is scheduled for completion in 1991. A second U.S. construction source also will be developed. Until the building programs for the MCM and MHC are well under way, the Navy must rely on

Avenger (MCM-1)

three active MSOs in the fleet and the 18 assigned to the Navy Reserve, which in time also will operate the new mine-warfare ships. Several of the MSOs were deployed to the Persian Gulf in the late summer of 1987 to sweep mines apparently planted by Iran.

Avenger Class

MCM-1 Avenger; Charleston, SC (MI 34090-1921)

Aggressive Class

MSO-443 Fidelity; Panama City, FL (MI 34091-1908)
MSO-448 Illusive; Charleston, SC (MI 34091-1910)
MSO-490 Leader; Charleston, SC (MI 34091-1917)

Leader (MSO-490)

MOBILE LOGISTIC SHIPS

Sacramento (AOE-1)

FAST COMBAT SUPPORT SHIPS (AOE)

Sacramento Class

DISPLACEMENT: approximately 53,000 tons full load.
LENGTH: 793 feet.
BEAM: 107 feet.
SPEED: 26 knots.
POWER PLANT: four boilers, geared turbines, two shafts, 100,000 shaft horsepower.
AIRCRAFT: two CH-46 Sea Knight helicopters.
ARMAMENT: four three-inch/50-caliber guns; rockets and two Phalanx CIWSs to be fitted.
COMPLEMENT: 594-621.
BUILDERS: AOEs 1, 3, 4, Puget Sound Naval Shipyard; 2, New York Shipbuilding; AOE 6, National Steel & Shipbuilding.

BRIEFING: These ships, the largest underway replenishment ships in the world, with capacities of more than 190,000 barrels of oil, 2,150 tons of ammunition, 500 tons of dry stores, and 250 tons of refrigerated stores, provide rapid replenishment of all these cargoes to Navy task forces. Ultimately, the Navy hopes to have 15 AOE/AOR ship types in the fleet and plans to seek funding for four AOEs in the FY 1987-1991 period. One was authorized in FY 1987, and is under construction; the second is being sought in FY 1989, and the last two will be sought in FY 1991.

Sacramento Class

AOE-1 Sacramento; San Diego, CA (SE 98799-3012)
AOE-2 Camden; Bremerton, WA (SE 98799-3013)
AOE-3 Seattle; Norfolk, VA (NY 09587-3014)
AOE-4 Detroit; Norfolk, VA (NY 09567-3015)

REPLENISHMENT OILERS (AOR)

DISPLACEMENT: 38,100 tons full load.
LENGTH: 659 feet.
BEAM: 96 feet.
SPEED: 20 knots.
POWER PLANT: three boilers, steam turbines, two shafts, 32,000 shaft horsepower.
AIRCRAFT: two CH-46 Sea Knight helicopters.
ARMAMENT: two Phalanx CIWSs, 20mm or 40mm gun, Sea Sparrow missiles.
COMPLEMENT: 445.
BUILDERS: 1-6, General Dynamics, Quincy; 7, National Steel and Shipbuilding.

BRIEFING: These large combination petroleum-munitions underway replenishment ships are smaller than AOEs but larger than almost all foreign ships with similar capability. They can carry 160,000 barrels of petroleum, 600 tons of munitions, 200 tons of dry stores, and 100 tons of refrigerated stores. They also have highly automated cargo-handling equipment. Although there are plans to build new AOEs, there are none at the moment to construct new AORs.

Wichita Class

AOR-1 Wichita; Oakland, CA (SF 96683-3023)
AOR-2 Milwaukee; Norfolk, VA (NY 09578-3024)
AOR-3 Kansas City; Oakland, CA (SF 96670-3025)
AOR-4 Savannah; Norfolk, VA (NY 09587-3026)
AOR-5 Wabash; Long Beach, CA (SF 96683-3027)
AOR-6 Kalamazoo; Norfolk, VA (NY 09576-3028)
AOR-7 Roanoke; Long Beach, CA (SF 96677-3029)

Kalamazoo (AOR-6)

Nitro (AE-23)

AMMUNITION SHIPS (AE)

Kilauea Class

DISPLACEMENT: approximately 20,000 tons full load.
LENGTH: 564 feet.
BEAM: 81 feet.
SPEED: 20 knots.
POWER PLANT: three boilers, geared turbines, one shaft, 22,000 shaft horsepower.
AIRCRAFT: two CH-46 Sea Knight helicopters.
ARMAMENT: four three-inch/50-caliber guns; two Phalanx CIWSs being fitted.
COMPLEMENT: 380.
BUILDERS: AE-26, 27, General Dynamics' Quincy Shipbuilding Division; 28, 29, Bethlehem Steel, Sparrows Point, Md.; 32-35, Ingalls Shipbuilding.

Suribachi and Nitro Class

DISPLACEMENT: 17,000 tons full load.
LENGTH: 512 feet.
BEAM: 72 feet.
SPEED: approximately 20 knots.
POWER PLANT: two boilers, geared turbines, one shaft, 16,000 shaft horsepower.
AIRCRAFT: none.
ARMAMENT: four three-inch/50 caliber guns.
COMPLEMENT: 349.
BUILDER: Bethlehem Steel, Sparrows Point, Md.

BRIEFING: Ammunition ships, like all of the other types of the Navy's major fleet-support ships, were in markedly increased demand after the upheaval in Iran and the Soviet invasion of Afghanistan. As a consequence, two Nitro-class ships which had been transferred to the reserve fleet were returned to the active fleet in 1982. A new class of AE is included in the Navy's long-range building plans, and the first was to have been sought in FY 1986. Now,

however, funds for it will be requested in FY 1991. *Kilauea* (T-AE-26) is operated by the Military Sealift Command and is unarmed.

Kilauea Class

AE-27 Butte; Earle, NJ (NY 09565-3005)
AE-28 Santa Barbara; Wpnsta, Charleston, SC (MI 34093-3006)
AE-29 Mount Hood; Concord, CA (SF 96672-3007)
AE-32 Flint; Concord, CA (SF 96665-3008)
AE-33 Shasta; Concord, CA (SF 96678-3009)
AE-34 Mount Baker; Wpnsta, Charleston, SC (MI 34092-3010)
AE-35 Kiska; Concord, CA (SF 96670-3011)

Nitro Class

AE-23 Nitro; Earle, NJ (NY 09579-3002)
AE-24 Pyro; Concord, CA (SF 96675-3003)
AE-25 Haleakala; Guam, MI (SF 96667-3004)

Suribachi Class

AE-21 Suribachi; Earle, NJ (NY 09587-3000)
AE-22 Mauna Kea; Concord, CA (SF 96672-3001)

FLEET OILERS (AO)

Cimarron Class (AO 177)

DISPLACEMENT: 27,500 tons full load.
LENGTH: 592 feet.
BEAM: 88 feet.
SPEED: 20 knots.
POWER PLANT: two boilers, one steam turbine, one shaft, 24,000 shaft horsepower.
AIRCRAFT: none.
ARMAMENT: two 20mm Phalanx CIWSs being fitted.
COMPLEMENT: 212.
CARGO CAPACITY: 120,000 barrels.
BUILDER: Avondale Shipyards.

Cimarron (AO-177)

Monongahela (AO-178)

Ashtabula Class

DISPLACEMENT: 34,750 tons full load.
LENGTH: 644 feet.
BEAM: 75 feet.
SPEED: 18 knots.
POWER PLANT: steam turbine, four boilers, two shafts, 13,500 shaft horsepower.
ARMAMENT: two 3''/50-caliber AA weapons.
AIRCRAFT: None. A small area for vertical replenishment is provided.
COMPLEMENT: 374.
BUILDER: Bethlehem Steel, Sparrows Point, MD.

BRIEFING: The number of Navy-manned fleet oilers has diminished steadily as more and more Military Sealift Command ships, all civilian manned and unarmed, have assumed responsibilities for supplying ships of the fleet. However, the Navy does plan to "jumboize" the five ships of the Cimarron class, all of which were commissioned between 1981-83. The first such conversion of a ship of this class is under way, a second was funded in FY 1988, and two more are to be sought in FY 1989.

Cimarron Class

AO-177 Cimarron; Pearl Harbor, HI (SF 96662-3018)
AO-178 Monongahela; Norfolk, VA (NY 09578-3019)
AO-179 Merrimack; Norfolk, VA (NY 09578-3020)
AO-180 Willamette; Pearl Harbor, HI (SF 96683-3021)
AO-186 Platte; Norfolk, VA (NY 09582-3022)

Ashtabula Class

AO-98 Caloosahatchee; Norfolk, VA (NY 09566-3016)
AO-99 Canisteo; Norfolk, VA (NY 09566-3017)

COMBAT STORES SHIPS (AFS)

Mars Class

DISPLACEMENT: approximately 16,000 tons full load.
LENGTH: 581 feet.
BEAM: 79 feet.
SPEED: 20 knots.
POWER PLANT: three boilers, steam turbines, one shaft, 22,000 shaft horsepower.
AIRCRAFT: two UH-46 Sea Knight helicopters.
ARMAMENT: four three-inch/50 caliber guns; two Phalanx CIWSs to be fitted.
COMPLEMENT: 436.
BUILDER: National Steel and Shipbuilding.

BRIEFING: Four of the seven ships of the Mars class are less than 20 years old and in excellent condition to respond to the additional logistics requirements placed on the Navy's auxiliary forces by the steady build-up toward a 600-ship Navy and the deployment of task forces to the Indian Ocean. However, no further acquisition of ships of this type is contemplated at this time.

Mars Class

AFS-1 Mars; Oakland, CA (SF 96672-3030)
AFS-2 Sylvania; Norfolk, VA (NY 09587-3031)
AFS-3 Niagara Falls; Guam, MI (SF 96673-3032)
AFS-4 White Plains; Guam, MI (SF 96683-3033)
AFS-5 Concord; Norfolk, VA (NY 09566-3034)
AFS-6 San Diego; Norfolk, VA (NY 09587-3035)
AFS-7 San Jose; Guam, MI (SF 96678-3036)

Mars (AFS-1)

MATERIAL SUPPORT SHIPS

SUBMARINE TENDERS (AS)

L.Y. Spear and Emory S. Land Classes

DISPLACEMENT: approximately 23,000 tons.
LENGTH: 644 feet.
BEAM: 85 feet.
SPEED: 20 knots.
POWER PLANT: two boilers, steam turbines, one shaft, 20,000 shaft horsepower.
AIRCRAFT: none.
ARMAMENT: two 40mm guns, four 20mm guns.
COMPLEMENT: ASs 36 and 37, 625; 39-41, 617.
BUILDERS: ASs 36, 37, General Dynamics' Quincy Shipbuilding Division; 39-41, Lockheed Shipbuilding.

Simon Lake Class

DISPLACEMENT: AS-33, 19,934 tons; 34, 21,089 tons.
LENGTH: 644 feet.
BEAM: 85 feet.
SPEED: 20 knots.
POWER PLANT: two boilers, steam turbines, one shaft, 20,000 shaft horsepower.
AIRCRAFT: none.
ARMAMENT: four 20mm guns.
COMPLEMENT: AS 33, 915; AS 34, 660.
BUILDERS: AS-33, Puget Sound Naval Shipyard; 34, Ingalls Shipbuilding.

Hunley Class

DISPLACEMENT: 19,000 tons full load.
LENGTH: 599 feet.
BEAM: 83 feet.
SPEED: 19 knots.
POWER PLANT: diesel-electric, one shaft, 15,000 brake horsepower.
AIRCRAFT: none.
ARMAMENT: four 20mm guns.
COMPLEMENT: AS 31, 612; AS 32, 659.
BUILDERS: AS-31, Newport News Shipbuilding; 32, Ingalls Shipbuilding.

Fulton and Proteus Classes

DISPLACEMENT: ASs 11 and 18, 16,230 tons full load; 19, 19,200 tons full load.
LENGTH: ASs 11 and 18, 530.5 feet; 19, 575 feet.
BEAM: 73 feet.
SPEED: 15.4 knots.
AIRCRAFT: none.
ARMAMENT: 4 20mm guns.
COMPLEMENT: approximately 573-706.
BUILDERS: AS-11, Mare Island, Calif., Navy Yard; 18, 19, Moore Shipbuilding and Drydock.

Spear (AS-36)

Canopus (AS-34)

BRIEFING: These four classes of ships reflect the difficulties encountered by the Navy over the years in acquiring enough modern, responsive support ships and in upgrading the capabilities of older ones to permit keeping pace with ever-changing fleet requirements. *Proteus* (AS 19), for example, joined the fleet in 1944 and then had to be modernized extensively 15 years later to give her the capability to service the first strategic nuclear missiles, the Polaris. Only four ASs were built between 1944 and 1970 when *Spear* (AS 36) was commissioned, and another eight years passed between the commissionings of the second ship of that class, *Dixon* (AS 37), and the *Emory S. Land* (AS 39). Meanwhile, capabilities of ships already operational were being improved upon constantly to cope with advances in missilery and nuclear propulsion. The Hunley, Simon Lake, and Proteus classes are configured especially to service ballistic-missile submarines. The Land and Spear classes were designed and fitted to accommodate SSNs, and can service simultaneously four submarines moored alongside.

Spear Class

AS-36 L.Y. Spear; Norfolk, VA (NY 09547-2600)
AS-37 Dixon; San Diego, CA (SF 96648-2605)

Emory S. Land Class

AS-39 Emory S. Land; Norfolk, VA (NY 09545-2610)
AS-40 Frank Cable; Charleston, SC (MI 34086-2615)
AS-41 McKee; San Diego, CA (SF 96621-2620)

Simon Lake Class

AS-33 Simon Lake; Holy Loch, Scotland (MI 34085-2590)
AS-34 Canopus; Kings Bay, GA (MI 34087-2595)

Hunley Class

AS-32 Hunley; Norfolk, VA (NY 09559-2580)
AS-32 Holland; Charleston, SC (MI 34079-2585)

Fulton Class

AS-11 Fulton; New London, CT (NY 09534-2565)
AS-18 Orion; La Maddalena, Italy (NY 09513-2570)

Proteus Class

AS-19 Proteus; Guam, MI (SF 96646-2575)

Puget Sound (AD-38)

DESTROYER TENDERS (AD)

Yellowstone and Samuel Gompers Class

DISPLACEMENT: approximately 22,500 tons full load.
LENGTH: 644 feet.
BEAM: 85 feet.
SPEED: 20 knots.
POWER PLANT: two boilers, steam turbines, one shaft, 20,000 shaft horsepower.
AIRCRAFT: none.
ARMAMENT: ADs 37 and 38, four 20mm guns; 41-43, two 40mm and two 20mm guns.
COMPLEMENT: 1,300-1,500, approximately.
BUILDERS: ADs 37, 38, Puget Sound Naval Shipyard; 41-43, National Steel and Shipbuilding.

Dixie Class

DISPLACEMENT: 18,000 tons full load.
LENGTH: 530 feet.
BEAM: 73 feet.
SPEED: 18.2 knots.
POWER PLANT: four boilers, geared turbines, two shafts, 12,000 shaft horsepower.
AIRCRAFT: none.
ARMAMENT: four 20mm guns.
COMPLEMENT: approximately 870.
BUILDERS: AD-15, New York Shipbuilding; 18, 19, Tampa Shipbuilding.

BRIEFING: These ships so vital to the fleet range in age from the venerable Dixie-class ship *Prairie* (AD 15), commissioned in 1940 and now the oldest active ship in commission in the Navy, to the new *Shenandoah* (AD 44), commissioned in late 1983. Because of the advent of nuclear power and the phenomenal advances in electronics and weaponry, AD capabilities have had to be vastly increased. The Gompers and Yellowstone classes are the first of post-World War II design; however, more than 15 years elapsed between the launching of the second of the Gompers class, *Puget Sound* (AD 38), and *Yellowstone* (AD 41). These classes, which have a helicopter platform and hangar and are equipped with two 30-ton and two 6½-ton cranes, can provide services simultaneously to as many as six destroyers moored alongside. Although earlier plans had called for additional ADs in the FY 1987 and 1988 budgets, none is included in the current five-year shipbuilding plan.

Yellowstone Class

AD-41 Yellowstone; Norfolk, VA (NY 09512-2525)
AD-42 Acadia; San Diego, CA (SF 96647-2530)
AD-43 Cape Cod; San Diego, CA (SF 96649-2535)
AD-44 Shenandoah; Norfolk, VA (NY 09551-2540)

Samuel Gompers Class

AD-37 Samuel Gompers; Alameda, CA (SF 96641-2915)
AD-38 Puget Sound; Norfolk, VA (NY 09544-2520)

Dixie Class

AD-15 Prairie; Long Beach, CA (SF 96639-2500)
AD-18 Sierra; Charleston, SC (MI 34084-2505)
AD-19 Yosemite; Mayport, FL (MI 34083-2510)

REPAIR SHIPS (AR)

Vulcan Class

DISPLACEMENT: approximately 16,270 tons full load.
LENGTH: 529 feet.
BEAM: 73 feet.
SPEED: 19.2 knots.
POWER PLANT: four boilers, steam turbines, two shafts, 11,000 shaft horsepower.
AIRCRAFT: none.
ARMAMENT: four 20mm guns.
COMPLEMENT: 841.
BUILDERS: AR-5, New York Shipbuilding; 6-8, Los Angeles Shipbuilding and Drydock.

BRIEFING: These relatively ancient ships, all of World War II vintage and funded under 1939 and 1940 shipbuilding programs spearheaded by the farsighted Georgia congressman, Carl Vinson, still serve a useful purpose. The ships can simultaneously repair a large number of ship systems and subsystems and would be invaluable in time of conflict.

Vulcan Class

AR-5 Vulcan; Norfolk, VA (NY 09548-2545)
AR-8 Jason; Pearl Harbor, HI (SF 96644-2560)

Jason (AR-8)

"Those who expect to reap
the blessings of freedom must, like men,
undergo the fatigues of supporting it."

Tom Paine
After the American defeat at the battle of Brandywine—1777

Peace, liberty, and security.

They depend upon a strong national defense. It is a lesson learned and relearned throughout 5,000 years of recorded history.

By far the least costly way to preserve freedom is to build and maintain an adequate defense.

Opinions may differ on what is "adequate," but informed men and women believe that it must include research and development of the most advanced defense systems. Equally, it requires the production and deployment of superior military equipment that will, if necessary, stand against any hostile force.

And, above all else, there is one essential element in America's national security system: the more than two million men and women who serve with distinction in our armed forces. It is their courage and dedication that are America's most certain guarantees of freedom.

Edenton (ATS-1)

SALVAGE SHIPS (ARS, ATS)

Safeguard Class

DISPLACEMENT: 2,880 tons full load.
LENGTH: 255 feet.
BEAM: 50 feet.
SPEED: 14 knots.
POWER PLANT: diesels, two shafts, 4,200 shaft horsepower.
AIRCRAFT: none.
ARMAMENT: two 20mm guns.
COMPLEMENT: 90.
BUILDER: Peterson Builders.

Edenton Class

DISPLACEMENT: 2,929 tons full load.
LENGTH: 282 feet.
BEAM: 50 feet.
SPEED: 16 knots.
POWER PLANT: four diesels, two shafts, 6,000 brake horsepower.
AIRCRAFT: none.
ARMAMENT: two 20mm guns.
COMPLEMENT: 115.
BUILDER: Brooke Marine, Lowestoft, England.

Bolster Class

DISPLACEMENT: 2,045 tons full load.
LENGTH: 213 feet.
BEAM: 44 feet.
SPEED: 14.8 knots.
POWER PLANT: diesel-electric, two shafts, 3,060 shaft horsepower.
AIRCRAFT: none.
ARMAMENT: two 20mm guns.
COMPLEMENT: ARS 41, 69; ARS 43, 103.
BUILDER: Basalt Rock Co.

BRIEFING: Following the commissioning of *Recovery* (ARS 43), the last of the Bolster class, in 1946, a quarter of a century passed before the Navy sought to modernize its salvage-ship capability with the three Edenton-class ships, one of two classes of ships built for the Navy in Great Britain in the last two decades. Then another decade passed before the keel laying of *Safeguard* (ARS 50). That ship and three sister ships, the last of which was delivered to the fleet in 1986, with the Edenton-class ships fulfill fleet salvage-ship

requirements for the immediate future, although one ARS is scheduled to be funded in FY 1990. The latter ships also have a rescue capability, can support diver operations to a depth of 850 feet, and can lift submerged objects weighing up to 300 tons from a depth of 120 feet. The Navy has a national responsibility for the salvaging of all U.S. ships, both government and private.

Salvor (ARS-52)

Safeguard Class

ARS-50 Safeguard; Pearl Harbor, HI (SF 96678-3221)
ARS-51 Grasp; Little Creek, Norfolk, VA (NY 09570-3220)
ARS-52 Salvor Pearl Harbor, HI (SF 96678-3222)
ARS-53 Grapple; Norfolk, VA (NY 09570-3223)

Edenton Class

ATS-1 Edenton; Little Creek, Norfolk, VA (NY 09568-3217)
ATS-2 Beaufort; Pearl Harbor, HI (SF 96661-3218)
ATS-3 Brunswick, Pearl Harbor, HI (SF 96661-3219)

Bolster Class

ARS-39 Conserver; Pearl Harbor, HI (SF 96662-3202)
ARS-41 Opportune; Little Creek, Norfolk, VA (NY 09581-3204)
ARS-43 Recovery; Little Creek, Norfolk, VA (NY 09586-3206)

Ortolan (ASR-22)

SUBMARINE RESCUE SHIPS (ASR)

Pigeon Class

DISPLACEMENT: 4,200 tons full load.
LENGTH: 251 feet.
BEAM: 86 feet.
SPEED: 15 knots.
POWER PLANT: four diesels, two shafts, 6,000 brake horsepower.
AIRCRAFT: none.
ARMAMENT: two 20mm guns.
COMPLEMENT: ship's company, 197; submersible operators, 24.
BUILDER: Alabama Drydock and Shipbuilding.

Chanticleer Class

DISPLACEMENT: 2,320 tons full load.
LENGTH: 251 feet.
BEAM: 44 feet.
SPEED: 15 knots.
POWER PLANT: diesel electric, one shaft, 3,000 brake horsepower.
AIRCRAFT: none.
ARMAMENT: two 20mm guns.
COMPLEMENT: 103.
BUILDERS: ASR-9, Moore Shipbuilding and Drydock; 13-15, Savannah Machine and Foundry.

BRIEFING: No submarine rescue ships were commissioned for more than a quarter of a century after *Sunbird* (ASR 15) joined the fleet in 1947. The two Pigeon-class ships are the first in the world to be built specifically for the submarine-rescue mission and, except for one Military Sealift Command Ship, are the first catamaran-hull ships to be built for the Navy since Robert Fulton's *Demologos* in 1812. They are capable of transporting, servicing, lowering, and raising two Deep Submergence Rescue Vessels (DSRV) and supporting saturation or conventional diving operations to depths of 850 feet. They can support divers indefinitely, lowering them to the ocean floor in pressurized transfer chambers for open-sea work periods. ASRs also serve as operational control ships for salvage operations. No new ASRs are included in the Navy's long-range shipbuilding plans.

Pigeon Class

ASR-21 Pigeon; San Diego, CA (SF 96675-3211)
ASR-22 Ortolan; Charleston, SC (MI 34092-3212)

Chanticleer Class

ASR-9 Florikan; Pearl Harbor, HI (SF 96665-3207)
ASR-13 Kittiwake; Norfolk, VA (NY 09576-3208)
ASR-14 Petrel; Charleston, SC (MI 34092-3209)
ASR-15 Sunbird; Groton, CT (NY 09587-3210)

MISCELLANEOUS AUXILIARY SHIPS

BRIEFING: *Coronado* (AGF-11) and *La Salle* (AGF-31) are converted LPDs which have been modified to serve as flagships. *La Salle* is a veteran of Middle East duty, having served as flagship of the Middle East force for more than a decade. She became the focus of unusual media attention following the attack on *Stark* (FFG-31) by an Iraqi aircraft in the Persian Gulf last May. Coronado also has seen Middle East duty as the relief of *La Salle,* when the latter was undergoing overhaul. She now is the flagship of Commander, Third Fleet, and is homeported in Hawaii. *Dolphin* (AGSS-555) is an experimental, deep-diving research submarine which reportedly has reached greater depths than any other operational submarine. She provides support to the Naval Ocean Systems Center and several other Navy research facilities. *Lexington* (AVT-16), commissioned in February 1943, is the only active ship of the 23 Essex-class carriers built from 1942-1946. She has been training pilots since 1962. She is scheduled for replacement by *Coral Sea* (CV-43) in 1991, 50 years after she was laid down. *Sphinx* (ARL-24) is the last of a number of LSTs that were converted into repair ships during World War II, and which, although limited in size and capability, performed yeoman service to the amphibious fleet in particular.

Miscellaneous Auxiliary Ships

Coronado (AGF-11); Pearl Harbor, HI (SF 96662-3330)
La Salle (AGF-31); Philadelphia, PA (NY 09577-3320)
Dolphin (AGSS-555); San Diego, CA (SF 96663-3400)
Lexington (AVT-16); Pensacola, FL (MI 34088-2700)
Sphinx (ARL-24); Key West, FL (NY 09587-2625)

NAVAL RESERVE FORCES

DESTROYER

Hull Class

DD-946 Edson; Newport, RI (NY 09568-1200)

FRIGATES

Knox Class

FF-1053 Roark; San Francisco, CA (SF 96677-1413)
FF-1054 Gray; San Francisco, CA (SF 96666-1414)
FF-1060 Lang; San Francisco, CA (SF 96671-1420)
FF-1061 Patterson; Philadelphia, PA (NY 09582-1421)
FF-1072 Blakely; Charleston, SC (MI 34090-1432)
FF-1091 Miller; Newport, RI (NY 09578-1451)
FF-1096 Valdez; Newport, RI (NY 09590-1456)

Oliver Hazard Perry Class

FFG-7 Oliver Hazard Perry; Philadelphia, PA (NY 09582-1465)
FFG-9 Wadsworth; Long Beach, CA (SF 96683-1467)
FFG-10 Duncan; Long Beach, CA (SF 96663-1468)
FFG-11 Clark; Philadelphia, PA (NY 09566-1469)
FFG-12 George Philip; Long Beach, CA (SF 96675-1470)
FFG-13 Samuel Eliot Morison; Charleston, SC (MI 34092-1471)
FFG-14 Sides; Long Beach, CA (SF 96678-1472)
FFG-15 Estocin; Philadelphia, PA (NY 09569-1473)
FFG-16 Clifton Sprague; Philadelphia, PA (NY 09587-1474)
FFG-19 John A. Moore; Long Beach, CA (SF 96672-1475)
FFG-20 Antrim; Mayport, FL (MI 34090-1476)
FFG-21 Lewis B. Puller; Long Beach, CA (SF 96675-1470)

LANDING CRAFT CARRIERS

Newport Class

LST-1190 Boulder; New York, NY (NY 09565-1811)
LST-1191 Racine; Long Beach, CA (SF 96677-1812)

MINESWEEPERS

Aggressive Class

MSO-427 Constant; San Diego, CA (SF 96662-1900)
MSO-433 Engage; Mayport, FL (MI 34091-1901)
MSO-437 Enhance; Tacoma, WA (SE 98799-1902)
MSO-438 Esteem Seattle, WA (SE 98799-1903)
MSO-439 Excel; San Francisco, CA (SF 96664-1904)
MSO-440 Exploit; Newport, RI (NY 09568-1905)
MSO-441 Exultant; Mayport, FL (MI 34091-1906)
MSO-442 Fearless; Charleston, SC (MI 34091-1907)
MSO-446 Fortify; Little Creek, Norfolk, VA (NY 09569-1909)
MSO-449 Impervious; Mayport, FL (MI 34091-1911)
MSO-455 Implicit; Tacoma, WA (SE 98799-1912)
MSO-456 Inflict; Little Creek, Norfolk, VA (NY 09574-1913)
MSO-464 Pluck; San Diego, CA (SF 96675-1914)
MSO-488 Conquest; Seattle, WA (SE 98799-1915)
MSO-489 Gallant; San Francisco, CA (SF 96666-1916)
MSO-492 Pledge; Seattle, WA (SE 98799-1918)

Acme Class

MSO-508 Adroit; Little Creek, Norfolk, VA (NY 09564-1919)
MSO-511 Affray; Newport, RI (NY 09564-1920)

FLEET SUPPORT SHIPS

Bolster Class

ARS-38 Bolster; Long Beach, CA (SF 96661-3201)
ARS-40 Hoist; Little Creek, Norfolk, VA (NY 09583-3203)
ARS-42 Reclaimer; Pearl Harbor, HI (SF 96677-3255)

Blakely (FF-1072)

Lang (FF-1060)

#100

On September 26, 1987, the *U.S.S. Leyte Gulf* — the 100th USN ship powered by GE LM2500 engines — joined the fleet.

The LM2500 thus continues a proud tradition of performance for the U.S. Navy: 6 PHM Hydrofoils, 51 FFG-7 Frigates, 31 DD-963 Destroyers, 4 DDG-993 Destroyers, and the balance in CG-47 AEGIS Guided Missile Cruisers. Throughout, the LM2500 has established a reputation as the most efficient and reliable gas turbine propulsion system in marine use.

The LM2500 also means cost effective performance. Unprecedented operating characteristics, like zero to full power in 90 seconds or less plus an availability of 99.9%, directly help the

The *U.S.S. Leyte Gulf* is powered by four GE LM2500 engines, giving it a top operating speed in excess of 30 knots.

U.S. Navy achieve a high order of mission readiness.

Based on this record, the LM2500 has also been selected as a preferred propulsion system by 16 other world navies, 31 different ship types, and a grand total of more than 230 ships.

We're proud of this record of acceptance. But beyond product, beyond engineering, beyond logistics, we believe it has everything to do with our sense of total commitment to the needs of the U.S. Navy.

For more information, contact Marketing Department, GE Marine & Industrial Engines, Mail Drop N158, One Neumann Way, Cincinnati, Ohio, USA 45215.

GE Marine & Industrial Engines

NAVAL FLEET AUXILIARY FORCE

The Military Sealift Command long has been assigned the responsibility for supporting all components of the Department of Defense, and occasionally those of other elements of the government as well, in both peacetime and wartime. However, it required the upheaval in Iran and the Soviet invasion of Afghanistan in the late 1970s to focus national attention on the inadequacies of the forces available for strategic sealift, and particularly in terms of supporting U.S. forces in the Indian Ocean area. The resulting close scrutiny of sealift forces and their capabilities also spotlighted the meager means available for handling cargo in areas where modern port facilities were almost nonexistent. The dismal overall sealift situation was worsened by two other factors: (1) The U.S. merchant marine had been, and still was, in a state of decline; (2) A large percentage of

modern merchant ships potentially available for sealift in time of emergency were containerships which were not configured to effectively handle military cargo. Since these deficiencies were faced up to, a number of actions have been taken both to add to the numbers of ships readily available for sealift and to greatly enhance the ability to both move and handle military cargo. Further emphasis was given to the importance of strategic sealift by its formal establishment by the Navy as one of the Navy's three primary functions; it joins sea control and power projection. As of 1 January 1988, the Military Sealift command controlled a force comprising more than 120 ships, including approximately 70 strategic sealift ships, in addition to the steadily increasing numbers of ships in the Ready Reserve Force.

Kaiser (TAO-187)

OILERS (TAO)

Henry J. Kaiser Class (TAO 187)

DISPLACEMENT: 40,000 tons full load.
LENGTH: 677.5 feet.
BEAM: 97.5 feet.
SPEED: 20 knots.
POWER PLANT: two fully automatic diesel engines, twin shafts, 32,540 shaft horsepower.
AIRCRAFT: none (landing platform for vertical replenishment provided).
CARGO CAPACITY: 180,000 barrels of gas-turbine and diesel fuel.
COMPLEMENT: 96 civilian, 21 Navy.
BUILDERS: 187-190, 193, 195, 197. Avondale Shipyards; 191-192, 194, 196, Pennsylvania Shipbuilding.

Mispillion Class (jumboized) (TAO 105)

DISPLACEMENT: Approximately 34,000 tons full load.
LENGTH: 644 feet.
BEAM: 75 feet.
SPEED: 16 knots.
POWER PLANT: Geared turbines, four boilers, two shafts, 13,500 shaft horsepower.
AIRCRAFT: none (landing platform for vertical replenishment provided).
CARGO CAPACITY: 150,000 barrels.
COMPLEMENT: 111 civilian, 21 Navy.
BUILDER: Sun Shipbuilding, Chester.

Neosho Class (TAO 143)

DISPLACEMENT: 38,000 tons full load.
LENGTH: 655 feet.
BEAM: 86 feet.
SPEED: 20 knots.
POWER PLANT: geared turbines, two boilers, two shafts, 28,000 shaft horsepower.
AIRCRAFT: none (landing platform for vertical replenishment provided).
CARGO CAPACITY: 180,000 barrels.
COMPLEMENT: 107 civilians, 21 Navy.
BUILDERS: 143: Bethlehem Steel, Quincy; 144-148, New York Shipbuilding, Camden.

BRIEFING: The *Henry J. Kaiser* (TAO-187), the first of what now appears will be an 18-ship class of oilers, was delivered in December 1986, three months late because of reduction-gear and logistics support problems. Three more of the class were delivered in 1987, two are scheduled for delivery this year, and five others are under construction. Authorization for the construction of two more was included in the FY 1988 defense budget. These ships will have a capacity for small quantities of fresh and frozen provisions, stores, and other materials which will permit full replenishment of some of their customers. As they join the fleet, Kaiser-class ships will permit retirement of some of the oilers of the 1940s (Mispillion class) and 1950s (Neosho class).

Pawcatuck (TAO-108)

Henry J. Kaiser Class

TAO-187 Henry J. Kaiser; No home port assigned. (NY 09576-4086)
TAO-188 Joshua Humphreys; No home port assigned.
TAO-189 John Lenthal; No home port assigned.
TAO-190 Andrew J. Higgins; No home port assigned.

Mispillion Class (Jumboized)

TAO-105 Mispillion; Oakland, CA (SF 96672-4030)
TAO-106 Navasota; Oakland, CA (SF 96673-4037)
TAO-107 Passumpsic; Oakland, CA (SF 96675-4044)
TAO-108 Pawcatuck; Bayonne, NJ (NY 09582-4045)
TAO-109 Waccamaw; Bayonne, NJ (MI 34093-4072)

Neosho Class

TAO-143 Neosho; Bayonne, NJ (NY 09579-4039)
TAO-144 Mississinewa; Bayonne, NJ (MI 34092-4031)
TAO-145 Hassayampa; Oakland, CA (SF 96667-4016)
TAO-146 Kawashiwi; San Diego, CA (SF 96670-4022)
TAO-147 Truckee; Bayonne, NJ (NY 09588-4068)
TAO-148 Ponchatoula; Oakland, CA (SF 96675-4046)

Prevail (TAGOS-8)

SURVEILLANCE SHIPS (TAGOS)

Stalwart Class

DISPLACEMENT: 2,285 tons full load.
LENGTH: 224 feet.
BEAM: 43 feet.
SPEED: 11 knots.
POWER PLANT: four diesel generators, two shafts, 3,200 brake horsepower.
AIRCRAFT: none.
COMPLEMENT: 25 civilians.
BUILDER: 1-12, Tacoma Boatbuilding Company; 13-18, Halter Marine.

TAGOS-19 Class

DISPLACEMENT: 4,200 tons full load.
LENGTH: 231 feet.
BEAM: 93 feet.
SPEED: 10.7 knots.
POWER PLANT: two Caterpillar diesel-General Electric generator combinations, one in each side of the hull, twin shafts, 1,600 shaft horsepower.
AIRCRAFT: none.
COMPLEMENT: 21 civilian, 13 Navy technicians.
BUILDER: McDermott Marine, Morgan City, La.

BRIEFING: These small, unarmed, civilian-manned auxiliary ships are destined to play a prominent role in augmenting overall ASW capability. They will tow sophisticated sonar gear (SURTASS) which will make possible a much broader area of coverage against forays by enemy submarines and more rapid transformation of information for analysis. Operational results from the deployment of the first group of the monohulled Stalwart (TAGOS-1) class were excellent;

however, their seakeeping qualities in the higher latitudes left something to be desired. Accordingly, in order to make possible more effective operation in these latitudes, the Navy elected to cease construction of the monohulled ships with the 18th ship, and to embark upon a program of construction of SWATH (small waterplane area twin hull) ships. A contract was awarded in October 1986 to McDermott Marine for construction of TAGOS-19, the first of this class, with an option for the construction of three others, which were scheduled for funding in FY 1989. The Navy's current five-year shipbuilding plan called for funding construction of three more in FY 1990 and two in FY 1991; that would bring the total TAGOS program to 27. However, Congress, obviously impressed with the operational performance of the Stalwart-class ships, advanced the construction timetable by including funds for two SWATH ships in the FY 1988 budget, even though the Navy had not requested any. TAGOS-19 currently is scheduled for delivery in July 1989, and the last of the monohulled surveillance ships in March 1990.

TAGOS-1 Stalwart; Little Creek, Norfolk, Va. (NY 09587-4077)
TAGOS-2 Contender; Pearl Harbor, Hawaii (SF 96682-4082)
TAGOS-3 Vindicator; Little Creek, Norfolk, Va. (NY 09590-4083)
TAGOS-4 Triumph; Pearl Harbor, Hawaii (SF 96679-4084)
TAGOS-5 Assurance; Pearl Harbor, Hawaii (SF 96660-4085)
TAGOS-6 Persistent; Little Creek, Norfolk, Va. (NY 09582-4047)
TAGOS-7 Indomitable; Pearl Harbor, Hawaii (SF 96668-4067)
TAGOS-8 Prevail; Little Creek, Norfolk, Va. (NY 09582-4002)
TAGOS-9 Assertive; Oakland, CA (SF 96660-4011)
TAGOS-10 Invincible; Little Creek, Norfolk, Va. (NY 09574-4041)

Sirius (TAFS-8)

COMBAT STORES SHIPS (TAFS)

Ex-British Lyness Class

DISPLACEMENT: 16,792 tons full load.
LENGTH: 524 feet.
BEAM: 72 feet.
SPEED: 18 knots.
POWER PLANT: one diesel, 11,520 brake horsepower.
AIRCRAFT: two UH-46 Sea Knight helicopters.
ARMAMENT: none.
COMPLEMENT: 25 civilian, 44 Navy.
BUILDER: Swan Hunter & Wigham Richardson Ltd., Wallsend-On-Tyne.

BRIEFING: These ships formerly were Royal Navy replenishment ships; they were purchased from Great Britain in 1982-83 because of the increased logistics requirements resulting from the decision to maintain two carrier battle groups in the Indian Ocean during, and for a considerable time after, the Iranian hostage crisis. They are slightly more than 20 years old and have been extensively modernized with improved communications and underway-replenishment facilities. They have proven to be welcome additions to the fleet, and became even more valuable when it was decided after the attack on the *Stark* to sharply increase the U.S. naval presence in and adjacent to the Persian Gulf.

TAFS-8 Sirius; Norfolk, VA (NY 09587-4064)
TAFS-9 Spica; Oakland, CA (SF 96678-4066)
TAFS-10 Saturn; Norfolk, VA (NY 09587-4052)

GREAT PR

ETENDER.

...ypifies the AAI philosophy in developing high-tech electronic and ...mechanical systems. Whatever the system, AAI designs it sensibly to meet ...r exceed standards without over-engineering for excess waste, weight or ...ost. This sensible approach to problem-solving has made AAI a major ...ontractor to industry and the Department of Defense.

AAI capabilities are worth inquiring about. Call or write our ...narketing director at AAI Corporation, Dept. 902, P.O. Box 126, Hunt ...alley, MD 21030. Phone (301) 666-1400. Telex 8-7849. For information ...n career opportunities, write or call the Personnel Department.

AAI

AAI Corporation, a subsidiary of United Industrial Corporation

THE SENSIBLE SOLUTION

Navajo (TATF-169)

FLEET OCEAN TUGS (TATF)

Powhatan Class

DISPLACEMENT: 2,260 tons full load.
LENGTH: 226 feet.
BEAM: 42 feet.
SPEED: 15 knots.
POWER PLANT: two diesels, two shafts, controllable pitch propellers.
COMPLEMENT: 17 civilian, four Navy.
BUILDER: Marinette Marine Corporation, Wisconsin.

BRIEFING: The seven ships in this class, the oldest of which was placed in service in July 1979, are the first fleet ocean tugs to be built by the Navy since the *Papago* (ATF 160) in 1945. They have a 300-brake-horsepower bow thruster, a 10-ton-capacity crane, and a 53.6 ton bollard pull. Space is provided for light armament in time of war. No other ships of this type are included in the five-year shipbuilding plan.

TATF-166 Powhatan; No home port assigned. (NY 09582-4048)
TATF-167 Narragansett; No home port assigned. (SF 96673-4035)
TATF-168 Catawba; No home port assigned. (SF 96662-4047)
TATF-169 Navajo; No home port assigned. (SF 96673-4036)
TATF-170 Mohawk; No home port assigned. (NY 09578-4033)
TATF-171 Sioux; No home port assigned. (SF 96678-4063)
TATF-172 Apache; No home port assigned. (NY 09564-4003)

FLEET BALLISTIC MISSILE SHIPS

Marshfield

DISPLACEMENT: 11,500 tons full load.
LENGTH: 455 feet.
BEAM: 28.5 feet.
SPEED: 17 knots.
POWER PLANT: steam turbine, two boilers, one shaft, 8,500 shaft horsepower.
CREW: 69 civilians, Navy security personnel.
BUILDER: Oregon Shipbuilding, Portland.

Vega

DISPLACEMENT: 18,365 tons full load.
LENGTH: 483 feet.
BEAM: 68 feet.
SPEED: 21 knots.
POWER PLANT: steam turbine, two boilers, one shaft, 12,500 shaft horsepower.
CREW: 67 civilians, 7 Navy.
BUILDER: Sun Shipbuilding and Drydock, Chester, Pa.

BRIEFING: *Marshfield* and *Vega* both are former merchant ships which have been converted to support SSBN tenders and have been fitted to carry 16 ballistic missiles.

Marshfield (TAK-282)

NAVAL FLEET MOBILITY ENHANCEMENT

MARITIME PREPOSITIONED SHIPS (MPS) (TAK)

MAERSK CONVERSIONS

DISPLACEMENT: 46,552 long tons full load.
LENGTH: 755 feet.
BEAM: 90 feet.
SPEED: 17.5 knots.
POWER PLANT: one diesel, one screw, 16,800 shaft horsepower.
ENDURANCE: 10,800 nautical miles.
AIRCRAFT: none.
ARMAMENT: none.
CAPACITY: bulk POL, 1.3 million gallons; water, 85,000 gallons; equipment and vehicles, 1/5 of Marine Amphibious Brigade (MAB).
COMPLEMENT: 27 civilians and 6 maintenance personnel.
CONVERTING SHIPYARD: Bethlehem Steel, Sparrows Point, MD (3); Beaumont, TX (2).

WATERMAN CONVERSIONS

DISPLACEMENT: 48,754 long tons full load.
LENGTH: 821 feet.
BEAM: 105.5 feet.
SPEED: 20 knots.
POWER PLANT: two geared turbines, two boilers, one screw, 30,000 shaft horsepower.
ENDURANCE: 13,000 nautical miles.
AIRCRAFT: none.
ARMAMENT: none.
CAPACITY: bulk POL, 1.5 million gallons; water, 91,938 gallons; equipment and vehicles, 1/4 of MAB.
COMPLEMENT: 29 civilians and 6 maintenance personnel.
CONVERTING SHIPYARD: National Steel and Shipbuilding.

AMSEA NEW CONSTRUCTION

DISPLACEMENT: 40,846 long tons full load.
LENGTH: 654.6 feet.
BEAM: 105.5 feet.
SPEED: 18 knots.
POWER PLANT: two diesels, one screw, 26,000 shaft horsepower.
ENDURANCE: 12,840 nautical miles.
AIRCRAFT: none.
ARMAMENT: none.
CAPACITY: bulk POL, 1.6 million gallons; water, 98,994 gallons; equipment and vehicles, 1/4 of MAB.
COMPLEMENT: 30 civilians and 6 maintenance personnel.
BUILDER: General Dynamics, Quincy.

BRIEFING: These 13 ships provide additional lift for Marine amphibious forces. Eight relatively new merchant ships were purchased for the purpose of conversion; the remaining five are new construction. They form three squadrons. The first, which was completed and loaded in 1984, operates in eastern and northern Atlantic waters. The second, which was completed and loaded in 1985, replaced five prepositioned ships in the Indian Ocean and operates in that area. The third, which was completed and loaded in 1986, operates in the western Pacific. Each squadron contains the equipment and 30 days of supplies for a Marine Amphibious Brigade and is capable of offloading at piers or from offshore with special equipment with which they have been fitted. However, the ships themselves have no amphibious capability. The prepositioning concept and the unique combined capabilities of these ships have been enthusiastically welcomed and supported by the Marine Corps.

TAK-3000 Cpl Louis J. Hauge, Jr.; No home port assigned. (SF 96667-7247)
TAK-3001 Pfc William B. Baugh; No home port assigned. (SF 96667-7250)
TAK-3002 Pfc James Anderson, Jr.; No home port assigned. (SF 96660-7258)

Baugh (TAK-3001)

TAK-3003 1st Lt Alex Bonnyman, Jr.; No home port assigned. (SF 96661-7260)
TAK-3004 Pvt Harry Fisher; No home port assigned. (SF 96665-7259)
TAK-3005 Sgt Matej Kocak; No home port assigned. (NY 09505-7248)
TAK 3006 Pfc Eugene A. Obregon; No home port assigned. (NY 09505-7253)
TAK-3007 Maj Stephen W. Pless; No home port assigned. (NY 09505-7209)
TAK-3008 Lt John P. Bobo; No home port assigned. (NY 09505-7255)
TAK-3009 Pfc DeWayne T. Williams; No home port assigned. (NY 09505-7210)
TAK-3010 1st Lt Baldomero Lopez; No home port assigned. (SF 96666-7223)
TAK-3011 1st Lt Jack Lummus; No home port assigned. (NY 09505-7232)
TAK-3012 Sgt William R. Button; No home port assigned. (NY 09505-7262)

Bobo (TAK-3008)

Capella (TAKR-293)

FAST LOGISTICS SHIPS (TAKR)

DISPLACEMENT: 55,350 long tons full load.
LENGTH: 946 feet.
BEAM: 105.5 feet.
SPEED: 33 knots maximum at full load.
POWER PLANT: two steam turbines, two boilers, two shafts, 120,000 shaft horsepower.
ENDURANCE: 12,000 nautical miles.
AIRCRAFT: can accommodate largest military helicopters.
COMPLEMENT: 42 civilians; 13 supercargos.
BUILDERS: 287, 289, 293: Rotterdamsche D.D. Maatshapp NV, Rotterdam; 288, 281; Rheinstahl Nordsweewerke, Emden, West Germany; 290, 292, 294: A.G. Weser, Bremen, West Germany.
CONVERSIONS: 287, 288, 292: National Steel and Shipbuilding; 289, 293: Pennsylvania Shipbuilding; 290, 291, 294; Avondale Shipyards.

BRIEFING: Originally built as containerships for Sea-Land Services, these eight high-speed ships subsequently were laid up as being uneconomical to operate. They ultimately were acquired by the Department of Defense in the 1981-82 sealift-enhancement program and modified to provide roll-on, roll-off, additional lift, and helicopter handling and storage facilities. The first of the eight conversions was delivered in June 1984, the last in May 1986. Together the ships can lift a full Army mechanized division. They have dramatically demonstrated their capabilities in major exercises involving overseas deployment. They will be manned and maintained in east- and Gulf-coast ports and kept in a reduced operating status but capable of being activated and ready to proceed to a loading berth in 96 hours.

TAKR-287 Algol; No home port assigned. (NY 09564-4081)
TAKR-288 Bellatrix; No home port assigned. (NY 09565-4078)
TAKR-289 Denobola; No home port assigned. (NY 09567-4019)
TAKR-290 Pollux; No home port assigned. (NY 09582-4062)
TAKR-291 Altair; No home port assigned. (NY 09564-4024)
TAKR-292 Regulus; No home port assigned. (NY 09586-4010)
TAKR-293 Capella; No home port assigned. (NY 09565-4079)
TAKR-294 Antares; No home port assigned. (NY 09564-4080)

PREPOSITIONED (PREPO) SHIPS (TAK, TAOT)

BRIEFING: In recognition of the acute shortage of sealift with which to move forces and equipment to the Indian Ocean area at the time of the Iranian hostage crisis and the invasion of Afghanistan, the Carter administration took action to preposition a small sealift force at Diego Garcia. That force now consists of nine ships in addition to MPS Squadron 2. Two ships also are stationed in the Philippines, and one provides extensive service in the Mediterranean area. One-third of this force is underway at all times, and all ships get underway every three months to take part in convoy operations.

LASH

TAK-2046 American Veteran; No home port assigned. (SF 96660-7240)
TAK-1015 Green Island; No home port assigned. (SF 96666-7218)
TAK-2049 Green Valley; No home port assigned. (SF 96666-7248)
TAK-2064 Green Harbour; No home port assigned. (SF 96666-7223)

FREIGHTERS

TAK-1010 American Trojan; No home port assigned. (SF 96660-7206)
TAK-2043 Letitia Lykes; No home port assigned. (SF 96671-7221)
TAK-2040 Elizabeth Lykes; No home port assigned. (NY 09577-7216) (Mediterranean Operations)

TANKERS

TAOT-1203 Overseas-Alice; No home port assigned. (SF 96674-7242) (in Philippines)
TAOT-1204 Overseas Valdez; No home port assigned. (SF 96674-7229)
TAOT-1205 Overseas-Vivian; No home port assigned. (SF 96674-7230) (in Philippines)
TAOT-1208 Falcon Leader; No home port assigned. (SF 06665-7217)

FLOAT ON/FLOAT OFF

TAK-2062 American Cormorant; No home port assigned. (SF 96660-7207)

American Veteran (TAK-2046)

ATLANTIC RESEARCH AND THE NAVY

. . . partners since 1949
on programs that include:

STANDARD MISSILE
TOMAHAWK
TRIDENT
AAAM

Drawing from a broad
technological base to meet
the Navy's needs.
Atlantic Research. Always there
with the right mix of technology,
facilities, and people to provide
quality solid rocket motors.
On time.
And within budget.

Atlantic Research Corporation
5945 Wellington Road
Gainesville, VA 22065

Photo: Launch of a Tomahawk cruise missile.

SPECIAL MISSION SUPPORT SHIPS

Lynch (TAGOR-7)

OCEANOGRAPHIC SHIPS

Silas Bent Class

DISPLACEMENT: 2,620 tons full load.
LENGTH: 287 feet.
BEAM: 48 feet.
SPEED: 14.5 knots, cruising.
RANGE: 7,000 nautical miles at cruising speed.
POWER PLANT: Diesel electric, one shaft, 3,600 shaft horsepower.
CREW: 47 civilians, 28 scientific personnel.
BUILDER: T-AGS 26, American Shipbuilding, Lorain, Ohio; 27, Christy Corporation, Sturgeon Bay, Wis.; 33-34, Defoe Shipbuilding, Bay City, Mich.

Conrad Class

DISPLACEMENT: 1,300 tons full load.
LENGTH: 208+ feet.
BEAM: 39 feet.
SPEED: 12 knots, cruising.
RANGE: T-AGOR 7, 12,000 nautical miles, 12-13, 9,000 nautical miles.
POWER PLANT: Diesel electric, one shaft, 1,200 shaft horsepower.
CREW: 26 civilian, 15 scientific personnel.
BUILDER: 7, Marietta Manufacturing, Point Pleasant, W. Va.; 12-13, Northwest Marine Iron Works, Portland, Ore.

Chauvenet Class

DISPLACEMENT: 4,000 tons full load.
LENGTH: 393 feet.
BEAM: 54 feet.
SPEED: 13 knots, cruising.
RANGE: 12,000 miles at cruising speed.
POWER PLANT: Geared diesel, one shaft, 3,600 shaft horsepower.
CREW: 69 civilian, 67 scientific personnel, 22 Coastal Survey Team personnel, 19 helicopter detachment.
BUILDER: Upper Clyde Shipbuilders, Glasgow, Scotland.

Bowditch Class

DISPLACEMENT: 13,050 tons full load.
LENGTH: 455 feet.
BEAM: 62 feet.
SPEED: 16.5 knots, cruising.
RANGE: 30,000 nautical miles at 14 knots.
POWER PLANT: Steam turbine, one shaft, 8,500 shaft horsepower.
CREW: 60 civilians, 38 scientific personnel.
BUILDER: Oregon Shipbuilding, Portland.

H.H. Hess

DISPLACEMENT: 17,874 tons full load.
LENGTH: 564 feet.
BEAM: 76 feet.
SPEED: 20 knots.
POWER PLANT: Steam turbine, two boilers, one shaft, 19,250 shaft horsepower.
CREW: 69 civilians, 14 scientific personnel, 27 Navy technicians.
BUILDER: National Steel and Shipbuilding.

BRIEFING: Ships of the Conrad class were the first ships built for the purpose of Naval Oceanography. Because they were completed over a seven-year period, and were subject to changes before and during construction, they vary in detail, with different bridge, side structure, mast, and laboratory arrangements. Three of the nine ships in the class were transferred to foreign governments, and three others are operated by U.S. academic institutions. Of the nine AGSs, *Bowditch* and *Dutton* are by far the oldest, having originally been Victory-type ships built in 1945. They were converted to deep ocean survey ships in 1958. They are scheduled to be replaced by two new construction AGSs, *Maury* and *Tanner,* which will be completed in mid-1988. The four Silas Bent-class ships were designed specifically for oceanographic survey operations. They were completed between 1965-1971. *Chauvenet* and *Harkness* are the largest coastal survey ships to be built specifically for that role. *H.H. Hess* is a converted merchant ship which was completed in 1964 and converted for deep ocean survey operations during 1975-1977. The Navy's overall oceanography program has continued to receive greatly increased emphasis from the current administration, as exemplified by the inclusion of an oceanographic research ship (AGOR-23) and two coastal hydrographic survey ships (TAGS-51/52) in the FY 1987 budget. Construction/conversion contracts for these ships are to be awarded early in 1988. Seven other oceanographic ships are currently included in the FY 1988-1992 shipbuilding program.

Silas Bent Class

TAGS-26 Silas Bent; No home port assigned. (SF 96661-4005)
TAGS-27 Kane; No home port assigned. (NY 09576-4021)
TAGS-33 Wilkes; No home port assigned. (NY 09591-4073)
TAGS-34 Wyman; No home port assigned. (NY 09594-4074)

Conrad Class

Tagor 7 Lynch; No home port assigned. (NY 09677-4025)
Tagor 12 De Steiguer; No home port assigned. (SF 96663-4012)
Tagor 13 Bartlett; No home port assigned. (NY 09565-4004)

Chauvenet Class

TAGS-29 Chauvenet; No home port assigned. (SF 96662-4009)

TAGS-32 Harkness; No home port assigned. (NY 09573-4015)

Bowditch Class

TAGS-21 Bowditch; No home port assigned. (NY 09565-4006)

TAGS-22 Dutton; No home port assigned. (NY 09567-4013)

TAGS-38 H.H. Hess; No home port assigned. (NY 09573-4018)

CABLE REPAIR SHIPS (TARC)

Neptune Class

DISPLACEMENT: 7,400 tons full load.
LENGTH: 369 feet.
BEAM: 47 feet.
SPEED: 14 knots.
POWER PLANT: Turbo-electric, two boilers, two shafts, 4,000 shaft horsepower.
CREW: 71 civilian, 6 Navy, 25 technicians.
BUILDER: Pusey and Jones, Wilmington, Delaware.

Zeus

DISPLACEMENT: 14,225 tons full load.
LENGTH: 511.5 feet.
BEAM: 73 feet.
SPEED: 15 knots.
POWER PLANT: diesel-electric, two shafts, 10,200 brake horsepower.
CREW: 88 civilian, 6 Navy, 30 technicians.
BUILDER: National Steel and Shipbuilding.

BRIEFING: The two ships of the Neptune class were built as Army cable ships; they were completed in 1946, laid up until the early 1950s, and then transferred to the Navy. They were transferred to the Military Sealift Command in 1973 and extensively modernized 1979-1982. Until their re-engining during this period, they were the last ships in the Navy with reciprocating engines. *Zeus* was the first cable ship built specifically for the Navy. She can lay up to 1,000 miles of cable in depths up to 9,000 feet. All three ARCs support the Navy's SOSUS system.

TARC-2 Neptune; No home port assigned. (SF 96673-4040)

TARC-6 Albert J. Myer; No home port assigned. (SF 96672-4034)

TARC-7 Zeus; No home port assigned. (SF 96687-4076)

UNDERSEA SURVEILLANCE SHIP (TAGOR)

Mizar

DISPLACEMENT: 4,942 tons full load.
LENGTH: 262 feet.
BEAM: 51.5 feet.
SPEED: 12 knots.
POWER PLANT: Diesel-electric, two shafts, 3,200 brake horsepower.
CREW: 46 civilians, 15 technicians, 5 Navy.
BUILDER: Avondale Shipyards.

BRIEFING: *Mizar* and a sister ship originally were built to carry cargo for Army projects in the Arctic. In 1964-1965 she received an extensive conversion to an AGOR. She was a key participant in the search for the sunken submarine *Thresher* (SSN-593) in 1964 and later helped to locate the sunken *Scorpion* (SSN-589) in the Atlantic and the Soviet Golf-class diesel submarine in the mid-Pacific. She also participated in the search for the hydrogen bomb lost at sea off Palomares, Spain, in 1966. She is operated by the Military Sealift Command for the Navy's Space and Naval Warfare Systems Command.

TAGOR-13 Mizar; No home port assigned. (SF 96672-4032)

NAVIGATION TEST SUPPORT SHIP (TAG)

Vanguard

This ship, more than 40 years old, served initially as a Navy oiler, and since has been converted twice, first to a missile-range instrumentation ship and then to a navigation research ship. She is operated by the Military Sealift Command for the Navy's Strategic System Project Office.

TAG-194 Vanguard; No home port assigned. (MI 34093-4072)

Zeus (TARC-7)

COMMON USER TRANSPORTATION

DRY CARGO SHIPS

BRIEFING: These ships, most of which are under long-term charter to the Military Sealift Command, provide point-to-point service to MSC customers all over the world. Several have been in MSC services for many years. When replaced, they could become part of the Ready Reserve Force.

ROLL ON/ROLL OFF

American Eagle; No home port assigned. (NY 09505-7201)
TAKR-10 Mercury; No home port assigned. (SF 96672-4028)

FREIGHTERS

Green Wave; No home port assigned. (NY 09505-7252)
Louise Lykes; No home port assigned. (SF 96605-7243)
Santa Adela; No home port assigned. (SF 96605-7251)
Santa Juana; No home port assigned. (SF 96605-7241)
Dawn; No home port assigned. (SF 96605-7214)

COMBINATION

Rover; No home port assigned. (NY 09505-7219)

TANKERS (TAOT)

BRIEFING: Augmenting and supporting fleet oilers in supplying fleet units and facilities with petroleum products are a number of classes of tankers. The most modern of these are the five ships of the T-5 class, the last two of which were delivered in 1986. The modified Falcon class of two and the nine-ship Sealift class were built specifically for the Military Sealift Command.

T-5 Class

DISPLACEMENT: 39,000 tons full load.
LENGTH: 615 feet.
BEAM: 90 feet.
SPEED: 16 knots.
POWER PLANT: one slow-speed diesel engine, one shaft, 15,300 brake horsepower.
CARGO CAPACITY: 238,400 barrels.
COMPLEMENT: 23.
BUILDER: TAOT 121-125, American Shipbuilding Co., Tampa.

Modified Falcon Class

DISPLACEMENT: 36,522 tons full load.
LENGTH: 666 feet.
BEAM: 84 feet.
SPEED: 16 knots.
POWER PLANT: diesel engines, one shaft, 14,000 brake horsepower.
AIRCRAFT: none.
CARGO CAPACITY: 224,000 barrels.
COMPLEMENT: 28.
BUILDER: Bath Iron Works.

Sealift Class

DISPLACEMENT: 34,100 tons full load.
LENGTH: 587 feet.
BEAM: 84 feet.
SPEED: 16 knots.
POWER PLANT: two turbo-charged diesels, one shaft, 19,200 brake horsepower.
AIRCRAFT: none.
CARGO CAPACITY: 225, 154 barrels.
COMPLEMENT: 32.
BUILDERS: TAOT 168-171, Todd Shipyards; 172-176, Bath Iron Works.

Bravado; No home port assigned. (SF 96605-7256)
Falcon Champion; No home port assigned. (NY 09505-7239)
TAOT-168 Sealift Pacific; New York, NY (NY 09587-4061)
TAOT-169 Sealift Arabian Sea; Wilmington, DE (NY 09587-4054)
TAOT-170 Sealift China Sea; Wilmington, DE (09587-4058)
TAOT-171 Sealift Indian Ocean; Wilmington, DE (09587-4056)
TAOT-172 Sealift Atlantic; Wilmington, DE (NY 09587-4056)
TAOT-173 Sealift Mediterranean; Wilmington, DE (NY 09587-4060)
TAOT-174 Sealift Caribbean; Wilmington, DE (NY 09587-4057)
TAOT-175 Sealift Arctic; Wilmington, DE (NY 09587-4055)
TAOT-176 Sealift Antarctic; Wilmington, DE (NY 09587-4053)
Susan Hanna/Barge 4882; No home port assigned.
TUG Seneca/Barge 255; No home port assigned. (SF 96605-7250)
TAOT-1121 Gus M. Darnell; Philadelphia, PA (NY 09505-7261)
TAOT-1122 Paul Buck; Philadelphia, PA (NY 09505-7211)
TAOT-1123 Samuel L. Cobb; Philadelphia, PA (NY 09505-7226)
TAOT-1124 Richard G. Mathieson; Philadelphia, PA (NY 09505-7227)
TAOT-1125 Lawrence H. Gianella; Philadelphia, PA (09505-7212)

Mercury (TAKR-10)

READY RESERVE FORCE

BRIEFING: Over the years, this force was permitted to decline to fewer than 25 ships. However, increased emphasis on sealift has resulted in decisions to increase it markedly. Its planned ultimate size had climbed each year for the past several years; the current goal is 120 ships by FY 1992. The Ready Reserve Forces ultimately will consist principally of dry cargo ships, but also will include tankers, auxiliary crane ships, containerships, roll on/roll off (RO/RO) ships, and aviation support ships. Most RRF ships will be maintained at the three National Defense Reserve Fleet sites, James River, VA, Beaumont, TX, and Suisun Bay, CA, in 10- and 20-day readiness status. However, more than 30 ships, including the TACS and certain general cargo ships, will be maintained in a five-day readiness status near load-out ports. Each RRF ship is designated to be crewed and operated by a particular shipping firm. Periodically ships are broken out to participate in readiness exercises or to carry out special missions. The Navy requested $43.4 million in FY 1988 and $35.4 million in FY 1989 in continued support for the program.

Keystone State (TACS-1)

AUXILIARY CRANE SHIPS (TACS)

DISPLACEMENT: 25,660 long tons full load.
LENGTH: 668.5 feet.
BEAM: 76 feet.
SPEED: 20 knots.
POWER PLANT: Geared steam turbine, one shaft, 19,250 shaft horsepower.
AIRCRAFT: none.
COMPLEMENT: 65 civilians (including crane operators).
CONVERTING YARDS: 1-2: DeFoe Shipbuilding Company, Bay City, Mich. 3: Dillingham Ship Repair, Portland, Ore. 4-6: NORSHIPCO, Norfolk, Va.

BRIEFING: These ships incorporate a unique capability stemming from the need to be able to offload containers and other heavy equipment from non-self-sustaining containerships in areas where port facilities range from meager to none. Each will have six cranes arranged in three pairs, all on the starboard side. Each crane can lift a 20-foot or a 40-foot container, each pair can lift an M-60 battle tank, and four working together can lift a 90-ton causeway. The cranes can handle loads in 3-5 foot seas. Five ships have been converted, a sixth joins the Ready Reserve Force early this year, two others are being converted, and funds for converting four more are being sought in the FY 1988-1989 budget. These ships will be maintained in a high state of readiness, but in a reduced operating status in the Ready Reserve Force.

AVIATION LOGISTICS SUPPORT SHIPS (TAVB)

DISPLACEMENT: 23,800 long tons full load.
LENGTH: 602 feet.
BEAM: 90 feet.
POWER PLANT: two boilers, geared steam turbine, one shaft, 30,000 shaft horsepower.
SPEED: 23 knots at 80 percent power.
AIRCRAFT: none.
COMPLEMENT: 41 civilians + 300 Marines (when fully manned).
CONVERTING YARD: Todd-Galveston.

BRIEFING: These converted ships provide the capability to load the vans and equipment of a Marine Corps aviation intermediate maintenance activity and transport them to the desired theater of operation. They have both a roll-on/roll-off and self-sustaining containership configuration which will permit them to offload both alongside and offshore. After the aviation equipment is offloaded, they can revert to a standard sealift role to carry 600 containers if required. The only two ships of this type completed conversion in 1987 and are being maintained in a reduced operating status in the Ready Reserve Force.

HOSPITAL SHIPS (TAH)

DISPLACEMENT: 69,360 long tons full load.
LENGTH: 894 feet.
BEAM: 106 feet.
SPEED: 17.5 knots.
POWER PLANT: Geared steam turbine, two boilers, one shaft, 24,500 shaft horsepower.
ENDURANCE: 13,420 nautical miles.
CAPACITY: 1,000 beds, 12 operating rooms.
COMPLEMENT: 1,207 (including 73 civilian crew, 387 Navy support and communications personnel, and 820 Naval medical personnel.
CONVERSION: National Steel and Shipbuilding Company.

BRIEFING: When the conversion of the first of these two San Clemente-class tankers was completed in the fall of 1986, the Navy had a hospital ship in its inventory for the first time in more than a decade. She is the *Mercy* (TAH-19). The last hospital ship to serve fleet personnel had been the *Sanctuary* (AH-17), commissioned in 1946, subsequently mothballed, then recalled from the Reserve Fleet for duty during the Vietnam War, and once again mothballed. Her overall poor condition ruled out modernization. The second conversion, completed late last year, became the *Comfort* (TAH-20), which will be based on the east coast. *Mercy* will be based on the west coast. Both ships will have skeleton crews and medical staffs aboard. They will be able to get underway in five days from notification of need. *Mercy* departed in February, even before she had completed her final contract trials, for the Philippines, where she provided medical care to civilians throughout many areas of the islands. She returned to the United States in July.

TAH-19 Mercy; Oakland, CA (SF 96672-4090)
TAH-20 Comfort; Baltimore, MD (NY—number not yet assigned)

Mercy (TAH-19)

(Ships in the Ready Reserve Force often are activated for special missions, overhaul and repair work, training, and participation in exercises. During those periods they would operate from areas other than the sites where they normally are maintained. However, in the listing that follows, RRF ships are placed in the areas to which they are assigned when inactive.)

EAST REGION

FREIGHTERS

TAK-1001 Admiral Wm. M. Callaghan
TAK-1809 American Victory
TAK-285 Southern Cross; No home port assigned.
TAK-5005 Adventurer; No home port assigned.
TAK-5006 Aide; No home port assigned.
TAK-5007 Ambassador; No home port assigned.
TAK-5008 Banner; No home port assigned.
TAK-5009 Cape Ann; No home port assigned.
TAK-5010 Cape Alexander; No home port assigned.
TAK-5011 Cape Archway; No home port assigned.
TAK-5012 Cape Alava; No home port assigned.
TAK-5013 Cape Avinof; No home port assigned.
TAK-5015 Agent; No home port assigned.
TAK-5016 Lake; No home port assigned.
TAK-5017 Pride; No home port assigned.
TAK-5018 Scan; No home port assigned.
TAK-5019 Courier; No home port assigned.
TAK-5030 Santa Barbara; No home port assigned.
TAK-5031 Santa Clara; No home port assigned.
TAK-5032 Santa Cruz; No home port assigned.
TAK-5033 Santa Elena; No home port assigned.
TAK-5034 Santa Isabel; No home port assigned.
TAK-5035 Santa Lucia; No home port assigned.
TAK-5037 Cape Canso; No home port assigned.
TAK-5040 Cape Canaveral; No home port assigned.
TAK-5042 Cape Carthage; No home port assigned.
TAK-5043 Cape Catoche; No home port assigned.
TAKR-5052 Cape Douglas; No home port assigned.
TAKR-5053 Cape Domingo; No home port assigned.
TAKR-5054 Cape Decision; No home port assigned.
TAKR-5055 Cape Diamond; No home port assigned.
TAKR-5066 Cape Hudson; No home port assigned.
TAKR-5067 Cape Henry; No home port assigned.
TACS-1 Keystone State; No home port assigned.
TAP-1000 Patriot State; No home port assigned.

GULF REGION

SEATRAIN SHIPS

TAK-5020 Washington; No home port assigned.
TAK-5021 Maine; No home port assigned.

TANKERS

TAOT-165 American Explorer; No home port assigned.
TAOT-181 Potomac; No home port assigned.

FREIGHTERS

TAK-2016 Pioneer Commander; No home port assigned.
TAK-2018 Pioneer Contractor; No home port assigned.
TAK-2019 Pioneer Crusader; No home port assigned.
TAK-2035 Gulf Shipper; No home port assigned.
TAK-2036 Gulf Trader; No home port assigned.
TAK-5000 Hattiesburg Victory; No home port assigned.
TAK-5022 Santa Ana; No home port assigned.
TAK-5026 Del Viento; No home port assigned.
TAK-5036 Cape Chalmers; No home port assigned.
TAK-5038 Cape Charles; No home port assigned.
TAK-5039 Cape Clear; No home port assigned.
TAK-5041 Cape Cod; No home port assigned.
TAK-5044 Gulf Banker; No home port assigned.

TAK-5045 Gulf Farmer; No home port assigned.
TAK-5046 Gulf Merchant; No home port assigned.
TAK-5049 Del Monte; No home port assigned.
TAK-5050 Del Valle; No home port assigned.
TAKR-5063 Cape May; No home port assigned.
TAKR-5064 Cape Mendocino; No home port assigned.
TAKR-5065 Cape Mohican; No home port assigned.
TAKR-5071 Cape Florida; No home port assigned.
TAKR-5072 Cape Fear; No home port assigned.
TAKR-5073 Cape Farewell; No home port assigned.
TAKR-5074 Cape Catawba; No home port assigned.
TAKR-5075 American Osprey

WEST REGION

TANKERS

TAOT-151 Shoshone; No home port assigned.

GASOLINE TANKERS

TAOG-78 Nodaway; No home port assigned.
TAOG-81 Alatna; No home port assigned.
TAOG-82 Chattahoochee; No home port assigned.

FREIGHTERS

TAKR-7 Comet; No home port assigned.
TAKR-9 Meteor; No home port assigned.
TAKR-11 Jupiter; No home port assigned.
TAK-184 Northern Light; No home port assigned.
TAK-5029 California; No home port assigned.
TAKR-5051 Cape Ducato; No home port assigned.
TAK-5056 Cape Breton; No home port assigned.
TAK-5057 Cape Bover; No home port assigned.
TAK-5058 Cape Borda; No home port assigned.
TAK-5059 Cape Bon; No home port assigned.
TAK-5060 Cape Blanco; No home port assigned.
TAK-5061 Austral Lightning; No home port assigned.
TAKR-5062 Cape Isabel; No home port assigned.
TAKR-5068 Cape Horn; No home port assigned.
TAKR-5069 Cape Edmont; No home port assigned.
TACS-2 Gem State; No home port assigned.
TACS-3 Grand Canyon State; No home port assigned.

The following ships are being readied for service in the Ready Reserve Force. Many will replace older ships already in the RRF; others such as seven merchantmen being converted to crane ships (TACS) will increase the size of the force. Almost all of the ships listed below will be renamed once they become a part of the RRF.

Ship Name	Type	RRF Entry	
American Altair	AK	9/89	(to become TACS-9)
American Banker	AK	2/89	(to become TACS-8)
American Draco	AK	11/89	(to become TACS-10)
Benjamin Harrison	LASH	To be decided.	
Buyer	AK	12/87	(replaces Santa Barbara)
Cornhusker State	TACS-6	3/88	(formerly Staghound)
Edward Rutledge	LASH	To be decided.	
Falcon Lady	AO	12/87	
Federal Lakes	AKR	To be decided.	
Federal Seaways	AKR	To be decided.	
Flickertail State	TACS-5	1/88	(formerly Lightning)
Gopher State	TACS-4	12/87	(formerly Export Leader)
Mormacsaga	AK	1/88	(replaces Santa Isabel)
Mormacsea	AK	1/88	(replaces Santa Clara)
President Adams	AK	12/87	
President Jackson	AK	12/87	
President Taylor	AK	11/88	
President Truman	AK	11/88	(to become TACS-7)
Rapid	AKR	12/87	
Spirit of Liberty	AO	11/87	
Tyson Lykes	AKR	8/87	

3 SECONDS

Backed by 3 Decades of Experience

When the catapult says, "Go!," Harris testing says, "You're ready." In just a few seconds, 30 tons of aircraft clear the deck—all systems checked for mission-readiness by our equipment.

For over 30 years, Harris has supplied automatic test systems to the U.S. Armed Forces. For the Navy, our computerized ATE systems have set the standards for cost-efficiency and reliability.

Now, our new generation of advanced systems has come aboard. With the ATS (V) 1, the ATS (V) 2, and the HTS, Harris will keep pace as the Navy upgrades its platforms. We'll support the complex testing needs of the F/A-18, F-14 A/D, S-3B, SH-60 B/F, A-6F, and V-22. As they join the fleet . . . and well beyond the year 2000.

At Harris, we test your future with our proven past.

Government Support Systems Division
6801 Jericho Turnpike
Syosset, NY 11791
1-800-4-HARRIS Ext. 2510

⊞ HARRIS

©Harris Corporation 1986

COMMENT: Many other kinds of ships and craft contribute immensely to the overall capability of the fleet. Prominent among them are submersibles, which are operated in support of search, rescue, research, and deep-ocean recovery activities. Two are nuclear powered. Two deep-submergence rescue vessels were developed and constructed after the loss of the submarine *Thresher* in 1963 to provide a capability for rescuing survivors from submarines disabled on the ocean floor above their hull collapse depth. The research submersible *Alvin*, which has made over 1,000 dives and made headlines during the mission to photograph the sunken liner *Titanic*, is operated by the Woods Hole Oceanographic Institute for the Office of Naval Research.

Also of great importance are large and medium harbor tugs, available in relatively large numbers and vital to harbor operations. Several WWII ships and craft have been converted to support weapons testing, research, and recovery operations. Patrol craft (YP) are used extensively to train future officers at the Naval Academy and at Officer Candidate School at Newport, RI. Utility landing craft (LCU) have served as real workhorses in the amphibious forces; several new classes have been built in the last three decades. A unique craft is the LWT, a warping tug designed to handle pontoon causeways and thus to make easier the offloading of ships in areas where port facilities are lacking.

Also contributing significantly to fleet operations are floating drydocks, which supplement fixed drydock facilities at major naval installations, support fleet ballistic missile submarines at forward bases, and provide repair capabilities in forward areas. The largest of those currently active, with a capacity of 40,000 tons, is at the Naval Base at Subic Bay in the Philippines.

The Navy has experimented in recent years with a few kinds of ships and craft representative of advanced technologies. Foremost among these have been ships and craft operating on the surface-effect principle, a principle the Soviet Union has made most effective use of. At one time plans to construct a 3,000-ton SES were well along, but skyrocketing costs forced cancellation of that project. Later, SES technology was incorporated into a proposed new class of minesweeper hunters (MSH), but the failure of a section of the hull of that ship to withstand shock tests resulted ultimately in cancellation of that program, too. SES technology has been successfully incorporated, however, in the new Marine Corps landing craft, air cushion (LCAC). The SWATH (Small Waterplane Area Twin Hull) principle is considered by many in the Navy to offer high potential for fleet operations and is being incorporated into surveillance ships (TAGOS); the first of these currently is under construction. The Navy also has sought bids on a new class of fast patrol boats with which to enable it to better counter threats of terrorism at sea.

Range Sentinel (TAGM-22)

Wilkes (TAGS-33)

Swath (artist concept)

Point Loma (AGDS-2)

ALLISON MARINE ENGINES HAVE BEEN PROVEN ONLY IN THE AREAS CAREFULLY MARKED IN BLUE.

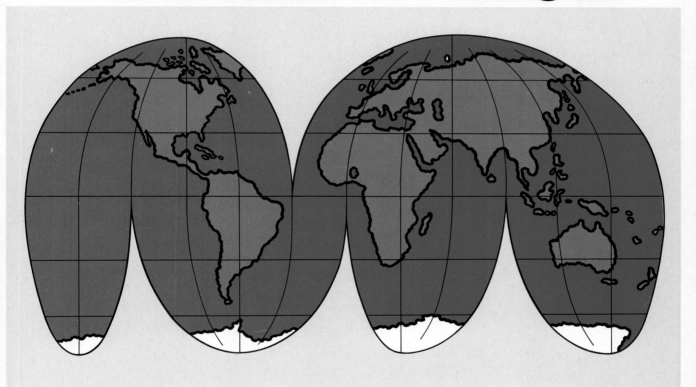

Since 1962, Allison engines have been called on for maritime propulsion and to create on-board electrical power in every corner of the globe.

The reason for all this is simple. We build reliability into each engine we make. Reliability that's been proven in harsh environments in the air, on land, and on the deepest, most hostile saltwater seas.

Allison engines have over 3,000,000 hours of cumulative maritime operating experience and over 100,000,000 hours of aviation and industrial experience. Our engines also have high maintainability plus worldwide support from our extensive parts and service network.

In addition, Allison is General Motors. So, the expertise of the world's largest engineering and manufacturing company is behind each engine.

Write to Allison Gas Turbine, General Motors Corporation, P.O. Box 420, U-6, Indianapolis, Indiana 46206 USA. Telex 6876054.

Allison
▲ ◼ GM

Hornet

Tomcat

AIRCRAFT/NAVY

F/A-18 HORNET

WING SPAN: 37.5 feet.
LENGTH: 56 feet.
HEIGHT: 15 feet, 3½ inches.
WEIGHT: fighter mission takeoff, 36,710 pounds; attack mission takeoff, 49,224 pounds.
SPEED: more than 1,360 mph.
CEILING: approximately 50,000 feet.
RANGE: fighter mission, 400 nautical-mile radius; attack mission, 575 nautical-mile radius; ferry range, more than 2,000 nautical miles.
POWER PLANT: two General Electric F404-GE-400 low-bypass turbofan engines; 16,000 pounds static thrust.
CREW: one.
CONTRACTOR: prime, McDonnell Douglas; airframe, Northrop.

BRIEFING: The Hornet, a multi-mission aircraft, was designed and developed as both a fighter and an attack aircraft which ultimately will replace both the A-7 and the F-4 in both the Navy and the Marine Corps. It can carry up to 17,000 pounds of armament, including Sparrow III and Sidewinder missiles, on nine stations. Its radar can track multiple targets and display up to eight. Almost all conventional instrumentation has disappeared from the cockpit, and all essential information is displayed at eye level so the pilot can be kept fully informed without taking his eyes off the target. Ease of maintenance also has been given careful consideration, and flight data after a year of deployment indicate that the F/A-18 requires less than half the maintenance hours of the aircraft it will replace while flying three times the number of hours those aircraft will before corrective maintenance is required. As a consequence, its squadrons can be manned with far fewer personnel than F-4 and A-7 squadrons. Its operations thus far have resulted in a 2% attrition rate, half the original estimate. The Navy now estimates that only 1,157 of these aircraft will be required, rather than the 1,366 projected earlier, because of a change in requirements reducing the total number of F/A-18 wings and the number of aircraft per squadron. A reconnaissance version of the aircraft is on schedule in both development and aircraft incorporation, and the first such aircraft is to be delivered in 1990. The first major upgrade of the F/A-18, with an October 1987 delivery, provided the Hornet with new weapons provisions, better survivability enhancements, and improved maintenance monitoring hardware. Continued improvements will give it a night-attack, under-the-weather capability by 1990. The proposed annual procurement rate has been sharply reduced; it was cut from 120 to 84 aircraft in FY 1987, and only 84 were sought in FY 1988. It is to be reduced to 72 in each of the four years following. The aircraft is being acquired by the air forces of Australia, Canada, and Spain.

F-14 TOMCAT

WING SPAN: 64 feet unswept; 38 feet swept.
LENGTH: 62.7 feet.
HEIGHT: 16 feet.
WEIGHT: Empty, 40,104 pounds; maximum take-off, 74,348 pounds.
SPEED: maximum, 1,544 mph; cruise, 576 mph.
CEILING: more than 56,000 feet.
RANGE: combat, 500 nautical miles; ferry range, 2,000 nautical miles.
POWER PLANT: two Pratt and Whitney TF-30-P412A turbofan engines with afterburners; 20,900 pounds static thrust; on remainder of F-14A+ aircraft and on F-14Ds, F-110-GE-400 augmented turbofan engines with afterburner and 27,000-29,000 pounds static thrust.
CREW: two.
CONTRACTOR: Grumman Aerospace.

BRIEFING: In 1969 Grumman was selected as the winner of a design competition to build the F-14 as a replacement for the F-4; after a somewhat stormy beginning it has emerged as a versatile and capable combat aircraft. The aircraft's sophisticated radar-missile combination enables it to simultaneously track 24 targets and attack six with Phoenix missiles while continuing to scan the airspace. It can select and destroy targets up to 100 miles away. Its original TF-30 engine's performance was deemed by the Navy to be far below desired standards, and in 1984 the Navy announced that the General Electric F110 turbofan engine had been selected to equip all future F-14A aircraft and the upgraded F-14D version. As of January 1988, two F110 engines had been installed in F-14As. The F-14D, which will have markedly improved computerization, radar, communications and electronics, and weaponry, also is expected to have avionics commonality of more than 80% with other first-line aircraft such as the F/A-18 and the A-6E upgrade. The first flight of the F-14D was scheduled in January 1988; its development is on schedule, and first deliveries are to commence in March 1990. The Navy's ultimate procurement goal is 304 aircraft. The final buy of five of the improved F-14A version also will be made in FY 1988.

F-4 PHANTOM II

WING SPAN: 38 feet.
LENGTH: 63 feet.
HEIGHT: 16 feet.
WEIGHT: empty, 30,328 pounds, combat takeoff, 41,487 pounds; maximum takeoff, 61,795 pounds.
SPEED: maximum at 36,000 feet, 1,630 mph; average, approximately 575 mph.
CEILING: 56,000 feet.
RANGE: area intercept, 683 nautical miles; defensive counter-air, 429 nautical miles; interdiction, 618 nautical miles; maximum, 1,718 nautical miles.
POWER PLANT: two General Electric J79-GE-17A turbojet engines with afterburner.
CREW: two.
CONTRACTOR: McDonnell Douglas.

BRIEFING: Developed as an all-weather fleet air defense fighter for the Navy, the F-4H prototype flew for the first time in 1958. It also was adopted by the Air Force, and the basic Air Force and Navy versions became the F-4B and the F-4C, respectively. In time, many updated and specialized-mission versions were developed. The F-4 subsequently became the mainstay of many foreign air forces, including those of Great Britain, West Germany, South Korea, Spain, Greece, and Turkey. F-4 production was halted in 1979 after delivery of more than 5,000 aircraft. With the phasing out in 1985 of the F-4 fleet replacement training squadron, only two active F-4 squadrons remained in the fleet, and those also were phased out in 1986.

Phantom II

Innovation

The U.S. Navy's Fleet Ballistic Missil
More than a quarter century of
effective deterrence.

Lockheed
Giving shape to imagination.

Corsair

A-7 CORSAIR

WING SPAN: 39 feet.
LENGTH: 46 feet.
HEIGHT: 16 feet.
WEIGHT: empty, 19,111 pounds; maximum takeoff, 42,000 pounds.
SPEED: maximum at 5,000 feet, with 12 Mk82 bombs, 646 mph; after dropping bombs, 684 mph.
CEILING: 35,500 feet.
RANGE: maximum ferry range with internal fuel, 1,981 nautical miles; with internal and external fuel, 2,485 nautical miles.
POWER PLANT: one Allison TF-41-A-2 non-after-burning turbofan engine.
CONTRACTOR: Vought.

BRIEFING: After two decades of service in the fleet, and also with the Air Force, the A-7 is being replaced with the F/A-18. Originally built on the F-8U Crusader airframe in order to keep costs down, the A-7 has gone through several modifications since the A-7A first was flown in 1965. The A-7E now carries varying payloads of bombs and missiles as well as a 20mm gun pod; its maximum payload of armament is more than 15,000 pounds. Six stations are available for ordnance. More than 1,500 A-7s have been built for the Navy, Air Force, and foreign air forces. No further purchases of the A-7 are contemplated, and the Navy does not plan to try to upgrade it. The last two A-7 squadrons will complete transition to F/A-18s during FY 1992.

A-6E INTRUDER

WING SPAN: 53 feet.
LENGTH: 55 feet.
HEIGHT: 16 feet.
WEIGHT: empty, 26,746 pounds; maximum catapult takeoff, 58,600 pounds.
SPEED: maximum at sea level, 647 mph; cruise at optimum altitude, 476 mph.
CEILING: 42,400 feet.
RANGE: 2,380 nautical miles ferry range; 878 nautical miles with maximum military load.
POWER PLANT: two Pratt and Whitney J52-P-8B turbojet engines; 9,300 pounds static thrust each. (For A-6F, two F-404-GE-400D augmented turbofan engines with 18,000 pounds static thrust.)
CREW: two.
CONTRACTOR: Grumman Aerospace.

BRIEFING: The several versions of the A-6 medium-attack, all-weather, day-night, carrier-based aircraft have been a mainstay of the Navy and Marine Corps air arms for more than two decades. Constantly being improved upon over this time span, it is used for close-air-support, interdiction, and deep-strike missions. Seven versions of the basic design have been built, with the EA-6B and the A-6E still being in production. The A-6E has an advanced electronics package, and can carry external weapons loads of 18,000 pounds; it is configured for both Harm and Harpoon missiles. At one time, the A-6E production line was a target for elimination by Congress; however, the aircraft's performance in recent years, and particularly during the 1986 attacks on Libyan targets, buttressed its reputation as an outstanding attack aircraft. The wings of the A-6E, however, are being replaced because of the discovery of cracks resulting from accelerated fatigue; the new aluminum composite wings were developed and are being produced by Boeing. The Navy had sought an improved version of the A-6E, the A-6F; however, after lengthy and complicated deliberations, the House and Senate Armed Services Committees balked at funding construction of A-6Fs and instead agreed on authorizing procurement of 11 A-6Es. Congress subsequently approved, and the President signed, the defense-authorizing legislation. At one time it appeared that neither A-6Es nor A-6Fs would be authorized, and that the Navy would have to rely on A-6Es currently in its inventory and those being built under prior year funding to meet operational requirements until the Advanced Tactical Aircraft (ATA) now under development was available for fleet use. The two Appropriations Committees, however, did not fund A-6Es, but instead put $587 million into the defense budget for construction of A-6Fs, with 12 aircraft expected to be built with those dollars. They also funded continued development of the ATA.

Intruder

Prowler

EA-6B PROWLER

WING SPAN: 53 feet.
LENGTH: 60 feet.
HEIGHT: 16 feet.
WEIGHT: empty, 32,162 pounds; maximum takeoff, 65,000 pounds.
SPEED: maximum at sea level, 651 mph; cruise, 481 mph.
CEILING: 38,000 feet, with five ECM pods.
COMBAT RANGE: 2,083 nautical miles with maximum external fuel.
POWER PLANT: two Pratt and Whitney J52-P-408 turbojet engines; 11,200 pounds static thrust.
CREW: four (including three electronic warfare officers).
CONTRACTOR: Grumman Aerospace.

BRIEFING: This slightly longer version of the A-6E, the extra length having been added to accommodate electronic-warfare personnel and equipment, is the Navy's first aircraft designed and built specifically for tactical electronic warfare. Its primary missions are active and passive defense of a task force and degradation and suppression of enemy defense systems by jamming. Avionics equipment has progressed through four generations of modernization; the latest modernization makes it possible for the aircraft to jam two different frequency bands simultaneously from each of its five wing- and fuselage-mounted pods. A fifth-generation modernization involves a major upgrade of the EA-6B's computer system, navigation/instruments equipment, and radar/communications jamming capability. The upgrade allows the crew to more rapidly evaluate and prosecute a larger number of threats; each of its five wing- and fuselage-mounted pods can jam two different frequency bands simultaneously. The Navy, after having had 12 aircraft funded in FY 1987, sought six in FY 1988 and nine in FY 1989. However, Congress, apparently deeming the FY 1988 buy insufficient to meet Navy and Marine Corps requirements, doubled it to 12.

E-2C HAWKEYE

WING SPAN: 81 feet.
LENGTH: 58 feet.
HEIGHT: 18 feet.
WEIGHT: empty, 37,678 pounds; maximum take-off, 51,569 pounds.
SPEED: maximum, 374 mph; cruise, 311 mph.
CEILING: 30,800 feet.
RANGE: 200 nautical-mile radius with six hours on station; ferry range, 1,525 nautical miles.
POWER PLANT: two Allison T56-A-422 turboprop engines.
CREW: five, including personnel assigned primarily to monitor various electronic systems.
CONTRACTOR: Grumman Aerospace.

BRIEFING: This durable carrier-based early warning aircraft has been improved upon constantly since the first E-2A flew in 1961. The E-2C, which made its first flight 10 years later, is equipped with radar capable of detecting targets anywhere within a three-million-cubic-mile surveillance envelope while simultaneously monitoring maritime traffic. Each E-2C also can maintain all-weather patrols, track, automatically and simultaneously, more than 600 targets, and control more than 40 airborne intercepts. An upgrading of its electronic suite and its engine, the latter to the T56-A-427 engine, began in 1986, with these actions aimed at ensuring its airborne-early-warning advantage through the 1990s. The E-2C dramatically demonstrated its capabilities in international incidents in 1985 and 1986, in particular during the 1985 intercept of the aircraft containing the hijackers of the liner *Achille Lauro* and during the 1986 attacks on Libyan targets. It also is being used effectively in the greatly expanded U.S. campaign against drug smugglers; the Customs Service and the Coast Guard each have been provided two E-2Cs with which to augment their efforts in that campaign. At the moment, annual production remains at six aircraft.

Hawkeye

Orion

P-3C ORION

WING SPAN: 100 feet.
LENGTH: 117 feet.
HEIGHT: 34 feet.
WEIGHT: maximum take-off, 142,000 pounds.
SPEED: maximum, 473 mph; cruise, 377 mph.
CEILING: 28,300 feet.
RANGE: maximum mission radius, 2,380 nautical miles; 3 hours on
station at 1,500 feet, 1,346 nautical miles.
POWER PLANT: four Allison T56-A-14 turboprop engines, 4,900
ehp each.
CREW: 10.
CONTRACTOR: Lockheed.

BRIEFING: In an era when aircraft development often is measured
by quantum jumps, it is fascinating to find a propeller-driven aircraft, the prototype of which first flew in 1958, still playing a major
ASW role for the Navy. Since the Orion's basic airframe first was
flown, more than half a dozen different improvement programs have
been incorporated; the most recent major equipment update significantly improves its ability to detect, track, and attack quieter, new-
generation submarines. Update III modernization is being incorporated into 133 older P-3s. Several P-3s have been converted to elec-
tronic-intelligence aircraft and now are in service, with more to
come. Modifying a number of P-3A aircraft with look-down, shoot-
down radar also has increased the ability of the Customs Service to
track drug smugglers flying low-flying aircraft. Concern about the
steadily increasing submarine threat has resulted in Navy plans to
incorporate a vastly improved avionics suite (Update IV) into 80
P-3Cs and 125 new Long Range ASW Capable Aircraft (LRAACA);
procurement is expected to commence in 1991. Boeing will produce
the avionics suite. The Navy plans to procure the new aircraft at a
rate of 25 per year commencing in 1990; competition for it will be
for a commercial or P-3 derivative at a cost comparable to the existing P-3 airframe.

C-130 HERCULES

WING SPAN: 133 feet.
LENGTH: 98-106 feet.
HEIGHT: 38 feet.
WEIGHT: empty, 75,331 pounds; maximum normal takeoff,
155,000 pounds; maximum overload takeoff, 175,000 pounds.
SPEED: maximum cruise, 374 mph; economical cruise, 345 mph.
CEILING: 33,000 feet.
RANGE: with maximum payload and allowance for 30 minutes at
sea level, 2,046 nautical miles; with maximum fuel and 20,000-
pound payload, 4,460 nautical miles.
POWER PLANT: four Allison T56-A-15 turboprop engines. Eight
JATO (Jet-Assisted Takeoff) units can also be carried.
CREW: four.
CONTRACTOR: Lockheed.

BRIEFING: The Hercules probably is the most versatile tactical
transport aircraft ever built. Its uses appear almost limitless: trans-

Hercules

port, electronic surveillance, search and rescue, space-capsule recovery, helicopter refueling, landing (with skis) on snow and ice, gun
ship, and special cargo delivery. It has even landed and taken off
from a carrier deck without benefit of arresting gear or catapults.
Its capabilities are appreciated worldwide; more than 50 countries
use at least one version of it. It still is serving as a VLF strategic
communications aircraft, communicating with ballistic-missile
submarines, under the TACAMO program. However, no purchases
of it for either the Navy or the Marine Corps are foreseen in the
immediate future.

S-3A VIKING

WING SPAN: 69 feet.
LENGTH: 53 feet.
HEIGHT: 23 feet.
WEIGHT: empty, 26,650 pounds; maximum takeoff, 52,539 pounds.
SPEED: 518 mph.
CEILING: 40,000 feet.
RANGE: more than 2,300 nautical miles.
POWER PLANT: two General Electric TF34-GE-2 turbofan engines.
ARMAMENT: various combinations of torpedoes, depth charges,
missiles, rockets, and special weapons.
CREW: four.
CONTRACTOR: Lockheed.

BRIEFING: A total of 187 of these carrier-based ASW aircraft were
built for the Navy, the last being delivered in 1978. The Navy currently is modernizing 160 of them at a rate of two per month. The
resultant S-3B will incorporate much improved technology for increased radar detection range and classification, advanced acoustic
processing, and support measures, and will have a Harpoon missile
capability. Mission-capable rates for the S-3A soared from 35 percent in 1981 to 77 percent in 1985, largely because of increased
availability of spare parts. Although the current modernization program, which is to be completed in FY 1993, is aimed at enabling
the S-3B to counter the submarine threat of the 1990s, it tentatively
is scheduled to be replaced by the V-22 Osprey in FY 1998.

Viking

Better training; faster training; more cost-effective training;

that's what's needed right now to help make the most of every defense dollar. And that's exactly what the T45 Training System's set to deliver for the Navy.

Developed to train tomorrow's pilots to higher standards in fewer flying hours, T45TS combines flight simulation and computer-based academics with practical instruction in the T-45A Goshawk, a new, versatile trainer developed from the highly successful British Aerospace Hawk.

Whether flying off a runway or a carrier d no trainer demands more of its pilot to help him ach the higher standards in airmanship and weapons syst management vital for tomorrow's sophisticated con aircraft. Yet no trainer's more forgiving of mistakes n along the way.

Then add into the equation a 42% reductic fuel use, a 46% reduction in support personnel requirements, and a need for 25% fewer flying ho and you end up with two things.

An overall 50% saving in training costs; and a

They'll come ready for action, delivered express, for just 50 cents in the dollar.

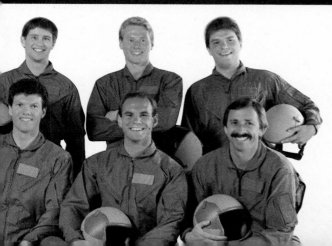

training system ideally suited for tomorrow's defense needs.

So no wonder the Navy's hooked on T45TS. It's the logical way forward into the 1990s for undergraduate jet flight training.

T45 TRAINING SYSTEM

The GE Team will save the Navy enough on CASS to pay all 12,000 Navy pilots.

For 6 years.

That's more than $3 billion—enough for pay and allowances for every Navy pilot—and what General Electric, teamed with Northrop and Honeywell, expects to save the Navy on the Consolidated Automated Support System.

Exceptional savings based on exceptional system architecture.

An architecture that replaces all electronic auto-mated test equipment with new technology that requires significantly less deck space and is far more reliable, more flexible, and is modular enough to meet all future weapons systems needs.

Compared to simply maintaining the present systems for the next 18 years, General Electric's CASS will save the Navy more than $3 billion for ATE development, operation and support.

GE Aerospace

Automated Systems Department
Burlington, MA 01803

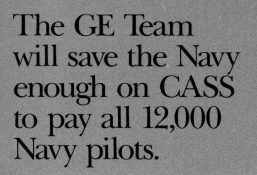

ASM-2

Greyhound

C-2A GREYHOUND

WING SPAN: 81 feet.
LENGTH: 57 feet.
HEIGHT: 16 feet.
WEIGHT: maximum take-off, 54,354 pounds.
SPEED: maximum, 352 mph; cruise, 296 mph.
CEILING: 28,800 feet.
RANGE: 1,440 nautical miles.
POWER PLANT: two Allison T56-A-8B turboprop engines; 4,050 shp. each.
CONTRACTOR: Grumman Aerospace.

BRIEFING: COD (Carrier On-board Delivery) aircraft transport personnel, key logistics items, mail, etc., between shore facilities and carrier task forces at sea. For years the C-1A was the Navy's only COD aircraft; now the Greyhound is the principal aircraft being used for that purpose. Since its basic airframe is that of the E-2C, also built by Grumman, production of the C-2A is not a problem. Nine C-2As were funded in FY 1987 and represent the last buy of these versatile aircraft for at least the next five fiscal years, barring unexpected operational losses.

C-9B SKYTRAIN II

WING SPAN: 93 feet.
LENGTH: 119 feet.
HEIGHT: 28 feet.
WEIGHT: empty, 65,283 pounds in passenger configuration, 59,706 pounds in cargo configuration; maximum takeoff, 110,000 pounds.
SPEED: maximum cruising speed, 576 mph; long-range cruising speed, 504 mph.
CEILING: 37,000 feet.
RANGE: at long-range cruising speed, 2,538 nautical miles.
POWER PLANT: two Pratt and Whitney JT8-D-9 turbofan engines.
PAYLOAD: 32,444 pounds of cargo or passengers.
CREW: two, plus cabin attendants.
CONTRACTOR: McDonnell Douglas.

BRIEFING: Although the Defense Department at one time sought to require all military airlift to come under the Military Airlift Command, and therefore to reduce the airlift capabilities of the individual services other than the Air Force almost to zero, it quickly became apparent that MAC could not possibly fulfill all individual service requirements. Among major Navy logistics requirements that could not be fulfilled was the airlifting of Naval Reservists to and from training sites. Ultimately, the Navy won approval for the acquisition of C-9 aircraft, the commercial version of which is the DC-9, to meet the airlift needs as the ancient C-118s being used for that purpose finally were being retired, the last in 1985. The Navy completed its buy of C-9Bs in FY 1985 and now has 27 in its transport

Skytrain

fleet. "Used" aircraft procured are undergoing a modernization program to allow their operational use beyond the year 2000. All are flown by Naval Reserve squadrons.

E6-A TACAMO

WING SPAN: 145 feet, 9 inches.
LENGTH: 153 feet.
HEIGHT: 42 feet, 5 inches.
WEIGHT: gross takeoff, 342,000 pounds.
CEILING: 42,000 feet; patrol altitude, 25,000-30,000 feet.
SPEED: 512 knots.
RANGE: unrefueled, 6,700 nautical miles with 16 hours on-station endurance.
POWER PLANT: CFM International F-108-CF-100 (CFM 56-24-2) turbofan engines.
CREW: Four flight crew, five mission crew.
CONTRACTOR: Boeing.

BRIEFING: A highly important but little-known Navy aircraft role is that of serving as the means of relaying VLF signals to strategic missile submarines. Currently, modified C-130 aircraft, EC-130Qs, are serving as the TACAMO (Take Charge and Move Out) platforms. The Navy plans to replace them with aircraft of the modified 707/C-137/E-3 design, two of which were funded in FY 1986. Three more were funded in FY 1987 and two in FY 1988. These aircraft will have an improved capability to communicate with Air Force AWACS aircraft and will contain the same basic equipment as the EC-130Cs, including 30,000 feet of trailing wire antenna. When replaced, the EC-130Cs will be modified for cargo and other support missions. The first E-6A production aircraft is scheduled for delivery in January 1989. No decision as to where these aircraft will be based has yet been agreed upon.

Tacamo

Osprey

V-22A OSPREY

BRIEFING: The joint-services tilt-rotor aircraft—the V-22 Osprey being developed by the Navy—took a long step toward complete development 2 May 1986 with the award of contracts for full-scale engineering development to a Bell Helicopter Textron-Boeing Vertol team and to the Allison Gas Turbine division of General Motors. The Bell-Boeing contract, a fixed-price-incentive pact for $1.714 billion to be fulfilled over a seven-year period, calls for ultimately building six prototype aircraft, with each firm assembling three prototypes. First flight of the V-22 is scheduled for June 1988, several months later than originally planned. Allison will receive $76.4 million for development of the T406 6,000-shaft horsepower turboprop engine. The Osprey, which will be the world's first production tilt-rotor aircraft, is designed to carry 24 combat-equipped troops or 10,000 pounds of cargo internally, and to attain speeds exceeding 300 mph, and altitudes close to 30,000 feet. At present, it is envisioned that at least 1,213 V-22s will be purchased by the nation's armed forces. The Marine Corps will require 552 to replace its CH-46E Sea Knight and CH-53A/D helicopters, the Army 231 to replace CH-47 helicopters, the Air Force 80 for replacement of HH-53 helicopters and C-130 aircraft used in special operations, and the Navy 50 to replace SH-3D helicopters and 300 for use on ASW aircraft. Extensive commercial utilization also is foreseen. Development of the aircraft appears to be on schedule; if development and initial-production plans are maintained, initial operational capability for the Osprey is envisioned for 1991. The entire Osprey program has received unusually close scrutiny both within the Department of Defense and the Navy and in Congress, but there now appears there is general agreement that it can live up to claims being made for it, and that the program is well managed and meeting its milestones.

BRIEFING: In June 1987, the Navy awarded a contract for $118.2 million to Westinghouse-Airship Industries, the latter a British company, for development of one airship. The contract award reflects the growing requirement for the Navy to acquire additional means of waging anti-submarine and anti-air warfare and stems from the 1983 Patrol Airship Concept Evaluation (PACE) program, which highlighted the advantages an airship would have over fixed-wing aircraft, including more time on station and greater endurance. The contract included full maintenance and support for the airship; in addition, another $50.7 million was included for the avionics suite, which will include either APS-125 or APS-139 radar. There also is an option for five additional airships. First flight of the operational development model (ODM) is scheduled for late 1990, with operational suitability trials to commence six months later and to continue for 18 months. The airship will be designed in the United Kingdom, and assembly of it will be carried out at Weeksville, NC, with logistics support to be provided there and at NAS, Lakehurst, NJ. The Naval Air Test Center at Patuxent River, MD, will be the prime ODM evaluation base. The airship will have a maximum flight speed, at stable equilibrium, of 82 knots, be able to attain an altitude of 14,000 feet, and have unrefueled endurance at 40 knots at 5,000 feet of 60.2 hours. It will be able to climb at a rate of 630 feet per minute, be propelled by two 1625-horsepower diesel cruise engines and one 1750-horsepower turboprop sprint engine, and manned by a crew of 12-15. The operational airship, which will be more than twice the size of the Goodyear airship seen on TV screens so often during major athletic events, will have a 30-day mission duration. A determination of the size of the proposed Navy airship fleet will not be made at least until the early 1990s, after the performance of the ODM has been extensively evaluated. However, it has been speculated that 40-50 airships will be acquired.

HELICOPTERS/NAVY

Super Stallion

CH/MH-53E SUPER STALLION

FUSELAGE LENGTH: 73 feet.
OVERALL LENGTH: 99 feet.
HEIGHT: 28 feet.
WEIGHT: empty, CH-53E, 33,226 pounds; MH-53E, 36,336 pounds; maximum loaded, 73,500 pounds.
SPEED: maximum at sea level, 196 mph; cruise, 173 mph.
CEILING: 18,500 feet.
RANGE: 1,120 nautical miles.
POWER PLANT: three General Electric T64-GE-416 turboshaft engines; 4,380 shp. each.
CREW: three.
CONTRACTOR: Sikorsky.

BRIEFING: The Super Stallion, the largest and most powerful helicopter yet put into production outside the Soviet Union, is designed to serve the Navy and Marine Corps in several roles. It can carry a 16-ton payload 50 nautical miles or a 10-ton payload 500 nautical miles. It can be used for vertical on-board delivery of personnel, supplies, and equipment; support of mobile construction battalions, and removal of damaged aircraft from carrier decks. It can carry 55 troops in an amphibious assault role for the Marines, as well as providing lift and movement of cargo. The first of these helicopters was delivered to the Marine Corps in 1981. The MH-53E minesweeping version, which is heavier and has a greater fuel capacity than the CH-53E, as well as sophisticated mine-countermeasures equipment, first flew in 1983. Deliveries began in FY 1986. The Navy had envisioned procuring 60 CH-53Es/MH-53Es through FY 1990; however, the minesweeping requirements in the Persian Gulf commencing in 1987 may result in more MH-53Es being procured to increase the Navy's airborne mine-countermeasures capability.

SH-60B/F SEAHAWK

FUSELAGE LENGTH: 50 feet.
OVERALL LENGTH: 64.8 feet.
HEIGHT: 17 feet.
WEIGHT: 18,000 pounds in Harpoon targeting role, 19,800 in ASW role, 21,000+ in utility role.
SPEED: maximum cruise at 5,000 feet, 155 mph.
RANGE: 50 nautical-mile radius with three hours on station; 150 nautical-mile radius with one hour on station.
POWER PLANT: two 1,690 shp T700-GE-401 turboshaft engines.
CREW: four.
CONTRACTORS: for entire LAMPS MkIII system, IBM; for helicopter, Sikorsky.

BRIEFING: The SH-60B Seahawk, better known as the LAMPS (Light Airborne Multipurpose System) Mk III helicopter, is a modified version of the Army's Black Hawk. It will be deployed on Ticonderoga-class cruisers, Burke-, Spruance-, and Kidd-class destroyers, and Perry-class frigates, and will provide all-weather capability for detection, classification, localization, and interdiction of ships and submarines. Its secondary missions include search and rescue, medical evacuation, vertical replenishment, fleet support, and communications relay. Since the first Seahawk squadron was formed in 1984, it has enjoyed remarkable success. Initial procurement of the SH-60B was set at 204 aircraft; that number was based on one aircraft per ship. Now, however, the Navy is modifying its Spruance- and Kidd-class destroyers to a dual RAST/LAMPS capability, and as a consequence the SH-60 overall procurement objective is expected to rise. The Navy also is acquiring a modified version of the Seahawk as its CV ASW helicopter as a replacement for the SH-3H Sea King. The SH-60F will operate from carriers to protect the inner zone of a carrier battle group from submarine attack. The first production model was delivered in late 1986. The Navy's procurement goal for the SH-60F is 175. SH-60Bs aboard ships operating in the Persian Gulf in 1987 were armed to make possible more effective defense against possible attacks on tankers being escorted by Navy ships and on Navy ships themselves.

Seahawk

Sea Stallion

CH-53 A/D SEA STALLION

FUSELAGE LENGTH: 67 feet.
LENGTH: 88 feet.
HEIGHT: 25 feet.
WEIGHT: gross, up to 50,000 pounds.
SPEED: 195 mph.
CEILING: 21,000 feet.
RANGE: 540 nautical miles; ferry range, 886 nautical miles.
POWER PLANT: several General Electric turboshaft engines have
    been used, with T64-GE-413 and T64-GE-415 the principal engines
    in Marine Corps and Navy versions.
CREW: three.
CONTRACTOR: Sikorsky.

BRIEFING: The prototype of this heavy assault helicopter, which
no longer is in production, first flew in 1964. It can carry 38 fully
equipped troops, 24 occupied stretchers and four corpsmen, or four
tons of freight. It also has been modified for use as a minesweeping
helicopter for the Navy, an aerospace rescue and recovery aircraft
for the Air Force, and an Alpine rescue helicopter for the Austrian
Air Force. Still another modification has given it enhanced night
and bad-weather capability for service in Europe.

Sea Knight

UH-46 SEA KNIGHT

FUSELAGE LENGTH: 45 feet.
LENGTH: 84 feet.
HEIGHT: 17 feet.
WEIGHT: gross, 23,000 pounds.
SPEED: 165 mph.
CEILING: 14,000 feet.
RANGE: 206 nautical miles; ferry range, 774 nautical miles.
POWER PLANT: two General Electric T58-GE-16 turboshaft en-
    gines.
CREW: three.
CONTRACTOR: Boeing Vertol.

BRIEFING: The Sea Knight is another example of a durable and
versatile aircraft that still is providing valuable services two decades
after it was first flown. Various versions of it have been flown by
both the Navy and the Marine Corps; the UH-46 by the Navy for
vertical replenishment, the CH-46 by the Marine Corps for troop
transport. It can carry approximately 10,000 pounds of cargo in a
sling beneath the fuselage. The CH—46E is equipped with an automatic navigation system, and has been modified with much more
powerful engines than earlier versions. Since the first flight of the
Sea Knight in 1962, it also has served the U.S. Army and the air
forces of Canada and Sweden. It has long been out of production.
There still are some 20 UH-46s in the Navy inventory, and those that
remain are programmed to remain through 1996.

SH-3H SEA KING

FUSELAGE LENGTH: 54 feet, nine inches.
OVERALL LENGTH: 73 feet.
HEIGHT: 17 feet.
WEIGHT: empty, 11,865 pounds; maximum takeoff, 21,000 pounds.
SPEED: maximum, 166 mph; cruise, 136 mph.
CEILING: 14,700 feet.
RANGE: 542 nautical miles.
POWER PLANT: two General Electric T58-GE-10 turboshaft engines.
CREW: four (including two sonar operators).
CONTRACTOR: Sikorsky.

BRIEFING: The first version of this workhorse ASW helicopter was
flown more than 20 years ago. The current model is equipped with
sonar, active and passive sonar buoys, magnetic anomaly detection
equipment, and electronic surveillance measures equipment, the latter adding an extra measure of missile-defense capability to the fleet.
A basic version of the Sea King was hurriedly converted for use by

"It was a scary experience, but the V-22 *Osprey* made it a short one."

"As I made my run on the target, I felt a big jolt — I'd been hit. Then things happened really fast ...

"Though close to the ground, I got a good 'chute. The fire was heavy, but no sooner had I hit the ground than I saw a V-22 hovering over me, lowering the hoist.

"What a beautiful sight! This was combat search and rescue at its finest, supported by the most versatile aircraft in the world — the HV-22A Osprey!"

That's no exaggeration. This Department of the Navy program is producing an aircraft that streaks forward at turboprop speeds, providing unmatched rapid-response capability. Yet, it takes off, hovers and maneuvers like a helicopter.

Credit the remarkable Bell Boeing TiltRotor Team for turning a challenging concept into a startling reality. The TiltRotor will bring speed and range you'd need in a fast combat transport. It can reach up high or race across the terrain at treetop level.

And it will rewrite mission profiles like no other aircraft in the world, ushering in a new era in combat rescue aviation.

Bell Boeing
THE TILTROTOR TEAM

Sea King

the British in the Falkland Islands operation and served as an early-warning and ASW helicopter for the Royal Navy's carrier task force. SH-60Fs began replacing SH-3Hs last year, and the Navy expects to have all of them replaced by 1999. Slightly more than 200 remained in the inventory as 1988 began.

Seasprite

SH-2F SEASPRITE

FUSELAGE LENGTH: 38 feet.
LENGTH: 53 feet.
HEIGHT: 15 feet, six inches.
WEIGHT: empty, 7,040 pounds; normal takeoff, 13,300 pounds.
SPEED: maximum, 164 mph; cruise, 150 mph.
CEILING: 22,500 feet.
RANGE: 367 nautical miles with maximum fuel.
POWER PLANT: two T58-GE-8F turboshaft engines.
CREW: three.
CONTRACTOR: Kaman.

BRIEFING: The prototype Seasprite flew for the first time in 1959. Since then, there have been many versions produced for the Navy under its LAMPS program to provide helicopters for ASW and anti-ship-missile defense operations. Almost every aspect of the helicopter and its equipment have been improved in one way or another over the years as the Navy gained more experience in its utilization. Avionics and equipment systems now installed include: surveillance radar, magnetic anomaly detectors, passive radiation detection receivers, active and passive sonobuoys, smoke markers, computer-

ized tactical navigation system, cargo hook for external loads, and a rescue hoist. Armament includes homing torpedoes; there also is a capability of carrying air-to-air missiles. In both FY 1986 and 1987, funding was included for six aircraft, but no further production is envisioned. Eight aircraft also will be modified between 1987 and 1990. The SH-2F, which operates from FF-1052, FF-1040, FFG-1, CG-25, and FFG-7 class ships, is expected to remain in service as an ASW helicopter until approximately 2010.

TH-57 SEA RANGER

FUSELAGE LENGTH: 33 feet.
OVERALL LENGTH: 42 feet.
HEIGHT: 10 feet.
WEIGHT: empty, 1,585 pounds; maximum takeoff, 3,200 pounds.
SPEED: cruise for maximum range, 117 mph; loiter for maximum endurance, 56 mph.
CEILING: 18,900 feet.
RANGE: maximum, 264 nautical miles.
POWER PLANT: one Allison T63-A-700 turboshaft engine.
CONTRACTOR: Bell Aircraft.

BRIEFING: These popular helicopters, used by the air forces and navies of several countries, also are a mainstay of the U.S. Army. They first saw action in Vietnam in 1969. They have been used by the Navy as trainers, but their procurement ended with the 36 included in the FY 1985 budget.

Sea Ranger

MISSILES/NAVY

AMRAAM

LENGTH: 11 feet, nine inches.
DIAMETER: seven inches.
WING SPAN: one foot, nine inches.
WEIGHT: 300 pounds.
SPEED: more than 760 mph.
RANGE: 39 nautical miles.
POWER PLANT: directed rocket motor.
WARHEAD: blast high explosive.
CONTRACTOR: Hughes Aircraft.

BRIEFING: Development of this advanced medium-range, air-to-air missile stems from a lengthy study of the likely air threat for the next 25-30 years, and the kind of beyond-visual-range weapon that could best meet such a threat. AMRAAM is the replacement for the venerable Sparrow missile and is to be deployed on F-14 and F/A-18 aircraft, as well as on Air Force and NATO fighters. It is smaller, faster, and lighter than the Sparrow and better able to attack at low level. The pilot will be able to aim at several targets simultaneously. Production of AMRAAM was scheduled to begin in 1984; however, development problems caused costs to soar, and Congress almost killed it in FY 1986. Subsequently, continued development, under severe restrictions imposed by Congress on expenditures, was authorized. In FY 1987 approval of limited production (180 missiles) of AMRAAM was granted. Funding for 630 more was provided in FY 1988; all these missiles, however, were for the Air Force, which is responsible for AMRAAM's development. The Navy hopes to acquire 50 in FY 1989. Raytheon has been certified as a second production source.

Harm

HARM

LENGTH: 13 feet, 8 inches.
DIAMETER: 10 inches.
WING SPAN: 3 feet, 8 inches.
WEIGHT: 807 pounds.
WARHEAD WEIGHT: 146 pounds.
SPEED: more than 760 mph.
RANGE: 22 nautical miles.
POWER PLANT: two-stage solid propellant rocket motor.
WARHEAD: laser terminal plus guidance-aided.
PRIME CONTRACTOR: Texas Instruments.

BRIEFING: Harm is one of the growing family of sophisticated missiles with which fleet aircraft are being equipped. A high-speed, anti-radiation missile, it succeeds Shrike and Arm as the primary anti-radiation, defense-suppression, air-to-surface missile. It is deployed on A-7E, F/A-18, EA-6B, and A-6E aircraft and has increased speed, greater range, improved sensitivity, and the frequency-band coverage needed to counter the current threat. Harm ws used effectively against Libyan targets in the Gulf of Sidra in 1986. Procurement of Harm dropped from 1,078 missiles in FY 1987 to 766 in FY 1988, but is scheduled to climb to 1,766 in FY 1989. Harm also is being procured by the Air Force and by West Germany.

Harpoon (Air)

HARPOON

LENGTH: surface/submarine-launched, 15 feet; air-launched, 12 feet, seven inches.
DIAMETER: missile body, 1 foot, 2 inches.
WING SPAN: 3 feet, with booster fins and wings.
WEIGHT: surface/submarine-launched, 1,450 pounds; air-launched, 1,160 pounds.
SPEED: 646 mph.
RANGE: surface/submarine-launched, 60 nautical miles; air-launched, 120 nautical miles.
POWER PLANT: turbojet and solid propellant booster for surface/submarine launch.
WARHEAD: 500 pounds, high explosive, blast penetrator.
CONTRACTOR: McDonnell Douglas.

BRIEFING: This highly reliable anti-ship missile has been in the fleet since 1977. Day-night and all-weather, it can be launched from most surface combatants, as well as from submarines and aircraft. Improvements to it will add to its range and also result in a decrease in altitude in its sea-skimming mode. The Harpoon was used effectively in attacks on Libyan targets during operations in the Gulf of Sidra in 1986. The Navy has under development a new infrared Harpoon called SLAM (Standoff Land Attack Missile), which should be ready to join the fleet in mid-1989. Total procurement of these missiles in FY 1988 will be 95 Harpoons and 25 SLAMs, the latter for continued development and testing.

Harpoon (Surface)

Understanding The Threat . . .

Applying The Technology

Phoenix

PHOENIX

LENGTH: 13 feet.
DIAMETER: 15 inches.
WING SPAN: 3 feet.
WEIGHT: 989 pounds.
SPEED: more than 3,040 mph.
RANGE: more than 104 nautical miles.
POWER PLANT: Rocketdyne Mk47, Mod. 0 solid propellant rocket.
WARHEAD: proximity fuse, high explosive; weight, 135 pounds.
CONTRACTOR: Hughes Aircraft, Raytheon.

BRIEFING: This long-range air-to-air missile is the mainstay of the weapons system of the F-14 Tomcat, the only Navy aircraft that can carry it. The initial version, the AIM-54A, was operational in the fleet for 10 years; however, it had been provided to the Iranian Air Force prior to the fall of the Shah of Iran in 1979 and was considered to have been compromised. Now out of production, it had enjoyed a success rate of 84 percent and had knocked down targets 120 miles away. It has been succeeded by the AIM-54C, an improved version which has encountered quality-control problems in its manufacture that have caused the Navy on several occasions to halt production of it. A new delivery schedule was renegotiated in early 1987 with Hughes, the initial production source, and monthly production of the missile was increased during the latter months of 1987. However, the delays in production also delayed certification of the second production source, which will be Raytheon. FY 1987 procurement was 205 missiles; the Navy hopes to more than double that to 430 in FY 1988. The FY 1988 budget also contained funds to begin competitive dual-source procurement of Phoenix. Six of these missiles can be carried by each F-14; they can be launched simultaneously against separate targets.

SIDEWINDER/SIDEARM

LENGTH: 9 feet, 6 inches.
DIAMETER: 5 inches.
WING SPAN: 2 feet, 1 inch.
WEIGHT: 165 pounds.
SPEED: 1,900 mph.
RANGE: more than 3.5 nautical miles.
POWER PLANT: Rocketdyne/Bermite single-stage, solid propellant motor.
WARHEAD: annular blast fragmentation; weight, 25 pounds.
CONTRACTORS: Raytheon and Ford Aerospace.

BRIEFING: Sidewinder is one of the oldest, least expensive, and most successful missiles in the entire U.S. weapons inventory. The prototype of this heat-seeking air-to-air missile first was fired more than 30 years ago; since then various versions of it have been produced for more than 27 nations. The latest Navy version introduced,

AIM-9M, has a significantly improved infrared countermeasure capability. However, Navy procurement of that version of Sidewinder is to end with the 288 missiles being funded in FY 1988. Procurement of the AIM-9R version is to commence in 1990. Early AIM-9C versions of Sidewinder are being converted into Sidearm missiles, short-range anti-radiation missiles that can be carried by most attack aircraft and helicopters and in particular Marine Corps AH-1 helicopters. Procurement will average slightly above 260 missiles over the FY 1987-1989 period.

Sidewinder

SPARROW

LENGTH: 12 feet.
DIAMETER: 8 inches.
WING SPAN: 3 feet, 4 inches.
WEIGHT: 510 pounds.
SPEED: more than 2,660 mph.
RANGE: more than 30 nautical miles.
POWER PLANT: Hercules Mk58, Mod. 0 solid propellant rocket.
WARHEAD: continuous rod, high explosive.
CONTRACTORS: Raytheon, General Dynamics' Pomona Division.

BRIEFING: Navy procurement of this highly successful air-to-air and surface-to-air missile ended with the 1,716 missiles funded in FY 1987. The AIM-7M version, the fifth model in the Sparrow family series, has considerably greater invulnerability to ECM, better target-tracking capability, and a new low-altitude active fuse. However, with the follow-on missile to it, AMRAAM, finally being approved for production, and faced with budget constraints, the Navy elected to convert the AIM-7M variant to RIM-7Ms as AMRAAM is delivered. The RIM-7M, with folding wings and clipped tail fins, is compatible with the NATO Sea Sparrow launcher; it also has a somewhat different rocket motor. Current improvements being made in it will be backfitted into the RIM-7M inventory. SPARROW still remains the primary weapon on aircraft of six foreign air forces and on NATO ships.

Sparrow

STANDARD

SM-1 MR, SM-2 MR

LENGTH: 14 feet, seven inches.
DIAMETER: 13.5 inches.
WINGSPAN: three feet, six inches.
WEIGHT: SM-1, 1,100 pounds; SM-2, 1,380 pounds.
SPEED: about 1,900 mph.
RANGE: SM-1, 15-20 nautical miles; SM-2, up to 90 nautical miles.
POWER PLANT: dual thrust, solid fuel rocket.
WARHEAD: proximity fuse, high explosive.
CONTRACTORS: General Dynamics' Pomona Division, Raytheon.

SM-2 ER

LENGTH: 26.2 feet.
DIAMETER: 13.5 inches.
WING SPAN: five feet, two inches.
WEIGHT: 2,980 pounds.
SPEED: more than 1,900 mph.
RANGE: approximately 65 nautical miles.
POWER PLANT: two-stage, solid-fuel rocket.
WARHEAD: proximity fuse, high explosive.
CONTRACTORS: General Dynamics' Pomona Division, Raytheon.

Standard

BRIEFING: The Standard family of missiles is one of the most reliable in the Navy's inventory. A two-model weapon which can be used against missiles, aircraft, and ships, it first came into the fleet more than a decade ago. It replaces Terrier and Tartar and now is part of the weapons suit of more than 100 U.S. Navy and 30 foreign ships. Standard is a superb example of a well-engineered weapon with excellent growth potential; it has encountered few problems during the development and production cycles of its various versions. Although more complex than the heralded Phoenix missile, it costs but 60% as much. Over the years range, speed, stability, maneuverability, fusing, accuracy, and overall performance constantly have been improved upon. SM-2 (MR), Blocks II and III, will be the primary air defense weapon for more than 100 ships, including Ticonderoga-class cruisers, Burke-class destroyers, California- and Virginia-class Tartar nuclear-powered cruisers with the New Threat Upgrade (NTU) conversion, Kidd-class destroyers with SM-2 conversion, and Perry-class frigates with SM-2 conversion. SM-2 (ER), Blocks II and III, will be the primary air defense weapon for Leahy-, Belknap-, Bainbridge-, Truxtun-, and Long Beach-class Terrier cruisers with NTU. An Aegis Extended Range version of SM-2, Block IV, is planned for deployment on future Ticonderoga-class cruisers and Burke-class destroyers. This vertically launched version will incorporate major guidance, airframe, and missile-booster improvements to permit using the full capabilities of the Aegis phased-array radar and combat system. Procurement of the various versions of Standard will rise steadily in the years immediately ahead, with almost $1.5 billion budgeted for that purpose in FY 1988-1989.

Tomahawk

TOMAHAWK

LENGTH: 18 feet, three inches: with booster, 20 feet, six inches.
DIAMETER: 20.4 inches.
WING SPAN: eight feet, nine inches.
WEIGHT: 2,650 pounds; 3,200 pounds with booster.
SPEED: about 760 mph.
RANGE: land attack, nuclear warhead, 1,500 nautical miles; land attack, conventional warhead, 700 nautical miles; anti-ship configuration, over 250 nautical miles.
POWER PLANT: Williams International F107-W-R-400 cruise turbofan; solid-fuel booster.
WARHEAD: conventional, 1,000 pounds high explosive.
CONTRACTORS: General Dynamics' Convair Division, McDonnell Douglas.

BRIEFING: Tomahawk is an all-weather, subsonic cruise missile that can be fired as a conventional anti-ship weapon or as a land-attack weapon using both nuclear and conventional warheads. All three versions—the anti-ship (T-ASM), the nuclear land-attack (T-LAM-N), and the conventional land-attack (T-LAM-C)—now are operational in the fleet. By 30 September 1987, there were 30 Tomahawk-capable surface ships, and by the end of the year 31 Tomahawk-capable SSN-688- and SSN-637-class submarines. Tomahawk's small cross section, ability to fly at low altitude, and low heat emission make it difficult to detect by infrared devices or by radar. It is scheduled for deployment in over 190 platforms, including the Navy's four battleships, Ticonderoga-class and five nuclear-powered cruisers, Burke- and Spruance-class destroyers, and Los Angeles- and Sturgeon-class submarines. Tests of both the surface-ship Tomahawk vertical launch system (VLS) and the submarine Tomahawk vertical launch system (CLS) have been successful aboard *Bunker Hill* (CG-52) and *Pittsburgh* (SSN-720), respectively; evaluation of these two launch systems continues. The Navy plans to buy more than 4,000 Tomahawks through 1992, and has been successful in bringing down costs of the missile through dual-source competition.

TRIDENT I

LENGTH: 34 feet.
DIAMETER: six feet, two inches.
WEIGHT: 70,000 pounds.
SPEED: not applicable.
RANGE: 4,000 nautical miles.
POWER PLANT: three-stage solid-fuel rocket, with inertial guidance.
WARHEADS: thermonuclear MIRV (Multiple Independently targetable Re-entry Vehicle) and MARV (Maneuverable Re-entry Vehicle) heads.
CONTRACTOR: Lockheed.

Trident

TRIDENT II

LENGTH: 44 feet.
DIAMETER: 83 inches.
WEIGHT: 126,000 pounds (approx.).
SPEED: not applicable.
RANGE: 6,000 nautical miles.
POWER PLANT: three-stage solid-propellant rocket, with inertial guidance.
WARHEADS: thermonuclear MIRV (Multiple Independently targetable Re-entry Vehicle) and MARV (Maneuverable Re-entry Vehicle) heads.
CONTRACTOR: Lockheed.

POSEIDON

LENGTH: 34 feet.
DIAMETER: Six feet, two inches.
WEIGHT: 65,000 pounds.
SPEED: not applicable.
RANGE: 2,170 nautical miles.
POWER PLANT: two-stage, solid-fuel rocket with inertial guidance.
WARHEAD: thermonuclear MIRV (Multiple Independently targetable Re-entry Vehicle).
CONTRACTOR: Lockheed.

BRIEFING: The Trident system makes possible deployment of an improved missile-carrying submarine, the Ohio class, with a much longer range strategic ballistic missile, offsetting improvements in Soviet ASW capability by vastly increasing the area in which submarines can operate and still have their missiles reach their targets. Trident I has a range almost double that of the Poseidon missile it replaces, and Trident II will have a 6,000-mile range. Trident Is will be deployed in the first eight submarines of the Ohio class and in 12 of the remaining 31 Franklin-class SSBNs remaining in the fleet. Trident IIs will be deployed on the ninth and succeeding Ohio-class ships and will be retrofitted into the first eight. Introduction of Trident II, which will weigh almost twice as much as Trident I and possess far greater warhead capability, is scheduled for 1989. Procurement commenced in FY 1987 with 21 missiles; 66 are to be acquired in FY 1988.

MAVERICK

LENGTH: eight feet, one inch.
DIAMETER: 11.8 inches.
WING SPAN: two feet, four inches.
WEIGHT: 459 pounds, 635 pounds with alternative warhead.
WARHEAD: 299 pounds high explosives.
RANGE: 12 nautical miles.
POWER PLANT: two-stage, solid-fuel rocket.
CONTRACTOR: Hughes Aircraft.

BRIEFING: There are two versions of the Maverick missiles. Laser Maverick is a short-range, air-to-surface weapon which will be used in close-air support and battlefield interdiction within amphibious objective areas and in deep support for destruction of targets outside objective areas. It is a variant of the Air Force's TV Maverick with a much larger warhead. It is planned primarily for Marine Corps use, although it is adaptable to Navy aircraft. 1099 missiles were sought in FY 1988. The second version, IIR Maverick, is an air-launched, direct-attack weapon for day or night use. It has an imaging infrared seeker and uses the same warhead as Laser Maverick. Production of IIR Maverick is scheduled to climb, with 601 missiles being sought in FY 1988. The Navy also seeks authority to produce IIR Maverick under a multiyear contract.

RAM

LENGTH: nine feet, two inches.
DIAMETER: five inches.
WING SPAN: one foot, five inches.
WEIGHT: 154 pounds.
SPEED: Supersonic.
RANGE: four-plus nautical miles.
POWER PLANT: solid propellant rocket.
WARHEAD: 25 pounds, conventional.
CONTRACTOR: General Dynamics, Pomona.

BRIEFING: The Rolling Airframe Missile (RAM) is a joint development and production program with West Germany of a high-fire-power self-defense system against anti-ship missiles. It uses the infra-red seeker of the Stinger missile and the rocket motor, fuse, and warhead from the Sidewinder. It can be fired from Sea Sparrow launchers and from a 21-cell stand-alone launcher, and will be installed aboard combatants, amphibious ships, and auxiliaries to complement other anti-missile systems. It will have an IOC in the Navy of 1990. Limited production of the missile was approved in April 1987, and 240 are being sought in FY 1988.

HELLFIRE

LENGTH: five feet, four inches.
DIAMETER: seven inches.
WING SPAN: 13 inches.
WEIGHT: 95 pounds.
POWER PLANT: solid-propellant rocket.
WARHEAD: conventional.
CONTRACTOR: Rockwell International.

BRIEFING: This air-to-surface, laser-guided, anti-armor missile was developed by the Army and has been adapted for use on the Marine Corps' AH-1T/J helicopter. The version to be used by the Marines has a longer range than the TOW missile which it replaces and permits greater aircraft maneuverability. No missiles were funded in FY 1987, but 1,393 are being sought in FY 1988 and a slightly larger number in FY 1989.

STINGER

LENGTH: five feet.
DIAMETER: 2.25 inches.
WING SPAN: eight inches.
WEIGHT: 34.5 pounds (including launch tube).
POWER PLANT: solid-propellant rocket.
WARHEAD: conventional high explosive.
RANGE: three miles.
CONTRACTOR: General Dynamics Pomona Division.

BRIEFING: This shoulder-held surface-to-air missile is the successor to the Army's Redeye Missile. It is an infrared homing weapon that can effectively engage jet or propeller-drive aircraft or helicopters at low altitudes. Used by the Marine Corps as well as the Army,

it was placed aboard a number of Navy ships in the Mediterranean in the winter of 1983-84 in reaction to threatened terrorist attacks. It also was used successfully by the Royal Navy in the Falklands operation in 1982. The Navy activated its first Stinger missile-armed detachment in the summer of 1987. Funding for 685 missiles was provided in FY 1987, and the final Navy buy of 425 will be made in FY 1988.

MARK 50 TORPEDO

LENGTH: 9.5 feet.
DIAMETER: 12.25 inches.
WEIGHT: 800 pounds (approximate).
SPEED: 40+ knots.
POWER PLANT: Stored chemical energy propulsion system; pump-jet.
GUIDANCE: Active/passive acoustic homing.
WARHEAD: Approximately 100 pounds conventional (shaped charge).
CONTRACTORS: Honeywell, Westinghouse.

BRIEFING: This successor to the Mark 46 torpedo is being developed for use from ships, aircraft, and submarines against the faster, deeper-diving, and more sophisticated submarines being developed and operated by the Soviet Union. It also will have the capability for use against slower, shallow-diving submarines and surface ships. The Mark 50 currently is in limited production, with only 39 torpedoes being procured in FY 1987. The Navy is restructuring the Mark 50 program to allow for more needed sea runs during the full-scale development phase. Technical evaluation is scheduled for early 1989, and operational evaluation for late 1989. Procurement is expected to rise slowly in FY 1988 and more rapidly in FY 1989. The Mark 50 also will provide the payload for the conventional variant of the submarine-launched ASW Standoff Weapon (Sea Lance). Wesinghouse was selected as the Mark 50 second source in April 1987; full competition is expected to begin in 1990.

Mark 48

MARK 48 TORPEDO

LENGTH: 19 feet.
DIAMETER: 21 inches.
WEIGHT: 3,520 pounds.
MAXIMUM SPEED: 55 knots.
POWER PLANT: piston engine; pump jet.
MAXIMUM RANGE: 23 miles.
MAXIMUM DEPTH: 500 fathoms.
WARHEAD: 650 pounds high explosives.
CONTRACTORS: Hughes, Gould Ocean Systems Division, Cleveland.

BRIEFING: A wire-guided torpedo, said to be the most complex torpedo ever developed, the Mark 48 is carried by all Navy attack and ballistic-missile submarines. Production of it, which commenced in 1972, is to end when the FY 1985 buy has been completed; however, all in the Navy's inventory but about 200 are to be upgraded. The latter improvement program is to be completed in 1990. An advanced-capability version, the Mark 48 ADCAP was scheduled to go into full production in 1987. However, that version, which came into being to permit countering the impressive capabilities of Soviet Alpha-class submarines and other advanced classes, has been plagued with delays and cost increases since development commenced in 1979. It now is undergoing operational testing; full production is scheduled to commence in August 1988. Only 50 Mark 48 ADCAP torpedoes were funded in FY 1987, and only 100 were sought in FY 1988, but the number being procured is expected to climb sharply in future years. The FY 1988 budget contains proposed funding to commence competitive dual-source procurement for the Mark 48 ADCAP.

MARK 46 TORPEDO

LENGTH: 8.5 feet; 14 feet, nine inches with ASROC booster.
DIAMETER: 12.8 inches.
WEIGHT: 508 pounds; 1,073 pounds with ASROC booster.
MAXIMUM SPEED: 40 knots.
RANGE: 12,000 yards.
POWER PLANT: piston engine (solid propellant) or cam engine (liquid propellant).
ACQUISITION RANGE: 500 yards.
WARHEAD WEIGHT: 96.8 pounds; high explosive.
CONTRACTOR: Honeywell.

BRIEFING: Since this lightweight torpedo first was introduced into the fleet in 1967, it has been acquired for use by the navies of 21 other countries. Twelve nations currently are buying the fifth modification of it. The Mark 46 can be launched from surface ships, fixed-wing aircraft, or helicopters against its primary target, submarines. Although the Mark 46 will be the backbone of the Navy's torpedo inventory well into the 1990s, and production is scheduled to continue until 1990, procurement ended with the 500 torpedoes funded in FY 1987. More than 1,300 are to be upgraded in capability to the fifth-modification level.

Mark 46

CAPTOR

LENGTH: 12.14 feet.
DIAMETER: 21 inches.
WEIGHT: 1,997 pounds, including torpedo and mooring.
CONTRACTOR: Goodyear Aerospace, Akron.

BRIEFING: Captor, whose name is a contraction of "encapsulated torpedo," is an anti-submarine system comprising a Mark 46 torpedo inserted in a mine casing. Normally deployed in deep water in the vicinity of routes traveled by enemy submarines, it has the ability to detect and classify submarine targets while surface ships are able to pass over it without triggering the torpedo. It can be launched by surface ships, submarines, and aircraft, including B-52s. Procurement of these torpedoes ended with the FY 1985 buy.

VERTICAL LAUNCH ASROC (VLA)

LENGTH: 15 feet.
DIAMETER: 12.75 inches.
WEIGHT: 1,000 pounds.
RANGE: Approximately 12 miles.
POWER PLANT: Solid-propellant rocket.
WARHEAD: Conventional, Mark 46 torpedo; nuclear depth bomb.
GUIDANCE: Terminal acoustic homing with Mark 46 torpedo.
CONTRACTORS: Honeywell, Martin-Marietta.

BRIEFING: ASROC is a ship-launched ballistic ASW weapon that can be fitted with a conventional torpedo or a nuclear depth charge. It entered service in 1961. The Vertical Launch ASROC (VLA), under development for some years, will be configured for either the Mark 46 or the Mark 50 torpedo. All those ships receiving the Vertical Launch System (VLS) will receive the VLA; these will include all Burke-class destroyers, all Ticonderoga-class cruisers from CG-52 on, and 24 Spruance-class destroyers. VLA will have increased range and effectiveness over the deck-launched ASROC. Martin-Marietta was selected in 1987 as the second production source. Although 200 VLAs were funded in FY 1987, and 260 are being sought in FY 1988, full production now is scheduled to commence in December 1989.

PHALANX CLOSE-IN WEAPONS SYSTEM

WEIGHT: 12,500 pounds, complete system.
GUN: M61A1 Vulcan (gatling-type).
AMMUNITION: 20mm with high-density penetrating projectile.
MAGAZINE CAPACITY: 989.
FIRING RATE: 3,000 rounds per minute.
CONTRACTOR: General Dynamics' Pomona Division, General Electric's Pittsfield Division.

BRIEFING: The Phalanx Close-In Weapons System (CIWS) is a last-ditch defense system against anti-ship missiles. It combines on a single mount fire-control radars and a six-barrel Gatling gun firing depleted-uranium projectiles at a theoretical rate of 3,000 rounds per minute. Its projectiles are 2.5 times heavier than those made of steel. A total, fully integrated weapons system, it automatically carries out search, detection, automatic threat evaluation, tracking, and firing. Its reliability has been increasing constantly. The Navy has installed or will install 672 systems aboard 44 classes of ships over the next 15-20 years and also has modified or is modifying over 400 of its CIWS installations to improve their capability with increased magazine capacity and enhanced operability, maintainability, and reliability. Competitive procurement is expected to commence during FY 1988, with General Electric's Pittsfield Division having been certified as the second source. Only five new systems for the Navy are included in the FY 1988 budget, although many others will be constructed under the Foreign Military Sales program.

Phalanx

SEA POWER:*MARINES*

As FY 1988 began, there were 199,600 Marines serving in the Fleet Marine Forces and at various USMC posts and stations around the world. About 1,470 Marines were assigned to security duty at American embassies, legations, and consulates in more than 100 countries. Other Marines were at sea with the U.S. Navy in shipboard detachments. Thirty-three Marine barracks, which traditionally have provided security forces at certain U.S. naval facilities in this country and overseas, are being reorganized into six barracks and 22 security force companies. Thousands served throughout the country as advisers to Marine Reserve units in inspector-instructor roles or on recruiting duty.

More than 9,777 women Marines serve in a wide range of occupational fields; they do not serve in combat arms.

The majority of Marines serve in the Fleet Marine Forces, which deploy units around the world throughout the year or to areas of crisis in preparation for commitment if required in the national interest. Following are the Corps' major commands and duty locations:

Fleet Marine Force Atlantic (FMFLANT), Norfolk, Va. Second Marine Division, Camp Lejeune, N.C.; 2d Marine Aircraft Wing, Cherry Point, N.C.; 2d Force Service Support Group, Camp Lejeune, N.C.

Fleet Marine Force, Pacific (FMFPAC), Camp Smith, Hawaii. First Marine Division, Camp Pendleton, Calif.; 3d Marine Aircraft Wing, El Toro, Calif.; 1st Force Service Support Group, Camp Pendleton, Calif.; 3d Marine Division, Okinawa; 1st Marine Aircraft Wing, Okinawa and Iwakuni, Japan; 3d Force Service Support Group, Okinawa; 1st Marine Brigade, Hawaii.

Marine Corps Development and Education Command, Quantico, Va.; Marine Corps Logistics Base, Barstow, Calif.; Marine Corps Logistics Base, Albany, Ga.; Marine Corps Recruit Depot, Parris Island, S.C.; Marine Corps Recruit Depot, San Diego, Calif.; Marine Corps Air-Ground Combat Center, Twentynine Palms, Calif.; 4th Marine Division/4th Marine Aircraft Wing (Headquarters), New Orleans, La.; 4th Force Service Support Group (Headquarters), Atlanta, Ga.

WORLD'S LARGEST COMBAT DIVISION

With over 17,000 Marines and sailors, the U.S. Marine division is the largest of the world's combat divisions.

Each of the Marine Corps' three active divisions and the reserve division is structured somewhat differently. But a division with the normal complement of three infantry regiments would typically be manned in this manner.
Marines: 1,055 officers, 16,903 enlisted personnel.
Navy: 74 officers, 847 enlisted personnel.
A Marine infantry regiment's complement:
Marines: 147 officers, 2,446 enlisted personnel.
Navy: 11 officers, 201 enlisted personnel.
In addition to the weapons organic to each of the regiment's infantry battalions, regimental headquarters maintains a number of crew-served weapons primarily for security of command posts, and an anti-tank platoon. A regiment's three battalions field a total of 24 81mm mortars, 27 60mm mortars, and 91 7.62mm machine guns. Their firepower has been increased with the addition of .50 caliber machine guns, 40mm machine guns, the new squad automatic weapon, shoulder-launched multi-purpose assault weapons, an increased number of M203 grenade launchers, and improvements to the present service rifle and the M60E3 machine gun.

A Marine infantry regiment comprises three infantry battalions and a headquarters company. The heavy anti-tank (TOW) weaponry of a Marine division has been doubled from 72 to 144 with the addition of a TOW platoon in each headquarters company infantry regiment. Through infantry battalions a regiment executes its mission, which is to locate, close with, and destroy enemy forces by fire and maneuver, or repel enemy forces by fire and close combat. Usually commanded by a colonel, a regiment can be completely transported by trucks, helicopters, fixed-wing aircraft, amphibious ships, vehicles, or ships.

With combat support a regiment reinforced becomes the ground combat element for a Marine Amphibious Brigade (MAB), which may be employed separately or as an advance force of a substantially larger Marine Amphibious Force (MAF). There are nine U.S. Marine infantry regiments in the active forces and three in the Marine Corps Reserve.

The 27th Marine Regimental (Nucleus) Headquarters was activated in December, 1981, in order to provide an interim ground combat element (GCE) for the 7th MAB and for the purpose of developing, testing, and evaluating Marine Corps doctrine in mechanized combined arms task force (MCATF) operations.

The 27 active Marine infantry battalions are built around the traditional 13-man rifle squad, composed of a squad leader and three four-man rifle teams. Battalion firepower has been increased 25% over the past four years.

The weapons used by a Marine infantry battalion range from the pistol and rifle to crew-served weapons, including machine guns, anti-tank weapons, and mortars.

The primary mission of a Marine infantry battalion, comprising three rifle companies, a weapons company, and a headquarters and service company, is the same as the infantry regiment's: to locate, close with, and destroy enemy forces by fire and maneuver, or to repel enemy assaults by fire and close combat. The battalion commander normally is a lieutenant colonel; his company commanders are captains.

A battalion usually moves on foot, but has a limited number of light vehicles assigned for transport of some weapons, communications equipment, ammunition, food, and water. The entire battalion and its weapons and equipment can be transported by helicopters or amphibious assault vehicles.

When reinforced with combat-support the battalion becomes the ground combat element of a Marine Amphibious Unit (MAU).

Marine Air-Ground Task Forces (MAGTFs) are combined arms teams of air and ground forces controlled by a single commander. They may deploy by sea or air, or by a combination of the two. Task organization is based on the mission assigned and the capabilities of opposing forces.

There are three basic types of Ma-

A Marine A-H1 Cobra helicopter provides cover for ground troops during Exercise Valiant Usher '87 in Western Australia.

rine air-ground task forces. The structure will vary depending on the mission assigned and other circumstances.

A Marine division usually has three infantry regiments; one of the three current active divisions, however, has only two regiments; what might be its third infantry regiment forms the nucleus of a separate brigade. In addition to its infantry regiments, a division also fields the following units:

Headquarters battalion. This unit provides command, control, and administrative services. It consists of a headquarters company, a service company, a truck company, a military police company, division headquarters, and a communications company. The headquarters company includes a photo-imagery interpretation unit, sensor control and maintenance platoon, and interrogator-translator teams. In addition to security duties, the military police provide beach and traffic control and guard prisoner-of-war stockades.

Artillery regiment. There are four Marine artillery regiments—one in each division. Each has its own unique structure. The 12th Marine Regiment, for example, is split, with one battalion assigned to support the 1st Marine Amphibious Brigade in Hawaii, and two direct-support battalions and one general support battalion with the 3d Marine Division on Okinawa. The 10th Marine Regiment—which is assigned to

the 2d Marine Division—provides an example of a regiment's typical firepower and structure. Commanded by a colonel, the regiment consists of a headquarters battery, three direct-support battalions, and two general-support battalions.

Direct-support battalions are assigned a total of 72 155mm howitzers (towed). One general-support battalion is equipped with 12 eight-inch howitzers (self-propelled), and 18 155mm howitzers (self-propelled). A second G/S battalion is equipped with 18 155mm howitzers (Towed). The artillery regiment is the primary source of fire support for the Marine division.

Reconnaissance battalion. This unit conducts ground reconnaissance and surveillance as part of the division. At full strength of 316 Marines, a battalion fields 36 four-man scout teams for reconnaissance behind enemy lines and along the forward edge of the battle area.

Tank battalion. A typical tank battalion consists of 1,291 Marines who are equipped with: 70 M60A1 105mm gun tanks; 72 Tube-launched, Optically tracked, Wire-command-link (TOW) guided missile systems; M88A1 tracked recovery vehicles, and four M60A1 armored vehicle-launched bridges (AVLB).

Assault amphibian battalion. This battalion transports landing forces

from amphibious ships to and across the beach, and provides transport in mobile operations ashore. A battalion usually consists of four assault amphibian companies and a headquarters and service company. A battalion is equipped with 187 assault amphibious vehicles (primarily for personnel transport), 15 assault amphibious vehicles equipped to serve as command and control vehicles, and six assault amphibious vehicles designed to retrieve damaged vehicles.

Combat engineer battalion. Four combat engineer companies, an engineer support company, and a headquarters and service company form this battalion of 800 Marines. They perform demolition missions, clear minefields, supervise booby-trap and mine emplacement, and build obstacles, rafts, bridges, and roads.

Force Service Support Group (FSSG). Marines provide combat service support to a MAF in garrison or while deployed. The FSSG is organized into a headquarters and several battalions: service, supply, maintenance, engineer support, motor transport, medical, dental, and landing support. From these units come elements that provide support for independently deployed battalion landing teams, regimental landing teams, Marine Amphibious Units, or Marine Amphibious Brigades.

The Fleet Marine Forces

The Fleet Marine Forces, a balanced blend of combined air and ground arms, are primarily trained, organized, and equipped for offensive amphibious employment. Each Fleet Marine Force normally consists of a headquarters unit, one or more Force Service Support Groups, one or more divisions, and one or more Marine aircraft wings; they also may have one or more brigades assigned.

There are two Fleet Marine Forces: Fleet Marine Force, Atlantic (FMFLANT) headquartered at Norfolk, Va.; and Fleet Marine Force, Pacific (FMFPAC) headquartered at Camp H.M. Smith, Hawaii. The two differ considerably in size. FMFLANT consists of the 2d Marine Division, 2d Marine Aircraft Wing, 2d Force Service Support Group (Reinforced).

The major units of FMFPAC are the 1st Marine Division, the 3d Marine Division, the 1st Marine Amphibious Brigade, the 3d Marine Amphibious Brigade, the 1st Marine Aircraft Wing, the 3d Marine Aircraft Wing, the 1st FSSG, the 3d FSSG, the 1st Radio Battalion, the 7th Communications

Battalion, the 1st Force Reconnaissance Company, the 1st Anglico Company, and a Headquarters and Service Battalion. The 1st Marine Amphibious Brigade includes a Marine aircraft group.

The primary mission of the Fleet Marine Forces is to seize objectives held by highly trained and well-equipped enemy forces. Primarily designed for offensive combat, the forces may also be used to defend advanced naval bases.

The forces are trained and equipped for immediate deployment by ship or by air anywhere in the world.

Marine Aircraft Wing

Capability to conduct tactical air operations is essential to the execution of an amphibious operation. To this end, the Marine Corps has pioneered an effective aviation combat arm capable of meeting all requirements of a landing force. These requirements call for a flexible, responsive Aviation Combat Element (ACE) specifically tailored to meet the anticipated tactical situation.

Current organization of Marine aviation consists of the Marine aircraft wing, which is the highest level tactical aviation command in the Fleet Marine Force. Each wing is task-organized with various groups, squadrons, light anti-aircraft missile battalions, and low-altitude air defense battalions. There are presently four wings, three in the regular forces and one in the reserves, each primarily designed to support one Marine division in an amphibious operation.

The mission of a Marine aircraft wing is to conduct air operations in support of Fleet Marine Forces to include offensive air support, anti-air warfare, assault support, aerial reconnaissance, electronic warfare, and control of aircraft and missiles. As a collateral function, the wing may participate as an integral component of naval aviation in the execution of such other Navy functions as the fleet commander may direct. The following aircraft are found in Marine aircraft groups of a typical Marine aircraft wing. Helicopter Group: CH-53 (heavy lift), CH-46 (medium lift), UH-1 (light lift utility), AH-1 (attack) helicopters as well as OV-10 (aerial reconnaissance/observation). Fixed-Wing Group: A-4, AV-8 (light attack), A-6 (all-weather attack), F/A-18 (all-weather fighter/attack), RF-4 (multi-sensor reconnaissance), EA-6 (electronic warfare) and KC-130 (air refueling).

Marine Amphibious Unit (MAU)

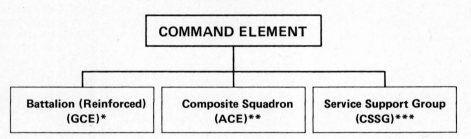

Usually sea-based, the MAU is the Marine Corps' most responsive air-ground task force. It normally is prepared to assault with 15 days of ammunition, food, fuel, water, and medical supplies available. It can be reinforced or resupplied rapidly. Usually embarked aboard three to five U.S. Navy amphibious ships, the MAU also may be airlifted. It most often is commanded by a colonel. Two to three MAUs usually are deployed forward or standing ready for immediate movement to forward combat areas or peacetime crisis points.

Personnel:

1,900 Marines; 100 U.S. Navy personnel assigned to Marine units (medical, dental, chaplain, etc.); 490 members of a Navy support element, explosive ordnance demolition teams, Sea-Air-Land teams ([SEALs], and other special-support units). Total: 2,490.

Aircraft and Missiles:

12 CH-46 medium-lift assault helicopters
4 CH-53 (D or E) heavy lift assault transport helicopters
4 UH-1 utility helicopters
4 AH-1 attack helicopters.
The squadron could be reinforced by one VMA Det (6 AV-8) Vertical/Short Takeoff and Landing (V/STOL) attack aircraft as the tactical situation dictates.
15 Stinger surface-to-air missile teams.

Major Ground Forces Equipment:

5 tanks
8 81mm mortars
32 Dragon missile launchers (anti-armor)
8 TOW missile launchers (tube-launched, optically sighted, wire-guided anti-armor)
14 amphibious assault vehicles
8 155mm howitzers
9 60mm mortars
20 .50-caliber machine guns
60 7.62mm machine guns
21 Smaws
26 40mm machine guns.

*GCE: Ground Combat Element
**ACE: Aviation Combat Element
***CSSG: Combat Service Support Group

EDITOR'S NOTE: The figures setting forth numbers of personnel and aircraft in these basic Marine units are in some instances sharply different from those contained in earlier editions of the *Almanac of Seapower*. The much greater numbers of personnel now comprising a Marine Amphibious Force result in part from the increased amount of amphibious lift now available to the Marine Corps, thus making it possible to lift more Marine combat and support forces to an objective area. That same increased lift makes possible the simultaneous lift of more units; as a consequence, the smaller figures listing the numbers of aircraft assigned to those units reflect the fact that more simultaneous moves can be made, and Marine aircraft assets would be allocated across a much broader spectrum. If only a single force were moved, however, its aircraft could be augmented from the assets of other units.

Marine Amphibious Brigade (MAB)

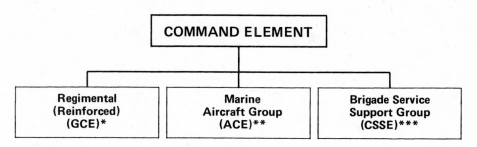

```
                    ┌─────────────────────────────┐
                    │      COMMAND ELEMENT        │
                    └─────────────────────────────┘
                                   │
        ┌──────────────────────────┼──────────────────────────┐
┌───────────────────┐    ┌───────────────────┐    ┌───────────────────┐
│    Regimental     │    │      Marine       │    │  Brigade Service  │
│   (Reinforced)    │    │  Aircraft Group   │    │   Support Group   │
│      (GCE)*       │    │     (ACE)**       │    │     (CSSE)***     │
└───────────────────┘    └───────────────────┘    └───────────────────┘
```

The MAB's GCE usually is composed of from two to five infantry battalions, an artillery battalion, a tank company, a combat engineer company, a reconnaissance company, an assault amphibian vehicle company, and a TOW platoon. Designed to operate for 30 days without resupply, the MAB quickly can establish procedures for resupply and for substantially longer periods of shore operations. It normally is commanded by a Marine brigadier general and is embarked aboard approximately 26 Navy amphibious ships. The MAB may be deployed forward as a floating ready force or may be airlifted forward rapidly. Three MAB command elements actively prepare for employment with the three maritime prepositioning ship squadrons in the Atlantic and Pacific Oceans. These ships carry substantial proportions of MAB equipment to forward assembly areas for link-up with airlifted personnel and essential equipment.

Personnel:

15,000 Marines; 700 U.S. Navy personnel (medical, dental, chaplain, etc.); 1,250 Navy support elements (UDTs, SEALs, beach support, etc.). Total, 16,950.

Aircraft and Missiles:

40 AV-8B V/STOL attack aircraft or 38 A-4 light attack aircraft
24 F-4 or F/A-18 fighter/attack aircraft
10 A-6E all-weather/night attack aircraft
4 EA-6B electronic warfare aircraft
4 RF-4B photo reconnaissance aircraft
5 OA-4 tactical control aircraft
6 KC-130 refueling aircraft
6 OV-10 observation aircraft
48 CH-46 medium-lift assault helicopters
16 CH-53D heavy assault transport helicopters
16 CH-53E heavy-lift, assault helicopters
12 AH-1T attack helicopters
12 UH-1N utility and command and control helicopters
12 Hawk surface-to-air missile launchers
45 Stinger surface-to-air missile teams

Major Ground Forces Equipment:

17 tanks
24 81mm mortars
72 Dragon missile launchers (anti-armor)
48 TOW missile launchers (anti-armor)
27 light armored vehicles (LAV) (Reinforced Company)
47 amphibious assault vehicles
24 155mm howitzers (towed)
6 155mm howitzers (self-propelled)
6 eight-inch howitzers (self-propelled)
27 60mm mortars
138 .50-caliber machine guns
255 7.62mm M60 machine guns
63 Smaws
114 40mm machine guns

*GCE: Ground Combat Element
**ACE: Aviation Combat Element
***CSSE: Combat Service Support Element

LCACs, which can operate at speeds in excess of 50 knots, speedily bring men and equipment to the beach.

Marine Amphibious Force (MAF)

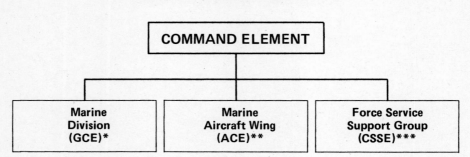

COMMAND ELEMENT

Marine Division (GCE)*	Marine Aircraft Wing (ACE)**	Force Service Support Group (CSSE)***

The MAF may range in size from less than one full division to several divisions and an aircraft wing or wings. The personnel, weapons, and equipment which illustrate this example of a MAF represent one consisting of one division and one wing; the ground combat element includes nine infantry battalions in three regiments. Normally, a force of this size also would include one artillery regiment, a tank battalion, an assault amphibian battalion, a LAV battalion, a combat engineer battalion, and a reconnaissance battalion. The Force Service Support Group could provide supplies, maintenance, engineering, motor transport, and medical and dental care for 60 days. Commanded by a Marine major general or lieutenant general, the MAF is the largest and most powerful of Marine air-ground task forces.

Personnel:

49,700 Marines; 2,600 U.S. Navy personnel (medical, dental, chaplain, etc.); 8,800 Navy support elements (SEALS, beach support, etc.). Total, 55,100.

Aircraft and Missiles:

60 AV-8 V/STOL attack aircraft or 57 A-4 light attack aircraft
48 F-4 or F/A-18 fighter/attack aircraft
20 A-6E all-weather/night attack aircraft
8 EA-6B electronic warfare aircraft
8 RF-4B photo reconnaissance aircraft
12 OV-10 observation aircraft
12 KC-130 refueling aircraft
9 OA-4 tactical control aircraft
60 CH-46 medium-lift assault helicopters
32 CH-53 (A or D) heavy assault transport helicopters
16 CH-53E heavy-lift assault helicopters

24 AH-1 (T and J) attack helicopters
24 UH-1N utility and command and control helicopters
24 Hawk surface-to-air missile launchers
90 Stinger surface-to-air missile teams

Major Ground Forces Equipment:

70 tanks
80 81mm mortars
216 Dragon missile launchers (anti-armor)
163 TOW missile launchers (anti-armor)
212 assault amphibious vehicles
110 light armored vehicles (LAV)
90 155mm howitzers (towed)
18 155mm howitzers (self-propelled)
12 eight-inch howitzers (self-propelled)
81 60mm mortars
701 .50-caliber machine guns
806 M60 machine guns
189 Smaws
631 40mm machine guns

*GCE: Ground Combat Element
**ACE: Aviation Combat Element
***CSSE: Combat Service Support Element

Maritime Prepositioning Ships Brigade

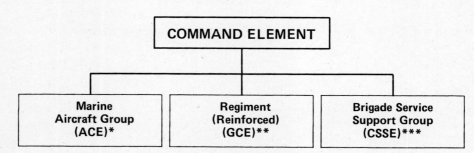

COMMAND ELEMENT

Marine Aircraft Group (ACE)*	Regiment (Reinforced) (GCE)**	Brigade Service Support Group (CSSE)***

Aircraft/Launchers:

40 AV-8 or 19 A-4 attack aircraft
24 F/A-18 or 24 F-4 fighter/attack aircraft
10 A-6E all-weather/night-attack aircraft
4 EA-6B electronic-warfare aircraft
4 RF-4B photo reconnaissance aircraft
5 OA-4 tactical control aircraft
6 KC-130 refueling aircraft
6 OV-10 observation aircraft
8 CH-53 heavy-lift assault helicopters
12 CH-53D heavy-lift assault helicopter transport helicopters.
12 UH-1N utility/command and control helicopters
12 AH-1T attack helicopters
12 CH-46 medium-lift assault helicopters

6 Hawk surface-to-air missile launchers
45 Stinger teams

Major Ground & Combat Equipment:

53 tanks
30 light armored vehicles (LAV)
24 81mm mortars
72 TOW missile launchers (anti-armor)
109 amphibious assault vehicles
24 155mm howitzers M198 (towed)
6 155m howitzers (self-propelled)
27 60mm mortars
303 .50 caliber machine guns
360 M-60 machine guns
6 8'' howitzers (self-propelled)
114 MK-19 40mm grenade launchers

*ACE: Aviation Combat Element
**GCE: Ground Combat Element
***CSSE: Combat Service Support Element

Approximate Personnel
USMC = 15,775
USN = 880

MARITIME PREPOSITIONING SHIPS

The advent of maritime prepositioning provides yet another capability to project power ashore or to demonstrate national resolve with naval forces.

In preparing for maritime prepositioning operations, the supplies (30 days' worth) and most of the equipment required for a powerful Marine Amphibious Brigade are loaded aboard specifically designated and configured merchant ships that are chartered and commanded by the Navy. These Maritime Prepositioning Ships (MPS) then are deployed to what are considered potential areas of conflict in which U.S. forces might become involved. They can reach these anticipated hot spots within seven days. If and when required, the ships proceed to a beach or port in the operating area, one perhaps secured by a 2,000-man forward-deployed Marime Amphibious Unit. Some 16,500 Marines and naval personnel are airlifted to nearby airfields at the same time. Meanwhile, the tactical aircraft of the MAB's aviation combat element flight-ferry to the area of employment.

Equipment and supplies quickly are offloaded from the MPS and married up with appropriate units. Now combat ready, the brigade moves on to its assigned objectives. It has arrived (anywhere in the world) within five days after the ships are offshore and is heavy enough in terms of firepower and sustainability to permit it to contribute mightily to achieving victory.

The first MPS squadron, consisting of four ships, has been deployed since April 1985 and is currently sailing in the eastern Atlantic. The 6th MAB is the headquarters element for the MPS brigade.

The second squadron, consisting of five ships, deployed in September 1985 and is homeported in Diego Garcia. The 7th MAB is the headquarters element for that MPS brigade.

The third squadron, consisting of four ships, completed loading out in the fall of 1986 and is deployed in the western Pacific. It is homeported at Guam/Tinian. The 1st MAB is the headquarters element for the third squadron's brigade.

NORWAY PREPOSITIONING PROGRAM

The Norway Prepositioning Program is a strategic mobility enhancement that reduces force closure time to Norway from weeks to days. It provides a creditable deterrent and expands the strategic options available for the rapid reinforcement of NATO's northern flank.

Prepositioning the equipment and supplies for a MAB in Norway facilitates this rapid reinforcement and reduces the MAB airlift requirements by about 4,000 sorties. The Norway Airlanded MAB will provide a credible, self-sustainable, and versatile force capable of executing current plans with minimal reliance on existing strategic airlift. It will be specifically tailored for this contingency and will be comprised of about 13,000 Marines, 150 aircraft, and, when combined with equipment and supplies carried by strategic airlift in the fly-in echelon, will be able to sustain itself for 30 days. The initial operating capability (IOC) of this program is late 1989.

This MAB is intended for use prior to hostilities and is not a substitute for amphibious assault. Further, it is not a change in traditional roles or missions of the Marine Corps in that it contributes to our maritime strategy designed to keep the vital U.S.-NATO Europe sea lanes of communication open.

COMBAT READINESS

A high level of combat readiness long has been the standard for the Marine Corps. As quality personnel are married up to new and improved equipment, readiness is sharpened to an even finer point. Training and readiness must remain synonymous if the Marine Corps is to continue to be "the force in readiness" and fight "in every clime and place." Marine Corps training demands the demonstration of performance standards at all levels of training, from the fighting skills of the individual Marine required for small unit tactics to those necessary to conduct task-force-level amphibious operations.

Marine Air-Ground Task Force (MAGTF) participate in a wide variety of exercises in virtually every corner of the globe. Since 1981, the Marine Corps has experienced a modest but steady increase in the number of MAGTF exercises conducted by Marine Amphibious Brigades (MAB) and Marine Amphibious Forces (MAF).

Marines and their equipment continue to be rigorously tested by participation in numerous joint-service exercises such as the U.S. Central Command's Gallant Eagle and Bright Star, the Atlantic Command's Solid Shield and Ocean Venture, and the Pacific Command's Team Spirit. These large-scale exercises sponsored by unified commanders include participation by all components, to include those associated with the Maritime Prepositioning Ships (MPS) program, and stress the interoperability among them.

In U.S. European Command exercises such as Northern Wedding and Bold Guard, the Marines have continued to strengthen their position in NATO. MAGTFs, utilizing the prepositioned equipment stationed in Norway, continue to prove that the Marine Corps is a very capable partner in the defense of Norway.

Forward deployed Marine Amphibious Units (MAU) regularly conduct amphibious landings and raids and noncombatant evacuation exercises to maintain their proficiency.

The Marine Corps provides realistic and challenging training under wartime conditions and allows commanders to exercise all supporting arms on a single range. Combined Arms Exercises (CAX) are conducted through a series of battalion and brigade live-fire exercises at the Marine Corps Air-Ground Combat Center, Twentynine Palms, CA.

In summary, Marine Air-Ground Task Forces continue to exercise more frequently and more realistically with elements of other services than at any time in the past. With the continued refinement of skills surrounding the utilization of Maritime Prepositioning Ships assets, and those assets prepositioned in Norway, the training readiness of the operational forces continues to reach new heights.

WEAPONS/MARINES

The following weapons and combat vehicles represent those items most common to Marine air-ground task forces or—where noted—which recently have been developed and will be in the hands of Marines in 1988.

M16A1 Rifle and M203 Grenade Launcher

M16A1 and M16A2 Rifles. A 5.56mm magazine-fed, gas-operated, air-cooled, shoulder-fired rifle, the M16A1 has been the standard rifle for Marines since the late 1960s. It can fire ball, tracer, or blank ammunition on automatic or semi-automatic and weighs 7.9 pounds when loaded with a 30-pound magazine. The M16A2, a substantially improved version of the M16A1, began entering the Marine Corps inventory in FY 1984. The M16A2 has a heavier barrel, improved handguards, a burst-control device (to limit automatic bursts to three rounds), a finger-operated windage and elevation knob, and a muzzle brake (to reduce muzzle rise when firing). The improvements were made by the rifle's original manufacturer, Colt Industries. The M16A2 has a maximum effective range of 800 meters (880 yards). A bayonet-knife, M7, may be mounted on the rifle.

Grenade Launcher, M203. Attached to the M16A1 or M16A2 rifle, the M203 can hurl several kinds of grenades beyond hand grenade range. Types include: high-explosive, white-star parachute illumination, white-star cluster illumination, tactical CS (riot-control gas), high-explosive airburst, high-explosive dual-purpose (for penetrating up to two inches of steel plate), multi-projectile (containing 20 projectiles about the size of No. 4 buckshot), and practice grenades. As Marine fire teams expand in size from four to five members, two grenade launchers per team will be assigned instead of one, as at present.

PERSONAL DEFENSE WEAPON. The caliber .45 M1191A1 pistol has served Marines as their primary sidearm for more than 70 years. Carried by officers, staff noncommissioned officers, and other Marines not armed with the rifle, the .45 weighs three pounds and has a maximum effective range of 50 meters (55 yards). A semi-automatic, recoil-operated, magazine-fed, self-loading weapon designed by Colt, it first was manufactured by Colt, then by Ithaca and Remington, for service use. Designed primarily for defense, it also has been used on attack missions on many occasions. Recently, however, there was a joint-service decision to replace the .45 with a 9mm pistol. Competition to select a replacement was completed in late 1984, with the winner being the Beretta 9mm semi-automatic M9 pistol. A five-year contract for production of the weapon was awarded to Beretta USA Corporation in April 1985.

M60 Machine Gun

Machine Gun, .50-Caliber M2. In use for more than 45 years, the .50-caliber machine gun is fired from a tripod as well as from mounts on vehicles and helicopters. It provides heavy automatic fire against personnel, vehicles, aircraft, and fortifications. Air-cooled and weighing 82 pounds, it is fed by metal link belts and has a maximum effective range of 2,000 meters (1.2 miles). The newly structured infantry battalion has eight M2s assigned to each of its weapons companies to give them enhanced coverage against air and ground targets—particularly against the threat of enemy helicopters. The M2 is manufactured by the Saco Defense Systems Division of Maremont Corp. The Marine Corps is participating in a product improvement program (PIP) through the Joint Service Small Arms Program (JSSAP) in an effort to reduce the weight of the M2 by 30 pounds while maintaining all other firing characteristics.

M16A2 Rifle

Machine Gun, M60. The gas-operated, belt-fed M60 provides a heavy volume of controlled fire over a maximum effective range of 1,100 meters (0.7 mile). It weighs 23.2 pounds and fires 7.62mm rounds at a cyclic rate of 550 to 600 rounds per minute. The "sustained" and "rapid" rates of fire are 100 and 200 rounds per minute, respectively. It uses tracer, ball, blank, armor-piercing, and armor-piercing incendiary ammunition. As infantry battalions are restructured, the six M60 machine guns now in each rifle company's weapons platoon will be replaced with newer M60E3s. The M60 is manufactured by the Saco Defense Systems Division of Maremont Corp.

Machine Gun M60E3. A product-improved version of the standard M60 machine gun. Manufactured by the Maremont Corporation, all major components of the M60E3 machine gun, including the barrel, are directly interchangeable with the standard M60 machine gun. Like the M60, the E3 model is an aircooled, link-belt-fed, gas-operated weapon designed to be fired from the shoulder, hip, sitting, or prone position. While the M60E3 retains the performance characteristics of the standard M60, it is 25% lighter, has the bipod mounted on the receiver instead of the barrel, has two pistol grips making it easier to handle during the assault, a swiveling trigger to permit the gun to be fired with heavy gloves or mittens, and a new feed cover to permit the gun to be cocked with the cover closed. These are among other new features which strengthened the weak points while retaining the strong points of the standard M60.

Mk19 Machine Gun Mod 3

Machine Gun, Mk19, Mod-3. Entering service in infantry battalions in 1985, the Mk19 fires M430 high-velocity 40mm grenades from linked belts. The grenades are configured in the form of armor-piercing rounds; their use is designed to counter the growing number of infantry fighting vehicles in the armed forces of potential enemies. The Mk19 has a cyclic rate of fire of 325 to 375 rounds per minute with an effective range of 1,600 meters (0.9 mile) and can be ground- or vehicle-mounted on a pedestal. The 75-pound gun also may be mounted on helicopter doors. It can be fired manually or electrically. The Mk19 is a developmental product of the Naval Ordnance Station, Louisville, Ky.

Squad Automatic Weapon (SAW), M249. The SAW began entering Marine rifle battalions in FY 1984. The SAW fires a 5.56mm round at a cycle rate of 850 to 950 rounds per minute. It may be fired

SAW

from the shoulder, hip, or underarm; its rate of fire can be increased to 1,100 rounds per minute. The weapon's molded plastic magazine holds 200 linked rounds; a 30-round box magazine may be used instead. With one SAW per fire team, the new weapon will fill a void in the Marine infantry battalion that has existed since the Browning automatic rifle was phased out 20 years ago. A product of Fabrique Nationale Herstal S.A., the SAW has a firing weight of just over 20 pounds.

Shoulder-launched Multi-purpose Assault Weapon (SMAW). Fielding of the SMAW began in 1984. Designed by McDonnell Douglas Astronautics Co. for breaching masonry structures and earth and timber bunkers, it is accurate up to 250 meters (275 yards). The warhead can differentiate between hard and soft targets—exploding on contact or penetrating before exploding. Fired from a reusable launcher, the 83mm projectile weighs 13.4 pounds and is aimed by use of a telescopic sight alone or by using the sight and a self-contained spotting rifle.

Starlight Scope. Night vision optics for the Marine Corps have been greatly improved. The AN/PVS-5A, individual night vision goggle (NVG) is a two-cell night-device that allows a commander, small-unit leader, and vehicle driver to operate during the hours of darkness. It provides a 40° field of vision and will operate for 12 hours on one disposable 2.7 volt DC battery. The AN/PVS-4 night vision sight is designed for the individual Marine's rifle. It replaces the AN/PVS-2 and is lighter, smaller, provides a better field of view, and has improved performance under more unfavorable environmental extremes.

Hand Grenades and Pyrotechnics. Marines have available for combat use a wide range of hand grenades, which are basically small bombs filled with explosives or chemicals. There are two types of fragmentation hand grenades—one weighing 16 ounces, the other 14 ounces. The 16-ounce M26 has a variety of fuse and safety clip configurations, including: delay fuse, no safety clip; delay fuse, safety clip; and impact fuse, safety clip. The M26 can be thrown 40 meters (44 yards) and has an effective casualty radius of 15 meters (16.5 yards), but some fragments may reach as far as 184 meters (about 200 yards). The M33 fragmentation grenade, two ounces lighter, has the same effective casualty radius. CS or riot-control grenades produce a thick cloud of irritant which causes tears and coughing. White-phosphorous grenades throw phosphorous over an area from 35 to 50 meters (115 to 165 feet) and are used for signaling, screening, incendiary purposes, or inflicting casualties. The AN-M14 incendiary (thermite) grenade weighs 32 ounces and contains a filler which burns for approximately 40 seconds at a temperature of 4,000 degrees. A portion of the filler turns into molten iron that produces intense heat, igniting or fusing whatever it touches. It can ignite combustible materials, destroy weapons and equipment, or burn holes in metal doors. Illumination grenades produce 55,000 candlepower for about 45 seconds and are used to illuminate small sections of the battlefield at night. M18 colored-smoke grenades produce a thick cloud of red, green, or yellow smoke and are used for signaling and screening. They are particularly useful in ground-to-air signaling and are frequently used to mark helicopter landing zones or to aid attack aircraft pilots in identifying friendly positions or lines. Hand-held, rocket-propelled signals are small rockets that are triggered by hand and reach a minimum height of 200 meters (220 yards) before igniting as single-star parachute flares, star-cluster flares, or smoke parachutes.

Mines. Explosive devices designed to kill or wound personnel or to destroy or damage equipment, mines may be set to detonate: by a controlled means, such as an electrical switch; by the actions of their victims; or by passage of time. They are considered both weapons and obstacles and may be laid in pattern or without pattern. The typical land mine contains a booster, body, detonator, fuse, and main charge. The M15 anti-tank mine is used against heavy tanks and can be fitted with a variety of fuses; a typical M15 can be initiated by a pressure of 565 pounds (plus or minus 174 pounds). The M16A1 series anti-personnel mine—commonly known as the "Bouncing Betty"—is a bouncing fragmentation mine which, when activated, pops from the ground to a height of about six feet and

detonates. Pressure of eight to 20 pounds on three prongs of the fuse, or a pull of between three and 10 pounds on a trip wire, activates the mine. The M18A1 anti-personnel mine—commonly known as the "Claymore"—is a directional fragmentation mine used primarily in protective minefields for defense of outposts and bivouac areas against infiltrators. It is also effective in ambush against personnel and vehicles such as jeeps and trucks. When detonated, by either electrical or non-electrical means, it fires a fan-shaped pattern of spherical steel fragments in a 60-degree horizontal arc at a height of two meters (6.6 feet) and can cause casualties in a radius of 100 meters (110 yards). Among other mines used by the Marines are the M19 and M21, designed for use against tanks and other heavy vehicles.

TOW

Dragon M47

Dragon M47. This surface-attack guided missile system is a recoilless, shoulder-fired, tube-launched, medium anti-tank assault weapon. One man can carry it, and it can be used in all weather conditions, as long as the target is visible. The Dragon M47 system consists of a day or night tracker and a round; the latter has two major components—the launcher and the missile. The day tracker weighs six pounds, the night tracker 22 pounds, and the round 25 pounds. Wartime plans call for 24 trackers to be assigned to the three sections of the Dragon platoon, a unit of the weapons company of the infantry battalion. The Dragon has an effective range of 1,000 meters (0.6 mile); it is manufactured by McDonnell Douglas Astronautics Co. A Dragon night tracker was fielded in FY 1984.

Light Anti-tank Weapon M72A2 (LAW). The LAW is a self-contained unit which consists of an expendable launcher and a rocket. The launcher consists of a fiberglass inner tube and an aluminum outer tube which telescopes from the carrying position into firing position. Carried by a Marine as an addition to rather than substitute for his own weapon, the LAW is considered, despite its name, to be a munition rather than a weapon. Launcher and rocket weight five pounds. The rocket will penetrate 12 inches of homogeneous steel. The maximum effective range is 150 meters (165 yards) against moving targets and 250 meters (275 yards) against stationary targets. Maximum range is 1,000 meters (0.6 mile).

TOW M22054. The Tube-launched, Optically tracked, Wire-command-link (TOW) guided missile system was developed as a heavy anti-tank or assault weapon and can be fired from a tripod, an LAV-AT, or a special truck mount. It can be employed in all weather conditions, as long as the gunner can see the target through the sights. It is the key weapon in the anti-tank company of the Marine tank battalion—three platoons of 24 launchers each—the TOW has a maximum range of 3,250 meters The TOW's high-explosive anti-tank round weighs 54 pounds and travels at a speed of 620 mph. The launcher weighs 173 pounds in the tripod configuration. The missile, designed by Hughes Aircraft Co., has a 20-year shelf life in its container and a 90-day life after the front handling is removed. The current TOW system was replaced by the TOW II in FY 1984.

60mm Mortar. The 60mm mortar is a smooth-bore, muzzle-loaded, high-angle, indirect-fire weapon consisting of a barrel, sight, bipod, and baseplate. Weighing 45.2 pounds, it can be used for direct or indirect fire missions. Maximum rate of fire is 30 rounds per minute, sustained rate of fire 18 rounds per minute. Its range using high-explosive ammunition is 3,600 meters (2.2 miles), 1,500 meters (0.9 mile) using smoke rounds, and 1,000 meters (0.6 mile) using illumination rounds. One round of high-explosive ammunition will neutralize an area 20 meters by 10 meters (66 feet by 33 feet); one mortar firing three rounds will neutralize an area 35 meters by 35 meters (115 feet by 115 feet).

81mm Mortar, M29. The 81mm mortar is a smooth-bore, muzzle-loaded, high-angle, indirect-fire weapon consisting of a barrel, sight, bipod, and baseplate. Unlike the 60mm mortar, which has a square baseplate, the 81mm mortar has a round baseplate and can fire in any direction. The barrel weighs 28 pounds and the M23A1 baseplate 48 pounds. Maximum rate of fire is 12 rounds per minute, the sustained rare of fire five or three rounds per minute, depending upon the charge used. The M29 fires high-explosive, smoke, illuminating, practice, and training ammunition. Its range using high-explosive ammunition is 3,650 meters (2.2 miles) for M362 rounds, 4,500 meters (2.7 miles) for M374 rounds. The M374 round has a bursting area in excess of 30 meters by 20 meters (99 feet by 66 feet) for its steel fragments. Fielding of the new 81mm mortar system will commence in FY 1989; it will be 17 pounds lighter and have a range of 5,600 meters (3.4 miles).

81mm Mortar, M29

ARTILLERY

Marine Corps artillery weapons are generically classified as cannon and are categorized according to caliber and means of transport. The cannon is a piece of fixed or mobile artillery that fires projectiles of various types. Its principal components are a breech, firing mechanism, and tube. The howitzer is a cannon with a barrel length usually between that of a gun and a mortar, capable of high- and low-angle fire, and with a medium muzzle velocity. Each type of Marine howitzer fires a variety of types of rounds, ranging from high-explosive to illumination to chemicals and, in the case of the 155mm and eight-inch howitzer nuclear ammunition.

Like the infantry battalion, the Corps' artillery regiments are in transition. Over the next several years, the M198 155mm howitzer (towed) will replace the 105mm howitzer in the Corps' reserve direct-support artillery battalions. This change will provide the units supported with a much greater degree of fire support over much greater range. The latter howitzer will remain in the inventory for contingency purposes. The table below shows some of the characteristics of each type of artillery in the Corps' inventory.

155mm Howitzer

Weapon	Weight (in pounds)	Range (high-explosive round; in kilometers)[1]	Rate of Fire (sustained; per minute)
M101A1 105mm howitzer (towed)	4,950	11.0	3 rounds
M114A2 155mm howitzer (towed)	12,700	14.6 19.7[2]	1 round
M198 155mm howitzer (towed)	15,740	30.1	2 to 4 rounds[3]
M109A3 155mm howitzer (self-propelled)	53,940	23.7 24.5[2]	1 round
M110A2 eight-inch howitzer (self-propelled)	62,100	20.5	0.5 round

[1] 1 km (0.6 mile).
[2] With rocket assist.
[3] Approximate.

COMBAT VEHICLES

Assault Amphibious Vehicles. The AAV7A1 family of assault amphibious vehicles can land troops and material, opposed or unopposed, through heavy, 10-foot surf. The AAVP7A1, the troop carrier, can transport 25 Marines, and a crew of three or 10,000 pounds of cargo with the crew of three; the AAVC7A1 is a mobile, moderately armored command and control center; the AAVR7A1 is a recovery vehicle used for retrieving vehicles of similar size and weight from the sea or beachhead. The basic AAVP7A1 weighs 38,450 pounds empty, is 26 feet long, and is powered by a turbocharged Cummins Diesel 400-horsepower engine which operates tracked running gear on land; two waterjets (3,025 pounds of force each) propel the vehicle through water. Fielding of the AA7A1 family of Assault Amphibian Vehicles began in 1983. The AAV7A1 is an improved version of the LVT7 family of vehicles. Improvements include a new power pack, secure voice communications system,

night vision driving device, nonintegral fuel tank, smoke generating system, ungunned weapons system, applique armor, and improved watertight integrity. The AAV7A1 will extend the Marine Corps organic amphibious assault capability into the late 1990s.

Main Battle Tank M60A1. The M60A1 main battle tank weighs 57.3 tons, has a maximum speed of 30 mph, and a 310-mile cruising range. It mounts a 105mm M68 main gun, a coaxial 7.62mm machine gun, and a dual-purpose .50-caliber machine gun. With gyro-stabilization added on, it can fire on the move. Powered by a 12-cylinder, 750-horsepower diesel engine that consumes 1.13 gallons of fuel per mile, or 20 gallons per hour, it has a road speed of 30 miles per hour. The M60A1 can carry 63 rounds of 105mm ammunition, 6,000 rounds of 7.62mm machine gun ammunition, and 900 rounds of .50-caliber ammunition.

Light Armored Vehicle (LAV). Light armored vehicles manufactured by General Motors of Canada began arriving in 1984; as of June 1987, 528 had been fielded. A total of 758 LAVs are to be procured, of which 425 will be primary assault vehicles (LAV 25s). Other variants will include recovery, primary assault, command and control, anti-tank, logistics, and mortar. The LAV 25s are armed with a 25mm chain gun and a 7.62mm machine gun as primary and secondary weapons. LAVs will be organized into three active and one reserve battalion; 90 also will be loaded into MPS ships. All LAVs were expected to be fielded by the end of 1987.

LAV

AIRCRAFT/MARINES

Skyhawk

A-4 SKYHAWK

WING SPAN: 28 feet.
LENGTH: 40 feet.
WEIGHT: empty, 10,465 pounds; full load, 24,500 pounds.
SPEED: maximum at sea level with 4,000-pound bomb load, 645 mph.
CEILING: 49,700 feet.
RANGE: 2,055 nautical miles with external fuel.
POWER PLANT: one Pratt and Whitney 152-P-408A turbojet engine.
ARMAMENT: several hundred variations of loads of more than 10,000 pounds of assorted rockets, bombs, torpedoes, and cannon.
CREW: one.
CONTRACTOR: McDonnell Douglas.

BRIEFING: This aircraft can perform a number of attack missions; it also may escort helicopters during assault operations. Marine A-4s are armed with two internally mounted 20mm cannons and can deliver conventional or nuclear weapons day or night. There are four A-4 attack squadrons, usually with 19 aircraft each, one training squadron, and five Reserve squadrons. A-4Ms from the active forces will replace the older model A-4s in the Reserve; these in turn subsequently will be replaced by F/A-18s.

A-6E INTRUDER

For specifications for the A-6E, see page 199.

BRIEFING: There are five squadrons of A-6s in the active Marine aircraft wings. The A-6, which can deliver both conventional and nuclear weapons, carries up to 14,000 pounds of armament. It provides ground forces with extremely accurate ordnance support during amphibious assault and extended operations inland during night and all weather conditions.

Intruder

AV-8C HARRIER

WING SPAN: 25 feet, three inches.
LENGTH: 45 feet, six inches.
HEIGHT: 11 feet, three inches.
WEIGHT: empty, 12,200 pounds; gross for vertical takeoff, 17,500 pounds; gross for short takeoff, 21,489 pounds.
SPEED: 637 mph at 1,000 feet.
RANGE: 200 nautical-mile radius with 2,500 pounds of ordnance; 400 nautical-mile radius (and one-hour loiter time) with two anti-air missiles.
POWER PLANT: one Rolls-Royce Pegasus Mk103 vectored thrust turbofan engine.
CREW: one.
CONTRACTOR: British Aerospace.

BRIEFING: Adopted in 1969 by the Marine Corps, the AV-8C became the first Vertical/Short Takeoff and Landing (V/STOL) jet aircraft to enter service with U.S. forces. The Marine Corps saw the aircraft as one with great potential in close-air support and air-defense missions. In close air support, the Harrier can land at relatively unprepared sites—and sometimes completely unprepared sites—early in an amphibious assault, making it quickly available for support missions. The British version of the aircraft saw combat in the Falklands in 1982. There are three Harrier squadrons, including one training squadron, in the active Marine aircraft wings.

AV-8B HARRIER

WING SPAN: 30 feet, three inches.
LENGTH: 46 feet, three inches.
HEIGHT: 11 feet, seven inches.
WEIGHT: empty, 12,800 pounds.
MAXIMUM WEIGHT: for short takeoff, 31,000 pounds.
MAXIMUM WEIGHT: for vertical takeoff, 18,900 pounds.
SPEED: 630 mph.
FERRY RANGE: 1,700nm unrefueled.
ARMAMENT: cluster, general purpose and laser-guided bombs, rockets, Maverick, Sidewinder, 25mm cannon.
MAXIMUM ORDNANCE: 16,500-pound bombs.
POWER PLANT: one Rolls-Royce Pegasus F-402-RR-404 vectored thrust turbofan engine.
CREW: one.
CONTRACTOR: McDonnell Douglas.

BRIEFING: The AV-8B is a V/STOL jet aircraft utilizing a vectored thrust turbofan engine. The normal mode of employment is the short take-off, which requires 300-1,200 feet of ground roll. Landings usually are in the vertical mode to minimize ground roll. The first AV-8B squadron stood up in 1985. Total procurement of AV-Bs for the Marine Corps is 328. These aircraft are phasing out AV-8C and A-4M aircraft. This will result in a modern light attack force for the Marine Corps in the 1990s.

Harrier

F-4 PHANTOM

For specifications for the F-4, see page 197.

BRIEFING: This all-weather multi-purpose fighter has been in Marine Corps service since the early 1960s. Its mission is to intercept and destroy enemy aircraft and to attack and destroy surface targets. The Phantom is being replaced by the F/A-18 Hornet. Production of the F-4 ended in 1979. A reconnaissance version, the RF-4, is operated by the Marine Corps' one photo-reconnaissance squadron. There are three Marine Reserve F-4 squadrons. The F-4s will be phased out by October 1991.

Phantom

STREET FIGHTER.

THE AV-8B—the Mean Machine. It thrives in tough neighborhoods.

It actually redefines the air base, operating from battle-scarred urban streets, jungle clearings, remote islands, damaged airfields—almost any small, unimproved site. Which makes it the ideal means of providing close air support for ground troops.

But basing flexibility is only part of the story. The AV-8B's weapon delivery system is the most accurate in the world. In fact, in the 1985 operational evaluation, an AV-8B dropped 24 bombs, only two of which hit more than 20 feet off the intended target.

With dramatically improved handling characteristics, the AV-8B is easy to fly. It offers longer range and a heftier payload. Performs well in extreme climate conditions. And all with minimal ground support and maintenance.

Put it all together and you find the AV-8B is more than a close air support aircraft. It's a surface attack, fleet defense, air-to-air combat and surveillance plane as well.

The AV-8B. "B" as in Big. Bad. Bold. Better. It's the Mean Machine.

MCDONNELL DOUGLAS

Hornet

F/A-18 HORNET

For specifications for the F/A-18, see page 197.

BRIEFING: The F/A-18 is replacing the F-4 Phantom in all 12 of the Marine Corps' fighter squadrons; it has been phasing into Marine Corps operations since 1982. Six F-4 squadrons have transitioned to the F/A-18.

Prowler

EA-6B PROWLER

For specifications for the EA-6B, see page 200.

BRIEFING: The EA-6B gives the landing force commander an excellent weapon against enemy air defenses. The earlier EA-6A entered Marine Corps service in 1966. The Corps operates one active EA-6B squadron in the Regular Forces and one EA-6A squadron in the Reserves.

KC-130 HERCULES

WING SPAN: 132 feet, seven inches.
LENGTH: 99 feet, 10 inches.
HEIGHT: 38 feet, three inches.
WEIGHT: empty, 75,368 pounds; loaded, 155,000 pounds.
SPEED: 348 mph at 19,000 feet; cruise, 331 mph.
RANGE: 2,160 nautical miles.
POWER PLANT: four Allison T56-A-15 turboprop engines.
CREW: two pilots, one navigator, one flight engineer, and one radio operator/loadmaster.
CONTRACTOR: Lockheed-Georgia.

BRIEFING: The KC-130 Hercules provides aerial refueling and "assault air" transport of Marines, equipment, and supplies in support of the Fleet Marine Forces. Other missions include air delivery of combat cargo, including resupply by parachute, and long-range delivery of high-priority cargo and personnel. The aircraft, which entered Marine Corps service in 1961, was combat proven in Vietnam. Configured to carry personnel, it can transport 92 Marines or

Hercules

64 parachutists; configured for cargo, it can transport 26,913 pounds of weapons, equipment, or other supplies. Carrying wounded, it can handle 74 litter patients. The Marine Corps operates three active KC-130 squadrons and one reserve squadron.

Bronco

OV-10 BRONCO

WING SPAN: 40 feet.
LENGTH: 42 feet.
HEIGHT: 15 feet, two inches.
WEIGHT: empty, 6,969 pounds; loaded, 14,466 pounds.
SPEED: 281 mph at sea level.
RANGE: 228 nautical-mile radius.
POWER PLANT: two Garrett T76-G-10/10A/12/12A turboprop engines.
CREW: one pilot, one observer.
CONTRACTOR: Rockwell International.

BRIEFING: The OV-10 is a multi-purpose, observation aircraft used primarily for reconnaissance missions, including control of artillery and naval gunfire spotting. The Bronco also escorts helicopters and is sometimes used for low-level photography. With the second seat removed, the Bronco can transport two litter patients, five parachutists, or 3,200 pounds of cargo. The Bronco is one of the ground force commander's most useful tools for battlefield reconnaissance and special missions. There are two active OV-10 squadrons and one Marine Air Reserve squadron.

HELICOPTERS/MARINES

Sea Cobra

AH-1T SEA COBRA

FUSELAGE LENGTH: 44 feet, 10 inches.
OVERALL LENGTH: 58 feet.
HEIGHT: 14 feet, two inches.
WEIGHT: maximum takeoff and landing, 14,000 pounds.
SPEED: maximum, 219 mph.
RANGE: 261 nautical miles.
POWER PLANT: two Pratt and Whitney T-400-WV-402 turboshaft
  engines.
CREW: one pilot, one gunner.
CONTRACTOR: Bell Helicopter Textron.

BRIEFING: The AH-1T provides fire support and fire support coordination to a landing force during amphibious assaults and shore operations. The aircraft is equipped with a 20mm XM197 gun in a nose turret, 2.75" and 5.0" rockets, Sidewinder air-to-air missiles, and a TOW missile system. The AH-1T and an older version, the AH-1J, are operated in six active composite squadrons of 12 AH-1 and 12 UH-1 aircraft. These units will be upgraded with the AH-1W, a growth version of the AH-1T, which will be equipped with two T700-GE-401 engines for enhanced high/hot operational capability, the HELLFIRE anti-mechanized missile for increased lethality, and a crashworthy fuel system for improved survivability. The active

force also operates one training squadron of 12 AH-1s and 8 UH-1s. The Marine Corps Reserves operate one attack helicopter squadron with 8 AH-1Js and will be building to two squadrons of 12 AH-1Js each as the active force transitions to the AH-1W.

UH-1N HUEY

FUSELAGE LENGTH: 45 feet, 10 inches.
OVERALL LENGTH: 57 feet, three inches.
WEIGHT: empty, 5,549 pounds; maximum weight loaded, 10,500
  pounds.
SPEED: 126 mph.
CEILING: 15,000 feet in horizontal flight; 12,900 feet hovering.
RANGE: 250 nautical miles.
POWER PLANT: two United Aircraft of Canada PT6 turboshaft
  engines.
CREW: two pilots, one crewman.
CONTRACTOR: Bell Helicopter Textron.

BRIEFING: One of the most widely used, versatile, and durable helicopters ever built, the Huey gives Marines support in the ship-to-shore phase of an amphibious assault in shore operations. Early models were used extensively in Vietnam for medical-evacuation and command-and-control missions. The UH-1 entered Marine Corps service in 1964. The UH-1N can carry 8-10 combat-loaded combinations of Marines and/or supplies. As a flying ambulance, it has room for six litter patients and one attendant. It may be armed with a 7.62mm M60 machine gun, a 7.62 GAU-2 B/A mini-gun, a .50 caliber machine gun, and 2.75" rockets. There are six composite UH-1/AH-1 squadrons with 12 UH and 12 AH aircraft each in the active forces, one training squadron, and three UH-1N Reserve units, one with 12 aircraft and two with six aircraft each.

CH-46 SEA KNIGHT

FUSELAGE LENGTH: 45 feet, three inches.
OVERALL LENGTH: 84 feet, four inches.
WEIGHT: empty, 12,112 pounds; loaded, 23,300 pounds.
SPEED: maximum, 166 mph; cruise, 140 mph.
RANGE: 160 nautical miles; ferry range, 620 nautical miles (with
  three internal tanks).
POWER PLANT: two General Electric T58-GE-16 turboshaft engines.
CREW: two pilots, one crewman.
CONTRACTOR: Boeing Vertol.

Huey

Sea Knight

BRIEFING: The CH-46 transports Marines ashore during an amphibious assault, or from one area of the beachhead to another during shore operations. It also moves equipment, weapons, and supplies, and serves as a search and rescue aircraft. The Marines' main assault helicopter during and since the Vietnam War, the CH-46 has been in USMC service since 1965. The CH-46E—the latest model—is expected to reach the end of its service life during the 1990s.

CH-53A/D SEA STALLION

FUSELAGE LENGTH: 67 feet, six inches.
OVERALL LENGTH: 88 feet, six inches.
WEIGHT: empty, 23,628 pounds; maximum weight loaded, 42,000 pounds.
SPEED: maximum, 196 mph; cruise, 173 mph.
CEILING: 21,000 feet in horizontal flight; 13,400 feet hovering.
RANGE: 250 nautical miles; ferry range, 886 nautical miles.
POWER PLANT: two General Electric T64-GE-413 turboshaft engines.
CREW: two pilots, one crewman.
CONTRACTOR: Sikorsky Aircraft.

BRIEFING: The heavy assault CH-53 Sea Stallion helicopter hauls supplies, equipment, and personnel from ship to shore during amphibious assault operations. The aircraft was designed and developed specifically for the Marine Corps by Sikorsky. Loading and unloading, including roll-on and roll-off of some vehicles, is speeded up through the use of a rear ramp. External loads can be carried in slings or nets. It can mount two .50-caliber machine guns. The CH-53, used extensively by the Marines during the Vietnam War, can transport 37 Marines or handle 24 litter patients and four attendants. Capable of lifting 8,000 pounds internally or externally under normal conditions, it can lift an additional 6,000 pounds in certain situations. The Marine Corps presently operates one Reserve and six active CH-53A/D squadrons.

CH-53E SUPER STALLION

FUSELAGE LENGTH: 73 feet, 4 inches.
OVERALL LENGTH: 99 feet, 1/2 inch.
WEIGHT: Empty, 33,236 pounds; maximum loaded, 73,500 pounds.
SPEED: Maximum, 196 mph; cruise, 173 mph.
CEILING: 27,900 feet in horizontal flight; 16,600 feet hovering.
RANGE: 254 nautical miles; ferry range, 942 nautical miles.
POWER PLANT: Three General Electric T64-GE-416 turboshaft engines.
CREW: Two pilots, one crewman.
CONTRACTOR: Sikorsky Aircraft.

BRIEFING: Able to transport 56 combat-ready Marines or 16 tons of cargo, the Super Stallion is the Marine Corps' most powerful helicopter. It can lift the Light Armored Vehicle (LAV), the 155mm howitzer, and that weapon's prime mover, the MN-923 five-ton truck. The CH-53E also can lift all Navy and Marine Corps fighter, attack, and electronic-warfare aircraft. It can refuel in flight from a KC-130 refueler aircraft. There are three CH-53E squadrons in the Marine Corps, with a goal of replacing all CH-53A/Ds with CH-53Es in the 1990s. A continuing series of accidents involving these aircraft, with most occurring during operations on the west coast, led to temporary grounding and to changes in operational procedures. Sikorsky also is making "fixes" which it hopes will markedly improve the aircraft's operational safety record.

Super Stallion

Sea Stallion

SEA POWER:*MARITIME*

The rise or decline in U.S. maritime industries over the years can best be shown through statistics. They effectively and often chronologically chart American shipping and shipbuilding activities and offer a means of comparison to other modes of transportation in U.S. foreign trade. They also show comparative data regarding the size and operation of foreign merchant fleets as well as other competitive factors that reflect upon national commercial and defense considerations. For example:

—Although ships transported more than half of American exports and imports, by 1987 only about 4 percent was moved on U.S.-flag ships. And that, of course, produced an adverse impact on the U.S. shipping balance of payments. The cost to the United States in dollar-exchange payments over receipts for such services reached a record high of $2.3 billion.

—In 1950, the U.S.-flag merchant marine ranked second to that of the United Kingdom in number and deadweight tonnage among the merchant fleets of the world. Since then, despite the tremendous rise in the volume and value of American oceanborne foreign trade, the U.S.-flag merchant fleet fell far behind in number and tonnage of ships, relative to other national registries. By 1987, the U.S.-flag merchant marine ranked in sixth place in tonnage and eighth place in number of ships. The merchant fleets registered under the flags of Liberia, Panama, Japan, Greece, and the U.S.S.R. outranked the United States.

—By 1987, there were 124 countries with merchant fleets comprising 25,238 merchant-type ships of 1,000 gross tons and over, totaling 640.9 million deadweight tons. Here is a table showing the development of the world merchant fleet since 1939:

Year	Countries	No. of Ships	dwt (millions)
1939 . .	49	12,798	80.6
1950 . .	60	13,282	107.2
1960 . .	74	17,317	171.9
1970 . .	96	19,980	327.0
1980 . .	121	24,867	654.9
1981[1] .	122	25,094	662.1
1982[2] .	121	25,482	671.0
1983[2] .	121	25,579	666.4
1984[2] .	121	25,424	656.4
1985[1] .	121	25,473	656.3
1986[1] .	145	25,238	640.9

[1] 1 July. [2] 1 January.

(More detailed tables on the merchant fleets of the world will be found on the following pages.)

Statistics show that America depends upon imports for numerous essential materials needed to fuel the nation's domestic economy and its defense industrial base. The lack of only 26 of the 91 materials considered critical and strategic, which the government stockpiles, determines, in large measure, as noted in *The United States Maritime Industry in the National Interest,* by Irwin M. Heine, ''. . . whether the United States can manufacture automobiles and trucks, railroad equipment, commercial and military aircraft, commercial ships and warships of all types, electronic equipment, radar, anti-friction bearings, computers, machine tools, telephones and other communications equipment, every type of arms and ammunition, petroleum refining and petrochemicals, as well as the thousands of civilian goods and military equipment that have become indispensable in the daily lives of the American people and for the security of the nation.''

Of the 26 representative essential materials, all must be imported in ships, and most of them in bulk lots.

Yet, since only a small percentage of these cargoes travel on U.S.-flag ships, the United States must depend upon the ships of foreign nations for the transportation of materials essential to the nation's industries and defense. The reliability of foreign ships in times of national emergency cannot always be taken for granted.

The impact of depressed domestic and world-wide economic conditions upon U.S. and foreign shipping operations is reflected in the statistics for ships laid up for lack of business. On 30 June 1987, there were 792 ships of all types, totaling 20.58 million deadweight tons, laid up through the world. This represents a sizable improvement since 30 June 1983, when 1,695 ships were laid up.

Seafaring employment has followed a similar decline, shown in the table: *Seafaring Employment on U.S.-Flag Ships.* An important factor in the decline of jobs has been the replacement of many smaller and less efficient ships by fewer, larger, and more productive ships that require smaller crews.

Table M-1

NEW NAVAL COMBATANT AND AUXILIARY VESSELS CONTRACTED FOR WITH PRIVATE U.S. SHIPYARDS

(1,000 Light Displacement Tons and Over)

Calendar Year	Total Vessels	Combatant	Auxiliary	Contract Yards	Light Displacement Tons	Initial Shipyard Contract $ Value
1965	23	10	13	9	158,249	476,579,120
1966	54	45	9	7	246,090	864,902,599
1967	8	1	7	4	50,030	188,549,396
1968	15	10	5	4	152,591	638,238,500
1969	6	6	0	3	79,533	453,180,000
1970	6	6	0	2	132,000	758,100,000
1971	15	15	0	3	88,044	1,055,000,000
1972	14	13	1	4	85,522	852,204,347
1973	7	7	0	2	38,727	512,345,000
1974	16	14	2	4	171,100	1,387,375,100
1975	16	13	3	6	106,197	1,677,241,000
1976	20	14	6	8	91,322	1,254,169,000
1977	15	12	3	8	88,616	1,575,271,000
1978	25	20	5	8	119,478	2,506,400,000
1979	13	11	2	6	60,646	1,356,752,936
1980	11	8	3	6	101,072	1,933,654,550
1981	28	13	15	10	97,307	2,842,300,500
1982	30	18	12	11	324,240	7,801,200,000
1983	27	12	15	10	431,760	5,041,400,000
1984	11	11	0	6	104,157	2,848,800,000
1985	11	4	7	7	92,320	1,679,400,000
1986	79	57	22	15	681,317	16,347,200,000
1987	84	61	23	15	726,043	17,464,750,000

Table M-2

MAJOR MERCHANT FLEETS OF THE WORLD—JULY 1, 1986

Country	No. of Ships[1]	Rank by No. of Ships	Deadweight Tons	Rank by Deadweight Tonnage
Liberia	1,783	3	113,856,000	1
Panama	3,611	1	70,379,000	2
Japan	1,572	5	59,394,000	3
Greece	1,756	4	57,524,000	4
U.S.S.R.	2,531	2	25,151,000	5
United States (privately owned)	468	13	20,790,000	6
United Kingdom	527	9	19,557,000	7
Norway	387	17	17,116,000	8
British Colonies	468	14	16,814,000	9
Cyprus	747	7	16,463,000	10
China (mainland)	1,048	6	15,989,000	11
Italy	573	8	12,557,000	12
France	260	24	11,887,000	13
Korea (Republic of)	487	10	11,150,000	14
Singapore	472	12	11,052,000	15
All Others[2]	8,734	—	136,726,000	—
Total	25,424		616,667,000	

[1] Oceangoing merchant ships of 1,000 gross tons and over.

[2] Includes 269 United States Government-Owned Ships of 3,597,000 dwt.

EMPLOYMENT IN THE SHIPYARD MOBILIZATION BASE

In 1982, the Maritime Administration (MARAD) of the Department of Transportation and the Naval Sea Systems Command defined the Shipyard Moblization Base (SYMBA) in specific terms. Their definition is as follows:

Any facility capable of constructing a vessel over 400 feet in length or having the drydocking capability to repair a vessel over 400 feet in length and any facility capable of performing topside repairs on vessels over 400 feet in length provided that water depth in the channel to the facility is at least 12 feet.

Since October 1982, MARAD has surveyed private United States shipyards which meet the above qualifications to determine production worker employment in the SYMBA. The table below shows results of the surveys. Please note that the total employment is estimated to be 125 percent of production worker employment.

THE U.S. MERCHANT MARINE ACADEMY

The U.S. Merchant Marine Academy, dedicated in 1943, is a tuition-free, four-year accredited college established to prepare young men and women as officers in the American merchant marine and for leadership positions in the maritime industry. Located on Long Island Sound at Kings Point, New York, the Academy is operated by the Maritime Administration of the U.S. Department of Transportation.

Candidates for admission must be nominated by a congressman or senator and must compete for vacancies allocated by state in proportion to its representation in Congress. Enrollment is approximately 885. In 1974 the academy became the first of the federal academies to admit women.

Graduates of the Academy have a variety of options open to them. These include serving as a shipboard merchant marine officer, selecting active military duty as an officer in some branch of the Armed Forces of the United States, or, when shipboard employment is not available, entering the shoreside sector of the maritime industry.

Degrees and Majors: The three basic courses of study, all leading toward a bachelor of science degree, are marine transportation, marine engineering, and the dual license program (which combines the first two curricula). Each graduate receives a merchant marine license certifying qualifications as a third mate, a third assistant engineer, or, in the case of a dual license candidate, both. In addition, each graduate receives a commission as ensign in the U.S. Naval Reserve.

Costs: Upon entrance, each midshipman pays a fee of $663 to cover student activities and personal services.

Financial Aid: The only pay received by a midshipman is $500 a month during two six-month training periods aboard ship.

Application Information: Candidates should contact congressmen and request applications at the end of their junior year in high school. For further information contact:

U.S. Merchant Marine Academy
Admissions Office
Kings Point, N.Y. 11024
Phone: (516) 773-5000

Government Agencies Concerned with Maritime Affairs

U.S. DEPARTMENT OF TRANSPORTATION
400 Seventh St. S.W.
Washington, D.C. 20590
(202) 366-4000

Maritime Administration
Maritime Administrator
(202) 366-5823
Office of Public Affairs
(202) 366-5807
Office of Maritime Labor and Training
(202) 366-5755
Office of Trade Analysis and Insurance
(202) 366-2400

U.S. Coast Guard
2100 Second St. S.W.
Washington, D.C. 20590
(202) 267-2229
Office of Merchant Marine Safety
(202) 267-2200
Office of Merchant Vessel Personnel
(202) 267-0214
Office of Merchant Vessel Inspection Division
(202) 267-2978

	Oct. 1983 101 Shipyards	Oct. 1984 95 Shipyards	Oct. 1985 83 Shipyards	Oct. 1986 74 Shipyards
East Coast	62,593	61,922	59,282	54,163
West Coast	18,392	15,701	13,213	11,609
Gulf Coast	15,835	16,591	14,269	15,369
Great Lakes	1,371	1,511	2,026	3,344
Non Contiguous	375	210	430	275
Total Production	98,566	95,935	89,220	87,760

Source: Shipbuilders Council of America

Table M-3

FY 1988-92 SHIPBUILDING PROGRAM

	FY 1988	FY 1989	FY 1990	FY 1991	FY 1992	FY88-92 Five-Year Total
	(Actual)		(Estimated)			
New Construction						
Trident (Ballistic Missile Submarine)	1	1	1	1	1	5
SSN-688 (Attack Submarine)	3	2	2	2	1	10
SSN-21 (Attack Submarine)	—	1	—	2	2	5
CVN (Aircraft Carrier)	—	—	1	—	—	1
CG-47 (Guided Missile Cruiser)	5	—	—	—	—	5
DDG-51 (Guided Missile Destroyer)	—	3	3	5	6	17
LHD-1 (Amphibious Ship)	1	1	—	1	—	3
LSD-41 (Landing Ship Dock-Cargo Variant)	1	—	1	1	2	5
MCM-1 (Mine Countermeasures Ship)	—	3	—	—	—	3
MHC-1 (Coastal Minehunter)	—	2	3	3	4	12
PXM (Patrol Craft)	—	—	1	—	4	5
AOE-6 (Fast Combat Support Ship)	—	1	—	2	—	3
AE-36 (Ammunition Ship)	—	—	—	1	1	2
ARS (Salvage Ship)	—	—	1	—	—	1
TAO-187 (Fleet Oiler)	2	2	2	1	—	7
TAGOS (Surveillance Ship)	2	1	3	2	—	8
AGOR (Research Ship)	—	1	2	4	—	7
	15	**18**	**20**	**25**	**21**	**99**
Conversions/SLEPs						
CV (Aircraft Carrier) SLEP	1	—	—	1	—	2
AO (Oiler) Conversion	1	2	1	—	—	4
TACS (Crane Ship) Conversion	2	2	—	—	—	4
	4	**4**	**1**	**1**	**0**	**10**

Source: Department of Defense

Table M-4

SEAFARING EMPLOYMENT ON U.S.-FLAG SHIPS 1945 TO 1987[2]
(privately owned merchant ships, by type of ship[2])

As of 30 September	Number of Operating Ships	Number of Shipboard Jobs			
		Total	Pass./Cargo	Cargo	Tanker
1945[4]	3,500	168,070	4,410	130,250	33,410
1950	1,082	53,506	8,435	27,851	17,220
1955	1,108	57,678	8,131	34,440	15,107
1960	945	48,846	8,863	28,442	11,541
1965	948	48,273	6,763	30,823	10,687
1970	770	36,168	2,178	23,488	10,502
1975	507	20,089	860	12,107	7,122
1980	527	19,362	617	10,184	8,561
1981	519	18,826	618	9,652	8,556
1982[1]	500	17,347	836	8,961	7,550
1983[1]	452	15,286	739	7,681	6,866
1984[1]	402	13,407	739	6,797	5,871
1985[1]	406	13,139	460	7,059	5,620
1986[2]	371	11,029	710	5,762	4,557
1987[2]	366	10,829	710	5,262	4,857

* Not available.

[1] As of 1 September.

[2] As of 1 June.

[3] Oceangoing ships of 1,000 gross tons and over.

[4] Estimated peak number of U.S.-flag ships in operation during World War II.

Source: Department of Transportation, Maritime Administration, Office of Maritime Labor and Training

FEDERAL MARITIME COMMISSION
1100 L St. N.W.
Washington, D.C. 20573
(202) 523-5707
Chairman
(202) 523-5911
Public Information Office
(202) 523-5707

U.S. DEPARTMENT OF COMMERCE
14th and E Sts. N.W.
Washington, D.C. 20230
(202) 377-2000

Bureau of the Census
Washington, D.C. 20233
(202) 763-4040

National Oceanic & Atmospheric Administration
National Ocean Survey
Office of Marine Operations
6001 Executive Blvd.
Rockville, Md. 20852
(301) 443-8910

Division of Foreign Trade
Transportation Branch (Shipping)
(202) 763-7770

U.S. DEPARTMENT OF THE NAVY
Military Sealift Command
Building 210
Washington Navy Yard
Washington, D.C. 20398-5100
(202) 433-0001
Office of Public Affairs
(202) 433-0330

U.S. DEPARTMENT OF LABOR
200 Constitution Ave. N.W.
Washington, D.C. 20210
(202) 523-7316

Bureau of Labor Statistics
441 G St. N.W.
Washington, D.C. 20212
(202) 523-1913

Federal Mediation and Conciliation Service
14th St. and Constitution Ave. N.W.
Washington, D.C. 20427
(202) 653-5290

U.S. DEPARTMENT OF THE TREASURY
15th St. and Pennsylvania Ave. N.W.
Washington, D.C. 20220
(202) 566-2111

U.S. Customs Service
1301 Constitution Ave. N.W.
Washington, D.C. 20229
(202) 566-3962

Table M-5

SHIPS LAID UP THROUGHOUT THE WORLD FOR LACK OF EMPLOYMENT

Comparison: 1973 to 1987

(dry cargo ships and tankers*; in millions of deadweight tons)

Date	Total		Dry Cargo		Tankers	
	No.	dwt	No.	dwt	No.	dwt
30 June 1987	792	20.58	638	6.38	154	14.20
31 December 1986	953	24.06	786	7.98	167	16.08
30 June 1986	1,021	36.4	795	8.2	226	28.3
31 Dec. 1985	1,212	54.3	913	9.8	299	44.4
30 June 1985	1,257	64.11	924	9.66	333	54.45
31 Dec. 1984	1,302	62.37	968	10.4	344	51.98
30 June 1984	1,471	71.3	1,099	13.1	372	58.2
31 Dec. 1983	1,663	79.8	1,245	16.4	418	63.3
30 June 1983	1,694	97.9	1,247	25.1	447	72.9
31 Dec. 1982	1,549	83.8	1,146	23.6	403	60.1
30 June, 1982	861	59.3	511	6.5	350	52.8
31 Dec. 1981	527	27.4	319	2.8	208	24.6
30 June 1981	414	17.3	287	1.9	127	15.4
31 Dec. 1980	402	9.2	325	2.2	77	7.0
30 June 1980	401	14.7	297	2.2	104	12.5
31 Dec. 1979	411	11.1	320	2.7	91	8.4
30 June 1979	507	21.4	363	4.9	144	16.5
31 Dec. 1978	593	30.2	370	7.0	223	23.2
30 June 1978	763	57.0	395	13.5	368	43.5
31 Dec. 1977	657	43.2	335	11.7	322	31.5
30 June 1977	544	37.1	217	6.0	327	31.1
31 Dec. 1976	595	35.7	236	5.3	359	30.4
30 June 1976	704	49.5	234	7.0	470	42.5
31 Dec. 1975	648	46.3	194	7.4	454	38.9
30 June 1975	531	33.4	163	6.0	368	27.4
31 Dec. 1974	154	2.0	108	0.4	46	1.6
30 June 1974	127	0.6	111	0.5	16	0.1
31 Dec. 1973	160	1.0	136	0.5	24	0.5

*Ships of 100 gross tons and over. Ships laid up in the U.S. Reserve Fleet and in the Eastern Bloc are excluded.

Source: "World Merchant Shipping Laid-up For Lack of Employment." Prepared monthly by the General Council of British Shipping, based on "Lloyd's Monthly List of Laid-up Vessels," published by Lloyd's of London Press Ltd.

U.S. DEPARTMENT OF STATE
2201 C St. N.W.
Washington, D.C. 20520
(202) 647-4000

Office of Citizen Consular Services
(202) 647-3666

*Office of Maritime
and Land Transport*
(202) 647-5840

**NATIONAL LABOR
RELATIONS BOARD**
1717 Pennsylvania Ave. N.W.
Washington, D.C. 20570
(202) 632-4952

**U.S. MARITIME TRADE
ASSOCIATIONS**

American Association of Port
Authorities (AAPA)
1010 Duke Street
Alexandria, Va. 22314
(703) 684-5700

American Institute of Merchant
Shipping (AIMS)
1000 16th St., N.W., Suite 511
Washington, D.C. 20036
(202) 775-4399

American Maritime Association
(AMA)
485 Madison Ave., 15th Floor
New York, N.Y. 10022
(212) 319-9217

American Maritime Officers Service
(AMOS)
Suite 3204, 490 L'Enfant Plaza, E, S.W.
Washington, D.C. 20005
(202) 479-1133

American Waterways Operators, Inc.
(AWO)
1600 Wilson Blvd., Suite 1000
Arlington, Va. 22209
(703) 841-9300

Boston Shipping Association
223 Lewis Wharf
Boston, Mass. 02110
(617) 523-3762

Council of American Flag Ship
Operators (CASO)
1627 K St. N.W., Suite 1200
Washington, D.C. 20006
(202) 466-5388

Council of North Atlantic
Shipping Association
600 Lafayette Building
Philadelphia, Pa. 19106
(215) 922-7510

Federation of American-Controlled
Shipping (FACS)
50 Broadway
New York, N.Y. 10004
(212) 344-1483

Joint Maritime Congress (JMC)
444 N. Capitol St., Suite 801
Washington, D.C. 20001
(202) 638-2405

Labor Management
Maritime Committee
100 Indiana Ave. N.W.
Washington, D.C. 20001
(202) 347-9771

Lake Carriers Association (LCA)
915 Rockefeller Building
Cleveland, Ohio 44113
(216) 621-1107

Marine Towing and Transportation
Employers Association
17 Battery Place, North, Room 1408
New York, N.Y. 10004
(212) 344-9097

Maritime Association of the
Port of New York/New Jersey
17 Battery Place
Suite 1006
New York, N.Y. 10004
(212) 425-5704

Maritime Institute of Research and
Industrial Development (MIRAID)
1133 15th St. N.W., Suite 600
Washington, D.C. 20005
(202) 463-6505

Maritime Service Committee
Mr. Edward Morgan
c/o Farrell Lines, Inc.
1 Whitehall St.
New York, N.Y. 10004
(212) 440-4868

Table M-6

NEW MERCHANT TYPE VESSEL CONTRACTS WITH U.S. PRIVATE SHIPYARDS*

(1,000 Gross Tons and Over)

Year	No.	G.T.	Construction Subsidy No.	G.T.	Contracted for Government Account No.	G.T.	for U.S. Flag No Subsidy No.	G.T.	For Foreign Registry No.	G.T.
1955	18	195,800	2	36,400	7	37,900	6	98,500	3	23,000
1956	57	1,324,600	2	30,000	1	16,500	37	777,800	17	500,300
1957	32	691,700	—	—	2	18,800	26	552,900	4	120,000
1958	22	176,000	19	167,600	—	—	3	8,400	—	—
1959	19	195,600	15	147,600	—	—	4	48,000	—	—
1960	23	269,700	23	269,700	—	—	—	—	—	—
1961	31	431,200	22	239,000	—	—	9	192,200	—	—
1962	15	173,500	14	147,500	—	—	1	26,000	—	—
1963	25	291,300	18	202,800	1	12,000	6	76,500	—	—
1964	18	277,200	17	240,200	—	—	1	37,000	—	—
1965	14	147,900	9	110,100	—	—	5	37,800	—	—
1966	16	244,400	14	202,600	—	—	2	41,800	—	—
1967	29	749,700	11	290,400	—	—	18	459,300	—	—
1968	23	614,400	11	209,800	—	—	12	404,600	—	—
1969	8	309,000	2	36,000	—	—	6	273,000	—	—
1970	13	579,500	8	358,100	—	—	5	221,400	—	—
1971	24	617,000	10	416,100	1	5,000	13	195,900	—	—
1972	47	1,537,900	25	1,218,400	—	—	22	319,500	—	—
1973	41	1,978,000	15	985,200	1	5,000	25	987,800	—	—
1974	15	1,113,300	2	398,000	—	—	13	715,300	—	—
1975	11	507,900	—	—	—	—	11	507,900	—	—
1976	16	339,400	6	120,300	—	—	10	219,100	—	—
1977	12	258,000	9	245,000	—	—	3	13,000	—	—
1978	30	394,000	10	196,500	—	—	20	197,500	—	—
1979	21	487,200	4	140,000	—	—	17	347,200	—	—
1980	7	116,200	—	—	—	—	7	116,200	—	—
1981	8	148,000	2	42,000	—	—	6	106,000	—	—
1982	3	12,200	—	—	—	—	3	12,200	—	—
1983	4	7,200	—	—	—	—	4	7,200	—	—
1984	5	227,400	—	—	—	—	5	227,400	—	—
1985	—	—	—	—	—	—	—	—	—	—
1986	—	—	—	—	—	—	—	—	—	—
1987	—	—	—	—	—	—	—	—	—	—

*New contracts that were cancelled are not included in this table.

Source: Shipbuilders Council of America

Mobile Steamship Association
Commerce Building, Suite 600
Mobile, Ala. 36633
(205) 432-3626

National Maritime Council
1748 N St. N.W.
Washington, D.C. 20036
(202) 785-3754

New Orleans Steamship Association
219 Carondelet St., Suite 300
New Orleans, La. 70130
(504) 522-9392

New York Shipping Association, Inc.
80 Broad St.
New York, N.Y. 10004
(212) 747-3700

The Tow Boat and
Harbor Carriers Association of NY/NJ
17 Battery Place, Room 1408
New York, N.Y. 10004
(212) 943-8480

Pacific Maritime Association (PMA)
635 Sacramento St.
San Francisco, Calif. 94111
(415) 362-7973

Pacific Merchant Shipping Association
635 Sacramento St.
San Francisco, Calif. 94111
(415) 986-7900

Philadelphia Marine Trade Association
Lafayette Building
Philadelphia, Pa. 19106
(215) 922-7510

Table M-7

INTERNATIONAL TRANSPORTATION TRANSACTIONS OF THE UNITED STATES, BY TYPE, 1981-1986

(millions of dollars)

Type of Transportation	1981	1982	1983	1984	1985	1986p
Total Receipts from Foreign Sources	15,671	15,491	15,627	16,837	17,106	18,752
Ocean passenger fares	*	*	*	*	*	*
Other ocean transportation	8,027	7,686	8,133	8,849	8,819	9,395
Freight	3,364	3,104	3,456	3,265	3,440	3,185
Port expenditures	4,552	4,468	4,562	5,457	5,247	6,070
Charter hire	111	114	115	127	132	140
Air passenger fares	3,111	3,174	3,037	3,028	3,040	3,562
Other air transportation	4,049	4,152	3,986	4,445	4,766	5,298
Freight	752	762	576	645	706	783
Port expenditures	3,297	3,390	3,410	3,800	4,060	4,150
Aircraft leasing						365
Miscellaneous Receipts	484	479	471	515	481	497
Total Payments to Foreign Sources	16,961	16,482	17,706	21,345	23,165	23,941
Ocean passenger fares	287	290	305	305	320	320
Other ocean transportation	8,613	8,017	8,319	10,255	10,890	11,640
Import freight	6,073	5,562	5,827	7,755	8,306	9,076
Port expenditures	2,054	1,957	1,980	1,972	2,048	2,026
Charter hire	486	498	512	528	536	538
Air passenger fares	4,200	4,482	5,179	6,197	6,993	6,522
Other air transportation	3,585	3,456	3,663	4,345	4,736	5,209
Import freight	671	725	1,066	1,633	1,683	2,059
Port expenditures	2,914	2,731	2,597	2,712	3,053	3,100
Aircraft leasing						50
Miscellaneous payments	276	237	240	243	226	250
Deficit	−1,290	−991	−2,079	−4,508	−6,059	−5,189

p Preliminary
* Less than $500,000

Source: U.S. Department of Commerce, Bureau of Economic Analysis, Balance of Payments Division, June 16, 1987

Table M-8

MERCHANT FLEETS OF THE WORLD
Oceangoing Steam and Motor Ships[1] of 1,000 Gross Tons and Over as of July 1, 1986
(Tonnage in Thousands)

Type of Vessel

	Total			Combination Passenger & Cargo			Freighters			Bulk Carriers			Tankers		
	No.	Gross Tons	dwt	No.	Gross Tons	dwt	No.	Gross Tons	dwt	No.	Gross Tons	dwt	No.	Gross Tons	dwt
All Countries	25,238	388,331	640,968	375	3,898	1,589	13,744	97,178	125,182	5,714	135,148	235,426	5,405	152,107	278,771
UNITED STATES	737	16,157	24,387	37	514	300	419	6,560	7,459	24	672	1,143	257	8,412	15,485
Privately Owned	468	13,203	20,790	8	139	74	207	4,500	4,817	24	672	1,143	229	7,892	14,755
Government Owned	269	2,954	3,597	29	375	226	212	2,059	2,642	—	—	—	28	520	729
Reserve Fleet	213	2,259	2,778	22	296	169	165	1,457	1,901	—	—	—	26	506	709
Other	56	695	819	7	79	56	47	603	741	—	—	—	2	14	21
*Albania	10	51	73	—	—	—	10	51	73	—	—	—	—	—	—
Algeria	61	810	967	1	4	—	38	205	292	4	57	93	18	544	580
Angola	13	69	107	—	—	—	12	68	105	—	—	—	1	2	2
Argentina	178	2,178	3,346	1	4	3	94	760	1,042	20	533	904	63	880	1,397
Aruba	1	127	257	—	—	—	—	—	—	—	—	—	1	127	257
Australia	76	1,997	3,223	—	—	—	24	241	285	33	1,090	1,805	19	666	1,132
Austria	24	120	203	—	—	—	19	47	79	5	73	124	—	—	—
Bahrain	3	22	38	—	—	—	2	5	5	1	17	29	—	—	—
Bangladesh	40	295	416	1	12	6	35	260	376	1	8	12	3	15	23
Barbados	2	3	7	1	—	—	1	3	7	—	—	—	—	—	—
Belgium	78	2,236	3,715	1	13	15	29	342	414	33	1,468	2,664	15	413	622
Benin	1	3	3	—	—	—	1	3	3	—	—	—	—	—	—
Bolivia	3	11	12	—	—	—	3	11	12	—	—	—	—	—	—
Brazil	344	6,087	10,025	3	5	4	164	1,157	1,529	92	2,801	4,768	85	2,124	3,725
*British Colonies	489	11,273	18,489	3	25	7	197	1,518	1,883	227	7,362	12,599	62	2,368	3,999
*Bulgaria	118	1,298	1,916	4	20	22	51	307	372	46	634	985	17	337	538
Burma	17	100	132	3	4	4	14	96	129	—	—	—	—	—	—
Cameroon	6	67	82	—	—	—	6	67	82	—	—	—	—	—	—
Canada	97	848	1,271	5	17	5	29	126	150	21	416	683	42	289	433
Cape Verde	4	8	14	—	—	—	4	8	14	—	—	—	—	—	—
Chile	36	508	895	—	—	—	20	131	190	12	314	604	4	63	101
*China (People's Republic)	1,055	10,599	16,125	12	127	77	714	5,135	7,241	189	3,751	6,243	140	1,587	2,564
China (Republic of)	210	4,504	7,017	1	2	1	130	1,578	1,899	62	2,341	4,075	17	584	1,043
Colombia	43	370	471	2	12	12	35	296	362	1	29	43	5	33	53
*Cuba	103	770	1,060	2	15	10	79	614	835	9	74	114	13	67	100
Cyprus	762	10,045	17,553	5	36	13	465	2,259	3,477	187	3,385	5,733	105	4,365	8,330
*Czechoslovakia	19	184	275	—	—	—	14	82	112	5	103	163	—	—	—
Denmark	250	4,328	6,642	3	7	3	160	1,690	1,823	13	316	556	74	2,315	4,260
Dominican Republic	10	32	54	1	11	19	9	21	35	—	—	—	—	—	—
Ecuador	58	453	653	2	3	1	34	238	288	2	13	24	20	199	340
Equatorial Guinea	2	6	3	—	—	—	2	6	3	—	—	—	—	—	—
Ethiopia	10	62	77	—	—	—	9	61	75	—	—	—	1	1	2
Fiji	5	14	13	—	—	—	2	9	7	—	—	—	3	5	6
Finland	103	1,329	2,102	2	31	7	53	358	476	18	168	228	30	771	1,392
France	252	6,019	9,989	6	38	16	138	1,537	1,861	32	998	1,698	76	3,446	6,414
Gabon	3	93	164	—	—	—	2	19	25	—	—	—	1	74	139
Gambia	1	1	3	—	—	—	1	2	3	—	—	—	—	—	—
*Germany Democratic Republic	161	1,348	1,805	2	26	5	133	890	1,119	22	382	605	4	50	75
Germany (Federal Republic)	529	4,783	6,559	7	63	37	416	3,056	3,751	23	633	1,007	83	1,031	1,764
Ghana	16	107	142	—	—	—	16	107	142	—	—	—	—	—	—
Greece	1,679	31,568	56,631	32	202	96	643	4,890	7,285	699	14,032	24,905	305	12,443	24,344
Greenland	1	1	2	—	—	—	1	1	1	—	—	—	—	—	—
Guatemala	4	9	13	—	—	—	4	9	13	—	—	—	—	—	—
Honduras	123	373	545	—	—	—	90	267	368	8	48	77	25	59	100
*Hungary	22	87	120	—	—	—	22	87	120	—	—	—	—	—	—
Iceland	29	58	93	1	—	1	26	55	87	—	—	—	2	3	5
India	346	6,362	10,493	5	33	26	167	1,543	2,232	115	2,948	5,080	59	1,839	3,156
Indonesia	336	1,542	2,314	9	66	35	230	774	1,136	12	139	207	85	563	935
Iran	115	2,793	4,904				40	405	560						

Country															
Japan	1,562	36,982	59,072				636	6,640	478	6,248	14,818	25,800	442	15,480	27,009
Jordan	3	36	57				1	10	2	14	26	43		59	114
Kenya	51	359	592	1	4	2	42	233	5	362	64	114	70	1,023	1,892
*Korea (People's Republic)	476	6,600	11,065				237	1,310	169	1,798	4,268	7,374	34	1,979	3,301
Korea (Republic of)	71	2,594	4,135				37	616		834			2		23
Kuwait	105	436	661		143	56	92	299	11	429	122	209	674	33,814	66,805
Lebanon	1,742	57,200	108,672	9			351	3,304	708	4,447	19,939	37,364	12	710	1,323
Liberia	27	781	1,417				15	71		94			2	9	13
Libya	13	63	87				10	54	22	74	465	792	39	609	787
Malagasy	177	1,609	2,315	2	5	4	114	530	5	733	55	88	3	9	1
Malaysia	23	113	170	1	4	5	16	53	58	75	1,057	1,776			
Maldives	185	2,200	3,642	2	19	6	114	614	58	893			11	510	968
Malta	1									1					
Mauritania	7	146	250	1	2	2	3	19	3	27	125	221	46	851	1,338
Mauritius	78	1,266	1,970				21	150	11	195	265	436	16	3	3
Mexico	1	3	5											163	272
Monaco	47	361	594				25	74	6	112	125	209	81	4,485	8,397
Morocco	8	16	23					16		23		58			
Mozambique	177	5,903	10,500	11	167	39	57	390	28	515	861	1,550	81		
Nassau Bahamas	6	65	92	2	9	8	16	18	2	25	37	58		629	1,186
Nauru	461	4,027	6,147	4	108	18	357	1,811	24	2,413	580	979	76	1,529	1,529
Netherlands	24	259	309				13	151	6	144	32	49	5	76	2,737
New Zealand	3	19	27				3	19		27				112	117
Nicaragua	30	493	739				25	277		322			9	470	203
Nigeria	352	9,468	15,370	22	358	68	120	960	74	1,175	2,918	5,081	136	5,233	9,047
Norway	2	130	257						1	21	12	17	1	126	256
Oman (Muscat)	39	439	638	4	32	1	33	352		500				43	89
Pakistan	3,593	42,209	69,277	38	507	224	2,025	13,107	944	18,102	17,902	31,039	586	10,693	19,912
Panama	9	20	14			4		9	1	14					
Papua New Guinea	9	20	28			9	4	20		28				130	223
Paraguay	53	582	922				31	247	12	344	205	356	10	629	1,186
Peru	463	6,495	10,942	13	55	32	209	1,091	195	1,548	4,720	8,177	46	308	1,529
Philippines	281	3,127	4,446	2	18	9	178	1,301	92	1,537	1,499	2,370	9	676	1,329
Poland	68	1,137	1,988	1	4	4	40	205	10	266	252	389	17	112	203
Portugal	16	316	470				13	205		267			9	470	846
Qatar	280	3,138	4,807	1	7	2	204	1,072	66	1,384	1,590	2,574	9	1,833	3,362
Romania	151	2,883	4,931	3	12	8	64	603	17	846	435	716	67		
Saudi Arabia	5	15	23	1	1	1	4	14		21			1		
Senegal	1									2					
Seychelles	465	6,680	11,121	1	2	2	278	2,267	88	3,125	2,450	4,362	98	1,961	3,632
Somalia	6	23	32				6	23	3	32	125	223	3	38	62
South Africa	16	463	570				10	300	73	286	1,293	2,309	95	2,545	5,098
Spain	457	4,735	8,776	1	3		288	894	9	1,368	242	393	4	137	255
Sri Lanka	41	613	948				28	233		300					
Sudan	11	93	123				11	93		123					
Surinam	3	7	9				1	9		9					
Sweden	188	2,013	2,681	2	12	3	106	1,102	19	1,208	301	481	61	598	990
Switzerland	32	344	538				13	65	12	83	264	428	7	15	27
Syria	15	43	60				14	40		56			1	1	4
Tanzania	5	31	45				4	30		43			1	3	2
Thailand	108	490	718				81	391	3	565	30	48	24	69	105
Togo	5	54	76				5	54		76					
Tonga	7	14	19	6	33		5	11	3	16	37	58	2	3	3
Tunisia	23	158	224	10	59	12	11	46	61	53	1,310	2,228	9	74	114
Turkey	329	3,490	6,010	52	478	49	207	693	15	1,064	323	524	55	1,454	2,706
U.A.R. (Egypt)	138	903	1,322			124	102	443	228	619	3,515	5,497	11	77	130
*U.S.S.R.	2,540	19,177	25,427	13	336	81	1,808	10,070		12,146	17	27	452	5,113	7,661
United Arab Emirates	49	621	970				29	240	88	313	2,340	4,091	18	364	630
United Kingdom	493	11,332	17,795				188	2,387		2,614			204	6,269	11,000
Uruguay	10	116	192				4	36		53	115	192	4	75	138
Vanuatu	11	153	261				36	41	6	65	92	150	1	556	4
Venezuela	79	930	1,415				46	282	9	389	150	23	24	34	875
Vietnam	61	283	431				53	235	2	352	14		6		55
Western Samoa	3	25	34				3	25		34					
Yemen	2	3	5	4	16	8				2			1	2	3
Yugoslavia	265	2,840	4,418	1	14	15	183	1,329	66	1,881	1,190	2,010	12	304	520
Zaire	7	70	104				6	56		89					

† Note: Tonnage figures may not be additive due to rounding.

* Source material limited.

Source: U.S. Department of Transportation, Maritime Administration, Office of Trade Studies and Subsidy Contracts

Table M-9

PRODUCTION WORKER EMPLOYMENT
IN MAJOR SHIPBUILDING & REPAIR FACILITIES

	Oct. 1982 110 Shipyards	Oct. 1983 100 Shipyards	Oct. 1984 94 Shipyards	Oct. 1985 83 Shipyards	Oct. 1986 74 Shipyards
East Coast	63,108	62,293	61,614	59,282	54,163
West Coast	23,724	18,392	15,701	13,213	11,609
Gulf Coast	22,886	15,835	16,591	14,269	15,369
Great Lakes	2,287	1,371	1,511	2,026	3,344
Non Contiguous.	450	375	210	430	275
Total Production	112,455	98,266	95,627	89,220	84,760

Source: Shipbuilders Council of America

The Kendall Whaling Museum
Stuart M. Frank, Director
P.O. Box 297
Sharon, Mass. 02067
(617) 784-5642

Maine Maritime Museum
John S. Carter, Director
963 Washington Street
Bath, Me. 14530
(207) 443-1316

Manitowoc Maritime Museum
Burt Logan, Director
75 Maritime Drive
Manitowoc, Wisc. 54220
(414) 684-0218

The Mariners' Museum
William D. Wilkinson, Director
Newport News, Va. 23606
(804) 595-0368

Maritime Museum Assn. of San Diego
Capt. Peter S. Branson, Director
1306 North Harbor Drive
San Diego, Calif. 92101
(619) 234-9153

Maritime Museum of the Atlantic
David B. Flemming, Director
1675 Lower Water Street
Halifax, Nova Scotia B3J 1S3 CANADA
(902) 429-8210

The M.I.T. Museum, Hart Nautical Collection
Warren A. Seamens, Director
265 Massachusetts Avenue
Cambridge, Mass. 02139
(617) 253-4444

Mystic Seaport Museum
J. Revell Carr, Director
Mystic, Conn. 06355
(203) 572-0711

Nantucket Historical Association
John N. Welch, Administrator
P.O. Box 1016
Nantucket, Mass. 02554
(617) 228-1894

National Maritime Museum at San Francisco
Glennie Wall, Manager, Maritime Unit
Golden Gate National Recreation Area
National Park Service
Ft. Mason, Bldg. 201
San Francisco, Calif. 94123
(415) 556-3002

The Navy Museum
Oscar P. Fitzgerald, Director
Bldg. 76, Washington Navy Yard
Washington, D.C. 20390
(202) 433-4882

North Carolina Maritime Museum
Charles R. McNeill, Director
315 Front Street
Beaufort, North Carolina 28516
(919) 728-7317

Old Dartmouth Historical Society
  Whaling Museum
Richard C. Kugler, Director
18 Johnny Cake Hill
New Bedford, Mass. 02740
(617) 997-0046

Peabody Museum of Salem
Peter Fetchko, Director
East India Marine Hall
Salem, Mass. 01970
(617) 745-1876

Penobscot Marine Museum
Robert D. Farwell, Director
Searsport, Me. 04974
(207) 548-2529

Philadelphia Maritime Museum
Theodore T. Newbold, President
321 Chestnut Street
Philadelphia, Pa. 19106
(215) 925-5439

Radcliffe Maritime Museum
Mary Ellen Hayward, Curator
The Maryland Historical Society
201 West Monument Street
Baltimore, Md. 21201
(301) 685-3750, Ext. 40

Sag Harbor Whaling and Historical Museum
George A. Finckenor, Sr., Curator
P.O. Box 1327
Sag Harbor, N.Y. 11796
(516) 567-1733

The Smithsonian Institution
Dr. Harold Langley
Curator of Naval History
National Museum of American History
Washington, D.C. 20560
(202) 357-2249

The Smithsonian Institution
Curator of Maritime History
Division of Transportation
National Museum of American History
Washington, D.C. 20560
(202) 357-2025

South Street Seaport Museum
Peter Neill, President
207 Front Street
New York, N.Y. 10038
(212) 669-9400

Suffolk Marine Museum
Roger B. Dunkerley, Director
Montauk Highway
West Sayville, N.Y. 11796
(516) 567-1733

Thousand Islands Shipyard Museum
Capt. Ferdinand Collins, Director
750 Mary Street
Clayton, N.Y. 13624
(315) 686-4104

U.S. Coast Guard Museum
Paul H. Johnson, Curator
U.S. Coast Guard Academy
New London, Conn. 06320
(203) 444-8511

U.S. Frigate Constellation
Herbert E. Witz, President
Constellation Dock
Baltimore, Md. 21202
(301) 539-1797

U.S. Naval Academy Museum
William W. Jeffries, Director
Annapolis, Md. 21402
(301) 267-2108

U.S.S. Constitution Museum Foundation
Richard C. Wheeler, Director
Boston Naval Shipyard
Boston, Mass. 02129
(617) 242-0543

Vancouver Maritime Museum
Robin R. Inglis, Director
1905 Ogden Street
Vancouver, British Columbia
V6J 3J9 CANADA
(604) 736-4431

Whaling Museum Society
Ann M. Gill, Director
Cold Spring Harbor, N.Y. 11724
(516) 367-3418

PORT AUTHORITIES

Officials at the port authorities listed below will advise on services available.

NORTH ATLANTIC
Eastport	(207) 853-4614
Portland	(207) 772-0690
Portsmouth	(603) 436-8500
Boston	(617) 973-5500
Fall River	(617) 674-5707
Providence	(401) 781-4717
New York/NJ	(212) 466-8337
Albany	(518) 445-2599
Philadelphia	(215) 928-9100
Camden	(609) 541-8500
Wilmington	(302) 571-4600

CHESAPEAKE AREA
Baltimore	(800) 638-7519
Norfolk	(804) 623-8000
Richmond	(804) 780-4326

GREAT LAKES
Buffalo	(716) 855-7411
Cleveland	(216) 241-8004
Toledo	(419) 243-8251
Detroit	(313) 259-8077
Green Bay	(414) 497-3265
Burns Harbor	(219) 787-8636
Chicago	(312) 646-4400
Milwaukee	(414) 278-3511
Duluth	(218) 727-8525
Kenosha	(414) 652-3125

SOUTH ATLANTIC
Morehead City	(919) 726-3158
Wilmington	(919) 763-1621
Georgetown	(803) 527-4476
Charleston	(803) 723-8651
Savannah	(912) 964-3811
Brunswick	(912) 264-7295
Fernandina Beach	(904) 261-0098
Jacksonville	(904) 630-3000
Canaveral	(305) 783-7831
Palm Beach	(305) 842-4201
Port Everglades	(305) 523-3404
Miami	(305) 371-7678

GULF COAST
Manatee	(813) 722-6621
Tampa	(813) 248-1924
Panama City	(904) 763-8471
Pensacola	(904) 435-1870

TABLE M-10

NEW NAVAL VESSELS 1,000 LIGHT DISPLACEMENT TONS AND OVER UNDER CONSTRUCTION OR ON ORDER IN U.S. PRIVATE SHIPYARDS

	1985		1986		1988	
	No.	LDT	No.	LDT	No.	LDT
Fast Combat Support Ship (AOE)					1	19,700
Repair Drydock (ARDM)	1	5,300	1	5,300		
Salvage Ship (ARS)	4	10,900	2	5,450		
Guided Missile Cruiser (CG)	14	124,740	12	106,920	3	26,730
Aircraft Carrier (Nuclear) (CVN)	3	213,000	3	213,000		
Guided Missile Destroyer (DDG)			1	8,300	1	8,300
Guided Missile Frigate (FFG)	10	27,270	5	13,635		
Dock Landing Ship (LSD)	6	66,600	7	77,700		
Amphibious Assault Ship (LHD)	1	28,500	1	28,500		
Mine Countermeasures Ship (MCM)	5	5,000	5	5,000		
Coastal Minehunter Ship (MNE)					1	780
Ballistic Missile Submarine (Nuclear) (SSBN) . .	6	75,000	5	62,500	1	12,500
Attack Submarine (Nuclear) (SSN)	18	108,000	15	90,000	4	24,000
Oiler (T-5)	5	45,000	2	18,000		
Ocean Surveillance Ship (T-AGOS)	9	14,400	7	11,200	3	4,800
Oceanographic Survey Ship (T-AGS)			2	17,620		
Prepositioning Ship (T-AKX)	5	113,500	2	45,400		
Fleet Oiler (T-AO)	4	38,000	7	66,500	2	19,000
USCG Medium Endurance Cutter (WMEC) . . .	9	10,800	8	9,600		
Totals.	**100**	**886,010**	**85**	**784,625**	**16**	**115,810**

Source: Shipbuilders Council of America

Mobile	(205) 690-6020	Los Angeles	(213) 519-3840
Pascagoula	(601) 762-4041	Long Beach	(213) 437-0041
Gulfport	(601) 865-4300	Hueneme	(805) 488-3677
New Orleans	(504) 522-2551	Richmond	(415) 620-6784
Baton Rouge	(504) 387-4207	San Francisco	(415) 391-8000
Lake Charles	(318) 439-3661	Oakland	(800) 227-2726
Beaumont	(409) 835-5367	Sacramento	(916) 371-8000
Port Arthur	(713) 983-2011	Stockton	(209) 946-0246
Houston	(713) 226-2100	Coos Bay	(503) 267-7678
Galveston	(713) 765-9321	Portland	(503) 231-5000
Freeport	(409) 233-2667	Vancouver	(206) 693-3611
Corpus Christi	(512) 882-5633	Longview	(206) 425-3305
Brownsville	(512) 831-4592	Tacoma	(206) 383-5841
PACIFIC COAST		Seattle	(206) 728-3400
San Diego	(800) 854-2757	Bellingham	(206) 676-2500

Table M-11

NEW MERCHANT TYPE VESSELS 1,000 GROSS TONS AND OVER UNDER CONSTRUCTION OR ON ORDER IN U.S. PRIVATE SHIPYARDS

	Jan. 1982		Jan. 1983		Jan. 1984		Jan. 1985		Jan. 1986	
	No.	G.T.	No.	G.T.	No.	G.T.	No.	G.T.	No.	G.T.
Ferry	2	7,930	1	2,930	2	3,215				
Passenger Vessel							1	1,100		
Passenger and Vehicle Ferry							1	2,100		
Tanker	10	258,400	7	176,300	3	75,000	2	179,400	2	179,400
Tug/Barge	9	195,000	4	100,000	2	50,000				
Containership	3	121,470	1	40,490			3	48,000	3	48,000
Container-Ro/Ro Ship	3	55,500	3	55,500						
Dry Bulk Carrier	2	47,000								
Hopper Dredge	3	20,000	1	6,000	1	3,000	1	3,000		
Tuna Purseiner	2	2,000								
Collier	1	23,000	1	23,000						
Incinerator Ship			2	9,700	2	9,700	2	9,700	2	9,700
Oceanographic Research			1	2,500						
TOTALS	35	730,300	21	416,420	10	140,915	10	243,300	7	237,100

Source: Shipbuilders Council of America

SEA POWER: *COAST GUARD*

The Coast Guard was established on 15 January 1915 as a merger of the Revenue Cutter Service (begun in 1790) and the Life-Saving Service (begun in 1848). It became a part of the newly formed Department of Transportation in 1967.

The strategic objectives of the Coast Guard are:

- To minimize the loss of life, personal injuries, and property damage on, over, and under the seas and waters subject to U.S. jurisdiction.
- To facilitate waterborne activity in support of national economic, scientific, defense, and social needs.
- To maintain an armed force prepared to carry out specific naval or military tasks in time of war or emergency.
- To assure safe and secure ports, waterways, and shoreside facilities.
- To enforce federal laws and international agreements on and under those waters subject to U.S. jurisdiction and on and under the high seas where authorized.
- To maintain or improve the quality of the marine environment.
- To cooperate with other government agencies—federal, state, and local—to assure efficient use of public resources.

The Coast Guard operates the world's largest Search and Rescue (SAR) organization. The search and rescue mission was one of the Coast Guard's earliest functions, and continues to be its most recognized. Ten Rescue Coordination Centers are maintained in the continental United States, Alaska, and Hawaii to coordinate the search and rescue efforts of 26 air stations, over 150 small boat stations, and all cutters assigned a SAR responsibility. About 71% of the Coast Guard's SAR cases involve recreational vessels. Almost 95% of all rescue missions take place within 20 miles of the shore.

A vital role in the SAR program is played by the Coast Guard Auxiliary, whose members participate in about 16% of the distress calls. Also playing a role is the Automated Mutual Assistance Vessel Rescue System, a voluntary movement report system that keeps records of the location of merchant vessels at sea to help mariners give assistance to one another.

ENFORCEMENT OF LAWS AND TREATIES

As the world's largest marine police force, the Coast Guard is charged with the enforcement of all applicable federal laws on the high seas and waters subject to U.S. jurisdiction. The USCG's "police work" ranges from interdiction of narcotics and illegal aliens to combating vessel thefts or hijackings and enforcing marine conservation laws. In order to do this, federal statutes allow Coast Guard personnel to board all U.S. vessels, foreign flag vessels within sovereign jurisdiction of the United States, and foreign vessels on the high seas in accordance with international law or specific special arrangements with the flag states.

In 1973, the Coast Guard seized six vessels loaded with marijuana. By 1986, the number of seizures had jumped to more than 300 annually. The Coast Guard estimates it interdicts between 15% and 20% of all illegal drugs coming into the United States by sea. The Coast Guard was heavily involved with policing the Cuban sealift in 1980, and since 1981 has been conducting a special operation to stop illegal Haitian emigration.

The Coast Guard has an extensive role in a major new initiative aimed at combating narcotics trafficking across the borders of the United States. In January 1982, the Vice President's Task Force on South Florida Crime was formed to take action against the severe problems faced in the maritime law enforcement efforts of the Southeast U.S. and the Caribbean Basin. Since then, the success of this task force led to the formation of the National Narcotics Border Interdiction Systems (NNBIS), with headquarters at St. Petersburg, FL, and regional centers located at Long Beach, CA; El Paso, TX; New Orleans, LA; Miami, FL; New York, NY; and Chicago, IL. And in October 1985, an NNBIS subregional center was established in Honolulu, HI. In coordinating the efforts of all the federal law enforcement agencies, these centers collate intelligence, assess threats, prioritize targets, maintain statistics, and coordinate special joint operations.

The legislative clarification of the Posse Comitatus Act, which heretofore limited military services from participating in law-enforcement activity, has enabled the other armed services to take an active role in assisting other federal agencies in the performance of the law enforcement mission. Coast Guard Law Enforcement Detachments (LEDETS) and Tactical Law Enforcement Teams (TACLETS) are now able to ride U.S. Navy ships to conduct

The Coast Guard continually protects U.S. resources within the 200-mile U.S. Economic Zone. Few foreign ships challenge the Coast Guard's authority.

Table CG-1

SEARCH AND RESCUE ACTIVITIES

	1981	1982	1983	1984	1985	1986
Search and Rescue Cases	71,781	68,552	63,980	57,431	70,062	58,259
Lives Saved	6,339	5,675	5,946	5,645	6,303	7,002
Persons Otherwise Assisted . . .	168,278	157,552	145,662	129,650	136,341	135,404
Property Loss Prevented (millions $)	955	524	615.3	801.8	820.3	1,002.2
Program Operating Expense (millions $)	334	397	410	415	386	319

Source: Coast Guard

boardings on suspected narcotics-smuggling-profile vessels at sea. The Navy and Air Force provide surveillance flights for both the Coast Guard and Customs Service, and the Army and Navy have loaned several aircraft to the Customs Service to bolster the air smuggling interdiction effort. As of 1 September 1987, Navy ships and aircraft have been involved in the seizure of 75 drug-smuggling vessels since the beginning of their active participation in the "War on Drugs" in December 1981.

The Coast Guard has primary responsibility for the at-sea enforcement of 28 fishery management plans and associated enforcement regulations which regulate domestic and foreign fishing in the U.S. Exclusive Economic Zone (EEZ) pursuant to the Magnuson Fisheries Conservation and Management Act (MFCMA). In addition, the Coast Guard is tasked with monitoring compliance with endangered species and marine sanctuary regulations, as well as certain international fishing agreements in waters beyond the limits of the U.S. EEZ.

Fisheries enforcement activities include surface and aircraft surveillance of major fishing areas and disputed regions as well as thorough boardings of domestic and foreign fishing vessels. A complete inventory of the hold of a foreign fishing vessel may require two or three days for a boarding team to complete.

During 1986, the Coast Guard conducted more than 373 boardings of foreign fishing vessels, issued 48 written warnings and 112 violations, and seized eight vessels for serious violations of the MFCMA. Some 3,109 boardings of domestic fishing vessels were carried out, resulting in 95 written warnings and 264 violations being issued. No domestic fishing vessels were seized in 1986.

In 1987, the Coast Guard expected to devote 45,000 cutter operating hours to fisheries enforcement and 227,000 cutter operating hours to general law enforcement.

AIDS TO NAVIGATION AND OTHER MISSIONS

To aid navigation, the Coast Guard locates and marks channels and buoys and manages the federal system of 48,072 lighthouses, buoys, daybeacons, fog signals, and radar reflectors. The Coast Guard manages 43,472 privately owned aids to navigation, as well as aids operated for the Department of Defense.

Because buoys are being replaced with less costly land-based or pile structures, the number of Coast Guard buoy tenders has been reduced significantly in recent years. The Coast Guard runs 14 manned and 445 unmanned lighthouses.

The Coast Guard also operates and maintains three types of radio-navigation aids throughout the United States and in other parts of the world:

- About 200 radio-beacons, which are simple and cheap non-directional radio transmitters. They allow vessels and aircraft to receive direction-finding information from 10 to 175 miles offshore.
- LORAN-C, a low-frequency, long-range navigational radio system that provides mariners with navigation data up to 1,500 miles offshore. The Coast Guard operates 25 domestic LORAN-C stations and 20 overseas (for U.S. military use).
- OMEGA, a worldwide, long-range radio-navigation system with eight transmitting and 50 monitoring stations. It is used for navigation by both sea and air travelers. The Coast Guard operates two OMEGA stations; six more are operated by host countries

under international agreements.

Other Coast Guard duties:

Port and environmental safety. Coast Guard officers, serving as Captains of the Port, and other employees at 46 Marine Safety and Inspection offices are charged with enforcing regulations governing waterfront safety and the anchorage of vessels with dangerous cargoes. USCG officers also are charged with ensuring the safe loading and stowage of explosives and other hazardous cargoes aboard ship.

Commercial vessel safety. The Coast Guard enforces safety standards in the design, construction, and equipping of vessels; examines foreign vessels to ensure compliance with U.S. statutes and international agreements; administers standards for licensed and unlicensed maritime personnel; investigates marine accidents; supervises the documentation of U.S. vessels and assignment of their official tonnage; and maintains merchant seamen's records.

The Coast Guard estimates in FY 1988 it will receive reports on 11,000 "marine incidents," inspect 16,000 commercial vessels, make 900 factory visits and inspections, board 35,000 boats, and monitor 2,500 loadings of explosives and other dangerous cargo.

Defense Readiness. The Coast Guard, by statute, always is an armed force of the United States, and shall operate as a service in the Navy in time of war or as the President so directs. In emergencies, Coast Guard vessels and aircraft, as well as specialty-skilled personnel, can be transferred to operational control of Navy commanders for special duties. Coast Guard forces are included in Navy fleet-commander contingency and war plans. In 1984 the new Office of Readiness and Reserve was established at Coast Guard headquarters to place further emphasis on the Coast Guard's commitment to both statutory and military missions in periods of heightened tension.

Building on the unique capabilities and responsibilities of both services, the Navy has established Maritime Defense Zones (MDZ) for the continental United States, Alaska, Aleutians, and Hawaii to provide for integrated coastal and harbor defense. The Maritime Defense Zone concept melds present Coast Guard command and control capabilities, active and Reserve Coast Guard forces and resources providing port security, maritime law enforcement, aids to navigation, surveillance and interdiction, and search and rescue with Navy and Naval Reserve anti-submarine warfare, inshore undersea war-

fare, mine countermeasures and other specialized units. The MDZ commanders are double-hatted. They currently are the commanders of Coast Guard Atlantic and Pacific areas, Coast Guard vice admirals, who are the senior operational commanders for peacetime Coast Guard operations. The MDZ commands have small Navy and Coast Guard staffs for peacetime planning, training, and exercising. The MDZs will interact with the Army in the land defense of North America, the Air Force for related air defense, and civilian agencies for optimum port utilization in supply/resupply efforts.

Planning, training, and exercising for wartime taskings are and will remain important among the Coast Guard's many peacetime missions. Both active and Reserve Coast Guard forces work together on all aspects of defense readiness. Major cutters participate in Navy fleet exercises. Harbor units routinely conduct mobilization and port breakout exercises. All commands down to port level play in Joint Chiefs of Staff command-post exercises.

Domestic ice operations. Domestic icebreaking is conducted for search-and-rescue missions and for the prevention of flooding caused by ice (an activity coordinated by the U.S. Army Corps of Engineers). These operations are conducted in direct support of the general public. Examples include opening channels to icebound communities which are in immediate need of food, winter fuel, or medical assistance. The Coast Guard will conduct icebreaking operations as needed to facilitate navigation, but it normally will not interfere with private enterprise in conducting icebreaking operations to facilitate navigation. If commercial icebreaking assistance is available and adequate, Coast Guard icebreaking assistance shall not be provided.

Guarding the marine environment. The Coast Guard responds to the accidental or intentional discharge—or substantial threat of discharge—of oil, hazardous substances, pollutants, and contaminants into U.S. waters. In 1986, more than 11,000 pollution incidents were reported to the Coast Guard. The Coast Guard investigated 8,114 oil spills and 650 chemical releases, supervised 257 oil and 27 chemical federally-funded cleanups and monitored 2,357 private-sector cleanups.

Marine science. The Coast Guard operates cutters and aircraft assigned to the International Ice Patrol, funded

jointly by 20 signatory nations to detect and predict the drift of icebergs in North Atlantic shipping lanes. The Coast Guard also provides oceanographic services and weather observations and reports in a cooperative program with the National Weather Service of NOAA and the Naval Oceanography Command, and assists other federal agencies in support of national marine science activities.

Waterways management. The Coast Guard's Vessel Traffic Services system coordinates vessel movements in or approaching a waterway to reduce congestion. Vessel Traffic Services are in: San Francisco, CA; Puget Sound, WA; Houston/Galveston, TX; New Orleans, LA; Prince William Sound, AK, and Berwick Bay, LA. Waterways management includes traffic routing, enforcement of speed limits, and limits on the size of vessels in certain waterways and harbors.

Bridge administration. The Coast Guard assumed responsibility for administering bridges over navigable U.S. waters in 1967, shortly after the Department of Transportation was formed. The Coast Guard is charged with ensuring safe and unobstructed navigation through or under bridges, while meeting the needs of other modes of transportation, such as car and truck traffic on the bridges. The Coast Guard determines whether a bridge unreasonably obstructs navigation; if so, federal funds to alter the bridge are requested. The Coast Guard also issues permits for bridge construction or modification and develops drawbridge regulations to ensure non-interference with commerce. It has responsibility for 18,000 bridges in the United States.

Recreational boating safety. The Coast Guard enforces construction and performance standards for recreational boats, educates the public about boat

safety, and enforces safety laws. The Coast Guard is the manager of a boating safety program, authorized by Congress, that encourages participation in boating safety by the states, the boating industry, and the boating public. As the states have increased their roles in enforcement and education, the Coast Guard has been able to reduce its direct involvement. The Coast Guard Auxiliary conducts boating education programs and examinations.

Polar ice operations. The Coast Guard supports and promotes national interests in both the Arctic and Antarctic by facilitating travel across ice-covered waters. The "national interests" supported include scientific study by the National Science Foundation, the Department of Defense, and the Coast Guard itself.

U.S. COAST GUARD ACADEMY

The U.S. Coast Guard Academy in New London, Conn., has an undergraduate enrollment of 800 men and women. This federal academy, situated along the Thames River, is halfway between New York and Boston.

Degrees and Majors: There are seven majors to choose from: electrical, civil, and marine engineering; government, management, applied science, and mathematics/computer sciences. Each graduate receives a bachelor of science degree and a commission as ensign in the Coast Guard.

Costs: A $500 deposit is required upon entrance to defray the cost of uniforms and educational equipment.

Financial Aid. Each cadet receives about $480 a month for uniforms, equipment, textbooks, and other training expenses.

Admission: Cadets are selected in an annual nationwide competition (no congressional appointments or geographical quotas). Eligibility requirements include satisfactory SAT or ACT scores, good scholastic records, and leadership potential. Each candidate must also pass a medical examination before being accepted.

Application Information: Applications, which are due the December before entrance of a new class in June, are available by contacting:

The Director of Admissions
U.S. Coast Guard Academy
New London, Conn. 06320-4195

or by calling: (203) 444-8500-8503.

COAST GUARD ACTIVE FLEET

Type of Cutter	No.
High Endurance Cutter (WHEC)	
Hamilton Class (378′)	12
Secretary Class (327′)	1
Casco Class (311′)	1
Medium Endurance Cutter (WMEC)	
Famous Class (270′)	13
Storis Class (230′)	1
Diver Class (213′)	3
Reliance Class (210′)	16
Cherokee and Achomawi Class (205′)	5
Balsam Class (180′)	3
Patrol Boats (WPB/WSES)	
Island Class (110′)	16
Cape Class (95′)	17
Point Class (82′)	53
Sea Bird Class (110′)	3

High-Endurance Cutters

Hamilton Class

CHASE
  (WHEC-718), New York, N.Y.
BOUTWELL
  (WHEC-719), Seattle, Wash.
GALLATIN
  (WHEC-721), New York, N.Y.
MORGENTHAU
  (WHEC-722), Alameda, Calif.
RUSH
  (WHEC-723), Alameda, Calif.
JARVIS
  (WHEC-725), Honolulu, Hawaii
MIDGETT
  (WHEC-726), Alameda, Calif.

In Modernization

HAMILTON
  (WHEC-715), Boston, Mass.
DALLAS
  (WHEC-716), New York, N.Y.
MELLON
  (WHEC-717), Seattle, Wash.
SHERMAN
  (WHEC-720), Alameda, Calif.
MUNRO
  (WHEC-724), Honolulu, Hawaii

Secretary Class

INGHAM
  (WHEC-35), Portsmouth, Va.

Casco Class

UNIMAK
  (WHEC-379), New Bedford, Mass.

Medium Endurance Cutters

Famous Class

BEAR
  (WMEC-901), Portsmouth, Va.
TAMPA
  (WMEC-902), Portsmouth, Va.
HARRIET LANE
  (WMEC-903), Portsmouth, Va.
NORTHLAND
  (WMEC-904), Portsmouth, Va.
SPENCER
  (WMEC-905), Boston, Mass.
SENECA
  (WMEC-906), Boston, Mass.
ESCANABA
  (WMEC-907), Boston, Mass.
TAHOMA
  (WMEC-908), New Bedford, Mass.

Under Construction or Approved:

CAMPBELL
  (WMEC-909), New Bedford, Mass.
THETIS
  (WMEC-910), Long Beach, Calif.
FORWARD
  (WMEC-911), Long Beach, Calif.
LEGARE
  (WMEC-912), Long Beach, Calif.
MOHAWK
  (WMEC-913), Long Beach, Calif.

Reliance Class

DILIGENCE
  (WMEC-616), Cape Canaveral, Fla.
VIGILANT
  (WMEC-617), New Bedford, Mass.
ACTIVE
  (WMEC-618), Port Angeles, Wash.
RESOLUTE
  (WMEC-620), Astoria, Ore.
VALIANT
  (WMEC-621), Galveston, Texas
STEADFAST
  (WMEC-623), St. Petersburg, Fla.
DAUNTLESS
  (WMEC-624), Miami Beach, Fla.
VENTUROUS
  (WMEC-625), Coast Guard Island, Calif.
DEPENDABLE
  (WMEC-626), Panama City, Fla.
VIGOROUS
  (WMEC-627), New London, Conn.
DECISIVE
  (WMEC-629), St. Petersburg, Fla.
ALERT
  (WMEC-630), Cape May, N.J.

In Modernization

RELIANCE
  (WMEC-615), Cape Canaveral, Fla.
CONFIDENCE
  (WMEC-619), New Bedford, Mass.
COURAGEOUS
  (WMEC-622), Key West, Fla.
DURABLE
  (WMEC-628), Brownsville, Tex.

Cherokee Class

UTE
  (WMEC-76), Key West, Fla.
LIPAN
  (WMEC-85), Ft. George, Fla.
CHILULA
  (WMEC-153), Atlantic Beach, N.C.
CHEROKEE
  (WMEC-165), Norfolk, Va.
TAMAROA
  (WMEC-166), New Castle, N.H.

Balsam Class

CLOVER
  (WMEC-292), Eureka, Calif.
EVERGREEN
  (WMEC-295), New London, Conn.
CITRUS
  (WMEC-300), Coos Bay, Ore.

Storis Class

STORIS
  (WMEC-38), Kodiak, Alaska

Diver Class

ESCAPE
  (WMEC-6), Charleston, S.C.
ACUSHNET
  (WMEC-167), Gulfport, Miss.
YOCONA
  (WMEC-168), Kodiak, Alaska

Icebreakers

Polar Class

POLAR STAR
  (WAGB-10), Seattle, Wash.
POLAR SEA
  (WAGB-11), Seattle, Wash.

Mackinaw Class

MACKINAW
  (WAGB-83), Cheboygan, Mich.

Wind Class

WESTWIND
  (WAGB-281), Mobile, Ala.
NORTHWIND
  (WAGB-282), Wilmington, N.C.

Surface Effect Ships

Sea Bird Class

SHEARWATER (WSES 2), Key West, Fla.
SEA HAWK (WSES 3), Key West, Fla.
PETREL (WSES 4), Key West, Fla.

Icebreaking Tugs

Bay Class

KATMAI BAY (WTGB 101), Sault Ste.
  Marie, Mich.
BRISTOL BAY (WTGB 102), Detroit,
  Mich.
MOBILE BAY (WTGB 103), Sturgeon Bay,
  Wis.
BISCAYNE BAY (WTGB 104), St. Ignace,
  Mich.
NEAH BAY (WTGB 105), Cleveland, Ohio
MORRO BAY (WTGB 106), Yorktown, Va.
PENOBSCOT BAY (WTGB 107), Governors
  Island, N.Y.
THUNDER BAY (WTGB 108), Portland,
  Maine
STURGEON BAY (WTGB 109), Portland,
  Maine

Patrol Boats

Island Class

FARALLON
  (WPB 1301), Miami Beach, Fla.
MANITOU
  (WPB 1302), Miami Beach, Fla.
MATAGORDA
  (WPB 1303), Miami Beach, Fla.
MAUI
  (WPB 1304), Miami Beach, Fla.
MOHEGAN
  (WPB 1305), Roosevelt Roads, P.R.
NUNIVAK
  (WPB 1306), Roosevelt Roads, P.R.
OCRACOKE
  (WPB 1307), Roosevelt Roads, P.R.
VASHON
  (WPB 1308), Roosevelt Roads, P.R.
ACQUIDNECK
  (WPB 1309), Portsmouth, Va.
MUSTANG
  (WPB 1310), Seward, Alaska
NAUSHON
  (WPB 1311), Ketchikan, Alaska
SANIBEL
  (WPB 1312), Rockland, Maine
EDISTO
  (WPB 1313), Crescent City, Calif.
SAPELO
  (WPB 1314), Eureka, Calif.
MATINICUS
  (WPB 1315), Cape May, N.J.
NANTUCKET
  (WPB 1316), San Juan, P.R.

Under Construction

ATTU
  (WPB 1317), St. Thomas, USVI
BARANOF
  (WPB 1318), Miami Beach, Fla.
CHANDELEUR
  (WPB 1319), Miami Beach, Fla.
CHINCOTEAGUE
  (WPB 1320), Mobile, Ala.
CUSHING
  (WPB 1321), Mobile, Ala.
CUTTYHUNK
  (WPB 1322)
DRUMMOND
  (WPB 1323)
LARGO
  (WPB 1324)
METOMKIN
  (WPB 1325)
MONOMOY
  (WPB 1326)
ORCAS
  (WPB 1327)
PADRE
  (WPB 1328)
SITKINIAK
  (WPB 1329)
TYBEE
  (WPB 1330)
WASHINGTON
  (WPB 1331)
WRANGELL
  (WPB 1332)
ADAK
  (WPB 1333)
LIBERTY
  (WPB 1334)
ANACAPA
  (WPB 1335)
KISKA
  (WPB 1336)
ASSATEAGUE
  (WPB 1337)

PRINCIPAL COAST GUARD OFFICES

Headquarters, U.S. Coast Guard
2100 Second St., S.W.
Washington, D.C. 20593-00001

Atlantic Area District Offices

Commander, Coast Guard Atlantic Area
and Maritime Defense Zone, Atlantic
Governors Island
New York, N.Y. 10004

Maintenance & Logistics Command,
Atlantic
Governors Island
New York, N.Y. 10004-5098

First Coast Guard District
408 Atlantic Avenue
Boston, MA 02210-2209

Second Coast Guard District
1430 Olive St.
St. Louis, Mo. 63101-2378

Fifth Coast Guard District
Federal Building
431 Crawford St.
Portsmouth, Va. 23704-5004

Seventh Coast Guard District
1018 Federal Building
51 S.W. First Ave.
Miami, Fla. 33130-1608

Eighth Coast Guard District
Hale Boggs Federal Building
500 Camp St.
New Orleans, La. 70130-3396

Ninth Coast Guard District
1240 E. Ninth St.
Cleveland, Ohio 44199-2060

Pacific Area District Offices

Commander, Coast Guard Pacific Area
and Maritime Defense Zone, Pacific
Government Island
Alameda, Calif. 94501

Maintenance & Logistics Command,
Pacific
Government Island
Alameda, Calif. 94501-5100

11th Coast Guard District
Union Bank Building
400 Oceangate Blvd.
Long Beach, Calif. 90822-5399

13th Coast Guard District
Federal Building
915 Second Ave.
Seattle, Wash. 98174-1067

14th Coast Guard District
Prince Kalanianaole Federal Building
300 Ala Moana Blvd., Ninth Floor
Honolulu, Hawaii 96850-4982

17th Coast Guard District
P.O. Box 3-5000
Juneau, Alaska 99802-1217

Regional Maintenance and Logistics Com-
mands (RMLC) have Nine (9) Support Cen-
ters located at:
  RMLC LANTAREA, (Command Head-
quarters), Governors Island, NY; Boston,
MA; Portsmouth, VA; Elizabeth City, NC;
New Orleans, LA.
  RMLC PACAREA, (Command Headquar-
ters), Alameda, CA; Kodiak, AK; Seattle,
WA; Terminal Island, CA.

SHIPS/COAST GUARD

Gallatin

HIGH-ENDURANCE CUTTERS

Hamilton Class

DISPLACEMENT: 3,050 tons full load.
LENGTH: 378 feet.
BEAM: 42.8 feet.
SPEED: 29 knots.
POWER PLANT: two diesel engines, 7,000 bhp, and two gas turbines, shp. Two controllable pitch propellers.
ARMAMENT: One Mk 75/76 Oto Malera, two 20mm, two triple torpedo tubes.
AIRCRAFT: One HH-52 or LAMPS I helicopter.
COMPLEMENT: 171.
BUILDER: Avondale Shipyards.

BRIEFING: The 12 ships in the Hamilton class, all commissioned in the late 1960s and early 1970s, are the most sophisticated high-endurance cutters. They are used for law enforcement, operational training, military-preparedness exercises, and search-and-rescue missions. During the last five years, a number of the class have been utilized extensively in drug-interdiction and immigrant-interception exercises in the Caribbean. Because of increased national emphasis on drug interdiction, it can be anticipated that operations in support of that goal will continue at an increased rate. In 1977 the *Gallatin* and the *Morganthau* became the first Coast Guard ships to have women assigned as permanent members of the crew. Commencing in October 1985, the *Hamilton* and the *Mellon* inaugurated an extensive FRAM (fleet rehabilitation and modernization) program which included upgrading these ships' radar, fire-control system, weapons, and flight-deck facilities to make them more compatible operationally with Navy ships. Soon after FRAMs are completed, these cutters will be equipped with Harpoon missiles and Phalanx CIWSs.

MEDIUM ENDURANCE CUTTERS

Famous Class

DISPLACEMENT: 1,780 tons full load.
LENGTH: 270 feet.
BEAM: 38 feet.
SPEED: 19.5 knots.
POWER PLANT: two diesels, two shafts, 7,000 bhp.
ARMAMENT: one 3″/76mm gun; space reserved for Phalanx CIWS and Harpoon missiles.
AIRCRAFT: one HH-52, HH-65A, or LAMPS I helicopter.
COMPLEMENT: 98.
BUILDERS: WMEC 901-904, Tacoma Boatbuilding Co.; 905-913, R.E. Dereckter of Rhode Island Inc., Middletown, R.I.

BRIEFING: There are eight Famous class cutters currently in commission; the first one, *Bear,* entered service in 1983. Five others are under construction and will be in service by the end of 1989. Famous class cutters are primarily assigned law-enforcement, defense-operations, and search-and-rescue missions. Their law-enforcement missions have included drug and illegal-immigrant operations and fisheries enforcement activities. These ships are the most modern and advanced medium endurance cutters. They are equipped with a sophisticated command, display, and control (COMDAC) computerized ship-control system which provides for maximum operational effectiveness with reduced crews. They also have a modern weapons and sensor suite and can support and hangar one HH-52A, HH-65A, or LAMPS I helicopter. These ships also can land LAMPS III helicopters. Famous class cutters are replacing aging WHECs and WMECs, all of which are over 40 years old.

Harriet Lane

Reliance Class

DISPLACEMENT: 907-1007 tons full load.
LENGTH: 210.5 feet.
BEAM: 34 feet.
SPEED: 18 knots.
POWER PLANT: two diesels, two shafts, 5,000 bhp.
ARMAMENT: one 3″/76 .50 cal., two .50 cal. machine guns.
AIRCRAFT: one HH-52 helicopter or one HH-65A.
COMPLEMENT: 70.
BUILDERS: WMEC 615-17, Todd Shipyards; 618 Christy Corp.; 620-24, 626-27, 630, American Shipbuilding; 619, 625, 628-29, Coast Guard Yard, Baltimore.

BRIEFING: The 16 Reliance class cutters are primarily assigned law-enforcement and search-and-rescue missions. These ships originally were classified as patrol craft (WPC), but their classification was changed to medium endurance cutters (WMEC) in 1966. They can support one HH-52 or HH-65A helicopter, but no hangar is provided. One 1 October 1984 *Active* entered an extensive Major Maintenance Availability (MMA), which now is complete, and the remaining ships of the class will undergo MMA during the next several years. The purpose of the MMA is to correct machinery and equipment problems in order that the class may remain mission capable, supportable, and reliable for the second half of its service life.

ICEBREAKERS

Polar Class

DISPLACEMENT: 12,087 tons full load.
LENGTH: 399 feet.
BEAM: 86 feet.
SPEED: 18 knots.
POWER PLANT: three gas turbines, six diesels, three shafts, 60,000 shp.
RANGE: 28,000 miles.
ARMAMENT: two 50 cal. guns.
AIRCRAFT: two HH-52 or HH-65A helicopters.
COMPLEMENT: 163.
BUILDER: Lockheed Shipbuilding, Seattle.

Wind Class

DISPLACEMENT: 6,515 tons full load.
LENGTH: 269 feet.
BEAM: 63 feet.
SPEED: 16 knots.
POWER PLANT: diesel-electric; four diesels, two shafts, 10,000 bhp.
RANGE: 16,000 at 16 knots.
ARMAMENT: two 40mm guns.
AIRCRAFT: two helicopters normally embarked.
COMPLEMENT: 135.
BUILDER: Western Pipe & Steel, San Pedro.

Mackinaw Class

DISPLACEMENT: 5,252 tons full load.
LENGTH: 290 feet.
BEAM: 74 feet.
SPEED: 18.7 knots.
POWER PLANT: two diesels with electric drive, three shafts (one forward, two aft), 10,000 bhp.
AIRCRAFT: one helicopter.
COMPLEMENT: 127.
BUILDER: Toledo Shipbuilding.

Polar Sea

BRIEFING: Aside from a small number of icebreaking tugs, five ships represent the nation's entire icebreaking capability. The two Polar Star-class ships are 10 and eight years old, and are the largest ships operated by the Coast Guard. *Glacier,* the only ship of its class, was 32 years old when decommissioned in 1987; *Mackinaw,* the only ship of its class, is 42 years old and designed and configured for use only on the Great Lakes. The two Wind-class ships, also 42 years old, are operational but are used sparingly. Congress perceives a need for additional icebreakers, and has directed that two new icebreakers be built; however, no firm plans for construction have been formalized. There also is some sentiment for having ships built by private firms and then leased by the Coast Guard. The Polar Star ships, capable of breaking ice six feet thick at a speed of three knots, have overcome a series of difficulties encountered in early voyages, including major problems with their controllable-pitch propellers.

Point Judith

PATROL BOATS

Island Class

DISPLACEMENT: 165 tons full load.
LENGTH: 110 feet.
BEAM: 21 feet.
SPEED: 26+ knots.
POWER PLANT: two Paxman Valento diesel engines, 5800 shp.
RANGE: 1,900 nautical miles.
ARMAMENT: one 20mm, two M-60 machine guns.
COMPLEMENT: 16.
BUILDER: Bollinger Machine Shop and Shipyard, Inc., New Orleans.

Cape Class

DISPLACEMENT: 106 tons full load.
LENGTH: 95.5 feet.
BEAM: 19 feet.
SPEED: 20 knots.
POWER PLANT: two Detroit diesels, 2470 shp.
RANGE: 1,900 nautical miles.
ARMAMENT: two .50 cal. machine guns, one M-60 machine gun.
BUILDER: U.S. Coast Guard Yard.

Point Class

LENGTH: 82 feet, 10 inches.
BEAM: 17 feet, 7 inches.
SPEED: 20 knots.
POWER PLANT: two Cummings diesels.
RANGE: 1,580 nautical miles.
ARMAMENT: two .50 cal. machine guns.
COMPLEMENT: 10.
BUILDER: U.S. Coast Guard Yard, except WPB 82345-82349, built by J. Martinac Shipbuilding.

BRIEFING: The primary missions of patrol boats are search and rescue, maritime law enforcement, and port security. The Cape Class WPBs were built between 1953-1959, and the Point class between 1960-1970. These cutters have seen service throughout the world. Several Point class WPBs conducted operations in Viet Nam, and some Cape class WPBs have been transferred to Ethiopia, Haiti, Thailand, and Saudi Arabia. Both classes of WPBs will continue in service through 1996. Twenty-one Island class WPBs are providing additional resources to stem the flow of illegal drugs into the United States, and 16 more are on the way. In addition to maritime law enforcement, these cutters will be used for search-and-rescue and defense operations.

SEAGOING BUOY TENDERS

Balsam Class

DISPLACEMENT: 1,025 tons full load.
LENGTH: 180 feet.
BEAM: 37 feet.
SPEED: 13 knots.
POWER PLANT: diesel electric, one shaft, 1,000-1,200 bhp.
ARMAMENT: unarmed except for five ships, which have two 20mm guns.
COMPLEMENT: 53.
BUILDERS: Various between 1942-45.

BRIEFING: The Coast Guard operates 28 ships of this class. All have been modernized once, and a SLEP program to extend their lives even further commenced in 1981. Despite their age, they have proven to be highly versatile, durable, reliable ships capable of performing a variety of missions at sea. Eleven of these ships have been configured for icebreaking. Also in service are several classes of coastal, inland, and river buoy tenders, most of which are 30 or more years old. All save one of the latter classes are under 500 tons displacement.

Salvia

Hammer

CONSTRUCTION TENDERS

BRIEFING: Performing a vital, if unsung, role for the Coast Guard are three classes of construction tenders, totaling 15 ships. Designed for the construction, repair, and maintenance of fixed aids to navigation, all operate in inland waters. One was built in the 1940s, 10 in the 1960s, and four in the mid-1970s. Their equipment includes piledrivers, cranes, and jetting equipment.

ICEBREAKING TUGS

Bay Class

DISPLACEMENT: 662 tons full load.
LENGTH: 110 feet.
BEAM: 37.6 feet.
SPEED: 14.7 knots.
POWER PLANT: diesel-electric, one shaft, 2,500 bhp.
COMPLEMENT: 17

BRIEFING: These small, multi-mission ships are especially configured for icebreaking on the Great Lakes, in coastal waters, and in rivers. Nine currently are in service. Eventually, they will replace the WYTM class of medium harbor tugs that now is over 40 years old. The Coast Guard also operates 14 small harbor tugs that are not configured for icebreaking.

Bristol Bay

Seabird

SURFACE-EFFECT SHIPS

Sea Bird Class

DISPLACEMENT: 145 tons full load.
LENGTH: 110 feet.
BEAM: 29 feet.
SPEED: 30 knots.
POWER PLANT: two diesels, propulsion; two diesels, two double-inlet, centrifugal fans, lift; two shafts, 3,200 bhp (propulsion), 736 bhp (lift).
ARMAMENT: two .50-caliber machine guns.
COMPLEMENT: 18.
BUILDER: Bell Halter, New Orleans.

BRIEFING: These three craft and a large Navy surface-effect ship are the only vessels of this type in government service, other than the Marines' LCACs, which are not designed for open-water operations. They use a cushion of air trapped between the sidewalls of the ships to lift much of the hull clear of the water, making possible speeds in excess of 30 knots. Used principally for drug interdiction, search and rescue, and missions connected with aids to navigation, they operate principally in Caribbean waters out of Key West, Fla. Although they have proven to be both versatile and effective, there are no plans for procurement of additional ones.

FAST ASSAULT PATROL BOATS

DISPLACEMENT: Maximum, 21,270 pounds, including 3,500 pounds of military payload.
LENGTH: 43 feet, six inches.
BEAM: nine feet, six inches.
SPEED: 48 knots at normal displacement, 42 knots at maximum displacement.
POWER PLANT: two 355hp Caterpillar diesels.
RANGE: 400 statute miles at normal displacement, 370 at maximum displacement.
ARMAMENT: No fixed armament; all small arms.
COMPLEMENT: two crew and a 10-man special combat unit.
BUILDER: Tempest Marine, Fort Lauderdale, FL.

BRIEFING: Because it has not had in its inventory a surface craft capable of intercepting "fast boats" (anything faster than 35 knots), the Coast Guard has procured four high-speed power boats that will enable it to better cope with speedy craft being used by drug smugglers. The enormity of the problem faced by the Coast Guard in seeking to intercept "fast boats" was dramatically illustrated in FY 1983-84. During that period, 255 surface craft of the "fast boat" category were encountered by Coast Guard forces, but only 61 seizures were made because of lack of speed by Coast Guard ships and craft. Further, 36 of the seizures resulted from the "fast boat" suffering a casualty. The four new power boats, which are capable of speeds in excess of 35 knots, were delivered in 1987 and now are stationed in Miami.

TRAINING CUTTER

BRIEFING: The Coast Guard's only training cutter, the sailing ship *Eagle*, is a former German training ship built by Blohm and Voss of Hamburg and launched in 1936. Accepted as reparation after World War II, it arrived at its homeport of New London, Conn., site of the Coast Guard Academy, in 1946. The 1,816-ton, three-masted ship, which recently was extensively overhauled, is 295 feet long, has a sail area of 21,351 feet, and, when the auxiliary diesel engine is used, a range of 5,450 miles at 7.5 knots. It is manned by a complement of 245. In September 1987, *Eagle* began a unique cruise to the Caribbean and the Pacific that is scheduled to take it to 17 foreign ports, including four in Australia, before it returns to the Coast Guard Academy in New London in May 1988.

Eagle

AIRCRAFT/COAST GUARD

Fixed-Wing	Number	Helicopter	Number
HC-130 Hercules	29	HH-3F Pelican	36
HU-25A Guardian	41	HH-52A Sea Guard	45
VC-11A	1	HH-65A Dolphin	52
VC-4A	1		
E-2C Hawkeye (on loan from Navy)	2		

Source: Public Affairs Division, Office of Boating, Public, and Consumer Affairs, U.S. Coast Guard

Hercules

HC-130 Hercules

BRIEFING: This extended-range version of the C-130 is a turbo-prop search aircraft which can transport up to 75 passengers, 50,000 pounds of cargo, or large quantities of rescue-survival and oil-pollution-control equipment. Its range with maximum payload is almost 2,500 miles, and with maximum fuel and light payload it can be extended to more than 5,000 miles. The Coast Guard has replaced all B, E, with H models of the aircraft. Fleet requirements are 41, with 25 ready for operation at any given time. However, budgetary problems may preclude that level being attained for several years.

HU-25A Guardian

BRIEFING: This twin-engine turbofan jet, deliveries of which were completed in 1983, is one of the few aircraft flown by the military services that is built by a foreign company, Dassault-Breguet of France. It is 56.25 feet in length, 17.6 feet in height, and has a crew of five. Its ceiling at Mach .855 is 42,000 feet, and it flies at 350 knots at sea level and 380 knots at 20,000 feet. It has advanced navigation, communications, avionics, and pollution-control equipment, and can deliver pumps, rafts, and rescue gear. Some problems still were encountered with its engines and in logistic support for them; however, corrections have been made. Its performance during its first years of service otherwise has been excellent.

Guardian

Pelican

HH-3F Pelican

BRIEFING: The Pelican is a Coast Guard version of the helicopter that acquired the familiar title of the Jolly Green Giant from its exploits across a wide spectrum of operations. U.S. production of this twin-turbine, amphibious, medium-range Sikorsky-built aircraft ended years ago. These most efficient workhorses can carry eight rescued persons or bulky cargo, including vehicles, in their search-and-rescue role. To eventually replace them, in 1986 a Navy-administered contract was awarded to Sikorsky for 48 medium-range recovery helicopters (MRR), 32 of which will be for the Coast Guard. They will be designed HH-60J and will be a variant of the Sikorsky basic "Hawk" series. The first of these is scheduled for delivery in 1990, with final delivery by 1993.

Dolphin

HH-65A Dolphin

BRIEFING: These short-range recovery aircraft finally were accepted by the Coast Guard late in 1984 after over two years of coping with a number of problems, including a major one caused by snow ingestion; an exhaust retrofit of the first 17 aircraft has corrected the problem. Meanwhile, they were introduced into full service in warmer operating areas. Manufactured by Aerospatiale of France, and intended as replacements for the HH-52A, they have sophisticated avionics and communications packages, including infrared sensors, to aid rescue operations in bad weather, darkness, or high seas. The initial requirement is for 96 aircraft. Fifty-two are presently on board.

Sea Guard

HH-52A Sea Guard

BRIEFING: The first of these helicopters flew its first mission for the Coast Guard a quarter century ago. Since then, this sturdy Sikorsky-built search-and-rescue aircraft has performed yeoman service indeed. However, its capabilities have been exceeded by those of more modern aircraft, and HH-52As are slowly being replaced in the Coast Guard inventory by HH-65A Dolphins.

SEA POWER: *OCEANOGRAPHY*

Ocean, or what oceanographers call "the world ocean," covers 71 percent of the Earth's surface, making the Earth the only "water planet" in the solar system. The dominant feature of this enormous water mass is the Pacific Ocean, which covers 34 percent of the world—more than all the land masses of the world put together.

Approximately seven percent of the ocean is less than 600 feet deep. The other percentages of depth:

Percent	Depth in feet
14	600 to 6,000
16	6,000 to 12,000
58	12,000 to 18,000
4	over 18,000

OCEAN WATER PRESSURE

Depth (in feet)	Pressure (lbs./sq. in.)
Ocean surface	14.7
600	269
1,200	536
3,000	1,338
7,200	3,208
18,000	8,019
30,000	13,363
36,000	16,124

Some other ocean statistics:

• The average depth of the world ocean is 12,500 feet. The deepest area is 36,000 feet, in the Challenger Deep near Guam. If the world's highest mountain, Mount Everest, were put into Challenger Deep, about a mile of water would cover the mountain.

• About three-fifths of the Northern Hemisphere and four-fifths of the Southern Hemisphere are covered by water.

• About 70 percent of the Earth's population live within 200 miles of a coast and 80 percent of the world's capitals are located within 300 miles of a coast.

• Two dominant features of the watery world, the polar ice caps, contain about 6.5 million cubic miles of fresh water in the form of ice; 90 percent of that total is in the Antarctic, where icebergs containing 300 cubic miles of ice are calved annually.

If both the Greenland and Antarctic icecaps should suddenly melt, the world ocean would rise about 200 feet. New York City would be submerged, with only the tops of the tallest buildings sticking out above the water.

According to *Facts About the Ocean* (the Institute for Marine and Coastal Studies), an iceberg one cubic mile in size contains enough fresh water to supply the needs of a city the size of Los Angeles for 10 years.

• Water pressure in the sea increases 14.7 pounds per square inch for every 33 feet in depth. At 30,000 feet, the pressure is more than six tons per square inch. This could be compared to having pressed against each square inch of your body the weight of an elephant.

THE NAVY AND THE OCEANS

What began in 1830, 16 years after Robert Fulton built the first steam warship, as the Depot of Charts and Instruments, later became the U.S. Navy Hydrographic Office and in 1962, the U.S. Naval Oceanographic Office. Here, data are collected from an environment that begins at the sea floor and ends far above the oceans at the earthward edge of outer space. To understand this environment and to operate in it, the Navy studies such phenomena as the propagation of

AREAS OF OCEANS AND PRINCIPAL SEAS

Area	Square Miles
Pacific Ocean	63,985,000
Atlantic Ocean	31,529,000
Indian Ocean	28,357,000
Arctic Ocean	5,541,000
Mediterranean Sea	1,145,000
South China Sea	895,000
Bering Sea	878,000
Caribbean Sea	750,000
Gulf of Mexico	700,000
Sea of Okhotsk	582,000
East China Sea	480,000
Yellow Sea	480,000
Hudson Bay	472,000
Sea of Japan	405,000
North Sea	221,000
Red Sea	178,000
Black Sea	168,500
Baltic Sea	158,000

Note: The Caspian Sea is normally classed as a lake rather than a sea, although its margins are claimed as territorial waters. Its area is 152,123 square miles.

Source: U.S. Department of State "Sovereignty of the Sea" Geographic Bulletin No. 3, revised October 1969

underwater sound, surf and near-shore wave activity (for planning amphibious landings), and the air and sea conditions that affect radar and sonar.

The Navy also accumulates information in many forms, and from numerous sources, on storms, wave heights, sea ice, cloud cover, fog, and other weather conditions to produce "optimum track ship routing" for the safe passage of Navy ships and "optimum path aircraft routing" for naval aircraft.

The Navy uses five major geophysical disciplines to collect and process information about the sea.

Hydrography measures the depth of the oceans and coastal areas for the production of charts that serve all warfare areas in terms of safety and accuracy of navigation. Ocean surveys also collect data on gravity and magnetic variations for the targeting of fleet ballistic missiles.

Oceanography is used for the collection of data on ocean chemistry, dynamics, geophysics, marine biology, temperature, salinity, and other physical characteristics of the oceans. The data are used to generate underwater acoustic predictions and for publication of atlases and other documentation of long-term ocean characteristics influencing submarine, anti-submarine, amphibious, surface, and mine warfare operations.

Meteorology investigates atmospheric conditions, collecting global data on winds, clouds, moisture, temperature, pressure systems, air masses, and upper-air winds for producing weather forecasts.

Chronometry keeps time by the operation of 22 atomic clocks which compare the resonant frequencies of cesium atoms, measuring time in increments of 1/25 millionth of a second and less.

Astronomy marks the movements of stars as the fundamental reference from which all precise time is established. Precise time and time-transfer services are essential to navigation and particularly to the targeting of long-range missiles and other weapons.

The Naval Observatory administers programs in chronometry and astronomy for the production of navigation aids and the measurement of precise time.

The Navy's oceanography program

provides precise information about the influences of the oceans on weapons design. Very little can be done to modify natural physical forces, but much can be done to overcome or employ those natural forces, if their effects are known ahead of time. The study of those forces and their effects is one of the principal purposes of the naval oceanography program. The program also focuses on the development of deep-ocean technology for search, rescue, and salvage operations.

A global communications system processes the flow of environmental data into production centers and, by way of oceanography centers, processes the flow of oceanographic products out to fleet operators.

By 1990 the Navy expects to launch the only U.S. oceanographic satellite, the Navy Remote Ocean Sensing System (N-ROSS). It will provide data on surface wind speed and direction, significant wave height, sea surface temperature, ice edge, and precipitation.

The Navy's oceanography program employs nearly 4,000 military and civilian personnel at production centers in Bay St. Louis, Miss., and Monterey, Calif., and at 70 oceanography centers around the world, at Navy shore stations, and aboard ships at sea. FY 1987 funding is nearly $400 million, with that sum including $36 million for shipbuilding. Funding at that level reflects a continued determination to strengthen the Navy's oceanographic program. This 25 percent increase in personnel and funding over the previous year represents, beyond inflation,

The United States has 14 different federal government departments/agencies with oceanography responsibilities. In order, by size of their oceanography budgets, they are:

Department of Defense (DOD)— Navy and Army (Corps of Engineers).
Department of Commerce (DOC) —National Oceanic and Atmospheric Administration (NOAA).
Department of the Interior (DOI) —U.S. Geological Survey (USGS) and the Minerals Management Service (MMS).
National Science Foundation (NSF).
Department of Transportation (DOT)—U.S. Coast Guard (USCG).
National Aeronautics and Space Administration (NASA).
Department of State (State).
Department of Energy (DOE).
Environmental Protection Agency (EPA).
Smithsonian Institution (SI).
The Department of Agriculture (USDA).

AN AERIAL VIEW of the internationally famous Woods Hole Oceanographic Institution of the Massachusetts Institute of Technology, where a new two-year master's degree program in oceanography is being sponsored by the Secretary of the Navy.

the determination of the Navy to regain the leadership in oceanography.

Toward this end, the Navy has established the position of Oceanographer of the Navy, has increased the number of ships and the number of personnel involved in the at-sea programs and has begun a modernization of the fleet.

Also, a two-year master's degree program in oceanography, sponsored by the Secretary of the Navy, can enroll about eight students a year. The program is administered jointly by Massachusetts Institute of Technology maritime academy and Woods Hole Oceanographic Institution in Woods Hole, MA.

During 1986 a robot camera developed by Woods Hole for the Navy was tested in an expedition photographing the remains of the passenger liner RMS *Titanic*, which had lain 12,500 feet down on the ocean floor since it sank 75 years ago after striking an iceberg. The 28-inch camera has a 170-degree view and operates from a 200-foot tether. The camera, named Jason Jr., was operated from the three-man submersible *Alvin*. The approximately $500,000 cost of the mission was underwritten by the Navy.

The MIT/Woods Hole facility probably is the best known of the nearly 300 sea-grant institutions preparing young people for careers in the ocean sciences. The National Sea Grant College Program was established 20 years ago to meet the growing challenges facing the nation's marine community in the same way that land-grant universities have helped America's agricultural community. The program is administered by the National Science Foundation.

RISE IN U.S. FISH CONSUMPTION CONTINUES

The fishing vessels that harvest the sea constitute another form of seapower in addition to that of warships and merchant ships. Although rarely numbered with the other fleets, this unglamorous fleet of more than 130,000 vessels brings in the fish Americans are eating in steadily increasing amounts.

According to the Department of Commerce, U.S. per capita consumption of commercially caught fish in 1986 was a record 14.7 pounds, up 0.2 pound from the previous year, and a pound during the last two years.

In 1986, the latest year for which Department of Commerce figures are available, the leading fish landed was menhaden, a marine fish that is a relative of the herring. Of the total menhaden landed, 99% were reduced to

meal, oil, and solubles; the rest were used for bait or canned for pet food. The other leading fish species were salmon (second in quantity and value), shrimp (third in quantity and first in value), crabs (fourth in quantity and third in value), sea herring (fifth in quantity and very low in value), and Alaska pollock (sixth in quantity and also low in value).

The U.S. commercial fish catch in 1986 was an estimated 6.0 billion pounds worth $2.8 billion, down 0.3 billion pounds from 1985, but up $500 million in value. Twelve years ago, the catch was 5 billion pounds worth about $932 million.

More than half of the 1986 catch— 3.4 billion pounds—was sold for human consumption. The rest was processed into meal, oil, and fish solubles or used as bait or as animal food.

The leading states in quantity of landings in 1986 were:

Louisiana. . . . . .1.7 billion
Alaska. . . . . .1.2 billion
Virginia. . . . . .528 million
Mississippi . . . . .418 million
California. . . . . .387 million

The United States imported a record $4.8 billion worth of edible fisheries products in 1986, compared with $4 billion the year before. U.S. exports of fishery products amounted to $1.3 billion, an increase of $0.3 billion over 1985.

The Soviet Union, with a fishing fleet that includes some 4,300 vessels 100 gross tons or over, consistently has been ahead of the United States in catch, but not in exports. In 1983, the most recent year for which figures are available, the United States ranked second among the leading nations in fishery commodity exports, while the Soviet Union ranked thirteenth.

FORECASTING THE WEATHER

The world's weather, and how it is created, are major concerns of oceanographic scientists because, as a National Science Foundation report says, "The . . . oceans and atmosphere are so closely linked that predicting climate changes requires in-depth knowledge about the dynamic processes affecting the mixing and circulation of heat and other ocean properties."

According to the National Advisory Committee on Oceans and Atmosphere, the federal government spends about $1 billion per year (distributed among several agencies) for weather

Table O-1
LEADING FISHING NATIONS, 1980-1985
(in millions of metric tons*)

1980

Country	Catch Size
Japan	10.41
U.S.S.R.	9.41
China	4.24
UNITED STATES	3.64
Chile	2.82
Peru	2.75
India	2.42
Norway	2.40
Republic of Korea	2.09
Denmark	2.03

1981

Country	Catch Size
Japan	10.66
U.S.S.R.	9.55
China	4.61
UNITED STATES	3.77
Chile	3.39
Peru	2.75
Norway	2.55
India	2.42
Republic of Korea	2.37
Indonesia	1.86

1982

Country	Catch Size
Japan	10.78
U.S.S.R.	9.96
China	4.93
UNITED STATES	3.99
Chile	3.67
Peru	3.48
Norway	2.50
India	2.34
Republic of Korea	2.28
Indonesia	2.00

1983

Country	Catch Size
Japan	11.25
U.S.S.R.	9.76
China	5.21
UNITED STATES	4.14
Chile	3.98
Norway	2.82
India	2.52
Republic of Korea	2.50
Thailand	2.25
Indonesia	2.11

1984

Country	Catch Size
Japan	12.00
U.S.S.R.	10.59
China	5.92
UNITED STATES	4.81
Chile	4.49
Peru	2.99
India	2.85
Republic of Korea	2.47
Norway	2.45
Thailand	2.25

1985

Country	Catch Size
Japan	11.44
U.S.S.R.	10.52
China	6.78
Chile	4.80
UNITED STATES	4.77
Peru	4.17
India	2.81
Republic of Korea	2.65
Thailand	2.12
Norway	2.11

*Weights shown are live weights. Figures do not include marine mammals or aquatic plants. Figures for the United States include the weight of clam, oyster, scallop, and other mollusk shells.

Source: U.S. Department of Commerce

forecasting, observation, research, and other services.

That figure does not seem exorbitant when balanced against the costs resultant from, and havoc created by, adverse weather conditions. The severe winter cold of 1976-77, for instance, resulted in direct losses to the nation of approximately $26.9 billion. The 1980 heat wave cost the economy between $15 billion and $20 billion.

The National Weather Service, founded in 1870 because of concern over storm losses on the Great Lakes and along the sea coasts, comes under the jurisdiction of the National Oceanic and Atmospheric Administration (NOAA). The cost of *not* having accurate forecasts available to ships was

already well recognized when the service was created. In 1868, for example, more than 1,000 ships were sunk or damaged and 321 lives lost on the Great Lakes. The next year nearly 2,000 ships suffered the same fate. Accurate weather prediction and quick dissemination of storm warnings might have prevented some of those losses.

The National Weather Service has come a long way since those days. Communications and technology have greatly improved since the times when "weather kiosks" were set up in some 50 cities to disseminate weather information.

Now, specialized weather services are provided by several federal agencies. The Department of Agriculture

provides special forecasts and warnings for farmers, for example. The U.S. Coast Guard marine information broadcasts forecast warnings affecting the operation of oil rigs off the coast of Nova Scotia and fishing off the coast of Alaska. Public television stations carry a daily 15-minute National Weather Service program.

The technology of forecasting also has greatly improved since the days when kites were used to carry weather instruments aloft.

Doppler radars today allow meteorologists to detect the beginning, growth, and intensity of tornadoes whose movements can thus be better predicted.

MINING THE OCEAN'S RICHES

The riches of the ocean come in many forms. In the United States, for example, it is estimated that marine recreational anglers add about $7.5 billion annually to the U.S. economy through direct and indirect expenditures associated with fishing (boats, equipment, fuel, tackle, lodging, etc.). Commerce Department statistics show that an estimated 17 million marine recreational anglers caught about 699 million pounds of finfish on approximately 72.4 million fishing trips in 1986. For some species, such as bluefish and spotted sea trout, the recreational catch greatly exceeded the commercial catch. Other common recreational catches include winter flounder, spot, saltwater catfish, and Atlantic croaker. Excluding catches of industrial species (such as anchovies and menhaden) and freshwater fish, the marine recreational catch comprised an estimated 30 percent of the total U.S. finfish landings used for food in 1986.

Other people fish for oil. One-fifth of the world's proven oil and gas reserves are in offshore fields. In 1984, the sea floor yielded 28 percent of all the oil and approximately 20 percent of all the gas produced in the world.

Veritable fortunes are spent—and earned—by those companies involved in the high-risk ventures to extract "black gold" from the oceanic seabeds. Gasoline shortages in the United States brought both rising fuel prices and a determination to become less dependent on foreign oil. The conditions were ideal for seeking new offshore sources of oil and gas. Between 1975-1980, more than $100 billion was invested worldwide in the explora-

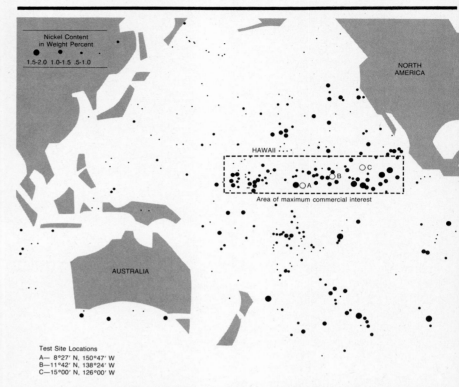

Test Site Locations
A— 8°27′ N, 150°47′ W
B—11°42′ N, 138°24′ W
C—15°00′ N, 126°00′ W

Area of manganese nodule maximum commercial interest and high nickel concentration in nodules with DOMES test site locations (Horn, Horn, and DeLach, 1972*).

*Geological data not subject to rapid changes.

Source: Deep Seabed Mining, U.S. Dept. of Commerce, NOAA—Office of Ocean Minerals and Energy, December 1981

tion and development of offshore oil and gas deposits.

Within the period from 1980-1982, the number of companies that manufacture drilling equipment jumped from 17 to more than 40. Within the same time frame, manufacturers of oil-well pumping units increased from four to an estimated 190 firms. A total of $6.5 billion in capital expansion was invested by publicly owned companies in this industry.

In 1980, there were 548 mobile rigs in existence; by 1984 the number had increased to 806. However, going into 1985, uncertainty over crude oil prices resulted in reduced offshore activity for the first quarter. By the second quarter, activity increased because there were some new oil fields in the Gulf of Mexico, and inactive holders of unexpired five-year drilling leases, issued in 1982 and 1983, began work to avoid losing their leases.

Falling oil prices in 1986, however, led most operators to cut expenses, including capital investment, equipment, staff, and operating expenses, from 35 to 50 percent. Volatile con-

ditions surrounding oil shipping in the Persian Gulf during 1987 resulted in increased interest in deep-water oil drilling and exploration in the Gulf of Mexico, and along the coasts of Brazil and Africa. Abundant surplus equipment makes it unlikely that the renewed activity will result in many, if any, orders for new drilling equipment during 1988.

Also, the Department of the Interior has adopted a new five-year Outer Continental Shelf (OCS) Oil and Gas Leasing Program for 1987-1991. This will be the third such program and is designed to slow the pace and scope of the OCS program by lengthening the period between sales in most areas from two to three years and reducing the amount of acreage offered for lease.

As we look toward the future, the deep seabed mining of minerals (at depths of three to three and a half miles) could turn out to be equally lucrative—and would have significant political ramifications. Manganese nodules, found in profusion on the sea floor at various locations throughout

the world, are a rich source of such metals as copper, nickel, cobalt, and manganese, all of which are essential for the production of steel, alloys, and other industrial products. The world's most valuable known supply of these fist-sized nodules lies deep in the international waters of the Pacific Ocean between Central America and Hawaii. (See map.)

According to *Deep Seabed Mining,* a special report to Congress, "Development of manganese nodule resources by the U.S. private sector would provide the United States with: (1) a stable supply of metals important to the economy at competitive prices; (2) a reduced annual balance of payments deficit; (3) increased investment in a basic industry; and (4) continued leadership in new ocean technologies."

Much also is at stake politically. The United States imports virtually all of its cobalt and manganese. The major sources of these minerals are Zaire and Zambia. By the end of the century, the Soviet Union and South Africa are expected to control virtually all of the world's manganese resources. Thus, access to oceanic mines closer to the United States would assure the United States a virtually uninterrupted supply of these valuable minerals, whatever the political situation in other countries.

Current international law provides no specific uniform regulations governing access to seabed mine sites. In the absence of clear-cut international regulations, Congress enacted the Deep Seabed Hard Minerals Resources Act to provide an interim legal framework. The National Oceanic and Atmospheric Administration (NOAA) has the authority to issue licenses to U.S. citizens for exploration, as well as permits for commercial recovery.

Authorities estimate that each deep seabed mining venture will require an investment of $1 billion to $1.5 billion.

The National Ocean Industries Association (NOIA) is the trade association and lobbying organization which represents ocean-oriented industries. According to NOIA, the range of companies involved in marine work runs the gamut, from the major oil companies and steel corporations to manufacturers of marine products and companies that provide housekeeping and catering services to offshore platforms.

The exploration and mining of oceanic resources require an innovative technology attuned to especially difficult environmental problems. One steel corporation, for instance, fabricated and installed the first all-weather drilling and production platform intended for use in the waters of Cook Inlet off the coast of Alaska. The platform had to be able to withstand the tremendous forces of ice floes and swift tidal currents—problems not encountered on shore.

Solutions for such problems are developed through application of advances in the field of oceanography, the scientific study of the ocean. This young, rapidly growing science is challenging many traditional views about the ocean.

In the summer of 1986, an expedition in the submersible *Alvin,* 1,800 miles east of Miami, discovered black and bluish-white geysers of mineral-rich steam shooting up from the ocean floor. The mineral-laden, 650-degree geysers affect the chemical composition of the ocean, but mining the minerals two miles deep would not be feasible at this time. NOAA scientists who made the find say the deposits found are a natural laboratory to study the process of ore formation in mineral deposits on land, which are similar.

Oceanography is an expensive science, heavily dependent upon the availability of ships and complex observing systems. But if the cost is high, so is the likelihood of important results. The broad applications of the oceanographic sciences are particularly important to the fields of national defense and weather forecasting, but also lead to a better understanding of major oceanic phenomena, improvements in fisheries, the development of aquaculture, and the study and fighting of pollution.

Most academic programs in oceanography are divided into five major areas: biological oceanography, ocean engineering, chemical oceanography, geological oceanography, and physical oceanography. Depending on the institution involved, there may be a sixth area emphasizing the social sciences—the economic and political aspects of problems associated with the use of the sea.

According to the Marine Technology Society, "More than 40% of the people in ocean careers work for the federal government . . . where the bulk of the money for ocean research has come from in the past." Job holders in oceanography include marine microbiologists; phycologists (specialists in algae); coastal, electrical, mechanical, and fisheries engineers; cartographers; meteorologists; and maritime lawyers.

For a complete listing of companies involved in commercial marine endeavors, contact the National Ocean Industries Association, 1050 17th St. N.W.,

Fairweather (S-220)

Table O-2

SIZE AND AGE OF UNIVERSITY OCEANOGRAPHIC RESEARCH FLEET (SURFACE VESSELS)

Length (in feet)	Name	Operator	"Full Utilization" days at sea per year[1]	Year Built	Desired Retirement[4]
245	MELVILLE[2]	University of California (Scripps Institute)	260	1970	2000
245	KNORR[2]	Woods Hole Oceanographic Institute	260	1969	1999
213	MOANA WAVE[2]	University of Hawaii	260	1973	2003
210	ATLANTIS II[3]	Woods Hole Oceanographic Institute	260	1963	1993
209	CONRAD[2]	Columbia University (Lamont-Doherty)	260	1962	1992
209	T.G. THOMPSON[2]	University of Washington	260	1965	1995
209	T. WASHINGTON[2]	University of California (Scripps Institute)	260	1965	1995
177	ENDEAVOR[3]	University of Rhode Island	240	1976	2006
177	OCEANUS[3]	Woods Hole Oceanographic Institute	240	1975	2005
177	WECOMA[3]	Oregon State University	240	1975	2005
174	GYRE[2]	Texas A&M University	240	1973	2003
170	COLUMBUS ISELIN[3]	University of Miami	240	1972	2002
170	NEW HORIZON	University of California (Scripps Institute)	240	1978	2008
165	FRED H. MOORE	University of Texas	220	1967	1997
135	POINT SUR[3]	California State University (Moss Landing)	220	1981	2011
135	CAPE HATTERAS[3]	Duke University	220	1981	2011
133	ALPHA HELIX[3]	University of Alaska	220	1965	1995
125	R.G. SPROUL	University of California (Scripps Institute)	220	1981	2011
120	RIDGELY WARFIELD[2]	Johns Hopkins University (Chesapeake Bay Institute)	220	1967	2005
80	LAURENTIAN	University of Michigan	200	1974	2004
72	BLUE FIN	University of Georgia (Skidaway Institute)	200	1972	2002
68	CALANUS[2]	University of Miami	200	1970	2000
64	C.A. BARNES[3]	University of Washington	200	1966	1996

[1] As defined by National Science Foundation in 1979.

[2] Ships owned by the U.S. Navy.

[3] Ships owned or constructed by the National Science Foundation.

[4] Based on a 30-year lifetime.

Suite 700, Washington, D.C. 20036, and ask for the NOIA membership directory. (There is a nominal charge for the directory.)

More than 300 colleges, universities, specialized schools, and other institutions offer programs in oceanic and marine studies. Some provide career-training programs, others offer certificates, but most of them grant degrees. Information about the broad spectrum of academic programs available can be obtained from the Marine Technology Society, 2000 Florida Ave., N.W., Suite 500, Washington, D.C. 20009.

Among the international organizations dedicated to the study of oceanography are the International Council for the Exploration of the Sea (Copenhagen), the International Hydrographic Bureau (Monaco), the Institute of Oceanology of the Academy of Science and the State Oceanographic Institute (Moscow), the German Hydrographic Institute (Hamburg), the Institut Oceanographique (Paris), the Ocean Research Institute of the University of Tokyo, and the Andhra University at Waltair (India).

Many nations cooperated in the International Decade of the Ocean Exploration (IDOE) which began in 1970. The efforts and resources of 52 countries were joined in a massive collaborative program for a full decade in a drive to discover more of the ocean's secrets.

The immense project produced, among other results, a map showing the distribution and composition of manganese nodules, potential sources of copper, nickel, and cobalt; studies revealing that dredging poses the greatest threat to valuable sea-grass resources by directly destroying substrates, the bases on which the grasses grow; a rich lode of basic data which should enhance forecasters' ability to predict large-scale weather or climate changes; and major studies on the effect of pollution on the ocean.

• Geosynchronous satellites provide information about small-scale destructive storms, such as thunderstorms and squall lines. The same satellites provide information on a continuing basis about the temperature and mass fields of life-threatening weather phenomena and about the rapidly changing nature of local, regional, and global weather conditions. The ability to forecast potential destructive weather events is greatly enhanced by these satellites.

• Next Generation Weather (NEX-RAD), a service planned to be in operation by about 1990, will track and analyze severe storms through the use of information not obtainable by present radars.

Today's seafarers have reliable sources of marine information. Marine Reporting (MAREP), in service for many years, has been expanded. The service relies not only on NOAA weather information, but on continuing reports from people in the marine environment. An increase in the number of recreational sail and fishing boats that need such information and the number of such boats that now have sophisticated radio capability, has brought greater cooperation and more accurate information.

Perhaps the most important development has been new satellite units that can be placed on ships at sea. The International Maritime Satellite Organization (INMARSAT), a private organization of more than 40 countries—including the United States, Canada, and Japan—collects and disseminates both weather and general information.

SEA POWER: *RESERVES*

The steady increase in the capabilities of regular forces and the improvement in their readiness continue to be matched by similar improvements in the nation's sea-service reserve forces. In addition, their numbers and responsibilities continue to grow, and, as has been the case with regular forces, the percentage of persons being retained in reserve forces continues to rise. However, the momentum which has led to this steady, and sometimes dramatic, increase in overall reserve-force capability may be slowed by increasing pressure to reduce national budget deficits and in turn to cut defense spending. At the same time, reserve participation in such national endeavors as drug interdiction and minesweeping in the Persian Gulf may be sharply increased.

The average authorized strength for the organized reserves of the three sea services at the end of FY 1987 was 149,486 for the Navy, 42,800 for the Marine Corps, and 13,500 for the Coast Guard. For FY 1988, the Navy was seeking an increase to 157,400, including 22,505 full-time support personnel (mostly TARS) for recruiting and training reservists and administering the overall program. That represented a proposed increase of 7,914. However, congressional action left the Navy far short of its goal. Congress authorized only 152,600, and reduced the requested number of support personnel to 21,991. The Marines fared better; they had requested 43,700, and Congress cut that request only 100, to 43,600.

The Naval Air Reserve continued its "horizontal integration" in FY 1987 with commencement of the transition to a second squadron of F/A-18s and of the remaining two VF squadrons to F-14s. The transition from A-7B to A-7E aircraft was completed, and the first Airborne Mine Countermeasures Squadrons, flying RH-53D helicopters, stood up. In FY 1988, the transition of the last two VF squadrons will be completed. Transition of the first squadron of A-7Es to KA-6Ds and A-6Es will commence, as well as the transition to the first squadron of P-3Cs. The last squadron of F-4 Phantoms, those reliable aircraft that have served the Navy so well for so many years, was phased out of the Naval Air Reserve in the spring of 1987; F-4s already had been phased out of regular forces.

The Navy Surface Reserve continues to grow in size, having received four Perry-class FFG-7 frigates and one Knox-class FF-1052 frigate in FY 1987 and being scheduled to receive four FFG-7s and one FF-1052 during FY 1988. These additions will bring the total number of frigates to 24. Five more Craft of Opportunity (COOP) units will be activated in FY 1988, increasing that total to 16. These units are utilized to augment mine countermeasures forces in time of war, and to train Naval Reservists and conduct route surveys in peacetime. A total of 22 COOP units are planned; they will be composed of patrol craft and converted fishing vessels. The first of 14 Mine Countermeasures Ships, the *Avenger* (MCM-1) will be introduced into the Naval Reserve in FY 1988; that ship was commissioned in September 1987. When MSOs were deployed from both fleets to the Persian Gulf in the summer of 1987, a number of Naval Reservists sailed with those ships, and still others

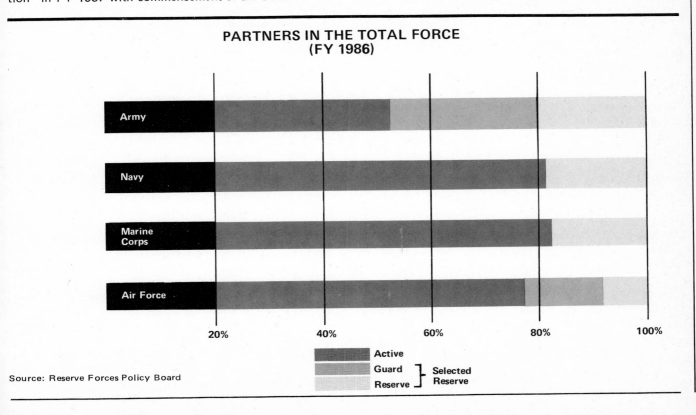

PARTNERS IN THE TOTAL FORCE
(FY 1986)

Army

Navy

Marine Corps

Air Force

20%   40%   60%   80%   100%

Active

Guard ⎤ Selected
Reserve ⎦ Reserve

Source: Reserve Forces Policy Board

volunteered for minesweeping duty aboard them. Eighteen of the Navy's 21 MSOs are in the Naval Reserve Force.

Three more Mobile Inshore Undersea Warfare (MIUW) units were activated in FY 1987, and two more are scheduled for activation during FY 1988, bringing the total to 23. Active MIUW-unit vans will be upgraded with AN/SQR-17 signal processors during FY 1988, markedly improving their capability. Also activated in FY 1987 was a 13th Cargo Handling Battalion, composed mostly of TAR and active-duty personnel. This battalion has the responsibility for training the other 12 and will have the same operational mission upon mobilization as the other battalions. Two more fleet hospitals will be activated during FY 1988, bringing the total to seven. The ultimate goal is 11.

The establishment of two Maritime Defense Zones (MDZs) already is having an impact on the Naval Reserve and, as missions and responsibilities become more clearly defined, is expected to involve Naval Reserve forces extensively. Coast Guard commanders based in New York and Alameda, CA, will be responsible for implementation of the operational concepts agreed upon by the Navy and the Coast Guard; these officers report to the Navy's fleet commanders in chief. Naval Reserve forces are particularly suited for many of the missions now assigned and expected to be assigned to commanders within the MDZs, and in some instances will be the only forces with necessary qualifications. Although much of the early emphasis has been on planning, the tempo of MDZ exercises is increasing sharply and can be expected to rise still further in the months to come.

Meanwhile, Naval Reservists already have been active in the national campaign against drug interdiction, with certain Reserve air units being employed extensively. That level of activity is expected to increase.

Operating out of 191 training centers in 46 states, the District of Columbia, and Puerto Rico, the Marine Corps Ready Reserve provides 25 percent of the wartime Fleet Marine Force structure. Consisting of two components, the Selected Marine Corps Reserve (SMCR) and the Individual Ready Reserve (IRR), it represents 33 percent of the trained manpower pool.

The principal components of the SMCR are the 4th Marine Division (Rein.), 4th Marine Aircraft Wing (MAW), and the 4th Force Service Support Group (FSSG). The 4th Marine Division is the largest in the Corps and is heavily reinforced to enhance its capability to augment and reinforce the active component. In addition to its regular complement, it includes an additional tank battalion, two force reconnaissance companies, two air-naval gunfire liaison companies, two civil-affairs groups, and a communications battalion. The 4th MAW, with 18 deployable squadrons, and the 4th FSSG, with additional beach and port and force engineer companies, represents substantial combat and combat service support capabilities. With over 42,700 currently in the SMCR, and projected growth to 48,000 by FY 1991, the SMCR will continue to represent a sizable portion of total Marine combat strength.

The IRR is the primary source of trained individuals for active and reserve units in the event of mobilization. With the increase in the military service obligation of new Marines from six to eight years, the IRR is expected to grow to approximately 85,000 men and women by FY 1991, a 63 percent increase from FY 1986. During FY 1987, one-day IRR recall screening resulted in over 78 percent of scheduled IRR personnel processed. This screening was conducted at 52 mobilization stations. This will be followed in FY 1988 with refresher training for volunteering IRR members.

A specific addition to the 4th MAW in FY 1987 was the Marine Corps adversary squadron in Yuma, AZ. Flying 13 F-21A Kfir fighters leased from Israel, it began operations in the fall of 1987. F-4 and A-4 squadrons will continue to be upgraded with F-4s and A-4M aircraft. Beginning in FY 1989, squadrons will be further upgraded with the F/A-18. A KC-130T squadron at Stewart Airport, New York, will be activated in late FY 1988. The wing received additional AH-1J attack helicopters throughout FY 1987, and plans call for a second AH-1J squadron to be activated by late FY 1988.

The 4th Marine Division completed its receipt of the M16A2 rifle and 9mm pistol and will begin receiving the M60E3 machine gun. The fielding of the M198 155mm howitzer commenced for the Reserves in FY 1985 and will continue through FY 1989. Upgrading of communications equipment, utility trucks, and vehicles continued through FY 1987 with the replacement of the M151 "jeep" with the MMMWV. By the end of FY 1989, the Marine Corps Reserve will have 97 percent of the dollar value of its wartime equipment.

Integrated training was intensified in FY 1987. Over 20,000 members of the SMCR had the opportunity to participate in 20 major exercises in nine different countries. Reserve/active force exercise integration was carried a step further in FY 1987 when for the first time a Marine Reserve Amphibious Brigade participated in a force-on-force exercise under the Commanding General, Fleet Marine Force, Atlantic. Reserve-alone exercises were used for combined arms training, cold-weather exercise training, and active-force standards training.

The Coast Guard Selected Reserve consists of 330 Reserve units organized into 60 Reserve Groups located in 42 states. The Coast Guard has been authorized 13,500 Reservists, but funding has been provided for only 12,850, and that funded level is not expected to rise in FY 1988. The goal is a Selected Reserve Force of 24,500 personnel by the end of FY 1997; whether that goal can be attained in an era of increasing austerity for military forces remains to be seen. The Coast Guard, more than the other services, is hampered by severe manpower shortages in the wartime mobilization force. It estimates that less than half the additional military manpower needed to perform Joint Chiefs of Staff high-priority wartime tasking is available from current mobilization manning resources. This adversely impacts on the Coast Guard's capability to implement Maritime Defense Zones, secure U.S. strategic ports, and protect water transportation systems. During 1987 Coast Guard Reservists participated in over 40 readiness exercises, of which nearly 90 percent also involved personnel from the other armed forces. These varied in scope from deployment to Jordan of a port-security unit to participating in three DOD exercises to offloading war materials from Military Sealift Command ships at the port of Jacksonville.

Index to Defense and Maritime Leaders

DEPARTMENT OF DEFENSE

Frank C. Carlucci, III
Secretary of Defense

William H. Taft, IV
Deputy Secretary of Defense

Fred C. Iklé
Under Secretary of Defense
for Policy

JOINT CHIEFS OF STAFF

Robert B. Costello
Under Secretary of Defense
for Acquisition

Admiral William J. Crowe, Jr.
Chairman
Joint Chiefs of Staff

Admiral Carlisle A.H. Trost
Chief of Naval Operations

General Larry D. Welch
Chief of Staff
of the Air Force

General Alfred M. Gray, Jr.
Commandant
of the Marine Corps

General Carl E. Vuono
Chief of Staff
of the Army

DEPARTMENT OF TRANSPORTATION

James H. Burnley, IV
Secretary of Transportation

Mimi W. Dawson
Deputy Secretary
of Transportation

MARITIME ADMINISTRATION

John Gaughan
Administrator
Maritime Administration

Elaine Chao
Deputy
Maritime Administrator

William A. Creelman
Deputy Maritime Adm.
for Inland Waterways
and Great Lakes

NAVY DEPARTMENT

James H. Webb, Jr.
Secretary of the Navy

H. Laurence Garrett, III
Under Secretary of the Navy

Robert H. Conn
Assistant Secretary
of the Navy
Financial Management

Everett Pyatt
Assistant Secretary
of the Navy
Shipbuilding & Logistics

Chase G. Untermeyer
Assistant Secretary
of the Navy
Manpower & Reserve Affairs

Dennis R. Shaw
Deputy Under Secretary
of the Navy, Policy

Seth Cropsey
Deputy Under Secretary
of the Navy, Special
Review and Analysis

(Nominations for the positions
of Assistant Secretary of the
Navy for Research, Engineering, and Systems, and General
Counsel of the Navy had not
been approved by Congress at
the time of publication.)

NAVY
LINE OFFICERS

ADMIRALS

William J. Crowe, Jr.
Chairman
Joint Chiefs of Staff

Carlisle A.H. Trost
Chief of Naval Operations

Kinnaird R. McKee
Director, Naval Nuclear
Propulsion Program

Ronald J. Hays
Commander in Chief
U.S. Pacific Command

Lee Baggett, Jr.
Supreme Allied Commander
Atlantic/CINC
U.S. Atlantic Command

James B. Busey
CINC, Allied Forces,
Southern Europe and
U.S. Naval Forces, Europe

Frank B. Kelso, II
CINC, U.S. Atlantic Fleet/
Deputy Commander in Chief
U.S. Atlantic Command

VICE ADMIRALS

Huntington Hardisty
Vice Chief
of Naval Operations

Powell F. Carter, Jr.
U.S. Representative
to NATO

David E. Jeremiah
Commander in Chief
U.S. Pacific Fleet

William H. Rowden
Commander
Naval Sea Systems Command

Nils R. Thunman
Chief
Naval Education & Training

James R. Hogg
Director, Naval Warfare
OPNAV

Edward H. Martin
Deputy Commander in Chief
U.S. Naval Forces Europe

Robert F. Dunn
Deputy Chief of
Naval Operations
Air Warfare

Henry C. Mustin
Deputy Chief of
Naval Operations
Plans, Policy, & Operations

Paul F. McCarthy, Jr.
Director
Research, Development,
and Acquisition, OPNAV

Kendall E. Moranville
Commander, Sixth Fleet
U.S. Atlantic Fleet

George W. Davis, Jr.
Commander
Naval Surface Force
U.S. Pacific Fleet

Joseph B. Wilkinson, Jr.
Commander
Naval Air Systems Command

William E. Ramsey
Deputy Commander in Chief
U.S. Space Command

Daniel L. Cooper
Commander
Submarine Force
U.S. Atlantic Fleet

Bruce DeMars
Deputy Chief of
Naval Operations
Submarine Warfare

Jonathan T. Howe
Assistant to the Chairman,
Joint Chiefs of Staff

Charles R. Larson
Commander, Second Fleet
U.S. Atlantic Fleet

Diego E. Hernandez
Commander, Third Fleet
U.S. Pacific Fleet

Paul D. Miller
Commander, Seventh Fleet
U.S. Pacific Fleet

Richard M. Dunleavy
Commander, Naval Air Force
U.S. Atlantic Fleet

Clyde R. Bell
Vice Director
Joint Strategic Target
Planning Staff

Walter T. Piotti, Jr.
Commander
Military Sealift Command

Jerry O. Tuttle
Director, J-6
Joint Chiefs of Staff

VICE ADMIRALS

John T. Parker, Jr.
Director
Defense Nuclear Agency

John H. Fetterman, Jr.
Commander
Naval Air Force
U.S. Pacific Fleet

John A. Baldwin, Jr.
Director, J-5
Joint Chiefs of Staff

William D. Smith
Director
Navy Program Planning
OPNAV

Albert J. Herberger
Deputy Commander in Chief
and Chief of Staff
U.S. Transportation Command

Leon A. Edney
Deputy Chief of Naval
Operations, Manpower
and Training

Joseph S. Donnell, III
Commander
Surface Force
U.S. Atlantic Fleet

John W. Nyquist
Deputy Chief
of Naval Operations
Surface Warfare

REAR ADMIRALS (Upper Half)

Stanley R. Arthur
Deputy Chief of Naval
Operations Logistics

David G. Ramsey
Chief of Staff
Supreme Allied Commander
Atlantic

Lawrence Layman
Director, Space, Command,
and Control, OPNAV

David L. Harlow
Chief of Naval
Technical Training

Robert C. Austin
Superintendent
Naval Postgraduate School
Monterey, CA

Benjamin T. Hacker
Commander
Naval Training Center
San Diego

John F. Addams
Commandant
National War College

Ronald J. Kurth
President
Naval War College

REAR ADMIRALS (Upper Half)

Edwin R. Kohn, Jr.
Assistant Deputy Chief
of Naval Operations
Air Warfare

Ronald F. Marryott
Superintendent
U.S. Naval Academy

James D. Williams
Director
Office of Program Appraisal
Office of SECNAV

Peter M. Hekman, Jr.
Deputy Commander
Surface Combatants
Naval Sea Systems Command

Ming E. Chang
Naval Inspector General
OPNAV

Daniel J. Wolkensdorfer
Commander
Operational Test and
Evaluation Force

Robert H. Shumaker
Director, Tactical Air,
Surface, & Electronic Warfare
Development Div., OPNAV

Richard C. Ustick
Chief of Staff
Commander in Chief
U.S. Southern Command

John S. Disher
Deputy Chief of Naval
Personnel/Commander
Navcal Mil. Pers. Command

James F. Dorsey, Jr.
Asst. Deputy Chief of
Naval Operations
Plans, Policy, & Operations

Ronald M. Eytchison
Director, Strategy Plans
& Policy Division
OPNAV

Dennis M. Brooks
Commander
Carrier Group FIVE
U.S. Pacific Fleet

William N. Fogarty
Director
Plans, Policy, and Programs
U.S. Central Command

James M.G. Seely
Director, Aviation Plans
and Requirements Division,
OPNAV

Harry K. Fiske
Vice Director, Strategic
Mobility & Resources
Joint Chiefs of Staff

Hugh L. Webster
Director for Logistics
& Security Assistance
U.S. Pacific Command

REAR ADMIRALS (Upper Half)

John R. Wilson, Jr.
Chief of Naval Research

Paul D. Butcher
Deputy & Chief of Staff
Commander in Chief
U.S. Atlantic Fleet

Dean R. Sackett, Jr.
JSC Representative
for Strategic Arms
Reduction Talks (START)

Jerry C. Breast
Director for Operations, J-3
U.S. Space Command

Jerome L. Johnson
Commander
Carrier Group FOUR
U.S. Atlantic Fleet

William T. Pendley
Commander
U.S. Naval Forces
Korea

Roger F. Bacon
Commander
Submarine Group EIGHT
U.S. Atlantic Fleet

Robert J. Kelly
Vice Director, J-3
Joint Chiefs of Staff

John F. Shaw
Commander
Cruiser Destroyer Group ONE
U.S. Pacific Fleet

Robert K.U. Kihune
Commander
Cruiser Destroyer Group FIVE
U.S. Pacific Fleet

Raymond P. Ilg
Commander
Carrier Group SIX
U.S. Atlantic Fleet

James G. Reynolds
Commander
Submarine Force
U.S. Pacific Fleet

Guy H. Curtis, III
Program Manager
SSN-21 Class Submarine
Naval Sea Systems Command

Henry H. Mauz, Jr.
Deputy Chief of Operations
Plans and Operations
U.S. Pacific Fleet

Theodore E. Lewin
Commander, U.S. Naval
Facility, Subic Bay
Republic of Philippines

Thomas R.M. Emery
Vice Commander
Defense Communications
Agency

REAR ADMIRALS (Upper Half)

Leonard G. Perry
Commander
Helicopter Wings
Atlantic

D. Bruce Cargill
Deputy Director
Space, Command, & Control
OPNAV

David F. Chandler
Director
Inter-American
Defense College

Robert H. Ailes
Deputy Commander
Weapons & Combat Systems
Naval Sea Systems Command

Thomas R. Fox
Assistant Deputy Director
International Negotiations
Joint Chiefs of Staff

Jeremy D. Taylor
Commander
Light Attack Wing
U.S. Pacific Fleet

Anthony A. Less
Commander
Carrier Group ONE
U.S. Pacific Fleet

Richard C. Gentz
Commander
Pacific Missile Test Center

Charles R. McGrail, Jr.
Deputy Director
Naval Warfare, OPNAV

James D. Cossey
Commander
U.S. Naval Forces Japan

Richard F. Pittenger
Director
Antisubmarine Warfare
Division, OPNAV

Stephen F. Loftus
Dir. of Budget & Reports
NAVCOMPT/Dir., Fiscal
Management Div., OPNAV

Salvatore F. Gallo
Commander
Fleet Air Mediterranean

Grant A. Sharp
Assistant Deputy Chief of
Naval Operations, Surface
Warfare, OPNAV

Michael C. Colley
Commander
Navy Recruiting Command

Richard H. Truly
Associate Administrator
for Space Flight, Office
of Space Flight, NASA

REAR ADMIRALS (Upper Half)   **REAR ADMIRALS** (Lower Half)

Raynor A.K. Taylor
Director, J-3
U.S. European Command

Burnham C. McCaffree, Jr.
Assistant Deputy Chief
of Naval Operations
Logistics

Gerald L. Riendeau
Chief, Military Assistance
Advisory Group, Spain

Oakley E. Osborn
Deputy Director
Defense Mapping Agency

"E" Inman Carmichael
Director
Logistics Plans Division
OPNAV

Willis I. Lewis, Jr.
Commander
Naval Logistics Command
U.S. Pacific Fleet

Robert J. Steele
Chief of Staff
U.S. Naval Forces
Europe

Charles H. Brickell, Jr.
Dir., Undersea & Strategic
Warfare & Nuclear Energy
Development Div., OPNAV

William J. O'Connor
Commander
U.S. Naval Forces
Caribbean

Chauncey F. Hoffman
Assistant Deputy Director
for Collection Management
Defense Intelligence Agency

Gerard J. Flannery, Jr.
Deputy Director for
Operations, NMCS, J-3
Joint Chiefs of Staff

Wendell N. Johnson
Commander
Naval Base, Charleston

Vernon C. Smith
Commander
Amphibious Group ONE
U.S. Pacific Fleet

John J. Higginson
Commander
Naval Surface Group
Long Beach

Dale N. Hagen
Commander
Naval Intelligence
Command

Thomas J. Johnson
Commander
Naval Base, Guam

REAR ADMIRALS (Lower Half)

Stanley E. Bump
Deputy Commander
Iberian Atlantic Area
Allied Forces, Atlantic

Norman D. Campbell
Ordered as Defense
Attache, Paris
ETA: June 1988

Denis T. Schwaab
Commander
Naval Safety Center

Harry S. Quast
Director
Information Services
Division, OPNAV

John W. Koenig
Commander
Naval Training Center
Orlando

Roger L. Rich, Jr.
Director of
Naval Communications
OPNAV

John W. Adams
Commander
ASW Warfare Wing
U.S. Pacific Fleet

Robert L. Toney
Commander Service Group
ONE & Naval Base
San Francisco

Ralph W. West, Jr.
Director, Personal Excellence
Program & Human Resources
Management Div., OPNAV

Gary F. Wheatley
Director, Office of
Technology Transfer &
Security Assistance, SECNAV

Francis R. Donovan
Commander
Amphibious Group THREE
U.S. Pacific Fleet

Raymond G. Zeller
Commander, Cruiser
Destroyer Group THREE
U.S. Pacific Fleet

Edward W. Clexton, Jr.
Director for Operations
Commander in Chief
U.S. Atlantic Fleet

John M. Kersh
Director, Strategic &
Theatre Nuclear Warfare
OPNAV

Henri B. Chase, III
Commander
Strike/Fighter Wing
Atlantic

Dwaine O. Griffith
Director, Deep Submergence
Systems Division
OPNAV

REAR ADMIRALS (Lower Half)

James E. Taylor
CMDR, Fighter Medium
Attack, Early Warning
Wings, Atlantic

Jimmy Pappas
Commander
Naval Base, Norfolk

Robert L. Leuschner, Jr.
Program Director for ASW
& Assault Programs
NAVAIRSYSCOM

William A. Dougherty, Jr.
Commander
Carrier Group EIGHT
U.S. Atlantic Fleet

Harold J. Bernsen
Commander
Middle East Force

Thomas W. Evans
Assistant Deputy Commander
ASW and Undersea Systems
NAVSEASYSCOM

David N. Rogers
Commander
Carrier Group THREE
U.S. Pacific Fleet

Thomas K. Mattingly, II
Director, Space and
Sensor Systems
NAVSPAWARSYSCOM

Robert T. Reimann
Commander
Naval Surface Group
Mid-Pacific

Daniel C. Richardson
Commander
Naval Surface Group
Western Pacific

Michael P. Kalleres
Commander
Cruiser Destroyer Group
TWELVE, U.S. Atlantic Fleet

Gerald E. Gneckow
Commander
U.S. Naval Forces
Southern Command

John F. Calvert
Commander
Naval Air Test Center

Eric A. McVadon, Jr.
Commander
Iceland Defense Force
Keflavik, Iceland

Lyle F. Bull
Commander
Carrier Group SEVEN
U.S. Pacific Fleet

Roland G. Guilbault
Director
Command & Control
Systems Division, OPNAV

REAR ADMIRALS (Lower Half)

Larry G. Vogt
Commander
Submarine Group TWO
U.S. Atlantic Fleet

Richard D. Milligan
Commander, Cruiser
Destroyer Group TWO
U.S. Atlantic Fleet

Jeremy M. Boorda
Commander
Cruiser Destroyer Group
EIGHT, U.S. Atlantic Fleet

John S. Yow
Commander
Patrol Wings
Atlantic

Virgil L. Hill, Jr.
Commander
Submarine Group FIVE
U.S. Pacific Fleet

John K. Ready
Commander
Carrier Group TWO
U.S. Atlantic Fleet

Henry G. Chiles, Jr.
Director
Strategic Submarine
Division, OPNAV

Cathal J. Flynn, Jr.
Director, J-6
U.S. Special Operations
Command

Wayne E. Rickman
Commander
Submarine Group NINE
U.S. Pacific Fleet

Ronald H. Jesberg
Commander
Helicopter Wings
Atlantic

William C. Francis
Commander
South Atlantic Force
U.S. Atlantic Fleet

Roberta L. Hazard
Director, J-1
(Manpower and Personnel)
Joint Chiefs of Staff

Philip D. Smith
Commander
Patrol Wings
U.S. Pacific Fleet

David R. Morris
Chief
Naval Air Training

Fredrick J. Metz
Cmdr., Medium Attack
Tact. Electronic Warfare
Wing, U.S. Pacific Fleet

Edward B. Baker, Jr.
Director, East Asia/
Pacific Region
OASD (ISA)

REAR ADMIRALS (Lower Half)

Peter G. Chabot
Inspector General
U.S. Atlantic Fleet

Jimmie W. Taylor
Deputy Chief
Naval Education
and Training

John F. Calhoun
Commander
Naval Training Center
Great Lakes

George H. Strohsahl, Jr.
Program Director
Tactical Aircraft
NAVAIRSYSCOM

Jesse J. Hernandez
Commander
Naval District
Washington

John W. Bitoff
Deputy Director for
Plans & Operations
U.S. European Command

David M. Bennett
Commander
Amphibious Group TWO
Atlantic Fleet

Thomas A. Mercer
Deputy Director, J-7
Joint Chiefs of Staff

Leighton W. Smith, Jr.
Director
Tactical Readiness
Division, OPNAV

Richard C. Macke
Commander
Naval Space Command

Henry C. McKinney
Deputy Chief of Staff
Logistics, CINCSOUTH

David R. Oliver, Jr.
Director
Force Level Plans
Division, OPNAV

Kenneth L. Carlsen
Director, Space Warfare
Systems Architecture
SPAWARSYSCOM

David B. Robinson
Director
Surface Warfare Division
OPNAV

George W. Davis, VI
Deputy Comptroller
of the Navy

Arlington F. Campbell
Commander
Naval Telecommunications
Command

REAR ADMIRALS (Lower Half)

Jerome F. Smith, Jr.
Director, POLMIL &
Current Plans Division
OPNAV

Stephen K. Chadwick
Director for Distribution,
NMPC-4, Naval Military
Personnel Command

Glenn E. Whisler, Jr.
Deputy Chief of Staff
for Plans and Policy
SACLANT

Craig E. Dorman
Program Director
ASW Warfare Systems
SPAWARSYSCOM

Geoffrey L. Chesbrough
Dir., Command & Control
Planning and Programming
Division, OPNAV

Grady L. Jackson
Director
Electronic Warfare
Division, OPNAV

James B. Greene, Jr.
Program Manager, AEGIS
Shipbuilding Project
NAVSEASYSCOM

Joseph P. Reason
Commander
Naval Base, Seattle

Eugene D. Conner
Commander, Military
Entrance Processing
Command, Chicago

Bobby C. Lee
Commander, Fleet Air
Western Pacific

Riley D. Mixson
Command Director
NORAD Combat
Operations Staff

Donald V. Boecker
Director
Navy Space Systems
OPNAV

Daniel P. March
Director, Program
Resource Appraisal
Division, OPNAV

Douglas Volgenau
Director
Submarine Combat Systems
NAVSEASYSCOM

William P. Houley
Director, Military
Personnel Policy
Division, OPNAV

Richard C. Allen
Director for Operations,
J-3, CINCLANT

REAR ADMIRALS (Lower Half)

Thomas A. Meinicke
Director
Attack Submarine Division
OPNAV

Raymond G. Jones, Jr.
Director, Total Force
Programming/Manpower
Division, OPNAV

Ronald C. Wilgenbusch
Deputy Program Director
Information Transfer
Systems, SPARWARSYSCOM

James B. Best
Commander, Fighter Airborne
Early Warnings Wings
U.S. Pacific Fleet

Jerry L. Unruh
Chief
Operational Readiness
Branch, SHAPE

Philip F. Duffy
Commander
U.S. Naval Forces
U.S. Central Command

Paul D. Moses
Commander
Service Group TWO
U.S. Atlantic Fleet

John R. Dalrymple, Jr.
Assistant VCNO
for Administration
OPNAV

Byron E. Tobin
Commander
Mine Warfare Command

Irve C. Lemoyne
Commander
Naval Special
Warfare Command

Walter L. Glenn, Jr.
Commander
Training Command
U.S. Pacific Fleet

George N. Gee
Director
Surface Combat Systems Div.
OPNAV

Peter H. Cressy
Director, Aviation,
Manpower, and Training
Division, OPNAV

Frederick L. Lewis
Director, Strike and
Amphibious Warfare
Division, OPNAV

William A. Owens
Commander
Submarine Group SIX
U.S. Atlantic Fleet

Phillip R. Olson
Deputy Director
NMCC, J-3
Joint Chiefs of Staff

REAR ADMIRALS (Lower Half)

Thomas C. Lynch
Chief
of Legislative Affairs

Joseph C. Strasser
Executive Assistant
to the Chairman,
Joint Chiefs of Staff

Photographs of the following
selectees for rear admiral
(lower half) were not available:

William C. Miller
Commanding Officer
Naval Research. Laboratory

Thomas D. Paulsen
Executive Assistant to
the Chief of Naval Operations

Raymond M. Walsh
Dir., Operations Division
Office of Budget & Reports
NAVCOMPT

RESTRICTED LINE (ENGINEERING DUTY)

VICE ADMIRAL

Glenwood Clark, Jr.
Commander
Space and Naval Warfare
Systems Command

REAR ADMIRALS (Upper Half)

Harold L. Young
Vice Commander
Naval Sea Systems Command

David P. Donahue
Fleet Maintenance Officer
U.S. Atlantic Fleet

Myron V. Ricketts
Director, Fleet Support
Atlantic

Malcolm MacKinnon, III
Deputy Cmdr. for Ships
Design and Engineering
Naval Sea Systems Command

Kenneth C. Malley
Director, Strategic
Systems Project Office
OPNAV

REAR ADMIRALS (Lower Half)

Lowell J. Holloway
Deputy Chief Engineer
for Combat Systems
Engineering, NAVSEA

Roger B. Horne, Jr.
Deputy Cmdr. for Facility
& Industrial Management
Naval Sea Systems Command

Thomas U. Seigenthaler
Fleet Maintenance Officer
U.S. Pacific Fleet

Robert L. Topping
Director, Warfare
Systems Engineering
SPAWARSYSCOM

REAR ADMIRALS (Lower Half)

George R. Meinig
Asst. Deputy Commander
Surface Warfare & AAW
Systems, NAVSEASYSCOM

Walter H. Cantrell
Deputy Commander
for Submarines
Naval Sea Systems Command

John S. Claman
Supervisor of Shipbuilding,
Conversion, and Repair
Groton

Robert E. Traister
Commander
Naval Shipyard
Pearl Harbor

RESTRICTED LINE (AVIATION ENGINEERING DUTY)

REAR ADMIRALS (Upper Half)

William J. Finneran
Vice Commander
Naval Air Systems Command

John C. Weaver
Vice Commander
Space and Naval
Warfare Systems Command

Richard D. Friichtenicht
Deputy Commander
for Plans and Programs
Naval Sea Systems Command

REAR ADMIRALS (Lower Half)

John H. Kirkpatrick
Assistant Commander for
Logistics & Fleet Support
NAVAIRSYSCOM

Thomas C. Betterton
Assistant Commander
for Space Technology
SPAWARSYSCOM

Larry E. Blose
Director
Joint Cruise Missile Project
Naval Air Systems Command

William C. Bowes
F-14 Program Manager
Naval Air Systems Command

SPECIAL DUTY (CRYPTOLOGY)

REAR ADMIRAL (Upper Half)   REAR ADMIRAL (Lower Half)

Charles F. Clark
Deputy Director
for Operations
National Security Agency

James S. McFarland
Commander
Naval Security
Group Command

INTELLIGENCE

REAR ADMIRAL (Upper Half)

REAR ADMIRALS (Lower Half)

Robert W. Schmitt
Deputy Director
Defense Intelligence Agency

William O. Studeman
Director
Naval Intelligence
OPNAV

Thomas A. Brooks
Deputy Director
for JCS Support
Defense Intelligence Agency

PUBLIC AFFAIRS

REAR ADMIRAL (Lower Half)

Edward D. Sheafer, Jr.
Director
for Intelligence, J-2
Commander in Chief, Atlantic

Jimmie B. Finkelstein
Chief of Information

OCEANOGRAPHY

REAR ADMIRAL (Lower Half)

**STAFF CORPS:
MEDICAL CORPS**

VICE ADMIRAL

John R. Seesholtz
Oceanographer of the Navy

James A. Zimble
Surgeon General of
the Navy/Director
of Naval Medicine

REAR ADMIRALS (Upper Half)

William M. Narva
Attending Physician
to Congress

Joseph S. Cassells
Commander
Naval Medical Command

Robert P. Caudill, Jr.
Deputy Director
Naval Medicine
OPNAV

Henry J.T. Sears
Commander
Naval Medical Command
Southwest Region

REAR ADMIRALS (Upper Half)   **REAR ADMIRALS (Lower Half)**

James K. Summit
Deputy Commander
Health Care Operations
Naval Medical Command

Lewis Mantel
Director of
Medical Practice
OPNAV

Russell L. Marlor
Fleet Surgeon
U.S. Pacific Fleet

Daniel B. Lestage
Fleet Surgeon
U.S. Atlantic Fleet

Donald F. Hagen
Director
Health Care Operations
OPNAV

William A. Buckendorf
Commander
Naval Medical Command
Mid-Atlantic Region

Donald L. Sturtz
Professor of Surgery
Uniformed Services,
Univ. of Health Services

Robert W. Higgins
The Medical Officer
U.S. Marine Corps

SUPPLY CORPS

REAR ADMIRALS (Upper Half)

David M. Lichtman
Head
Orthopedic Department
Naval Hospital, Bethesda

Robert B. Halder
Commanding Officer
Naval Hospital
Naples, Italy

Edward K. Walker, Jr.
Commander, Naval Supply
Systems Command & Chief
of the Supply Corps

Carl R. Webb, Jr.
Director
Material Division
OPNAV

Daniel W. McKinnon, Jr.
Deputy Director for
Acquisition Management
Defense Logistics Agency

Robert B. Abele
Vice Commander
Naval Supply
Systems Command

James B. Whittaker
Assistant Commander
Inventory & Systems
Integrity, NAVSUP

REAR ADMIRALS (Lower Half)

Rodney K. Squibb
Commander
Naval Resale and
Services Support Office

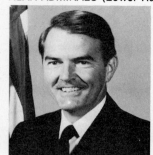

Phillip F. McNall
Commanding Officer
Naval Aviation
Supply Office

Robert A. Phillips
Commanding Officer
Navy Ships Parts
Control Center

James E. Miller
ACOS/Logistics
Fleet Supply Officer
U.S. Atlantic Fleet

William E. Powell, Jr.
Commanding Officer
Naval Supply Center
Norfolk

James E. Eckelberger
Executive Director
Supply Operations
Defense Logistics Agency

Brady M. Cole
Force Supply Officer
COMNAVLOGPAC

Peter DeMayo
Asst. Deputy Commander
for Depot Management
Naval Air Systems Command

Francis L. Filipiak
Assistant Comptroller
Financial Management
OPNAV

William H. Hauenstein
Deputy Commander
for Contracts
Naval Sea Systems Command

Robert M. Moore
Competition
Advocate General
of the Navy, SECNAV

CHAPLAIN CORPS

REAR ADMIRAL (Upper Half)

John R. McNamara
Chief of Chaplains/Director
of Religious Ministries
OPNAV

REAR ADMIRALS (Lower Half)

Alvin B. Koeneman
Deputy Chief of Chaplains/
Deputy Director of
Religious Ministries

CIVIL ENGINEER CORPS

REAR ADMIRALS (Lower Half)

Benjamin F. Montoya
Cmdr., Naval Facilities Engi-
neering Command/Chief of
Civil Engineers of the Navy

Arthur W. Fort
Commander
Pacific Region
NAVFACENGCOM

Frederick G. Kelley
Vice Commander
Naval Facilities
Engineering Command

David E. Bottorff
Commander
Atlantic Division
NAVFACENGCOM

Jon R. Ives
Deputy Commander
for Planning
NAVFACENGCOM

JUDGE ADVOCATE GENERAL CORPS

REAR ADMIRALS (Upper Half)

Hugh D. Campbell
Judge Advocate General
of the Navy

REAR ADMIRALS (Lower Half)

DENTAL CORPS

REAR ADMIRALS (Upper Half)

Everette D. Stumbaugh
Deputy Judge Advocate
General of the Navy

John E. Gordon
Commander, Naval Security
& Investigative Command

Richard G. Shaffer
Cmdr., Nav. Med. Command,
Natl. Capital Region, and
Chief of the Dental Corps

REAR ADMIRALS (Lower Half)

Henry J. Sazima
Deputy Commander
Readiness & Logistics
Naval Medical Command

Robert W. Koch
Director, Dental Care
Operations Division
Naval Medical Command

Milton C. Clegg
Director
Resource Division
OPNAV

A photograph of rear admiral
selectee James C. Doebler
(CEC), Director, Shore Activities Planning & Programming
Division, OPNAV, was not
available.

MEDICAL SERVICE CORPS

REAR ADMIRAL (Lower Half)

Donald E. Shuler
Chief of the Medical
Service Corps/Vice Cmdr.
Naval Medical Command

NURSE CORPS

REAR ADMIRALS (Lower Half)

Mary F. Hall
Deputy Commander for
Personnel Management/Dir.,
Navy Nurse Corps

Joseph P. Smyth
Commander
Naval Medical Command
European Region

NAVAL RESERVE (TAR)

REAR ADMIRALS (Lower Half)

Albert E. Rieder
Commander, Naval Base
Philadelphia

Richard K. Chambers
Deputy Commander
Naval Reserve Force

NAVAL RESERVE (RECALL)

REAR ADMIRAL (Lower Half)

Francis N. Smith
Chief of Naval Reserve

NAVY (RETIRED-RECALL)

REAR ADMIRAL (Lower Half)

John D. Bulkeley
President
Board of Inspection
and Survey

MASTER CHIEF PETTY OFFICER OF THE NAVY

William H. Plackett
Master Chief Petty Officer
of the Navy

NAVAL RESERVE CORPS

Each Naval Reserve flag officer ultimately is given a mobilization assignment. However, since these assignments often change during the years an officer remains active in the Naval Reserve in flag rank, they are not included in the listing which follows.

REAR ADMIRALS (Upper Half)

Lemuel O. Warfield
934 Coachway
Annapolis, MD 21401

Vincent J. Anzilotti, Jr.
572 Moraga Way
Morinda, CA 94563

Richard E. Young
2345 Elm Street
Denver, CO 80207

Tammy H. Etheridge
135 Woodland Circle
Jackson, MS 39216

LeRoy Collins, Jr.
418 Blanca Avenue
Tampa, FL 33606

Frederick P. Bierschenk, Jr.
8315 Burning Tree Drive
Franktown, CO 80116

John E. Love
1002 Spokane Street
Garfield, WA 99130

John D. Summers
3666 Partridge Lane
Roanoke, VA 24017

John J. Sweeney
351 Williams Road
Wynnewood, PA 19096

Kenneth E. Myatt
2841 Cravey Drive
Atlanta, GA 30345

Jack S. Smith
1070 Mountain Creek Trail
Atlanta, GA 30328

REAR ADMIRALS (Lower Half)

Martin W. Leukhardt
5 Crystal Lane
Latham, NY 12110

Burton O. Benson
5 Evans Place
Orinda, CA 94563

James M. Strickland
133 Belmont Court
Redlands, CA 92373

John W. Gates, Jr.
32 Carroll Drive
Foxboro, MA 02035

REAR ADMIRALS (Lower Half)

Stephen G. Yusem
Township Line Road
Gwynedd Valley, PA 19437

Richard S. Fitzgerald
Route 1, Box 108
Catlett, VA 22019

Samuel E. McWilliams
1859 Vallejo Street
San Francisco, CA 94123

Richard K. Maughlin
707 Meadow Lake Lane
Great Falls, MD 20634-9728

David A. Janes
1721 La Ramada Avenue
Arcadia, CA 91006

Wallace N. Guthrie, Jr.
1618 Wood Duck Drive
Winter Springs, FL 32708

Larry B. Franklin
2801 Altagate Court
Louisville, KY 40206

Jimmie W. Seeley
2538 Foxwood Road South
Orange Park, FL 32073

ENGINEERING DUTY

REAR ADMIRALS (Lower Half)

William P. O'Donnell, Jr.
113 Countryside Drive
Chagrin Falls, OH 44022

Wilson F. Flagg
63 Scott Ridge Road
Ridgefield, CT 06877

Paul K. Arthur
2050 San Acacio
Las Cruces, NM 88001

AVIATION ENGINEERING

REAR ADMIRAL (Upper Half)

Clay W.G. Fulcher
18710 Point Lookout
Houston, TX 77058

Brian T. Sheehan
387 Mosely Road
Hillsborough, CA 94010

CRYPTOLOGY

REAR ADMIRAL (Upper Half)

William J. Miles
2009 N. Kensington Street
Arlington, VA 22205

INTELLIGENCE

REAR ADMIRALS (Upper Half)

Robert P. Tiernan
1747 Calle Arrayo
Diablo, CA 94528

PUBLIC AFFAIRS

REAR ADMIRAL (Lower Half)

Robert A. Ravitz
5 Westview Lane
South Norwalk, CT 06854

Gene P. Dickey
2214 Scarlet Lane
Grand Prairie, TX 75050

MEDICAL CORPS

REAR ADMIRALS (Upper Half)

James A. Austin
3601 La Colmena Way
Los Alamitos, CA 90720

John D. Tolmie
1543 Abbey Court
Winston-Salem, NC 27103

James G. Roberts
3040 Octavia Street
New Orleans, LA 10125

REAR ADMIRALS (Lower Half)

James J. Cerda
3332 N.W. 133rd Street
Gainesville, FL 32601

Robert L. Summitt
3102 Glennfinnan Road
Memphis, TN 38128

Robert C. Nuss
8151 Blue Jay Lane
Jacksonville, FL 32216

Horace MacVaugh, III
116 Spruce Street
Philadelphia, PA 19106

SUPPLY CORPS

REAR ADMIRALS (Upper Half)

Paul T. Kayye
Route 1, Box 343C
Angier, NC 27501

Thomas G. Lilly
4408 Deer Creek Drive
Jackson, MS 39211

Delbert H. Beumer
452 University Avenue
Los Altos, CA 94022

REAR ADMIRALS (Lower Half)

Donald G. St. Angelo
15126 Williston Lane
Minnetonka, MN 55345

Philip A. Whitacre
1541 Brickell Avenue
Miami, FL 33129

Henry C. Amos, Jr.
6116 Glennox Lane
Dallas, TX 75214

James H. Mayer
6 Mockingbird Court
Movato, CA 94947

CHAPLAIN CORPS

REAR ADMIRAL (Lower Half)

J. Ronald Denney
800 Pebble Hill Road
Doyleston, PA 18901

Vance H. Fry
1404 Rowewood Drive
Chattanooga, TN 37421

Aaron Landes
8372 Fisher Road
Elkins Park, PA 19117

CIVIL ENGINEERS CORPS

REAR ADMIRAL (Upper Half)

REAR ADMIRAL (Lower Half)

David O. Smart
5607 West 98th Street
Overland Park, KS 66204

Paul C. Rosser
64 West Brookhaven Drive
Atlanta, GA 30319

JUDGE ADVOCATE GENERAL'S CORPS

REAR ADMIRAL (Upper Half)

DENTAL CORPS

REAR ADMIRAL (Upper Half)

Robert E. Wiss
2864 Sheridan Place
Evanston, IL 60201

Edward J. O'Shea, Jr.
7 West Gate Lane
Setauket, NY 11733

REAR ADMIRAL (Lower Half)

William B. Finagin
6 Romar Drive
Annapolis, MD 21403

MARINE CORPS

GENERALS

Alfred M. Gray, Jr.
Commandant of the
Marine Corps

George B. Crist
Commander in Chief
U.S. Central Command
MacDill AFB, FL

Thomas R. Morgan
Assistant Commandant

LIEUTENANT GENERALS

Keith A. Smith
Deputy Chief of Staff
for Aviation

Joseph J. Went
Deputy Chief of Staff
for Installations
and Logistics

John Phillips
Deputy Chief of Staff
for Plans, Policy, & Operations

Frank E. Petersen, Jr.
Commanding General, Marine
Corps Development &
Educational Center, Quantico

Stephen G. Olmstead
Deputy Assistant Secretary
of Defense for Drugs, Policy
and Enforcement

Anthony Lukeman
Deputy Assistant Secretary
of Defense, Military Man-
power & Personnel Policy

Edwin J. Godfrey
Commanding General
Fleet Marine Force
Pacific

Louis H. Buehl, III
Chief of Staff

Ernest T. Cook, Jr.
Commanding General
Fleet Marine Force
Atlantic

John I. Hudson
Deputy Chief of Staff
for Manpower

MAJOR GENERALS

Wesley H. Rice
Inspector General
of the Marine Corps

James J. McMonagle
Commanding General
I Marine Amphibious Force/
1st Marine Division

Richard M. Cooke
Deputy Commander
Fleet Marine Force
Pacific

Donald J. Fulham
Commanding General
Marine Corps Recruit Depot
San Diego, CA

Jacob W. Moore
Deputy Chief of Staff
Reserve Affairs

William G. Carson, Jr.
Commanding General
Marine Corps Logistics Base
Albany, GA

William R. Etnyre
Deputy Chief of Staff
Requirements and Programs

Charles H. Pitman
Assistant Deputy
Chief of Staff, Aviation

Norman H. Smith
Commanding General
III Marine Amphibious Force/
3rd Marine Division

Ray "M" Franklin
Deputy Chief of Staff
Research, Development
Studies

John R. Dailey
Commandant
Armed Forces Staff College
Norfolk, VA

James E. Cassity
Commanding General
Marine Corps Base
Camp Lejeune, NC

Carl E. Mundy, Jr.
Director, Operations
Division, Plans, Policy,
and Operations

John P. Monahan, Assistant
Chief of Staff, C-5, Com-
bined Forces, Korea/J-5,
U.S. Forces, Korea

Richard A. Gustafson
Deputy Commander
U.S. Forces, Japan

Edmund P. Looney, Jr.
Director, Logistics Plans,
Policy, and Strategic
Mobilization Div., I&L

MAJOR GENERALS

Orlo K. Steele
Commanding General
2d Marine Division/Dep.
Cdr., II Marine Amphib. Force

Hollis E. Davison
Commanding General
4th Marine Division

Robert F. Milligan
Commander
U.S. Forces
Caribbean

Gene A. Deegan, Command-
ing Gen., Marine Corps Air/
Ground Combat Center,
Twentynine Palms, CA

Joseph P. Hoar
Commanding General
Marine Corps Recruit Depot
Parris Island, SC

Royal N. Moore, Jr.
Director, Operations
U.S. Pacific Command

Donald E.P. Miller
Commanding General
3rd Marine Air Wing/
Deputy Cmdr., I MAF

BRIGADIER GENERALS

Michael K. Sheridan
Director, Plans Division
Headquarters, USMC

Robert R. Porter
Director
Naval Council of
Personnel Boards

Robert J. Winglass
Ordered as Commanding
General, Marine Corps
Logistics Base, Albany, GA

Jim R. Joy
Director, Personnel
Procurement Division
Headquarters, USMC

James M. Mead
Commanding General
Marine Corps Air Station
Cherry Point, NC

Frederick E. Sisley
Deputy Chief of Staff
for Training
Headquarters, USMC

James D. Beans
Commanding General
5th Marine
Amphibious Brigade

Michael P. Sullivan
Commanding General
2d Marine Air Wing

BRIGADIER GENERALS

Jarvis D. Lynch, Jr.
Commanding General
2d Forward Support
Services Group

John I. Hopkins
Dir., Marine Corps Research,
Development, & Acquisition
Command, Quantico

Ronald L. Beckwith
Commanding General
4th Marine Air Wing

Ross S. Plasterer
Commanding General
1st Marine Air Wing/
Deputy Cmdr., III MAF

Matthew T. Cooper
Commanding General
Marine Corps Base
Camp Pendleton, CA

Gail M. Reals
Director, Manpower Plans
& Policy Division
Headquarters, USMC

Matthew P. Caulfield
Commanding General
4th Marine
Amphibious Brigade

Henry C. Stackpole, III
Director, Plans & Policy
Directorate, Commander
in Chief, Atlantic

Frank J. Breth
Director
Intelligence Division
Headquarters, USMC

David M. Brahms
Director
Judge Advocate Division
Headquarters, USMC

James E. Sniffen
Commanding General
Marine Corps Logistics Base
Barstow, CA

John S. Grinalds
Dep. Dir., Force Structure
Resource & Assessment
J-8, Joint Chiefs of Staff

David V. Shuter
Commanding General
Marine Corps Air Station
El Toro, CA

Bobby G. Butcher
Commanding General
6th Marine
Amphibious Brigade

George L. Cates
Commanding General
1st Marine
Amphibious Brigade

Richard H. Huckaby
Commander, Defense
Electronics Supply Agency
DLA, Dayton, OH

BRIGADIER GENERALS

Jeremiah W. Pearson, III
Commander, Forward
Headquarters Element
U.S. Central Command

Walter E. Boomer
Director
Public Affairs Division
Headquarters, USMC

Frank A. Huey
Commanding General
Camp Smedley D. Butler
Okinawa

John A. Studds
Deputy Director, J-3
U.S. European Command

William M. Keys
Director, Personnel
Management Division
Headquarters, USMC

William P. Eshelman
Asst. Division Commander
1st Marine Division

Lloyd G. Pool
Assistant Wing Commander
3d Marine Air Wing

Donald R. Gardner
Assistant Division Commander
2d Marine Division

Harry W. Jenkins, Jr.
Legislative Assistant
to the Commandant

Michael P. Mulqueen
Commanding General
3rd Forward Support
Services Group

John P. Brickley
Dir., Education Center
Marine Corps Education
& Development Ctr., Quantico

Michael P. Downs
Director, Facilities
& Services Division, I&L
Headquarters, USMC

Duane A. Wills
Deputy Director, J-3
National Military
Command Center, JCS

Richard L. Phillips
Director
C-4 Systems Division
Headquarters, USMC

Robert B. Johnston
Asst. Division Commander
3rd Marine Division

Peter J. Rowe
Assistant Chief of Staff
Operations Division
Allied Forces North, Oslo

RIGADIER GENERALS

Clyde L. Vermilyea
Assistant Wing Commander
2nd Marine Air Wing

Francis X. Hamilton, Jr.
Commanding General
1st Forward Support
Services Group

SERGEANT MAJOR OF THE MARINE CORPS

David W. Summers
Sergeant Major
of the Marine Corps

MARINE CORPS RESERVE

each Marine Corps Reserve eneral officer is given a mobization assignment. However, ecause these assignments are ubject to frequent changes, ney are not reflected here; nly those general officers curently active in the Reserve nd their home addresses are sted.

MAJOR GENERALS

John J. Salesses
89 Peleg Road
Portsmouth, RI 02871-4507

Ronald K. Nelson
649 Woodward Drive
Huntingdon Valley, PA
19006-4057

C. Dean Sangalis
1204 Theresa Drive
Schererville, IN 46375-1547

BRIGADIER GENERALS

Charles S. Bishop, Jr.
1735B Wildberry Drive
Glenview, IL 60025-1726

Richard P. Trotter
2965 307 S. Pharr Court, NW
Atlanta, GA 30305

Jerome G. Cooper
1208 Palmetto Street
Mobile, AL 36604-2645

G. Richard Omrod
100 Gill Road
Haddonfield, NJ 08033-3404

Mitchell J. Waters
347 Shoreline Road
Lake Barrington Shores, IL
60010-1627

John F. Cronin
6333 Silverado
Bend, OR 97702

(A photograph of MGEN William H. Cossell, USMCR, 14303 Juniper Cove, Farmers Branch, TX 75234-2211, was not available.)

COAST GUARD

ADMIRAL

Paul A. Yost, Jr.
Commandant

VICE ADMIRALS

James C. Irwin
Vice Commandant

John D. Costello
Commander, Pacific Area
and U.S. Maritime Defense
Zone, Pacific

REAR ADMIRALS

Donald C. Thompson
Commander, Atlantic Area
and U.S. Maritime Defense
Zone, Atlantic

Clyde T. Lusk
Chief of Staff

William P. Kozlovsky
Commander, Fourteenth
Coast Guard District

Richard P. Cueroni
Superintendent
Coast Guard Academy

Kenneth G. Wiman
Chief
Office of Engineering

Edward Nelson, Jr.
Commander, Seventeenth
Coast Guard District

Clyde E. Robbins
Chief
Office of Operations

Theodore J. Wojnar
Commander, Thirteenth
Coast Guard District

Arnold M. Danielsen
Commander, Ninth
Coast Guard District

Howard B. Thorsen
Commander, Seventh
Coast Guard District

Alan D. Breed
Commander, Fifth
Coast Guard District

John W. Kime
Chief, Office of
Marine Safety, Security,
& Environmental Protection

EAR ADMIRALS

Robert L. Johanson
Commander, First
Coast Guard District

William F. Merlin
Chief, Office of
Command, Control, and
Communications

Arnold B. Beran
Commander, Eleventh
Coast Guard District

Peter J. Rots
Commander, Eighth
Coast Guard District

Thomas J. Matteson
Chief
Office of Personnel

Richard I. Rybacki
Comptroller

Martin H. Daniell, Jr.
Chief
Office of Navigation

Robert T. Nelson
Commander, Second
Coast Guard District

Marshall E. Gilbert
Chief, Office of
Boating, Public and
Consumer Affairs

Joseph E. Vorbach
Chief Counsel

George D. Passmore, Jr.
Commander, Maintenance
and Logistics Command,
Atlantic

Ernest B. Acklin
Chief
Office of Acquisition

Paul A. Welling
Chief
Office of Readiness
and Reserve

Walter T. Leland
Commander, Maintenance
and Logistics Command,
Pacific

Edward F. Blasser, USPHS
Chief
Office of Health Services

Allen W. Thiele
Master Chief Petty Officer
of the Coast Guard

COAST GUARD
RESERVE

REAR ADMIRALS

Daniel J. Murphy
90 Sunview Drive
San Francisco, CA 94131

Bennett S. Sparks
3233 Wonder View Drive
Hollywood, CA 90068

NOAA

Francis D. Moran
Director
NOAA Corps

Wesley V. Hull
Director
Charting & Geodetic Services
National Ocean Service

Robert L. Sandquist
Dir., Pacific Marine Center
& Act. Dir., Office of Marine
Operations, Natl. Ocean Serv.

Ray E. Moses
Director
Atlantic Marine Center
National Ocean Service

KEY PERSONNEL LOCATOR
DEPARTMENT OF THE NAVY — WASHINGTON AREA ORGANIZATIONS

SECRETARY OF THE NAVY

HON JAMES H WEBB JR	4E686	695-3131
EXECUTIVE ASSISTANT & NAVAL AIDE		
CAPT T M Daly	4E686	695-4603
SPECIAL ASSISTANT & MARINE CORPS AIDE		
COL H Peirpan USMC	4E686	695-5133
ADMINISTRATIVE AIDE		
CDR T W La Fleur	4E687	695-5410
SPECIAL ASSISTANT PUBLIC AFFAIRS		
CDR M D Neuhart	4E733	697-7491
SPEC ASST & SPEECH WRITER TO SECNAV & UNSECNAV		
LCDR M B Rosel	4D723	694-4926
SPEC ASST (LEGAL & LEGISLATIVE AFFAIRS)		
CAPT D Williams	4E725	697-6935

UNDER SECRETARY OF THE NAVY

HON H L GARRETT III	4E714	695-3141
EXECUTIVE ASSISTANT & NAVAL AIDE		
CAPT N Ray	4E714	695-2140
SPECIAL ASSISTANT & MARINE CORPS AIDE		
COL T Steele USMC	4E714	695-2002
DEPUTY UNDER SECRETARY (POLICY)		
Mr D Shaw	4E725	694-6122
DEPUTY UNDER SECRETARY (SPECIAL RESEARCH & ANALYSIS)		
Mr S Cropsey	4E780	697-6684
DEPUTY ASST SECRETARY (TECH TRANSFER & SECURITY AFFAIRS)		
Mr R Levine	CP-6 580	692-7260
DIR NAVAL INDUSTRIAL IMPROVEMENT PROGRAM		
Mr W Lindahl	5E689	875-2028
AUDITOR GENERAL		
Mr R L Shaffer NASSIF	501A	756-2117
ASSISTANT FOR ADMINISTRATION		
Mr O R Ashe	4E752	694-5032

OFFICE OF THE SECRETARY OF THE NAVY

OFFICE OF THE GENERAL COUNSEL

VACANT	4E724	694-1994
(General Counsel)		
PRINCIPAL DEPUTY GENERAL COUNSEL		
Vacant	4E724	694-2307
DEPUTY GENERAL COUNSEL (LOGISTICS)		
Mr H J Wilcox	CP-5 480	692-7136
ASSOCIATE GENERAL COUNSEL (MANAGEMENT)		
Mr F A Phelps	CP-5 480	692-7328
ASSOCIATE GENERAL COUNSEL (LITIGATION)		
Mr C J Turnquist	CP-6 1024	746-1000
ASSISTANT GENERAL COUNSEL (ACQUISITION)		
Mr E L Saul	CP-5 480	692-7186
ASSISTANT GENERAL COUNSEL CIVILIAN PERSONNEL LAW)		
Ms M Harris	CP-5 480	692-7155

ASSISTANT SECRETARY OF THE NAVY
(FINANCIAL MANAGEMENT)

HON R H CONN	4E768	697-2325
(Comptroller)		
EXECUTIVE ASST & NAVAL AIDE		
CAPT A Combe	4E768	697-2325
SPECIAL ASST & MARINE AIDE		
LTCOL N M Murray III	4E768	695-7925
DIR DON INFORMATION RESOURCES MGMT		
RADM H S Quast	53731	695-0103

OFFICE OF THE COMPTROLLER OF THE NAVY

RADM G W DAVIS VI	4E768	695-3377
(Deputy Comptroller)		
EXECUTIVE ASST		
CDR G H Huban Jr	4E768	695-3377
SPECIAL ASST		
CDR R J Colucci	4E768	695-3377
COUNSEL		
Mr P M Hitch	4E765	697-5588
ADMIN/FISCAL DIV		
Ms V S Allen	2C317	694-3443
DIRECTOR OF BUDGET & REPORTS		
RADM S F Loftus	4C736	697-7105
ASST COMPTROLLER CM-3 (FIN MGMT SYSTEMS)		
RADM F L Filipiak	425	697-3195

ASSISTANT SECRETARY OF THE NAVY
(SHIPBUILDING AND LOGISTICS)
(CP-5)

HON E PYATT	266	692-2202
EXECUTIVE ASST & NAVAL AIDE		
CAPT G R Fister	266	692-3272
SPECIAL ASST FOR LEGAL AFFAIRS		
CDR A J Haiman	266	692-3233
SPECIAL ASST & MARINE AIDE		
LTCOL J E Parker	266	692-2204
PRIN DEP ASST SEC (S&L)		
Mr K Eastin	266	692-3227
ADMINISTRATIVE ASST		
CDR P Brawley	266	692-3232
DIR SMALL & DISADVANTAGE BUS UTILIZATION		
Mr D L Hathaway	120	692-7122

DIR INSTALLATIONS & FACILITIES		
Mr F Sterns	218	692-7076
DIR SHIPBUILDING		
Mr R Kiss	250	692-7083
DIR AVIATION & ORDNANCE PROGRAMS		
Mr F W Swofford	236	692-4983
DIR INTERNATIONAL PROGRAMS		
Mr F Beer	368	692-2247
DIR RESOURCE & POLICY EVALUATION		
Mr R O Thomas	244	692-2355
COMPETITION ADVOCATE GENERAL		
RADM R M Moore	310	692-3202
DIR SUPPLY SUPPORT		
CDR D A Hempson	236	692-1806
DIR CONTRACTS & BUSINESS MGT		
Mr G Cammack	578	692-3555
SPECIFICATION CONTROL ADVOCATE GENERAL		
Mr G Hoffman	334	692-3201
DIR RELIABILITY MAINT & QUAL ASSUR		
Mr W J Willoughby	348	692-9058

ASSISTANT SECRETARY OF THE NAVY
(RESEARCH, ENGINEERING & SYSTEMS)

MR R L RUMPF (Acting)	4E732	695-6315
EXECUTIVE ASST		
CAPT D R Eaton	4E732	695-6315
SPECIAL ASST & MARINE CORPS AIDE		
COL Terry Crews USMC	4E732	697-2674
PRIN DEP ASST SECY (RE&S)		
Mr R L Rumpf	4E741	697-4928
DEP ASST SECY (ACQ MGT, INTL PGM & CONG SUPP)		
Mr J E Gaines	5E813	697-1710
DEP ASST SECY (SURF WARF)		
Vacant	5E731	694-4794
DEP ASST SECY (C³IS)		
Dr E Ann Berman	4D745	695-0023
CHIEF OF NAVAL DEVELOPMENT		
RADM J R Wilson Jr—BT 1	907	696-4258
DEP ASST SECY (AIR)		
Mr W J Schaefer Jr	4E748	694-7793
DIR STRATEGIC PGMS		
Dr W H Smith	5E683	694-4480
DIR ASST SECY (SUB/ASW)		
Mr J Keane	5E779	694-0957

OFFICE OF THE CHIEF OF NAVAL RESEARCH
(Ballston Centre Tower Bldg. 1)

RADM J R WILSON JR	907	696-4767
Chief		
ASST CHIEF		
CAPT G T A Wagner	907	696-4261
COUNSEL		
Mr W G Rae	207	696-4271
INTELLIGENCE ADVISOR		
CAPT T M Murdock	1022	696-4275
SPECIAL ASST FOR MARCORPS MATTERS		
COL F J Kirchner USMC	507	696-4771
PUBLIC AFFAIRS OFFICER		
CAPT J H Barrett	921	696-4917
DIR FINANCIAL MGMT/COMPTROLLER		
Mr G T Maupin	924	696-4277
DIR OPERATIONS, RESOURCES & MGMT		
Dr J J Shepard	502	696-4264

OFFICE OF NAVAL RESEARCH

DIR OFFICE OF NAVAL RESEARCH		
Dr F E Saalfield	907	696-4517
DEP DIR ONR/PLANNING & ASSESSMENT		
Dr B B Robinson	907	696-4484
DIR CONTRACT RESEARCH DEPT		
Vacant	528	696-4101
DIR APPLIED RESEARCH & TECH		
CAPT R W Klementz	819	696-4224
DIR OCEAN SCIENCE & TECH		
Mr R Nagelhout	907	696-5084
DIR UNIVERSITY BUSINESS AFFAIRS		
Mr T J Dolan Jr	BT3 341	696-4601
DIR ACQUISITION		
Mr J T Bolos	724	696-4607

OFFICE OF NAVAL TECHNOLOGY

DIR OFFICE OF NAVAL TECHNOLOGY		
Dr P A Selwyn	907	696-5115
DEP DIR ONT/PLANNING & ASSESSMENT		
Mr R P Moore	907	696-5117
DIR ANTI-AIR WARFARE ANTI-SURFACE WARFARE SURFACE-AEROSPACE TECH		
Dr E Zimet	507	696-4771
DIR SUPPORT TECH		
Mr G R Spalding	503	696-4844
DIR ASW UNDERSEA TECH		
Dr A J Faulstich	503	696-5120
DIR LOW OBSERVABLES		
CAPT D W Cook	507	696-4251
DIR INDUSTRY RESEARCH & DEVELOPMENT		
Dr R M Culpepper	BT3 1212	696-4448

ASSISTANT SECRETARY OF THE NAVY
(MANPOWER AND RESERVE AFFAIRS)

HON C UNTERMEYER	4E788	697-2179
EXECUTIVE ASST & NAVAL AIDE		
CAPT L C Wilmot	4E788	695-4537
SPECIAL ASST & MARINE CORPS AIDE		
CAPT L C Wilmot	4E788	695-4537
(PERS & FAMILY MATTERS)		
LTCOL M A Rietsch USMC	4E778	697-0975
SPECIAL ASST MILITARY LAW		
CDR C W Tucker	5E823	697-6454
LTCOL J P Hertel USMC	5E825	695-0865
SPECIAL ASST NAVY PERSONNEL		
CDR W H Gay Jr	5E825	697-0891
SPECIAL ASST MARINE PERSONNEL		
MAJ F D Stephens USMC	5E825	697-0640
DIR HEALTH AFFAIRS		
CAPT R F Hopkins	5D820	694-0855
DEPUTY ASST SECY (PERS & FAMILY MATTERS)		
Mrs A M Stratton	4E777	694-3553
DEPUTY ASST SECY (RESERVE AFFAIRS)		
Mr L H McRoskey Jr	4E775	697-7506
DEPUTY ASST SECY (MANPOWER)		
Dr R E Elster	4E789	695-4350
DIR (CIVPERS POLICY/EQUAL EMPLOY OP)		
Mr A R DiTrapani	4E789	695-2248

(The principal organizational changes that have taken place since the locator was printed 1 October are reflected. However, not all changes could be made prior to publication.)

BOARD FOR CORRECTION OF NAVAL RECORDS
Mr W D PFEIFFER (Exec Dir)   AA 2432 694-1402
Mr R D Zsalman
(Dep Exec Dir)   AA 2432 694-1402
NAVDEPT BOARD OF DECORATIONS & MEDALS
RADM M E Chang
(Sen Mbr)   WNY 200 433-2000
COUNCIL OF PERSONNEL BOARDS
BGEN R E Porter   BCT 2 918 696-4355
CAPT J L Kuhn   BCT 2 918 696-4365

OFFICE OF CIVILIAN PERSONNEL

MANAGEMENT

(Ballston Centre Tower – 1)

MS D M MELETZKE   1104   696-4546
Director
EXEC ASST & NAVAL AIDE
CDR W Howell   1104   696-4546
SPEC ASST TO DIRECTOR
Ms J Guilford   1104   696-4546
COUNSEL
Ms J Gnerlich   BCT 3 110 696-4717
SPEC ASST FOR EXEC PERSONNEL
Mr M Duggins   1106   696-5165
DEPUTY EEO
Ms M McGoldrick   1212   696-4476
DIR CLASS COMP & INFO DEPT
Mr R C Burow   1205   696-4833
DIR SKILLS ACQ DEPT
Ms C C Clark   1217   696-4074
DIR WORK FORCE RELATIONS DEPT
Mr T J Haycock   1113   696-6597
DIR MGMT & ASSESSMENT DEPT
Mr M Marchesani   1103   696-6272

OFFICE OF PROGRAM APPRAISAL

RADM J D WILLIAMS   4D730   697-9396
Director
DEPUTY DIRECTOR
CAPT E R Losure   4D730   697-9396
EXECUTIVE ASST
CDR T W Wilt   4D730   697-9396
DEPUTY FOR USMC MATTERS
COL D B Herbert   4D735   695-7343

OFFICE OF LEGISLATIVE AFFAIRS

RADM T LYNCH   5C760   697-7146
(Chief of Legislative Affairs)
DEPUTY COMREL
CAPT C R Testa   5C760   697-7146
EXECUTIVE ASST
CDR J A Russack   5C760   697-7146
OPS AND LEGIS SUPPORT
LT D Gallo   5C765   697-4451
PUBLIC AFFAIRS
LCDR J CARMAN   5C768   695-0395
SENATE LIAISON DIV
CAPT J I Maslowski   OSOB182 475-1682
HOUSE LIAISON DIV
CAPT F P Moosally   RHOB B324 475-1672
NAVY PROGRAMS
CAPT J H Findley   5C840   697-3212
LEGISLATION DIV
CAPT R F Pitkin   5C800   695-5276

OFFICE OF THE JUDGE ADVOCATE GENERAL

(Hoffman Bldg 2)

RADM H D CAMPBELL (JAGC)   5D840   694-7420
(Judge Advocate General)
DEPUTY
RADM E D Slater (JAGC)   9N27   325-9823
EXECUTIVE ASST
LDCR S W Horton (JAGC)   5D840   694-7420
SPECIAL ASSISTANT
LCDR J Suszan (JAGC)   922   325-9820
ASSISTANT JAG FOR OPS & MGMT
RADM J E Gordon (JAGC)   3E966   697-5381
PRIN DEP ASST JAG FOR OPS & MGMT
CAPT H D Bohaboy (JAGC)   9N21   325-9850
ASSISTANT JAG FOR CIVIL LAW
CAPT J L Hoffman Jr (JAGC)   9N21   325-9850
ASSISTANT JAG FOR MILITARY LAW
COL C H Mitchell USMC   9N21   325-9850
SPECIAL ASST TO JAG (INSPECTOR GENERAL)
CAPT M J Gormley III (JAGC)   8N15   325-6117
SPECIAL ASSISTANT TO JAG (COMPTROLLER)
Mr D J Oppman   8N45   325-0786

OFFICE OF INFORMATION

RADM J B FINKELSTEIN   2E340   697-7391
(Chief of Information)
DEPUTY CHINFO
CAPT O J Resweber   2E340   697-6724
EXECUTIVE ASST
CDR J S Zakem   2E340   697-7391
ADMINISTRATIVE FLAG AIDE
Vacant   2E340   697-7391

SPECIAL ASST FOR MANPOWER
CDR M W Doubleday   2D327   695-5630
ASST CHINFO (RESOURCE MGMT)
CAPT R A Bennett   2E352   695-3161
ASST CHINFO (MEDIA OPERATIONS)
CDR K M Pease   2D341   697-2904
ASST CHINFO (FIELD OPS/RESERVE PROGS)
CAPT R A Bennett   2E352   695-3161
ASST CHINFO (INTERNAL RELATIONS)
CDR D W Thomas   CWB1046 696-6915
ASST CHINFO (PLANS & POLICY & COMREL)
CDR J F Britt   2E325   697-0250
ASST CHINFO (RADIO & TV)
Mr H R Hiner   EADS ST 692-6556

OFFICE OF THE NAVAL INSPECTOR GENERAL

(Washington Navy Yard Bldg 200)

RADM M E CHANG   112   433-2000
DEPUTY NAVAL INSPECTOR GENERAL
CAPT R W McFerren   113   433-2000
*DEPUTY NAVAL INSPECTOR GENERAL
FOR MARCORPS MTRS*
BGEN W H Rice   Arl Annex 2233   694-1533
INVESTIGATIONS OVERSIGHT DIV
CDR B Patton   210   433-4537
INSPECTIONS DIV
CAPT J D Curry   108   433-2144
SPECIAL INVESTIGATIONS DIV
CAPT B W Strong   211   433-4548
PLANS, ANALYSIS AND ACQUISITION DIV
CAPT J H McCorry   109   433-2268
HEALTH CARE REVIEW DIV
CAPT C A Brown   300   433-2688

OFFICE OF THE CHIEF NAVAL OPERATIONS

CHIEF OF NAVAL OPERATIONS

ADM C A H TROST   4E660   56007
CAPT T D Paulsen   4E672   55664
(Exec Asst)
CDR N R Ryan Jr   4E674   53567
(Admin Asst)
CDR L C Mason   4E658   70651
(Naval Aide)
LT D Murphy   4E658   70651
(Naval Aide)
MCPON W H Plackett   AA1056   44854

VICE CHIEF OF NAVAL OPERATIONS

ADM H HARDISTY   4E644   78347
CAPT W R McGowen   4E636   53193
(Exec Asst)
LT J Ackerson   4E644   78347
(Aide)
CAPT M E Clark   4E644   78347
(USMC Aide)
CDR J B Mayberry   4E636   53193
(Admin Asst)
YNCM G H Eaton   4E632   53193
(Staff Secy)
CWO M Hurlen   4E632   53193
(Staff Secy)

DEPUTY CHIEFS OF NAVAL OPERATIONS

DCNO (MANPOWER, PERSONNEL AND TRAINING)/CHNAVPERS

VADM L A EDNEY   AA2072   41101
CAPT C R Cramer   AA2075   42340
(Exec Asst)
ADCNO (MPT)
RADM J S Disher   AA2068   43051
TOTAL FORCE TRNG & EDUC DIV
CAPT G R Norrington   AAG831   45216
TOTAL FORCE PROG MPW DIV
RADM (Sel) R G Jones   AA2821   45097
MIL PERS POLICY DIV
RADM W P Houley   AA1825   45571
CIVPERS POL DIV/ADCNO (CIVPERS/EEO)
Mr G Steinhauer   SKYL-6   756-8480
HRM DIV
RADM R W West   AA1070   44259
TOTAL FORCE INFO RES & SYS MGMT DIV
Mr D Skeen   AA1052   41012

DCNO (SUBMARINE WARFARE)

VADM B DeMARS   4E524   50058
ADCNO (SUBMARINE WARFARE)
                                 4E524   50061
STRATEGIC SUBMARINE DIV
RADM H G Chiles Jr (Dir)   4D534   70886
ATTACK SUBMARINE DIV
CAPT T A Meinicke   4D482   71981
DEEP SUBMERGENCE SYS DIV
RADM D O Griffith (Dir)   4D462   72040
SUB MPWR & TRNG DIV
CAPT E D Hux   4E453   51515

DCNO (SURFACE WARFARE)

VADM J W NYQUIST   4E552   7746
ADCNO (SURFACE WARFARE)
RADM G A SHARP   4E552   5461
SURF WARF PROG & BUDGET DIV
CAPT M C Foote (Dir)   4D481   7451
SPEC WARFARE DIV
CAPT M Jukoski (Dir)   4D537   7780
SURFACE WARFARE DIV
RADM D B Robinson (Dir)   4D547   7146
SURFACE COMBAT SYS DIV
CAPT G N Gee (Dir)   4B545   5764
COMBAT LOG, AUX, AMPHIBS & MINE WARF DIV
CAPT T Triplett (Act Dir)   4A720   7689
SURF WARF MPWR & TRNG RQMTS DIV
Capt J D Pearson (Dir)   4C520   7679

DCNO (LOGISTICS)

VADM S R ARTHUR   4E606   521
ADCNO (LOGISTICS)
RADM E I Carmichael   4E606   551
ASST FOR CIVIL ENG
CAPT P W Drennon Hoff Bldg 2 10N59 325-05
ASST FOR PPBS
CAPT R Vanni   4C521   548
NAVAL RESERVE COORD (LOGISTICS)
CAPT R L Dooley   4C527   543
LOGISTIC PLANS & PROG DIV
RADM B C McCaffree Jr (Dir)   4B546   428
MATERIEL DIV
RADM C R Webb (Dir)   4B470   540
STRATEGIC SEALIFT DIV
Mr J D Kaskin (Dir)   BD766   540
ACQUISITION LOG & ASSESS DIV
Mr E D Cale (Dir)   4B546   4372
SHORE ACTIVITIES DIV
CAPT J C Doebler (Dir)   4B473   428
ENVIR PROT SAFETY & OCCUP HLTH DIV
CAPT G F Everhart   219   433-20

DCNO (AIR WARFARE)

VADM R L DUNN   4E394   5237
ADCNO (AIR WARFARE)
RADM E R Kohn Jr   4E394   5262
ADCNO (MARINE AVIATION)
LGEN K A Smith   AA   2335 4102
AVN PLANS & REQS DIV
RADM J M G Seely (Dir)   4E384   7144
NAVAL AVN MAINT PROG (NAMP) DIV
CAPT J L Young (Dir) (Actg)   4E360   7550
MARINE AVN PLANS & PROGS DIV
LGEN K A Smith   AA   2335 4102
CARRIER & AIR STATION PROG DIV
CAPT J H Springer (Dir) (Actg)   4E391   7935
AVN MPWR & TRNG DIV
CAPT P H Cressy (Dir)   4E424   5056

DCNO (PLANS, POLICY AND OPERATIONS)

VADM H C MUSTIN   4E592   5370
ADCNO (PLANS, POLICY AND OPS)
RADM J F Dorsey   4E592   5508
STRAT PLANS AND POLICY DIV
RADM R M Eytchison   4E566   5562
POLITICO-MILITARY POL & CUR PLAN DIV
RADM J F Smith (Dir)   4E572   5245
FLT OPS & READINESS DIV
CAPT M D Bruce (Dir)   4D600   76033
STRAT & THEATER NUCLEAR WARF DIV
RADM J M Kersh (Dir)   4E572   54402

DIRECTORS, MAJOR STAFF OFFICES

DIRECTOR, NAV PROGRAM PLANNING

VADM W D SMITH   4E620   50346
CAPT D C Blair   4E620   50347
(Exec Asst)
GENERAL PLANNING & PROGRAMMING DIV
RADM S R Arthur (Dir)   4D662   70517
PROGRAM RESOURCE APPRAISAL DIV
RADM D P March (Dir)   4A530   70831
FISCAL MANAGEMENT DIV
RADM S F Loftus (Dir)   4C736   77105

DIRECTOR, NAVAL MEDICINE/ SURGEON GENERAL

VADM J A ZIMBLE (MC)   4E436   70587
CAPT G S Harris (MSC)   4E436   70587
(Exec Asst)
DEPUTY DIRECTOR, NAVAL MEDICINE
RADM R P Caudill Jr (MC)   4E436   76201
DEPUTY DIRECTOR FOR MARINE CORPS MATTERS
RADM J K Summitt (MC)   AA 2229 44477
DEPUTY DIRECTOR FOR MEDICAL PRACTICE
RADM L Mantel (MC)   NMCNR 295-0006
DEPUTY DIRECTOR FOR NAVAL RESERVES
RADM J G Roberts (MC)   4C475   72311
RESOURCES DIV
RADM M C Clegg (DC)   4C461   51921
PLANS & POLICY DIV
CAPT W E Hirschfeld (DC)   4C457   71460
HEALTH CARE OPERATIONS DIV

RADM D F Hagen (MC)   PA#6 653-1727
DUCATION & TRAINING DIV
CAPT P M Curran (MSC)   PA#6 653-1752

DIRECTOR, SPACE, COMMAND AND CONTROL

ADM L LAYMAN	4C679	53239
RADM B D Cargill	4C679	53668
(Dep Dir)		
2 PLANNING AND PROGRAMMING DIV		
RADM G L Chesbrough (Dir)	5B730	76441
AVAL COMMUNICATIONS DIV		
RADM R L Rich Jr (Dir)	5A718	57284
2 SYS DIV		
RADM R G Guilbault (Dir)	5E569	56667
AVY SPACE SYS DIV		
RADM D V Becker (Dir)	4C668	70761
IFO SYS DIV		
RADM H S Quast (Dir)	5B731	50103

DIRECTOR, NAVAL WARFARE

ADM J R HOGG	4E536	71098
CAPT F L Bowman	4E536	71098
(Exec Asst)		
RADM C R McGrail Jr	4E536	73408
(Dep Dir)		
ORCE LEVEL PLANS & WARF APPRAISAL DIV		
RADM D Oliver (Dir)	4E482	53777
NTI SUBMARINE WARFARE DIV		
RADM R F Pittenger	5D589	51767
ACTICAL READINESS DIV		
RADM L W Smith Jr (Dir)	5D566	75857
TRIKE AND AMPHIBIOUS WARFARE DIV		
RADM F L Lewis (Dir)	5E613	71466
NTI AIR WARFARE DIV		
CAPT E E Kilinger (Dir)	2C340	47274
LECTRONIC WARFARE DIV		
RADM G Jackson (Dir)	4C652	59590

DIRECTOR, RESEARCH, DEVELOPMENT AND ACQUISITION

ADM P F McCARTHY	5C686	75533
RADM C H Brickell	5C686	74532
(Dep Dir)		
ES & DEV PROGRAMMING & BUDGETING DIV		
Mr W G MacLean (Dir)	5C724	50611
NDERSEA & STRATEGIC WARFARE & NUCLEAR ENERGY DEVELOPMENT DIV		
RADM W C Miller (Dir)	5C675	52905
ACT AIR SURF & ELECTRONIC WARF DEV DIV		
RADM R H Shumaker (Dir)	5C711	52865
EST AND EVAL DIV		
CDR R T Fuller (Dir)	5C736	74402
ECH ASSESSMENT DIV		
Dr F Shoup (Dir)	5D760	79726

CNO/VCNO STAFF ASSISTANTS

CHIEF OF INFORMATION

RADM J B FINKELSTEIN	2E340	77391
NAVY INTERNAL RELATIONS ACTIVITY		
CDR D W Thomas	CMWLTH BLDG	66876
NAVY BROADCASTING SERVICE		
Mr H R Hiner	Bldg 168 ANA	433-6550

DIRECTOR, NAVAL NUCLEAR PROPULSION PROGRAM

(National Center 2)

ADM K R McKEE		23887

ASSISTANT FOR SAFETY MATTERS

RADM D T SCHWAAB	4A452	57500

ASSISTANT FOR LEGAL SERVICES

RADM H D CAMPBELL (JAGC)	5D840	47420

ASSISTANT FOR NAVAL INVESTIGATIVE MATTERS AND SECURITY

(Suitland Federal Center)

RADM J E GORDON	310	763-3750

DIRECTOR, RELIABILITY, MAINTAINABILITY & QUALITY ASSURANCE

CP-5

MR W J WILLOUGHBY JR	348	29058

ASSISTANT VICE CHIEF OF NAVAL OPERATIONS

RADM J R DALRYMPLE	4E623	54337
CAPT P L Gruendl	4E623	54336
(Exec Asst)		
ASST FOR CIVPERS AND SES POLICY		
Ms J Eul	4B531	58784
ASST FOR EEO		
Ms S A Lee	2B328	78203
ASST FOR FIELD SUPPORT		
Mr R B Keller	Bldg 150 ANA	433-3037
DIR OF NAVAL HISTORY		
Dr R Spector	Bldg 57 WNY	433-2210
ASST FOR LEGAL LEGIS MATTERS		
CDR D J Guter	4E629	53480
OPNAV CAREER COUNSELOR		
NCC S J Facsko	4C549	57787
OPNAV COMMAND MASTER CHIEF		
RMCM R J Sunday	4C549	57787
NAVAL IMAGING MGMT DIV		
CAPT B A Gastrock (Dir)	Bldg 168 ANA	433-2102
ORG & OPNAV RESOURCE MGMT DIV		
CAPT C A Preston (Dir)	4D435	70282
OPNAV SERVICES & SECURITY DIV		
Mr H J Loeper III (Dir)	5E595	54253
INTERNAL CONT SYS MGT DIV		
Mr N J Cook (Dir)	Bldg 159 WNY	433-5950

CHIEF OF CHAPLAINS/ DIRECTOR OF RELIGIOUS MINISTRIES

RADM J R MCNAMARA	AAG842	44043
CAPT R H Dressler Jr	AAG840	44326
(Exec Asst)		
RADM A B Koeneman	AAG841	44326
(Dep Chief of Chaplains)		

DIRECTOR OF NAVAL RESERVE

RADM F N SMITH	4E466	55353
CAPT J D Olson	4E466	44605
(Dep Dir)		
AIR PROG MGMT DIV		
Vacant (Dir)	4E478	55517
SURF PROG MGMT DIV		
CAPT J B Doolittle (Dir)	4E427	74551
FINANCIAL MGMT DIV		
CAPT A M Shriver (Dir)	4E458	52859
PLANNING & PROG DIV		
CAPT B E Bennett (Dir)	4B489	58970
PLANS & READINESS DIV		
Vacant (Dir)	4B536	75201
MPWR, PERS & TRAINING POL DIV		
CAPT H E Glad (Dir)	4E433	70075

OCEANOGRAPHER OF THE NAVY

(Naval Observatory, Bldg 1)

RADM J R SEESHOLTZ		653-1299
CAPT A L Cheaure		653-1491
(Dep)		
TECHNICAL DIRECTOR		
Mr R Winokur		653-1536

NAVAL INSPECTOR GENERAL

(Washington Navy Yard)

RADM M E CHANG	200	433-2000

DIRECTOR OF NAVAL INTELLIGENCE

RADM W O STUDEMAN	5C564	53944
CAPT M W Cramer	5C564	50124
(Exec Asst)		
DEPUTY DIRECTOR		
RADM J S McFarland	5C564	52988
DEPUTY DIRECTOR		
Mr R L Haver	5C600	44408
SPECIAL ASSISTANT		
CAPT I C Cole	5C564	52988
ADMINISTRATION		
LCDR D J Maresh	5C564	50124
OPERATIONAL SUPPORT		
CAPT C L Moore	5D660	74199
CURRENT INTELLIGENCE		
CDR D L Herrington	4D642	72196
LEGAL AFFAIRS		
LCDR P A Genzler	5C558	70045
INTERAGENCY COORDINATION		
CAPT D G Wilbourne	5D660	54819
FOREIGN LIAISON		
CAPT M W Bronson	5C565	55333
PLANS AND POLICY		
CAPT J C Clark	5B688	40277
RESOURCES		
CAPT T P Lapierre	5B681	52907
SPECIAL PROGRAMS		
Mr E J Gallaher	5D600	72070
RESERVE AFFAIRS		
CAPT D R Zickafoose	5B680	56255
FOREIGN COUNTERINTEL		
RADM C L Flynn Jr	NIC 1	763-3750
ANALYSIS		
CAPT J M Eglin	5B674	54468

SYSTEMS COMMANDS

NAVAL AIR SYSTEMS COMMAND HEADQUARTERS

(Jefferson Plaza Bldg 1 & 2)

VADM J B WILKINSON	JP-1	1200	22260
(Commander NAVAIR)			
CDR J A Cook	JP-1	1200	22260
(Exec Asst)			
VICE COMMANDER			
RADM W J Finneran	JP-1	1200	22270
DEPUTY COMMANDER			
Mr R V Johnson	JP-1	1200	24156
EEO OFFICE			
Mr W L Hawk	JP-1	1176	25538
SAFETY OFFICER			
CDR C H Yates	JP-2	942	21234
INSPECTOR GENERAL			
CAPT D L Osburn	JP-2	124	28582
RESEARCH & TECH DIRECTORATE			
CAPT H G Chalkey	JP-1	412	27439
LEGIS & PUBLIC AFF OFFICE			
Mrs D C Prince	JP-1	1244	746-3785
READINESS RELIAB & MAINT OFF			
CAPT E E Chelton	JP-2	230	28521
CORP MGMT DIRECTORATE			
Mr M G Akin	JP-1	1276	746-3713
DEP COM FOR PROGRAMS SUPPORT			
RADM R D Frúchtenicht	JP-1	1186	22280
DEPUTY ACQUISITION EXEC			
Mr O L Talbot	JP-1	1186	22283
PDA FOR JOINT CRUISE MISSILE			
RADM L E Blose	CG-4	632	27409
PDA FOR TACTICAL AIRCRAFT PROG			
RADM G H Strohsahl	JP-1	1186	22282
PDA FOR WEAPONS PROGRAMS			
Mr W L Wagner	JP-1	1186	27988
PDA FOR EW & MISSIONS SUPPORT PROG			
Mr J Goldfarb	JP-1	1186	22283
PDA FOR ASW & ASSAULT PROGRAMS			
RADM R L Leuschner	JP-1	1186	27989
ASST COM FOR CONTRACTS			
CAPT W Morris	JP-1	116	20916
ASST COM FOR FLEET SUPPORT & FA MGT			
RADM J H Kirkpatrick	JP-2	460	22690
ASST COM FOR SYS & ENGR			
VADM J R Wilson Jr	JP-2	1240	23827
COMPTROLLER			
RADM R G Milligan	JP-1	1114	2392

NAVAL SEA SYSTEMS COMMAND HEADQUARTERS

(National Center Bldgs 2 & 3 Crystal Park Bldg 1)
(Crystal Plaza Bldg 5 Jefferson Plaza Bldg 1)

VADM W H ROWDEN	NC-3	12E10	23381
(Commander NAVSEASYSCOM)			
CAPT D S Bill III	NC-3	12E10	23327
(Exec Asst)			
LCDR T G Briggs	NC-3	12E10	23328
(Flag Admin Off)			
LCDR J Wilson	NC-3	12E10	23328
(Flag Aide)			
VICE COMMANDER			
RADM H L Young	NC-3	12E10	23681
DEPUTY COMMANDER			
Mr J N Shrader	NC-3	12E10	26163
CHIEF ENGINEER			
RADM H L Young	NC-3	4E60	22746
DEP COM COMPTROLLER			
CAPT J E Hancock	NC-3	12E24	23438
DEP COM CONTRACTS			
RADM(Sel) W H Hauenstein	NC-3	5E58	27977
DEP COM FOR SHIP DESIGN & ENG			
RADM M Mackinnon III	NC-3	10E08	22438
DEP COM FOR WPNS & COMBAT SYS			
RADM R H Ailes	NC-2	9W62	20913
ASST DEP COM FOR AAW & SURFACE WARF			
RADM G R Meinig Jr	NC-2	7S06	27190
ASST DEP COM FOR COMBAT SYS ENGR			
Mr O F Braxton (Actg)	NC-2	9S06	22591
ASST DEP COM FOR ASW & UNDERSEA WARF			
RADM T W Evans	NC-2	12N06	28826
ASST DEP COM FOR SUB COMBAT SYSTEMS			
CAPT D Volgenau	NC-3	6E08	746-0006
ASST DEP COM FOR ELECTRICAL WARFARE			
Mr P Prikals (Actg)	JP-1	586	22525
DEP COM FOR INDUSTRIAL & FACILITY MGMT			
RADM R B Horne	CP-5	1174	28551
DEP COM FOR NUCLEAR PROP			
ADM K R McKee	NC-2	3N06	23887
DEP COM FOR ACQ, PLANNING & APPRAISAL			
Mr W A Tarbell	CPK-1	1102	746-3000
DEP COM FOR SURFACE COMBATANTS			
RADM P M Hekman Jr	NC-3	9S08	22072
DEP COM FOR SUBMARINES			
RADM W J Cantrell	NC-3	7S18	21564
DEP COM FOR AMPHIB, AUX, MINE & SEALIFT SHIPS			
CAPT J F King	NC-3	8E34	26918
PROG MANAGER AEGIS SHIPBUILDING PROG			
RADM J B Greene	NC-2	10N18	23795
PROG MANAGER SSN-21 ACQUISITION PROG			
RADM G H Curtis	NC-3	7N24	27200

SPACE AND NAVAL WARFARE SYSTEMS COMMAND HEADQUARTERS

(National Center Bldg 1)

VADM G CLARK JR   9E44   23006
  (Commander SPAWARSYSCOM)
  CAPT D W Cook   9E44   23006
  (Exec Asst)
VICE COMMANDER
  RADM J C Weaver   9E44   28960
DEP COM FOR FIN CONTRACTS & MGMT
  Mr R E Doak   9E44   23008
COUNSEL
  Mr H J Nathan   9W80   28458
INSPECTOR GENERAL
  CAPT D W Cook   9W44   28958
ASST COM FOR ACQ & LOGS PLANNING
  RADM R J Grich   5E08   28480
ASST COM FOR SPACE TECH
  RADM T C Betterton   NRL-33   767-2040
DIR OF NAVY LABS
  Vacant   CP-5   866   22766
COMPTROLLER
  CAPT W M Stanley   9N20   23260
ASST COM FOR CONTRACT
  CAPT J A Schroeder   7E08   27777
DIR OF WARF SYS ARCH & ENG
     10N08   29223
DIR OF SPACE & SENSOR SYS PROG
  RADM T K Mattingly II   3N20   22182
DIR OF INFORMATION TRANS SYS PROG
  CAPT C A Rose Jr   6S08   28873
INFO MGMT SYS PROG
  CAPT S V Holmes   8N20   28964
MARCORPS SYS PROG
  COL B J Speights   5S20   28880
ASW SYS PROG
  RADM C E Dorman   5D616   74737

NAVAL SUPPLY SYSTEMS COMMAND HEADQUARTERS

(Crystal Mall Bldg 3)

RADM E K WALKER JR (SC)   622   54009
  (Commander NAVSUPSYSCOM)
  CDR P J Brown (SC)   622   54922
  (Exec Asst)
VICE COMMANDER
  RADM R B Abele (SC)   622   54493
DEPCOM HUMAN RESOURCES DIV
  Mr N J Suszynski   504   56984
RESALE & SERV SUPP PROG
  CDR W T Kaloupek   606   44034
SMALL/DISADVANTAGED BUSINESS UTIL
  Mr R F Quinn   606   55952
CIVILIAN PERSONNEL PROG OFF
  Mr B DaRosa   634   74795
MANAGEMENT INFORMATION CENTER
  Ms D Brown   624   55351
PUBLIC AFFAIRS OFFICE
  Ms N Dimond   638   73795
INSPECTOR GENERAL NAVSUPSYSCOM
  CAPT G W Willis (SC)   520   55391
OFFICE OF COUNSEL
  Mr C J McManus   625   55519
FLEET HOSPITAL PROGRAM OFFICE
  CAPT D A Ringberg (MC)   221   52136
NAVY SPARES COMPETITION & LOGS TECH PROG MGT OFF
  Mr J J Genovese   CSQ 5 Rm 511   22269
SUPPLY CORPS PERSONNEL
  CAPT F S Garner (SC)   2501AA   48765
DEPCOM FIN MGT COMPTROLLER
  CAPT E M Straw (SC)   730   55545
DEPCOM CONTRACTING MGMT
  CAPT J C Cheney (SC)   619   54377
DEPCOM FL SUPP CORP PLANS & LOGS
  CAPT A J Nissalke (SC)   608   73922
ASSTCOM INVENTORY & SYS INTEGRITY
  RADM J B Whittaker (SC)   718   53824
DEPCOM INVENTORY & INFO SYS DEV
  CAPT K E Kittock (SC)   718   56976
DEPCOM TRANSPORTATION
  CAPT C J Nichols (SC)   CM 2 Rm 112   52954
DEPCOM PHYSICAL DISTRIBUTION
  CAPT W S Draper (SC)   714   53181
DEPCOM SECURITY ASSISTANCE
  CAPT L S Frieberg (SC)   522   50753
DEPCOM ADMIN MGMT
  Mr J Browne   700   56087
DEPCOM NAVY PUBS & PRINTING PROG
  Mr J L Cherny   Bldg 157-3 WNY   433-2261
DEPCOM NAVY RESALE & SERV SUPP PROG
  RADM R A Squibb (SC)   NYC AV8-456-2444/5
DEPCOM NAVY FOOD SERV SYS OFF
  CAPT J F Anderson (SC)   166-2 WNY   433-3701
DEPCOM NAVY FUEL MGMT SYSTEM
  CAPT D W Falconer (SC)   CAMSTA   274-7467

NAVAL FACILITIES ENGINEERING COMMAND HEADQUARTERS

(Hoffman Bldg 2)

RADM B F MONTOYA (CEC)   11N37   325-0400
  (Commander NAVFACENGCOM)
  CDR J P Collins (CEC)   11N37   325-0403
  (Exec Asst)
VICE COMMANDER
  RADM F G Kelley (CEC)   11N37   325-0402
DEP COM FOR FAC ACQ
  CAPT E R Wilson   11S59   325-9484

DEP COM FOR FAC MGMT
  CAPT C M Maskell   11N57   325-8541
DEP COM FOR PUB WORKS CNTRS
  CAPT G Weigle   12N37   325-8548
MILITARY JUDGE STAFF ADVOCATE
  CAPT J M Dougherty   10N59   325-0056
DEP COM FOR MPWR & ORG
  CAPT W C Hilderbrand   12S25   325-8543
COUNSEL
  Mr M K McElhaney   11N69   325-9067
INSPECTOR GENERAL
  CAPT W M Bell   12N33   325-8548
SMALL BUSINESS ECONOMIC UTILIZATION & CONTRACTOR LIAISON OFF
  Ms R Dubuisson   11N59   325-8549
DIRECTOR OF PROG & COMPT
  CAPT L A Fermo (CEC)   11N19   325-8577
DEP COM FOR CONTRACTS
  Mr P P Buonaccorsi   11S67   325-9121
ASST COM FOR R&D
  CAPT W K Goodermote   12N45   325-9014
ASST COM FOR ENG & DESIGN
  Mr H H Zimmerman   12S55   325-0032
ASST COM FOR CONSTRUCTION
  CAPT R P Dillman   11S59   325-9484
DEP COM FOR MIL READINESS (SEABEES)
  CAPT D J Nash   12S33   325-8555
ASST COM FOR HOUSING
  CAPT A Moyle   10N41   325-9246
ASST COM FOR FAC & TRANSP
  Mr A S Bradford   10N07   325-0028
ASST COM FOR ENERGY & ENVIRONMENT
  CDR R Rice (CEC)   10S23   325-0295
ASST COM FOR PUBLIC WORKS CTRS
  CAPT G B Estes   10S03   325-8194
ASST COM FOR FAC PLAN & REAL ESTATE
  CAPT J M Dougherty (CEC)   10N59   325-0556
ASST COM FOR MILCON PROGRAMMING
  CAPT B F Folsom   10S55   325-8600

NAVY COMMANDS AND ACTIVITIES

MILITARY SEALIFT COMMAND HEADQUARTERS

(Bldg 210 WNY)

VADM W T PIOTTI JR   404   433-0001
  (Commander MSC)
VICE COMMANDER
  Mr W Sansone   404   433-0007
DEPUTY COMMANDER
  CAPT F M Williamson (Actg)   405   433-0005
LEGISLATIVE & PUBLIC AFF OFF
     243   433-0330
COMMAND DEPUTY EEO OFF
  Vacant   Wolfe Bldg 246   427-5559
FLAG SECRETARY
  CDR R H Enderly   419   433-0004
INSPECTOR GENERAL
  CAPT F M Williamson   267   427-5475
  Wolfe Bldg
PERSONNEL, MPWR, & MGMT OFF
  Mrs M L Lewis   Bldg 219   324   433-0445
READINESS & PRO INTRODUCTION OFF
  CAPT L Magner   300   433-0497
OPERATIONS OFF
  CAPT J C Toland   339   433-0075
ENGINEERING OFF
  Mr T W Allen   131   433-0170
FORCE MEDICAL OFF
  CAPT J L Hauser (MC) Wolfe Bldg 206   427-5612
SUPPLY OFF
  CAPT A K Paszly   120   433-0116
COMPTROLLER
  Mr. W D Savitsky   Wolfe Bldg   160   427-5615
STRATEGIC MOBILITY OFF
  COL J A Weiss USA   232   433-0296
COUNSEL
  Mr R S Haynes   425   433-0140
COMMAND INFO SYS OFF
  Mr B Genzlinger   244   433-0320
CONTRACTING OFF
  CAPT H R Boalick   456   433-0315

NAVAL INTELLIGENCE COMMAND HEADQUARTERS

RADM D N HAGEN   S200   763-3552
  (Commander NAVINTCOM)
DEPUTY COMNAVINTCOM
  CAPT W H Cracknell   S200   763-3553
DEP DIR
  Mr D P Harman   S210   763-3555
INSPECTOR GENERAL
  Mr J Runyon   S207   763-3557
DEPUTY EEO OFFICER
  Mr F L Antoine   S212   763-3540
COMMAND MASTER CHIEF
  ISCM L E Fish   S208   763-3551
PJO/JNIDS
  CAPT J E Ripple   S241   763-3462
ASST FOR PROCESSING SYS

  CAPT F W Levin   S235   763-356
SPEC ASST FOR R&D
  Mr P Lowell   5D675   695-92
ACNIC MP&T
  CAPT T D Buckley   S218   763-35
ATTACHE AFFAIRS
  CDR C W Cushman Jr   S232   763-344
ACNIC FIN MGMT/COMPT
  Ms B P Swift   S164   763-341
ACNIC OPERATIONS CTF-168
  CAPT R A Saenz   S246   763-359
ACNIC SECURITY
  CAPT M Pelensky   S282   763-358
ACNIC DATA PRODUCTION
  CAPT B J Kennelly   S214   763-361

NAVAL MILITARY PERSONNEL COMMAND

(Arlington Annex)

RADM J DISHER   2068   4224
  (Commander NMPC)
  LCDR L W Biegler   2068   4147
  (Admin Asst)
CHIEF OF STAFF/EXEC ASST
  CAPT G Rheinstrom   2068   4825
DIR CLASSIFICATION SYSTEM
  CAPT E L Naro   ANA   433-548
DIR ADMIN OFFICE
  CAPT T J Williams   2705   4110
RESOURCE MGMT OFFICE
  Mr T C Fiocchi   2058   4352
DIR MIL CORRES & CONG LIAISON OFF
  CAPT W P Cooper   2625   4137
NAVY UNIFORM MATTERS OFFICE
  CDR D O Richey   1055   4507
PUBLIC AFFAIRS OFFICE
  CAPT G I Peterson   1074   4200
OFFICE OF LEGAL COUNSEL
  CAPT R E Coyle   2708   4515
DIR NAVY PASSENGER TANS OFFICE
  Mr J H Brown   2711   4362
DIR CAREER PROGRESSION DEPT
  CAPT F J Ferry   4637   4111
DIR MIL PERS RECORD DATA MGMT DEPT
  CAPT M Yeoman   4074   4276
DIR DISTRIBUTION DEPT
  RADM S K Chadwick   3072   4345
DIR PRIDE PROFESSIONALISM & PERSONAL EXCEL DEPT
  RADM R W West   1070   4425
DIR MPN FINANCIAL
  Mr F Robenhymer   1733   4566
DIR MIL PERS PERFORMANCE & SEC DEPT
  CAPT T W Hutt Jr
DIR TOTAL FORCE AUTOMATED SYS DEPT
  Mr D Skeen   1050   41012

NAVAL SECURITY GROUP COMMAND HEADQUARTERS

(3801 Nebraska Ave NW Wash DC)

RADM J S MCFARLAND   17137   282-0444
  (Commander NAVSECGRU)
DEPUTY COMNAVSECGRU
  CAPT S W Jacobs   17137   282-0444
FORCE MASTER CHIEF
  CTOCM R R Adams   17133   282-0264
INSPECTOR GENERAL
  CAPT F R Demech   17133   282-0306
ASST COMMANDER (FT MEADE)
  CAPT G E Huke   8A164   688-6446
ASST FOR ADMIN
  LTJG T W Chapman   17118   282-0272
ASST FOR PPB & RM/COMPTROLLER
  CAPT C J Malloy   17201   282-0491
ASST FOR MARCORPS MATTERS
  LTCOL P Brown   1118   282-0251
ASST FOR PERS & TRAINING
  CAPT D L Currie   1112   282-0459
ASST FOR TELECOM/ADP SYS
  CAPT J A Leonard   17045   282-0758
ASST FOR LOGISTICS & MATERIEL
  CAPT J H Gates   2393   282-0851
ASST FOR SPECIAL OPERATIONS
  CAPT F T Stevens   1220   282-0236
ASST FOR TECH DEVELOPMENT
  CAPT J W Moffat   20209   282-0630
ASST FOR RESERVE PLANS & READINESS
  RADM W J Miles   17123   282-0201

NAVAL SECURITY AND INVESTIGATIVE COMMAND

(Suitland Federal Ctr)

RADM J E GORDON   763-3750
  (Commander)
DEPUTY COMMANDER
  COL G Connell USMC   763-3754
DIR NIS
  Mr J B McKee   763-3751
CHIEF OF STAFF
  CAPT J E Ulmer   763-3751
INSPECTOR GENERAL
  Mr P Reilly   763-3755

JTY EEO OFFICER
s I Robison		763-3454

NFO SECURITY
R Allen	Wolfe Bldg	427-5900

FOR COUNTERINTELLIGENCE
W A Worochock		763-3758

FOR CRIMINAL INVEST
R Powers		763-3759

FOR LAW ENFORCE/PHY SEC
J O'Hara		763-3390

T DIR CAREER SERV
W K Sumner		763-3768

T DIR TECH SERV
G Aldridge		763-3775

T DIR INFO SYS
J T Oney		763-3777

T DIR ADMIN
R E Childs		763-3783

CAF
G Jackson	Wolfe Bldg	427-6026

T DIR TRAINING
D W Dykes		763-3770

TASK FORCE
L McCullah	Half St	475-1057

NAVAL TELECOMMUNICATIONS
COMMAND HEADQUARTERS
(4401 Mass Ave NW Washington DC)

M A F Campbell	19119	282-0550

ommander NAVTELCOM)
G AIDE

S A MacDonald	19127	282-0691

UTY COMNAVTELCOM
APT W May	19119	282-0356

F CHIEF OF STAFF MPWR. PERS. TRAINING,
ADMIN AND RESERVE AFFAIRS
APT R H Pewett	19124B	282-0262

F CHIEF OF STAFF OPERATIONS AND
READINESS
R W Hill	19235A	282-0821

F CHIEF OF STAFF ENGINEERING AND
FACILITIES
APT C Street	19351	282-2500

F CHIEF OF STAFF PLANS, INTEG AND MGMT
APT J F Gamboa	19317D	282-0719

F CHIEF OF STAFF SUPPLY BUDGET AND PROG
CDR J M Dykes	19413	282-0545

TELCOM INSPECTOR GENERAL
APT R W Michaux	19231A	282-0495

UTY EEO OFFICER
W B Gentry	19110	282-0420

CE MASTER CHIEF
MCM T E Hayden	19117A	282-0466

CIAL ASSISTANT FOR FREQUENCY MGMT
H W Holsopple	19435	282-0581

Y COML COMM OFF
R Connatser	19105	282-0577

ECTOR OFC OF NAVY TELCOM CONTRACTING
D V White	19101	282-2544

(Cheltenham, MD)

ECTOR NAVAL TELCOM SYSTEM INTEGRATION
ENTER
R J Lynch	(Bldg 1)	238-2456

ECTOR NAVAL TELCOM AUTOMATION SYS CTR
W C Bryson	(Bldg 31)	238-2170

NAVAL CIVILIAN PERSONNEL CENTER
(6 Skyline Place)

G P Steinhauer	701	756-8447

irector)
DIR
R M Felton	701	756-8450

T PLANS PROG & ADMIN
s J M Wenger	701	756-8450

DS PROJECT MANAGER
F T Catenaccio	515	756-8477

NAVAL DATA AUTOMATION
COMMAND HEADQUARTERS
(Bldg 166 Washington Navy Yard)

K B HANCOCK		433-4067

(Commander NAVDAC)
DEPUTY COMMANDER
CAPT E J Bendar		433-4067

CHNICAL DIRECTOR
Mr L Meador		433-4911

SPECTOR GENERAL
CDR B Sharpe		433-4309

UNSEL
Mr D Andross		433-4025

MMAND DEPUTY EEOO
Ms H A Wilson		433-2041

MPTROLLER
Mr C Bolter		433-4299

R SYS EVAL & POL
Mr W O'Brien		433-2872

R COMMAND SUPPORT
Mr J Markland		433-4967

R DATA COMMUNICATIONS
CAPT S R Cablk		433-4996

DIR COMPUTER PROG DEVELOP
CAPT K VanLue		433-2241

DIR COMPUTER SYS OPS
Mr R W White		433-4917

DIR NAVY DIRECTIVES, POSTAL &
RECORDS MGMT
CDR R Glass		433-2434

DIR ADVANCE TECH, PLAN & MKTING
Mr S Greenblatt		433-3528

BOARD OF INSPECTION & SURVEY
(Potomac Annex)

RADM J D BULKELEY	6002	653-1133

(President)
DEPUTY
CAPT D J Klinkhamer	6003	653-1136

NAVAL LEGAL SERVICE COMMAND

RADM H D CAMPBELL (JAGC)	5D840	694-7420

(Commander NAVLEGSVCCOM)
VICE COMMANDER
RADM E D Stumbaugh (JAGC)	9N27	325-9823

ASSISTANT COMMANDER (OPS & MGMT)
CAPT H D Bohaboy (JAGC)	9N21	325-9850

DEP ASST TO COMMANDER (INSPECTIONS)
CAPT M J Gormley III (JAGC)	8N15	325-6117

DEP ASST TO COMMANDER (COMPTROLLER)
Mr D J Oppman	8N45	325-0786

NAVAL MEDICAL COMMAND
(Potomac Annex)

RADM J S CASSELS (MC)		653-1144

(Commander NAVMEDCOM)
CAPT L L Biesiadny (MSC)		653-1146

(Exec Asst)
VICE COMMANDER
RADM D E Shuler (MSC)		653-1145

DEP COM FOR FIN MGMT
Mr J Radcliffe		653-1074

DEP COM FOR FLT READINESS & SUPP
CAPT R A Nelson (MC)		653-1241

DEP COM FOR HEALTH CARE OPS
RADM M Nieubowicz (NC)		653-1176

DEP COM FOR READINESS & LOGS
RADM H Sazima (DC)		653-1202

DEP COM FOR PERSONNEL MGMT
CAPT R H Bodenbender (MC) (Actg)		653-1168

DEP COM FOR DENTAL CARE
RADM R W Koch		653-1170

NAVAL SPACE COMMAND
(DAHLGREN)

RADM R C MACKE	101	663-7841

(Commander NAVSPACECOM)
DEPUTY COMMANDER
COL P D Williams (USMC)		663-7841

TECHNICAL DIRECTOR
Dr W E Howard III	104	663-7841

STRATEGIC SYSTEMS PROGRAM
COMMAND HEADQUARTERS
(Crystal Mall Bldg 3)

RADM K C MALLEY	1142	52064

(Director)
DEPUTY DIR
CAPT W Taylor	1142	52158

DIR PLANS & PROG
Mr G Keightley	1140	53013

DIR TECHNICAL DIV
CAPT J Mitchell	1136	52964

HEADQUARTERS
US MARINE CORPS

COMMANDANT OF THE MARINE CORPS

GEN A M GRAY	2004	42500
COL H C Barnum Jr	2001	42500
(Military Secretary)		
SGTMAJ D W Sommers	2038	42475
(SGTMAJ of the Marine Corps)		

ASSISTANT COMMANDANT OF THE MARINE CORPS

GEN T R MORGAN	2003	41201
LTCOL R W Hodory	2102	41201
(Executive Assistant)		

CHIEF OF STAFF

LTGEN L H BUEHL, III	2010	42541
LTCOL J M Strickland	2010	42828
(Secretary of the General Staff)		

SPECIAL PROJECTS DIRECTORATE

COL H C BARNUM JR	2108	41515
(Dir)		

(Arlington Annex)
SEPARATE OFFICES

LEGISLATIVE ASSISTANT
BGEN H W JENKINS	3026	41686

COUNSEL FOR THE COMMANDANT
Mr P M MURPHY	2119	42150

THE MEDICAL OFFICER
RADM J S SUMMITT	2229	44477

THE DENTAL OFFICER
CAPT R E WILLIAMS	2227	44477

THE CHAPLAIN
CAPT W A HISKETT (CHC) USN	1022	44491

MARINE CORPS UNIFORM BOARD
CAPT J A SCARBOROUGH	201 HH	42086

DEPARTMENTS AND DIVISIONS

PLANS, POLICIES AND OPERATIONS DEPARTMENT
LTGEN J PHILLIPS	2018	42503
DC/S for Plans Pol & Ops		
BGEN M K Sheridan	2020	42833
Dir Plans Div		
MGEN C E Mundy	2208	43554
Dir Ops Div		

AVIATION DEPARTMENT
LTGEN K A SMITH	2335	41022
(DC/S for Aviation)		
BGEN L G POOL	2333	41021
(Dir PPR)		

MANPOWER DEPARTMENT
LTGEN J I HUDSON	4020	48003
(DC/S for Manpower)		
BGEN W M KEYS	4000	42533
(Dir Pers Mgmt Div)		
BGEN J R Joy	4102	42508
(Dir Pers Procurement Div)		
BGEN G M Reals	4026	42518
(Dir Manpower Plans & Pol Div)		
COL P Angle	102 HH	45105
(Dir Mor Spt Div)		
COL D J Cassady	4304	42890
(Dir Hum Res Div)		

INSTALLATION & LOGISTICS DEPARTMENT
LGEN J J WENT	562 CWB	42755
(DC/S for Install & Log)		
BGEN R J Winglass	376 CWB	41969
(Dir Materiel Div)		
BGEN M P Downs	744 CWB	42588
(Dir Facilities & Serv Div)		
Mr P E Zanfagna Jr	660 CWB	42403
(Dir Contracts Div)		

TRAINING DEPARTMENT
BGEN F E Sisley	3333	42540
(DC/S Trng)		

RESEARCH, DEVELOPMENT
AND STUDIES DIVISION
MGEN R "M" FRANKLIN	2042	42871
(DC/S for Research Dev and Studies)		

REQUIREMENTS & PROGRAMS DIV
MGEN W R ETNYRE	2114	43435
(DC/S for Rqmts and Programs)		

RESERVE DIVISION
MGEN J W MOORE	1114	41161
(DC/S for Reserve Affairs)		

INSPECTION DIVISION
BGEN W H RICE	2233	41533
(Inspector General)		

FISCAL DIVISION
Mr E T COMSTOCK	3000	42590
(Dir)		

COMMAND, CONTROL, COMMUNICATIONS &
COMPUTER (C4) SYSTEMS DIVISION
BGEN R R PORTER	3020	48010
(Dir)		

DIVISION OF PUBLIC AFFAIRS
BGEN W E BOOMER	1134	42958
(Dir)		

JUDGE ADVOCATE DIVISION
BGEN D M BRAHMS JR	1000	42737
(Dir)		

INTELLIGENCE DIVISION
BGEN F J BRETH	3233	42443
(Dir)		

HEADQUARTERS SUPPORT DIVISION
Mr L J KELLY	1026	41837
(Dir)		

HISTORY AND MUSEUMS DIVISION
BGEN E H SIMMONS (RET)	Bldg 58 WNY	433-2273

SEAPOWER: Fiction, Fact, and Opinion

1987: A Smorgasbord For Seagoing Readers

By BROOKE NIHART

The cargo of purely naval books this year is relatively light. Of course, there are the usual yearbooks updated and expanded. *Jane's Fighting Ships,* for 90 years the standard by which all others are measured, heads the list. *Weyer's Warships of the World 1988/89* is a German publication in English translation with foreword by the ubiquitous Norman Polmar. It is complete yet a handier size than the massive *Jane's. The Ships and Aircraft of the U.S. Fleet,* now in its 14th edition and edited by Polmar, is the standard reference on the U.S. Navy and comes from the Naval Institute Press. *U.S. Naval Developments,* now in its 3rd printing and also with a foreword by Polmar, brings ships, aircraft, missiles, and fleets alive with a thorough discussion of today's American naval scene. Publisher is the Nautical & Aviation Publishing Co., which is almost as prolific in the field as the Naval Institute Press.

In the ships department there are three of note from the Naval Institute Press: *Battleship New Jersey* traces its history from World War II to its illconceived strike in Lebanon and is as massive as the ship itself. *The Little Giants: U.S. Escort Carriers Against Japan* should appeal to those who served on, or with, the jeep carriers as well as today's advocates of small carriers and through-deck cruisers. *U.S. Small Combatants: An Illustrated Design History,* is a much-needed documentation of such smallfry as PTs, SCs, and other patrol craft.

Like Mark Twain's weather, everybody talks about the demise of America's merchant marine but nobody (read Congress) does anything about it. This year's plaintive cry in the wilderness comes from the Center for Strategic and International Studies in Washington and is titled *U.S. Maritime Industries: Down for the Third Time?* Anyone out there listening? Longtime *Jane's Fighting Ships* editor, Capt. John E. Moore, RN (Ret.), presents a British view of the world submarine-warfare scene in *Submarine Warfare: Today and Tomorrow* while our own Adm. I.J. Galantin writes of his experience in the gallant USS *Halibut* in *Take Her Deep! A Submarine Against Japan in World War II.* On the naval aviation side, *On Yankee Station: The Naval Air War Over Vietnam* tells with candor the story of carrier air in that war. We must applaud the Naval Institute Press's reissue in its "Classics of Naval Literature" series of *The Quiet Warrior: A Biography of Admiral Raymond A. Spru-*

BROOKE NIHART, the compiler, describes himself as a Marine who reads and writes (but who uses a hand calculator for arithmetic) and in his dotage runs the Marine Corps museums. Successful open-heart surgery interrupted his preparation of the introduction to his bibliography, but failed to deter him in his completion of it.

---

ance. The life and victories of this consummate practitioner of modern naval warfare has much to say to today's naval leaders. A broader biographic study is *Commander in Chief: Franklin Delano Roosvelt, His Lieutenants, and Their War* in which a naval-oriented President chose, and used, his top wartime military and naval leaders. We must note the publishing of Forest Pogue's 4th and final volume of his biography of *George C. Marshall* subtitled *Statesman 1945-1959.* Marshall's career as soldier-statesman touched us all during the mid-20th century.

Books on history as history continue to proliferate and World War II continues to be told and retold. Master storyteller Robert Leckie's *Delivered From Evil: The Saga of World War II* is hailed as the first complete one-volume history of that war and it comes at an opportune time for the younger generation to learn about the central event of the 20th century won by their grandfathers. A more general work and of particular interest to the Navy and Marine Corps personnel who participated in most of the actions described is Edwin Hoyt's *America's Wars: And Military Excursions* which recounts small wars and expeditions largely forgotten.

As in recent years, matters of nuclear warfare, the arms control concomitant, and the Strategic Defense Initiative or space shield come in for extensive treatment from left, right, and center. The list is extensive and we refer the reader to it: "You pay your money and take your choice." Meanwhile, we recommend Edward Teller's *Better a Shield Than a Sword: Perspectives in Defense and Technology* as a mature and authoritative discussion of a subject of overarching importance. In the related area of high technology.

This year didn't see many books that could be conveniently placed under "national defense." Two, however, deserve a second look. First, Tom Allen, who is no stranger to these pages having co-authored with Polmar the definitive Rickover biography, has dissected modern war games in *War Games: The Secret World of the Creators, Players, and Policy Makers Rehearsing World War III Today.* It makes a fascinating introduction to the subject for any military man who expects to become involved in this arcane art, and most sooner or later do so. Although pre-Summit, William G. Hyland's *Mortal Rivals: Superpower Relations From Nixon to Reagan* draws the provocative conclusion that the Soviet position has so deteriorated that it may embark on an adventurist foreign policy. That is still a possibility that must be borne in mind.

The "threat" continues to be the "Evil Empire," Russia, officially but inaccurately known as the Soviet Union. Books exposing its aims and practices continue to roll off the presses. Heading the list this year is *Soviet Global Strategy* by Col. Dr. Ambassador and cold warrior William R. Kintner. Once again the Russian empire expansionist program is exposed in great detail by an expert. Of use to penetrate the mysteries of Russian "public relations" are *Soviet Strategic Deception, The Soviet Propaganda Machine, Soviet Military Deception,* and *The Pattern of Soviet Conduct in the*

Third World. All serve as handboo[k] understanding.

As with books on "the threat," wor[k] "terrorism" pour forth from the publi[sh] houses. Noteworthy is Col. John C[?] *Green Berets, SEALs, and Spetsnaz:[?] and Soviet Special Military Opera[?]* which inventories these forces and dis[c] their operations. *Modern Irregular [War]fare: In Defense Policy and as a Mi[litary] Phenomenon* by retired West German[?] von der Heydte is an indepth analysis [of] subject in classical form. *Wars Wi[?] Splendor: The U.S. Military and Low-Conflict* by Ernest Evans prescribes[?] measures America must take.

As usual, the list of books on i[ntelli]gence matters bulks large. While not st[?] speaking a naval matter, the Navy[?] Marine Corps have from the beginning[?] involved in intelligence and special [opera]tions as consumers and as operator[s,] sailors, intelligence and counterintelli[gence] should be regarded as basic as seama[nship] and gunnery. Allen and Polmar poin[t?] that our counterintelligence has [?] us. This is partly from naivete, p[artly] from fear of seeming paranoid. But the[re are] traitors and enemy agents out there. [?] second line of defense" against these [is?] awareness of the threat and how it ope[rates] by all hands, not just the CI people, [and] willingness to report suspicious [beha]vior.

The Walker Navy family is a ca[se in] point and that story is covered in deta[il in] *Pledge Allegiance ... The True Stor[y of] the Walkers, An American Spy Family,* [and] in *Breaking The Ring: The Bizarre Ca[se of] the Walker Family Spy Ring.* Sad, distu[rbing] reading but instructive in how such [?] works.

The Iran-contra contretemps is [too] recent to be fully covered, although [Bob] Woodward's CIA-bashing and controv[ersial] *Veil: The Secret Wars of the CIA 1981-[?]* touches upon it as do *Presidents' S[ecret] Wars, Witness: From the Shah to the S[?] Arms Deal,* and *The Crimes of Patriots.*

These, then, comprise the sea [?] of books from 1987, light on purely [naval?] subjects, but long on matters of equ[ally] greater importance: the Soviet t[hreat,] Soviet-sponsored terrorism, and intellig[ence] which is both our shield and a swor[d to] penetrate the chinks in our armor.

AVIATION

Wings of the Navy: Flying Allied Carrier[?] craft of World War II, by Capt. Eric Br[own,] RN, Naval Institute Press, $19.95. E[valu]ations of 16 carrier aircraft, cockpit v[iews] and cutaway drawings.

On Yankee Station: The Naval Air War [Over] Vietnam, by Cmdr. John B. Nichols, [?] and Barrett Tillman, Naval Institute [Press,] $16.95. Candid look at naval air in [Viet]nam, strengths and shortcomings of [?] doctrine, political conduct of the war [and] opposition.

Skyraider: The Douglas A-1 "Flying D[ump] Truck," by Capt. Rosario Rausa, US[N,] Nautical & Aviation Publishing Comp[any,] $19.95. From the AD of 1944 co[mbat] and the Korean War to the "Spad" o[f?]

Vietnam, by a man who flew them.

Marine Corps Aviation: 1912 To The [pre]sent, by Peter B. Mersky, Nautical & [Avi]ation Publishing Company, $22.95. [Thi]s second revised edition includes oper[atio]ns in Grenada and Libya.

[Attac]k Helicopters, by Cmdr. Howard Wheel[er,] USN, Nautical & Aviation Publishing [Com]pany, $22.95. The gunship as devel[ope]d by America, exploited by Russia in [Afg]hanistan, and used by France, Britain, [and] Germany.

[Mes]serschmitts Over Sicily, by Gen. Johan[nes] Steinhoff, Nautical & Aviation Pub[lishi]ng Company, $19.95. Two months in [194]3 that convinced a young Luftwaffe [maj]or that the war was lost.

[Histo]ry of Marine Corps Aviation in WWII, [by] Robert Sherrod, Foreword by Brig. [Gen]. Edwin H. Simmons, USMC, Nautical [& A]viation Publishing Company, $24.95. [A n]ew edition of a classic by a war cor[resp]ondent and historian.

[Flyin]g Boats and Amphibians Since 1945, [by] David Oliver, Naval Institute Press, [$19].95. The story of 11 aircraft from seven [cou]ntries since 1945 with technical details [and] over 200 photographs.

[Mode]rn Combat Aircraft Design: Technol[ogy] and Function, by Klaus Hunecke, Na[val] Institute Press, $28.95. Publicly una[vail]able information from a German indus[try] authority.

[A F]orce Spoken Here: General Ira Baker [and] the Command of the Air, by James [Par]ton, Adler & Adler, $24.95. An uncrit[ical] biography of the wartime commander [of] the Mediterranean Allied Air Forces, [the] Eighth Air Force, and then deputy [com]mander of the Army Air Forces.

[The] Smithsonian Book of Flight, by Walter [J. B]oyne, Orion Books, Division of Crown [Pub]lishers, $35.00. Lavishly illustrated [and] tightly written by the former director [of] the National Air and Space Museum, [on] the meaning of flight for the human [spi]rit—the inventiveness, the craftsman[shi]p, the daring achievements, and the ad[ven]ture.

[The] Early Birds, by Capt. Joe Hill, USN, [Sun]flower University Press, $19.95. Flying [boy]s from Pearl Harbor to VJ Day.

[Whit]tle: The True Story, by John Golley, [Smi]thsonian Institution. The complete [sto]ry of Frank Whittle's invention and [dev]elopment of the turbojet engine in the [19]30s and 1940s.

[BIO]GRAPHY

[The] Quiet Warrior: A Biography of Admiral [Ra]ymond A. Spruance, by Thomas B. [Bu]ell, Naval Institute Press, $21.95. Win[ne]r of the Mahan Award for Literary [Ac]hievement in 1974, this classic biogra[ph]y of a master of strike warfare is reis[su]ed in the "Classics of Naval Literature" [for]mat.

[Ike:] His Life and Times, by Piers Brendon, [Ha]rper & Row, $21.95. Witty, perceptive, [bu]t cynical British view of Eisenhower.

[Win]ston S. Churchill: Volume Seven—Road [to] Victory 1941-1945, by Martin Gilbert, [Ho]ughton Mifflin, $40. A convenient [ab]ridgement of Churchill's own multivol[um]e work.

[Com]mander in Chief: Franklin Delano [Ro]osevelt, His Lieutenants, and Their [Wa]r, by Eric Larrabee, Harper & Row, [$2]5. Roosevelt's strategic skills lay in [ch]oosing well his leaders and strategists.

[Mont]y: Final Years of the Field Marshal, [19]44-1976, by Nigel Hamilton, McGraw-

Hill, $29.95. A warts-and-all account of one of the most brilliant—and certainly one of the quirkiest—generals of this century.

The World and Richard Nixon, by C.L. Sulzberger, Prentice Hall, $18.95. The author holds that Nixon enjoyed more foreign policy triumphs than most presidents.

George C. Marshall: Statesman 1945-1959, by Forrest C. Pogue, foreword by Drew Middleton, Viking Press, $29.95. Fourth and final volume of the monumental study of one of the greatest figures in 20th-century American history.

Ike the Soldier: As They Knew Him, by Merle Miller, Putnam's. Eisenhower's military career based on interviews with contemporaries plus unpublished diaries, letters, and memoirs.

War Bird: The Life and Times of Elliott White Springs, by Burke Davis, University of North Carolina Press, $19.95. WWI double ace, novelist, adman, and industrialist.

FICTION

Patriot Games, by Tom Clancy, Putnam, $19.95. Protagonist is a former Marine. Trade experts say technically flawed but good plot.

Occupation, by John Toland, Doubleday. A sequel to the saga of Marines in the Pacific War.

South to Java, by Vice Adm. William P. Mack and William P. Mack, Jr., Nautical & Aviation Publishing Co., $19.95. A four-piper destroyer of the Asiatic Fleet escapes from the Philippines.

HISTORY

Delivered From Evil: The Saga of World War II, by Robert Leckie, Harper & Row. Billed as the first complete one-volume history, it well may be as it begins with the war's origins in the Versailles Treaty.

The Mask of Command, by John Keegan, Viking Press, $18.95. Alexander the Great, Wellington, U.S. Grant, and Hitler studied as commanders in an ill-masked pacifist tract.

Behind Japanese Lines: An American Guerrilla in the Philippines, by Ray C. Hunt and Bernard Norling, University Press of Kentucky, $20. A P-40 mechanic turns guerrilla on Luzon and is unprepared for the ruthlessness of guerrilla war, difficult decisions of eliminating spies, and the poisoned legacy left to successor civilian societies.

Portrait of the Enemy, by David Chanoff and Doan Van Toai, Random House, $17.95. Oral history of the other side in wartime Vietnam.

In the Field of Fire, edited by Jeanne Van Buren Dann and Jack Dann, Tor/St. Martin's Press, $8.95 (paper). Anthology of 22 stories about Vietnam by sci-fi writers.

Embattled Courage: The Experience of Combat in the American Civil War, by Gerald L. Linderman, The Free Press, $22.50. What made Civil War soldiers fight probed through their letters, diaries, and memoirs. Closer to a true understanding of the Civil War than that so far available.

America's Wars: And Military Excursions, by Edwin P. Hoyt III, McGraw-Hill, $24.95. Small wars and skirmishes at home and abroad.

Hollywood Goes to War, by Clayton R.

Koppes and Gregory D. Black, The Free Press, $22.50. Appropriateness of governmental coercion and censorship of a private medium to mobilize America for war, and the consequences of these ways for the peace, is questioned.

Remaking Japan: The American Occupation as New Deal, by Theodore Cohen, edited by Herbet Passin, The Free Press, $27.50. Cohen, who headed MacArthur's labor division, holds that New Dealers in Washington directed economic policies. Actually, and what is omitted, MacArthur's political reforms facilitated the kind of capitalism that Japan had favored since the Meiji Restoration.

The 25-Year War: America's Military Role in Vietnam, by Gen. Bruce Palmer, Jr., University Press of Kentucky, $24. Sound analysis of U.S. military, political, and diplomatic results in Vietnam.

Maverick Marine: General Smedley D. Butler and the Contradictions of American Military History, by Dr. Hans Schmidt, University Press of Kentucky, $28. How Butler, disappointed at his non-selection to Marine Corps commandant, turned against the establishment.

Bitter Victory, by Robert Shaplen, Harper & Row, $16.95. The author reported from Indo-China for the past 40 years. He tells how North Vietnam fought the war and how it is failing in the peace.

Arlington National Cemetery: Shrine To America's Heroes, by James Edward Peters, Woodbine House, $9.95. Complete facts, figures, names, and maps.

The U.S. Marine Corps Story, by J. Robert Moskin, McGraw-Hill, $14.95 (paper). The definitive history of the U.S. Marines revised and updated to 1987 and to include Lebanon and Grenada.

December 7, 1941: The Day the Japanese Attacked Pearl Harbor, by Gordon Prange, McGraw-Hill, $22.95. Culmination of Prange's Pearl Harbor trilogy—*At Dawn We Slept* and *Pearl Harbor: The Verdict of History.*

The Landing at Veracruz 1914, by Jack Sweetman, Naval Institute Press, $21.95. The intervention from both sides plus the eyewitness account of the author's father.

The Marines in China 1927-1928, by Gen. David M. Shoup, USMC, edited with an introduction by Howard Jablon, Archon Books, $19.50. Young Lt. Shoup's journal of Marines protecting Americans and national interests against revolution and anarchy.

The Russian Civil War, by Evan Mawdsley, Allen & Unwin, $49.95, $14.95 (paper). Hailed as the best book written on the subject.

The Killing Ground: The British Army, the

Western Front and the Emergence of Warfare, 1900-1918, by Tim Travers, Allen & Unwin, $34.95. How the British army developed its WWI ideas, tactics, and strategies from original sources.

The Dogma of the Battle of Annihilation: The Theories of Clausewitz and Schlieffen and Their Impact on the German Conduct of Two World Wars, by Jehuda L. Wallach, Greenwood Press, $45. An Israeli military scholar critiques Germany's misapplication of Clausewitz.

The Long Peace: Inquiries Into the History of the Cold War, by John Lewis Gaddis, Oxford University Press, $24.95. Deterrence and how we didn't fall into nuclear war.

The Korean War, by Max Hastings, Simon and Schuster. Command decisions are integrated with combat descriptions in a British view that may not be palatable to all Americans.

Military Effectiveness, Vol. 1 The First World War, Vol. 2 The Interwar Period, Vol. 3 The Second World War, edited by Allan R. Millet and Williamson Murray, Allen & Unwin, $50 each volume. Twenty-four eminent scholars examine the performance of seven major powers' military institutions from 1914 to 1945.

The Texas Navy: In Forgotten Battles and Shirtsleeve Diplomacy, by Jim Dan Hill, State House Press, Austin. A facsimile reprint of a 1937 classic. The 10-year history of a force that protected Sam Houston's flank at the small Battle of San Jacinto and served until the Republic became a state.

U.S. Marines in Grenada 1983, by Lt. Col. Ronald H. Spector, USMCR, History and Museums Division, HQMC, Government Printing Office. The Marines' participation in the Grenada intervention, based on interviews and action reports.

U.S. Marines in Lebanon 1982-1984, by Benis M. Frank, History and Museums Division, HQMC, Government Printing Office. Insertion, presence, and withdrawal of Marine Amphibious Units during the Arab-Israeli War. Written from interviews and after-action reports. Includes the Long Commission's conclusions and recommendations.

HIGH TECH

A Race on the Edge of Time, by David E. Fisher, McGraw-Hill, $19.95. A major work of scientific and political history which presents an absorbing examination of the development of radar from its inception in the 1930s to its present role in SDI, and our military and political environment.

Rabi: Scientist and Citizen, by John S. Rigden, Basic Books, $21.95. I.I. Rabi, a Brooklyn-born nuclear physicist, opposed development of the H-bomb and stood by Oppenheimer in his trials.

Alvarez: Adventures of a Physicist, by Luis W. Alvarez, Basic Books, $19.95. The California-born autobiographer favored the H-bomb and testified against Oppenheimer.

Manufacturing Matters: The Myth of the Post-Industrial Economy, by Stephen S. Cohen and John Zysman, Basic Books, $19.95. The United States cannot hope to pay for its manufactured imports by selling services abroad. We need too many goods, and there are not enough services in demand.

Creating the Computer: Government, Industry, and High Technology, by Kenneth Flamm, Brookings Institution, $28.95,
$10.95 (paper). Identifies and analyzes the origins of technologies important to the development of computers and the government role in their development.

INTELLIGENCE

Merchants of Treason: America's Secrets for Sale, From the Pueblo to the Present, by Thomas B. Allen and Norman Polmar, Delacorte Press, $19.95. The first comprehensive analysis of why we are losing the game of counterespionage on the battlefields of the new cold war. March 1988 is the publication date.

Klaus Fuchs, Atom Spy, by Robert Chadwell Williams, Harvard University Press, $25. Scholarly and definitive account of a German Communist Party man from youth through his days at Los Alamos where he passed information to Russia, to his trial and life in prison, and to his present East German Communist Party-line anti-nuclear activism.

On The Run, by Philip Agee, Lyle Stuart, $19.95. The 20-year run of a traitor, Communist, and defector from the CIA who has caused incalculable damage to national interests. One wonders why his "run" was not long since terminated with extreme prejudice.

Veil: The Secret Wars of the CIA 1981-1987, by Bob Woodward, Simon & Schuster, $21.95. Hailed as technically flawed and a melange of truth, fiction, and innuendo, it does shed some light on clandestine activity of the 1980s, if the truth can be shredded out.

I Plege Allegiance . . . The True Story of the Walkers: An American Spy Family, by Howard Blum, Simon & Schuster, $18.95. The shift from the previous spy of mindless ideology to a nautical lumpen proletarian tribe, rootless, bored, resentful, and mercenary. Best characterized by one commentator as, "bumbling adolescents at play in the fields of Armageddon" and with near catastrophic results.

The Crimes of Patriots: A True Tale of Dope, Dirty Money, and the CIA, by Jonathan Kwitny, W.W. Norton & Co., $19.95. A secret government and the pressures of opportunity for profit are alleged and related to the Iran-contra affair.

Greek Memories, by Compton Mackenzie, University Publications of America, $27.50. Banned in Britain since 1933 under the Official Secrets Act, it reveals the amateurish bumbling of MI5 operations in Greece during World War I. The banned portions are shaded in gray.

Sleeping With Moscow: The Authorized Account of the KGB's Bungled Infiltration of the FBI by two of the Soviet Union's Most Unlikely Operatives, by Anatole Verbitsky and Dick Adler, Shapolsky Publishers, $14.95. Two of the most inept Soviet spies meet one of America's dumbest FBI agents in Los Angeles.

Spy Tech: A Look at the Fascinating Tools of the Espionage Trade, by Graham Yost, Facts on File, $17.95. From the simple garrote to the infrared reconnaissance satellite.

Foreign Intelligence Organizations, by Jeffrey T. Richelson, Ballinger Publishing, $16.95 (paper). Origins, structure, operations, and performance during actual missions of eight major intelligence services.

The Secret War in Central America: Sandinista Assault on World Order, by John Norton Moore, University Publications
of America, $17.95. Argues convinc[...] that U.S. aid to contras is justified [...] legal because the Sandinistas are w[...] secret war on their democratic neigh[...]

Sword and Shield: The Soviet Intellig[...] and Security Apparatus, by Jeffr[...] Richelson, Ballinger Publishing, $[...] (paper). Russia's well-hidden and gr[...] technical espionage activities from su[...] lance to ELINT trawlers, HUMINT [...] active measures.

Traitors: The Anatomy of Treason[...] Chapman Pincher, St. Martin's [...] $19.95. Exhaustively researched stu[...] the most heinous kind of spy—one [...] betrays his own country's secrets—[...] the Rosenbergs and Sir Anthony [...] to the Walkers and dozens of othe[...] cluding "agents of influence" in high [...] and Lenin's "useful idiots" in low.

Spycatcher: The Candid Autobiography[...] Senior Intelligence Officer, by Peter W[...] Viking Press, $19.95. Revelations of [...] tish counterintelligence officer; the [...] is in violation of the Official Secret[...] but has been published in America.

My Dear Alex: Letters From the KGB, e[...] by Dinesh D'Souza and Gregory Foss[...] Regnery Gateway, $14.95. A not so r[...] *a clef*—although some such as Ant[...] Lewis are mentioned—about how Ru[...] agents manipulate the contemporary [...] for disinformation.

Cloak & Gown: Scholars in the Secret [...] 1939-1961, by Robin W. Winks, Wi[...] Morrow & Co., $22.95. Yale Universi[...] a recruiting ground for the OSS and [...]

Conspiracy of Silence: The Secret Li[...] Anthony Blunt, by Barrie Penrose [...] Simon Freeman, Farrar, Straus, & Gi[...] $22.95. Exposed by Margaret Thatch[...] 1979, Blunt had penetrated royal c[...] as art historian to the Queen's Colle[...] and was one of the leaders of the "[...] bridge Conspiracy" which recruited [...] gess, MacLean, and other traitor spies.

Mayday: The U-2 Affair, by Michae[...] Beschloss, Harper & Row, $8.95. D[...] mented account of the 1 May 1960 s[...] down of Gary Powers and his U-2 r[...] naissance plane over Russia. Both th[...] and political history.

Disinformation, Misinformation, and [...] "Conspiracy" to Kill JFK, by Ar[...] Moss, Archon Books, $22.50. Were al[...] conspiracies really Russian disinforma[...]

The Red and the Blue: Cambridge, Tre[...] and Intelligence, by Andrew Sinclair, [...] tle, Brown, $17.95. The Communist[...] Cambridge University who became [...] moles inside Britain's government and [...] telligence services.

The Second Oldest Profession: Spies [...] Spying in the Twentieth Century, by [...] lip Knightley, W.W. Norton & Co., $19[...] The subtitle of the British edition [...] "The Spy as Bureaucrat, Patriot, Fanta[...] and Whore." The author holds that spy[...] is unnecessary and wasteful. Is this disa[...] ing disinformation?

Operation GARBO, by Juan Pujol with N[...] West, Random House, $17.95. A W[...] double agent deception operation [...] convinced Hitler that the imminent Al[...] landing would be elsewhere than Norm[...] dy.

The Spy Story, by John G. Cawelti [...] Bruce A. Rosenberg, University of Chic[...] Press, $22.50. History of spying in [...] and fiction.

The CIA and The U.S. Intelligence Syst[...] by Scott D. Breckinridge, Westview Pr[...] $30. Objective, professional, informa[...]

ege textbook.

*Cambridge Apostles: A History of
[Cam]bridge University's Elite International
[Sec]ret Society,* by Richard Deacon, Farrar,
[Stra]us, & Giroux, $19.95. From the be-
[ginn]ing in 1820 to the "Cambridge Con-
[spir]acy" of the 1930s.

*[Mo]ss: From the Shah to the Secret Arms
[Deal], An Insider's Account of U.S. Involve-
[men]t in Iran,* by Mansur Rafizadeh, Wil-
[liam] Morrow & Co. By the former chief
[of S]AVAK and a CIA mole.

*[Break]ing The Ring: The Bizarre Case of the
[Walk]er Family Spy Ring,* by John Barron,
[Hou]ghton Mifflin. For 17 years Russia
[kne]w every military move we made.

*[Deep] Black: Space Espionage and National
[Secu]rity,* by William E. Burrows, Random
[Hou]se, $19.95. The principal source of
[U.S.] strategic intelligence.

[The F]BI-KGB War: A Special Agent's Story,
[by]Robert J. Lamphere and Tom Shacht-
[man], Random House, $18.95. Breaking
[the]Rosenberg network and others in the
['40]s through '50s.

[GC&R]: The Secret Wireless War, 1900-86,
[by]Nigel West, Weidenfeld and Nicolson,
[$24.]95. Best published account of British
[SIG]INT currently available.

[The N]ew KGB: Engine of Soviet Power, by
[Willi]am R. Corson and Robert T. Crowley,
[Willi]am Morrow & Co. $10.95 (paper). A
[new] edition with fresh material on the
[KGB]-Gorbachev link.

*[Presid]ents' Secret Wars: CIA and Pentagon
[Cove]rt Operations Since World War II,* by
[John] Prados, William Morrow & Co.,
[$19.]95. Can be seen as a continuation of
[the]leftist assault on the executive as,
[see]n in the context of the time, these
[war]s" were neither whims nor aberrations
[but]withstanding the ineptitude of some.

*[Sea]son of Inquiry: The Senate Intelligence
[Inve]stigation,* by Loch K. Johnson, Uni-
[ver]sity Press of Kentucky, $31. Ac-
[cou]nt of the Church Committee of the
['70]s which gutted American intelligence,
[by o]ne of the staffers.

[NATI]ONAL DEFENSE

*[War G]ames: The Secret World of the Crea-
[tors,]Players, and Policy Makers Rehears-
[ing]World War III Today,* by Thomas B.
[Alle]n, McGraw-Hill, $19.95. The fascinat-
[ing s]tory of today's top-level war games,
[their] utility, and their dangers and pitfalls.

*[To Ch]ain the Dog of War: The War Powers
[of C]ongress in History and Law,* by Fran-
[cis]D. Wormuth and Edwin B. Firmage,
[Sout]hern Methodist University Press,
[$24.]50. Argues that the Constitution
[prov]ides massive powers to Congress in
[forei]gn policy, with regard to both ends
[and]means, but that these powers have
[been] allowed to atrophy from lack of use.

*[To A]rm A Nation: Rebuilding America's
[End]angered Defenses,* by Richard Hallo-
[ran,]MacMillan, $21.95. Among other
["ref]orms" proposed by the author, Hallo-
[ran]would return most overseas troops to
[the]US and merge the Marines to the
[Arm]y.

*[The S]trategic Dimension of Military Man-
[powe]r,* edited by Gregory Foster, et al.,
[Balli]nger Publishing, $24.95. For scholars
[and]practitioners who will be involved
[in]future defense manpower problems.

*[Mor]tal Rivals: Superpower Relations From
[Nixo]n to Reagan,* by William G. Hyland,
[Rand]om House, $19.95. Analyzes and
[fin]ds Kissingerian detente and con-
[clude]s that the Soviet position has weak-

ened and so the Soviet Union may embark
on an adventurist foreign policy.

Ideology and U.S. Foreign Policy, by Michael H. Hunt, Yale University Press, $22.50.
History of the ideas of revolution, race,
and liberty that have influenced policy.

*Superpower Competition and Security in
the Third World,* edited by Robert S. Lit-
wak and Samuel F. Wells, Jr., Wilson Cen-
ter/Ballinger Publishing, $29.95. Where
the Western alliance and the Russians
may meet and conflict.

*Watershed in Europe: Dismantling the East-
West Military Confrontation,* by Jonathan Dean, Lexington Books, $29, $9.95
(paper). A negotiator looks at the inter-
play between Western Europe and the
United States in arms control, and their
sometimes conflicting aims.

NAVY

Battleship New Jersey, by Paul Stillwell,
Naval Institute Press, $36.95. Voluminous
and well-illustrated history of the battle-
wagon from World War II to Lebanon.

*The Little Giants: U.S. Escort Carriers
Against Japan,* by William Youngblood,
Naval Institute Press, $28.95.

Seamanship, by Robin-Knox Johnston,
W.W. Norton & Co., $22.95. A useful
compendium of lore, law, techniques, and
practices of the sea.

*U.S. Small Combatants: An Illustrated De-
sign History,* by Norman Friedman, Naval
Institute Press, $46.95. All about PT
boats, subchasers, and the brown-water
navy.

*The Navy V-12 Program: Leadership for a
Lifetime,* by James G. Schneider, $29.95.
How the Navy got its officers in the
second half of World War II from Johnny
Carson and Jack Lemmon, to William
Webster, Howard Baker, and Mel Laird.

*U.S. Maritime Industries: Down for the Third
Time?,* by Robert Hilton et al., CSIS Significant Issues Series, $6.95. The demise
of an essential national and naval asset.

*Citizen-Sailors in a Changing Society: Policy
Issues for Manning the United States Naval
Reserve,* edited by Louis A. Zurcher, et al.,
Greenwood Press, $35. Recruitment, man-
power, training, mobilization, readiness,
retention, organization relevance, and
societal relevance are covered.

*U.S. Army Ships and Watercraft of World
War II,* by David H. Grover, Naval Institute Press, $44.95. The Army's "navy" of
980 ships of over 1,000 tons and 126,000
small craft, barges, tugs, and dredges.

NUCS, SDI, AND ARMS CONTROL

*Better a Shield Than a Sword: Perspectives
in Defense and Technology,* by Edward
Teller, The Free Press, $19.95. The father
of the H-bomb and early protagonist of
SDI says, "No one can be happy about
the balance of terror that followed the
development of thermonuclear weapons,
but a Soviet monopoly on intercontinental missiles carrying thermonuclear
weapons would have been worse." To
counter this "balance of terror" he advocates defense through SDI.

*Stemming the Tide: Arms Control in the
Johnson Years,* by Glenn T. Seaborg with
Benjamin S. Loeb, Lexington Books,
$24.95. A study of bureaucratic give-and-
take that illuminates the ambivalence that
ran throughout the administration.

The Arms Control Delusion, by Sen. Malcolm Wallop and Angelo Codevilla. Arms-

control advocates have sacrificed real U.S.
security for the false security of arms control by insisting that the process survive at
all costs. Contains text of still-classified
August 1985 NSDD 192 which lays
groundwork for looser interpretation of
the ABM treaty.

*Blundering Into Disaster: Surviving the First
Century of the Nuclear Age,* by Robert S.
McNamara, Pantheon, $5.95 (paper). With
a new introduction by the author, one of
the blunderers who also gave us the Edsel,
MAD, and body count.

The SDI Challenge To Europe, by Ivo H.
Daalder, Ballinger Publishing. A Dutchman
with London's IISS examines the different
aims and perspectives troubling U.S.-NATO
relations over SDI.

The Making of the Atomic Bomb, by Richard Rhodes, Simon and Schuster, $22.95.
A political history of the wartime race for
atomic weapons, an institutional history
of the Manhattan Project, a history of
nuclear physics and engineering, and a
personal account of the men who made
the bomb possible and then made it happen.

*Peace in a Nuclear Age: The Bishops' Pastor-
al Letter in Perspective,* edited by Charles
J. Reid, Jr., Catholic University of America Press, $44.95. Pro and con in 24 essays,
mainly from Roman Catholic academics
and policy consultants. *General conclusion: The Bishops generally ignore the
reality of the Soviet threat.*

*Prophecy and Politics: Militant Evangelists
on the Road to Nuclear War,* by Grace
Halsell, Lawrence Hill & Co., $16.45. The
scary prospect of TV evangelists, including
Pat Robertson, affecting U.S. Middle East
policy by their belief that nuclear Arma-
geddon will begin in that region.

*A Very Special Relationship: Britain's
Atomic Weapon Trials in Australia,* by
Lorna Arnold, Ministry of Defence, HMSO.
A definitive account of Britain's nuclear test
program in Australia in the 1950s and how
only the special relationship with non-
nuclear Australia made it possible.

*Policy Versus the Law: The Reinterpretation
of the ABM Treaty,* by Raymond L. Gart-
hoff, Brookings Institution, $8.95 (paper).
A negotiator of the treaty says it does ap-
mly to systems based on new technologies.
The USSR takes the opposite view.

The ABM Treaty and Western Security, by
William J. Durch, Ballinger Publishing,
$19.95. The SDI vs. ABM Treaty debate
is not about hardware feasibility, but
about the future nuclear strategies of East
and West.

Nuclear Blackmail and Nuclear Balance, by
Richard K. Betts, Brookings Institution,
$28.95, $10.95 (paper). Examines crises
involving nuclear threats—Berlin, Korea,
Taiwan Straits, and Middle East.

Space and National Security, by Paul B.
Stares, Brookings Institution, $28.95,
$10.95 (paper). Assesses the costs and
benefits of developing anti-satellite weapons and the feasibility of alternative
policies, and advocates negotiated limitations.

*Nuclear Fallacy: Dispelling the Myth of
Nuclear Strategy,* by Morton H. Halperin,
Ballinger Publishing, $19.95. Would remove
nuclear weapons from the military and
put them under a separate command reporting directly to the President.

Star Wars: The Economic Fallout, by Rosy
Nimroody, foreword by Paul C. Warnke,
Ballinger Publishing, $19.95. The liberal
media approach, "Star Wars" in the title

rather than the correct SDI tells all. Cost of the program, an unresolved and controversial area, and the alleged displacement of other programs are stressed while the economic impact of technological spinoffs on the order of those from the Manhattan Project and the space program are down played.

The Medical Implications of Nuclear War, edited by Frederic Solomon and Robert Q. Marston, National Academy Press, $33.50. Focuses exclusively on the effects of weapons and ignores the political realities of how nuclear weapons came to be relied upon for deterrence and possible alternatives. "Disarmament is worth any price. Science says nuclear weapons are bad; therefore, get rid of them."

Superpower Arms Control: Setting the Record Straight, edited by Albert Carnesale and Richard N. Haass, Ballinger Publishing, $34.95, $14.95 (paper). Perceptions about the potential benefits or drawbacks of arms control are in fact misperceptions. Examines a long list of negotiations and treaties with the Russians.

American Lake: Nuclear Peril in the Pacific, by Peter Hayes, Lyuba Zarsky, and Walden Bello, Penguin, $6.95 (paper). This tract against American nuclear deterrence was released last year in New Zealand and Australia and no doubt has much to do with New Zealand's subsequent rejection of our Navy ships with nuclear capabilities.

Going Nuclear: The Spread of Nuclear Weapons, 1986-1987, by Leonard S. Spector, Ballinger Publishing, $29.95, $9.95 (paper). Nuclear proliferation and the ambitions of developing countries with implications for the major powers.

Managing Nuclear Operations, edited by Ashton B. Carter, John D. Steinbruner and Charles A. Zraket, Brookings Institution, $39.95, $18.95 (paper). Examines U.S. nuclear operations and command and control, peacetime safety and control, survival under nuclear attack of command authorities, deterrence theory, and war termination.

The New Maginot Line, by Jon Connell, Arbor House, $18.95. Asserts the West's nuclear and high-tech response to the Soviet threat is a "New Maginot Line" and doomed to fail because conventional forces are neglected. The flaw: The Maginot Line was not high tech and the French did not stint conventional forces; leadership, will, doctrine, and doctrine were at fault.

The Nuclear Connection, edited by Alvin Weinberg, Marcelo Alonso, and Jack N. Barkenbus, Paragon House, $27.95, $19.95 (paper). Explores the problems of how man can benefit from the vast energy potential of the peaceful atom without the concurrent development of the military atom.

Strategic Nuclear War: What the Superpowers Target and Why, by William C. Martel and Paul S. Savage, Greenwood Press, $35. Purports to reveal many of the most troubling and dangerous weaknesses in U.S. nuclear planning.

The Price of Peace: Living With the Nuclear Dilemma, by Lawrence Freedman, Henry Holt, $18.95. The professor of War Studies at London University endorses arms control efforts and strengthening conventional forces, while eschewing nuclear superiority and the Strategic Defense Initiative.

Star Wars: The Strategic Defense Initiative Debates in Congress, by Sen. Larry Pressler, Praeger, $19.95. Sets forth both sides of the U.S. controversy, plus Soviet capabilities from congressional hearings.

Nuclear Winter, Deterrence, and the Prevention of Nuclear War, edited by Peter C. Sederberg, Praeger, $33.95. Essays urge an assessment of the impact of the flawed nuclear winter hypothesis on current ideas of nuclear deterrence, limited nuclear war, and war-fighting doctrines.

Strategic War Termination, edited by Stephen J. Cimbala, Praeger, $37.95. Explores present U.S. policy on termination and recommends strategies for improving it.

The Logic of Nuclear Terror, edited by Roman Kolkowicz, Allen & Unwin, $39.95, $14.95 (paper). As MAD erodes, these essays present a critical review of the premises, concepts, and policy prescriptions of deterrence theories and doctrines.

REFERENCE

Weyer's Warships of the World 1988/89, edited by G. Albrecht, foreword by Norman Polmar, Nautical & Aviation Publishing Co., $74. Standard reference, portable size, 1,582 superb detailed drawings of all ships, 747 photos, in English and German.

The Ships and Aircraft of the U.S. Fleet, Fourteenth Edition, edited by Norman Polmar, Naval Institute Press, $29.95. Fahey's old standard reference from the 1940s upgraded and updated. Essential.

Handbook of the Nautical Rules of the Road, by Christopher B. Llana and Cmdr. George P. Wisneskey, USCG (Ret.), Naval Institute Press, $16.95. International and inland rules side-by-side with the high points and rationale of each.

U.S. Naval Developments, third printing, by Jan S. Breemer, foreword by Norman Polmar, Nautical & Aviation Publishing Co., $24.95. Detailed and thorough description of today's Navy, people, politics, ships, aircraft, armament, and future plans.

The Mariner's Pocket Companion 1988, by Wallace E. Tobin III, Naval Institute Press, $6.95. The Bluejacket's Manual won't fit the pocket; the *Companion* does.

Naval Leadership: Voices of Experience, edited by Karel Montor et al., Naval Institute Press, $24.95. The Leadership and Law Department of USNA have compiled the thoughts of more than 100 distinguished international naval leaders addressing the issues 2,700 JOs thought were most important in a survey.

MILSPEAK: The Dictionary of Military Acronyms and Abbreviations, compiled by Andy Lightbody and Joe Poyer, North Cape Publications, $5.95 (paper). Originally an in-house staff guide at International Combat Arms: Journal of Defense Technology. Over 4,000 entries.

The ACCESS Resource Guide: An International Directory of Information on War, Peace, and Security, edited by William H. Kincade and Priscilla Hayner, Ballinger Publishing, $32, $14.95 (paper). Resources by name, subject, country, project, etc.

SUBMARINES

Take Her Deep! A Submarine Against Japan in World War II, by Adm. I.J. Galantin, Algonquin Books, $17.95. Submarines accounted for more than half the Japanese merchant ships and men-of-war sunk by the United States, but the submarine service had only 2 percent of the sailors. This is the story of the USS *Hailbut,* one of the more successful boats. The cause and cure of the notorious Mark XIV tor-

pedo also is well covered.

Submarine Warfare: Today and Tomo by John E. Moore and Richard Com Hall, Adler & Adler, $22.50. A B point of view with universal applica Russian use of mini-subs receives attention.

Shinano!, by Capt. Joseph F. Enrigh Martin's Press. In 1944, Japan's mig aircraft carrier was attacked and sunk a spread of four torpedoes on her secret maiden voyage by the USS A Fish.

U-BOATS UNDER THE SWASTIKA

Jak. P. Mallmann Showell

U-Boats Under the Swastika, by Ja Mallmann Showell, Naval Institute $19.95. New edition of a 1973 c with new material from recently u ered archives—from pre-war to the surrender.

Submarines of the Imperial Japanese by Dorr Carpenter and Norman Po Naval Institute Press. Developmen 1941 with detailed data on World W subs and operations.

TERRORISM

The Financing of Terror, by James Ad Simon & Schuster, $18.95. Document shift from governmental financing o rorists to their self-financing. Today' rorists have become "better capita who manage their own portfolios.

The Master Terrorist: The True Story Be Abu Nidal, by Yossi Melman, A Books, $16.95. Al-Fatah's 100 terr and the future of Arab terrorism.

Alchemists of Revolution: Terrorism i Modern World, by Richard E. Ruben Basic Books, $17.95. "Our policy mu to uproot the causes of terrorism by ting an end to American-sponsored op sion of classes, nations, and ethnic munities . . ." Enough said.

The American Connection: U.S. Guns, ey, and Influence in Northern Irelan Jack Holland, Viking Press, $19.95. tributions to NORAID go straight t IRA.

Terrorism: The Solutions, by Michael nor, Paladin Press. Advice on avoiding ations conducive to terrorist violence a full range of countermeasures, per to governmental.

From the Barrel of a Gun, by An James Joes, Pergamon-Brassey's Int tional Defense Publishers. The relatio between revolutionary and military fo

Wars Without Splendor: The U.S. Mi and Low-Level Conflict, by Ernest E Greenwood Press, $27.95. The U States must overcome the lingering

of Vietnam that denigrate the effec-
ss of a good special operations force
ernational stability, the suspicions
ulars of elite units, and U.S. reluc-
to engage in low-tech, low-intensity
e.

rectory of International Terrorism,
orge Rosie, Paragon House, $18.95.
he organization names, acronyms,
, and usual suspects.

Berets, SEALs, and Spetsnaz: U.S.
oviet Special Military Operations,
l. John M. Collins, Pergamon-Bras-
International Defense Publishers,
) ($15.95 paper). Generally accurate
nformative comparison of U.S. and
n special operations forces capabili-
d limitations. Conclusion: our limi-
s are many and our understanding of
plications and application of this
t new form of warfare is low.

etsnaz Threat: Can Britain be De-
?, by Col. Michael Hickey, London
te for European Defence & Strate-
udies, $8.00. Britain provides the
az with the most tempting, strategi-
aluable, and vulnerable target of all
ATO countries.

orists: Their Weapons, Leaders and
, revised edition, by Christopher
n and Ronald Payne, Facts on File,
 ($9.95 paper). Every aspect of ter-
described in chilling detail.

ng Nuclear Terrorism: The Report
pers of the International Task Force
vention of Nuclear Terrorism, edited
ul Leventhal and Yonah Alexander,
ton Books, $22.95 (paper). The
 of illegal building of a nuclear
the theft of one, or of sabotage of
mic power plant.

attack: The West's Battle Against
ists, by Christopher Dobson and
 Payne, Facts on File, $6.95 (paper).
ng, armament, leadership, and tac-
 U.S. anti-terror teams, U.K. SAS,
Sayaet Matla, West German GSG9,
hers are examined.

Irregular Warfare: In Defense Pol-
d as a Military Phenomenon, by
Professor Friedrich August F. von
eydte, translated by George Gregory,
Benjamin Franklin House, $9.95
). English translation of a 1972 Ger-
lassic. A Clausewitzian exposition of
es and practice of guerrilla warfare
rrorism today and its sources.

porary Terrorism, edited by William
idge, Facts on File, $21.95 (9.95
. Brings together a number of the
significant studies on terrorism pub-
in recent years by the Institute for
udy of Conflict in London.

t: The Incredible Pursuit of A CIA
 Turned Terrorist, by Peter Maas,
$3.95 (paper). Background to the
ontra affair. Many of the names and
nships are the same. The story of
 Wilson and his arms dealing with
 and Arab terrorist networks until
 down, captured, tried, and sen-
 to 52 years.

ok of International Terrorism and
al Violence, by Timothy M. Laur,
Press International, $55. First an-
comprehensive guide with over 40
y files, organization and leader
key dates for travel planning, per-
anticipation, and protection.

rorism Survival Guide: 101 Travel
n How Not to Become a Victim,
ndy Lightbody, North Cape Publi-
s, $3.95. How to blend, mask your

identity, and establish seeming rapport
with your captors.

*The New Battlefield: The United States
and Unconventional Conflicts,* by Sam
Sarkesian, Greenwood Press, $37.95.
The essential features of the "new battlefield" and why responding to it has been,
and remains, such a problem for this country.

*The New Battlefield: The United States and
Unconventional Conflicts,* by Sam C. Sarkesian, Greenwood Press, $37.95. A study
of the problems faced by the United States
in irregular warfare and terrorism, and
possible solutions.

THE THREAT

*The Wolf of the Kremlin: The First Biogra-
phy of L.M. Kaganovich, The Soviet
Union's Architect of Fear,* by Stuart Ka-
han, William Morrow & Co. As Stalin's
brother-in-law and closest confidant, he
was one of the world's most powerful
and dangerous men.

Reagan and Gorbachev, by Michael Mandel-
baum and Strobe Talbot, Council on Foreign Relations/Vintage, $5.95. Gorbachev's
high-tech goals and how and why Reagan's
SDI plans have him worried.

*Shadows and Whispers: Power Politics Inside
the Kremlin From Brezhnev to Gorbachev,*
by Dusko Doder, Random House, $19.95.
The Washington Post's Moscow correspondent looks over *Glasnost* and *Perestroika*
and concludes that Gorbachev is trying to
reform the world's most comprehensive
welfare state. His chances are left unans-
wered.

*The Last Empire: Nationality and the Soviet
Future,* edited by Robert Conquest, Hoover Institution, $27.95. The Russian Em-
pire's major problem of assimilating the
non-assimilatable ethnic minorities.

Chernobyl and Nuclear Power in the USSR,
by David R. Marples, St. Martin's Press,
$35 ($14.95 paper). Russia's coverup of
the accident and the low-tech reactor that
caused it. Also the remarkable Russian
preparations for coping with radiation
accidents once the decision was made.

*The Berlin Wall: Kennedy, Khrushchev, and
a Showdown in the Heart of Europe,* by
Norman Gelb, Times Books, $19.95. How
the Wall was necessary for the Russians to
save East Germany for communism and
how it led to West Germany's *Ostpolitik.*

Liberation Theology, by Phillip Berryman,
Pantheon, $6.95. Mis-subtitled "The Essen-
tial Facts about the Revolutionary Movement in Latin America and Beyond."
"Non-facts" would be more accurate,
since the real truths such as how liberation
theology was exported by European Marxist academics, not home grown by Latin
American peasants and their priests, are
not told.

*Will it Liberate? Questions About Liberation
Theology,* by Michael Novak, Paulist Press,
$14.95. America's leading lay Catholic
scholar mounts an effective intellectual
attack.

*Soviet Expansion in the Third World: Afghan-
istan, a Case Study,* by Nasir Shansab, Bart-
tleby Press, $15.95. Soviet strategy is in a
military holding action while sowing dis-
sension among resistance groups and driving a wedge between them and foreign
supporters.

Soviet Strategic Deception, edited by Brian
D. Daily and Patrick J. Parker, Hoover
Press/Lexington Books, $49. Lenin's "use-
ful idiots" who want to believe that free

men and Communists share common aspi-
rations for peace and justice are easily
duped by propaganda that tells them what
they want to hear.

*Armed Truce: The Beginnings of the Cold
War, 1945-1946,* by Hugh Thomas, Athen-
eum, $27.50. How Roosevelt's concessions
at Yalta and Stalin's Russian and Communist expansionist dynamic ensured the
Cold War.

The Soviet Propaganda Machine, by Martin
Ebon, McGraw-Hill, $22.95. Extensive
background information, detailed historical context, penetrating analysis.

*Gorbachev's Challenge: Economic Reform
in the Age of High Technology,* by Marshall I. Goldman, W.W. Norton & Co.,
$16.95. How the Soviet economy grew in-
to such a behemoth of inefficiency, and
a guide to correction by Harvard's number
two Soviet scholar.

*A Question of Trust: The Origins of U.S.-
Soviet Diplomatic Relations,* by Loy W.
Henderson, Hoover Institution, $44.95.
Stationed in Moscow more than 50 years
ago, Henderson recounts deception, dissim-
ulation, obstructionism, and duplicity in
early diplomatic exchanges which have
continued to this day.

*Ethiopia, The United States, and the Soviet
Union,* by David A. Korn, Southern Illinois University Press, $24.95. The forced
famine of the Ukraine in the 1930s as a
system of political control repeated in
Ethiopia.

Soviet Military Deception, by David Thomas,
CSIS Washington Papers/Praeger, $9.95.
Maskirovka, camouflage, concealment, and
deception as a strategy and its dangerous
application to the deployment of the new
Soviet ICBM, the SS-25, a mobile system.

*The Pattern of Soviet Conduct in the Third
World,* edited by Walter Laqueur, Praeger,
$27.95. Use of Communist parties, ideol-
ogy, front-organizations, nationalism, and
religion by the Soviets in the third world.

*Soviet Submarine Operations in Swedish
Waters,* by Milton Leitenberg, CSIS Washington Papers/Praeger, $9.95. Preparing
the way for a Soviet invasion.

Military Objectives in Soviet Foreign Policy,
by Michael McGwire, Brookings Institution, $39.95, $18.95 (paper). New input
into the U.S. debate over Soviet military
policy.

*Stalin's War: A Radical New theory of the
Origins of the Second World War,* by
Ernst Topitsch, translated by A. Taylor
and B.E. Taylor, St. Martin's Press, $19.95.
Holds that Stalin was going to attack Germany should Hitler have become involved
in England, but Hitler pre-empted him.

Soviet Global Strategy, by William R. Kintner, American Security Council, Boston,
Virginia, $24.95. Army colonel, Ph.D. and
ambassador exposes Russian Empire expan-
sionism; "We must not forget that he
(Gorbachev) is a protege of Andropov,
former head of the KGB."

*The Sixth Continent: Russia and the Making
of Mikhail Gorvachev,* by Mark Frankland,
Harper & Row, $22.95. The Soviet Union
under Gorbachev is just as defensively self-
righteous about its place in the world as
Russia under the Czars. How Gorbachev's
rise was the direct result of Brezhnev's failure to deal with the consequences of Sta-
linism.

*Perestroika: New Thinking for Our Country
and the World,* by Mikhail Gorbachev,
Harper & Row. Gorbachev's very own disinformation on his re-structuring of Soviet
society and its significance for the world.

INDEX

Index to Advertisers